THE HANDBOOK OF
COUNTRY RISK
2004–2005

A Guide to International Business and Trade

coface

KOGAN
PAGE

London & Sterling, VA

Publisher's note

Every possible effort has been made to ensure
that the information contained in this book is
accurate at the time of going to press, and the
publishers cannot accept responsibility for
any errors or omissions, however caused.
No responsibility for loss or damage occasioned
to any person acting or refraining from action,
as a result of the material in this publication,
can be accepted by the editor, the publisher or
any of the authors.

First published in 1999 by Kogan Page Limited
Sixth edition published in 2004

120 Pentonville Road   22883 Quicksilver Drive
London N1 9JN   Sterling VA 20166-2012
United Kingdom   USA
www.kogan-page.co.uk

© Coface and Kogan Page Limited, 2004

ISBN 0 7494 4198 4

British Library Cataloguing-in-Publication Data

A CIP record for this book is available from the British Library

Typeset by Saxon Graphics Ltd, Derby
Printed and bound in Great Britain by Thanet Press Ltd, Margate

Contents

CONTENTS

■ THE AMERICAS
The Economic Outlook for the Americas in 2004 128

Experts from Oxford Analytica, London

The Range of Country @ratings in the Americas ...134

Sylvia Greisman and Olivier Oechslin, *Coface Country Risk and Economic Studies Department, Paris*

■ ASIA
Economic Prospects for South and South-East Asia in 2004 196

Experts from Oxford Analytica, London

The Range of Country @ratings in Asia.................200

Sylvia Greisman and Pierre Paganelli, *Coface Country Risk and Economic Studies Department, Paris*

Acknowledgements

The publisher wishes to thank the Oxford Analytica and Coface country risk and short-term experts (Nathalie Ballage, Angélique Bougeard, Jean-Louis Daudier, Dominique Fruchter, Bernard Lignereux, Catherine Monteil, Olivier Oechslin, Pierre Paganelli, Jean-François Rondest and Yves Zlotowski) who have contributed to *The Handbook of Country Risk 2004*.

Our thanks are also extended to Stanley Glick (Lingua Franca), Govind Bhinder (FEAT – Financial and Economic Authors and Translators) and Coface's Communication Department.

Recovery is Here

François David, *Chairman and Chief Executive, Coface*

After three years of stagnation, economic recovery finally emerged in 2003 despite geopolitical tensions and the sudden crisis triggered by the SARS pandemic. Besides prompting a return of confidence in financial markets, that recovery could mark the start of a new expansion phase if we give credence to economic cycle theories. The upturn should go hand in hand with improvement in company solvency, already evident in the United States, and a lasting reduction of payment incidents.

The recovery is nonetheless not risk-free considering the major tensions and imbalances marking the world economic and geopolitical environment. Moreover, it has remained very uneven across world regions, within both industrialized and emerging countries.

In the United States, company profitability has improved, creating an environment conducive to a growth recovery also largely spurred by expansionary monetary and fiscal policy. In Japan, growth has returned, buoyed by steady US and Chinese demand. Conversely, in West Europe, low company profitability, a lack of room for manoeuvre on fiscal policy, and the euro's appreciation have contributed to stagnation of the region's main economies. Microeconomically, those divergent macroeconomic trends have resulted in a sharp improvement in US-company payment behaviour with default frequency stabilizing at a level still high in Europe.

Emerging countries have benefited from strong North American and Chinese demand, financial market confidence and, for oil-exporting countries, continuing high barrel prices. Regional disparities have nonetheless persisted with the dynamism of Asian countries or Russia still in contrast to economic activity in Latin America hampered by

the need to maintain financial equilibriums and by geopolitical tensions in the Near and Middle East. Company payment behaviour has been clearly reflecting those disparities. While payment incidents are still commonplace in the main South American economies, Asian company solvency has remained relatively steady. Those persistent imbalances could impede the spread, albeit essential, of recovery across all regions.

In the United States, the excessive fiscal and trade imbalances incurred for over three years now could trigger brutal adjustments apt to impede economic activity. An increase in interest rates resulting from the public sector's growing financing needs and a loss of confidence by foreign investors would undermine consumer-spending dynamism and limit the financing capacity of companies.

In Europe, the euro's appreciation could reduce company competitiveness, thus hampering the expected export recovery and increasing competition in the domestic market. Despite some recent easing of the situation regarding fiscal-imbalance levels, there is little likelihood of economic policy being capable of massively stimulating GDP growth.

Affected by regional geopolitical instability, Near and Middle Eastern countries may again be subject to an investment slump with oil revenues, after an exceptional year in 2003, likely to fall due to a price and quantity decline and, especially, a return to more customary production levels. That situation would limit the stimulatory capacity of economic policy.

In South America, persistent financial constraints that impose economic austerity policies coupled with an insufficient growth recovery could spur discontent after the hopes inspired by election of representatives of the most disadvantaged classes. That could affect financial market confidence.

INTRODUCTION

The Outlook for 2004–05

Jonathan Reuvid, *Consultant Editor, Global Market Briefings, Kogan Page*

The introduction to this book normally takes the form of an eco-political *tour d'horizon* of the regions, focusing first on the United States and the Americas and then on the other regions in turn in the order in which the book's contents are arranged. For this edition, a more pragmatic approach is adopted. Against the background of almost unanimous predictions of blossoming global economic recovery in 2004 and a less certain outlook for world security, it seems more relevant to concentrate instead on the principal causes of friction between what we characterized in a previous edition as the 'tectonic plates of the geopolitical and geo-economic environment'.

The analysis that follows is predicated on the United States' military hegemony and its dominating influence on other countries' economies and world trade, which were both prominent in 2003 and likely to remain so under the realpolitik of the 2004 US presidential election year. An emerging influence on the world economy, also discussed in this introduction, is that of China in terms of high domestic growth and its increased impact on world trade since WTO entry. The case that US military supremacy will have a mollifying effect on threats to global security is debated. The likely influences of both US and Chinese trade and currency policies on European and other economies worldwide are also discussed. Finally, likely causes of friction in the cockpit of an enlarged European Union, which have emerged in 2003, are noted.

◼ RISKS TO INTERNATIONAL SECURITY

If for nothing else, 2003 will be remembered as the year when the world came to terms with the truth that a US president, with popular domestic support

and determined upon military action, could not be controlled by the peer pressure of a UN Security Council majority in opposition. It is doubtful that the decision to invade Iraq would have been voided in the absence of support from the UK and other UN allies. Claims about the presence of remaining weapons of mass destruction (WMD) or Iraq's intention to manufacture them, which failed to convince Security Council members, are now shown to have been on slender intelligence or false premises. However unwelcome the realization may be to the United States' NATO allies, their collective influence on US foreign policy towards any regime that it may target in its 'war against terror' is slight. It seems likely that the UK prime minister's moderating influence on US actions in Iraq has been overstated.

Coalitions of the willing

However, there is a more encouraging reverse side to the prospect of living with 'coalitions of the willing' – a euphemism for US unilateralism – in place of Security Council resolutions. The present administration's manifest willingness to engage without tangible provocation in non-nuclear, high-tech military action against regimes having, or believed to have, WMD capabilities or to be harbouring terrorists seems to have paid dividends in the closing months of 2003.

Some regimes on President Bush's hit list for pre-emptive action, specifically Libya, North Korea and Iran, have reacted to the destruction visited on Saddam Hussein's Ba'athist regime by seeking an accommodation with the United States and opening their WMD facilities to UN inspectors or other observers. It is true that Libya, in spite of the Qaddafi regime's long-standing history of terrorist acts, was not named in President Bush's 'axis of evil', the premier league of threats to US security, and that Iran's decision to invite UN inspection was triggered by a joint Franco-British-German diplomatic initiative. However, the deterrent effect of the US coalition's enforced regime change in Iraq was surely a root cause of both welcome developments and, therefore, a justification of US foreign policy. The same deterrent factor has played an important part in the bizarre nuclear poker game that Mr Kim Jong Il launched in North Korea well before the start of the Iraq invasion following its inclusion as an 'axis of evil' member. In this evolving drama the key diplomatic role was taken by China, which successfully initiated six-party discussions with North Korea as a substitute for the bilateral negotiation with the United States on which Mr Kim originally insisted.

Other conflicts

These three encouraging signs of movement in the geopolitical tectonic plates are supplemented by more hopeful scenarios elsewhere. The United States can take credit for a vital role in promoting the lessening of tensions between India and Pakistan following the recent rapprochement between Mr Atal Behari Vajpayee and General Pervez Musharraf at a summit meeting of South Asian leaders on 6 January 2004, which has resulted in agreement to discuss all outstanding issues including the future status of Kashmir beginning in February. This will be a long, difficult and highly vulnerable process, which could be blown apart by a single bomb placed by Pakistan-based terrorists in a well-chosen Indian civilian location. General Musharraf is also personally at risk following his decision to support the United States in Afghanistan and abandon the Taliban.

Another promising development is the growing possibility of an end to the civil war in the Sudan where the government has taken a major step towards peace by proposing a government of national unity with the Sudan People's Liberation Army, the rebel opposition. However, this long-running war of attrition has little relevance to international security on a global scale, and local conflicts generally, unless they occur in the oil-producing states of Eastern Europe, the Middle East and Africa, are unlikely to engage interventionist action by the US and its retinue of supporters or the UN Security Council.

A by-product of al-Qaeda's success in disseminating fear and discord in the West has been the absorption in terrorist-related areas of risk to the near exclusion of Western willingness to engage in other issues. The electorate of Georgia were fortunate in having a champion with strong US connections in their overthrow of an oppressive regime. No such good fortune attends the electorate of Zimbabwe, which can only cling to the supine sympathy of the Commonwealth.

How goes the war on terror?

It has become important to define more clearly the battleground for the 'war on terror'. The strategy of 'incapacitation' applied to al-Qaeda, which began with the expulsion of the Taliban regime from Afghanistan, has achieved the capture or death of more than 3,000 operatives, according to US claims, and two-thirds of the senior leadership. It continues today with the disruption of terrorist cells across Europe and in previously less committed countries, notably Saudi Arabia where anti-terrorist action was the riposte to the targeting of Muslim allies. Preventative action against terrorist strikes now involves the public at large with the introduction of safety measures on airlines and their passengers entering the United States.

Nevertheless, categorizing conflicts founded on local issues as a part of the general war on terror is unhelpful to broader political understanding. Both the Chechen uprising within the Russian confederacy and the Palestine–Israel conflict are based on local or regional political issues, although both involve persistent acts of terrorism on the one side and oppression on the part of the dominant protagonist.

The unresolved security and sovereignty issues of Israel and Palestine remain the stumbling block to Middle East peace and to overarching political reconciliation between Muslim states and the West. So long as the United States is regarded as the 'bully on the block' and a supporter of intransigent Israeli leadership, it is unlikely that further significant progress can be made in the renunciation of WMD or the outlawing of Osama bin Laden's philosophy and the works of al-Qaeda. Unfortunately, the Middle East 'road map', once a beacon of hope, seems to be consigned to the glove compartment of President Bush's election-year limousine.

The US coalition won the war in Iraq but it remains uncertain that it will win the peace. The successful installation of a form of democratic government in both Afghanistan and Iraq is essential to long-term acceptance of non-authoritarian government as a standard throughout the region. In Afghanistan, approval of the new constitution by the US-installed assembly (*loya jirga*) is good news although enforcement will be a difficult process, starting with elections for president in 2004 and parliament in 2005. In Iraq, under pressure from Grand Ayatollah Ali Sistani, the country's foremost Shia religious authority, the United States modified its plans to select a national assembly through a process of regional caucuses, which has made it less likely that sovereignty can be handed over to a transitional administration appointed by the assembly by 30 June 2004 . The invitation to examine whether elections are feasible or find room for compromise gives the UN its first significant role in post-war Iraq and could restore its credibility.

Therefore, President Bush can reasonably claim a degree of success in the war on terror through progress in reducing the risks from the deployment of WMD by 'rogue' states. Major obstacles remain to the completion of this task, which will probably not be hurdled in 2004–05.

Is the world a safer place than it was a year ago?

It is impossible for ordinary citizens to judge how well Western intelligence has penetrated al-Qaeda communications, although the growing frequency of security alerts implies success. Certainly, up to now, the terrorist network has been driven to repeated attacks on civilians in 'soft' target countries such as Kenya, Morocco and Turkey. On balance, international security has improved and the risks may be reduced. However, Secretary of State Colin Powell's dictum that, in the last analysis, the United States may be relied upon to pursue its self-interest seems rather less reassuring than it did.

■ THE WORLD ECONOMY IN 2004–05

The economic outlook for each of the regions is reviewed thoroughly by Oxford Analytica in the regional overviews that follow, as are the economies of individual countries by Coface analysts. It is common ground that the recovery that took hold in the United States in early 2003 producing GDP growth in the fourth quarter of 8.2 per cent over quarter 3 will continue through 2004 and 2005 and has played an important role in pulling the OECD countries generally out of stagnation. The current OECD growth forecast for the United States of 4.2 per cent for 2004 compares with 2.9 per cent achieved in 2003 and far exceeds forecasters' expectations for the euro zone of less than 2.0 per cent and much the same for Japan. The UK may do rather better with GDP growth of around 2.8 per cent.

The OECD also takes an uncharacteristically optimistic view of the recovery's sustainability with GDP growth for all OECD countries of 3.1 per cent in 2005 (2004: 3.0 per cent), only a slight slowdown in the United States to 3.8 per cent and further improvement in the euro area to 2.5 per cent. Under this scenario, inflation continues to present no problem, falling slightly to 1.4 per cent in both 2004 and 2005 from 1.8 per cent in 2003.

The US recovery

However, the US recovery has been driven by an expansionary policy since 2002, which has encouraged both the public sector budget deficit and the trade deficit to rise to the level of 5.0 per cent with the former forecast to increase further to perhaps 5.3 per cent during 2004. In absolute terms, the trade deficit for the 12 months ended November 2003 was almost US$550 billion against a Japanese surplus of US$102 billion and a euro zone surplus of US$86 billion. This profligacy, which is unlikely to be addressed before the November 2004 presidential election, is unsustainable in the long term and makes the US economy vulnerable to external events. Unlike the late 1990s when the current account deficit was funded largely by private capital, the present US deficit is supported by flows from the foreign exchange reserves of China, Japan and other Asian countries.

The US recovery appears relatively robust although job growth has been slower than in most previous upturns. Unemployment fell from 5.9 per cent in November to 5.7 per cent in December 2003 but only 1,000 new jobs were created against the 150,000 expected by forecasters. More encouragingly, the merchandise trade deficit narrowed unexpectedly in November to US$44 billion, the lowest level in over a year, with the weakening dollar helping to stimulate exports and dampen imports. Against the 2003 experience of the EU and Japan, foreign direct investment (FDI) into the United States almost trebled to US$86.6 billion although still well below the 2001 peak of US$144 billion.

The fall in the dollar continues to be a double-edged sword, benefiting the United States but posing problems for Europe. It fell 17 per cent against the euro in 2003 and continued its downward path until 12 January when the euro peaked at almost US$1.29. In the week that followed, the European Central Bank (ECB) succeeded in talking the euro down to a more modest US$1.235 but the relief will be no more than temporary and ECB intervention in the currency markets is widely expected in the coming months. The United States itself is highly unlikely to take corrective action, not just because the low dollar helps to reduce the current account deficit but also because it addresses the concerns of farmers, steelmakers and others claiming support from the administration against lower-priced imports. The lower dollar exchange rate was certainly a factor in President Bush's eleventh-hour decision to call off its breach of WTO commitments in respect of steel. Nor can the US proposal to fellow WTO members this January to revive the stalled round of Doha negotiations – one of the international community's conspicuous failures in 2003 – by focusing on the issue of agricultural export subsidies be unconnected.

The European upturn

The former chief economist of the International Monetary Fund (IMF), Ken Rogoff, anticipates a further rise in the euro to US$1.40 and stated in mid-January that the euro at US$1.50 or even US$1.60 is not impossible. At that level the nascent recovery of European economies, particularly that of Germany whose GDP fell 0.1 per cent in 2003,

could be seriously damaged by the friendly fire of the falling dollar. Similarly, a rise in sterling past the US$2 mark might sabotage the relatively bullish outlook for the UK economy where storm clouds are gathering in the form of deteriorating terms of trade and a growing budget deficit.

In abandoning the Maastricht stability pact with the complicity of fellow members, both France and Germany have given themselves some freedom to pursue more aggressive economic policies. However, as members of the euro zone their monetary policy is in the hands of the ECB and they are unable to act with the same expansionary abandon as the United States.

Global FDI remained flat in 2003 at US$653 billion, only just above the 2002 level and less than half the record US$1.4 trillion registered in 2001. FDI into the EU declined from US$374 billion in 2002 to US$342 billion in 2003 with particularly large falls in France and Germany. Ireland was the only EU member to experience an increase, with its FDI inflows more than doubling to almost US$42 billion. However, the United Nations Conference on Trade and Development (UNCTAD), whose statistics are quoted, expects faster economic growth in 2004, particularly in the automotive, electronics and services sectors.

The more encouraging outlook for foreign investment in the EU, both FDI and portfolio investment, is also vulnerable to the higher euro- and sterling-to-dollar exchange rates. Investors will need to be convinced both that their asset values will be sustained and that the exports from foreign-financed manufacturing and service operations will be competitive.

China's banquet

The significant impact of China's economy on the world economy can no longer be denied. Indeed, the contentious 'coupling' effect of the US economic cycle on the European cycle finds echoes in the connection of the US economy to China's foreign trade and the deployment of its currency reserves. The problem for the United States lies in the pegging of China's remnimbi to the US dollar at a rate that is generally considered to overvalue the Chinese currency. So long as this link persists there is no relief for the United States in the competitiveness of Chinese imports as the dollar decreases in value, and the impact of cheap Chinese exports on to the euro zone and other countries whose currencies appreciate is aggravated.

The growth of the Chinese economy remains robust with GDP growth at 8 per cent or above since 2002 and expected to continue at that level through to 2005. Its public sector deficit is maintained below 3 per cent and the current account balance is being managed to decline gently towards US$25 billion. Although the US failure to close the massive gap between its imports from China and its exports to China (estimated at US$125 billion for 2003) causes continuing criticism of the pegged exchange rate and conflict between the administrations, China has continued to deposit a high proportion of its US$400 billion currency reserves in dollar securities, making a major contribution towards the US current account deficit.

There is no prospect of China revaluing its currency in 2004 and little likelihood of a realignment in 2005. Allowing the remnimbi to trade freely would imperil China's big four state banks and risk undermining sovereign creditworthiness. However, the Chinese government is in the process of restructuring its banks and grooming the first two, China Construction Bank and Bank of China, for flotation from 2005 and has injected US$45 billion of its currency reserves in long-term capital to offset the balance sheet effects of their non-performing loans. Reassuringly, the funds were promptly reinvested in US securities. The downside of removing the dollar peg in the future is that less of China's foreign currency reserves may be invested in dollar securities.

The effects of China's growing share of world trade are not confined to the United States and Europe. The engine of industrial expansion demands fuelling in raw materials, in particular coal and mineral base metals, and the shift from an agricultural to an industrial community has generated demand for food basics such as soya bean. Imports of these commodities from Brazil and Argentina is already having a beneficial effect on their economies but elsewhere, as in Mexico, manufactured goods such as clothing and textiles

have lost competitiveness to China in the North American market. These trends will continue to affect world trade for the foreseeable future.

■ EUROPEAN ENLARGEMENT

The formal entry of the EU's 10 new members on 1 May 2004 was meant to be cause for celebration throughout the Community. The one-step enlargement remains a major achievement giving all the countries involved the opportunity through peaceful means to maintain a permanent political and economic union in which democratic rights are respected and the principles of a common market economy prevail. However, the warm glow that the successful conclusion of final negotiations in December 2002 generated has faded somewhat in the dimmer light of less satisfying developments.

First, the sluggish economic performance of the present EU's largest economies throughout 2003 and the outlook for less-than-dynamic euro zone growth through 2005 compare unfavourably with the United States, South-east Asia and most of the new member states. Indeed, study of the comparison gives a quite new meaning to the concept of a two-speed European Community.

Second, the abandonment of the Maastricht budget deficit criterion for euro zone membership, although entirely justifiable in relation to the realities of the French and German economies, has removed the imperative that new member states had accepted to achieve the compliance of their debt ratios for euro zone entry themselves.

The four larger Central European states are all forecast to continue exceeding the 3 per cent Maastricht criterion in 2004. The peevish reaction of Brussels bureaucrats towards the Council of Ministers, which sanctioned France's and Germany's default, has done nothing to foster good relations within the EC itself. Understandably, the governments of the Central European states now joining are refocusing on the growth and expansion of their economies rather than the early euro zone to which they had previously committed. The sense of urgency that they might have felt in completing the harmonization of their tax and accountancy regimes with EC directives may also have been blunted.

Third, the breakdown in the debate to approve the draft EU constitution may have broken the mould of how EU disagreements are habitually resolved through compromise. The new Irish presidency has expressed quiet confidence that it can achieve member state consensus on the constitution during its term of office, but there is no reason to think that any change of position on the voting rights issue is likely among the more intransigent protagonists. If some kind of compromise or interim solution is achieved in 2004 it will probably lack the elegant congruity of Mr Giscard d'Estaing's revised draft.

Finally, discussion on the next EU budget, its allocation and members' contributions is due to begin soon. A degree of generosity towards entry states is expected, but the flaccid economic condition of the larger economies among the established membership will make generosity politically difficult. By the end of another protracted negotiation process, the new members may be reflecting on their entry experience in the light of the adage that it is sometimes 'better to travel in hope than arrive'.

The @rating System

In 2000, Coface introduced the first worldwide insurable company rating scheme. The @rating system assesses the ability of a company to meet its short-term business obligations vis-à-vis customers and suppliers. International businesses can now log on to www.cofacerating.com or any of the national websites (eg www.cofacerating.fr) and access the three following rating systems.

@rating credit opinion indicates the recommended credit exposure for a company using a very simple assessment scale (1 @ = €20,000, 2 @ = €50,000, 3 @ = €100,000, etc). Credit exposure arising from BtoB credit transactions is insurable by Coface. An @rating credit opinion is assigned to some 44 million companies worldwide (including French firms), reflecting Coface's dual expertise in corporate information and credit insurance.

@rating score, which was launched in October 2002 by Coface and Coface Scrl, measures a company's default risk over one year. It comprehensively and accurately rates 4.5 million large, medium and small-sized French companies. @rating score is used not only by different-sized companies but also by financial institutions looking to develop a rating system that complies with new banking regulations (McDonough ratio). Measuring credit risk among companies is an important exercise when addressing not only traditional needs (bank loans to firms, BtoB credit and market credit) but also emerging needs created by new instruments such as loan securitizations and new banking solvency regulations (McDonough ratio). While scepticism over accounting practices persists, companies and banks have an even greater need for reliable tools to benefit from the recovery while keeping risks under control.

Country @rating, another of Coface's key achievements, allows people and businesses engaged in international trade to strengthen the security of their transactions. It continuously tracks a series of indicators for 144 countries, evaluating political factors, the risk of currency shortage, the ability of a government to meet its international obligations, the risk of devaluation following massive capital withdrawals, the risk of a systemic crisis in the banking sector and payment behaviour for short-term transactions. An aggregate rating is assigned to each of the 144 countries monitored on the basis of seven risk categories. As in the approach used by rating agencies, there are seven different rating grades from A1 to A4 for investment-grade risks and B, C, D for 'speculative' risks. This classification is used for each of the countries covered by this guide.

Country @rating Definition

Economic liberalization has led to a boom in BtoB trade, with 70 per cent of accounts being settled by short-term instruments. It is therefore vital to assess the risk associated with such transactions. Country @rating addresses this need by evaluating the extent to which a firm's financial commitments in a given country are influenced by that country's economic, financial and political prospects. Log on to cofacerating.com to access country @rating, the supplement to company @rating.

A1 The highly stable political and economic situation has a favourable effect on corporate payment behaviour, which is generally good. The likelihood of default is very low.

A2 The likelihood of default is low, even if the country's economic and political environment or corporate payment behaviour is somewhat shakier than in countries rated A1.

A3 Payment behaviour in these countries – generally less satisfactory than in A1 and A2 countries – could be affected by shifts in the economic and political climate, although defaults remain unlikely.

A4 Payment behaviour is often rather mediocre and could be affected by an economic downturn or deteriorating political climate, although the risk of default remains acceptable.

B The uncertain economic and political environment is likely to affect corporate payment behaviour, which is often mediocre.

C The highly uncertain economic and political environment could worsen the payment behaviour of companies that already often have a bad track record.

D The economic and political environment represents a very high risk that could worsen corporate payment behaviour, which is generally deplorable.

Sectoral Overview

Sylvia Greisman and Dominique Fruchter
Coface Country Risk and Economic Studies Department, Paris

Sectoral activity has been slowly improving in a more favourable macroeconomic environment. Although some sectors like new information and communication technology have been contributing to the recovery registered in the United States and Asia, others have been struggling to emerge from the cyclical downturns gripping them.

Moreover, regional disparities in production costs and the very uneven strength of demand have been accelerating the delocalization process. Like the macroeconomic environment, sectoral business conditions have been exhibiting marked disparities between emerging Asia, where performance has been remarkable in most sectors, and the rest of the world. As such, improvement in company profitability in many sectors has often been the result of restructuring and delocalization rather than a firm world demand recovery.

1. Electronics and, to a lesser extent, the computer and telecommunications sectors have been enjoying a recovery buoyed by innovation and equipment renewal after several slump years. The outlook is still bright.

World economic conditions in the **electronics** sector have been improving rapidly, due notably to its Asian component. World electronic component sales grew markedly in 2003, gaining about 14 per cent. The upward phase will continue in 2004. Consumer electronics demand, representing one-fifth of the total market, has been benefiting from the revolution involving digitization of all applications: video cameras, still cameras, flat-screen television and DVD. Demand from the telecommunications (one-fifth of sales) and computer sectors (nearly half the market) has not been outdone, thanks to the strong recovery of mobile telephony handset sales and upturn of computer deliveries. Sales growth has nonetheless been weaker than that registered during the last upward phase. Furthermore, the improvement has been much more pronounced in the Asia-Pacific region than in the United States, Europe or Japan, due to increasing delocalization towards Asia and the concentration of consumer product manufacturers in that region.

The **computer** sector has been recovering progressively although with sharp disparities by segment and by region. The **personal computer** segment has thus made significant progress towards recovery. In 2003, world sales rose by 12 per cent in volume, accelerating in the last months of the year. That growth notably benefited from robust demand from households and public institutions, spurred by the Internet's development, whereas company demand has been lagging behind. The craze for portables has also been a major positive factor, with office computer sales remaining relatively sluggish. Peripherals like multifunction printers and flat screens have also been trending up. Deliveries have been increasing much faster in the Asia-Pacific region than in Europe, the United States or Japan. Sales should continue to grow in 2004, still buoyed by tax incentives in the United States and the continued fall of prices, amplified in Europe by the dollar's sharp decline. However, in conjunction with this favourable environment,

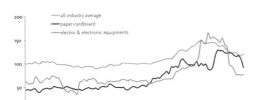

PAYMENT INCIDENTS INDEX
(12 months moving average - base 100 : World 1995)

players in the sector have been contending with shrinking margins, squeezed between the continued decline of sales prices and increased component prices. In the **applications and IT services** segment, the upturn has been slower, gaining 2 per cent in 2003, based on sharp growth in computer-site security, facilities management and applications maintenance but a decline in consulting, development and technical assistance.

In **telecommunications**, progressive improvement in the financial situation of the sector's various players has resulted partly from a mobile telephone sales recovery but particularly from restructuring efforts by both operators and equipment manufacturers. **European telecommunication-service operators** have substantially improved their situation by recentring their business in geographic and core-business terms, selling off assets, restructuring debt, cutting back drastically on investments and focusing more on profitability than just on gaining market share. They have generally been running large cash surpluses permitting them to reduce debt despite fixed telephony's decline and mobile telephony's more moderate growth. Development of high-bandwidth Internet access has been providing them with additional revenues. **North American operators** have had to contend with the moderate growth of traffic in a more competitive market. Long-distance operators and local-alternative operators, Bell companies or even cable operators have been competing for markets. The prospective development of Internet telephony will only sharpen the competition. In Asia, **mobile telephone operators**, benefiting from rapidly growing markets and higher revenues per subscriber due to the popularization of third-

generation services, have been sustaining good profitability.

After three years of sharply declining business, **telecommunication infrastructure manufacturers** should finally achieve stabilization or at worst drop slightly in 2004. Much restructuring has taken place, often accompanied by delocalizations to South-east Asia, which has permitted manufacturers to lower the profitability threshold and restore their cash positions despite severe price pressure. Recovery will nonetheless remain unlikely before 2005. Mobile telephony equipment should then benefit from an investment upturn in connection with the launch of new services and progressive introduction of 3G networks. Fixed telephony infrastructures will benefit from expansion of broadband Internet access (ADSL). An upturn will come later for the optical fibre segment, due to continued overcapacity in the United States and in underwater cables, and for specialized transmission and connection equipment for local networks.

World **mobile handset** sales have been recovering (up 15 per cent in 2003) buoyed by replacement purchases in mature markets linked to development of new functionalities (like imaging, the Internet or games) and by mobile telephony's booming development in China, India and Central and East Europe. However, the increased volumes have not produced entirely comparable gains in value terms due to the growing share of emerging markets where demand has been focusing mainly on bottom-of-range models. Large traditional European and US manufacturers have been contending with fierce competition in that market segment from Chinese manufacturers and for sophisticated handsets from Japanese and Korean manufacturers, where the domestic markets have been fond of that type of product for a longer time.

2. Although pharmaceuticals and mass distribution have continued to benefit from generally strong demand, price constraints have been increasing. Despite the presence of major international players, competition has been fierce with sharp regional disparities.

The major **pharmaceuticals** markets have continued to trend up. Although two-digit growth

PAYMENT INCIDENTS INDEX
(12 months moving average - base 100 : World 1995)

— all-industry average
— pharmaceuticals, perfumery
— food

is no longer feasible, growth has remained robust. However, the general price level has been increasing very little due to pressure from bodies responsible for reimbursing medical costs, generics and parallel imports. That pressure has been affecting industrial margins. Supplying drugs to emerging countries at realistic prices, acceptable to all concerned, and growing competition from countries like India also constitute challenges.

Although sales growth has slowed markedly in the **United States**, which represents half the world market, it nonetheless reached an estimated 9 per cent in 2003. New drug launches have been less frequent and expirations of patents on very profitable products more numerous. The importance acquired by generics (40 per cent of prescriptions) could affect the sector. On that score, the recent authorization of drugs re-imports from Canada and other industrialized countries could contribute to accelerating the price decline.

In **West Europe**, which represents a quarter of the market, sales rose about 5 per cent in 2003 but with large geographic disparities. While growth reached about 9 per cent in Spain, the United Kingdom and Germany, it was flat in Italy and France due to price reductions and changes in reimbursement terms imposed by public health insurance officials.

In **Japan**, sales virtually stabilized, notably due to price reductions imposed by public authorities and changes in reimbursement terms. The market has remained extremely fragmented and thus coveted by large Western laboratories.

In **Latin America**, the market has continued to sag in Brazil and Argentina while growing in Mexico. That situation should persist in coming months.

The existence of international giants has not prevented **mass distribution** from being subject to fierce competition and sharp regional disparities linked to household spending.

In the **United States**, strengthening consumer confidence and the expected decline in unemployment have created a favourable environment. Business has been improving in almost every retail segment. In general, however, all have been contending to various degrees with competition from Wal-Mart, which now operates a wide range of sales outlets and has been gaining market share in many segments like food, clothing, household appliances and consumer electronics.

In **Japan**, sluggish consumer spending has persisted. Department stores have been hampered by their insufficient number of points of sale and the insufficient profitability of sales of food, furniture and household appliances, which nonetheless still represent a substantial portion of their turnover. Specialized chains and neighbourhood stores seem much better positioned.

In **West Europe**, retail trade has also been suffering from sluggish household spending. Underlying this overall assessment, the trends have varied widely by country, type of merchandise and point-of-sale format. Although faring well in general, food retailing has been subject to growing pressure from hard discount. Megastore business has tended to drop in favour of supermarkets and mini-markets. The consequences of that competition have nonetheless been limited since, in many countries, the same players control all sales formats. Owing to fierce competition in Germany and the Netherlands, the situation in those countries has appeared much shakier than in France or the United Kingdom where the limited number of players and the regulations on installing sales outlets have somewhat frozen market positions.

Despite economic 'accidents', emerging markets (Argentina, Brazil, Poland) have remained very attractive to large European and North American groups, which have been competing for shares of those markets. However, the difficult context has been compelling foreign players to squeeze prices and develop hard discount. They also have to

PAYMENT INCIDENTS INDEX
(12 months moving average - base 100 : World 1995)

— all-industry average
— chemicals
— mechanical equipment

2004, buoyed by a world industrial investment upturn. Machine tools and equipment linked to automation and energy production will be the main beneficiaries. Only farm machinery should continue to suffer due to consequences of the 2003 summer heat wave and despite sales growth in Central and East Europe. The euro's appreciation against the dollar will not impede export growth, due to the technical nature of the products. Increased sales volumes should offset the consequences of tighter export margins.

In the **United States**, the sector's profitability remained poor in 2003 due to increased costs (energy, raw materials, labour), which it could not pass on to customers due to the sluggishness of demand for most of the year. The acceleration of activity that developed in the second half only had limited positive effects with production capacities still far from saturation and the wait-and-see attitude of decision makers. The situation should improve markedly in 2004 due not only to the combined effects of the world recovery and dollar depreciation but also to an investment upturn that will notably benefit equipment intended for mining, hydrocarbon exploration and exploitation, and semi-conductor manufacturing. The civil engineering sector's steadiness will continue to buoy heavy construction equipment.

In **Japan**, the sector's activity trended strongly up in 2003, fuelled both by robust sales to regional countries, particularly China, and by recovery of sales to exporting companies. The outlook for 2004 is not quite as bright due to an investment slowdown. The yen appreciation should have little impact on exports even though it may slightly affect unit margins.

Economic conditions in the **chemicals** sector have been progressively improving since the 2003 second half. Robust activity in Asia and the United States will particularly buoy the continued improvement expected in 2004.

In **West Europe**, there was hardly any growth in 2003. User sectors like household appliances, civil engineering and the car industry have been flat. Although the euro appreciation and development of petrochemical production capacity in the Middle East and Asia have been hampering exports, large

search for lower-cost suppliers locally to meet the competition of small domestic chains and circumvent the impact of local-currency devaluations. The increase in purchasing power has prompted market players to broaden their product lines beyond food and move outside large urban centres. Those markets have remained relatively accessible except in **Asia** where public authorities often give preference to national groups.

3. Mechanical engineering, chemicals and paper should benefit from the investment upturn and increasingly dynamic world demand.

The **mechanical engineering** sector has finally begun breaking out of its slump even if the situation has varied by region. While Japanese mechanical engineering has been benefiting from the robust Asian context, the other regions have barely emerged from the downturn. Considering the wariness of companies and the 6- to 12-month lag between orders and deliveries, 2004 should be a transition year. A fully fledged recovery will be unlikely to develop before 2005.

In **West Europe**, the situation remained difficult in 2003, notably due to low domestic investment. Reduced volumes and increased production costs have resulted in a further decline in profitability. Machine tools (affected by the sluggish transportation industry), printing equipment, farm machinery, pumps and compressors particularly suffered. Only heavy civil engineering equipment, food-industry equipment and textiles machinery, due to sales in Asia, achieved good performance. The improvement that developed in late 2003 should intensify in

European groups have not been losing market share, thanks to the factories they operate in the various world regions. The sector's players have also been contending with high hydrocarbon prices, which they have been unable to pass on entirely to customers due to demand sluggishness. That situation has been squeezing margins, with all segments, including fine and specialized chemicals, affected. Only industrial gases, phenol and acrylics have registered satisfactory results. In 2004, growth should accelerate slightly (up 2 per cent), thanks notably to an export upturn, with robust demand from Asia and the United States likely to offset partly the negative impact of unfavourable exchange rates. Profitability should also improve provided hydrocarbon prices ease. However, adoption of REACH, the European chemicals directive proposal intended to increase awareness of the environmental impact of substances, could ultimately generate cost increases.

In the **United States**, growth has been slightly stronger than in Europe amid more robust regional demand. Moreover, the dollar's sharp decline has eased competition from European imports. Even more than in Europe, however, due to the proportion of gas in their purchasing, industrialists have had to contend with high energy prices, which they have been unable to pass on entirely to customers due to the relative sluggishness of demand. The continued acceleration of growth in 2004 should produce a marked improvement in the sector, whose production should gain 4 per cent.

The **Asian market**'s growth has been benefiting from the explosion of demand from China, which has been a windfall for the chemical industry not only in the region but also in the Middle East. Western groups have been benefiting indirectly from that situation via facilities they operate in the region. The coming start-up of new petrochemical production units in China will not cover all the needs and will thus not eliminate all the opportunities. However, the greater quantities available on the Chinese market could put some pressure on prices. Meanwhile, the **Japanese market** should remain slack, as should Japanese exports, due to increasing delocalizations.

The improvement in conditions in the **paper** sector developed during the 2003 second half and only concerned the North American and Asian markets with the European market remaining in a cyclical downturn. The recovery should firm up in 2004 provided general economic activity continues to accelerate.

In **Europe**, paper prices stabilized at a low level reflecting the sluggish economic activity in 2003. The slight improvement in the confidence of companies and their order books towards year-end rested mainly on exports. The situation has remained difficult for paper intended for commercial printing, advertising, catalogues and office use as well as for packaging materials. Buoyed by accelerated growth in 2004, the recovery will be very progressive. However, the euro appreciation and the continued presence of overcapacity in art paper will affect price levels and thus margins.

In the **United States**, in conjunction with the economic upturn, the papermaking situation improved during the last months of 2003, notably via sharply higher demand for packaging and newsprint buoyed by an advertising upturn. Low stock levels and the control over production capacity resulting from the broad process of concentration carried out in recent years have contributed to price increases for those products. A favourable macroeconomic outlook and the dollar's sharp decline augur continuation of that upward trend in 2004. **Canadian** producers have been in a more perilous situation with the Canadian dollar's appreciation against the US dollar reducing accordingly the value of sales to their neighbour. Moreover, their lumbering activities have been suffering from compensatory duties imposed by the United States on imports of wood and derivatives from Canada.

In **Asia**, the explosion of Chinese demand, which domestically developed capacity has been unable to satisfy, has been driving the market. The region's papermaking industries have been benefiting from that imbalance and from ready raw material supplies. That has been notably true for **Japanese papermakers**, which, moreover, have been unable to count either on domestic demand dynamism or, amid growing pressure from imports, on price increases.

PAYMENT INCIDENTS INDEX
(12 months moving average - base 100 : World 1995)

In **Latin America**, Brazilian and Chilean pulp exporters have been benefiting from competitiveness enhanced by favourable exchange rates and low-cost raw materials. Their situation should further improve with the continuing rise of world prices and growing Asian needs. Conversely, papermakers focusing on the regional market and particularly those not integrating pulp production have been suffering from still-sagging local demand and rising pulp prices billed to them in dollars.

4. The car industry has been contending with flagging demand in many regions, a trend that should persist in 2004. The construction sector, almost overheating in some markets, should also suffer a slowdown after several years of robust growth.

The stabilization or even decline of **automobile** registrations in most Western markets has contrasted with continued robust demand in Asia. Despite very progressive improvement expected in industrialized countries in 2004 and the dollar's depreciation, the sector's industrialists in the United States will still have to cope with strong pressure on margins.

Although remaining at high levels, passenger car sales have continued to dwindle in the **United States**, down 1.2 per cent in 2003 despite tax incentives and promotional offers. Market share for the three major domestic manufacturers fell below the 60 per cent threshold under the pressure of Asian competition, which now extends to the sector's very profitable pick-up and truck segments. They have been less profitable than the competition due to commercial discounts, lower productivity linked to the age of their facilities,

overstaffing and pension fund commitments. The sales recovery expected in 2004 (up 2 per cent), linked to improvement in the employment situation and rental company purchases, may not suffice to restore their profitability. Parts manufacturers have suffered indirectly from their clients' shrinking margins even though elimination of customs surtaxes and quotas on their steel imports should reduce the cost of their purchases. A utility-vehicle sales recovery (up 9 per cent) should also develop due to the ageing of vehicles in circulation, clarification of the new environmental standards, and especially the economic recovery.

In **West Europe**, the decline of passenger car sales (down 1.2 per cent) has particularly affected the French, Belgian and Dutch markets, which suffered a sharp decline, while the United Kingdom, Germany and Italy registered virtual stability and Spain posted growth. Like their US counterparts, and despite the production stoppages marking the second half, European manufacturers had to begin offering discounts, which affected their nonetheless generally satisfactory profitability. Similarly, European carmakers have been facing increasing competition from Asian manufacturers, who alone enjoyed strong sales growth. European carmakers will continue to come up against competition with the euro appreciation squeezing their margins.

In **Latin America**, subsidiaries of the world's major manufacturers have continued to suffer from the Brazilian market's failure to recover (down 10 per cent in 2003 after shedding 7 per cent in 2002). Except for Fiat, whose vehicles have a very high local integration rate, carmakers have been contending with losses attributable to the increased cost of imported parts caused by the devaluations. Although certainly suffering from the decline of both production and the parts/accessories market, local parts-makers should ultimately benefit from the increasing integration of local production. The only positive element in 2003 was the Argentine market's strong recovery, gaining 40 per cent although from a very low starting point, essentially concentrated on low-priced vehicles. In 2004, those two markets could gain about 10 per cent.

In **Asia**, the main sales drivers have been the booming Chinese and Indian markets. Amid the strong development potential linked to high growth and the emergence of middle classes, foreign manufacturers have been forging ahead, generally in joint ventures with local players, creating very real risks of overcapacity emerging to meet solvent demand. Although the **Japanese market** has remained stable, local manufacturers have been benefiting from their excellent export performance and the robust activity of their factories abroad.

Influenced by the economic environment and the level of interest rates, the **construction** sector's activity is also very dependent on specific local factors and thus tends to vary widely by region.

In **West Europe**, although activity stagnated in 2003, it should grow slightly in 2004, notably in the civil engineering segment. In the non-residential construction segment, office property could decline again due to sluggish investment by companies, the decline in rental levels and extent of vacancies, whereas commercial construction should fare better. Residential construction, representing about half of total investments, should continue to trend up provided unemployment remains under control and interest rates remain low. That situation nonetheless obscures disparities, the dynamism of Greece, Spain and Italy contrasting with decline in Portugal and the Netherlands and tentative recovery in Germany where the sector's players have remained weak.

In **North America**, the sector grew 2 per cent in 2003 with a sharp decline in civil engineering and a new upsurge in the residential segment. The situation should stabilize in 2004. A non-residential recovery, essentially commercial and office space, will offset a progressive slowdown in residential construction resulting from saturation of needs, high price levels and increased long-term interest rates.

In **Japan**, the sector will continue to decline (down 3 per cent in 2004 after shedding 4 per cent in 2003). Burdened by heavy debt, public institutions have been reducing their investments. Meanwhile, the private-housing construction situation has stabilized albeit at a low level. The renovation segment has even been growing. Facing a slack domestic market, some actors have been developing business abroad benefiting from the construction boom in other **Asian countries**, notably China.

With regard to other emerging regions, the situation is likely to remain bleak in **South America**, although it should improve in **Central and East Europe**. Activity in that region stabilized in 2003 after declining since 2001, due to the recessive Polish market, and should progress in 2004.

5. Above all, steel, textiles and clothing have had to contend with the increasing success of emerging countries, with price pressure prompting extensive restructuring. Here again, Asia's dynamism has contrasted with performance in the rest of the world.

To meet increased Asian demand, world **steel** production registered sharp growth in 2003, gaining an estimated 7 per cent. Prices and profits rose. Although that trend will persist in 2004, it will incorporate substantial regional disparities.

In **Asia**, production grew strongly, gaining an estimated 13 per cent in 2003, in response to robust local demand. The Chinese market, where user sectors (construction, mechanical engineering, automobile) have been experiencing a remarkable boom, has been notably buoying the regional steel industry. Local prices have thus remained very high. The inadequacy of China's domestic supply despite rapid development of production capacity has greatly benefited Japanese, Korean and Taiwanese steelmakers.

In **North America**, production stagnated in 2003, with local demand only growing weakly. The protectionist customs barriers introduced in March 2002 have nonetheless facilitated the price increases necessitated to meet higher production costs. They also coincided with restructuring programmes intended to make the sector more concentrated and reduce payroll costs by cutting staff and transferring pension commitments to the federal government. Discontinuation of those same measures in December 2003 should not alter the situation in coming months, with the dollar's sharp decline, the increasing cost of sea transport, strong Chinese demand, and continued anti-dumping duties continuing to deter imports and support prices. A return to satisfactory profitability for

PAYMENT INCIDENTS INDEX
(12 months moving average - base 100 : World 1995)

— all-industry average — yarn
— textile fiber — fabrics
— clothing

integrated steelmakers will depend largely on continued restructuring.

In **West Europe**, production has been stable due to essentially sluggish demand. User sectors (automobile, household appliances, tubes, non-residential construction) have lacked dynamism. However, thanks to good control over the steel supply and strong Asian demand, price levels have remained satisfactory. The situation could nonetheless deteriorate if the dollar's sharp decline against the euro intensifies.

In **Central and East Europe**, production has markedly increased buoyed by growing domestic demand and development of exports. That robust market should nonetheless not obscure the inadequate productivity levels and the restructuring needed for many production units.

In **Latin America**, production has been growing strongly, particularly in Brazil, essentially in response to an export boom, buoyed by favourable exchange rates and low production costs. Benefiting from relatively high average world prices, local producers have been making comfortable profits permitting them to reduce their substantial debt burdens.

In industrialized countries, **textiles and clothing** have been contending with increasing competition from imports from low-production-cost countries, especially China. The end of the Agreement on Textiles and Clothing in January 2005 has been overhanging the industry, with common law then to apply to commercial matters in the industry.

In the **United States**, industrial activity in the sector has continued to decline whereas imports, notably from China, have continued to expand. Shutdowns, often due to bankruptcy, have been numerous. Difficulties previously concentrated on clothing-article production have tended to move upstream in the industry (spinning and weaving) with the increased imports from Asia often coming at the expense of products originating in Mexico and the Caribbean, which generally contain thread and fabric produced in the United States. In 2004, sales prices and profitability should improve in the sector amid robust consumer spending.

In **West Europe**, the situation has not been very different. However, since the difficulties began earlier in time, the delocalization process has progressed further. Here again, the downstream industry has not been suffering alone, with spinning and weaving now obliged to follow their customers and delocalize to new production sites. Moreover, the euro's appreciation against the dollar and Asian currencies, coupled with weak consumer spending, has been exacerbating competitive pressures. Italy and Spain, which had been faring relatively well, have been experiencing increasing difficulties.

The textile industry in many **emerging countries** should also suffer from the end of the Agreement on Textiles and Clothing. Although Turkey seems well prepared to withstand the competition, that is not the case for countries like Mexico, Morocco and Tunisia, which are moreover already faced with the increasing world market share of Chinese production.

Oxford Analytica

Our corporate goal: *to be the information industry standard for strategic analysis of geopolitical, macroeconomic and social developments.*

Founded in 1975, *Oxford Analytica* is an international consulting firm providing business and political leaders with timely analysis of worldwide political, economic and social developments.

Oxford Analytica acts as a bridge between the world of ideas and the world of enterprise. One of its major assets is an extensive international network that draws on the scholarship and expertise of over 1,000 senior members at Oxford University and other leading universities around the world, as well as think-tanks and institutes of international standing.

Clients of *Oxford Analytica* are able to integrate the judgements drawn from this unparalleled resource into their own decision-making process. Clients include multinational corporations, major banks, national governments and international institutions in more than 40 countries.

Global strategic analysis

© Oxford Analytica Ltd • 5 Alfred Street, Oxford OX1 4EH, United Kingdom
Tel: +44 (0)1865 261600 • Fax: +44 (0)1865 242018
• E-mail: oa@oxford-analytica.com • Website: www.oxan.com

Europe

1

The Economic Outlook for Europe in 2004

Experts from Oxford Analytica, Oxford

The low point in the economic cycle for the euro area would seem to have been reached in 2003, with indicators pointing to a steady improvement in economic output in 2004. However, recovery will remain modest. By contrast, the eight accession states' economies have proved resilient during the global slowdown, and growth in the region as a whole will accelerate in 2004, not least reflecting the economic recovery in Poland.

EURO AREA

The forecasts by leading European and international institutions are all predicting acceleration in the growth of real GDP in the euro area during 2004. The IMF expects growth of 1.9 per cent, the OECD and the European Commission 1.8 per cent, and Consensus Forecasts 1.7 per cent. This follows marked downward revisions of 2003 growth predictions:

- In autumn 2002, the IMF predicted growth of 2.3 per cent for 2003; the Fund suggests 0.5 per cent is now likely.
- Germany's major institutes are even less confident, estimating 0.4 per cent growth in 2003 (after forecasting 1.8 per cent in November 2002).

After the marked disparity between forecast and estimated outcome for 2003, there are clear reasons for suggesting that predictions for 2004 may be just as fragile.

■ Positive signs

Certainly, there are a number of positive signs:

- The results of the European Commission's Business and Consumer Survey have shown a slow but steady improvement over the last four months. November results show industrial confidence, consumer confidence, construction confidence and service sector confidence all pointing upwards, albeit from a low cyclical base. Only retail confidence had slipped back, with retail trade declining during the third quarter.
- Improvements in order books, in particular for export orders, were evident from both EU surveys and national surveys in Belgium, Denmark, France and Germany.
- After rises in industrial production in the third quarter of 2003, capacity utilization has also begun to rise in the euro area for the first time since the autumn of 2002.
- Unit wage costs have risen only marginally as a result of both modest wage settlements and improving levels of productivity.
- While the annual euro area inflation rate was 2.0 per cent in October (estimated at 2.2 per cent in November), the October industrial producer price index (up 0.9 per cent year on year) points towards the continuing price competitiveness of goods within the euro area. Furthermore, the rise in the euro exchange rate and the accompanying fall in import prices will put additional downward pressure on the

inflation rate. Above all, the fall in the price of crude oil, along with other dollar-denominated basic materials, will also enhance the competitiveness and profitability of euro area enterprises from the cost side. This could explain the clear rise in the price confidence indicator in the Commission's November Business and Consumer Survey.

- The framework conditions for corporate costs are also improved by the European Central Bank (ECB) setting relatively low refinancing rates for bank lending as well as by corporate cost relief through planned reductions in non-wage labour costs in core euro area economies, notably Germany.

■ Demand-side factors

Such positive supply-side factors have contributed to optimism about corresponding improvements on the demand side. These are in part indicated in slight but noticeable improvements in demand factors in the second half of 2003:

- Third-quarter GDP growth came out at 0.4 per cent quarter on quarter, accompanied by upward movements in the demand for investment goods within the euro area and for imported basic materials and semi-finished goods, mirroring the rise in production levels and capacity utilization. In turn, investment demand in the euro area is expected to reverse the negative trend (–2.6 per cent in 2002 and –1.3 per cent in 2003) and improve by some 1.9 per cent in 2004.
- Consumer demand is set to rise by a modest 1.4 per cent in 2003, but after very weak growth in 2002 (0.4 per cent). Forecasts for increased consumer spending show a further – albeit modest – rise to 1.6 per cent.
- The main vehicle for demand growth is euro area trade. The slump in export orders (and value) in the first half of 2003 was followed by a marked improvement in the third quarter, driven by corresponding improvements in demand from the United States and from the still-dynamic economies of Central and Eastern Europe. While the aggregate outcome for exports in 2003 will remain negative, forecasters have predicted strong growth of both exports (3.5 per cent) and imports (3.7 per cent) in 2004.

■ Grounds for caution

Notwithstanding the modest levels of growth predicted for 2004, there are significant grounds for expressing caution over the reliability of such outcomes:

- All the upward indicators are moving from an extremely low base. The Commission's confidence surveys are only just approaching the long-term average, having been stuck below that average for two full years. Likewise, capacity utilization levels in the euro area's manufacturing sector (81 per cent) are still below the long-term average for the period since 1991 (82 per cent). Apart from Spain, all euro area member states are a long way off their maximum historical levels. Some, like the Netherlands, Austria, Italy, Finland and Ireland, are languishing close to minimum historical levels.
- The strength of the recovery in the US economy has yet to be tested over the medium term, and there are doubts about its sustainability.
- One major forecast (Germany's six economics institutes) assumes a euro–dollar rate of no more than 1.15, as the basis for 1.7 per cent real GDP growth. However, given the size of the US current account deficit, the likely outcome could be higher. This would begin to have a severe effect on euro area exports to the United States and the wider dollar zone, which had boomed when the rate was below par. At the time of writing, levels had already reached 1.22. While euro area price competitiveness will in part be offset by the reduced cost of imported materials and semi-finished goods, appreciation beyond 1.15 will still reduce the attractiveness of euro area exports, but particularly if US growth falters and budgetary consolidation at state, corporate and household level sets in.

- The fragility of export performance as the vehicle for macroeconomic expansion in 2004 was demonstrated by figures released recently by Germany's national statistics office, indicating that exports in October 2003 fell by a seasonally adjusted 6.6 per cent from September and stood 1.2 per cent below October 2002 levels. A combination of normalized US demand levels and the appreciation of the euro are certainly responsible for this sudden reversal.
- There would seem to be few grounds to assume that supply conditions, much less demand factors, will improve to such a degree as to motivate euro area companies significantly to raise their levels of investment in either fixed or movable assets. At most, equipment purchases are likely to be driven by productivity considerations, rather than by the desire to extend capacity.
- The states of the euro area remain fixed on budgetary consolidation, particularly those with budget deficits above 3 per cent. Lower-than-predicted growth, as in 2003, together with lower-than-predicted revenue, will increase the pressure on states to pursue further austerity measures, in part weakening recovery on the demand side. Most market analysts remain sanguine about the breaches of the Stability and Growth Pact and there are no indications of any significant capital flight nor of reduced market confidence in euro-denominated securities. Rather, the problem remains the funding of the US current account deficit by capital imports as the dollar slides.

ACCESSION COUNTRIES

The IMF's *World Economic Outlook*, released in September 2003, forecasts real GDP growth of 4.1 per cent in the EU candidate states, excluding Turkey, in 2004 – over twice the rate projected for the 12-member euro area. While the region's projected average rate of inflation (4.8 per cent) and current account deficit (4.5 per cent of GDP) remain well above EU levels, macroeconomic trends in the region on the eve of accession are generally favourable.

Indeed, the IMF's projections may appear rather downbeat in light of generally strong third-quarter 2003 growth figures. However, country-specific obstacles, combined with a still-poor outlook for the euro area economy, mean that their caution appears justified.

Real GDP growth

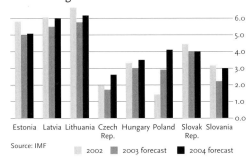

Estonia Latvia Lithuania Czech Hungary Poland Slovak Slovania
Rep. Rep.

Source: IMF   2002   2003 forecast   2004 forecast

1. Czech Republic

The IMF projects a 2004 GDP growth rate of 2.6 per cent, the lowest of the eight Central European and Baltic (CEB) accession states. Recently released results, showing growth accelerating to 3.4 per cent in the third quarter, and second-quarter figures revised up to 2.4 per cent from 2.1 per cent, provide grounds for a modest upward revision of this forecast. However, the growth trajectory remains weak, reflecting:

- a cautious economic reform strategy, particularly in public utility and infrastructure privatization;
- cuts in government expenditure to reduce the budget deficit, which at 6.7 per cent of GDP in 2002 is one of the largest in the region; and
- sluggish exports to the euro area, which account for 30 per cent of GDP.

The primary bright spot in the Czech economy is foreign direct investment (FDI). Owing to a series of lump-sum multinational investments, the country has overtaken Hungary as Eastern Europe's leader in FDI per capita (nearly US$3,000) and approaches Poland in FDI stock (US$38.5 billion), despite its much smaller population. This surge has created an installed foreign investment base of original equipment manufacturers (OEMs) and supplier firms, promising sequential investments.

These will position the Czech Republic as one of Europe's leading sites for advanced manufacturing and bode well for the country's medium- and long-term growth path.

2. Hungary

At 3.5 per cent, Hungary's projected GDP growth rate in 2004 represents only a modest improvement over the country's growth performance in 2003 (an expected 3.0 per cent) and 2002 (3.3 per cent). This trajectory places Hungary with the Czech Republic and Slovenia among the slowest-growing economies in CEB. Three factors limit Hungary's capacity to achieve more robust economic growth:

- From its position as Eastern Europe's foreign investment champion of the 1990s, Hungary has incurred a sharp fall-off in FDI. Equally significantly, Hungary now ranks behind both Poland and the Czech Republic in AT Kearney's annual FDI Confidence Survey of global corporate executives.
- The authorities will struggle to restore investor confidence in the economy after a series of policy blunders generated by efforts to align Hungary with ERM II. Concerns remain about Hungary's ability to finance its large current account deficit (projected at 5.4 per cent of GDP in 2004).
- The government is increasingly committed to pursuing a fairly austere budgetary policy to lower Hungary's budget deficit (likely to reach around 5–6 per cent of GDP in 2004) to the 3 per cent Maastricht threshold and enable admission to the euro area in 2008. This will hamstring it from using fiscal policy to stimulate economic growth.

3. Poland

Following its anaemic performance of 2000–02, Poland's economy is set to grow by 4.1 per cent in 2004. This growth path promises little relief for the country's unemployment rate (around 18 per cent), which emanates chiefly from structural conditions rather than GDP growth factors. However, possessing CEB's largest market and a large FDI stock, Poland is well positioned for solid if not spectacular growth as it enters the EU. Sustainable growth will encounter policy challenges:

- Poland's outsized farm sector needs restructuring. Warsaw's resistance to efforts by the European Commission to realign the December 2002 Copenhagen agreement on agriculture with the EU's more recent reform to the Common Agricultural Policy could impede this.
- Warsaw's tough stance on voting rights in negotiations on the new EU Constitution presages an assertiveness that will bring policy clashes between Poland and other EU members in coming years and may damage Poland's economic interests.
- Doubts remain over the ability of Prime Minister Leszek Miller's government to pursue necessary reforms.

4. Slovakia

Slovakia's solid GDP growth rate (4.0 per cent projected in 2004), strong FDI performance and aggressive economic reform programme (including the introduction of a unified tax regime in January 2004) validate the EU's decision to include the country in its 'big bang' enlargement. Slovakia has clearly reoriented towards Europe following the political drift of the 1990s. Key economic challenges remain:

- High rates of unemployment (around 18 per cent) and inflation (8.1 per cent projected in 2004) bring policy-making difficulties.
- The country's heavy industries face competitive obstacles as EU accession proceeds.

5. Slovenia

At 3.0 per cent, Slovenia's projected 2004 growth rate falls below the regional average and significantly below the rates of the comparably sized Baltic states. The chief impediments to stronger growth are twofold:

- The inflation rate (estimated at 5.9 per cent in 2003) impairs the country's export competitiveness.

- While labour costs remain substantially lower than those of Germany, Austria and other EU countries, the country's relatively high per capita income, combined with its tiny size, hinders its ability to compete with other emerging markets for FDI.

6. Estonia

The economy is expected to grow by 5.1 per cent in 2004, placing it in the top tier of CEB economies. Its stable economic policy, which reflects years of policy discipline and which enables the country plausibly to aspire to early membership of the euro area, augurs favourably for the continuation of this growth trajectory. However, two factors loom as potential obstacles:

- The appreciation of the euro, to which the Estonian kroon is pegged, has caused real currency appreciation that threatens the competitiveness of Estonia's export sector.
- With a population of just 1.4 million, one of Europe's lowest fertility rates and meagre levels of immigration, Estonia faces a demographic crisis that imperils its long-term growth prospects.

7. Latvia

With its supply of skilled low-cost labour and favourable geographical position between Russia and the Baltic Sea, Latvia is well poised to continue its strong GDP growth, projected to reach 6.0 per cent in 2004. The primary obstacles to sustained growth are political: the country's eurosceptic camp, which remains the strongest in CEB, and complicated citizenship issues, with continued ambiguities over the status of the large Russian-speaking minority, could disrupt the reform process.

8. Lithuania

With 6.2 per cent projected GDP growth in 2004, Lithuania is the fastest-growing state in CEB. Moreover, the overwhelming approval of Lithuania's EU referendum promises a politically smoother accession process than in Latvia, notwithstanding the controversy surrounding President Rolandas Paksas.

As in Latvia, Lithuania's low labour costs and favourable geographical location offer important advantages to foreign investors seeking manufacturing, processing and transshipment hubs in north-eastern Europe. However, Russia's Kaliningrad region is a potential liability – uncertainty persists over the spillover effects of the enclave's notorious organized crime network, pervasive drug trafficking, high incidence of AIDS and other social maladies.

While there are clear signs of an upturn in the euro area economy, these are generally from a low base and heavily dependent on export growth in the absence of a clear pick-up in domestic demand. Euro area recovery could be threatened if global trade growth is less robust than generally anticipated and/or if the dollar continues to slide against the euro. Given these factors, growth of 1.0 per cent appears to be a realistic expectation. Fulfilment of growth projections for CEB in 2004 depends largely on the EU's economic developments, whose export markets represent a major share of GDP in CEB, and whose currency appreciation has impaired the wider export competitiveness of accession candidates anchored to the euro.

The Range of Country @ratings in Europe

Sylvia Greisman, Jean-Louis Daudier, Dominique Fruchter and Yves Zlotowski
Coface Country Risk and Economic Studies Department, Paris

COUNTRY @RATING SCALE

A regional country risk @rating represents an average of country @ratings weighted according to their contribution to the region's production.

A Country @rating measures the average level of short-term non-payment risk associated with companies in a particular country. It reflects the extent to which a country's economic, financial and political outlook influences financial commitments of local companies. It is thus complementary to @rating Credit Opinions on companies.

In 2004, growth should progressively recover in West Europe after a year marked by economic sluggishness and a continued high rate of company payment incidents. The quality of risks improved in the region during the second half of 2003. That permitted removing the ratings of the United Kingdom (A1) and Spain (A1) from negative-watchlist status. Meanwhile, France, Germany and the Netherlands have retained their A2 ratings with Italy's A2 rating negative-watchlisted. Overall, the level of risk has remained higher than that registered in 2000.

Conversely, the quality of risks improved in Central Europe in the run-up to European Union accession for many countries. The ratings of the Czech Republic and Slovakia were respectively upgraded to A2 and A3. The continued A4 rating of Poland with the region's largest economy reflects the persistent weakness of many companies.

The average level of risk across the entire Community of Independent States has remained stable, although at a level still substantially higher than the emerging-country average.

Although the European Union country-risk index has been trending down, dropping 12 per cent in the 2003 second half, it has remained substantially (46 per cent) higher than its December 2000 level.

Growth should progressively recover in 2004 after a year marked by economic sluggishness. Strong American and Asian demand should buoy export recovery despite the pressure exerted by the euro

	Jan 2002	Jan 2003	Jan 2004
Spain	A1	A1↓	A1
United Kingdom	A1↓	A1↓	A1
Germany	A1	A2	A2
France	A1↓	A1↓	A2
Netherlands	A1	A2	A2
Italy	A2	A2	A2↓
Portugal	A1↓	A2	A2↓
Hungary	A2	A2	A2
Czech Republic	A3	A3	A2
Slovakia	B	A4	A3
Poland	A4↓	A4↓	A4
Russia	B	B	B
Romania	C	B	B

↑: positive-watchlisted rating
↓: negative-watchlisted rating

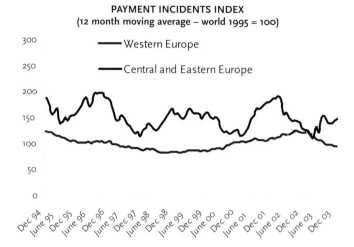

PAYMENT INCIDENTS INDEX
(12 month moving average – world 1995 = 100)

— Western Europe

— Central and Eastern Europe

appreciation on European-product competitiveness. However, public sector deficits will continue to necessitate fiscal austerity policies and economic activity will vary by country. The United Kingdom and Spain will again enjoy growth much higher than that of France, Italy or Germany.

In Central Europe, economic activity was upbeat in 2003, buoyed by steady domestic demand or surging exports linked to competitiveness gains. Re-emergence of exchange-rate tensions, notably in **Hungary** and **Poland**, nonetheless marked the year. In 2004, regional growth should accelerate slightly amid improved economic conditions in West Europe. Although the economic outlook has remained bright with the prospect of European Union membership in May 2004, weaknesses have persisted. The region has fallen behind on reforms and implementation of management and control tools meeting European standards. Current account deficits have remained high with countries struggling to reduce their public sector debt. Such imbalances have been generating appreciable vulnerability to currency crises, which should only ease with the new members' progressive integration into the euro zone.

Further east, economic and financial conditions in **Russia** have continued to improve. Although the country has been benefiting from high oil prices and the euro appreciation, two factors unlikely to last, the business climate has remained uncertain.

The relatively strong growth rates registered by Central and East European countries have gone hand

in hand with generally improved payment behaviour. Payment incident indices in the region have nonetheless remained above those of West European companies, reflecting the still insufficient restructuring of the productive apparatus. Improved macroeconomic performance has prompted Coface to upgrade the ratings of some countries in the region.

■ **Countries rated A1**
Very stable political and economic conditions favourably influence generally good company payment behaviour. Moreover, a satisfactory legal framework ensures protection of creditors and the effectiveness of collection procedures. That generally favourable environment nonetheless does not exclude either disparities in growth or occasional risks of payment default.

In the **United Kingdom**, growth has been steady, buoyed by robust private and public spending. Conversely, despite stronger demand from the United States, exports declined again, affecting industrial activity. Economic growth should nonetheless accelerate in 2004 with exports benefiting from the delayed effects of the pound sterling's decline against the euro. However, household spending and especially residential investment should stabilize under the effect of rising interest rates with households carrying heavy debt burdens at variable rates.

Despite slight improvement in company solvency, weaknesses have generally persisted in industry, particularly in textiles, clothing, metals, furniture, printing and mechanical engineering.

Spain's robust growth has been in contrast with the sluggishness of neighbouring countries. The economy has benefited from infrastructure and housing investment and from buoyant consumer spending. Meanwhile, there has been a noticeable tourism rebound. In 2004, the continued positive trend of domestic demand components should again contribute to fuelling growth. Moreover, improved economic conditions in Europe will contribute to acceleration of exports.

The deterioration of company solvency, resulting from the economic slowdown that began in 2002, changed direction in the 2003 second half thanks to the improved economic climate. That trend should continue in 2004. The textile and clothing sector has nonetheless remained shaky.

■ Countries rated A2

Default likelihood has remained low on average even though a country's economic and political environment or local company payment behaviour is slightly less good than in countries rated A1.

In **Germany**, the first-half recession in 2003 gave way to a timid year-end recovery amid improvement in confidence indicators. That recovery should intensify in 2004, buoyed by exports, which will benefit from improved world demand despite the strong euro. Increased industrial production will prompt an investment upturn that rising stock-market prices and increased bank support should help finance. Conversely, a fiscal context constrained by the sizeable deficit will impede the household spending recovery.

The sluggish conditions of 2003 have continued to affect company solvency, prompting numerous payment incidents. Although already perceptible in the Coface payment-incident index decline in late 2003, the improvement expected in 2004 will only develop progressively.

In **France**, after the economic stagnation of 2003, growth should progressively firm up in 2004, buoyed by exports, which will benefit from the improved world economic environment despite the euro appreciation. Conversely, amid continued high unemployment, households will prove to be relatively insensitive to the small tax cuts permitted in a tight fiscal situation and their spending will barely

COFACE MAP OF COUNTRY @RATINGS

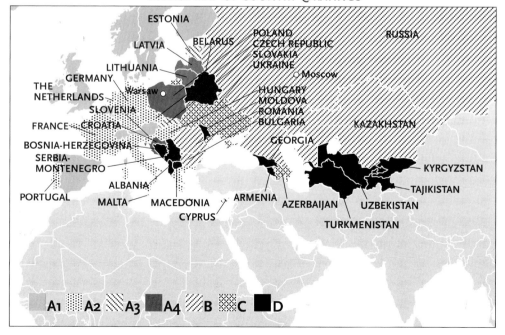

9

increase. The deterioration of company payment behaviour noted by Coface has been consistent with the bankruptcy rate. The improvement expected in 2004 will be very progressive.

Italy's economy (with a negative-watchlisted rating) endured a difficult year in 2003. With exports falling sharply, household spending suffered from the decline of real disposable income. At the year-end, furthermore, the Parmalat affair nourished doubts about the transparency of company accounts. A modest upturn is nonetheless expected in 2004 with exports benefiting from stronger world demand and improved competitiveness linked to easing inflation, the euro's appreciation notwithstanding. However, cancellation of the income tax reduction, necessitated by deterioration of public finances, will hardly be favourable to a consumer spending recovery.

Payment incidents have remained commonplace in Italy and much more frequent than the European average. Moreover, their frequency rose in 2003. The risk level should remain high this year considering the moderate economic recovery. Companies in the clothing, electronics, mechanical engineering and printing/publishing sectors have remained the most vulnerable.

In the **Czech Republic**, growth recovered in 2003 at a moderate pace, buoyed by private consumption. The slight exchange rate decline, low interest-rate levels and progressive recovery of foreign demand should bolster the economy in 2004. Concurrently, foreign direct investment inflows, among the highest in Central Europe, will permit covering the still-sizeable current account deficit and limit recourse to foreign debt. Moreover, the government has obtained adoption of tax reform that augurs gradual improvement in public sector accounts, also substantially in deficit.

Hungary, meanwhile, had to contend with an economic slowdown in 2003 attributable to a loss of competitiveness and sagging foreign demand. Despite those poorer conditions, company payment behaviour remained good. An upturn should develop in 2004, benefiting from the exchange rate depreciation and improved economic conditions in Europe. Although the public sector deficit has declined since the slippage registered in 2002, the objective of bringing it below 3 per cent of GDP within two years will prove difficult to achieve. Moreover, external accounts have markedly deteriorated with weak sales abroad compounded by

COFACE MAP OF MEDIUM- AND LONG-TERM COUNTRY RISK

ESTONIA
LATVIA
LITHUANIA
BELARUS
POLAND
CZECH REPUBLIC
SLOVAKIA
UKRAINE
RUSSIA
Moscow
Warsaw
SLOVENIA
CROATIA
BOSNIA-HERZEGOVINA
SERBIA
MONTENEGRO
ALBANIA
MALTA
MACEDONIA
CYPRUS
GREECE
ARMENIA
HUNGARY
MOLDOVA
ROMANIA
BULGARIA
GEORGIA
AZERBAIJAN
TURKMENISTAN
KAZAKHSTAN
UZBEKISTAN
KYRGYZSTAN
TAJIKISTAN

Very low risk
Low risk
Quite low risk
Moderately high risk
High risk
Very high risk

an import surge. That deterioration has generated increased external financing needs and, due to the low level of foreign investment, covering them will mainly depend on additional debt. Although debt service level has not been a source of concern, volatile capital – responsible for periodic tensions on the foreign exchange market – has been a weakness.

■ Countries rated A3

Company payment behaviour is poorer than in the two higher categories and could be affected by a change in the country's economic and political environment, although the likelihood of that leading to widespread payment defaults remains relatively low.

Slovakia has confirmed its good economic performance, posting growth rates among the highest in the region. Driven mainly by exports, notably automobiles, the economy should strengthen slightly in 2004, thanks to continued sales growth abroad and a domestic demand recovery. Maintenance of growth at satisfactory levels coupled with planned cuts in social spending should permit the country to meet Maastricht fiscal criteria ahead of its neighbours. Moreover, robust exports have permitted reducing the current account deficit and improving foreign debt ratios. Nonetheless, the deficits and foreign debt have remained relatively high in relation to GDP. Furthermore, the exchange rate appreciation could ultimately erode the country's competitiveness.

■ Countries rated A4

These countries often present fairly mediocre payment behaviour that could be affected by an economic downturn, although the probability of that causing a large number of payment defaults remains moderate.

In **Poland**, the economy recovered in 2003, fuelled by a strong export surge linked to the zloty's depreciation and moderate growth of domestic demand. Inflation thus remained low and the current account deficit declined. However, doubts about fiscal-policy management have affected market confidence. Parliamentary approval of the government's tax reform programme has appeared uncertain, which could postpone the necessary consolidation of public finances. In 2004, an investment upturn should contribute to a slight

acceleration of growth with exports remaining robust and permitting stabilization of the current account deficit. External financing needs will remain moderate and the expected increase in foreign direct investment after two poor years should facilitate meeting them. In an improving economic context, payment incidents have remained commonplace, reflecting the weaknesses of many companies undermined by foreign competition, two years of virtual stagnation, and the necessary restructuring.

■ Countries rated B

A precarious economic environment could affect company payment behaviour, which is often poor.

The electoral context has been marking **Russia**'s situation. With the party in power, United Russia, having claimed a sweeping victory in the December 2003 legislative elections, the legislature will continue to follow the Kremlin's directives scrupulously. Although the Yukos affair has destabilized stock markets and should impede the expected return of foreign investment, its economic consequences have been limited thus far. Despite recurrent discord between clans, the economic and financial situation has continued to improve rapidly. A continued current account surplus and strong growth – underpinned by strong domestic demand – would suggest that the improvement has been benefiting many economic sectors. Official statistics reflect a sharp improvement in company payment behaviour in domestic commerce. The stock of payment defaults in relation to GDP fell from 50 per cent in 1998 to 14 per cent in 2003. Growth has nonetheless remained vulnerable to oil price fluctuations. Implementation of reforms has continued to pose problems. The banking system has remained very shaky due to the increasingly lagging pace of reform. Furthermore, the business climate has remained uncertain with companies once again assuming massive debt burdens on international capital markets.

In **Romania**, after a slight slowdown in early 2003, industrial activity and exports have strengthened. Moreover, with confidence growing in business circles and disinflation continuing, the rise of real wages and the expansion of credit to companies have spurred domestic demand. European Union membership, scheduled for 2007, has remained a top government priority. Although the economic outlook has remained bright, that has to be put into the perspective of the need for substantial catch-up development. Furthermore, public authorities have been struggling to reduce the public finance imbalance. The country has a lot of ground to make up in restructuring the energy sector, which has continued to suffer large losses. Meanwhile, the current account deficit has begun to grow again and, concomitantly, so have external financing needs. Nonetheless, the strengthening of market confidence and growth of direct investment inflows coupled with low debt and satisfactory currency reserve levels have been limiting the country's external vulnerability.

PAYMENT-INCIDENT RATE BY ECONOMIC SECTOR

Continuing to suffer more amid sagging consumer spending, clothing article manufacturing and distribution have remained the sectors most exposed to payment incidents. Moreover, the difficulties have tended to spread to weaving and spinning, segments affected by competition from low-wage countries via finished product imports.

The industrial recovery's slow pace and the extent of available production capacity have been impeding investment and the restocking of intermediary products. The chemical, paper and steel industries in the United Kingdom and Italy have thus been slow to return to optimal payment conditions with the situation deteriorating instead.

After a third year of declining investment in West Europe, the capital goods industry, notably metal processing and mechanical engineering, has been encountering difficulties. That has been particularly true for Italian, French and British manufacturers whereas their German counterparts have succeeded in capitalizing on robust Asian demand.

The food, glass and pharmaceuticals industries, less affected by the consumer spending slowdown, have continued to present relatively lower risk levels.

PAYMENT INCIDENT RATE BY SECTOR

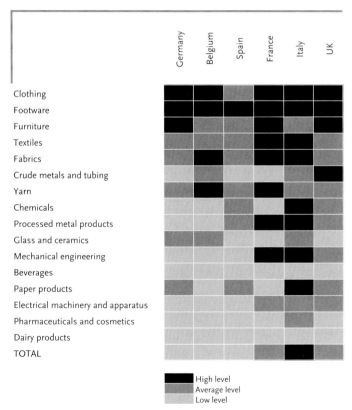

Albania

Population (million inhabitants)   3.2
GDP (million USD)   4,114
GDP per capita (USD)   1,286

Coface analysis

Short-term: **D**

Medium-term:
Very high risk

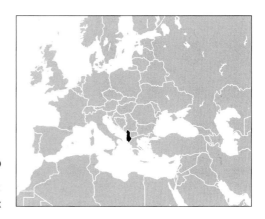

RISK ASSESSMENT

Growth has returned to a relatively high level with the difficulties encountered in 2002 partially dispelled. Industrial activity has recovered due to improvement in the supply of electricity. Agriculture, meanwhile, has benefited from the repair of damage caused by the flooding. Public-sector investment should also have a positive impact despite the need to limit government spending under the agreement concluded with the IMF. Severe constraints should nonetheless continue to impede growth including political instability, the slow pace of reform implementation, unresolved energy problems and the weakness of the European recovery. Albania has remained one of Europe's poorest countries with much work still to be done

on infrastructure, education and health. It also needs to combat fraud and corruption effectively to improve the business climate.

On external accounts, the current account deficit has remained high although expatriate worker remittances and tourism revenues have been partly offsetting deterioration of the trade balance. Moreover, the country has remained dependent on official transfers and multilateral loans to cover its external financing needs.

Infighting within the Socialist Party in power has continued to mark the political situation. The resulting slow pace of reforms could notably jeopardize the signing of a stabilization and association agreement with the European Union.

MAIN ECONOMIC INDICATORS						
US$ million	1999	2000	2001	2002	2003 (e)	2004 (f)
Economic growth (%)	8.9	7.7	6.8	4.7	6.0	6.0
Inflation (%)	0.4	0.0	3.1	5.4	3.0	3.0
Public-sector balance/GDP (%)	−11.8	−8.9	−8.2	−6.9	−6.4	−6.0
Exports	275	255	305	330	391	430
Imports	938	1,076	1,332	1,485	1,683	1,806
Trade balance	−663	−821	−1,027	−1,155	−1,292	−1,376
Current account balance	−272	−274	−263	−440	−471	−482
Current account balance/GDP (%)	−7.7	−7.1	−6.2	−9.1	−8.5	−8.0
Foreign debt	1,109	1,173	1,199	1,183	1,321	1,488
Debt service/Exports (%)	2.8	2.2	2.3	3.3	2.8	3.2
Currency reserves (import months)	5.0	4.9	5.0	4.7	4.3	4.1

e = estimate, f = forecast

Armenia

Population (million inhabitants)	3.8
GDP (million USD)	2,118
GDP per capita (USD)	557

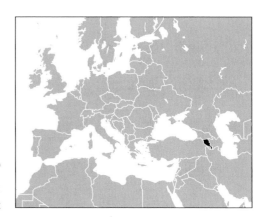

Coface analysis

Short-term: **D**

Medium-term:
Very high risk

RISK ASSESSMENT

Growth has been accelerating thanks to the precious and semi-precious metal export sector's firmness (over 50 per cent of total exports), with most sales going to Belgium and Israel. The retail sector has also been a growth engine. Moreover, monetary stabilization has been progressing with inflation and the fiscal deficit relatively contained thanks to prudent economic policy. That has permitted renewed IMF backing.

The current account deficit, which has remained too high, has been declining slowly thanks to export dynamism and the high level of private transfers (expatriate worker remittances). Although debt service seems to be under control, the country has remained dependent on multilateral-institution backing. It has nonetheless

continued to benefit from a strategic alliance with Russia, which has been firming up both financially and militarily. However, relations with the European Union and the United States could suffer from Western demands for political reforms.

As such, the domestic political situation has remained unstable. The opposition has been contesting Robert Kotcharian's re-election as president in March 2003 and his camp's victory in the May 2003 legislative elections and seeks a referendum on confidence in the president. Moreover, persistent poverty (the European Bank for Reconstruction and Development has estimated that over 80 per cent of the population lives below the poverty line) has been forcing Armenians to live off expatriate income and fostering political instability.

MAIN ECONOMIC INDICATORS						
US$ millions	1999	2000	2001	2002	2003 (e)	2004 (f)
Economic growth (%)	3.3	6	9.6	12.9	10	8
Inflation (%)	2.1	0.4	2.9	2	2	3
Public-sector balance/GDP (%)	−7.2	−6.4	−3.8	−0.6	−2.5	−2.5
Exports	247	310	353	458	583	639
Imports	721	773	773	847	945	1,014
Trade balance	−474	−463	−420	−389	−362	−375
Current account balance/GDP (%)	−16.6	−14.5	−9.5	−8.4	−6.5	−5.9
Foreign debt	855	862	905	1,025	999	1,060
Debt service/Exports (%)	14.3	10.6	9.7	10.5	11.6	6.5
Currency reserves (import months)	4.0	3.9	4.0	4.1	4.6	4.6

e = estimate, f = forecast

Austria

Population (million inhabitants)	8.1
GDP (million USD)	204,100
GDP per capita (USD)	25,077

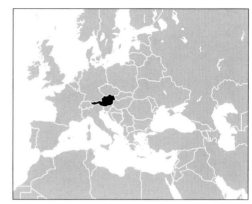

Coface analysis　　　　Short-term: **A1**

RISK ASSESSMENT

In 2003, Austria's economy again registered weak growth despite a year-end upturn. Relatively steady exports to Central and East European countries and tourist activity were not enough to offset the negative effects of poor international economic conditions, particularly in Germany. Furthermore, amid concerns over pension reform, households only increased their current spending slightly despite higher social security benefits. Investment has nonetheless benefited from tax incentives granted to companies and from dynamic public infrastructure spending and motor vehicle purchasing.

The stronger growth should continue in 2004. Improvement in the German and Swiss economies and the European Union's enlargement to the east will buoy exports while investment will become even more dynamic amid the continuing public infrastructure programme and strengthening domestic demand. Private consumption will grow moderately in a globally neutral tax context.

The essentially sluggish economic conditions have not undermined company solvency with the number of bankruptcies dropping about 4 per cent in 2003. Despite persistent difficulties in some sectors like textiles/clothing, paper, capital goods and metals, the Coface payment-incident index, already well below the world average, has been trending down and should continue to do so in 2004.

MAIN ECONOMIC INDICATORS

%	1999	2000	2001	2002	2003 (e)	2004 (f)
Economic growth	2.7	3.4	0.8	1.4	0.9	1.8
Consumer spending (% change)	2.4	3.3	1.4	0.8	1.2	1.7
Investment (% change)	4.6	12.2	2.0	−2.6	2.7	4.9
Inflation	0.8	1.4	2.2	1.1	1.3	1.2
Unemployment rate	5.3	4.7	4.8	5.3	5.4	5.3
Short-term interest rate	3	4.4	4.2	3.3	2.3	2.1
Public-sector balance/GDP (%)	−2.4	−1.6	0.1	−0.4	−1.3	−1.2
Public-sector debt/GDP (%)	67.5	67	67.1	66.7	67.1	66.1
Exports (% change)	8.7	13.4	7.5	3.7	0.8	5.6
Imports (% change)	8.8	11.5	5.9	1.2	1.1	5.8
Current account balance/GDP (%)	−3.2	−2.6	−2	0.4	0.2	−0.2

e = estimate, f = forecast

PAYMENT AND COLLECTION PRACTICES

■ Payment

Bills of exchange and cheques are neither widely used nor recommended as they are not always the most effective means of payment.

To be valid, bills of exchange must meet strict criteria. This deters business people from using them. Cheques need not be backed by funds at the date of issue, but must be covered at the date of presentation. Banks generally return bad cheques to their issuers, who may also stop payment on their own without fear of criminal proceedings for misuse of this facility.

Bills of exchange and cheques are more commonly employed for repayments where the counterparties have agreed to their use.

Conversely, SWIFT transfers are widely used for domestic and international transactions and offer a cost-effective, rapid and secure means of payment.

■ Debt collection

As a rule, the collection process begins with the debtor being sent a demand for payment by registered mail, reminding the debtor of his or her obligation to pay the outstanding sum plus default interest in accordance with the sales agreement.

Where there is no interest rate clause in the agreement, the rate of interest applicable from 1 August 2002 is the Bank of Austria's base rate, calculated by reference to the European Central Bank's refinancing rate, marked up by eight basis points.

For claims that are certain, liquid and uncontested, but below 10,000 euros (formerly 130,000 Austrian schillings), creditors may seek a fast-track court injunction (*Mahnverfahren*) from the district court by submitting a pre-printed form.

An amendment to the code of civil procedure (ZPO), in force since 1 January 2003, allows creditors to seek a fast-track injunction for claims of up to 30,000 euros. Under this procedure, the judge serves the debtor with an order to pay the outstanding amount, plus legal costs. If the debtor does not appeal against the injunction, the order is enforceable relatively quickly.

A special procedure (*Wechselmandantverfahren*) exists for unpaid bills of exchange under which the court immediately serves a writ ordering the debtor to settle within two weeks. Should the debtor contest the claim, the case will be tried through the normal channels of court proceedings.

Where no settlement can be reached, or where a claim is contested, the last remaining alternative is to file an ordinary action (*Klage*) before the district court (*Bezirksgericht*) or the regional court (*Landesgericht*) depending on the amount claimed or the type of claim.

A separate commercial court (*Handelsgericht*) exists in the district of Vienna alone to hear commercial cases (commercial disputes, unfair competition suits, insolvency petitions, etc).

During the preliminary stage of proceedings the parties must make written submissions of evidence and file their respective claims. The court then decides on the facts of the case presented to it, but does not investigate cases on its own initiative. At the main hearing, the judge examines the evidence submitted and hears the parties' arguments as well as witnesses' testimonies.

An enforcement order can usually be obtained in the first instance within 10 to 12 months.

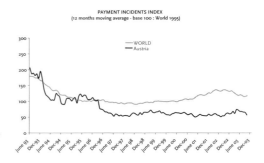

PAYMENT INCIDENTS INDEX
(12 months moving average - base 100 : World 1995)

Azerbaijan

Population (million inhabitants)	8.1
GDP (million USD)	5,585
GDP per capita (USD)	690

Coface analysis

Short-term: **C**

Medium-term:
High risk

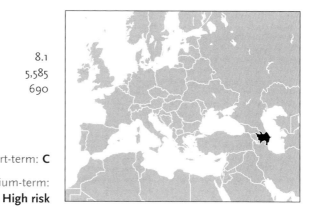

1

RISK ASSESSMENT

After the presidential elections held in October 2003, Ilham Aleev succeeded his father, Heydar Aleev, who had led Azerbaijan since independence in 1991. The country should therefore continue its development policy focused on opening the oil sector to foreign investors. However, Ilham Aleev's authority is still shaky in the face of the elite and a population aspiring to more equitable distribution of oil export revenues.

Economic conditions have nonetheless remained favourable. Buoyed by increasing investment in oil production and transportation, the very high growth rate will not be overly sensitive to oil prices in the short term. The current account deficit is very large with the oil sector's technology and service imports remaining massive. Foreign direct investment inflows have been amply covering external imbalances while permitting oil production to gain 10 per cent since 2000. Those investments should continue to flow in and thus bolster the economy.

MAIN ECONOMIC INDICATORS

US$ millions	1999	2000	2001	2002	2003 (e)	2004 (f)
Economic growth (%)	7.4	11.1	9.9	10.6	10	8
Inflation (%)	−0.5	2.2	1.5	3.2	3.5	3.5
Public-sector balance/GDP (%)	−5.5	0.4	1.2	−0.4	−1.5	−2
Exports	1,027	1,877	2,046	2,305	2,780	2,624
Imports	1,433	1,539	1,465	1,823	2,416	3,261
Trade balance	−406	338	581	482	364	−637
Current account balance/GDP (%)	−13	−3	−1	−13	−21	−37
Foreign debt	926	1,171	1,267	1,384	1,452	1,542
Debt service/Exports (%)	4.3	4.9	5.5	5.3	5.6	4.9
Currency reserves (import months)	4.1	3.5	3.5	2.5	2.0	1.8

e = estimate, f = forecast

Belarus

Population (million inhabitants)	10
GDP (million USD)	12,219
GDP per capita (USD)	1,222

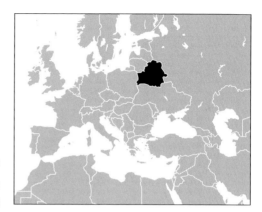

Coface analysis

Short-term: **D**

Medium-term:
Very high risk

RISK ASSESSMENT

With high, stable growth, a current account deficit essentially under control and limited debt, the country's economic and financial situation appears in decent shape. However, it still largely rests on an obsolete industrial sector sustained by lax monetary policy and indirect subsidies. The public deficit has apparently been contained but only by exempting social funds from taxation. Moreover, the government has sold industrial assets to the Russian private sector to provide financing for pubic-sector accounts. A lack of reform and opening up of the economy has made the country increasingly dependent on its Russian neighbour, which has been absorbing half Belarus's exports and, as its sole energy supplier, representing up to 65 per cent of total imports.

The Kremlin has thus been envisioning the proposed Russia–Belarus union more as the smaller country's integration in the Russian Federation than as a union of equals, which is favoured by President Loukashenko. Moscow's will to impose unsubsidized energy prices on Minsk reflects the pressures being applied. Belarus has nonetheless remained an important country for oil and gas transit, which has tended to limit Russia's room for manoeuvre. The international stigmatization focused on President Loukashenko has ultimately had little impact on the solidity of his position. He has continued to exercise power with an iron fist and enjoy a fair degree of public support.

MAIN ECONOMIC INDICATORS

US$ millions	1999	2000	2001	2002	2003 (e)	2004 (f)
Economic growth (%)	3.4	5.8	4.7	4.7	4	3.5
Inflation (%)	251	168.6	61.1	42.6	29.2	18.3
Public-sector balance/GDP (%)	−2	−1	−3.1	−1.9	−4	−4
Exports	5,949	6,641	7,256	7,727	7,901	8,125
Imports	6,700	7,525	8,063	8,265	8,956	9,304
Trade balance	−751	−884	−807	−538	−1055	−1,179
Current account balance	−700	−323	−285	8	−377	−533
Current account balance/GDP (%)	−1.6	−2.5	−2.3	0.1	−2.4	−3.1
Foreign debt	2,395	2,053	2,428	2,757	3,049	3,666
Debt service/Exports (%)	3.5	1.7	2.5	2.4	2.4	2.4
Currency reserves (import months)	0.5	0.6	0.5	0.9	0.6	0.5

e = estimate, f = forecast

Belgium

Population (million inhabitants)	10.3
GDP (million USD)	245,400
GDP per capita (USD)	23,897

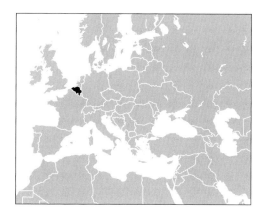

Coface analysis   Short-term: **A1**

STRENGTHS

- Situated in the heart of the major European economic region, Belgium is also at the crossroads of many communication channels, whether road, rail or water transport.
- Multiculturalism and multilingualism fostered by proximity to a range of countries and the presence of European and international institutions have facilitated the entry of foreign companies and trade relations in general.
- The country just posted its fifth straight year with a balanced budget.

WEAKNESSES

- The country's regionalized political organization, whether institutions or, more recently, political parties, has reduced central government prerogative, complicating matters in smoothing regional disparities.
- The economy's extreme openness, a consequence of the domestic market's narrowness, has made it subject to external influences and led to the takeover of large companies by foreign interests.
- Labour market inflexibility has contributed to the persistence of high unemployment notably attributable to low employment rates among the least skilled and older segments of the working population.
- The balanced budgets have not permitted sufficient reductions in a public-sector debt struggling to get below the 100 per cent of GDP threshold but which must come down with the prospect of an ageing population.

RISK ASSESSMENT

In 2003, growth remained sluggish for the third consecutive year with exports affected by both the gloomy international context and a loss of competitiveness attributable to the euro's marked appreciation and high unit labour costs. Sluggish foreign trade, whose GDP contribution has been particularly high, has prompted a stagnation of investments. Despite a rising unemployment rate, private spending has improved with households benefiting from an increase in purchasing power resulting from easing inflation and income tax reductions.

In 2004, Belgium's strong position in semi-finished products should permit it to benefit from the European recovery. The recovery of exports and industrial production will buoy an economic upturn whereas investments will remain sluggish due to the low production capacity utilization rate. Consumer spending, meanwhile, should continue to trend upward with household confidence buoyed by higher real wages. Conversely, the plan to introduce public return-to-work and hiring incentives may only have limited effect on unemployment, which will remain high.

Despite the sluggish economic context in 2003, payment incidents have remained relatively rare as evidenced by the low Coface payment-incident index and moderate increase in bankruptcies. The recovery expected in 2004 should further that trend. Some sectors have nonetheless remained particularly risky, like clothing, wood processing and tanning.

MAIN ECONOMIC SECTORS

■ Construction

After two consecutive years of decline, the construction sector essentially stabilized in 2003. The decline of mortgage rates and a prospective rise in prices have spurred increased renovation and residential construction activity. However, non-residential construction has been stagnating, as have public works, which continue to suffer from budgetary constraints. Increased consumer confidence and advantageous tax reforms should permit the sector to perform better in 2004.

■ Mass distribution

Mass-distribution turnover growth accelerated in 2003 at the expense of specialized retailers and small stores. Moreover, the branch became more concentrated with the sale of Laurus Belgium stores to the Colruyt and Carrefour groups. The vitality of mass distribution, which now controls half the retail market, is attributable not only to the business dynamism of the groups but also to the ineluctable ascendancy of discounters. This trend should persist in 2004 with stiff price competition between Carrefour and Colruyt.

■ Textiles

The sector declined less in 2003 than the European average. The drop in turnover, of which two-thirds derives from exports, is attributable to price pressure spurred by international competition, the euro's appreciation and the decline of sales in West Europe not yet offset by booming Central and East European markets. The trends have nonetheless diverged by product group: technical textiles have been gaining with interior textiles, the branch's main export product, and textiles for clothing declining sharply. In 2004, this activity will be subject to the conflicting effects of rising demand and less favourable exchange rates.

■ Information and communication technologies

In 2003, telecommunications registered a progressive and moderate recovery, nonetheless marked by the contrast between the positive growth of services, buoyed by mobile telephony and high-bandwidth Internet access, and further decline of equipment demand. That trend should continue in 2004, fuelled by increased investments by operators.

MAIN ECONOMIC INDICATORS

%	1999	2000	2001	2002	2003 (e)	2004 (f)
Economic growth	3.2	3.7	0.7	0.7	0.8	1.9
Consumer spending (% change)	2.3	3.4	0.9	0.4	1.8	2
Investment (% change)	2.5	4.6	2.5	−2.2	−0.1	1.9
Inflation	1.2	2.3	2.5	1.7	1.5	1.6
Unemployment rate	8.6	6.9	6.7	7.3	8	8.1
Short-term interest rate	3	4.4	4.2	3.3	2.3	2.1
Public-sector balance/GDP (%)	−0.4	0.1	0.5	0	0.1	0.0
Public-sector debt/GDP (%)	114.8	109.6	108.5	106.1	102	99
Exports (% change)	5.3	8.5	1.3	0.8	−1	4.3
Imports (% change)	4.3	8.3	1.1	1.1	−0.2	4.7
Current account balance/GDP (%)	5.1	4.1	4	4.7	4.9	5

e = estimate, f = forecast

The situation in the computer sector has remained uneven with all equipment segments declining except printers, laptops and flat screens amid a wait-and-see attitude on the part of companies attributable to the lack of economic visibility. Conversely, IT services have benefited from stabilization of their activity due to the increasing complexity of software. In 2004, the sector's growth will largely depend on innovations and investment decisions by companies intended to improve efficiency.

■ Steel

In a difficult economic context, steel companies were able to sustain their turnover in 2003 thanks to better control over supply, which permitted them to effect price increases. Nonetheless, the wait-and-see stance of user sectors, notably the car industry, resulted in a decline of real consumption, causing stock levels to rise and volume sales to fall. Furthermore, imports from countries outside Europe rose, spurred not only by the euro's appreciation but also by the Brazilian real's devaluation. Business should nonetheless improve from the first quarter of 2004, buoyed by the European and international economic upturn.

PAYMENT AND COLLECTION PRACTICES

■ Payment

The bill of exchange is a common means of payment in Belgium. In the event of default, a protest may be drawn up through a bailiff within two days of the due date whereby the bearer can initiate proceedings against the bill's endorsers.

The National Bank of Belgium publishes a list of protests that can be consulted by the public at the office of the clerk of the commercial court and in some business and financial newspapers (*Journal des protêts*, *Echo de la Bourse*). Such publication is an effective means of pressuring debtors to settle disputes because of the possibility that they might be refused credit by banks and suppliers.

Cheques are commonly used, but to a lesser extent than bills of exchange. Issuing uncovered cheques is a criminal offence. The Belgian public prosecutor's office is frequently willing to press criminal charges for claims over 5,000 euros (formerly about 200,000 Belgian francs). Uncovered cheques (like protested drafts) are equivalent to an acknowledgement of debt and, when needed, can be used to obtain an attachment order.

Although bank transfers are the fastest means of payment (all major Belgian banks use the SWIFT system), they do not offer a foolproof guarantee of payment as the transaction is very much dependent on the buyer's good faith. They should, therefore, be used where background financial information on the buyer is known to the seller.

■ Debt collection

Out-of-court collection begins with the debtor being sent a demand by registered letter for settlement of the outstanding principal, plus late interest or application of a penalty clause (*clause penale*) provided for in the terms and conditions of sale.

In the absence of a prior contractual agreement, interest on an unpaid invoice is automatically applicable from the day following the due date at a rate set by the Ministry of Finance on a six-monthly basis by reference to the European Central Bank's refinancing rate plus seven basis points (Act on combating late payments in commercial transactions of 2 August 2002, enacted 7 August 2002).

Summary proceedings resulting in an injunction to pay in respect of claims under 1,860 euros (formerly 75,000 Belgian francs) fall within the sole jurisdiction of a justice of the peace. They must be supported by a document drawn up by the debtor pointing to the undisputed nature of the claim. But owing to their excessive formalism, summary proceedings are little used. Moreover, they require a lawyer's signature.

Where debtors fail to settle amicably or respond to a formal demand, creditors can initiate ordinary proceedings against them in which they are summoned to appear before the competent commercial court. For undisputed claims, rulings are usually delivered either immediately from the bench or within a month of the final hearing.

For disputed claims, proceedings can take up to two years (especially in the event of an appeal). However, under the Belgian Code of Civil Procedure the judge may set a deadline for the submission of arguments and evidence at the request of the parties.

The Bankruptcy Act of 8 August 1997 (amended by the law of 4 September 2002) and the Composition Act of 17 July 1997 – both of which came into force on 1 January 1998 – recognize retention of property rights in specific cases and circumstances. For instance, an action for recovery is only admissible if initiated before the registered list of admitted debts is drawn up (*procès-verbal de vérification de créances*).

Another safeguard for creditors is the right granted to them in respect of debtors' movable property stipulated under article 20-5 of the mortgage law – this concerns all durable equipment employed directly in an industrial, commercial or craft activity and generally considered as 'real estate' by incorporation or economic destination. A creditor may act on this right during a five-year period, a debtor's bankruptcy notwithstanding, provided he or she has registered certified true copies of invoices with the clerk's office of the commercial court within 15 days of delivery of the goods.

PAYMENT INCIDENTS INDEX
(12 months moving average - base 100 : World 1995)

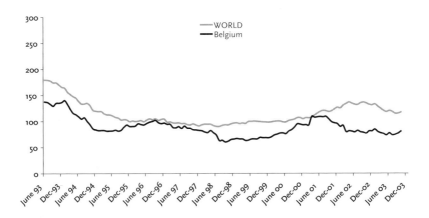

Bosnia and Herzegovina

Population (million inhabitants)	4.1
GDP (million USD)	4,769
GDP per capita (USD)	1,163

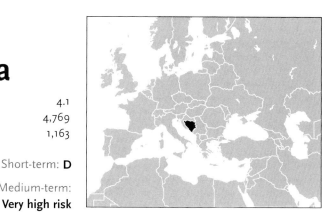

Coface analysis

Short-term: **D**

Medium-term:
Very high risk

RISK ASSESSMENT

The tightening of credit and fiscal policy resulted in an economic slowdown in 2003. Furthermore, many reconstruction projects are now complete and agriculture has suffered from drought. In 2004, more dynamic domestic demand and an upturn in Europe should permit stronger growth. External account imbalances should stabilize although remaining at very high levels. Foreign exchange reserves should remain at a comfortable level.

The foundations of that performance have nonetheless remained fragile. Fiscally, the country will have to settle substantial payment and wage arrears compounded by the cost of reforms and returning refugees. Meanwhile, the backing of international donors, which has been contributing substantially to financing deficits until now, has tended to decline. Growth will depend on progress on reforms, notably concerning the business environment and privatizations where much lost ground has to be made up. The socio-political context has hardly been conducive to implementing the needed reforms. The government coalition led by nationalist parties has remained shaky. The country's multi-ethnic confederal structure is complex and the unemployment level has remained very high.

The country is still very dependent on international financial aid with preserving the peace still depending on the presence of United Nations soldiers.

MAIN ECONOMIC INDICATORS

US$ millions	1999	2000	2001	2002	2003 (e)	2004 (f)
Economic growth (%)	9.6	5.5	4.4	5.5	3.5	5.1
Inflation (%)	3.4	5.0	3.2	0.3	0.4	1.0
Public-sector balance/GDP (%)	−22.4	−16.3	−10.4	−7.1	−3.4	−3.3
Exports	852	932	957	1,059	1,273	1,460
Imports	2,600	2,610	2,750	3,148	3,417	3,567
Trade balance	−1,748	−1,678	−1,793	−2,089	−2,144	−2,107
Current account balance/GDP (%)	−8.2	−12.9	−15.8	−18.5	−17.5	−15.9
Foreign debt	3,196	2,804	2,326	2,177	2,466	2,605
Debt service/Exports (%)	5.2	4.3	3.7	5.3	5.6	5.0
Currency reserves (import months)	1.9	2.1	5.0	4.7	4.1	4.2

e = estimate, f = forecast

Bulgaria

Population (million inhabitants)	8
GDP (million USD)	13,553

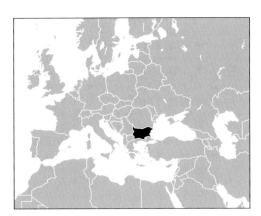

Short-term: **B**

Medium-term:
Moderately high risk

Coface analysis

STRENGTHS

- The country boasts a skilled labour force.
- It enjoys the backing of multilateral organizations and is actively engaged in the European Union accession process.
- Implementation of reforms and pursuit of prudent economic policy have led to an improvement in the economic situation and a reduction of the public debt burden.
- The banking sector is solid.

WEAKNESSES

- Strong demand for imported products linked to an economy in transition has generated major external imbalances.
- The level of development has remained low amid insufficient savings and continued high unemployment.
- Substantial work remains necessary on reforms, particularly to restructure the energy sector and improve the business climate.
- Such progress on reforms would notably permit attracting foreign direct investment unrelated to the privatization process, which will ultimately dry up.

RISK ASSESSMENT

Bulgaria has been posting good macroeconomic results. Fixed investment, private consumption and exports have been sustaining growth. Inflation has remained under control within a currency board system, and the prudent fiscal policy pursued by authorities has been sharply improving the government's solvency.

Concerning external accounts, the development of subcontracting and steadiness of tourism have contributed to expanding goods and services exports, although less rapidly than imports. Capital inflows have nonetheless been amply covering the country's current account deficit and permitting it to increase its foreign exchange reserves.

However, in a less-favourable political context marked by the government's sagging popularity

and disunity, important reforms have been delayed like restructuring public administration and the energy sector, privatizations and modernizing the legal system. Those reforms, which should nonetheless continue to progress in the run-up to European Union membership in 2007, are necessary to ensure renewal of foreign direct investments and sustain strong growth. They are all the more necessary with the country having adopted a particularly inflexible exchange system, whose durability has depended on regular capital inflows.

In an overall context of steady economic activity, textiles, pharmaceuticals, cosmetics and mobile telephony have been faring best. However, company payment behaviour has continued to suffer from substantial delays.

MAIN ECONOMIC INDICATORS

US$ millions	1998	1999	2000	2001	2002 (e)	2003 (f)
Economic growth (%)	2.3	5.4	4.1	4.8	5.0	5.0
Inflation (%)	2.6	10.3	7.4	5.8	1.5	4.3
Public-sector balance/GDP (%)	−0.9	−0.6	−0.6	−0.6	−0.8	−0.7
Unemployment rate (%)	16.0	16.4	19.5	16.8	14.3	14.8
Exports	4,006	4,825	5,113	5,688	6,780	7,790
Imports	5,087	6,000	6,693	7,281	8,930	10,240
Trade balance	−1,081	−1,176	−1,581	−1,593	−2,150	−2,450
Current account balance	−704	−679	−843	−677	−1,100	−1,180
Current account balance/GDP (%)	−5.4	−5.4	−6.2	−4.3	−5.5	−5.3
Foreign debt	10,914	11,202	10,619	10,946	11,669	12,119
Debt service/Exports (%)	17.2	13.6	15.5	10.4	7.9	7.0
Currency reserves (import months)	5.2	4.8	4.4	5.4	5.2	4.8

e = estimate, f = forecast

CONDITIONS OF ACCESS TO THE MARKET

■ Market overview

With a population of around 8 million and one of the lowest per capita GDPs in Europe, Bulgaria is still grappling with the effects of transition. There are widespread income disparities: the average monthly wage is US$120, 80 per cent of Bulgarians live in hardship if not poverty, while 5 per cent earn more than the European average.

■ Means of entry

The country now has a market economy. The banking sector has been completely privatized and government monopolies in energy and telecommunications are undergoing privatization.

Customs duties on industrial products from the EU were abolished in 2002. Foreign companies do not have major difficulties doing business in Bulgaria. There is room for improvement in the country's intellectual property legislation.

■ Attitude towards foreign investors

The government is extremely investment-friendly. The volume of FDI, which has been climbing sharply since 1992, stands at US$5,316 million today. A bill introduced before parliament at the end of October 2003 aims to simplify administrative and registration formalities for foreign companies.

OPPORTUNITY SCOPE

Breakdown of internal demand (GDP + imports) %
- Private consumption   44
- Public spending   10
- Investment   12

Exports: 56% of GDP   Imports: 63% of GDP

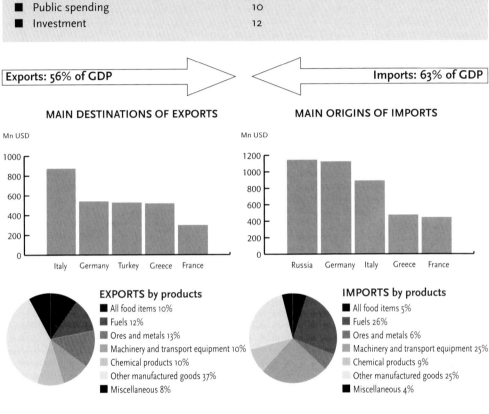

MAIN DESTINATIONS OF EXPORTS

Mn USD

Italy Germany Turkey Greece France

MAIN ORIGINS OF IMPORTS

Mn USD

Russia Germany Italy Greece France

EXPORTS by products
- All food items 10%
- Fuels 12%
- Ores and metals 13%
- Machinery and transport equipment 10%
- Chemical products 10%
- Other manufactured goods 37%
- Miscellaneous 8%

IMPORTS by products
- All food items 5%
- Fuels 26%
- Ores and metals 6%
- Machinery and transport equipment 25%
- Chemical products 9%
- Other manufactured goods 25%
- Miscellaneous 4%

STANDARD OF LIVING / PURCHASING POWER

Indicators	Bulgaria	Regional average	DC average
GNP per capita (PPP dollars)	6740	8420	6778
GNP per capita (USD)	1650	3544	3568
Human Development Index	0.795	0.810	0.708
Wealthiest 10% share of national income	24	25	33
Urban population percentage	67	61	60
Percentage under 15 years old	15	19	31
number of telephones per 1000 inhabitants	359	280	157
number of computers per 1000 inhabitants	44	101	66

Croatia

Population (million inhabitants)	4.4
GDP (million USD)	20,260

Coface analysis

Short-term: **A4**

Medium-term:
Moderately high risk

STRENGTHS

- Reforms have helped bolster market confidence.
- Foreign direct investment inflows, although declining, have permitted a partial restructuring of the economy.
- Croatia enjoys substantial tourist potential.
- The coalition government's policy of opening up internationally has permitted Croatia to achieve greater integration into the international community and to move closer to the European Union, which it hopes to join in the 2007 enlargement wave.

WEAKNESSES

- The public deficit and debt burden remain heavy.
- The contribution of foreign investments to covering external financing needs has been falling, which tends to increase the country's dependence on foreign borrowing.
- The weakness of the coalition government has been impeding progress on reforms.
- Besides progress on reforms, acceptance of the country's European Union candidacy will depend on improved cooperation with the International Criminal Tribunal.

RISK ASSESSMENT

Although credit expansion has fuelled growth, it has also been responsible for a notable worsening of the current account deficit, compelling authorities to adopt cooling-off measures. In the medium term, growth prospects will depend on the government's capacity to sustain the reform process, notably durably to absorb the fiscal deficit and improve the business climate.

The country has been facing growing external financing needs with foreign direct investment declining. Although the rapidly growing external debt burden has been high in proportion to GDP, covering those financing needs has not been a major problem so far and foreign exchange reserves have been increasing. Reducing the country's external vulnerability has nonetheless become a priority.

After its victory in the November 2003 legislative elections, the HDZ party (the Croatian Democratic Union) has promised to break with its nationalist past and reaffirmed its pro-European declarations. The European Union, which is supposed to decide in 2004 on opening membership negotiations, has been exhorting authorities to push ahead with the reform process and cooperate fully with the International Criminal Tribunal for former Yugoslavia. Benefiting from an already advanced level of development and economic convergence, the country should be well placed to negotiate its European Union accession rapidly. This would substantially enhance the country's attractiveness to foreign investors.

CONDITIONS OF ACCESS TO THE MARKET

■ Market overview

Of an estimated population of 4.44 million, 1.53 million are employed. The average unemployment rate was 21.8 per cent in July 2003. Average take-

27

MAIN ECONOMIC INDICATORS						
US$ millions	1999	2000	2001	2002	2003 (e)	2004 (f)
Economic growth (%)	−0.9	2.9	3.8	5.2	4.2	4.5
Inflation (%)	4.1	6.2	4.9	2.2	2.3	2.6
Public-sector balance/GDP (%)	−8.2	−6.5	−6.8	−4.8	−4.6	−4.5
Unemployment rate (%)	20.8	22.6	23.1	22.0	n/a	n/a
Exports	4,395	4,567	4,759	4,995	5,861	6,090
Imports	7,693	7,771	8,860	10,274	11,883	12,394
Trade balance	−3,299	−3,204	−4,101	−5,279	−6,022	−6,304
Current account balance	−1,397	−459	−725	−1,547	−1,502	−1,569
Current account balance/GDP (%)	−7.0	−2.5	−3.7	−6.9	−5.5	−5.3
Foreign debt	9,976	11,079	11,641	15,616	17,483	18,819
Debt service/Exports (%)	18.3	19.1	21.7	23.8	18.1	18.0
Currency reserves (import months)	3.5	4.1	4.8	5.2	5.1	5.1

e = estimate, f = forecast

home pay, estimated at 525 euros in August 2003, rose by 4.8 per cent over the previous year against a background of price stability (1.7 per cent inflation).

Imports, whose rise has been somewhat slowed by the Central Bank's credit-tightening measures, are normally exempt from prior approval, except for products governed by international agreements (arms, gold, works of art, etc) or subject to public health restrictions (foodstuffs, etc). Under the most favoured nation system, applicable since WTO accession, customs duties continue to be lowered. The stabilization and association agreement with the European Union, in force since 1 January 2002, provides for the zero rating of the vast majority of products. Croatia has signed 36 free trade agreements with its trading partners and joined EFTA in March 2003. It has also officially applied for membership of the European Union, pending a decision by the Commission sometime in spring 2004.

For industrial products, 68 per cent of tariffs are 5 per cent or less. The average tariff for agri-foodstuffs should have been gradually cut to 16.4 per cent by 2005, but the government has asked for transition status and for the deadline to be put back to 2007.

All means of payment are used in Croatia. For private purchases, credit cards are more widely used than cheques, which are not all that common. Cash payment often attracts a 10 per cent discount. Money orders can be used to settle government invoices. For business transactions, the most widely used instruments are bank transfers, bank guarantees confirmed by a foreign bank and cheques drawn on a recognized local bank.

■ **Attitude towards foreign investors**
Croatian law guarantees foreign investors equality of treatment with locals, despite a small number of practical difficulties. The uncertainty surrounding land and property rights creates a climate of insecurity that the judicial system is struggling to address (lengthy court procedures, non-enforcement of court orders, lack of independence of the judiciary). Between 1993 and the second quarter of 2003, foreign direct investment amounted to US$8.4 billion. The year 2003 was a promising one, with US$1 billion of FDI in the period to June alone. The three leading investors over the last 10 years are Austria (24.7 per cent), Germany (21.95 per cent) and the United States (16.87 per cent). France accounts for 1.1 per cent of FDI (US$92.5 million).

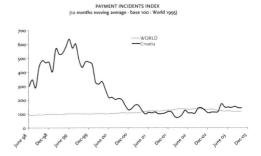

PAYMENT INCIDENTS INDEX
(12 months moving average - base 100 : World 1995)

■ Foreign exchange regulations

The national currency, the kuna, is not convertible outside the country. Foreign companies must open a foreign currency account and a kuna account to do business in the country.

The central bank (HNB) has adopted a slightly overvalued floating exchange rate for the kuna, which it regulates by intervening on the currency market. At 21 October 2003, the exchange rate was 7.6 kunas to the euro.

OPPORTUNITY SCOPE

Breakdown of internal demand (GDP + imports)	%
■ Private consumption	38
■ Public spending	16
■ Investment	16

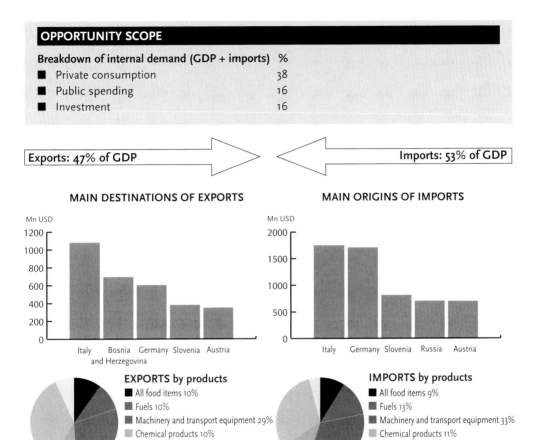

Exports: 47% of GDP   Imports: 53% of GDP

MAIN DESTINATIONS OF EXPORTS

Mn USD — Italy, Bosnia and Herzegovina, Germany, Slovenia, Austria

MAIN ORIGINS OF IMPORTS

Mn USD — Italy, Germany, Slovenia, Russia, Austria

EXPORTS by products
- ■ All food items 10%
- ■ Fuels 10%
- ■ Machinery and transport equipment 29%
- ■ Chemical products 10%
- ■ Other manufactured goods 34%
- ■ Miscellaneous 7%

IMPORTS by products
- ■ All food items 9%
- ■ Fuels 13%
- ■ Machinery and transport equipment 33%
- ■ Chemical products 11%
- ■ Other manufactured goods 30%
- ■ Miscellaneous 4%

STANDARD OF LIVING / PURCHASING POWER

Indicators	Croatia	Regional average	DC average
GNP per capita (PPP dollars)	8930	8420	6778
GNP per capita (USD)	4550	3544	3568
Human Development Index	0.818	0.810	0.708
Wealthiest 10% share of national income	25	25	33
Urban population percentage	58	61	60
Percentage under 15 years old	17	19	31
number of telephones per 1000 inhabitants	365	280	157
number of computers per 1000 inhabitants	86	101	66

Cyprus

Population (inhabitants)	790,000
GDP (million USD)	9,149
GDP per capita (USD)	11,581

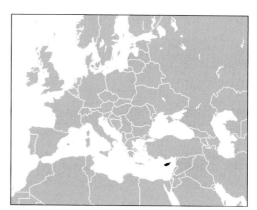

Short-term: **A3**

Medium-term:

Coface analysis **Low risk**

RISK ASSESSMENT

Richest of the European Union's 10 new member countries (with per capita GDP representing 70 per cent of the average for the Fifteen), Cyprus's growth has sagged since the end of 2001 with a severe slowdown in tourism, the island's primary source of revenue. Authorities have nonetheless attempted to stem the downturn by adopting more accommodating fiscal policy.

Although the foreign demand recovery should fuel growth in 2004, it will depend mainly on the British economy's dynamism with the United Kingdom the island's main trading partner and the country of origin of half its tourists. The government should concurrently initiate a public finance consolidation plan to reduce public-sector debt exceeding 60 per cent of GDP. Rising tourism revenues should also notably spur improvement in external accounts.

Meanwhile, with the United Nations' efforts to reunify the island having failed so far, only the Greek portion will be joining the European Union at this juncture. Chances for settling the Cyprus question are being compromised by the very close results of the December 2003 legislative elections.

MAIN ECONOMIC INDICATORS						
US$ millions	1999	2000	2001	2002	2003 (e)	2004 (f)
Economic growth (%)	4.8	5.2	4.0	2.2	1.9	3.7
Inflation (%)	1.7	4.1	2.0	2.8	4.2	3.4
Public-sector balance/GDP (%)	−4.0	−2.7	−2.8	−3.6	−5.4	−3.7
Exports	1,000	951	977	845	1,028	1,125
Imports	3,310	3,557	3,527	3,703	4,536	4,882
Trade balance	−2,309	−2,606	−2,550	−2,857	−3,508	−3,757
Current account balance	−217	−456	−395	−543	−746	−562
Current account balance/GDP (%)	−2.3	−5.1	−4.3	−5.3	−6.0	−4.1
Foreign debt/GDP (%)	49.0	50.0	57.8	62.3	53.7	50.4
Debt service/Exports (%)	6.0	7.5	9.1	7.4	6.4	5.7
Currency reserves (import months)	4.5	4.0	5.1	5.5	4.6	4.2

e = estimate, f = forecast

Czech Republic

Population (million inhabitants)	10.2
GDP (million USD)	56,784

Short-term: **A2**

Medium-term:

Coface analysis **Low risk**

STRENGTHS

- The Czech industrial sector has great potential.
- The country benefits from one of the highest rates of foreign direct investment in Central Europe.
- Foreign exchange reserves have been at comfortable levels with a moderate foreign debt burden.
- The country's accession to the European Union in May 2004 will bolster its stability and the continuity of its political and economic options.

WEAKNESSES

- The public finance deficit, exacerbated by bank restructuring costs, remains the economy's main weakness.
- Economic activity is still very dependent on the health of the country's main trading partners (particularly Germany).
- The current account deficit has worsened under the effect not only of less favourable economic conditions but also of increased revenue payments to foreign investors.

RISK ASSESSMENT

Affected in 2002 by the European Union's economic slowdown, the August floods and the koruna's appreciation, growth only recovered slowly in 2003 fuelled by private consumption, itself buoyed by increases in real wages and credit. Conversely, low investment and foreign demand levels have impeded growth. The slight weakening of the koruna, low interest rates and progressive recovery of foreign demand should somewhat bolster growth in 2004.

Meanwhile, foreign direct investment inflows among the highest in the region will permit financing the still-sizeable current account deficit and limiting recourse to foreign debt. Moreover, despite tensions within the centre-left coalition, the government succeeded in having tax reform adopted, which augurs gradual improvement in public accounts, which have also been substantially in deficit.

In a context of moderate growth in 2003, the Coface payment-incident index has remained at risk levels below the world average. The automobile, cosmetics and household appliance sectors have been dynamic with agriculture, steel, textiles and leather continuing to encounter difficulties. More sustained growth in 2004 will nonetheless not exclude the possibility of occasional payment incidents in the weakest sectors.

CONDITIONS OF ACCESS TO THE MARKET

■ Means of entry

There are no tariff barriers for industrial products imported from the European Union. Customs duties and permanent quotas for EU agricultural products will be abolished from 1 May 2004. Current tariff and quota levels for these products range from 25 per cent for wines to 9 per cent for prepared meats.

MAIN ECONOMIC INDICATORS

US$ billions	1999	2000	2001	2002	2003 (e)	2004 (f)
Economic growth (%)	0.5	3.3	3.1	2.0	2.5	3.0
Inflation (%)	2.1	3.9	4.7	1.8	0.2	1.7
Public-sector balance/GDP (%)	-3.4	-4.6	-5.3	-6.7	-7.6	-6.3
Unemployment rate (%)	8.6	9.0	8.6	9.3	10.0	n/a
Exports	26.3	29.1	33.4	38.2	46.5	50.9
Imports	28.2	32.2	36.4	40.5	49.5	53.4
Trade balance	-1.9	-3.1	-3.1	-2.3	-3.0	-2.5
Current account balance	-1.5	-2.7	-3.3	-4.5	-5.6	-5.3
Current account balance/GDP (%)	-2.7	-5.4	-5.7	-6.5	-6.7	-6.0
Foreign debt	22.6	21.4	22.4	26.3	29.9	31.3
Debt service/Exports (%)	13.6	13.2	9.8	8.4	5.8	5.3
Currency reserves (import months)	4.1	3.8	3.7	5.3	4.9	4.6

e = estimate, f = forecast

Attitude towards foreign investors

The government pursues a proactive investment promotion policy, mainly via the investment promotion agency, Czechinvest. Investments relating to start-ups and the modernization and extension of existing plant and machinery for the purposes of creating a new production line are eligible for grants. To qualify, companies must invest a minimum of 350 million koruna (10.2 million euros), or 100 million koruna (3.1 million euros) if their activity is based in a high-unemployment region. Given the high eligibility thresholds, the current investment incentives law tends to favour foreign investors. Newly formed entities pay no corporation tax for 10 years, while existing entities are granted a five-year partial tax exemption. The new law also provides for other forms of assistance, including job creation subsidies, training allowances and infrastructure development grants.

Companies investing in the strategic services and technology sectors (computer software, NICT, e-solutions, high-tech, audit and consultancy) are eligible for additional government grants, provided they invest a minimum of 50 million koruna (1.5 million euros) in strategic services or 15 million koruna (470 million euros) in technology centres, create 50 new jobs over three years and generate half their turnover abroad.

Foreign exchange regulations

The Czech koruna is fully convertible. Business transactions are usually settled by bank transfer in euros or koruna. The majority of payments between French and Czech companies doing business together on a regular basis are made by SWIFT transfer and pass off smoothly. However, for initial business transactions or large orders, it is advisable to use documentary credit (payable by buyer's bank upon presentation of proof of export by seller).

PAYMENT AND COLLECTION PRACTICES

■ Payment

The bill of exchange and the cheque are not widely used as they must be issued in accordance with certain criteria to be valid.

For unpaid and protested bills of exchange (*směnka cizí*), promissory notes (*směnka vlastní*) and cheques, creditors may access a fast-track procedure for ordering payment under which, if the judge admits the plaintiff's application, the debtor has only three days in which to contest the order against him or her.

Bank transfers are by far the most widely used means of payment. Leading Czech banks – after an initial phase of privatization and a second phase of concentration – are now linked to the SWIFT system, which provides an easier, quicker and cheaper method for handling domestic and international payments, as well as CERTIS, a clearing interbank local payments system.

Inspired by EU regulations, a new payment systems law setting out the conditions for making funds tranfers in the enlarged European area and empowering the Czech National Bank (Ceská Národni Bank) to oversee the use of electronic payment instruments locally was enacted on 1 January 2003.

■ Debt collection

It is advisable, as far as possible, not to initiate recovery proceedings locally because of the country's cumbersome legal system, the high cost of legal action and the slowness of court procedures – it takes almost three years to obtain a writ of execution due to a lack of judges properly trained in the rules of the market economy and proper equipment.

Following the service of final demand for payment, supported by proof of debt, creditors are advised to seek an out-of-court settlement based on a schedule of payment, preferably drawn up by a notary public, accompanied by an enforcement clause that allows them, in the event of default by the debtor, to go directly to the enforcement stage, provided the binding nature of this document is admitted by the courts.

Where creditors have significant proof of claim (unpaid bills of exchange or cheques, acknowledgement of debt, etc), they may obtain an injunction to pay (*platební rozkaz*) under a fast-track procedure, which can take anything from one month to one year depending on the workload of the courts, but which does not necessitate a hearing as long as the claim is sufficiently well founded.

Where a debtor contests the injunction, the parties are summoned to a hearing where they must produce evidence on the basis of which the judge decides whether to throw out the plaintiff's application or to order the debtor to pay principal and costs.

The written part of ordinary proceedings consists in the filing of submissions by the parties and supporting original case documents, whereas the oral part involves a hearing of the parties and their witnesses on the main hearing date.

Any settlement reached between the parties during these proceedings and ratified by the court is tantamount to a writ of execution, in the event of non-compliance at a later date.

Commercial disputes are heard by civil courts (district courts and regional courts) since the abolition, in January 2001, of the country's only regional commercial courts in Prague, Brno and Ostrava.

To speed up enforcement of court orders (there were more than 400,000 cases awaiting enforcement at the end of June 2002), a new body of bailiffs (*soudní exekutor*), with less formal enforcement powers, was created in May 2001. The new bailiffs should help improve enforcement in the future.

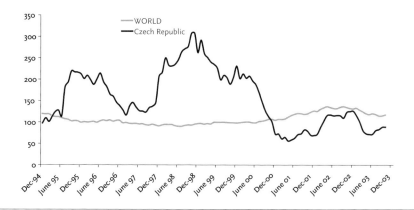

PAYMENT INCIDENTS INDEX
(12 months moving average - base 100 : World 1995)

OPPORTUNITY SCOPE

Breakdown of internal demand (GDP + imports) %
- Private consumption   30
- Public spending   11
- Investment   17

Exports: 71% of GDP   Imports: 74% of GDP

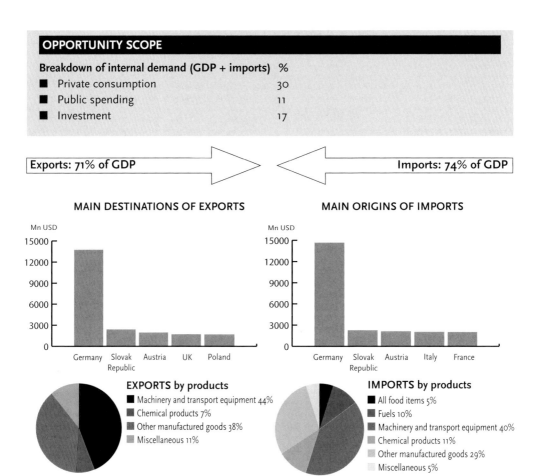

MAIN DESTINATIONS OF EXPORTS

Mn USD

Germany, Slovak Republic, Austria, UK, Poland

MAIN ORIGINS OF IMPORTS

Mn USD

Germany, Slovak Republic, Austria, Italy, France

EXPORTS by products
- Machinery and transport equipment 44%
- Chemical products 7%
- Other manufactured goods 38%
- Miscellaneous 11%

IMPORTS by products
- All food items 5%
- Fuels 10%
- Machinery and transport equipment 40%
- Chemical products 11%
- Other manufactured goods 29%
- Miscellaneous 5%

STANDARD OF LIVING / PURCHASING POWER

Indicators	Czech Republic	Regional average	DC average
GNP per capita (PPP dollars)	14320	8420	6778
GNP per capita (USD)	5310	3544	3568
Human Development Index	0.861	0.810	0.708
Wealthiest 10% share of national income	22	25	33
Urban population percentage	75	61	60
Percentage under 15 years old	16	19	31
number of telephones per 1000 inhabitants	375	280	157
number of computers per 1000 inhabitants	146	101	66

Denmark

Population (million inhabitants)	5.4
GDP (million USD)	172,900
GDP per capita (USD)	32,173

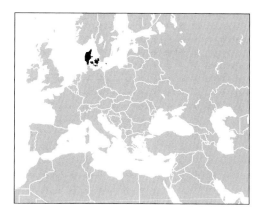

Coface analysis   Short-term: **A1**

RISK ASSESSMENT

Growth slowed in 2003 with exports rising only slightly, hampered by sluggish European demand. Increased unemployment had a negative impact on household spending and, with weak demand, investment declined.

Growth should accelerate in 2004 with tax reductions and low interest rates buoying domestic demand. Furthermore, progressive easing of unemployment should in turn contribute to stimulating household consumption. Exports will grow at a more sustained pace spurred by the European demand recovery and good levels of productivity and competitiveness.

The Coface default index for Danish companies has been reflecting a default frequency substantially below the world average and consistent with an estimated 4 per cent decline in bankruptcies in 2003. That situation should persist in 2004.

MAIN ECONOMIC INDICATORS						
%	1999	2000	2001	2002	2003 (e)	2004 (f)
Economic growth	2.6	2.9	1.4	2.1	1	2.2
Consumer spending (% change)	0.7	−1.9	0.4	1.9	1	2.4
Investment (% change)	1.9	8.9	4.8	−0.7	−5.5	2.2
Inflation	2.4	3.5	2.6	2.4	2.1	1.8
Unemployment rate	4.8	4.4	4.3	4.5	5.8	5.6
Short-term interest rate	3.3	4.9	4.6	3.5	2.4	2.6
Public-sector balance/GDP (%)	3.2	2.5	2.8	2	1.1	1.3
Public-sector debt/GDP (%)	61.1	54.3	53.8	51.7	50.9	49.9
Exports (% change)	12.3	13.1	3	5.8	1.3	3.7
Imports (% change)	5.5	11.9	1.9	4.2	−0.5	3.7
Current account balance/GDP (%)	1.7	1.5	3.1	2.5	3	3.1

e = estimate, f = forecast

PAYMENT AND COLLECTION PRACTICES

■ Payment

Like the cheque, the bill of exchange is not frequently used in Denmark. Both are an embodiment and, therefore, an acknowledgement of debt.

Accepted but remaining unpaid bills and cheques are legally enforceable instruments that exempt creditors from obtaining a court judgment. In such cases, a judge–bailiff (*Fogedret*) is appointed to oversee enforcing attachment. First, however, the debtor is summonsed to declare his or her financial situation for the purposes of determining ability to repay the debt. It is a criminal offence to make a false statement of insolvency.

Bank transfers are the most commonly used means of payment. All major Danish banks use SWIFT – a rapid and efficient international funds transfer service.

■ Debt collection

Out-of-court collection begins with the creditor or his or her legal counsel sending the debtor a final demand for payment by registered or ordinary mail in which the latter is given 10 days to settle the principal amount, plus any interest penalties provided for in the agreement.

Where there is no such clause, the rate of interest applicable to sales agreements contracted after 1 August 2002 is the Danish National Bank's benchmark (or lending) rate in force on 1 January or 1 July of the year in question, plus seven basis points.

It should also be noted that, where the due date for payment is not complied with, any settlement or acknowledgement of debt negotiated at this stage of the recovery process is directly enforceable, on condition that an enforcement clause is duly included in the new settlement or agreement.

For claims that are not settled out of court, creditors usually engage a lawyer to defend their interests, even though Danish law allows plaintiffs and defendants direct representation in court.

Unlike other countries, Denmark has only one type of legal professional: lawyers (ie there are no notaries, barristers, bailiffs-at-law, etc).

Where debtors fail to respond to a demand for payment or where the dispute is not serious, creditors may obtain, usually after three months of proceedings, a judgment following an adversarial hearing or a judgment by default ordering the debtor to pay, within 14 days, the principal amount plus court fees and, where applicable, a proportion of the creditor's legal costs.

Complex or disputed claims of up to 1 million Danish krone are heard by the court of first instance (*Byret*). The proceedings at this level are predominantly oral, rather than written. Claims above this amount are heard by one of two regional courts: the Vestre Landsret in Viborg or the Østre Landsret in Copenhagen. The proceedings here involve a series of preliminary hearings, in which the parties present written submissions and proofs, and a plenary hearing, in which the court hears witness testimonies and the parties' arguments.

Denmark does not have a system of commercial courts outside the Copenhagen area, which has a maritime and commercial court (Sø- og Handelsretten) presided over by a panel of professional and non-professional judges who have jurisdiction over insolvency actions as well as commercial and maritime disputes.

PAYMENT INCIDENTS INDEX
(12 months moving average - base 100 : World 1995)

Estonia

Population (million inhabitants)   1.4
GDP (million USD)   5,525

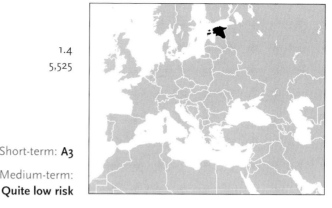

Short-term: **A3**

Medium-term:
Quite low risk

Coface analysis

STRENGTHS

- The country's successful transition to a market economy has permitted it to focus effectively on the dynamic services sector.
- A climate conducive to foreign investment has fostered rapid modernization of industry and reorientation of foreign trade towards Scandinavian markets.
- The banking system is sound.
- Confidence in the currency board is still high.
- Public-sector debt and the country risk premium have been low.

WEAKNESSES

- With the country's very open trade policy, growth depends on international economic conditions.
- The high import content of exports (subcontracting activity) partially explains the current account deficit's size, which has made the country more vulnerable to crises.
- The domestic savings rate is low.
- The foreign debt burden is high in relation to GDP.

RISK ASSESSMENT

Growth has held up relatively well amid the sluggish economic conditions in Europe and decline of transit activities, attributable to robust domestic demand (consumer spending and investment). Spurred by surging imports, the current account imbalance and external financing needs have nonetheless reached record levels. Since 2002, foreign debt has notably increased, exacerbated by the decline of foreign direct investment. However, although the stock of debt has remained high in relation to GDP (nearly 70 per cent), favourable borrowing terms have kept debt service low.

In 2004, growth should accelerate and the current account deficit decline slightly amid strengthening foreign demand. That deficit will nonetheless remain high due notably to the subcontracting industry's size (electronics and telecommunications).

Politically, discord over fiscal policy within the centre-right coalition could prompt its restructuring, which should not jeopardize either current economic options or the reform programme. A desire to harmonize the economy with that of the European Union will remain the government's central focus.

CONDITIONS OF ACCESS TO THE MARKET

■ Market overview

At purchasing power parity, per capita GDP in 2002 was 10,380 euros, the highest among the Baltic states. The average wage in 2003 was 450 euros.

■ Means of entry

Estonia's ultra-liberal trade policy is the cornerstone of its programme to develop a market economy. The country will join the EU on 1 May 2004. Until 2000, there were no import duties. From 1 July 2002, Estonia introduced the EU's common external tariff

MAIN ECONOMIC INDICATORS						
US$ millions	1999	2000	2001	2002	2003 (e)	2004 (f)
Economic growth (%)	−0.6	7.3	6.5	6.0	4.5	5.5
Inflation (%)	3.3	4.0	5.8	3.6	1.1	3.0
Public-sector balance/GDP (%)	−4.6	−0.7	0.4	1.2	0.3	0.0
Unemployment rate (%)	12.2	13.7	12.6	10.3	10.0	10.0
Exports	2,453	3,311	3,360	3,518	4,360	4,782
Imports	3,331	4,080	4,148	4,621	5,834	6,292
Trade balance	−878	−768	−789	−1,104	−1,474	−1,510
Current account balance	−295	−294	−339	−802	−1,053	−874
Current account balance/GDP (%)	−5.7	−5.7	−6.1	−12.3	−12.8	−9.6
Foreign debt	3,052	2,992	3,311	4,233	5,694	6,261
Debt service/Exports (%)	7.0	6.5	6.5	6.9	7.2	7.6
Currency reserves (import months)	2.3	2.1	1.7	1.8	1.5	1.5

e = estimate, f = forecast

for non-EU goods. Trade with EU countries is exempt from customs duties. Excise duties are levied on certain products without any distinction between domestic and imported goods. The duty charged on each import or export transaction for the purposes of self-financing customs procedures is 100 Estonian kroon (6.4 euros). Estonia administers a system of non-tariff barriers based on automatic licensing for some products (wines and spirits, lubricants, medicines). The same licensing rules apply to domestically produced goods. There are no ceilings.

The veterinary authorities are over-cautious about issuing certificates and, accordingly, have banned beef and pork imports from France. Wine registration formalities are long-winded and complicated. These barriers should be lifted with EU accession. The country's standards legislation does not contain any restrictions of note that might serve to protect local industry. Although down-payments are advisable for initial business transactions, 30- or 60-day credit is the most widely used method of payment. Credit cover is advisable. The Estonian banking industry is perfectly sound. The two leading banks are owned by Swedish banks and account for 85 per cent of the country's banking assets.

■ **Attitude towards foreign investors**

In September 1991, Estonia passed a foreign investment law that provides for simple and non-

discriminatory company registration procedures. A foreign company may hold a 100 per cent stake in a local company. There is no special incentives scheme and foreigners are accorded the same treatment as nationals in matters of direct taxation. There are no restrictions on the repatriation of profits after tax, dividends or proceeds from the sale or liquidation of an investment. Estonia has concluded a mutual investment promotion and protection agreement and a dual taxation agreement with France. Both agreements are still in force. Income tax and corporation tax are levied at a flat rate of 26 per cent. The rate will be cut to 24 per cent in 2004, 22 per cent in 2005 and 20 per cent in 2006. Retained earnings have been exempt from tax since 1 January 2000. One of the the country's chief assets for foreign investors is its highly qualified yet cheap labour. Social security contributions, borne entirely by employers, amount to 33 per cent of wages, including 13 per cent for health insurance and 20 per cent for pensions. An unemployment contribution – 0.5 per cent of an employee's wage borne by the employer and 1 per cent by the employee – was introduced on 1 January 2002. A pension fund, the second pillar of the country's pension system, was launched on 1 April 2002.

■ **Foreign exchange regulations**

Introduced in June 1992, with a parity unchanged to this day of 8 kroon to the deutschmark, the

Estonian currency is freely convertible and consequently enjoys de facto parity with the euro (1 euro = 15.64664 kroon). Estonia has abolished exchange controls and local banks accept accounts in both local and foreign currency. The Estonian government is looking to join the EMU and will probably adopt the euro on 1 January 2007.

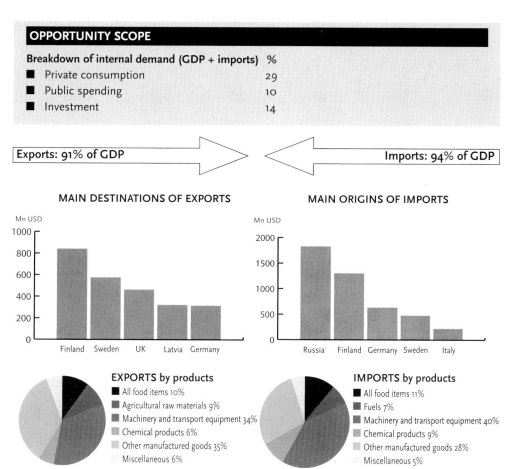

OPPORTUNITY SCOPE

Breakdown of internal demand (GDP + imports)	%
▪ Private consumption	29
▪ Public spending	10
▪ Investment	14

Exports: 91% of GDP → ← Imports: 94% of GDP

MAIN DESTINATIONS OF EXPORTS

Mn USD

Finland, Sweden, UK, Latvia, Germany

MAIN ORIGINS OF IMPORTS

Mn USD

Russia, Finland, Germany, Sweden, Italy

EXPORTS by products
- ▪ All food items 10%
- ▪ Agricultural raw materials 9%
- ▪ Machinery and transport equipment 34%
- ▪ Chemical products 6%
- ▪ Other manufactured goods 35%
- ▪ Miscellaneous 6%

IMPORTS by products
- ▪ All food items 11%
- ▪ Fuels 7%
- ▪ Machinery and transport equipment 40%
- ▪ Chemical products 9%
- ▪ Other manufactured goods 28%
- ▪ Miscellaneous 5%

STANDARD OF LIVING / PURCHASING POWER

Indicators	Estonia	Regional average	DC average
GNP per capita (PPP dollars)	9650	8420	6778
GNP per capita (USD)	3870	3544	3568
Human Development Index	0.833	0.810	0.708
Wealthiest 10% share of national income	30	25	33
Urban population percentage	69	61	60
Percentage under 15 years old	17	19	31
number of telephones per 1000 inhabitants	352	280	157
number of computers per 1000 inhabitants	175	101	66

Finland

Population (million inhabitants)	5.2
GDP (million USD)	131,500
GDP per capita (USD)	25,288

Coface analysis   Short-term: **A1**

RISK ASSESSMENT

The moderate expansion registered in 2003 is attributable to the strong euro and difficult world economic conditions, which have limited export growth, particularly in the wood sector and new information and communication technologies. The export slowdown has caused a slight deterioration of the current account balance, which has nonetheless remained substantially positive. Investment has declined with existing production capacity under-utilized. In that difficult context, the main growth driver has been private consumption stimulated by tax cuts. Despite those recent tax cuts, however, public accounts have continued to post large surpluses and inflation has remained moderate – below 2 per cent.

Considering the Finnish economy's openness, GDP growth in 2004 will be very dependent on the world economic recovery, particularly in the telecommunications sector, which represents 28 per cent of exports. Exports should grow faster, thereby permitting GDP growth to accelerate. Although the unemployment rate has remained high despite government job-creation measures, domestic consumption should remain steady thanks to the new tax reductions announced.

The economic slowdown has not undermined company solvency with payment incidents remaining rare. The decline of bankruptcies (a 5.5 per cent drop estimated in 2003) reflects the strength of Finnish companies in the face of unfavourable economic conditions.

MAIN ECONOMIC INDICATORS						
%	1999	2000	2001	2002	2003 (e)	2004 (f)
Economic growth	3.4	5.1	1.2	2.2	1.4	2.9
Consumer spending (% change)	3.5	3.1	2	1.5	2.8	2.7
Investment (% change)	0.9	6.8	10.4	−9	−4.9	6
Inflation	1.2	3.7	3.4	3	1.5	1.4
Unemployment	10.3	9.8	9.1	9.2	9.2	9.2
Short-term interest rate	3	4.4	4.2	3.3	2.3	2.1
Public-sector balance/GDP (%)	2.2	7.1	5.1	4.2	3.0	2.5
Public-sector debt/GDP (%)	56.2	53.5	51.8	53.6	51.6	52
Exports (% change)	6.5	19.3	−0.8	4.9	2.3	4.5
Imports (% change)	3.5	16.9	0.2	1.3	2.3	3
Current account balance/GDP (%)	6.1	7.6	7.2	7.6	6.3	6.5

e = estimate, f = forecast

PAYMENT AND COLLECTION PRACTICES

■ Payment

Bills of exchange are not commonly used in Finland because, as in Germany, they signal the supplier's distrust of the buyer. A bill of exchange primarily substantiates a claim and constitutes a valid acknowledgement of debt.

Cheques, also little used in domestic and international transactions, only constitute an acknowledgement of debt. However, cheques that are uncovered at the time of issue can result in the issuer's being liable to criminal penalties. Moreover, as the timeframe for cashing cheques is particularly long in Finland (20 days for domestic and European cheques, 70 days for cheques issued outside Europe), they are not recommended.

Conversely, SWIFT bank transfers are increasingly used to settle commercial transactions. Finns are familiar with this efficient method of payment. When using this instrument, sellers are advised to provide full and accurate bank details to facilitate timely payment, which, it should not be forgotten, is ultimately dependent on the buyer's good faith.

■ Debt collection

Out-of-court collection begins with the debtor being sent a final demand for payment by registered or ordinary mail in which he or she is asked to pay the outstanding principal together with any contractually agreed interest.

In the absence of an interest rate clause in the agreement, interest automatically accrues from the due date of the unpaid invoice at a rate equal to the Bank of Finland's (Suomen Pankki) six-monthly rate, calculated by reference to the European Central Bank's refinancing rate, plus seven basis points (Interest Act Amendment, effective since 1 July 2002). The Interest Act (*Korkolaki*) of 20 August 1982 already requires debtors to pay up within contractually agreed timeframes or become liable to interest penalties.

For documented and undisputed claims, creditors may resort to the fast-track procedure resulting in an injunction to pay (*Suppea*

haastehakemus). This is a simple written procedure based on submission of whatever documents substantiate the claim (invoice, bill of exchange, acknowledgement of debt, etc). Creditors do not need a lawyer to initiate such an action.

The reform of civil procedure, enacted on 1 December 1993, requires plaintiffs to submit all supporting documents and evidence substantiating a claim before the debtor is asked to provide, in response, a written statement explaining his or her position.

During the preliminary hearing, the court bases its deliberations on the parties' written submissions and supporting case documents. Thereafter, the litigant's arguments are heard. Where the dispute remains unresolved after this preliminary hearing, plenary proceedings are held before the court of first instance (*Käräjäoikeus*), with one to three presiding judges depending on the case's complexity. During this hearing, the judges examine the documentary evidence and hear the parties' witnesses before rapidly delivering their verdict. The average timeframe for obtaining a writ of execution is 10 months.

Commercial cases are generally heard by civil courts, although a 'Market and Competition Court' (*Markkinatuomioistuin*) located in Helsinki has been in operation as a single entity since 1 March 2002. This court is competent to examine fraudulent business practices, denounce unfair trading, investigate corporate mergers, deliver prohibition orders against such practices and impose fines on offenders.

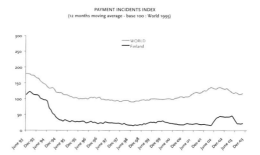

PAYMENT INCIDENTS INDEX
(12 months moving average - base 100 : World 1995)

France

Population (million inhabitants)	59.5
GDP (million USD)	1,431,300
GDP per capita (USD)	24,063

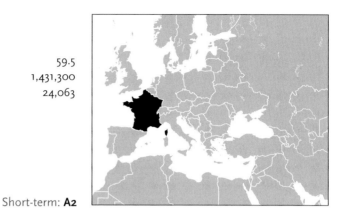

Coface analysis   Short-term: **A2**

STRENGTHS

- The levels of work productivity and skilled labour are excellent.
- The quality of transportation, water and energy infrastructure is good.
- The country has initiated structural reforms intended to absorb additional costs resulting from demographic imbalances that will peak towards 2030–40.
- Creation of an autonomous agency to oversee government interest holdings should enhance public-sector effectiveness.

WEAKNESSES

- Persistent public-sector deficits will be a major handicap considering the expected growth of spending due notably to the ageing population.
- Although the decentralization process has been going forward, reform of taxation and national and local civil-service structures has stalled.
- High unemployment has been undermining social security system accounts and consumer spending.
- Despite institution of networks allying industrialists and public research laboratories, discoveries and their authors are still insufficiently rewarded.
- Regulation on operating large sales outlets has limited competition in retail distribution.

RISK ASSESSMENT

The economic slowdown intensified in 2003. Rising unemployment and uncertainties surrounding the social protection system notably affected household confidence. Exports suffered from the strong euro and difficult international economic conditions. Despite low interest rates, company investment declined again amid stagnating domestic and foreign demand and shrinking margins squeezed between higher raw material prices and limited increases in sales prices.

Growth should strengthen progressively in 2004 buoyed by exports benefiting from improvement in the world economic environment but nonetheless threatened by risks of an overly strong euro. Despite income tax reductions, household spending should remain sluggish amid continuing high unemployment. While residential investment will still benefit from low interest rates, two factors will impede the growth of company investment: still-low production capacity utilization rates and continuing pressure on margins. Despite adjustments to the Stability Pact, the government's room for manoeuvre on fiscal policy will remain limited.

The deterioration of company payment behaviour observed by Coface in 2003 is consistent with the increase in bankruptcies. Some sectors like textiles, foundry and mechanical engineering have been particularly shaky. The improvement expected in 2004 will be very progressive.

MAIN ECONOMIC INDICATORS

%	1999	2000	2001	2002	2003 (e)	2004 (f)
Economic growth	3.2	4.2	2.1	1.3	0.2	1.7
Consumer spending (% change)	3.5	2.9	2.8	1.5	1.4	1.5
Investment (% change)	9.2	9.7	3.1	−2.3	−1.9	2.3
Inflation	0.2	1.2	1.4	1.8	2.2	1.8
Unemployment rate	10.7	9.4	8.7	9	9.6	9.8
Short-term interest rate	3	4.4	4.2	3.3	2.3	2.1
Public-sector balance/GDP (%)	−1.8	−1.4	−1.5	−3.1	−4	−3.8
Public-sector debt/GDP (%)	66.2	65.2	64.5	67.1	69	69.3
Exports (% change)	4.2	13.7	1.8	1.3	−1.6	5
Imports (% change)	6.1	15	1.4	0.8	1.1	5
Current account balance/GDP (%)	2.9	1.3	1.6	2	1.2	1.5

e = estimate, f = forecast

MAIN ECONOMIC SECTORS

■ Steel

In 2003, real domestic consumption declined again due to the poor economic conditions in metal construction and the car industry. The strong euro and sluggish European demand hampered exports. Despite a brighter growth outlook for 2004, production will only rise moderately in the sector in the face of uncertain demand and prices undermined by competition from imports.

■ Chemicals

The sector posted moderate volume growth of about 2.2 per cent in 2003 but only 1.1 per cent excluding pharmaceuticals. Moreover, companies suffered from high raw-material costs with sluggish demand making it difficult to increase sales prices. The pharmaceuticals sector has also been contending with increased price pressure resulting from the development of generic drugs. Despite still-uncertain economic conditions, the French chemicals industry should recover slightly in 2004 with growth near 3 per cent, or 2.4 per cent excluding pharmaceuticals.

■ Construction and civil engineering

In 2003, there were disparate trends in the sector. New home construction benefited from the dynamism of housing starts evidenced by an increase of about 7 per cent in the number of building permits granted. Conversely, the non-residential segment declined sharply. Civil engineering benefited from the road and motorway recovery as well as from local community investments. In 2004, activity will stabilize due to steady public-sector orders, a smaller decline in non-residential property and the housing segment's continued steadiness despite sagging prices.

■ Textiles – clothing

The production decline registered in 2003 resulted from sagging foreign demand and increased imports. Exports suffered from the poorer international economic conditions and a loss of competitiveness by French products linked to the euro's appreciation, which also prompted distributors to shop in the dollar zone, notably Asia, in meeting household demand that has been stable but increasingly drawn to low-priced products. A slight improvement is expected in 2004 buoyed mainly by mass distribution, which will benefit both from a shift in buying towards bottom-of-range products and the possibility of purchasing stocks at low cost in delocalization areas.

■ Mechanical engineering

Traditionally very cyclical, the sector has suffered from the sharp industrial-investment decline in

43

France and from the euro's rise. With improved economic conditions in 2004, the slight recovery expected will depend on possible revision of investment programmes in France and on exchange-rate trends. Only precision mechanical engineering should enjoy continued growth thanks to dynamic domestic demand.

■ **Car industry and parts-makers**

After an uninterrupted decline since early 2003 and a vertiginous drop in August, the market stabilized due partly to discounts offered by all brands. The decline in registrations nonetheless reached almost 6 per cent in 2003. That persistent weakness has affected French parts-makers, notably that part of their production not yet delocalized. In 2004, car manufacturers will be banking on a slight recovery (up about 2 per cent) buoyed by improved demand and especially by the introduction of many new models.

PAYMENT AND COLLECTION PRACTICES

■ **Payment**

The cheque remains the most widely used payment instrument in France, representing 43.5 per cent of payments in value terms, or about 1,835.5 billion euros in 2001.[1] For cheques remaining unpaid over 30 days from the date they were first presented for payment, a creditor may immediately obtain an enforcement order (without need of further procedural act or cost) based on a certificate of non-payment provided by his or her banker after a second unsuccessful presentation of the cheque for payment and where the debtor has not provided proof of payment within 15 days of formal notice to pay served by a bailiff (article L 131-73 of the monetary and financial code).

Bills of exchange, a much less frequently used mode of payment than cheques, have been in virtually constant decline although total volume remained steady in value terms year on year in 2001 at an estimated 453.6 billion euros.[1] Bills of exchange are attractive for companies in so far as they may be discounted or transferred, thus providing a valuable source of short-term financing. Moreover, they allow creditors to bring legal recourse in respect of exchange law (*droit cambiaire*) and are particularly suitable for successive instalment payments.

Although lagging behind cheques, the number of common bank transfer operations has continued to rise every year, increasing 4.9 per cent year on year in 2001. Concurrently, however, volume declined 10 per cent in value terms to 1,367 billion euros.[1]

Bank transfers can be made within France or internationally via the SWIFT network, which offers a reliable platform for timely payment subject to mutual trust and confidence between suppliers and their customers.

■ **Debt collection**

Since the new economic regulations law of 15 May 2001, commercial debts automatically bear interest from the day after the payment due date shown on the invoice. Unless the terms and conditions of sale stipulate interest rates and conditions of application, the applicable rate will be the European Central Bank's refinancing rate, increased by seven basis points. Formal notice to pay nonetheless remains a precondition for creditors to instigate any legal action.

Where a debt results from a contractual undertaking and is undisputed, creditors may obtain an injunction to pay (*injonction de payer*). This relatively straightforward system does not require creditors to argue their case before the appropriate commercial court (the court having jurisdiction in the district where the debtor's registered offices are located) and enables them rapidly to obtain a court order to be served thereafter by a bailiff.

Summary proceedings (*référé-provision*) offer a rapid and effective means of debt collection, even in routine cases, provided the claims are not subject to dispute. However, the presence of an attorney is required at the proceedings to represent the creditor in court.

[1] Source for 2001 figures: Conseil national du crédit et du titre.

If a claim proves to be litigious, the judge competent to rule on special urgency summary proceedings (*juge des référés*) evaluates whether the claim is well founded. As appropriate, the judge may then declare him- or herself incompetent and invite the plaintiff to seek a ruling on the substance of the case through the formal court process.

Formal procedures of this kind permit having the validity of a claim recognized by the court, a relatively lengthy process lasting about a year or more owing to the numerous procedural phases involved in the French legal system and the emphasis placed on the adversarial nature of proceedings.

If justified by a claim's size and the uncertain solvency of the debtor, legal action may include a petition to obtain an attachment order on available assets and thereby protect the plaintiff's interests pending completion of the proceedings and enforcement of the court's final verdict.

PAYMENT INCIDENTS INDEX
(12 months moving average - base 100 : World 1995)

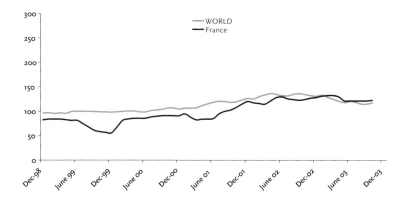

Georgia

Population (million inhabitants)	5.3
GDP (million USD)	3,138
GDP per capita (USD)	592

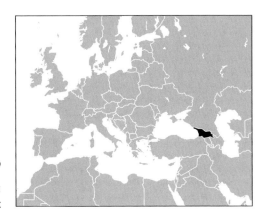

Coface analysis

Short-term: **D**

Medium-term:
Very high risk

RISK ASSESSMENT

Edward Chevardnadze, Georgia's head of state since 1992, had to step down as president in November 2003 after legislative elections contested by the opposition. New elections will be held and the opposition could win. That political transition has been playing out in a context of territorial disintegration and government weakness with much of Georgian territory escaping from effective government control. Nothing currently augurs a durable return to political stability.

International tensions could develop with Russia again should those in power appear too close to the United States. Moscow has concluded agreements on energy with Tbilisi and appears to have played a role in the former president's departure. With military advisors present in the country, the United States will also expect to gain influence in the region. That rivalry has undoubtedly contributed to the country's recurrent instability.

The economy, which has been registering respectable growth, could further benefit from the recently confirmed construction of a pipeline from Azerbaijan to Turkey. However, the economy is not very diversified and has been hampered by infrastructure in poor condition and an extensive grey market. Moreover, the financial situation has been shaky. With the country posting record current account deficits financed by multilateral organizations on which it is completely dependent and with which it has strained relations, Georgia has thus been verging on payment default.

MAIN ECONOMIC INDICATORS						
US$ millions	1999	2000	2001	2002	2003 (e)	2004 (f)
Economic growth (%)	3.0	1.9	4.7	5.6	4.8	4.5
Inflation (%)	19.1	4	4.7	5.6	4.4	5
Public-sector balance/GDP (%)	−6.7	−4	−2	−2	−1.4	0.2
Exports	477	528	473	469	521	556
Imports	1,013	937	935	944	1,240	1,312
Trade balance	−536	−409	−462	−475	−719	−756
Current account balance/GDP (%)	−7.8	−5.8	−5.6	−6.0	−11.1	−10.8
Foreign debt	1,706	1,613	1,712	1,858	1,958	1,941
Debt service/Exports (%)	6.0	9.3	6.4	10.5	14.9	16.2
Currency reserves (import months)	1.2	0.9	1.4	2	1	1

e = estimate, f = forecast

Germany

Population (million inhabitants)   81.6
GDP (million USD)   1,986,200
GDP per capita (USD)   24,350

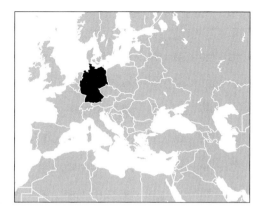

Coface analysis   Short-term: **A2**

STRENGTHS

- The German economy will benefit from the accession of Central and East European countries to the European Union.
- Industrial exports remain competitive and contribute to generating substantial current account surpluses.
- Extensive unionization and company co-management have fostered social cohesion, even if that can sometimes slow the decision-making process.
- The compromise reached by the government with the opposition should permit pursuing the Agenda 2010 reforms notably intended to increase labour market flexibility and 'restore the social security system's financial equilibrium'.

WEAKNESSES

- Ageing demographics have been impeding growth and will jeopardize the social welfare system.
- Unemployment has remained high despite the low proportion of women in the labour force.
- Public finances have been running large structural deficits.
- The banking sector's still-insufficient profitability and implementation of Basle II solvency criteria could increase the cost and selectivity of credit, particularly for small and medium-sized companies.

RISK ASSESSMENT

The German economy's stagnation in 2003 obscured contrasting trends marked by a first-half recession and timid recovery towards year-end accompanied by improving confidence indicators. Amid rising unemployment, sagging household confidence affected consumer spending whereas exports suffered from the sharp euro appreciation and difficult international economic conditions. Moreover, the sluggish demand deterred investment, which declined for the third consecutive year despite low interest rates.

The recovery should intensify in 2004, buoyed by exports, which will benefit from improving world demand, the strong euro notwithstanding.

Higher industrial production will fuel an investment upturn, which rising stock-market prices and increased support from banks should help finance. On the contrary, household spending will be limited.

The gloomy economic conditions affected company solvency in 2003, reflected by the continued high level of the Coface payment-incident index, which remained 40 per cent above 1999/2000 levels. Bankruptcies continued to increase (up 10 per cent). The improvement expected in 2004, although already perceptible with the Coface payment-incident index falling in recent months, will nonetheless be very progressive.

MAIN ECONOMIC INDICATORS

%	1999	2000	2001	2002	2003 (e)	2004 (f)
Economic growth	1.9	3.1	1	0.2	0	1.7
Consumer spending (% change)	3.6	2.2	1.5	−1	0.2	1.2
Investment (% change)	4.6	7.7	−2.9	−7.2	−2.4	2.3
Inflation	0.3	1.5	1.6	1.3	1.1	1.3
Unemployment rate	8	7.3	7.4	8.1	10.3	10.2
Short-term interest rate	3	4.4	4.2	3.3	2.3	2.1
Public-sector balance/GDP (%)	−1.5	1.3	−2.8	−3.5	−4.2	−3.8
Public-sector debt/GDP (%)	61.2	60.5	60.2	62.4	63.7	65
Exports (% change)	5.1	14.4	6.1	3.4	0.9	5.4
Imports (% change)	8.1	11	1.2	−1.6	2.7	5.1
Current account balance/GDP (%)	−1.2	−1.4	0.2	2.7	2	2.4

e = estimate, f = forecast

MAIN ECONOMIC SECTORS

■ Car industry

The industry registered little growth in 2003 due notably to domestic market sluggishness. Recovery is expected this year, buoyed by a catch-up effect and an investment and spending upturn. Exports to Asia, Central and East Europe and North America should remain robust despite the strong euro. Parts manufacturers will also benefit from that bright period with carmaker pressure on prices easing considerably with parts-makers playing an increasingly crucial role in manufacturing vehicles.

■ Mechanical engineering

With 2003 finishing better than it started, that trend should substantially firm up this year with a sharp increase in both foreign and domestic demand. The buoyant demand and technical nature of the products will mitigate the effects of the surging euro. The already marked improvement in machine tools, robotics and automation will spread to the other segments.

■ Wood pulp, paper and printing

Since 2004 began, wood pulp producers have been benefiting from a better price trend. Further downstream, it is necessary to distinguish between high-end paper used in printing and writing, where conditions have been slow to improve, and material used in packaging and newspapers, already benefiting from a demand recovery. Wholesalers have been suffering from stiff price competition and the numerous bankruptcies of printers, which assumed large debts to invest in new machinery whereas demand has been sagging due to reduced advertising budgets. The entire sector should nonetheless benefit from improved business conditions this year.

■ Computers and telecommunications

In 2003, the IT sector improved slightly, mainly in laptops. Turnover for office computers declined, meanwhile, due to falling prices, notwithstanding the increase in the number of units sold. That trend should continue this year with companies and public administrations needing to modernize now obsolete equipment. Increased volumes should more than offset the continuing decline of prices. Telecommunications have been following a similar trend with improvement deriving essentially from increased mobile handsets while investments linked to networks have remained slow to recover.

■ Construction

The sector continued to sag in 2003. The downward trend could nonetheless bottom out this year with the resulting stabilization masking moderate growth in the west and further decline in the east. All segments will benefit from that relative improvement except for residential construction, which will continue its downturn. With overall turnover not expected to rise until 2005, the bankruptcy rate will remain high in the sector.

■ Distribution

Retailers have been suffering from the ageing of the population, sluggishness of housing construction and the increased share of household budgets devoted to leisure. Stiff price competition accompanied by the growing market shares of discount and mail order and increases in store sizes despite the business decline have been squeezing profitability. After falling for three years, turnover should nonetheless grow slightly in 2004.

PAYMENT AND COLLECTION PRACTICES

■ Payment

Standard payment instruments such as the bill of exchange and cheque are not so widely used in Germany. For Germans, a bill of exchange implies a precarious financial position or distrust on the part of the supplier.

Cheques are not considered a payment as such but an 'attempt at payment'. As German law ignores the principle of covered cheques, the issuer can cancel payment at any time and on any ground. Bounced cheques are therefore fairly common.

Bills of exchange and cheques clearly do not seem to be effective payment instruments even though they entitle creditors to access a fast-track procedure for debt collection.

Bank drafts (*Überweisung*), by contrast, remain the prevalent means of payment. Leading German banks are connected to the SWIFT network, which enables them to provide a quick and efficient funds transfer service.

■ Debt collection

The recovery process begins with the debtor being sent a final demand for payment, via ordinary or registered mail, reminding the debtor of his or her obligations. The law on 'speedier matured debts', in force since 1 May 2000, states that, where the due date is not specified in the conditions of sale, the customer is deemed a defaulter if he or she does not pay up within 30 days of receipt of the invoice or a demand for payment, and is liable to interest penalties thereafter.

From 1 January 2002, the benchmark default interest rate is the Bundesbank's six-monthly base rate, calculated by reference to the European Central Bank's refinancing rate, plus eight basis points for commercial enterprises and five basis points for non-commercial ones.

If payment or an out-of-court settlement is not forthcoming despite this approach, the creditor must initiate court proceedings. If the claim is not disputed, the creditor can seek an injunction to pay (*Mahnbescheid*) through a simplified and inexpensive procedure involving the use of pre-printed forms and resulting in a writ of execution fairly quickly. Foreign creditors must file their claim with the Schöneberg court in Berlin, which, after examining the claim, may deliver an injunction to pay. The debtor is given two weeks to pay up or challenge the ruling.

Ordinary legal proceedings tend to be oral, with the judge reaching a decision on the arguments presented by both parties present in court. If the case is contested, the judge hears the litigants or their lawyers and asks them to submit any evidence deemed relevant by the judge, which the judge alone is then authorised to appraise. The adverse parties are requested also to submit a pleading memorandum outlining their claims within the specified time limit.

Once the claim has been properly examined, a public hearing is held at which the court hands down a well-founded judgment.

The reform of civil procedure, enacted on 1 January 2002, is designed to give all German citizens quick and effective access to law. The new measures encourage parties to attempt conciliation before resorting to legal action and give the district courts (*Amtsgerichte*) stronger powers. They also require the majority of cases to be settled in first instance, either through an out-of-court settlement or through a court decision. The role of the appeal courts is limited to verifying whether the facts of the case have been properly appraised and the law correctly applied.

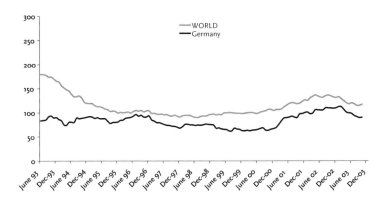

PAYMENT INCIDENTS INDEX
(12 months moving average - base 100 : World 1995)

Greece

Population (million inhabitants)	10.7
GDP (million USD)	132,800
GDP per capita (USD)	12,462

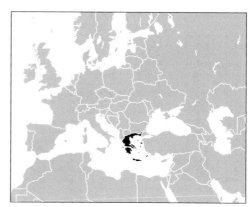

Coface analysis   Short-term: **A2**

RISK ASSESSMENT

Growth remained robust in 2003, buoyed by the prospect of the upcoming Olympic Games in Athens. Remaining the engine of economic activity, investment has posted spectacular gains, notably in the public and construction sectors, which have benefited from European subsidies. Household spending has remained buoyant despite continuing high inflation and unemployment. Conversely, exports fell again, hampered by the euro's appreciation, whereas imports rose under the pressure of energy prices and purchases necessary in organizing the Olympics. The combined effect of those trends has kept the current account deficit at high levels.

The economic dynamism will continue in 2004. Besides the very favourable growth effect of staging the summer Olympics, consumer spending should be steady thanks to the likelihood of favourable wage negotiations in the run-up to legislative elections in spring 2004. However, once the Olympic Games effect peters out, a growth slowdown will be likely with external and public-sector imbalances prompting an inevitable adjustment. Public-sector reform will have to continue with the goal of increasing effectiveness.

In that favourable economic context, and despite the weaknesses of the clothing, weaving, metals and alcohol sectors, the Coface company payment-incident index has remained below the world average while trending down. Company payment behaviour will nonetheless bear watching from the 2004 second half when exceptional factors will no longer be spurring the economy.

MAIN ECONOMIC INDICATORS

%	1999	2000	2001	2002	2003 (e)	2004 (f)
Economic growth	3.4	4.4	4	3.8	3.8	3.9
Consumer spending (% change)	2.5	2	2.8	2.8	3	3.2
Investment (% change)	16.7	9.4	8.6	6.1	8	7
Inflation	2.3	3.3	3.4	3.6	3.6	3.7
Unemployment rate	11.9	11.1	10.4	10	9.5	9.2
Short-term interest rate	8.9	4.4	4.2	3.3	2.3	2.1
Public-sector balance/GDP (%)	−1.8	−2	−1.4	−1.5	−1.7	−2.2
Public-sector debt/GDP (%)	105.1	106.2	107	104.9	102	101
Exports (% change)	18.1	14.1	−1.1	−7.7	−1	4.5
Imports (% change)	15	8.9	−3.4	−4.7	2.2	5.2
Current account balance/GDP (%)	−4.3	−6.9	−6.2	−6.4	−6	−5.4

e = estimate, f = forecast

PAYMENT AND COLLECTION PRACTICES

■ Payments

Bills of exchange are widely used by Greek companies in domestic and international transactions and, along with promissory notes, are no longer subject to stamp duty from 1 January 2002. In the event of payment default, a protest certifying the dishonoured bill must be drawn up by a notary public within two working days of the due date.

Cheques, on the other hand, are less widely used in international transactions. For domestic transactions, the practice is to use cheques as a credit rather than payment instrument. Post-dated cheques endorsed by several creditors are fairly common. Furthermore, issuers of dishonoured cheques may be liable to prosecution if a complaint is lodged.

'Promissory letters' are another means of payment widely used by Greek companies in international transactions. They are a written acknowledgement of an obligation to pay issued to the creditor by the customer's bank committing the maker to pay the creditor at a contractually fixed date. Although 'promissory letters' are a sufficiently effective instrument in that they constitute a clear acknowledgement of debt on the part of the buyer, they are not deemed a bill of exchange and so fall outside the scope of the exchange law (*droit cambiare*).

SWIFT bank transfers are used to settle a growing proportion of transactions and offer a quick and secure method of payment.

■ Debt collection

The recovery process commences with the debtor being sent a final demand for payment by registered mail reminding the debtor of his or her payment obligations, including any interest penalties that may have been contractually agreed or, failing this, those accruing at the legal rate of interest. Under a presidential decree passed on 5 June 2003, interest is due from the day following the date of payment fixed in the sales agreement at a rate, unless the parties agree otherwise, equal to the European Central Bank's refinancing rate plus seven basis points.

Creditors may seek an injunction to pay (*diataghi pliromis*) from the court via a lawyer under a fast-track procedure that generally takes one month from the date of lodging the petition and, for undisputed claims, results in immediate enforcement of the court order, which generally does not have suspensive effect. To do so, creditors must submit documentary evidence equivalent to an acknowledgement of debt by the customer or a bill of exchange, such as an accepted and protested bill, an unpaid promissory note or an unpaid promissory letter, an acknowledgement of debt established by private deed, or an original invoice featuring the goods sold as well as the buyer's signature certifying receipt of delivery.

From 1 October 2003, claims of up to 12,000 euros are heard by a justice of the peace (*Eirinodikeio*), and those above this amount but under 80,000 euros by a court of first instance presided over by a single judge (*Monomeles Protodikeio*). Claims above 80,000 euros are heard by a panel of three judges (*Polymeles Protodikeio*).

Where creditors do not have a written acknowledgement signed by the debtor, or where the claim is disputed, the only remaining alternative is to obtain a summons under ordinary proceedings. Such litigation generally takes over a year, or even two years, depending on the backlog of cases in each jurisdiction, the complexity of the action and whether it requires extensive evidence – such as examination of all the documents related to a commercial transaction – or multiple witness testimonies.

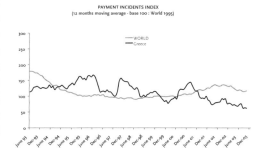

PAYMENT INCIDENTS INDEX
(12 months moving average - base 100 : World 1995)

Hungary

Population (million inhabitants) 10.2
GDP (million USD) 51,926

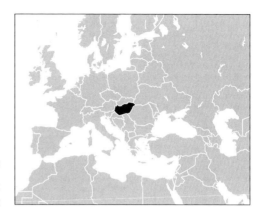

Short-term: **A2**

Medium-term:
Low risk

Coface analysis

STRENGTHS

- Hungary is one of Central Europe's most advanced countries in reform terms.
- Its financial system is one of the most developed in the region.
- The prospect of European Union accession in 2004 has been enhancing the country's political and economic stability.

WEAKNESSES

- With a very open economy, Hungary has become dependent on business conditions in the European Union, its main trading partner.
- The expansionary policy linked to elections held in 2002 was responsible for some fiscal slippage.
- The country's trade deficits have been recurrent due to the import content of exports.
- The relatively high level of external debt in relation to GDP has also constituted a constraint.

RISK ASSESSMENT

Growth sagged in 2003 affected by a loss of competitiveness and sluggish external demand. However, the increase in bankruptcies has not caused a significant deterioration of company payment behaviour. The sectors continuing to perform well include chemicals, wood, consumer electronics and household appliances whereas farming, construction, textiles and paper have been facing difficulties. Economic activity should nonetheless accelerate in 2004 thanks to an exchange-rate depreciation and improved business conditions in Europe.

Although the public deficit has narrowed since the slippage registered in 2002, the objective of bringing it below 3 per cent of GDP within two years, in the run-up to euro zone integration by 2008, will nonetheless be difficult to achieve.

Moreover, external accounts have notably deteriorated amid weak sales abroad coupled with surging imports. That deterioration has caused an increase in external financing needs, which the country will have to cover with additional debt due to the low level of foreign direct investment. Although servicing that debt has not been giving any cause for concern, volatile capital, which has been responsible for periodic tensions on the foreign exchange market, has been a definite weakness.

MAIN ECONOMIC INDICATORS

US$ billions	1999	2000	2001	2002	2003 (e)	2004 (f)
Economic growth (%)	4.2	5.2	3.8	3.3	2.5	3.5
Inflation (%)	10.0	9.8	9.1	5.3	4.5	5.0
Public-sector balance/GDP (%)[1]	n/a	–3.0	–4.7	–9.3	–5.0	–3.8
Unemployment rate (%)	7.0	6.4	5.7	5.8	6.0	n/a
Exports	25.6	28.7	31.1	34.8	41.4	45.1
Imports	27.7	31.6	33.3	36.9	45.7	49.5
Trade balance	–2.2	–2.9	–2.2	–2.1	–4.3	–4.4
Current account balance	–2.4	–2.6	–1.4	–2.5	–4.8	–4.6
Current account balance/GDP (%)	–5.0	–5.6	–2.8	–3.8	–5.8	–5.0
Foreign debt	29.0	30.0	32.7	39.8	47.3	50.9
Debt service/Exports (%)	13.8	14.9	13.4	12.9	13.2	12.3
Currency reserves (import months)	3.7	3.4	3.1	2.6	2.6	2.5

[1] According to the European System of Integrated Economic Accounts definition (ESA 95)   e = estimate, f = forecast

CONDITIONS OF ACCESS TO THE MARKET

■ Means of entry

The tariff peaks in force for agri-foodstuffs will be abolished when Hungary joins the EU on 1 May 2004. Trade barriers, in the form of long and costly certification procedures, remain in force, especially for consumer goods, but in this field too the situation should be sorted out with EU entry. Public procurement procedures lack transparency. Although a new EU-compliant public procurement law is under preparation and should be passed by 1 May 2004, its implementation is bound to take time.

■ Attitude towards foreign investors

Investment in Hungary is unrestricted, regardless of source of funding and size of foreign shareholding. The system of tax incentives was revised in 2002 to bring it into line with EU competition and government subsidy law. The new system of investment subsidies is based on three types of incentive: tax exemption, new direct grants – in particular for infrastructure development, education and vocational training – and investment-friendly administrative procedures (one-stop shop).

Restrictions on the acquisition of secondary residences by EU nationals and EU-incorporated firms are to be lifted no later than May 2009. Hungary has also obtained a transition period until May 2011 to relax its ban on the acquisition of farmland and forests by foreign persons and companies.

Tax, health and environmental authorities at central and local levels tend to be over-zealous when enforcing regulations against foreign-held companies.

■ Foreign exchange regulations

Since the widening of the forint's fluctuation band to +/–15 per cent in May 2001, it has been more difficult to forecast the movement of the currency. The forint rose in January 2003, then fell. The central rate was cut by 2.26 per cent to 282.36 forints to the euro in June 2003.

PAYMENT INCIDENTS INDEX
(12 months moving average - base 100 : World 1995)

OPPORTUNITY SCOPE

Breakdown of internal demand (GDP + imports) %
- Private consumption — 39
- Public spending — 7
- Investment — 17

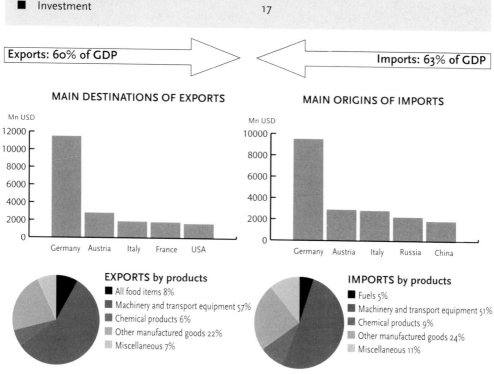

Exports: 60% of GDP

Imports: 63% of GDP

MAIN DESTINATIONS OF EXPORTS

Mn USD (Germany, Austria, Italy, France, USA)

MAIN ORIGINS OF IMPORTS

Mn USD (Germany, Austria, Italy, Russia, China)

EXPORTS by products
- All food items 8%
- Machinery and transport equipment 57%
- Chemical products 6%
- Other manufactured goods 22%
- Miscellaneous 7%

IMPORTS by products
- Fuels 5%
- Machinery and transport equipment 51%
- Chemical products 9%
- Other manufactured goods 24%
- Miscellaneous 11%

STANDARD OF LIVING / PURCHASING POWER

Indicators	Hungary	Regional average	DC average
GNP per capita (PPP dollars)	11,990	8420	6778
GNP per capita (USD)	4830	3544	3568
Human Development Index	0.837	0.810	0.708
Wealthiest 10% share of national income	21	25	33
Urban population percentage	65	61	60
Percentage under 15 years old	17	19	31
number of telephones per 1000 inhabitants	374	280	157
number of computers per 1000 inhabitants	100	101	66

Iceland

Population (inhabitants)	288,000
GDP (million USD)	8,400
GDP per capita (USD)	29,167

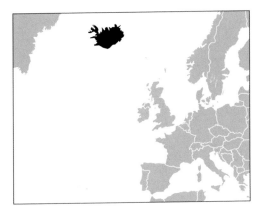

Coface analysis   Short-term: **A1**

RISK ASSESSMENT

In 2003, Iceland's economy resumed moderate growth, buoyed mainly by two factors: investment, spurred by a vast development project in the aluminium industry associated with the implementation of new energy installations, and household spending, which has benefited from the rise of real wages caused by easing inflation. Increased imports, particularly of capital goods, again inflated the current account deficit already affected by a drop in fish exports attributable to the simultaneous decline of prices and quotas.

In 2004, growth acceleration will rest on robust expansion of investment linked to

continuation of the development project launched in 2003. It will also depend on the unrelenting dynamism of private consumption, fuelled by the increased confidence of households and an unemployment decline. That substantial dynamism will nonetheless continue to cause some imbalances like an increased external-account deficit and inflationary pressures. Those imbalances will necessitate adoption of more disciplined monetary and fiscal policy to keep the economy from overheating again.

Reflecting the brighter economic conditions, bankruptcies began a marked decline in the 2003 second half, a trend that should persist in 2004.

MAIN ECONOMIC INDICATORS						
%	1999	2000	2001	2002	2003 (e)	2004 (f)
Economic growth	4	5.6	3.1	−0.2	2	3.8
Consumer spending (% change)	7.3	4	−3	−1.1	3.9	4
Investment (% change)	−5.8	14.9	−13.4	−20.5	14	18.8
Inflation	2.6	4.5	8.1	3.6	2	2.5
Unemployment rate	2	2.3	2.2	3.3	3.3	2.5
Short-term interest rate	8.6	11.2	11	8	5.7	7.1
Public-sector balance/GDP (%)	2.4	2.5	0.3	−1	−0.8	0.3
Public-sector debt/GDP (%)	44.8	42.2	46.1	44.1	40.2	37.5
Exports (% change)	4	5	7.7	3.7	0.2	4.2
Imports (% change)	4.2	8	−9	−2.3	5.9	6.5
Current account balance/GDP (%)	−7	−10.3	−4	−0.1	−3	−3.2

e = estimate, f = forecast

Ireland

Population (million inhabitants)   3.9
GDP (million USD)   121,700
GDP per capita (USD)   31,229

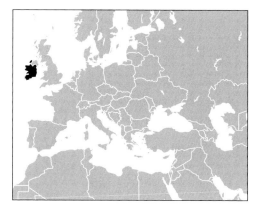

Coface analysis   Short-term: **A1**

RISK ASSESSMENT

Ireland's growth has been flagging, posting its lowest level in over a decade in 2003. Exports have suffered both from the depressed technology sector – which has constituted the country's main activity and remained very dependent on decisions by foreign companies, notably North American – and a loss of competitiveness due to the euro's sharp appreciation. The consequent weakness of foreign demand has caused a sharp cutback in investments. A slight household spending slowdown, attributable to slower wage growth, and a higher savings rate have contributed to easing inflationary pressures, which have nonetheless remained significant.

In 2004, growth acceleration will rest on joint recovery of exports buoyed by a favourable international context and foreign investment inflows sustained by low interest rates. Moreover, private consumption should strengthen, benefiting from both higher wages and resumption of job creation. Conversely, budget restrictions imposed by deterioration of public accounts should continue to impede public sector demand.

The Coface payment-incident index has remained generally below the European average. However, disparities between sectors have increased. With pharmaceuticals, medical equipment and high technology driving the economy, other, more traditional, sectors like clothing, metals, transportation and food service have become more risky.

MAIN ECONOMIC INDICATORS

%	1999	2000	2001	2002	2003 (e)	2004 (f)
Economic growth	11.3	10.1	6.2	6.9	2.2	3.7
Consumer spending (% change)	8.3	10	4.8	2.7	2.2	3.3
Investment (% change)	14.6	1.4	−1.9	−0.9	−9	3.5
Inflation	3.5	4.9	5.5	6.1	3.6	3
Unemployment rate	5.6	4.3	3.9	4.5	4.6	4.7
Short-term interest rate	3	4.4	4.2	3.3	2.3	2.1
Public-sector balance/GDP (%)	2.3	4.4	0.9	−0.2	−1.1	−1.4
Public-sector debt/GDP (%)	48.6	38.8	36.5	32.4	34.4	34
Exports (% change)	15.2	20.6	8.3	6.2	−5.7	4
Imports (% change)	12.1	21.3	6.5	2.3	−8	3
Current account balance/GDP (%)	0.3	−0.4	−0.8	−0.7	−1	−0.9

e = estimate, f = forecast

PAYMENT AND COLLECTION PRACTICES

■ Payment

Bills of exchange are little used in domestic commercial transactions and only occasionally used in international trade. The cheque, defined as 'a bill of exchange drawn on a bank and payable on demand', is more widely used for commercial transactions, but does not provide a foolproof guarantee as issuing a bouncing cheque is not a criminal offence.

On the other hand, SWIFT bank transfers are widely used as they are quick and efficient.

Payment orders issued via the website of the client's bank are a rapidly growing instrument.

■ Debt collection

The collection process usually begins with the debtor being sent a final demand, or 'seven-day' letter, by registered mail asking him or her to pay the principal along with any contractually agreed default interest. Where there is no specific interest clause, the rate applicable to commercial contracts concluded after 7 August 2002 (Regulation number 388, 2002) is the benchmark rate, ie the European Central Bank's refinancing rate, in force before 1 January or 1 July of each year, marked up by seven basis points.

For claims of 1,270 euros (formerly 1,000 punt) or more, creditors may threaten debtors with a statutory demand for the winding up of their business if they fail to pay up within 21 days of a final demand for payment being sent to them (21-day notice). Thereafter the debtor is regarded as insolvent.

Irish law and the Irish legal system are mainly founded on British 'common law' inherited from the past, although separate national legislation has subsequently been developed.

In ordinary proceedings, creditors who hold material evidence of their claim (contractual documents, acknowledgement of debt, unpaid bills of exchange) may seek a summary judgment from the court where their claim is not contested. This allows them to obtain a writ of enforcement more quickly. If a debtor fails to respond to a civil summons before the district court or a civil bill before the circuit court, the creditor may obtain a judgment by default based on the submission of an affidavit of debt without a court hearing. An affidavit of debt is a sworn statement that substantiates the outstanding amount and cause of the claim. It bears a signature attested by a notary or an Irish consular office.

Cases are heard by either a district court, a circuit court or a high court depending on the amount of the claim. Similarly, each court may hand down a summary judgment where justified by the circumstances of the petitioner's claim. Where defendants answer a summons but refuse to settle their debt, plenary proceedings are instituted in which the court gives equal importance to the case documents submitted by the parties and barristers' arguments as to the oral evidence presented at the main hearing.

For claims brought before the district courts (ie below 6,348.69 euros, formerly 5,000 punt), there is a simplified written procedure, but the accent is mainly on hearing respective litigants' witnesses.

PAYMENT INCIDENTS INDEX
(12 months moving average - base 100 : World 1995)

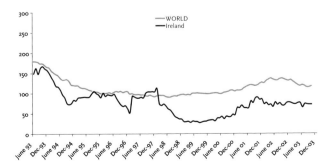

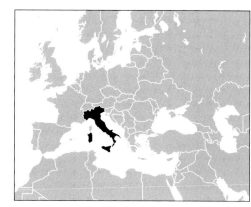

Italy

Population (million inhabitants)	57.5
GDP (million USD)	1,184,300
GDP per capita (USD)	20,606

Coface analysis   Short-term: **A2**

STRENGTHS

- The 'Pact for Italy' adopted in 2002 by public authorities, labour and management should permit continuing labour market reform while strengthening labour policy effectiveness.
- The many regional networks of small and medium-sized companies have tended to foster dynamism and entrepreneurial spirit, even if their limited resources have not always permitted development to proceed in the most effective way.
- Privatization has been changing the country's economic environment with liberalization of several sectors (energy, telephony, for example) endowing it with renewed vigour by fostering competition.
- Despite some occasional foot-dragging, the savings and gains in effectiveness resulting from Italian civil service reform should continue to grow, particularly in a context of greater political stability.

WEAKNESSES

- Despite some progress, the market has not always exercised enough control over company financing and management, with bankruptcy law no longer adequate.
- Progress on pension and health system reform has been insufficient with measures taken in that regard remaining too limited considering the low birth rate and rapidly ageing population.
- Public accounts are still structurally in deficit, which has not permitted a significant reduction of the imposing public-sector debt.
- The underground economy's impact, notably in southern regions, has remained substantial with its integration remaining very progressive despite recent incentive measures.
- Economic disparities between the country's northern and southern regions remain too great.

RISK ASSESSMENT

Despite a slight year-end recovery, the Italian economy nonetheless suffered in 2003. Exports fell sharply, affected by the euro's appreciation and sluggish foreign demand. Moreover, the decline of real disposable income impeded household spending. That decline is attributable to wage stagnation, increased inflation and a persistent lack of confidence linked to both continued high unemployment and uncertainties about the pension reform programme announced by the government.

Faced with sluggish demand, companies have continued to reduce investments.

Economic activity should be steadier in 2004. Despite the euro's appreciation, exports should benefit from both stronger world demand and improved competitiveness linked to easing inflation. However, cancellation of the planned income tax reduction, made necessary by deterioration of public finances, will not help consumer spending. In spite of this, investment should recover.

MAIN ECONOMIC INDICATORS

%	1999	2000	2001	2002	2003 (e)	2004 (f)
Economic growth	1.7	3.3	1.7	0.4	0.4	1.7
Consumer spending (% change)	2.6	2.7	1.1	0.4	1.7	1.8
Investment (% change)	6.1	9	1.7	0.2	−3.5	2.8
Inflation	2.1	2.9	2.7	3	2.8	2.1
Unemployment rate	11.5	10.7	9.6	9.1	8.7	8.5
Short-term interest rate	3	4.4	4.2	3.3	2.1	2.3
Public-sector balance/GDP (%)	−1.8	−0.7	−2.7	−2.5	−2.7	−2.2
Public-sector debt/GDP (%)	125	120.4	117.8	117.4	117.3	117
Exports (% change)	0.1	11.7	1.1	−1	−2.4	5.1
Imports (% change)	5.5	8.9	1	1.5	1.8	5.9
Current account balance/GDP (%)	0.7	−0.6	−0.1	−0.6	−1.3	−1.3

e = estimate, f = forecast

Payment defaults by Italian companies have remained commonplace and far above the European average. Moreover, default frequency increased in 2003 as reflected by the Coface payment-incident index. The level of risk should remain high this year amid a moderate economic recovery. Companies in the clothing, electronics, mechanical engineering and printing/publishing sectors have remained the weakest.

The Parmalat affair has reinforced doubts about the transparency of accounts.

MAIN ECONOMIC SECTORS

■ Car industry

The disappearance of tax incentives has not caused the domestic market to sag due to promotional offers by dealers and carmakers. However, carmakers will suspend such offers when new models go on sale. The Fiat Group is counting on the complete overhaul of its range to overcome the crisis. Its slower sales decline in late 2003 is encouraging for 2004. It is nonetheless too soon to affirm that the situation has recovered with that group's Italian market share remaining far below the 30 per cent objective targeted by management.

■ Paper/cardboard

A production and price decline marked the sector in 2003 due to sluggish domestic demand and with the euro's appreciation affecting foreign orders. Producers of packaging for the food, pharmaceuticals and cosmetics industries have nonetheless suffered less with demand from those sectors not very cyclical. Conversely, those working for the printing/publishing sector have been suffering greatly. An upturn in 2004 will remain dependent on European growth.

■ Chemicals/pharmaceuticals

Activity in the chemicals sector has been stagnating due to sluggish demand (particularly from the car industry and textiles) and an overly strong euro. Slow payments by the public sector have also been affecting some companies. In 2004, the expected moderate recovery could improve results especially if energy and raw material prices were to ease. In the more dynamic pharmaceuticals industry, revenues and orders have been growing. That situation should persist in 2004 although the government's strict austerity measures on health spending could affect company profitability.

■ Construction

Overall, 2003 was a good year. Elimination of the tax exemptions provided by the 'Tremonti' law slightly affected performance in the non-residential construction and civil-engineering segments.

However, in the residential segment, performance remained at acceptable levels and should register comfortable growth in 2004.

■ Electrical and electronic capital goods

Industrial activity has continued to trend down with computers and telecommunications posting the worst performance. Some manufacturers of equipment for the energy, rail and residential construction sectors have nonetheless registered respectable results. Moderate growth is expected in 2004.

■ Mechanical engineering

This sector has been showing no signs of recovery with the level of activity in decline. The poor growth prospects have not been encouraging companies to invest. The euro's appreciation has only made things worse. That situation should persist in 2004.

■ Textiles – clothing

Results in 2003 were just as bad as in the previous year with the textile and shoe industries nonetheless suffering more than clothing. Forecasts for 2004 have hardly been brighter. Although recovery of the American, Asian and, to a lesser extent, European economies could spur demand for all product categories, the dollar's weakness and competition from Chinese products will continue to affect Italian companies. Moreover, many manufacturers have been planning to delocalize production facilities.

PAYMENT AND COLLECTION PRACTICES

■ Payment

Trade notes (*cambiali*) are available in the form of bills of exchange or promissory notes. *Cambiali* must be duly accepted by the drawee and stamped locally at 12/1,000 of their value or at 6/1,000 if stamped beforehand in France. In the event of default, they constitute a *de facto* enforcement order as they are automatically admitted by the courts as a writ of execution (*ezecuzione forzata*) against the debtor.

Signed bills of exchange are a fairly secure means of payment but are rarely used on account of the high stamp duty, the somewhat lengthy cashing period and the drawee's fear of damage to his or her reputation caused by the recording and publication of protested unpaid bills at the chambers of commerce.

Cheques too are in widespread use since the legislation on cheque amounts was relaxed in April 1990. However, to be cashed abroad, they must bear the wording *non trasferibile* and include the date and place of issue.

Bank vouchers (*ricevuta bancaria*) are not a means of payment, but merely a notice of bank domicile drawn up by the creditor and submitted by the creditor to his or her own bank for presentation to the debtor's bank for the purposes of payment (the vouchers are also available in electronic form, in which case they are known as *Ri.Ba. elettronica*). Bank vouchers may be accepted by the courts as an admission of debt if they are signed by the buyer. However, they do not have the force of a writ of execution.

Bank transfers are widely used (90 per cent of payments from Italy are made by bank transfer). SWIFT transfers are gaining popularity as they are considerably faster than ordinary transfers. The bank transfer is a cheap and secure means of payment once the contracting parties have established mutual trust.

■ Debt collection

As elsewhere, an out-of-court settlement is always preferable to legal action. Demands and telephone dunning are quite effective, as are on-site visits that provide an opportunity to restore dialogue between supplier and customer and so to conclude a settlement.

Settlement negotiations focus on payment of the principal, plus any contractual default interest that may be provided for in writing and accepted by the buyer. Where there is no such agreement, the rate applicable to sales agreements concluded after 8 August 2002 (Decree-law of 9 October 2002) is the six-monthly rate set by the Ministry of Economic Affairs and Finance by reference to the European Central Bank's refinancing rate, marked up by seven basis points.

Where an out-of-court settlement cannot be reached with the customer, the type of legal remedy varies with the type of document used to justify the claim. In the case of *cambiali* notes (bills of exchange, promissory notes) and cheques, creditors may obtain a writ of execution in the form of a demand for payment (*atto di precetto*) delivered by a bailiff, prior to attachment of the debtor's property.

Creditors may obtain an injunction to pay (*decreto ingiuntivo*) by way of a fast-track procedure if they can produce written proof of their claim. This helps them avoid taking ordinary legal action, still perceived as slow despite the reform of civil procedure adopted in May 1995. Ordinary proceedings can take up to two years, although creditors may obtain, in the first instance, a provisional payment order that serves as a writ of execution.

PAYMENT INCIDENTS INDEX
(12 months moving average - base 100 : World 1995)

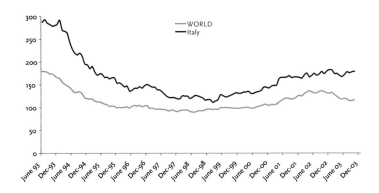

Kazakhstan

Population (million inhabitants)	14.9
GDP (million USD)	22,389

Coface analysis

Short-term: **B**

Medium-term:
Moderately high risk

STRENGTHS

- Kazakhstan's natural resource potential is substantial and diversified (oil, metals).
- The start-up of the CPC pipeline linking the Caspian Sea to the Russian Black Sea port of Novorossisk has permitted an increase in oil exports.
- The country has been claiming 40 per cent of investments flowing to the Community of Independent States.
- Good relations with Russia, China and Western countries have contributed to Kazakhstan's development and political stability.

WEAKNESSES

- Development of sectors other than raw materials, like farming and process industries, has been lagging.
- Economic conditions will ultimately be vulnerable to raw material prices.
- The country's landlocked situation could limit its export capacity.
- President Nazerbaev's administration has been contending with growing political opposition.

RISK ASSESSMENT

Kazakhstan's economic and financial situation has remained satisfactory. Ever-increasing investment in the oil sector has been buoying growth. Direct investment inflows in crude extraction and transport are likely to continue, justifying hopes for sustained high growth. Existing imbalances in productive structures could nonetheless undermine economic activity with the farming and manufacturing sectors lagging increasingly and disturbingly far behind the energy sector. Moreover, the country is dependent on Russia for providing inputs and forwarding its oil to viable markets.

Financially, the country has been pursuing a stringent fiscal policy with establishment of an oil-reserve fund constituting real progress. Although foreign debt seems high, it includes intercompany loans from parent companies to subsidiaries, which represent 59 per cent of total foreign debt.

The political situation is stable with President Nazerbaev tightening his grip on the political system by muzzling opposition. Furthermore, relations with foreign companies have been erratic. Those weaknesses are nonetheless unlikely to shake foreign investor confidence.

MAIN ECONOMIC INDICATORS

US$ millions	1999	2000	2001	2002	2003 (e)	2004 (f)
Economic growth (%)	2.7	9.8	13.5	9.5	8	8
Inflation (%)	17.8	9.8	6.4	6.6	5.5	5.0
Public-sector balance/GDP (%)	−5	−0.8	2.7	1.4	4.1	2.1
Exports	6,123	9,468	9,124	10,186	12,467	13,133
Imports	5,645	6,848	7,607	7,646	8,651	9,444
Trade balance	478	2,620	1,517	2,540	3,816	3,689
Current account balance	−37	880	−879	−473	441	127
Current account balance/GDP (%)	−0.2	4.8	−4.0	−1.9	1.6	0.4
Foreign debt	12,034	12,616	15,130	17,377	18,403	18,944
Debt service/Exports (%)	19.3	25.9	26.4	25.9	21.6	23.2
Currency reserves (import months)	3.2	2.8	2.9	3.3	3.8	3.9

e = estimate, f = forecast

CONDITIONS OF ACCESS TO THE MARKET

■ Market overview

Nearly 11 years after gaining independence on 16 December 1991, Kazakhstan has yet to complete its reform programme, despite its 'good pupil' image. A candidate for WTO accession, the country is crippled by corruption, bureaucracy, an inefficient tax system and widening social cleavages. However, it has made excellent headway in public-sector privatization, albeit in somewhat non-transparent conditions, and trade liberalization. According to experts, net foreign direct investment at end 2002 amounted to US$18–22 billion. The country's foreign trade surplus continues to grow on the back of strong oil, mineral and metal exports.

■ Means of access

Despite its designation as a market economy by the European Union in 2000 (and by the United States in 2002) and its weak protectionist policies, landlocked Kazakhstan remains a difficult place in which to do business. Customs duties continue to be lowered, with the average rate standing at below 7.8 per cent. There is also 16 per cent non-refundable VAT calculated on the customs value. However, customs clearance is riddled with illegal practices

and tariff hikes persist. A number of products are also subject to certification. The fact that certificates from non-CIS countries are not valid in Kazakhstan significantly slows import formalities. Foreign business persons should make allowance for corruption, even though it is not systematic.

■ Attitude towards foreign investors

At end 2002, Kazakhstan attracted the biggest volume of foreign direct investment in the CIS after Russia. Foreign investor interest is driven by the country's oil and gas reserves and unquestionable political stability. The new law of January 2003, however, strengthens the government's interventionist powers during a downturn. The sustained improvement in the country's economic situation, which is extremely vulnerable to international economic trends and fluctuations in the price of oil, has generally set foreign investors at loggerheads with the government. Paradoxically, the government's awareness of the country's potential has been accompanied by a gradual deterioration in business relations with government and semi-public bodies, in sharp contrast to the private sector and the retail trade, both of which have benefited from the country's strong growth over the last three years.

OPPORTUNITY SCOPE

Breakdown of internal demand (GDP + imports) %
- Private consumption   40
- Public spending   11
- Investment   17

| Exports: 46% of GDP | Imports: 49% of GDP |

MAIN DESTINATIONS OF EXPORTS

MAIN ORIGINS OF IMPORTS

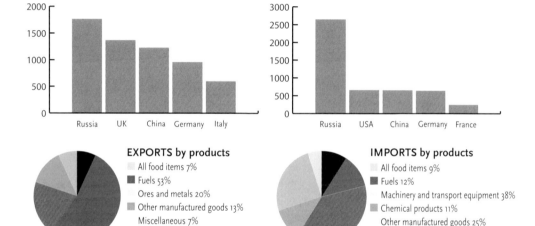

EXPORTS by products
- All food items 7%
- Fuels 53%
- Ores and metals 20%
- Other manufactured goods 13%
- Miscellaneous 7%

IMPORTS by products
- All food items 9%
- Fuels 12%
- Machinery and transport equipment 38%
- Chemical products 11%
- Other manufactured goods 25%
- Miscellaneous 5%

STANDARD OF LIVING / PURCHASING POWER

Indicators	Kazakhstan	Regional average	DC average
GNP per capita (PPP dollars)	6150	8420	6778
GNP per capita (USD)	1350	3544	3568
Human Development Index	0.765	0.810	0.708
Wealthiest 10% share of national income	24	25	33
Urban population percentage	56	61	60
Percentage under 15 years old	26	19	31
number of telephones per 1000 inhabitants	113	280	157
number of computers per 1000 inhabitants	n/a	101	66

Kyrgyzstan

Population (million inhabitants) 5
GDP (million USD) 1,525
GDP per capita (USD) 305

Coface analysis

Short-term: **D**

Medium-term:
Very high risk

RISK ASSESSMENT

An industrial production recovery and rising gold prices have permitted a growth upturn after the slight recession registered in 2002. Gold has remained an essential element of growth with precious metals representing 35 per cent of exports. Electrical energy and agriculture (40 per cent of GDP), two other important sectors for the economy, have been suffering from the lagging pace of their modernization.

Despite progressive fiscal-deficit reduction and the debt structuring accorded by the Paris Club in 2002, the country's financial situation has remained dependent on multilateral institutions. The opening up of the economy and substantial reforms augur well for uninterrupted IMF backing. Internationally, the country has been maintaining good relations with all great powers. It has hosted a US base since the military operations in Afghanistan and also a Russian military base since October 2003, reflecting Moscow's renewed influence in the country. Domestically, the government has hardened its stance in the face of gains by the opposition. With President Akaev having announced that he will step down in 2005, the struggle for the succession could cause some political instability in this context.

MAIN ECONOMIC INDICATORS

US$ millions	1999	2000	2001	2002	2003 (e)	2004 (f)
Economic growth (%)	3.7	5.4	5.3	−0.5	4	3
Inflation (%)	39.9	9.6	3.70	2	4	4
Public-sector balance/GDP (%)	−12.6	−9.9	−5.5	−5.3	−4.7	−4.2
Exports	463	510.9	480.3	502.4	567.2	571.5
Imports	547	506.9	440.3	554.5	604.6	639.8
Trade balance	−84	4	40	−52.1	−30.7	−30.7
Current account balance/GDP (%)	−15.6	−6.6	−3.3	−2.6	−3.4	−4.8
Foreign debt	1,359	1,779	1,629	1,740	1,800	1,801
Debt service/Exports (%)	21.7	22.5	28.0	26.0	20.0	20.0
Currency reserves (import months)	3.4	4.4	3.9	4.3	4.5	4.6

e = estimate, f = forecast

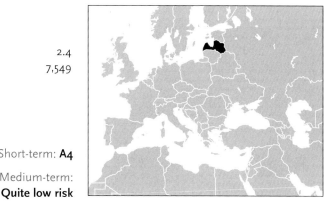

Latvia

Population (million inhabitants)   2.4
GDP (million USD)   7,549

Coface analysis

Short-term: **A4**

Medium-term:
Quite low risk

STRENGTHS

- Well positioned geographically, the country boasts skilled, low-cost labour.
- Prospective European Union accession has been shaping the reform process and economic policy.
- Latvia has been benefiting from appreciable foreign direct investment inflows.

WEAKNESSES

- Strong demand for imported products partly explains the sizeable current account deficit.
- The country has remained dependent on Russia for its transit business, notably for energy products.
- The external debt burden has been high in relation to GDP.
- Discord within the government coalition has been impeding reforms.

RISK ASSESSMENT

Latvia has been posting high growth rates buoyed by strong domestic demand, which should remain the principal economic driver in 2004. The economy should also benefit from strengthening demand from the Community of Independent States, other Baltic countries and the European Union. Development of Russia's port capacity should not yet significantly affect transit business, which has been an appreciable GDP component.

The country's main weakness has been its sizeable current account deficit, inflated by strong demand for imported products linked to consumer spending dynamism and facilities modernization. Thus far, however, that has not been jeopardizing the country's macroeconomic stability with capital inflows, notably foreign direct investment, permitting it to offset the imbalance. The foreign debt burden has nonetheless appeared high in relation to GDP (70 per cent) due to the amount of short-term debt, largely comprising non-resident deposits, mainly Russian. However, the corresponding debt service has remained at reasonable levels.

Politically, discord over reforms has persisted within the centre-right coalition. Progress is still needed in combating corruption, managing the government and improving the legal and social systems. Moreover, despite some easing of the situation, ambiguities still surround the large Russian-speaking minority's status.

MAIN ECONOMIC INDICATORS						
US$ millions	1999	2000	2001	2002	2003 (e)	2004 (f)
Economic growth (%)	2.8	6.8	7.9	6.1	6.0	6.3
Inflation (%)	2.4	2.6	2.5	1.8	2.9	3.4
Public-sector balance/GDP (%)	−3.9	−3.2	−2.2	−2.7	−3.2	−2.9
Unemployment rate (%)	9.1	7.8	7.7	7.6	n/a	n/a
Exports	1,889	2,058	2,216	2,576	3,021	3,542
Imports	2,916	3,116	3,567	4,020	4,918	5,522
Trade balance	−1,027	−1,058	−1,351	−1,444	−1,897	−1,980
Current account balance	−654	−495	−732	−659	−866	−884
Current account balance/GDP (%)	−9.8	−6.9	−9.6	−7.8	−9.0	−8.3
Foreign debt	3,821	4,714	5,570	6,334	6,950	7,240
Debt service/Exports (%)	16.8	20.3	19.6	19.4	16.7	14.9
Currency reserves (import months)	2.7	2.5	3.1	3.0	2.7	2.5

e = estimate, f = forecast

CONDITIONS OF ACCESS TO THE MARKET

■ Market overview

The Latvian market is open and highly competitive. There are no special protectionist measures in place. Latvia is one of 10 countries admitted to the European Union. Talks since March 2000 have speeded up harmonization of the country's legislation, and compliance of its administrative procedures, with EU rules and integration criteria. Latvia completed accession talks on 13 December 2002. On 16 April 2003 it signed the Treaty of Accession, which was ratified by parliament on 30 October 2003. EU entry, set for 1 May 2004, was approved by a referendum held on 20 September 2003, with 67 per cent in favour of membership.

■ Means of entry

Following WTO membership in February 1999, Latvia signed free-trade agreements with various countries, which were revoked by the government on the eve of EU membership. However, they will remain in force until entry. Except for agricultural products, still protected by customs duties at an average rate of 18.6 per cent and a top rate of 50 per cent, trade with the EU and the country's Baltic neighbours is not liable to customs duty. There is a ban on imports of beef, mutton and goatmeat, as well as products containing these meats, on account of BSE. Imports of pigmeat from Lorraine are also prohibited. The country's intellectual property laws are inadequate. Depending on relations with the customer, prepayments are common, as are 30- to 45-day documentary credit and bank transfers. Payments can be made in lats or in foreign currency. The euro has overtaken the dollar as the leading currency of payment, with 55.2 per cent of trade denominated in euros during the first half of 2003, compared with 27.1 per cent in dollars. There are no restrictions on capital transfers. Information on the creditworthiness of Latvian companies can be obtained from the credit information firm IGK BALT, a local subsidiary of Coface IGK Holding.

■ Attitude towards foreign investors

The country is open to foreign investors, with foreign direct investment accounting for 5 per cent of GDP in the first half of 2003. After cutting corporation tax from its current rate of 19 per cent to 15 per cent in 2004, Latvia will have one of the lowest corporation tax rates in Europe. The new Labour Code, adopted in 2002, is in line with European directives. Proposals to cut social security contributions (currently 35.09 per cent of wages, with 26.09 per cent borne by the employer and 9 per cent by the employee) have been indefinitely postponed. A bilateral tax agreement has been in force since 1 May 2001.

■ Foreign exchange regulations

Pegged to special drawing rights since February 1994, the lat's value fluctuates in tandem with the currencies comprising the SDRs. In the first half of 2003, the lat fell against the euro and rose against the dollar. At 5 November 2003, the exchange rate was 1.67 euros to the lat. There are no foreign exchange controls in Latvia.

The Latvian Central Bank plans to join the European Exchange Rate Mechanism (ERM II) on 1 January 2005 and adopt the euro on 1 January 2008.

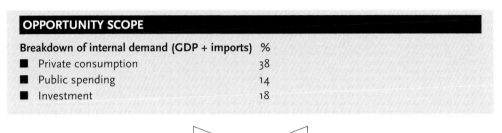

OPPORTUNITY SCOPE

Breakdown of internal demand (GDP + imports)	%
■ Private consumption	38
■ Public spending	14
■ Investment	18

Exports: 46% of GDP   Imports: 54% of GDP

MAIN DESTINATIONS OF EXPORTS

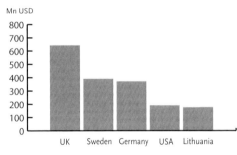

Mn USD — UK, Sweden, Germany, USA, Lithuania

MAIN ORIGINS OF IMPORTS

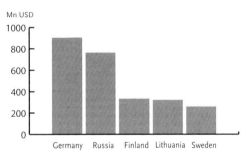

Mn USD — Germany, Russia, Finland, Lithuania, Sweden

EXPORTS by products
- ■ All food items 9%
- ■ Agricultural raw materials 26%
- ■ Machinery and transport equipment 8%
- ■ Chemical products 6%
- ■ Other manufactured goods 44%
- ■ Miscellaneous 7%

IMPORTS by products
- ■ All food items 12%
- ■ Fuels 11%
- ■ Machinery and transport equipment 30%
- ■ Chemical products 12%
- ■ Other manufactured goods 32%
- ■ Miscellaneous 3%

STANDARD OF LIVING / PURCHASING POWER

Indicators	Latvia	Regional average	DC average
GNP per capita (PPP dollars)	7760	8420	6778
GNP per capita (USD)	3230	3544	3508
Human Development Index	0.811	0.810	0.708
Wealthiest 10% share of national income	26	25	33
Urban population percentage	60	61	60
Percentage under 15 years old	17	19	31
number of telephones per 1000 inhabitants	308	280	157
number of computers per 1000 inhabitants	153	101	66

Lithuania

Population (million inhabitants)   3.5
GDP (million USD)   11,992

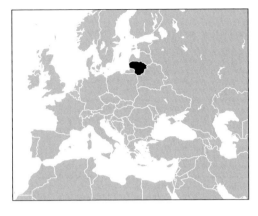

Coface analysis

Short-term: **A4**

Medium-term:
Quite low risk

STRENGTHS

- The country boasts skilled, low-cost labour and is well positioned geographically.
- Prospective European Union accession has been shaping the reform process.
- Prudent economic policy and the local currency's successful re-pegging to the euro in February 2002 should facilitate future adoption of the single currency.
- An ethnically homogeneous population has contributed to the country's stability.

WEAKNESSES

- The litas's prolonged appreciation could affect competitiveness with robust imports already keeping the current account deficit at high levels.
- That imbalance has been the country's main weakness, increasing its dependence on foreign capital inflows.
- Lithuania has been notably lagging in combating corruption and organized crime.

RISK ASSESSMENT

Lithuania boasts one of the region's most dynamic economies. Investment, private consumption, and steady demand from Russia and other Baltic countries fuelled growth in 2003. Economic recovery in Europe and continued steady domestic demand should underpin strong GDP expansion in 2004.

However, the continued import surge, driven by industrial sector restructuring and robust consumer spending, should further exacerbate the external account deficit. Covering that deficit has not given cause for concern so far with the country enjoying both favourable access to international capital markets and appreciable foreign direct investment inflows.

Politically, the likely initiation of impeachment proceedings against President Rolandas Paksas, accused of links with Russian organized crime, and the run-up to legislative elections (October 2004) will disrupt parliament's work and could thus impede progress on reforms. The reform effort must continue in several areas including anti-corruption measures, public finance consolidation, energy sector privatization, the pension system and farm sector restructuring.

MAIN ECONOMIC INDICATORS						
US$ millions	1999	2000	2001	2002	2003 (e)	2004 (f)
Economic growth (%)	−1.8	4.0	6.5	6.7	7.0	6.2
Inflation (%)	0.8	1.0	1.3	0.3	0.0	2.5
Public-sector balance/GDP (%)	−8.5	−2.8	−2.0	−1.2	−1.8	−3.0
Unemployment rate (%)	10.0	12.6	12.9	10.9	9.4	n/a
Exports	3,147	4,050	4,889	6,028	8,033	8,760
Imports	4,551	5,154	5,997	7,343	9,695	10,684
Trade balance	−1,405	−1,104	−1,108	−1,315	−1,662	−1,924
Current account balance	−1,194	−675	−574	−721	−1,006	−1,164
Current account balance/GDP (%)	−11.2	−6.0	−4.8	−5.2	−5.7	−5.9
Foreign debt	4,528	4,856	5,268	6,199	6,874	7,376
Debt service/Exports (%)	17.4	19.3	32.6	37.1	18.2	17.3
Currency reserves (import months)	2.5	2.5	2.7	3.3	2.7	2.6

e = estimate, f = forecast

CONDITIONS OF ACCESS TO THE MARKET

■ Market overview

Purchasing power has been steadily rising for several years. The average wage was about 335 euros at the end of 2002, up almost 5 per cent on the previous year. The growth of Lithuania's economy depends on exports, investment and household spending. The country has a highly competitive and fast-growing mass food retail sector.

■ Means of entry

Compliance with EU integration criteria is largely responsible for turning Lithuania into a highly open market. The only duties that remain in force are excise duties for products such as alcoholic beverages, meat, sugar, cigarettes and oil. Certain products may be imported only by holders of an ad hoc licence. The conditions for obtaining such licences have been greatly relaxed, and the price of import licences, particularly for alcoholic beverages, slashed. The ban on French beef imports is gradually being lifted. These last remaining barriers will be dismantled when the country joins the European Union on 1 May 2004. A new EU-compliant public procurement law abolishing, among other things, the national preference principle has been in force since early 2003. But the administrative machinery would need to be cranked up for the purposes of enforcement.

Standards harmonization is making good progress and it is not difficult to obtain the relevant certificates as long as the products in question comply with a European standard. Competition law is also broadly in line with EU criteria. For payments, short-term credit is increasingly used and has all but replaced prepayment and documentary credit.

■ Attitude towards foreign investors

Foreign investors are treated on an equal footing with Lithuanian nationals, with no cases of discrimination reported. Lithuanian legislation offers foreign investors a number of incentives, including 15 per cent corporation tax. Foreign investors may freely repatriate profits, income and dividends derived from their activities upon meeting their tax obligations. The workforce is highly skilled (technicians, engineers, scientists) and wage costs low. Law and financial services firms offer the highest wages. Employer and employee social security contributions are 31 per cent and 3 per cent of gross wages respectively. Contributions are paid to the country's social security agency, Sodra.

Foreign investors by and large appreciate the overall business climate in Lithuania. A combination of factors makes the country attractive: proper regulatory framework, good infrastructure, low taxation, skilled labour and low labour costs.

■ **Foreign exchange regulations**

After being pegged to the dollar, the Lithuanian currency, the litas, has been tied to the euro since 1 February 2002 by a fixed rate (1 euro = 3.4528 litas). Numerous Lithuanian firms hold euro-denominated accounts. Lithuania plans to join the euro zone in early 2007.

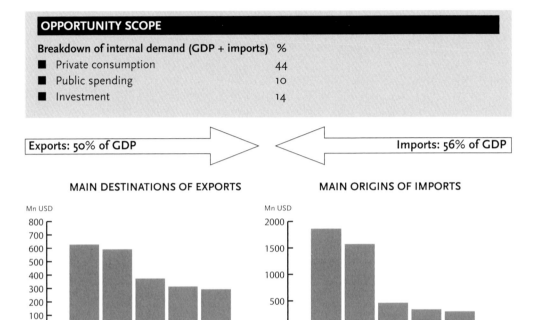

OPPORTUNITY SCOPE

Breakdown of internal demand (GDP + imports)	%
■ Private consumption	44
■ Public spending	10
■ Investment	14

Exports: 50% of GDP ⟹ ⟸ Imports: 56% of GDP

MAIN DESTINATIONS OF EXPORTS

Mn USD
(bar chart: Latvia, Germany, UK, Poland, USA)

MAIN ORIGINS OF IMPORTS

Mn USD
(bar chart: Russia, Germany, Italy, Poland, France)

EXPORTS by products
- ■ All food items 12%
- ■ Fuels 23%
- ■ Machinery and transport equipment 20%
- ■ Chemical products 7%
- ■ Other manufactured goods 31%
- ■ Miscellaneous 7%

IMPORTS by products
- ■ All food items 9%
- ■ Fuels 20%
- ■ Machinery and transport equipment 28%
- ■ Chemical products 12%
- ■ Other manufactured goods 24%
- ■ Miscellaneous 7%

STANDARD OF LIVING / PURCHASING POWER

Indicators	Lithuania	Regional average	DC average
GNP per capita (PPP dollars)	8350	8420	6778
GNP per capita (USD)	3350	3544	3568
Human Development Index	0.824	0.810	0.708
Wealthiest 10% share of national income	25	25	33
Urban population percentage	69	61	60
Percentage under 15 years old	19	19	31
number of telephones per 1000 inhabitants	313	280	157
number of computers per 1000 inhabitants	71	101	66

Luxembourg

Population (inhabitants)	444,000
GDP (million USD)	21,000
GDP per capita (USD)	47,297

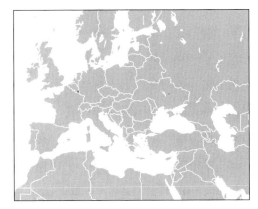

Coface analysis   Short-term: **A1**

RISK ASSESSMENT

Despite a year-end upturn, growth remained weak in 2003. Private consumption fell sharply amid surging unemployment attributable to a delayed employment adjustment to a long-past economic slowdown. Investment only averted a decline thanks to increased public spending facilitated by the virtual absence of public-sector deficits or debt and the sizeable fiscal reserves amassed during good years. Meanwhile, the decline of financial-service exports, linked to the widespread drop in market activity, weighed on total exports.

A moderate upturn should develop in 2004. Strengthening international demand and the continued recovery of financial markets should spur goods and services exports with public-sector spending continuing to buoy investment. However, consumer spending will remain affected by the persistent rise of unemployment attributable to continuing cost reductions in the financial sector and the fact that job creations have been more beneficial to cross-border workers than residents.

Despite the sluggish growth, Coface's payment experience remained at satisfactory levels in 2003, a trend consistent with the stable bankruptcy rate. The good business conditions enjoyed in commerce and company services offset the shakier situation in finance and non-residential construction. The improved economic conditions expected this year should consolidate those results.

PAYMENT INCIDENTS INDEX
(12 months moving average - base 100 : World 1995)

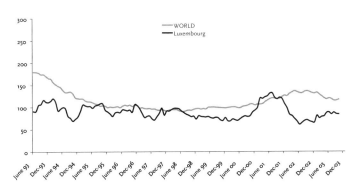

MAIN ECONOMIC INDICATORS

%	1999	2000	2001	2002	2003 (e)	2004 (f)
Economic growth	7.8	9.1	1.2	1.3	1.2	2
Consumer spending (% change)	2.6	4.6	4.5	2.3	1.6	1.9
Investment (% change)	14.6	−3.5	10.1	−1.4	0.7	2.2
Inflation	1.5	2.6	3.3	2.3	2	1.8
Unemployment rate	2.9	2.6	2.6	3	3.8	4.2
Short-term interest rate	3	4.4	4.2	3.3	2.3	2.1
Public-sector balance/GDP (%)	3.5	6.4	6.2	2.4	−0.6	−0.8
Public-sector debt/GDP (%)	6	5.5	5.5	5.7	5.1	5.7
Exports (% change)	14.8	16.7	2.6	−0.3	1.4	3.8
Imports (% change)	14.6	14.8	4.8	−1.6	1.8	4
Current account balance/GDP (%)	8.9	13.7	9	7.2	6.9	7.6

e = estimate, f = forecast

Macedonia

Population (million inhabitants) 2
GDP (million USD) 3,426
GDP per capita (USD) 1,713

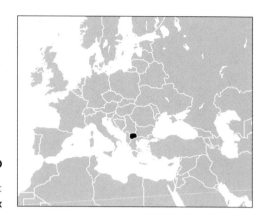

Short-term: **D**

Medium-term:
Very high risk

Coface analysis

RISK ASSESSMENT

Concentrated on a small number of exporting companies, the growth upturn has remained shaky. However, tight fiscal policy along with a decline of food prices and appreciation of the euro – to which the denar is pegged – has permitted the controlling of inflation.

Moreover, the export recovery should stop the current account deficit from growing. The imbalance has nonetheless remained substantial amid low levels of foreign direct investment attributable to high political risk and an unfavourable business climate. Implementation of major reforms will be necessary notably to strengthen the banking sector and improve health and pension system management. The country benefits from an IMF loan and has remained dependent on international aid.

Over two years after signature of the Ohrid agreement in August 2001, which brought the civil war to an end, the peace has remained shaky. Although consultations between political parties have been occurring more regularly, the coalition government's position is still precarious. The social climate has remained tense with unemployment affecting over 30 per cent of the working population. Moreover, insecurity and inter-ethnic tensions between the Slavic majority and substantial Albanian minority could boil over at any time. Negotiations on defining municipal boundaries in the framework of administrative and fiscal decentralization will be a major test for continued political dialogue.

MAIN ECONOMIC INDICATORS						
US$ millions	1999	2000	2001	2002	2003 (e)	2004 (f)
Economic growth (%)	4.3	4.5	−4.5	0.7	2.8	3.0
Inflation (%)	−0.7	5.8	5.3	2.4	1.8	2.5
Public-sector balance/GDP (%)	0.0	1.8	−7.2	−5.7	−2.5	−2.5
Exports	1,190	1,321	1,155	1,113	1,354	1,443
Imports	1,686	2,011	1,677	1,877	2,123	2,202
Trade balance	−496	−690	−521	−764	−769	−759
Current account balance/GDP (%)	−0.9	−2.1	−6.8	−8.6	−6.3	−7.0
Foreign debt/GDP (%)	1,493	1,487	1,368	1,507	1,583	1,710
Debt service/Exports (%)	9.6	9.6	15.1	11.9	10.0	10.1
Currency reserves (import months)	2.7	3.5	4.5	3.9	3.9	3.8

e = estimate, f = forecast

Malta

Population (inhabitants)	390,000
GDP (million USD)	3,633
GDP per capita (USD)	9,315

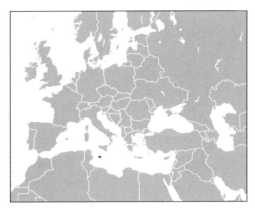

Short-term: **A3**

Medium-term:

Coface analysis   **Low risk**

RISK ASSESSMENT

The Central Bank reduced its key interest rates in 2003. Several factors have facilitated that policy including the weakness of inflationary pressures and strengthening of the foreign exchange regime's credibility (pegging of the Maltese lira to a currency basket where the euro represents 70 per cent) after confirmation of the country's admission to the European Union. However, growth has failed to accelerate due notably to the sagging international economic environment. External accounts have deteriorated. Moreover, public finances have continued to register severe imbalances with concomitant growth of already high government debt.

An investment upturn and strengthening foreign demand should nonetheless drive growth in 2004. With capital goods imports rising, the trade deficit will nonetheless remain high, only partly offset by the growing services balance surplus fuelled by a slight tourism recovery. Although foreign debt, due in part by banks, will remain substantial in relation to GDP, it has to be put into the perspective of the substantial assets held by the banking system abroad.

MAIN ECONOMIC INDICATORS						
US$ millions	1999	2000	2001	2002	2003 (e)	2004 (f)
Economic growth (%)	4.1	6.4	−1.2	1.2	1.5	3.3
Inflation (%)	2.1	2.4	2.9	2.2	1.0	1.2
Public-sector balance/GDP (%)	−7.8	−5.5	−5.2	−6.2	−7.0	n/a
Exports	2,017	2,479	2,002	2,150	2,408	2,521
Imports	2,680	3,232	2,568	2,653	3,232	3,413
Trade balance	−663	−754	−566	−503	−824	−892
Current account balance	−122	−470	−165	−151	−240	−250
Current account balance/GDP (%)	−3.3	−13.1	−4.5	−3.9	−5.2	−5.1
Foreign debt/GDP (%)	128.7	113.3	113.4	108.6	93.5	87.2
Debt service/Exports (%)	11.2	15.6	15.4	15.1	13.0	12.5
Currency reserves (import months)	4.6	3.5	4.9	6.3	6.0	6.4

e = estimate, f = forecast

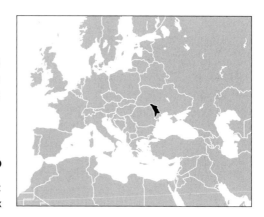

Moldova

Population (million inhabitants)	4.3
GDP (million USD)	1,479
GDP per capita (USD)	344

Short-term: **D**

Medium-term:

Coface analysis **Very high risk**

RISK ASSESSMENT

Although the economy has been growing at a good pace, it has been essentially catch-up growth after a severe recession in the 1990s. Moreover, it has remained particularly dependent on economic growth in Russia, Moldova's main trading partner. Meanwhile, the economy has been undermined by its dependence on both agriculture (25 per cent of GDP) and the food sector (40 per cent of exports) and the country's very limited industrial diversification, linked to the low level of private investment.

Economic policy has been prudent with the fiscal deficit under control but not without recourse to

budgetary sequestration amid limited revenues from tax collection and privatizations. With the current account deficit remaining too high considering Moldova's capacities, the country had to restructure its sole eurobond in 2002. Hampered by non-negligible debt service and its limited currency reserves, the country has not been able to rely on regular backing by international financial institutions. Despite pro-European pronouncements, the current communist government has carried out very incomplete reforms. Finally, political risk has remained high with the country divided on the linguistic issue and the virtually autonomous Transnistria region's future still uncertain.

MAIN ECONOMIC INDICATORS

US$ millions	1999	2000	2001	2002	2003 (e)	2004 (f)
Economic growth (%)	−3.4	2.1	6	7	6	5
Inflation (%)	43.8	18.5	6	6	12	13
Public-sector balance/GDP (%)	−5.3	−2.0	−0.7	−2.3	−1.0	−1.2
Exports	474	477	567	660	800	910
Imports	611	771	879	1,038	1,320	1,430
Trade balance	−137	−294	−311	−378	−520	−520
Current account balance	−79	−107	−105	−109	−150	−140
Current account balance/GDP (%)	−3.6	−8.4	−7.4	−8.0	−8.1	−6.6
Foreign debt	1,000	1,200	1,200	1,400	1,411	1,451
Debt service/Exports (%)	25.1	14.1	15.9	14.0	14.9	13.3
Currency reserves (import months)	2.9	2.7	2.5	2.6	2.3	2.2

e = estimate, f = forecast

The Netherlands

Population (million inhabitants)	16.1
GDP (million USD)	418,500
GDP per capita (USD)	25,986

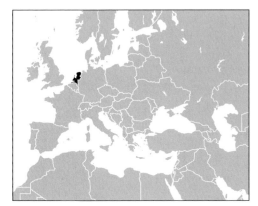

Coface analysis   Short-term: **A2**

RISK ASSESSMENT

Despite a slight recovery in the last quarter, recession took hold in 2003. With domestic demand sagging, exports have been suffering from both the persistent sluggishness of European demand, particularly from Germany, and the strong euro. Confronted with a loss of competitiveness resulting from the rapid rise of labour costs, companies have been cutting back on investments and personnel. Amid increasing unemployment and slower wage growth, meanwhile, households have been saving more and spending less.

Improvement of economic conditions in 2004 will primarily depend on an international trade recovery, notably in Europe. With the public sector again in deficit, the government should reduce spending, cut social services and increase taxes while attempting to increase the flexibility of an employment market marked by a high unemployment rate. Household consumption should remain sluggish due to the tightening of fiscal policy, rapid increase in unemployment and a loss of purchasing power.

Those economic difficulties compounded by the loss of competitiveness by Dutch companies have resulted in a sharp increase in bankruptcies, rising an estimated 26 per cent in 2003.

MAIN ECONOMIC INDICATORS

%	1999	2000	2001	2002	2003 (e)	2004 (f)
Economic growth	4	3.5	1.2	0.2	−0.7	1.1
Consumer spending (% change)	4.7	3.5	1.4	0.8	−0.6	0.8
Investment (% change)	9.9	1	−1.9	−6.5	−3.1	1.7
Inflation	1.9	3.3	4.6	3.5	2.1	1.7
Unemployment rate	3.2	2.6	2	2.3	4.3	5.8
Short-term interest rate	3	4.4	4.2	3.3	2.3	2.1
Public-sector balance/GDP (%)	0.7	2.2	0.1	−1.6	−2.4	−2.4
Public-sector debt/GDP (%)	63.1	55.8	52.8	52.7	53.5	54.3
Exports (% change)	5.1	11.3	1.7	−0.1	1	5.3
Imports (% change)	5.8	10.6	2.4	−0.2	1.5	4.8
Current account balance/GDP (%)	3.8	2.2	2.0	1.4	2.3	3.5

e = estimate, f = forecast

PAYMENT AND COLLECTION PRACTICES

■ Payment

Bills of exchange are rarely used in the Netherlands because it is not standard business practice to do so. As in Germany, they signal mistrust on the part of the supplier and so are incompatible with the climate of trust needed to maintain a stable business relationship.

Cheques too are little used. They are an unreliable means of payment as they can be cashed only if covered. Consequently, issuing an uncovered cheque is not a criminal offence and those on the receiving end of a bounced cheque incur high bank charges.

Under Dutch law, bills of exchange and cheques serve mainly to substantiate the existence of a debt.

By contrast, bank transfers ('Bankgiro') are by far the most common means of payment. All leading Dutch banks use the SWIFT network, which offers a cheap, flexible and quick international funds transfer service.

Centralizing accounts, based on a centralized local cashing system and simplified management of fund repatriation, are also widely used.

■ Debt collection

The collection process begins with the debtor being sent a formal demand for the payment of principal plus accrued interest. This is followed, where necessary, by the service of a summons via a bailiff or solicitor. Where the sales agreement makes no mention of the interest rate, from 1 December 2002 the rate of interest applicable is the European Central Bank's refinancing rate, marked up by seven basis points. The rate in force before the first day of the six-monthly period in question applies throughout that period.

In the absence of payment or an agreement, creditors may engage a local lawyer to initiate legal proceedings. The Dutch legal system allows lawyers to act as both barristers and solicitors: as solicitors they practise within the jurisdiction of their registration; whereas as barristers they may plead cases before any court in the country.

Before initiating legal proceedings, effective pressure can be brought to bear on a debtor by means of a winding-up petition. For undisputed claims, this can be obtained without much difficulty, provided the creditor produces evidence of payment default. Such petitions are filed in a civil court (there being no commercial courts), but require the existence of a second claim of any kind (commercial, alimony, tax debt and so on) in order to be admissible.

Ordinary proceedings in which both parties are heard are for the most part based on written submissions. They consist in a simplified procedure being brought before a district court (*kantongerecht*) for claims under 5,000 euros (formerly 10,000 guilders). Larger claims are heard by a court of first instance (*Rechtbank*), whereby both parties argue their case via written submissions. Unless the parties expressly request the right to make oral arguments, which is rarely the case, the judge bases his or her ruling on the principal case documents submitted by the parties after they have appeared in court (primarily to seek an amicable settlement).

For complex cases requiring special examination, the judge will follow a more formal procedure based on the examination of each adversary's brief and counter-briefs. In such matters, the judge will carefully assess the parties' compliance with the general terms and conditions of sale appearing on invoices and purchase orders, which form the legal framework of the commercial contract.

Finally, recourse to arbitration is common in the Netherlands. Most arbitration bodies work in specific fields and abitrators are often selected from among specialist lawyers. Arbitral awards tend to be based on equity rather than on legal considerations.

PAYMENT INCIDENTS INDEX
(12 months moving average - base 100 : World 1995)

Norway

Population (million inhabitants)	4.5
GDP (million USD)	190,500
GDP per capita (USD)	41,979

Coface analysis   Short-term: **A1**

RISK ASSESSMENT

Growth was very sluggish in 2003 despite increased public sector spending financed by higher oil revenues and robust household spending buoyed by increased disposable income. Exports, which represent 40 per cent of mainland Norway's economy, suffered from still-difficult international economic conditions and a loss of competitiveness by companies attributable to increased production costs. Faced with sluggish foreign demand, companies were unable to capitalize on the second-half interest-rate decline to increase their investments.

Growth should register a sharp rebound in 2004 thanks to more favourable interest-rate and

krone exchange-rate levels and a budget including both sharp income tax reductions and increased public-sector spending. The foreseeable halt of the unemployment rise and greater control over inflation will further bolster household confidence and consumption. Household spending should thus continue to drive growth. Exports, meanwhile, will recover buoyed by a more favourable international context and the krone's depreciation.

The company bankruptcy rate increased sharply in 2003, rising an estimated 18 per cent, reflecting the Norwegian economy's difficulties. A progressive improvement in the company financial situation should accompany the recovery expected in 2004.

MAIN ECONOMIC INDICATORS

%	1999	2000	2001	2002	2003 (e)	2004 (f)
Economic growth	2.1	2.8	1.9	1	0.3	2.4
Consumer spending (% change)	3.3	3.9	2.6	3.6	2.8	3.7
Investment (% change)	−8.6	−4	−7.8	−4.3	2	2.7
Inflation	2	3	2.4	0.7	2.4	1.6
Unemployment rate	3.2	3.4	3.5	4	4.5	4.4
Short-term interest rate	6.5	6.7	7.2	6.9	4.2	3.4
Public-sector balance/GDP (%)	6.1	15	13.7	10.9	9	6.7
Public-sector debt/GDP (%)	26.8	30	27.3	26	25	25
Exports (% change)	2.8	4	4.1	−0.5	0.1	2.1
Imports (% change)	−1.8	2.7	0.9	1.7	3.2	2.7
Current account balance/GDP (%)	5.3	15	15.3	13.2	12	11.2

e = estimate, f = forecast

PAYMENT AND COLLECTION PRACTICES

■ Payment

Bills of exchange and cheques are neither widely used nor recommended as they must meet a number of formal requirements in order to be valid. In addition, creditors frequently refuse to accept cheques as a means of payment. As a rule, both instruments serve mainly to substantiate the existence of a debt.

Conversely, promissory notes (*gjeldsbrev*) are much more common in commercial transactions and offer superior guarantees when accompanied by an acknowledgement of debt from the buyer as, in the event of default, such an admission allows the beneficiary to obtain a writ of execution from the competent court (*Namrett*).

Bank transfers are by far the most widely used means of payment. All leading Norwegian banks use the SWIFT network, which offers a cheap, flexible and quick international funds transfer service.

Centralizing accounts, based on a centralized local cashing system and simplified management of fund transfers, are also fairly widely used.

Electronic payments, involving the execution of payment orders via the website of the client's bank, are rapidly gaining popularity.

■ Debt collection

The collection process commences with the debtor being sent a demand for the payment of the principal amount, plus any contractually agreed interest penalties, within 14 days. Where there is no specific interest clause in the agreement, interest starts to accrue one month after the demand is sent at a rate set by royal decree under the Late Interest Act of 17 December 1976 (*lov om renter ved forsinket betaling m.m*).

In the absence of payment or an agreement, creditors may go before the Conciliation Board (*Forliksrådet*), an administrative body presided over by non-professional judges, to obtain a quick and inexpensive ruling. In this event, they must submit documents authenticating their claim, which should be denominated in Norwegian kroner. The Conciliation Board then summons the debtor at short notice to acknowledge or dispute the claim before hearing the parties, either in person or through their official representatives (*Stevnevitne*). At this stage of proceedings, lawyers are not required.

If a settlement is not forthcoming, the case is referred to the court of first instance for examination. However, for claims found to be valid, the Conciliation Board has the power to hand down a decision which has the force of a court judgment.

Where a defendant fails to respond to the arbitrator's summons or appear at the hearing, the Board passes a ruling in default, which also has the force of a court judgment.

More complex or disputed claims are heard by the court of first instance (*Byret*). The plenary proceedings of this court are based on oral evidence and written submissions. The court examines the arguments and hears the parties' witnesses before delivering a verdict.

Norway does not have a system of commercial courts, but the probate court (*Skifteret*) is also competent to rule on insolvency proceedings.

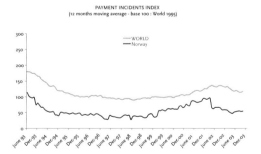

PAYMENT INCIDENTS INDEX
(12 months moving average - base 100 : World 1995)

Poland

Population (million inhabitants)	38.6
GDP (million USD)	176,256

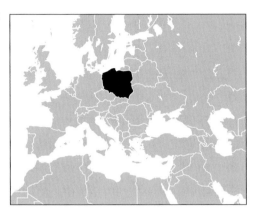

Coface analysis

Short-term: **A4**

Medium-term:
Quite low risk

STRENGTHS

- The country's scheduled admission to the European Union in May 2004 has been enhancing its growth prospects.
- Foreign direct investment has permitted a continued modernization of the country's manufacturing sector.
- Foreign debt remains at sustainable levels.
- Moderate external financing needs and comfortable foreign exchange reserves tend to reduce the country's vulnerability to a crisis of confidence.

WEAKNESSES

- Poland has been lagging seriously in its preparation for European Union membership (particularly in the agricultural sector).
- The size of the public-sector deficit has been undermining market confidence.
- Structural rigidities have been impeding growth (the country has been particularly lagging in loss-making company restructuring, privatizations and labour-market reform).
- Private foreign debt has grown strongly in recent years.
- The coalition government's weakness and social tensions have been complicating matters in implementing economic policy and reforms.

RISK ASSESSMENT

Growth rebounded in 2003, buoyed by a strong export surge attributable to the zloty's depreciation and a moderate increase in domestic demand. Inflation has remained weak and the current account deficit has narrowed. However, uncertainties surrounding the conduct of fiscal policy have undermined market confidence. The social democrat coalition has lost its majority and is suffering from a lack of popularity. A substantial part of the government's tax reform could fail to gain approval, delaying the necessary consolidation of public accounts.

In 2004, an investment upturn, which should result from the European recovery in particular, will contribute to a slight acceleration of growth. The sustained rise of sales abroad should permit stabilization of the current account deficit despite increased imports. An increase in amortization of the foreign debt will nonetheless inflate financing needs. However, those needs have remained moderate and the expected increase in foreign direct investment, after two sub-par years, should help cover them.

In an improving economic context, payment incidents have become less frequent. However, the Coface payment-incident index remains above the world and regional averages, reflecting the weaknesses of many companies undermined by foreign competition and two years of virtual stagnation. Some companies have been experiencing solvency problems. The situation has remained difficult in sectors like shipyards, steel, mass distribution, construction and textiles.

MAIN ECONOMIC INDICATORS

US$ billions	1999	2000	2001	2002	2003 (e)	2004 (f)
Economic growth (%)	4.1	4.0	1.0	1.4	3.5	3.8
Inflation (%)	7.3	10.2	5.5	2.0	0.8	2.0
Public-sector balance/GDP (%)	−3.2	−2.6	−5.1	−6.5	−6.7	−8.3
Unemployment rate (%)	13.1	16.0	18.5	20.0	19.5	19.0
Exports	30.1	35.9	41.7	46.7	60.9	70.9
Imports	45.1	48.2	49.3	54.0	66.2	75.5
Trade balance	−15.1	−12.3	−7.7	−7.2	−5.3	−4.6
Current account balance	−12.4	−10.0	−5.3	−5.0	−4.2	−4.5
Current account balance/GDP (%)	−8.0	−6.1	−2.9	−2.7	−2.0	−2.0
Foreign debt	65.4	69.5	71.8	81.9	89.6	91.6
Debt service/Exports (%)	11.1	13.7	18.2	11.9	9.8	10.3
Currency reserves (import months)	5.8	5.2	4.9	5.1	4.8	4.4

e = estimate, f = forecast

CONDITIONS OF ACCESS TO THE MARKET

■ Market overview
From 1 January 2003, the minimum gross wage has been 800 zlotys (about 180 euros). At the end of 2003, the average wage was 2,300 zlotys (about 500 euros).

■ Means of entry
Sweeping reforms in the laws and regulations governing the terms of access to the Polish market have brought Poland closer into line with European Union standards. In matters of trade policy, Poland continues to harmonize its trade arrangements with EU integration criteria and, through the WTO, coordinate its actions and policies with those of the European Union.

From 1 May 2004, there will be no more customs duties between Poland and the European Union. Transitional measures, however, will remain in place for medical equipment (until the end of 2005) and human and veterinary medicines, with approval of their release on to the market withheld until the end of 2008.

■ Attitude towards foreign investors
Drawing on the country's clear competitive edge, the Polish government had already attracted US$68 billion in foreign direct investment by mid-2003. But the pace of privatization has slowed since 2001, even though many leading companies in the energy, banking, petrochemicals, heavy industry, defence and food sectors still have to be sold.

The new business law, in force since 1 January 2001, places domestic and foreign companies on an equal footing. Almost all restrictions on foreign investment have been abolished – except for the acquisition of farmland – and the number of activities subject to approval reduced. Safeguards for foreign investors have also been strengthened. There are no restrictions on the repatriation of dividends. However, the administrative service continues to be marred by lack of transparency, red tape and, in some cases, corruption. Administrative procedures, especially the process for obtaining court rulings, remain long and complex.

■ Foreign exchange regulations
The zloty's exchange rate is determined by the market, with a central peg set daily by the National Bank of Poland. Since 1 October 2002, the zloty has been fully convertible.

PAYMENT AND COLLECTION PRACTICES

■ Payment

Bills of exchange and cheques are not widely used as they must meet a number of formal issuing requirements in order to be valid. Nevertheless, for dishonoured and protested bills and cheques, creditors may resort to a fast-track procedure resulting in an injunction to pay.

Until now, cash payments were commonly used in Poland by individuals and firms alike, but under the new Business Act (*Działalność gospodarczy*), which came into force on 1 January 2001, companies are required to make settlements via a bank account for transactions exceeding the equivalent in zlotys of 3,000 euros.

One highly original instrument is the *weksel in blanco*, an incomplete promissory note bearing only the term *weksel* and the issuer's signature at the time of issue. The signature constitutes an irrevocable promise to pay and this undertaking is enforceable upon completion of the promissory note (amount, place and date of payment) in accordance with a prior agreement between issuer and beneficiary. *Weksels in blanco* are widely used as they also constitute a guarantee of payment in commercial agreements and the rescheduling of payments.

Bank transfers are by far the most widely used means of payment. Leading Polish banks – after an initial phase of privatization and a second phase of concentration – use the SWIFT network, which offers a cheap, flexible and quick domestic and international funds transfer service.

■ Debt collection

It is advisable, as far as possible, not to initiate recovery proceedings locally due not only to the cumbersome formalities and the high cost of legal action but also to the country's lengthy court procedures: it takes almost two years to obtain a writ of enforcement due to the lack of judges adequately trained in the disciplines of the market economy and proper equipment.

A demand for payment, accompanied by proof of debt, serves to remind the debtor of his or her obligation to pay the outstanding sum, plus accrued interest. From 1 January 2004, interest may be claimed as of the 31st day following delivery of the product or service, even where the parties have agreed to a longer time limit for payment. From the 31st day till the contractual payment date the rate of interest applicable is the legal interest rate in force. Thereafter, in the case of late payment, the higher tax penalty rate is applicable.

It is advisable to seek an amicable settlement based on a schedule of payment, preferably drawn up by a notary public, which includes an enforcement clause that allows creditors, in the event of default by the debtor, to go directly to the enforcement stage, subject to acknowledgement by the courts of the binding nature of this document.

Creditors may seek an injunction to pay (*nakaz zapłaty*) via a fast-track and less expensive procedure, provided they produce positive proof of debt (bill of exchange, cheque, unpaid *weksel in blanco*, acknowledgement of debt, etc). If the judge is not convinced of the substance of the claim – a decision the judge alone is empowered to make – he or she may refer the case to full trial.

The written part of ordinary proceedings consists in the filing of submissions by the parties and supporting case documents, and the oral part in the hearing of parties and their witnesses on the main hearing date. At such legal proceedings, the judge is required, as far as possible, to attempt conciliation between the parties.

Commercial disputes are generally heard by the commercial courts (*Sąd Gospodarczy*), which fall under the jurisdiction either of the district courts or of the regional courts (*Voivodies*) depending on the size of the claim.

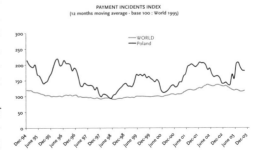

PAYMENT INCIDENTS INDEX
(12 months moving average - base 100 = World 1995)

OPPORTUNITY SCOPE

Breakdown of internal demand (GDP + imports)	%
■ Private consumption	50
■ Public spending	13
■ Investment	17

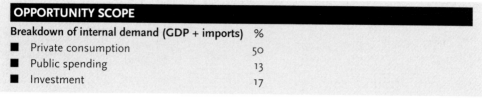

Exports: 29% of GDP   Imports: 33% of GDP

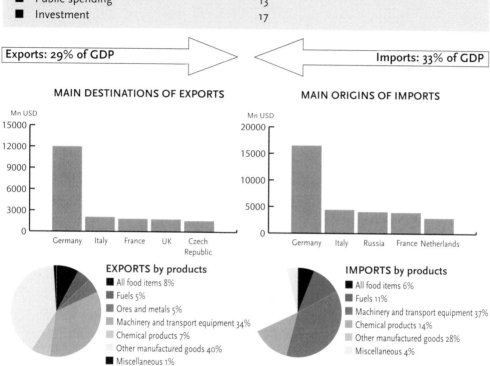

MAIN DESTINATIONS OF EXPORTS

Mn USD
Germany, Italy, France, UK, Czech Republic

MAIN ORIGINS OF IMPORTS

Mn USD
Germany, Italy, Russia, France, Netherlands

EXPORTS by products
- ■ All food items 8%
- ■ Fuels 5%
- ■ Ores and metals 5%
- ■ Machinery and transport equipment 34%
- ■ Chemical products 7%
- ■ Other manufactured goods 40%
- ■ Miscellaneous 1%

IMPORTS by products
- ■ All food items 6%
- ■ Fuels 11%
- ■ Machinery and transport equipment 37%
- ■ Chemical products 14%
- ■ Other manufactured goods 28%
- ■ Miscellaneous 4%

STANDARD OF LIVING / PURCHASING POWER

Indicators	Poland	Regional average	DC average
GNP per capita (PPP dollars)	4230	8420	6778
GNP per capita (USD)	9370	3544	3568
Human Development Index	0.841	0.810	0.708
Wealthiest 10% share of national income	25	25	33
Urban population percentage	63	61	60
Percentage under 15 years old	19	19	31
number of telephones per 1000 inhabitants	295	280	157
number of computers per 1000 inhabitants	85	101	66

Portugal

Population (million inhabitants)	10.4
GDP (million USD)	121,700
GDP per capita (USD)	11,724

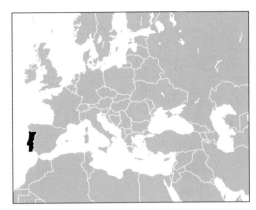

Coface analysis   Short-term: **A2**

RISK ASSESSMENT

In 2003, the economy continued to pay for the past decade's excesses. Economic stagnation thus gave way to recession. Domestic demand remained hampered by continuing austere fiscal policy (increased VAT and reduced spending) intended to bring the deficit back down below the 3 per cent threshold. Furthermore, household spending declined due to a sharp rise in unemployment, slower wage growth and a still-troubling inflation rate that caused a further loss of purchasing power. Meanwhile, the euro's appreciation and weak foreign demand prevented exports from really taking off. Facing sluggish domestic and foreign demand, companies cut back further on their investments.

Although the economy should strengthen in 2004, the recovery will doubtless only be moderate.

Improving European demand should spur exports with slightly lower inflation and interest rates buoying private consumption. After declining in 2002 and 2003, investments should moderately recover.

Companies in most sectors suffered from the negative effects of the depressed context of the past two years. Their payment behaviour deteriorated as evidenced by the Coface payment-incident index trend. Despite the upturn expected in 2004, company solvency will remain shaky particularly with European Union enlargement increasing competitive pressure on many products and necessitating a major effort on productivity to offset higher payroll costs compared to Central Europe. On that score, companies in the textiles and clothing sector will be the most vulnerable to competition.

MAIN ECONOMIC INDICATORS						
%	1999	2000	2001	2002	2003 (e)	2004 (f)
Economic growth	3.8	3.4	1.7	0.4	−0.8	1.7
Consumer spending (% change)	5.1	2.9	1.3	0.6	−0.9	1.5
Investment (% change)	6.4	4.4	0.1	−5.2	−6	2.5
Inflation	2.1	3.3	4.4	3.7	3	2.5
Unemployment rate	4.4	4	4.1	5.1	6.5	6.5
Short-term interest rate	3	4.4	4.2	3.3	2.3	2.1
Public-sector balance/GDP (%)	−2.9	−2.9	−4.3	−2.7	−2.9	−3.3
Public-sector debt/GDP (%)	54.3	53.3	55.5	58.1	60	60
Exports (% change)	2.9	7.8	1.8	2.1	2	5.5
Imports (% change)	8.4	5.4	0.9	−0.4	−5	2
Current account balance/GDP (%)	−8.5	−10.9	−9.4	−7.1	−7.7	−6

e = estimate, f = forecast

PAYMENT AND COLLECTION PRACTICES

■ Payment

Bills of exchange are widely used for commercial transactions in Portugal. In order to be valid, however, they are subject to stamp duty whose rate is set each year in the country's budget. The current rate of stamp duty is 0.5 per cent of the amount of the bill, or a minimum of 1 euro. A bill of exchange is generally deemed independent of the contract to which it relates.

While creditors, in the event of payment default, are not required to issue a protest notice before bringing an action to court, such a notice can be used to publicize payment default and pressure the debtor to honour his or her obligations, albeit belatedly.

Cheques too are widely used. They are payable on presentation and subject to the minimum stamp duty that is borne by the bank. It is no longer an offence to issue uncovered cheques as a guarantee for staggered payments.

In the event of default, cheques, bills of exchange and promissory notes offer effective guarantees to creditors as they are enforceable instruments in law and entitle holders to initiate executory proceedings. Under this process, creditors may petition the court to issue a writ of execution and notify the debtor of such an order. Where the debtor still fails to pay up, creditors may request the court to issue an attachment order against the debtor's property.

SWIFT bank transfers, which are both flexible and efficient, also account for a growing proportion of payments.

■ Debt collection

Out-of-court collection starts with the debtor being sent a final demand for the payment of the principal amount, plus any default interest that may have been agreed between the parties, within eight days. Save as otherwise provided in the agreement, from 18 February 2003 the rate of interest applicable is the European Central Bank's refinancing rate marked up by seven basis points. The Ministerial

Order of April 1999, which is still in force, sets the legal default interest rate at 12 per cent for commercial debt and 7 per cent for other debt.

In addition to the fast-track procedure (injunction to pay – *injunção*) in respect of undisputed claims arising from civil or commercial contracts (regardless of amount from 19 March 2003), which must be initiated at the court in whose jurisdiction the obligation is enforceable, creditors may bring an action under the somewhat costly and protracted 'declarative proceedings' (*acção declarativa*), which take a year or more, in order to obtain a ruling establishing their right to payment. Thereafter, they have to bring 'enforcement proceedings' (*acção executiva*) to enforce the court's ruling.

Under the revised Code of Civil Procedure introduced in January 1996, any original deed established by private seal (ie any written document issued to a supplier) in which the buyer unequivocally acknowledges his or her debt is henceforth deemed an instrument enforceable by law. This provision aims to encourage buyers to comply with contractual undertakings and offers creditors a safeguard against protracted legal action.

As Portugal does not have commercial courts (other than those in Lisbon and Oporto, which deal with insolvency proceedings and dissolution of companies), civil courts (*Varas Cíveis*), presided over by a collegial panel of three judges, rule on business-related claims over 14,963.94 euros (formerly 3 million escudos).

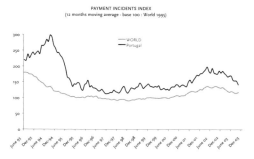

PAYMENT INCIDENTS INDEX
(12 months moving average - base 100 : World 1995)

Romania

Population (million inhabitants)   22.4
GDP (million USD)   38,718

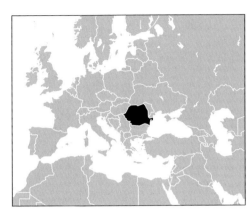

Short-term: **B**

Medium-term:
Coface analysis   **Moderately high risk**

STRENGTHS

- The country's pending admission to the European Union, scheduled for 2007, has been enhancing its economic prospects.
- Romania boasts a significant domestic market (22 million inhabitants).
- The country's labour force is skilled and low-cost.

WEAKNESSES

- The country has become more dependent on foreign capital due to increased external financing needs.
- The country has been lagging in restructuring and privatizing its industrial sector. The corporate environment is insufficiently developed.
- International backing and market confidence will remain dependent on the continuation of reform efforts.

RISK ASSESSMENT

After a slight slowdown in early 2003, industrial activity and exports have regained their dynamism. Moreover, rising real wages and increased loans to companies, in conjunction with the climate of confidence developing in business circles and continued disinflation, have spurred domestic demand.

The economic outlook has remained bright but has to be put into the perspective of the need for substantial catch-up development. Moreover, authorities have been struggling to reduce the public finance imbalance. The country has to make up a lot of ground in restructuring the energy sector, which has continued to post large losses. Concurrently, the current account deficit has begun to grow and, in consequence, so have external financing needs. Nonetheless, firm sales abroad, increased market confidence and rising foreign direct investment in conjunction with low debt and satisfactory foreign exchange reserves have been limiting the country's external vulnerability.

The Social Democratic Party in power has remained the favourite in the legislative elections to be held at the end of 2004, despite the social cost of restructuring. Accession to the European Union, scheduled for 2007, remains the government's priority.

In that favourable macroeconomic context, the sectors demonstrating above-average dynamism include textiles, pharmaceuticals and cosmetics, car manufacturers and parts-makers. However, company payment delays have remained substantial and incidents commonplace, even if they often give rise to collections.

MAIN ECONOMIC INDICATORS

US$ billions	1999	2000	2001	2002	2003 (e)	2004 (f)
Economic growth (%)	−1.2	2.1	5.7	4.9	4.7	5.0
Inflation (%)	45.8	45.7	34.5	22.5	15.1	12.0
Public-sector balance/GDP (%)[1]	n/a	−8.7	−8.1	−5.1	−5.6	−5.5
Unemployment rate (%)	11.8	10.5	8.6	8.1	8.0	8.0
Exports	8.5	10.4	11.4	13.9	17.4	19.0
Imports	9.6	12.1	14.4	16.5	21.1	22.9
Trade balance	−1.1	−1.7	−3.0	−2.6	−3.7	−3.9
Current account balance	−1.3	−1.4	−2.2	−1.6	−2.6	−2.9
Current account balance/GDP (%)	−3.6	−3.7	−5.5	−3.4	−4.8	−4.8
Foreign debt	9.8	10.9	12.4	15.8	18.9	21.2
Debt service/Exports (%)	25.0	13.7	16.7	15.9	15.2	12.5
Currency reserves (import months)	1.6	2.0	2.7	3.7	3.7	3.8

[1] general government deficit + public energy-sector losses

e = estimate, f = forecast

CONDITIONS OF ACCESS TO THE MARKET

■ Market overview

The conclusion of an association agreement with the European Union in 1995 and subsequent talks on the country's admission to the EU, under way since 2000, have promoted liberalization of the Romanian market. In 2002, the EU accounted for 68 per cent of the country's foreign trade. Trade liberalization is proceeding more slowly in the farm sector, as it is in a particularly difficult phase of restructuring.

■ Means of entry

Goods can be traded freely as import–export licences are required for only a handful of products (agricultural products, used equipment). Imports of beef from countries with reported cases of BSE are now admitted subject to certain conditions set out in the animal and public health certificate (RO VFA OCT 02).

Certain agricultural products are protected by customs duties that range from 9 per cent to 45 per cent. However, there is a provision for waiving duties on products imported under a quota system. Customs duties on industrial products imported from the European Union have been phased out in stages in accordance with the Association Agreement concluded in 1995. The payments system is undergoing modernization, with the adoption of bank transfers and bills of exchange as means of payment. Cheques are virtually non-existent. The use of charge cards is growing steadily.

When dealing with clients for the first time, it is advisable to use documentary credit for payments. Documents against payment/acceptance are also used. Some large banks offer factoring services.

The banking sector restructuring programme is at an advanced stage. Leasing is enjoying a boom in the industrial and capital goods sectors. Payment prior to shipment is frequently accepted in Romania.

■ Attitude towards foreign investors

The law of July 2001 defines the legal framework for foreign investment in excess of US$1 million and enshrines the principle of non-discrimination between foreign and domestic investors. It also regulates SME investments. Foreign investments schemes over US$10 million are eligible for special benefits. Since August 1993, all profits have been freely transferable. Profits repatriated by foreign investors in the form of dividends are subject to 10 per cent tax. The new constitution, voted recently, provides for land ownership by foreigners.

■ Foreign exchange regulations

Romanian importers have immediate access to foreign exchange through their banks. Business persons and private individuals can open foreign currency accounts with approved Romanian and foreign banks. Romanian and foreign business persons are allowed to hold and freely dispose of all their foreign currency earnings.

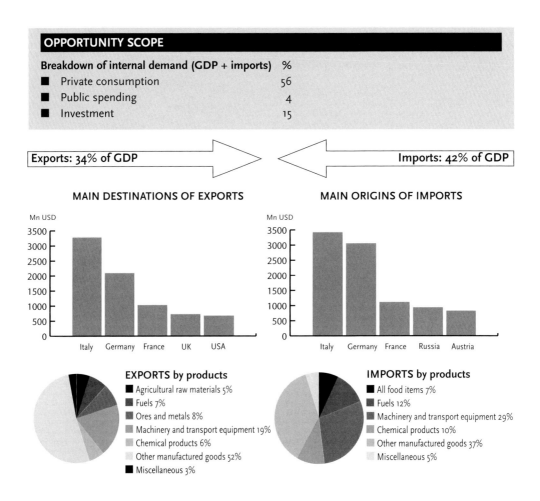

OPPORTUNITY SCOPE

Breakdown of internal demand (GDP + imports) %
- Private consumption 56
- Public spending 4
- Investment 15

Exports: 34% of GDP   Imports: 42% of GDP

MAIN DESTINATIONS OF EXPORTS

Mn USD
(bar chart: Italy, Germany, France, UK, USA)

MAIN ORIGINS OF IMPORTS

Mn USD
(bar chart: Italy, Germany, France, Russia, Austria)

EXPORTS by products
- Agricultural raw materials 5%
- Fuels 7%
- Ores and metals 8%
- Machinery and transport equipment 19%
- Chemical products 6%
- Other manufactured goods 52%
- Miscellaneous 3%

IMPORTS by products
- All food items 7%
- Fuels 12%
- Machinery and transport equipment 29%
- Chemical products 10%
- Other manufactured goods 37%
- Miscellaneous 5%

STANDARD OF LIVING / PURCHASING POWER

Indicators	Romania	Regional average	DC average
GNP per capita (PPP dollars)	5780	8420	6778
GNP per capita (USD)	1720	3544	3568
Human Development Index	0.773	0.810	0.708
Wealthiest 10% share of national income	24	25	33
Urban population percentage	55	61	60
Percentage under 15 years old	18	19	31
number of telephones per 1000 inhabitants	184	280	157
number of computers per 1000 inhabitants	36	101	66

Russia

Population (million inhabitants)   144.8
GDP (million USD)   309,951

Coface analysis

Short-term: **B**

Medium-term:
Moderately high risk

STRENGTHS

- Russia boasts many natural resources and a skilled workforce.
- The country's regional and nuclear power status has strengthened since Vladimir Putin took office.
- Vladimir Putin has initiated many legislative changes.
- The political stability resulting from the federal government's reassertion of authority over the federation, parliament and the oligarchs has begun to influence economic behaviour.

WEAKNESSES

- The industrial sector is not particularly open to foreign investment, which remains very limited.
- Dominated by raw materials, the economy has remained vulnerable to world price swings with pressure on the real exchange rate hampering national production.
- Implementation of reforms adopted is uncertain with economic and regional players not always considering application of new rules to be in their interest.
- Reforms regarding property rights and financial transparency of firms are still insufficient to improve the business climate.

RISK ASSESSMENT

Russia's financial situation has continued to improve rapidly. The maintenance of a current account surplus for the fourth consecutive year, and strong economic growth – sustained by dynamic internal demand – suggest that many economic sectors have been improving. Official statistics have been reflecting a clear improvement in company payment behaviour in the domestic economy. In percentage of GDP terms, the stock of defaults fell from 50 per cent in 1998 to 14 per cent in 2003.

Growth has nonetheless remained shaky with the economy's increasing dependence on raw-material exporting sectors tending to make the growth rate very vulnerable to swings in oil-barrel prices. Economic activity has been buoyed by exogenous factors – high oil prices and a strengthening euro – that may not be durable.

Moreover, the business climate has remained uncertain. The legal action taken against the Yukos Company and its managers could deter foreign investment projects and reflects the continuing discord between clans. Implementation of reforms has remained uncertain and the next elections, although unlikely to cause a political upheaval, are not conducive to renewed action on that score. Companies have begun going deeply into debt again on international capital markets while the banking system has remained very shaky due to the lagging pace of reforms.

MAIN ECONOMIC INDICATORS						
US$ billions	1999	2000	2001	2002	2003 (e)	2004 (f)
Economic growth (%)	5.4	9	5	4.3	6.5	4.7
Inflation (%)	36.5	20.2	19	15.0	13.1	13.0
Public-sector balance/GDP (%)	−1.6	1	3	1	1	1
Exports	63.6	91.2	86.5	91.0	107.7	104.9
Imports	29.2	31.4	40.7	49	64	74
Trade balance	34.4	59.8	45.8	42.2	43.8	30.8
Current account balance	22	44.2	30.0	27	27.7	12.6
Current-account balance/GDP (%)	11.5	17	9.7	8	5	2.6
Foreign debt	159	140.1	131.4	146.3	165.3	175.9
Debt service/Exports (%)	27.4	21.5	20.2	18.7	16.1	19.6
Currency reserves (import months)	2	5.1	5.7	6.8	8.6	9.3

e = estimate, f = forecast

CONDITIONS OF ACCESS TO THE MARKET

■ Market overview

The situation remains precarious and calls for wide-ranging structural reforms. The banking sector is in urgent need of sweeping reforms, significant investment is required to develop the country's infrastructure, especially in the field of energy, and greater transparency in the country's somewhat ineffectual business legislation is called for.

■ Means of entry

The root-and-branch reforms implemented in such varied fields as customs procedures, taxation, land ownership and administrative practices aim to bring Russia's economic mechanisms into line with international standards and practices. This should promote the exchange of goods and strengthen investor confidence. Only continued and proper implementation of the reforms, spurred by the prospect of Russia's WTO accession, will significantly enhance the business climate and boost foreign investor confidence.

Since January 2001, Russia has carried out a series of customs reforms designed to lower and unify customs duties. Despite these improvements, customs procedures remain lengthy and costly due to chaotic customs reorganization and rigid customs clearance procedures. The new customs code, which came into effect on 1 January 2004,

should ease imports, in particular by reducing clearance times and setting in place simplified customs clearance procedures. Nevertheless, only effective implementation will deliver the expected returns.

■ Attitude towards foreign investors

The revised tax code, by far the most important piece of legislation between 2000 and 2001, has introduced across-the-board tax cuts. In addition, corporation tax has been slashed from 35 per cent to 24 per cent (standard rate), the turnover-based toll tax on motorway users was abolished on 1 January 2003, and personal income tax has been reduced to 13 per cent (standard rate). From 1 January 2004, sales tax will have been abolished and VAT cut from 20 per cent to 18 per cent. The new land ownership law, in force since 30 October 2001, authorizes the sale of urban, industrial and commercial land, but not farmland. It gives foreign businesses and persons almost the same property rights as Russian nationals, including the ownership of land in all but a few cases.

A series of reforms designed to streamline investment regulations was carried out in early 2001. The measures simplify licensing, investment registration (via a one-stop shop) and product certification. The growing awareness in the last few years of the usefulness of intellectual property protection has resulted in the introduction of better legal safeguards under the amended Brands and Denominations of Origin Act passed on 16 December 2002. However, only proper implementation of the new provisions will help combat the alarming level of infringements.

While there has been a marked improvement in investment legislation, some negative signs are starting to emerge. For instance, from autumn 2002 the foreign business community has been subject to unnecessary red tape to obtain visas and work permits.

■ **Foreign exchange regulations**

Exchange controls were eased slightly in 2001. Under a law dating back to 1992, Russian-based exporters must convert 75 per cent of their income – generally generated in dollars – into roubles within 14 days of receiving payment. The conversion threshold was lowered to 50 per cent from 1 January 2002 and then to 30 per cent under the Foreign Exchange Control Act signed by President Putin on 15 December 2003, and the new Act provides for the gradual abolition of this requirement.

OPPORTUNITY SCOPE

Breakdown of internal demand (GDP + imports) %
- Private consumption 41
- Public spending 11
- Investment 18

Exports: 37% of GDP ⟩ ⟨ Imports: 24% of GDP

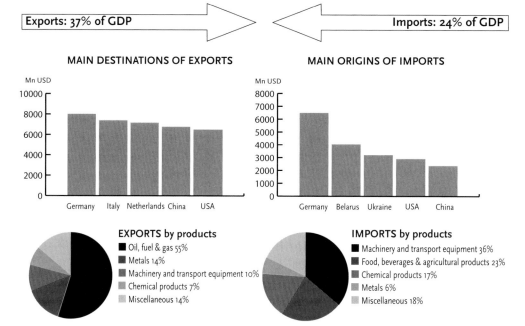

MAIN DESTINATIONS OF EXPORTS

Mn USD

Germany, Italy, Netherlands, China, USA

MAIN ORIGINS OF IMPORTS

Mn USD

Germany, Belarus, Ukraine, USA, China

EXPORTS by products
- Oil, fuel & gas 55%
- Metals 14%
- Machinery and transport equipment 10%
- Chemical products 7%
- Miscellaneous 14%

IMPORTS by products
- Machinery and transport equipment 36%
- Food, beverages & agricultural products 23%
- Chemical products 17%
- Metals 6%
- Miscellaneous 18%

STANDARD OF LIVING / PURCHASING POWER

Indicators	Russia	Regional average	DC average
GNP per capita (PPP dollars)	6880	8420	6778
GNP per capita (USD)	1750	3544	3568
Human Development Index	0.779	0.810	0.708
Wealthiest 10% share of national income	36	25	33
Urban population percentage	73	61	60
Percentage under 15 years old	18	19	31
number of telephones per 1000 inhabitants	243	280	157
number of computers per 1000 inhabitants	50	101	66

Serbia and Montenegro

Population (million inhabitants)	10.7
GDP (million USD)	10,861

Short-term: **D**

Coface analysis

Medium-term:
Very high risk

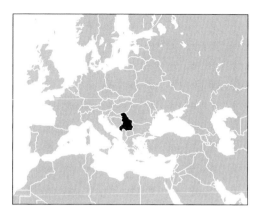

STRENGTHS

- Serbia and Montenegro boasts a well-trained, low-cost labour force.
- Regime change in Belgrade in October 2000 permitted the country to reintegrate all international organizations and break out of a decade of isolation.
- The new authorities have undertaken an economic reform programme permitting the country to earn broad international community backing, including Paris Club debt cancellation.

WEAKNESSES

- With 10 years of conflicts and international sanctions having drained the economy, the country has to make up a lot of ground in the transition process.
- Restructuring costs and social needs have been severely undermining public finances.
- An obsolescent productive apparatus and firming domestic demand have pushed the current account deficit to very high levels.
- The political situation has remained very unstable, impeding reform efforts and undermining democracy.
- The challenges concerning territorial integrity have persisted notwithstanding near-term containment of Montenegro's vague yearnings for independence.

RISK ASSESSMENT

An unstable political environment has continued to affect the country. In Serbia, the prime minister was assassinated in March 2003, and the presidential election was invalidated for the third time, in November 2003, after the radical nationalists defeated the reformers. Moreover, the coalition government's lack of cohesiveness has prompted organization of early legislative elections. Living standards have remained low and unemployment high with the economic transition's initial results having disappointed the public.

The political environment has continued to impede growth with production remaining at low levels after a decade of disinvestment and conflict. Agriculture and industry registered poor performance in 2003 due to drought, low investment and a strong dinar. Despite expected export growth, which should benefit from the restructuring accomplished thus far and the international environment's progressive improvement, the current account deficit will remain substantial. The external debt burden will remain at a relatively high level despite the arrangements that international commercial banks (London Club) may grant the country.

MAIN ECONOMIC INDICATORS						
US$ millions	1999	2000	2001	2002	2003 (e)	2004 (f)
Economic growth (%)	−18.0	5.0	5.5	4.0	3.0	4.0
Inflation (%)	42.1	69.9	91.1	21.2	12.5	10.0
Public-sector balance/GDP (%)	n/a	−2.9	−1.4	−4.5	−4.5	−4.3
Unemployment rate (%)	n/a	25.9	27.0	28.9	n/a	n/a
Exports	1,676	1,923	2,003	2,412	3,185	3,796
Imports	3,295	3,711	4,837	6,320	7,935	8,648
Trade balance	−1,619	−1,788	−2,834	−3,908	−4,750	−4,852
Current account balance[1]	−764	−610	−1,119	−2,007	−2,272	−2,218
Current account balance/GDP (%)[1]	−7.5	−7.1	−9.7	−12.8	−10.9	−10.2
Foreign debt	10,744	11,403	11,948	11,839	12,795	11,440
Currency reserves (import months)	0.9	1.4	2.5	3.7	3.7	3.7

[1] before grants

e = estimate, f = forecast

CONDITIONS OF ACCESS TO THE MARKET

■ Market overview

Foreign remittances and income from the grey economy have spurred consumer demand, reflected in the surge of imports and the recent emergence of mass retailing. Multilateral and bilateral assistance for the country's reconstruction make sectors such as transport, energy, water and the environment especially attractive. The buoyant office and residential construction market offers building equipment suppliers good opportunities. Restructuring of major state-owned enterprises and a flurry of privatizations have also opened up a market for capital goods.

■ Means of entry

The measures adopted by the Serbian government to ease foreign trade include a reduction in the number of rates of import duty from 36 to 6 (0, 1, 5, 10, 20 and 30 per cent). Seventy-three per cent of products are subject to rates ranging from 1 per cent to 10 per cent, and 50 per cent to rates between 1 per cent and 5 per cent.

The conditions of access to the Serbian and Montenegrin market should gradually improve with the harmonization of customs duties between the two republics. Harmonization is a precondition for the commissioning of a feasibility study on a stabilization and association agreement with the European Union. Ninety-three per cent of tariff categories have already been harmonized through rate cuts in Serbia and rate increases in Montenegro. The remaining 7 per cent should be harmonized in the next three to five years. The failure to agree on the status of 56 agricultural products, considered strategic for the Serbian economy, remains a stumbling block to progress in harmonization.

Talks on the conclusion of a free trade agreement between the countries of the region are making headway, but their outcome is to some extent dependent on the total harmonization of tariff categories. Following the adoption of the constitutional charter redefining the respective powers of the two republics (Serbia and Montenegro) and the union, Montenegro demanded that amendments on issues of concern to it be appended to the agreements. Its partners have accepted these amendments and agreements with Bulgaria, Moldova and Albania were signed on 13 November 2003. An agreement with Romania is due to follow. Croatia raises a legal problem as it has already ratified the agreement it had signed with the former Federal Republic of Yugoslavia. A public procurement law, 90 per cent of which is based on the EU model, was voted for by the Serbian parliament in August 2002.

■ Attitude towards foreign investors

The sizeable current account deficit of Serbia and Montenegro is mainly funded by bilateral and multilateral financing, grants and foreign remittances, with direct investment accounting for only 23 per cent of all funding. In 2002, direct investment surged by 188 per cent to US$475 million on the back of privatizations. Despite this spectacular increase, it remains small in volume terms – a legacy of 10 years of war, isolation and an economic embargo, whose lifting after political normalization in October 2000 has done little to restore investor confidence.

■ Foreign exchange regulations

The two republics have separate currencies: Montenegro has opted for the euro, while Serbia has retained the dinar. Since 2002, the dinar has been convertible and exchange controls on foreign payments made by individuals and companies have been abolished. At the end of 2003, the dinar was trading at 67 dinars to the euro.

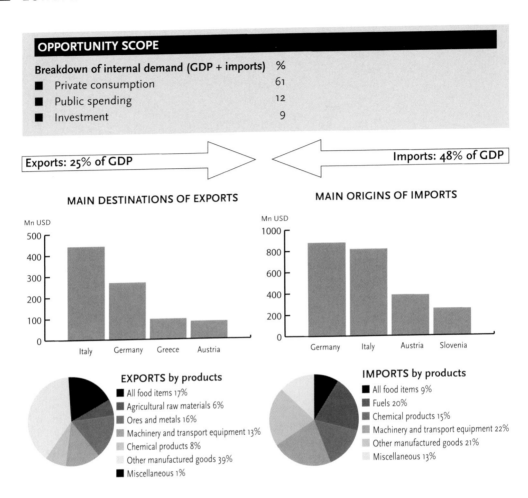

OPPORTUNITY SCOPE

Breakdown of internal demand (GDP + imports) %
- Private consumption 61
- Public spending 12
- Investment 9

Exports: 25% of GDP   Imports: 48% of GDP

MAIN DESTINATIONS OF EXPORTS

Mn USD

Italy — Germany — Greece — Austria

MAIN ORIGINS OF IMPORTS

Mn USD

Germany — Italy — Austria — Slovenia

EXPORTS by products
- All food items 17%
- Agricultural raw materials 6%
- Ores and metals 16%
- Machinery and transport equipment 13%
- Chemical products 8%
- Other manufactured goods 39%
- Miscellaneous 1%

IMPORTS by products
- All food items 9%
- Fuels 20%
- Chemical products 15%
- Machinery and transport equipment 22%
- Other manufactured goods 21%
- Miscellaneous 13%

STANDARD OF LIVING / PURCHASING POWER

Indicators	Serbia & Montenegro	Regional average	DC average
GNP per capita (PPP dollars)	n/a	8420	6778
GNP per capita (USD)	930	3544	3568
Human Development Index	n/a	0.810	0.708
Wealthiest 10% share of national income	n/a	25	33
Urban population percentage	52	61	60
Percentage under 15 years old	20	19	31
number of telephones per 1000 inhabitants	229	280	157
number of computers per 1000 inhabitants	23	101	66

Slovakia

Population (million inhabitants)   5.4
GDP (million USD)   20,459

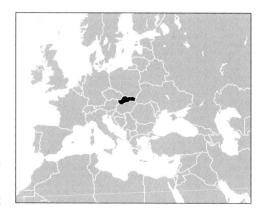

Short-term: **A3**

Medium-term:

Coface analysis   **Quite low risk**

STRENGTHS

- The prospect of European Union admission in May 2004 has been bolstering the country's economic and financial situation.
- Foreign direct investment linked to privatizations or greenfield ventures has enhanced the country's economic potential.
- Foreign exchange reserves are at comfortable levels.
- Slovakia is well positioned geographically at the crossroads of Central Europe.

WEAKNESSES

- Substantial fiscal and external deficits continue to encumber the economy.
- The Slovak koruna's appreciation could hamper the country's competitiveness.
- Foreign debt has remained relatively high in relation to GDP.
- The unemployment level remains high.

RISK ASSESSMENT

Growth continued at a relatively fast pace in 2003, fuelled mainly by exports. Inflation rose essentially because of price deregulation and increases in indirect taxes. In 2004, economic activity should benefit from the continued growth of sales abroad and a domestic demand recovery. In this favourable economic context, company solvency has been good overall with the Coface payment-incident index remaining at risk levels below the world average. Sectors like the car industry, energy and mobile telephony have been very dynamic whereas the situation has remained notably difficult in textiles, health and food.

With growth remaining at satisfactory levels and the programmed reduction of social spending, the country should be able to meet Maastricht fiscal criteria more rapidly than its neighbours. Moreover, export dynamism has permitted reducing the current account deficit and improving external debt ratios with currency reserves remaining at comfortable levels. One of the main challenges facing authorities concerns the exchange rate appreciation linked to sustained foreign direct investment inflows, which could erode the country's competitiveness.

MAIN ECONOMIC INDICATORS

US$ millions	1999	2000	2001	2002	2003 (e)	2004 (f)
Economic growth (%)	1.3	2.2	3.3	4.4	4.0	4.2
Inflation (%)	10.6	12.0	7.1	3.3	8.4	7.5
Public-sector balance/GDP (%)	−3.5	−3.8	−5.4	−7.2	−5.0	−3.9
Unemployment rate (%)	16.2	18.6	19.2	18.5	n/a	n/a
Exports	10,229	11,870	12,631	14,365	20,780	24,060
Imports	11,321	12,786	14,766	16,497	22,370	26,060
Trade balance	−1,092	−917	−2,135	−2,131	−1,590	−2,000
Current account balance	−820	−622	−1,678	−1,832	−1,210	−1,590
Current account balance/GDP (%)	−4.1	−3.2	−8.2	−7.7	−3.6	−4.0
Foreign debt	10,518	10,804	11,269	13,188	15,141	15,637
Debt service/Exports (%)	15.0	17.4	14.3	12.3	12.2	9.1
Currency reserves (import months)	2.9	3.2	2.9	5.4	4.8	4.8

e = estimate, f = forecast

CONDITIONS OF ACCESS TO THE MARKET

■ Market overview

At 17 per cent in August 2002, unemployment was alarmingly high. In addition, the job market is affected by strong regional disparities. Despite substantial wage increases in 2002, the average monthly wage is a mere 310 euros. With banking sector restructuring and partial privatization of gas and electricity supply companies now completed, the ongoing privatization of the Slovak electricity utility SE and the water supply company marks the last stage in Slovakia's economic liberalization programme. While the expanding consumer goods market clearly offers many business opportunities, industrial joint ventures – subcontracting agreements, manufacturing under licence and, above all, joint start-ups – offer the greatest growth prospects.

■ Means of entry

Customs duties on industrial products have been lifted, but agricultural products do not qualify for exemption and continue to be charged duty. The last remaining barriers, in the form of certification and technical standards, are gradually being dismantled as Slovakia moves closer towards compliance with EU integration criteria. Although the Slovak customs code, in force since 1 August 2001, is in line with European Union legislation, goods entering the country are subject to clearance by a sworn customs official. The most widely used means of payment are SWIFT transfers, bills of exchange and documentary credit. Disputes and litigation are relatively rare.

■ Attitude towards foreign investors

Slovakia's liberal legislation permits investors wholly to own a local company. A 34 per cent stake constitutes a blocking minority. The law establishes equality of treatment between Slovak and foreign investors. The Slovak investment and trade development Agency, SARIO, is now more proactive in the development of Slovak industrial areas. The new government's resolutely liberal policies, which include the lifting of restrictions on foreign shareholdings in so-called strategic sectors (such as energy), will help boost foreign direct investment in the country.

■ Foreign exchange regulations

The Slovak koruna, which enjoys stable parity with the euro, is freely convertible but rarely traded abroad. Since the abolition of exchange controls and the introduction of a new banking law, the accent is on simplifying international commercial settlements.

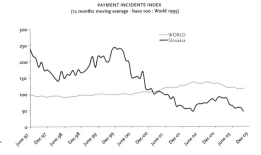

PAYMENT INCIDENTS INDEX
(12 months moving average - base 100 : World 1995)

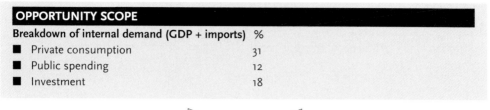

OPPORTUNITY SCOPE

Breakdown of internal demand (GDP + imports) %

- Private consumption — 31
- Public spending — 12
- Investment — 18

Exports: 74% of GDP   Imports: 82% of GDP

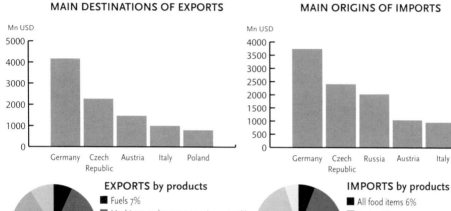

MAIN DESTINATIONS OF EXPORTS

Mn USD

Germany, Czech Republic, Austria, Italy, Poland

MAIN ORIGINS OF IMPORTS

Mn USD

Germany, Czech Republic, Russia, Austria, Italy

EXPORTS by products
- Fuels 7%
- Machinery and transport equipment 39%
- Chemical products 7%
- Other manufactured goods 38%
- Miscellaneous 9%

IMPORTS by products
- All food items 6%
- Fuels 15%
- Machinery and transport equipment 38%
- Chemical products 10%
- Other manufactured goods 26%
- Miscellaneous 5%

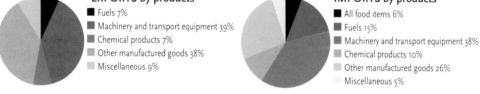

STANDARD OF LIVING / PURCHASING POWER

Indicators	Slovakia	Regional average	DC average
GNP per capita (PPP dollars)	11,780	8420	6778
GNP per capita (USD)	3760	3544	3568
Human Development Index	0.836	0.810	0.708
Wealthiest 10% share of national income	21	25	33
Urban population percentage	58	61	60
Percentage under 15 years old	19	19	31
number of telephones per 1000 inhabitants	288	280	157
number of computers per 1000 inhabitants	148	101	66

Slovenia

Population (million inhabitants)   2
GDP (million USD)   18,810

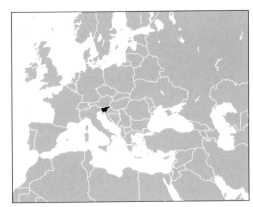

Short-term: **A2**

Medium-term:
Coface analysis   **Low risk**

STRENGTHS

- Slovenia benefits from a stable macroeconomic and political environment.
- It boasts Central Europe's highest level of wealth.
- Prospective European Union accession has been enhancing the country's medium-term outlook.
- Public and external finances are sound.
- The country is ethnically homogeneous.

WEAKNESSES

- High inflation has been undermining export competitiveness.
- With a small and open economy, the country is dependent on international economic conditions.
- Slovenia must contend with competition from emerging countries, which benefit from lower production costs.
- Reforms still remain to be initiated or expanded (privatization, promotion of competition, labour market flexibility).

RISK ASSESSMENT

Growth sagged slightly in 2003. The steady pace of investments was insufficient to offset the decline of exports to European Union countries amid relatively stable household spending. Industrial production has dropped markedly since 2001 with its reorientation towards higher value-added sectors still not having borne fruit.

The economy should gain momentum in 2004 buoyed by increased private consumption, the granting of funds for residential construction, and continuation of the motorway construction programme. Furthermore, sales abroad should benefit from improved economic conditions in Europe. Meanwhile, the conclusion of wage negotiations and continued slowdown of the exchange rate depreciation should contribute to easing inflation. Despite a widening trade deficit, the current account balance will remain nearly in balance due to increased current transfers and service exports. After stalling in 2003, furthermore, foreign direct investment inflows should increase again with the sale of the telecommunications company.

MAIN ECONOMIC INDICATORS

US$ millions	1999	2000	2001	2002	2003 (e)	2004 (f)
Economic growth (%)	5.9	4.1	2.9	2.9	2.4	3.4
Inflation (%)	6.1	8.9	8.4	7.5	5.6	4.7
Public-sector balance/GDP (%)	−0.6	−1.4	−1.4	−2.9	−1.9	−1.8
Unemployment rate (%)	7.6	7.0	6.4	6.2	6.3	6.2
Exports	8,623	8,808	9,343	10,473	11,856	13,218
Imports	9,858	9,947	9,962	10,716	12,439	14,037
Trade balance	−1,235	−1,139	−620	−243	−583	−819
Current account balance	−698	−548	31	375	16	14
Current account balance/GDP (%)	−3.5	−2.9	0.2	1.7	0.1	0.0
Foreign debt	5,400	6,217	6,717	8,799	10,638	12,156
Debt service/Exports (%)	7.6	9.0	13.9	13.6	14.7	15.2
Currency reserves (import months)	3.2	3.3	4.4	6.4	6.3	6.1

e = estimate, f = forecast

CONDITIONS OF ACCESS TO THE MARKET

■ Means of entry

Average customs duty for goods imported from the EU is 1 per cent. Most consumer goods are dutiable at this rate, except milk and meat, which are liable to duties of up to 10.9 per cent and 30 per cent respectively. Cosmetics and drugs are subject to high rates of duty and cumbersome customs procedures.

Public tenders are now officially open to EU firms. There is a tendency towards arbitrary enforcement of certification rules and standards. In addition, excessive food inspections and plant health tests have been in force since 2001, but there are continual moves towards greater harmonization with EU criteria.

SWIFT transfers are a common means of payment. Many Slovenian companies settle their invoices through deferred payment arrangements, thanks to their creditworthiness and good credit rating. Debt collection firms are efficient, although court procedures are generally slow.

The lack of competitively priced and timely sources of local finance is a major obstacle to the growth of both Slovenian and foreign businesses.

■ Attitude towards foreign investors

Investment is unrestricted, except in armaments, compulsory pension funds and health insurance. However, there are no special incentives for foreign investment. Government approval is required to acquire over 25 per cent of a Slovenian company with a capital of 800 million tolars or more (approximately 400 million euros). Foreign companies enjoy equal access to tax-free trade areas in Maribor, Celje and the fast-expanding port of Koper. The market is by and large open, although in a number of sectors (retail, locally manufactured consumer goods, financial services) Slovenian companies fiercely resist foreign competition. However, the situation is changing as compliance with EU integration criteria grows. There is still a deplorable lack of transparency in the way public tenders are conducted, with public opinion and the government supporting cartels in public works and construction, telecommunications, etc.

■ Foreign exchange regulations

The tolar is a fully convertible, floating currency and is due to join ERM II by the end of 2004 and be replaced by the euro in 2007.

PAYMENT INCIDENTS INDEX
(12 months moving average - base 100 : World 1995)

— WORLD
— Slovenia

OPPORTUNITY SCOPE

Breakdown of internal demand (GDP + imports) %
- Private consumption   34
- Public spending   13
- Investment   17

Exports: 59% of GDP   Imports: 63% of GDP

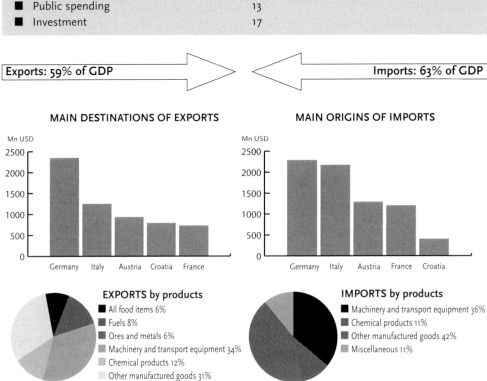

MAIN DESTINATIONS OF EXPORTS

Mn USD

Germany Italy Austria Croatia France

MAIN ORIGINS OF IMPORTS

Mn USD

Germany Italy Austria France Croatia

EXPORTS by products
- All food items 6%
- Fuels 8%
- Ores and metals 6%
- Machinery and transport equipment 34%
- Chemical products 12%
- Other manufactured goods 31%
- Miscellaneous 3%

IMPORTS by products
- Machinery and transport equipment 36%
- Chemical products 11%
- Other manufactured goods 42%
- Miscellaneous 11%

STANDARD OF LIVING / PURCHASING POWER

Indicators	Slovenia	Regional average	DC average
GNP per capita (PPP dollars)	17,060	8420	6778
GNP per capita (USD)	9760	3544	3568
Human Development Index	0.881	0.810	0.708
Wealthiest 10% share of national income	23	25	33
Urban population percentage	49	61	60
Percentage under 15 years old	16	19	31
number of telephones per 1000 inhabitants	401	280	157
number of computers per 1000 inhabitants	276	101	66

Spain

Population (million inhabitants) 40.5
GDP (million USD) 653,100
GDP per capita (USD) 16,108

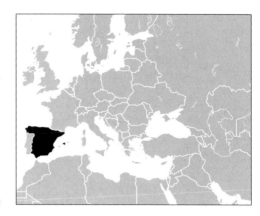

Coface analysis   Short-term: **A1**

STRENGTHS

- Public accounts have remained in balance thanks to social security surpluses generated by increased employment and to the law prohibiting autonomous communities and municipalities from running deficits.
- Continued public infrastructure investment, bolstered by European subsidies, has permitted the country to make up ground in communication networks.
- Spain remains a primary tourist destination, which allows it to offset its trade deficit.
- Market liberalization has been continuing even if privatizations and the breaking up of monopolies have not spelt the end of national champions and their influence.

WEAKNESSES

- Anaemic demographics have been undermining an already insufficient health insurance and retirement system.
- Despite reforms undertaken, labour legislation has remained too rigid, thus contributing to sustaining still-high structural unemployment.
- Low productivity, wage indexation, and European monetary policy unsuited to Spain's case have been spurring inflationary pressures.
- A property boom, responsible for high housing prices and household debt, has led to formation of a speculative bubble.

RISK ASSESSMENT

Spain's dynamic growth, which even accelerated sharply towards year-end, has contrasted with the sluggishness of neighbouring countries. Infrastructure and housing investment buoyed that growth, benefiting from low interest rates, increased public spending and financial aid from the European Union. Domestic consumer spending also fuelled growth, itself stimulated by lower inflation, tax breaks and job creation. Moreover, goods and services exports also rebounded thanks mainly to tourism revenues.

In 2004, favourable trends for all demand components should contribute to spurring growth. Investment will continue to trend up thanks to expansion of infrastructure projects facilitated by the public account surplus, which will offset a decline in residential construction after the excesses of recent years. Despite high household debt, consumer spending should remain robust, buoyed by easing unemployment. Moreover, improvement in European economic conditions will contribute to a new export surge.

As evidenced by the Coface payment-incident index, the deterioration of company solvency resulting from the economic slowdown that began in 2002 changed directions in the 2003 second half amid improvement in the economic climate. That trend should continue in 2004 even if persistent structural weaknesses of some companies may impede it. The clothing sector will remain shaky due to pressure from imports and bankruptcies precipitated by adoption of new, stricter bankruptcy law.

MAIN ECONOMIC INDICATORS						
%	1999	2000	2001	2002	2003 (e)	2004 (f)
Economic growth	4.2	4.2	2.8	2	2.3	2.8
Consumer spending (% change)	4.7	4	2.8	2.6	3.2	3.3
Investment (% change)	9.7	7.9	3.8	−1	2.9	3.9
Inflation	2.4	3.2	3.3	3.5	2.9	2.6
Unemployment rate	12.8	11	10.5	11.4	11.4	10.8
Short-term interest rate	3	4.4	4.2	3.3	2.3	2.1
Public-sector balance/GDP (%)	−1.2	−0.8	−0.3	0.1	0.2	0.3
Public-sector debt/GDP (%)	75.6	72.4	68.4	65.9	63	60.5
Exports (% change)	7.6	10.1	3.6	0	5.4	6.4
Imports (% change)	12.8	10.6	4	1.8	6.8	7.2
Current account balance/GDP (%)	−2.3	−3.4	−2.8	−2.4	−3.1	−3

e = estimate, f = forecast

Textiles

The sector has been shaky as evidenced by its high bankruptcy rate, with pressure from Asian imports a major contributing factor. An industrial fabric dominated by small and medium-sized companies, and with underground workshops serving established firms, has also been a factor. Although business improved slightly in 2003 and the trend may intensify in 2004, that will only mitigate the difficulties that will re-emerge with the lifting of quotas in early 2005.

Steel

Domestic demand growth has been buoying the market. That trend has been benefiting imports, which the investments under way to increase domestic capacity will be unlikely to jeopardize. It is nonetheless necessary to distinguish between long steel products benefiting from infrastructure projects and special or flat steel products intended for the car industry, which have suffered from declining sales and margins. Companies operating in the latter segment could present potential risks.

Construction

This is still Spain's most dynamic sector. Although residential construction has been sagging, public works and non-residential construction activity have remained robust. Those business conditions have fostered mergers between builders and promoters, and their diversification into road infrastructure concessions and telecommunications services as well as their penetration of East European markets. Risks have been centred on medium-sized companies focusing on residential construction outside large urban centres and tourist areas. Those companies could thus suffer should a sharp downturn develop. In that case, the difficulties would spread rapidly to construction material wholesalers.

Car industry

With 80 per cent of domestic production exported to Europe, the sector suffered from that market's new decline in 2003 with carmakers nonetheless partially offsetting the damage via increased domestic sales. That was not the case for their subcontractors, which had to contend with price pressure as their sales fell in the wake of sagging vehicle sales. Cable and carburettor manufacturers in particular have been the most vulnerable. However, their situation should slowly improve as the market becomes progressively more dynamic and since carmakers have entrusted local factories with the production of new models.

Computers

Except for services, the IT sector showed signs of recovery in 2003. That improvement should continue in 2004 with company investment accelerating. Uncertainties have nonetheless persisted. It has thus remained open to question whether small local assemblers that won significant market share over the years will be able to withstand the counter-attack of major world leaders. It is uncertain whether they possess the resources needed to make essential investments in research and development.

■ Distribution

Mass food distribution has been registering good performance, even if the economic slowdown has affected earnings growth. Actors in the sector have the means to extend their presence throughout the country by opening new sales outlets or buying out competitors. Conversely, retail distribution of cosmetics and perfume has remained very fragmented despite the growing presence of new entrants, notably the major European specialists in the segment. Wholesalers will be the first to suffer from an emerging concentration process with traditional boutiques ultimately disappearing.

PAYMENT AND COLLECTION PRACTICES

■ Payment

The bill of exchange is frequently used for commercial transactions in Spain. In the event of default, it offers creditors certain safeguards, including access to the new exchange procedure (*juicio cambiario*) introduced by the recent civil procedure rules under which, based on his or her appraisal of the documents submitted, a first-instance judge (*juzgado de primera instancia*) may order debtors to pay up within 10 days and have their property attached. Where a claim is contested, a court hearing is held to examine both parties' arguments and a judgment is handed down within 10 days of the hearing.

Widely accepted though somewhat difficult to obtain, the bill of exchange guranteed by a bank limits the risk of payment default by offering creditors additional recourse to the endorser of the bill.

The cheque, which is less widely used than the bill of exchange, offers similar legal safeguards under the 'exchange procedure' (*procédure cambiaire*) in the event of default.

The same is true of the promissory note (*pagaré*), which, like the bill of exchange, is an instrument enforceable by law. However, defaults on this instrument are not recorded in the bad debts register, RAI (*Registro de Aceptationes Impagadas*), where banks and other financial institutions may look up the credit history of a firm before deciding whether or not to extend credit to it.

SWIFT bank transfers, widely used by Spanish banks, are a quick, fairly reliable and cheap instrument, provided the purchaser, in good faith, orders payment. If the buyer fails to order a transfer, the legal remedy consists in instituting ordinary proceedings for non-payment of the invoice.

■ Debt collection

To speed up court procedures and modernize the obsolete code of civil procedure dating back to February 1881, new rules of civil procedure (*Ley de Enjuiciamento Civil*) were introduced on 8 January 2001. The rules cut the time taken up by litigation significantly and give oral arguments priority over written submissions – the cornerstone of the previous system – even though the authentication of large numbers of documents remains a requirement.

Where sellers cannot reach an amicable settlement with a buyer, they may enforce their right to payment through the new civil procedure (*juicio declarativo*), divided into ordinary proceedings (*juicio ordinario*) for claims over 3,000 euros (formerly 500,000 pesetas) and oral proceedings (*juicio verbal*) for claims under 3,000 euros. The aim of the new procedure is to speed up delivery of enforcement orders by reducing and simplifying the stages of the old procedure.

In addition, for commercial claims under 30,000 euros (formerly 5,000,000 pesetas) a more flexible special procedure (*juicio monitorio*), by way of pre-printed form, has been introduced, under which the judge of first instance may order the debtor to pay up within 20 days of an application and supporting documents being lodged with the court.

This innovative law, which brings Spanish judicial practice into line with the rest of Europe, is slowly gaining ground as it breaks with the tradition of formalism acquired by the Spanish judiciary over several decades.

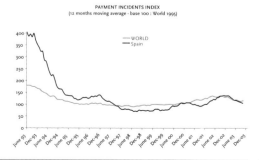

PAYMENT INCIDENTS INDEX
(12 months moving average - base 100 : World 1995)

Sweden

Population (million inhabitants)	8.9
GDP (million USD)	240,300
GDP per capita (USD)	26,924

Coface analysis   Short-term: **A1**

RISK ASSESSMENT

Although only moderate in 2003, the growth rate again exceeded the European average. Despite slight improvement, consumer spending remained insufficient to stimulate the economy with rising unemployment undermining consumer morale. Company investment declined again. Conversely, exports remained relatively robust despite a sluggish European context.

The situation should be brighter in 2004. Improved business conditions in the paper and telecommunications sectors should drive the economy. Exports will thus be more dynamic, confirming the mild impact of the failure of Sweden's euro-adoption referendum. Meanwhile,

the continuous fiscal surpluses posted since 1998 will permit the pursuit of accommodating economic policy. The environment will thus be conducive to a household spending recovery.

Although generally sound and competitive, Swedish companies suffered from the economic slowdown in 2003 with the bankruptcy rate increasing by 5 per cent over the year. Although the situation has already begun to improve in the wood pulp, telecommunications equipment, automobile and retail sectors, it has nonetheless remained difficult in construction, wood and metals. However, the expected economic expansion should benefit all branches with the Coface payment-incident index remaining substantially below the world average.

MAIN ECONOMIC INDICATORS

%	1999	2000	2001	2002	2003 (e)	2004 (f)
Economic growth	4.6	4.4	1.1	1.9	1.6	2.5
Consumer spending (% change)	3.8	4.9	0.2	1.3	1.9	2.4
Investment (% change)	8.5	9.5	−0.1	−6.3	0.3	2.6
Inflation	1.1	1.2	2.1	2.0	2.1	1.4
Unemployment rate	5.6	4.7	4.0	4.0	4.8	4.7
Short-term interest rate	3.1	4.0	4.0	4.1	3.0	3.1
Public-sector balance/GDP (%)	1.3	3.4	4.6	1.1	0.2	0.5
Public-sector debt/GDP (%)	71.5	64.2	63.2	60.1	62.5	59
Exports (% change)	7.4	11.3	−0.8	0.4	3.6	4.9
Imports (% change)	4.8	11.5	−3.5	−2.7	3.8	4.8
Current account balance/GDP (%)	4.2	3.9	3.9	4.1	3.7	4.0

e = estimate, f = forecast

PAYMENT AND COLLECTION PRACTICES

■ Payment

Bills of exchange and promissory notes are neither widely used nor recommended as they must meet a number of formal requirements in order to be valid. Just as the rules for issuing cheques have become more flexible, so the sanctions for issuers of uncovered cheques have been relaxed in recent years.

Conversely, the use of the SWIFT system by Swedish banks ensures a secure, efficient and fairly cheap domestic and international funds transfer service. However, as payment is dependent on the buyer's good faith, sellers are advised to take great care to ensure that their bank account details are correct if they wish to receive timely payment.

■ Debt collection

As a rule, the collection process begins with the debtor being sent a final demand by registered mail asking him or her to pay the principal amount together with any contractually agreed interest penalties. Where there is no specific interest clause in the contract, the rate of interest applicable from 1 July 2002 is the Bank of Sweden's (Sveriges Riksbank) six-monthly benchmark (*reporäntan*) rate, plus eight basis points. Under the Swedish Interest Act (*räntelag*, 1975, last amended in 2002), interest starts to accrue 30 days after the invoice date or after a demand for payment is sent to the debtor by registered mail.

Where claims meet certain requirements – denominated in Swedish krona, certain, liquid and indisputable – creditors can obtain an injunction to pay (*Betalningsföreläggande*) within about four months from the Enforcement Service, set up in 1992.

This Enforcement Service (Kronofogde-myndigheten) may order a debtor to settle the claim or justify late payment within two weeks. If the debtor fails to respond after one month, the service issues a writ of execution at the creditor's request. While formal, this system offers a relatively straightforward and quick remedy in respect of undisputed claims and has greatly freed up the courts. Creditors are not required to engage a lawyer but, in some circumstances, would be well advised to do so.

Where claims are disputed or where buyers fail to enter into an agreement to pay, the Enforcement Service has no jurisdiction. Creditors must obtain legal remedy through the ordinary court process by bringing their claims before a court of first instance (*Tingsrätt*). It should be noted that civil courts are also competent to hear commercial disputes.

Proceedings at this court involve a preliminary hearing in which the judge attempts to reconcile the parties after examining their case documents, evidence and arguments. If the dispute remains unresolved, the proceedings continue with written submissions and oral arguments until the main hearing, where the accent is on counsels' pleadings (defence and prosecution) and examination of witnesses' testimonies. In accordance with the 'immediacy of judgment' principle, the court bases its decision exclusively on the evidence presented at the proceedings.

It takes about 10 months on average to obtain a writ of execution in the first instance, bearing in mind that there is a widespread tendency in Sweden to appeal against judgments.

PAYMENT INCIDENTS INDEX
(12 months moving average - base 100 : World 1995)

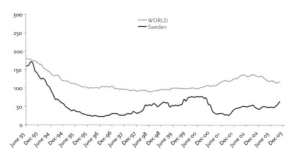

Switzerland

Population (million inhabitants)	7.3
GDP (million USD)	267,400
GDP per capita (USD)	36,375

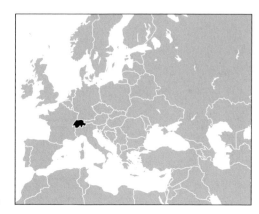

Coface analysis　　　　Short-term: **A1**

STRENGTHS

- Switzerland's industrial and financial fabric has performed particularly well in many economic sectors.
- Labour market flexibility and a highly skilled workforce have consistently ensured high employment and relatively low jobless rates compared to neighbouring countries.
- An effective pension system meets the needs imposed by an ageing population.
- A stable political environment (that the populist UDC party's recent breakthrough should not jeopardize) in conjunction with low taxes and a sound currency has continued to attract investors.

WEAKNESSES

- Non-member status of both the European Union and European Economic Area has tended to limit competition and sustain resistance to change, notably on company ownership.
- That situation has been affecting the competitiveness of economic players too focused on the domestic market.
- There exists jurisdictional overlapping and disparities between cantons. This should be reduced by the allocation of tasks between the confederation and the cantons as well as the sharing of the relevant financing.

RISK ASSESSMENT

Growth sagged in 2003 due to the decline of exports (45 per cent of GDP including 60 per cent going to the European Union) hampered by a strong franc and weak demand from Switzerland's main trading partners. Investment was down for the third consecutive year. Rising unemployment and slower growth of real wages have been a drag on spending by households, which have also been facing higher healthcare costs. In those crisis conditions, the public-sector deficit has widened.

In 2004, a modest growth recovery will depend on slight improvement in exports, particularly in the financial services area, and stabilization of company capital-goods investments. With no inflationary pressures, the Central Bank should continue pursuing its expansionary monetary policy. That essentially modest improvement will nonetheless not suffice to revive significantly the employment market or consumption.

In that hardly favourable environment, bankruptcies have been increasing – up an estimated 14 per cent in 2003 – and company payment behaviour, which was still excellent only recently, has been deteriorating. Facing sluggish demand, companies have had to squeeze prices, which has been undermining their profitability. The solidarity system that welds the economic fabric has been cracking. The difficulties have been affecting several sectors. While watchmaking, textiles, printing, mechanical engineering, retail trade and tourism have been suffering most, chemicals and machine tools have been registering good performance.

MAIN ECONOMIC INDICATORS

%	1999	2000	2001	2002	2003 (e)	2004 (f)
Economic growth	1.5	3.2	0.9	0.2	−0.4	1.5
Consumer spending (% change)	2.2	2	2.1	0.7	0.5	1.0
Investment (% change)	1.3	5.3	−4.3	−5.1	−3.2	1.5
Inflation	0.3	1.0	0.7	0.8	0.6	0.6
Unemployment rate	2.9	2.5	2.5	3.1	3.8	4.1
Short-term interest rate	1.4	3.2	2.9	1.1	0.3	0.6
Public-sector balance/GDP (%)	−0.2	2.6	0.2	−0.9	−2.1	−1.9
Public-sector debt/GDP (%)	51.4	51.2	51.3	55.2	49.3	47.8
Exports (% change)	5.1	10	−0.1	0.4	−1.8	1.5
Imports (% change)	7.4	8.4	−0.3	−2.6	−1.1	2.3
Current account balance/GDP (%)	11.7	13.2	8.9	9.3	10.6	11.6

e = estimate, f = forecast

MAIN ECONOMIC SECTORS

■ Construction

Despite the upward trend registered in housing construction, that sector should generally continue to suffer from the decline in investment spending by companies and public authorities and from pressure on prices. To cope with fluctuations in business conditions and shrinking margins, companies have been moving towards concentration or vertical integration while resorting to lay-offs to reduce costs.

■ Tourism

The reduced flow of tourists from Germany, the United States and Japan due to competition from other destinations, poor international economic conditions and the strong franc have affected this sector's performance in 2003. The slight increase in domestic tourism has not sufficed to stem the difficulties of a sector characterized by low productivity and overcapacity problems and where small, independent companies predominate.

■ Watchmaking

This major export sector has suffered relatively little from the reduced demand caused by the tourism decline, reduced traffic in airport duty-free areas and the strong franc. The luxury sector, little affected by economic conditions, has been posting good results with the mid-range and low-end segments even expecting increased demand from China, Russia and India. The situation has nonetheless remained difficult for independent watchmakers and subcontractors.

■ Chemicals and pharmaceuticals

Despite an export decline and pressure on prices, the chemicals sector has been posting satisfactory results thanks to cost savings and synergies on research. Buoyant European sales have been offsetting the poor performance registered in North America due to unfavourable exchange rates and the sector's growing maturity. High specialization and continued R&D investments have permitted pharmaceutical laboratories to withstand economic fluctuations and preserve high profits.

■ Capital goods

This export sector, which sells 75 per cent of its production abroad with one-third going to Germany, has suffered a sharp drop in turnover resulting from declines in both volumes and prices. Except for large companies capable of maintaining their performance thanks to strict cost control and the dynamism of electrical appliance sectors, no improvement is likely in 2004.

111

■ Retail trade

With the process of concentration continuing and the arrival of foreign companies increasing competition, the lower propensity to spend has had relatively little effect on this sector. Tobacco, health and beauty care, and electronics have been posting better-than-average performance, whereas turnover has declined in the clothing and consumer durable goods sectors. In 2004, performance should remain stable.

■ Food industries

Except for the uncompetitive dairy sector recently opened to European competition, foods industries have withstood the economic slowdown relatively well. Facing a saturated domestic market, the sector can only count on quality products and sales growth abroad hindered nonetheless by prices averaging 50 per cent higher than those of their European counterparts.

PAYMENT AND COLLECTION PRACTICES

■ Payment

Bills of exchange and cheques are not commonly used owing to prohibitive banking and tax charges; the stamp duty on bills of exchange is 0.75 per cent of the principal amount for domestic bills, and 1.5 per cent for international bills. Similarly, commercial operators are particularly demanding as regards the formal validity of cheques and bills of exchange as payment instruments.

SWIFT bank transfers are the most commonly used payment system. Most Swiss banks are connected to the SWIFT network, which facilitates rapid and effective payments.

■ Debt collection

The Swiss legal system presents technical specificities, as follows:

- The existence of an administrative authority (eg Office des poursuites et des faillites or Betreibungs und Konkursamt) in each canton, which is responsible for executing court orders and whose functioning is regulated by federal law. Interested parties may consult or obtain extracts of the Office's records.
- Specific rules for legal procedure prevail in each canton (there are 26 different codes of civil procedure), which sometimes vary greatly depending on the legal doctrine that has inspired them. As such, before instigating actions, plaintiffs should ensure that their counsel is familiar with the law of the concerned jurisdiction as well as the language to be used before the court (French, German or Italian). These two key constraints hamper the swift course of justice and a project to harmonize these various procedures is under review.

The debt collection process commences with the issuing of notice to pay by ordinary mail or registered letter (thus enabling interest penalties to be charged). This gives the debtor two weeks in which to pay the principal amount, plus – unless otherwise agreed by the parties – interest penalties equivalent to the bank rate applicable in the place of payment.

Where no payment is received after this 14-day period, the creditor may return a form to the *Office des poursuites et des faillites*, which then serves the debtor with a final order to pay within 20 days. This procedure, which is relatively simple to implement, nevertheless affords debtors the possibility of opposing the order without having to provide grounds. Where a claim is thus disputed, the only alternative for creditors is to seek redress through the courts.

Conversely, where a seller holds an unconditional evidence of debt signed by the buyer (any original document in which the buyer recognizes his or her debt, bill of exchange, cheque, etc), the seller may request the temporary lifting of the debtor's opposition without having to appear before the court. This is a summary procedure, quick and relatively easy to obtain, in which the court's decision is based upon the documents submitted by the seller.

Once this lifting order has been granted, the debtor has 20 days in which to refer the case before the judge ruling on the merits of the matter, to obtain the debt's release and obtain an executory order. This entails instigating a formal procedure, with a written phase followed by a court hearing, lasting from one to three years depending upon the canton involved. Legal costs vary, also, in each canton.

Once the court has handed down its definitive ruling, the *Office des poursuites et des faillites* delivers an execution order or, in the case of traders, a winding-up petition (*commination*). In all cases, the law decides which measure – execution order or winding-up petition – is applied. Procedures are heard by either a court of first instance or a district court. Commercial courts, presided over by a panel of professional and non-professional judges, exist in the cantons of Aargau, Berne and Zürich.

Once an appeal has been entered with the cantonal court (regarding the cantons that have a second-instance court), cases in the final step are heard by the Swiss Federal Court (the only federal court of justice) in Lausanne.

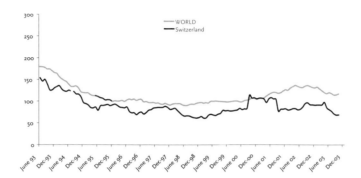

PAYMENT INCIDENTS INDEX
(12 months moving average - base 100 : World 1995)

Tajikistan

Population (million inhabitants)	6.2
GDP (million USD)	1,056
GDP per capita (USD)	170

Short-term: **D**

Medium-term:
Coface analysis   **Very high risk**

RISK ASSESSMENT

After emerging from a record recession exacerbated by a long civil war in the 1990s, the country has posted strong catch-up growth, which has nonetheless been tending to slow down. Economic activity has remained subject to an agricultural sector that has undergone little reform and still employs 60 per cent of the country's labour force. Moreover, the country has continued to suffer from persistent poverty and the lowest living standards in the Community of Independent States. Although Tajikistan has been making progress towards macroeconomic stabilization with IMF backing, the debt burden has

been undermining its solvency with the country remaining very dependent on official financing.

Politically, relations between President Rakhmonov and the Islamist opposition have been increasingly strained, which could jeopardize the newly restored political stability. The country has nonetheless remained flanked by the great powers with very close ties to Moscow, both militarily – with Russia stationing large numbers of troops there – and in trade terms. The Tajikistan authorities have also maintained good relations with the United States as evidenced by Washington's status as the country's main donor.

MAIN ECONOMIC INDICATORS						
US$ millions	1999	2000	2001	2002	2003 (e)	2004 (f)
Economic growth (%)	3.7	8.3	10.2	7.5	6	6
Inflation (%)	30.1	60.6	12.5	13	7	6
Public-sector balance/GDP (%)	−3.1	−0.6	−0.1	−0.3	−0.5	−1
Exports	666	788	652	699	766	826
Imports	693	834	773	823	864	917
Trade balance	−27	−46	−121	−124	−99	−91
Current account balance	−36	−62	−74	−33	−67	−68
Current account balance/GDP (%)	−3.4	−6.5	−7.1	−2.8	−5	−4.8
Foreign debt	1,233	1,226	1,017	976	1,049	1,124
Debt service/Exports (%)	5.4	9.6	25.2	23.4	17.1	13.2
Currency reserves (import months)	1.7	2.1	1.9	1.8	2.1	2.5

e = estimate, f = forecast

Turkmenistan

Population (million inhabitants)	5.4
GDP (million USD)	5,962
GDP per capita (USD)	1,104

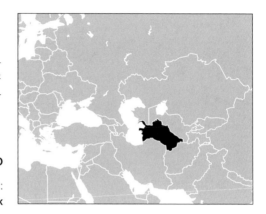

Short-term: **D**

Medium-term:

Coface analysis **Very high risk**

RISK ASSESSMENT

Growth has been very high, at least according to official statistics, with the gas sector representing over 60 per cent of exports and continuing to dominate the economy. Agriculture (notably the cotton sector), representing over one-quarter of GDP, has undergone little modernization and has thus remained vulnerable to variable factors affecting harvests.

The country's reluctance to undertake economic or political reforms along with its isolation has been seriously impeding growth and development. Its dependence on the Russian pipeline network has been undermining exploitation of gas export income. The country's traditional trading partners have been CIS countries (Ukraine

takes 46 per cent of Turkmenistan's exports) that have experienced solvency problems. However, the general improvement in CIS economies and the conclusion of bilateral agreements have permitted resolving the payment difficulties.

Relations with Moscow have thus been crucial. Tensions nonetheless developed in 2003 when Turkmen authorities announced their intention of calling into question the dual nationality of Russian citizens in Turkmenistan. They had to back down, however, which attests to Russian influence beyond Gazprom's interest in Turkmenistan's hydrocarbon sector. Domestically, the frequent purges and tensions within President Niazov's regime would suggest that the country's political stability may be shakier than it seems.

MAIN ECONOMIC INDICATORS

US$ millions	1998	1999	2000	2001	2002 (e)	2003 (f)
Economic growth (%)	5	16	17.6	10	16	8
Inflation (%)	19.8	21.2	7.4	8	10	12
Public-sector balance/GDP (%)	−2.6	0	0.4	−1	−10	−10
Exports	614	1,187	2,506	2,620	2,700	2,800
Imports	1,137	1,478	1,785	2,349	2,400	2,400
Trade balance	−523	−291	721	271	300	400
Current account balance	−934	−864	611	−149	−210	−250
Current account balance/GDP (%)	−32.2	−22.2	13.9	−2.5	−3.2	−3.9
Foreign debt	2,259	2,015	2,300	2,350	2,500	2,600
Debt service/Exports (%)	97.0	43.7	22.7	25.1	35.0	40.0
Currency reserves (import months)	10.3	9.4	8.9	6.2	6.1	6.1

e = estimate, f = forecast

Ukraine

Population (million inhabitants)	49.1
GDP (million USD)	37,588

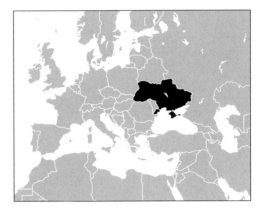

Short-term: **C**

Medium-term:
Very high risk

Coface analysis

STRENGTHS

- Ukraine benefits from transit-fee revenues on Russian gas exports to West Europe.
- The economy is relatively diversified (food sector, heavy and light industries).
- Soon to share borders with the European Union, the country is strategically placed.

WEAKNESSES

- Restructuring of the metallurgy sector – which represents 40 per cent of exports – has been progressing very slowly.
- Ukraine has remained dependent on Russia for energy inputs and a large proportion of its metal exports.
- With political instability impeding economic reforms, foreign investment has been very limited.

RISK ASSESSMENT

Economic activity has been dynamic, fuelled by buoyant domestic demand and strong exports. Regarding external solvency, the current account has continued to post surpluses and the external financial situation has been improving. Despite the unfinished status of tax reforms, fiscal policy has remained relatively disciplined with Ukraine emerging from its over-indebted situation.

Considering its very marked specialization in metals and the low rate of investment, Ukraine's performance has remained shaky and dependent on progress on tax reforms, privatization and broad improvement in the legal framework. However, recurrent political problems have limited the authorities' capacity to pursue sustained reform policy as evidenced by its erratic relations with the IMF. The prospect of presidential elections at the end of 2004 could spur the conflicts between political and economic clans. Relations with the United States have improved. Despite border tensions with Russia around the Black Sea, the general trend is towards progressive reconciliation with Moscow while the insufficiency of reforms has continued to limit Ukraine's European Union moorings.

MAIN ECONOMIC INDICATORS

US$ billions	1999	2000	2001	2002	2003 (e)	2004 (f)
Economic growth (%)	−0.2	5.9	9.2	4.8	6	5
Inflation (%)	19.2	25.8	6.1	−0.6	6.0	4.0
Public-sector balance/GDP (%)	−1.4	0.2	−1.7	0.2	−1.0	−1.5
Exports	12.5	15.7	17.1	18.7	19.5	20.4
Imports	12.9	14.9	16.9	18.0	19.3	20.7
Trade balance	−0.5	0.8	0.2	0.7	0.2	−0.2
Current account balance	0.8	1.5	1.4	3.2	2.6	1.6
Current account balance/GDP (%)	2.6	4.7	3.7	7.7	6	4
Foreign debt	12.5	10.4	10.1	10.2	9.0	9.1
Debt service/Exports (%)	8.9	10.4	6.7	5.4	8	8.4
Currency reserves (import months)	0.7	0.9	1.7	2.3	2.5	2.7

e = estimate, f = forecast

CONDITIONS OF ACCESS TO THE MARKET

■ Market overview

Ukraine's rising standard of living is reflected in the pick-up in domestic consumer demand (up 13.5 per cent in the first half of 2003) and the 18 per cent increase in the average wage to US$80. This trend should continue with the introduction of a 13 per cent standard rate of personal income tax, against a marginal rate of 40 per cent. Private investment has grown on the back of easier availability of medium-term credit, the cut in interest rates to 17 per cent and the restoration of local investor confidence. The local currency (hryvnia) has been stable for two years at around 5.33 to US$1, but could rise by the end of the year. At US$6.6 billion, the country's foreign currency reserves have been strengthened in line with IMF prudential standards. The mechanical engineering, pharmaceuticals, transport and construction sectors are growing. Trade is up 28 per cent, but the trade surplus could shrink by the end of the year because of the growth in imports caused by the poor harvest and the pick-up in investment. The country posts a balance-of-payments surplus.

■ Means of entry

The market remains difficult to penetrate mainly on account of high tariff and non-tariff barriers. Progress has been made in dismantling some obstacles, but others have sprung up in their place

(special inspection procedures, tax incentives law). The adoption in January 2004 of a customs code and a trade code should make the system a little less unsettled. On the other hand, the calendar of planned tax reforms for 2003 (reduction of VAT to 17 per cent) has been upset by the upcoming presidential elections in October 2004. Product certification procedures remain long-winded and often unfair despite a number of improvements (reduction of the list of products subject to compulsory certification, better terms for pharmaceuticals). Ukraine is stepping up intellectual property protection through its inclusion in the civil code and greater harmonization with the TRIPS and WTO agreements (heavier penalties). But the overall result remains unsatisfactory as far as the international community is concerned.

The Financial Action Task Force (FATF) has acknowledged the progress made by Ukraine in the introduction of legislation to combat smuggling and money laundering (tax deductions for previously undeclared income, the setting up in October 2003 of an inter-ministerial money-laundering study group). Although the additional countermeasures imposed in 2002 have been lifted, Ukraine remains on the FATF's blacklist.

■ Attitude towards foreign investors

Officially, the government has adopted measures to erase differences between foreign and local investors (Russia and the CIS included), with a similar tax system and exchange controls for foreigners and locals (2000), investment safeguards for foreigners guaranteed by bilateral treaties, and ownership by foreigners of companies and non-agricultural land (2002). Nevertheless, a number of obstacles remain, including acquisition of farmland by Ukrainians alone, exemption from customs duties for some Russian products (in contradiction to the GATT agreements) and limited participation of foreign bidders in the privatization programme. The most-favoured-nation clause continues to be applied to the CIS although it was due to be abolished in 1998, while the law providing tax exemption for foreign-held companies has been revoked. Because of lack of transparency, the special economic areas have mostly benefited Ukrainian companies close to the local authorities. Nevertheless, large foreign companies continue to expand their presence. Foreign investment has risen to US$736 million in six months, against US$688 million in 2002, but remains small in overall terms. The climate for foreign investment is still far from satisfactory as Ukraine lacks a long-term strategy in this respect. The government is therefore planning to set up a national investment promotion agency in January 2004 to stimulate foreign direct investment and promote the country's image.

OPPORTUNITY SCOPE

Breakdown of internal demand (GDP + imports) %
■ Private consumption   36
■ Public spending   15
■ Investment   13

Exports: 56% of GDP   Imports: 54% of GDP

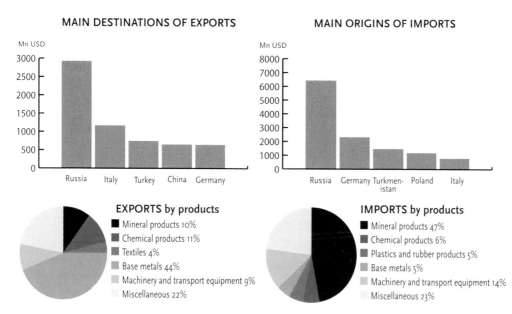

MAIN DESTINATIONS OF EXPORTS

Mn USD

Russia Italy Turkey China Germany

MAIN ORIGINS OF IMPORTS

Mn USD

Russia Germany Turkmen- Poland Italy
                 istan

EXPORTS by products
■ Mineral products 10%
■ Chemical products 11%
■ Textiles 4%
■ Base metals 44%
■ Machinery and transport equipment 9%
□ Miscellaneous 22%

IMPORTS by products
■ Mineral products 47%
■ Chemical products 6%
■ Plastics and rubber products 5%
■ Base metals 5%
■ Machinery and transport equipment 14%
□ Miscellaneous 23%

STANDARD OF LIVING / PURCHASING POWER

Indicators	Ukraine	Regional average	DC average
GNP per capita (PPP dollars)	4270	8420	6778
GNP per capita (USD)	720	3544	3568
Human Development Index	0.766	0.810	0.708
Wealthiest 10% share of national income	23	25	33
Urban population percentage	68	61	60
Percentage under 15 years old	17	19	31
number of telephones per 1000 inhabitants	212	280	157
number of computers per 1000 inhabitants	18	101	66

United Kingdom

Population (million inhabitants)	59.0
GDP (million USD)	1,564,100
GDP per capita (USD)	26,507

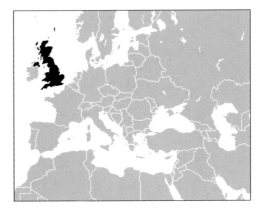

Coface analysis   Short-term: **A1**

STRENGTHS

- Despite re-emergence of a deficit, the public finance situation has remained satisfactory amid low debt and compliance with the rule calling for equivalence between debt contracted and investments made over a given cycle.
- The unemployment rate has been relatively low thanks to labour market flexibility and employment office effectiveness.
- Fiscal moderation, procedural simplicity and a central position in the English-speaking world have contributed to making the country a destination of choice worldwide for foreign direct investment.
- Although traditional industries have been in decline, higher value-added sectors like chemicals, pharmaceuticals, aviation, automobile engines and electronics have been developing rapidly.

WEAKNESSES

- Public services like transportation, health and education have been struggling to fulfil their roles despite substantial public funding recently granted to them, and their productivity has generally reflected this situation.
- The dichotomy between the continued dynamism of the services and housing sectors and the difficulties hampering most industries has not been facilitating the Bank of England's task in setting interest rates.
- Although the persistent euphoria surrounding residential property has been buoying consumer-spending dynamism via a wealth effect and mortgage loans, there is nonetheless a major economic-downturn risk due to the sizeable, mostly variable-rate, household debt burden.
- Northern Ireland has remained a thorny problem for the public authorities as evidenced by the results of the last local elections, which will still not permit constitution of an assembly capable of managing the region.

RISK ASSESSMENT

In 2003, growth held up well, fuelled by dynamic private and public consumption. Households benefited from the creation of public-sector jobs and concomitant wage rises. Moreover, continued low interest rates, by fostering property market dynamism and higher housing prices, generated an increase in mortgage loans that further stimulated consumer spending. Conversely, despite resumption of strong growth in the United States, exports continued to decline, which has tended to impede industrial production and investment.

In 2004, growth should accelerate amid a sharp industrial export recovery, spurred by improved world economic conditions and delayed effects of the pound's weakening against the euro. Despite a

MAIN ECONOMIC INDICATORS

%	1999	2000	2001	2002	2003 (e)	2004 (f)
Economic growth	2.8	3.8	2.1	1.7	2	2.7
Consumer spending (% change)	4.4	4.6	3.1	3.6	2.4	2.2
Investment (% change)	2.2	4.8	3.6	−3.5	1.6	2.8
Inflation	1.7	1.1	2.2	1.3	1.3	1.8
Unemployment rate	6	5.5	5.1	5.2	5.1	5
Short-term interest rate	5.4	6.1	5	4	3.7	4.3
Public-sector balance/GDP (%)	1.1	3.9	0.7	−1.5	−3.0	−3.1
Public-sector debt/GDP (%)	55.8	55.6	50.4	52	54	55
Exports (% change)	4.3	9.4	2.5	−0.9	−1	6
Imports (% change)	7.9	9.1	4.5	3.6	1	6.5
Current account balance/GDP (%)	−2.3	−2.1	−1.8	−1.8	−2.1	−2

e = estimate, f = forecast

still-low unemployment rate, household spending and especially residential investment should stabilize. Rising interest rates could strongly contribute to that result considering the extent of variable-rate household debt.

The slight improvement registered by the Coface payment-incident index in 2003, borne out by an approximate 10 per cent drop in bankruptcies,

would tend to suggest that the difficulties endured by British industry have been progressively easing, even if the situation has remained difficult in textiles, clothing, metals, furniture, printing and mechanical engineering. Metal, paper, alcohol, fruit and vegetable wholesalers and electrical installation, as well as hotels and food service, have also been causing problems.

MAIN ECONOMIC SECTORS

■ Steel

Players in this sector endured another difficult year in 2003. The gradual shrinking of British industrial production, pressure on margins and an export decline have been the main causes of the problems encountered at all industry levels, from steelmakers to wholesalers, processors and user sectors. Among user sectors, the mechanical engineering sector thus posted very poor performance resulting in some resounding bankruptcies. Construction, meanwhile, has continued to trend up due to steady public investment, both direct and delegated to the private sector via the Private Finance Initiative.

■ Wood and furniture

Wood trading benefited from a revival during the past year. Buoyed by the abrupt halt of the price decline for soft wood, low interest rates and the

construction-sector boom, profitability and confidence rose. However, the news from user industries has been less favourable. Furniture industry production thus declined in the face of increased competition from products from East European countries, steady household demand notwithstanding. The sector has remained dominated by family-owned companies, often undercapitalized, that would have difficulty withstanding an economic downturn. Hopes are for a new generation of managers taking control.

■ Paper

British papermakers continued to face foreign competition in 2003 even if the pressure eased somewhat towards year-end with the pound sterling's decline. Most paper consumed in the United Kingdom is now produced abroad and the trend should continue to develop. Wholesalers have continued to struggle in a highly competitive market, decimated by the steady decline of printing and subject to the will of manufacturers on price. The prospect of price rises in 2004 initiated by wholesalers not manufacturers has thus been good news.

■ Printing

British printers have remained in a downward spiral reflected in the increased bankruptcies registered in the sector with no sign of improvement in sight. Costly investments made to keep pace with technological progress, although not justified by business volumes, have been the sector's Achilles heel. Margins have remained under pressure attributable both to the stiff competition that has plunged the actors into a suicidal price war to gain market share, and to debt service bloated by their disproportionate investments. Shrinking advertising budgets have only exacerbated the difficulties.

■ Textiles and clothing industry

The sector has continued to suffer from competition from Asian countries, price pressure exerted by the major distributors of clothing articles, and continued delocalizations to East Europe and the Maghrib. In 2004, the manufacturer situation will continue to deteriorate, particularly due to the higher minimum legal wage enacted in October. That new minimum wage will increase production costs and result in a loss of competitiveness for companies employing low-skilled labour.

■ The fresh-produce markets

The British fresh-produce industry's turnover rose in 2003. As expected, the mass-distribution share in its total market outlets continued to rise thus tending to reduce the industry's room for manoeuvre in negotiations. Facing mass distributors that are increasingly omnipresent, concentrated and in direct contact with producers, both locally and abroad, the situation of importers and wholesalers has also deteriorated. Wholesalers, moreover, have been contending with reorganizations in process or planned on the premises of several wholesale markets with a reduction in the number of actors a likely corollary.

PAYMENT AND COLLECTION PRACTICES

■ Payment

Cheques are widely used, but do not provide total security as non-payment of a cheque is not a criminal offence (cheques do not have to be covered at the time of issue). The drawer of a cheque may refuse payment at any time. Cheques can be presented for cashing a second time under the RDPR (Refer to Drawer Please Re-present) option.

The bill of exchange, while rare in commercial transactions, is used in special cases. If a foreign bill remains unpaid at maturity, it must be protested. Centralized accounting helps reduce costs and cashing times.

Bank transfers, particularly by SWIFT, are regularly used for domestic and international settlements. Leading British companies also use two other highly automated interbank transfer systems – BACS (Bankers' Automated Clearing Services) and CHAPS (Clearing House Automated Payment Systems).

■ Debt collection

Debt collection agencies or solicitors handle the recovery of overdue payments, which begins with the issue of a reminder. Under the Late Payment of Commercial Debts (Interest) Act 1998, small companies are entitled – from 1 November 1998 – to demand default interest from large companies, both public and private. This law, introduced in successive stages with the last stage coming into effect on 7 August 2002, now permits all commercial companies to bill interest in cases of late payment. Save as otherwise provided between the parties, the applicable rate of interest is the Bank of England's base rate (dealing rate) plus eight basis points.

The legal recovery process is designed to enable creditors to obtain a ruling after lodging a 'claim form' with the appropriate legal authority.

Summary judgments, while quicker to obtain through ordinary proceedings, are more difficult to obtain if contested by the defendant. The reform of the judicial process (or the Lord Woolf reform), which saw the introduction of new Civil Procedures Rules with effect from 26 April 1999, is considered by lawyers to be a major breakthrough in dealing with disputed claims.

The new rules of procedure have gradually cut litigation time as parties seek ways of coming to a settlement either directly or through mediation (ie ADR: Alternative Dispute Resolution).

Devices to speed up proceedings include the establishment of three separate 'tracks' – small claims track, fast track and multi-track – based on the size of the claim and the drawing up of a timetable of hearing dates by the courts.

Judgments are enforced either through conventional methods (service by bailiff, attachment of debtor assets with subsequent auction) or directly through an order of 'statutory demand' giving the debtor 21 days to settle his or her debt or face a winding-up petition. At the end of an additional 21-day period and in the absence of a serious payment proposal from the debtor, the creditor may file a liquidation order in the court, as the debtor is regarded as insolvent. This enforcement procedure may, in some cases, be directly used to recover undisputed claims, without requiring a prior ruling.

PAYMENT INCIDENTS INDEX
(12 months moving average - base 100 : World 1995)

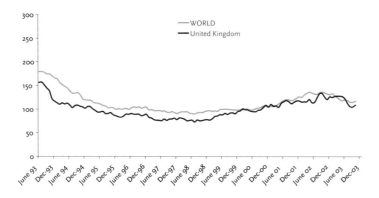

Uzbekistan

Population (million inhabitants)	25.1
GDP (million USD)	11,270

Short-term: **D**

Coface analysis

Medium-term:
Very high risk

STRENGTHS

- Uzbekistan boasts natural wealth, mainly cotton and gold.
- The country has been attempting to diversify towards other raw materials (oil and gas) and industry (automobiles).
- As Central Asia's most populated country with over 25 million inhabitants, it offers attractive market potential.
- The country hosts US bases since the military campaign in Afghanistan with official financial assistance gradually increasing.

WEAKNESSES

- The country's sources of wealth are subject to exogenous factors like world prices and weather conditions.
- Its limited progress on reforms could deter backing by multilateral bodies.
- Centralized decision making and the state-controlled economy have been impeding growth.
- Notwithstanding the repression of Islamism, the causes of its expansion (like the social situation) are still present.

RISK ASSESSMENT

Economic conditions and the financial situation have been benefiting from the improvement in cotton and gold prices. However, the government's pervasive intermediary role has been discouraging producers, notably in the farm sector. Moreover, the import reduction policy has prompted disinvestment in the manufacturing sector. Although that policy has certainly permitted current account improvement, it has also progressively undermined exports.

The country has been posting low external debt ratios. Since the devaluations, however, companies have been having difficulty repaying currency loans obtained with a sovereign guarantee. Although the government possesses the means to offset those difficulties considering its disciplined fiscal policy, a lack of transparency and likely instances of capital flight would suggest that the financial situation is less solid than it may seem.

A scenario of renewed emphasis on reforms appears hardly likely. Although the authorities have begun to liberalize the exchange system under IMF urging, they have concurrently consolidated their control over trade, which has seriously undermined their credibility. Despite closer ties with the United States – with the presence of US troops in Uzbekistan – progress on political and economic reforms has been too limited to attract new investments.

MAIN ECONOMIC INDICATORS

US$ millions	1999	2000	2001	2002	2003 (e)	2004 (f)
Economic growth (%)	4.1	3.3	4.1	3.2	1.8	4.1
Inflation (%)	25.2	48.5	51.6	26.9	30	25.2
Public-sector balance/GDP (%)	−2.8	−2.4	−1.5	−1.8	−1.4	−2.8
Exports	2,671	2,935	2,740	2,510	2,837	2,671
Imports	2,594	2,441	2,554	2,186	2,311	2,594
Trade balance	77	494	186	324	526	77
Current account balance	−203	216	−113	222	375	−203
Current account balance/GDP (%)	−2.0	1.6	−1.0	2.3	4.3	−2.0
Foreign debt	4,163	4,234	4,279	4,363	4,122	4,163
Debt service/Exports (%)	16.3	25.7	25.8	23.4	24.8	16.3
Currency reserves (import months)	2.6	6.1	5.4	6.5	6.0	2.6

e = estimate, f = forecast

CONDITIONS OF ACCESS TO THE MARKET

■ Market overview

Uzbekistan signed Article 8 of the IMF charter on 15 October 2003, while declaring its currency officially and freely convertible. The fact that this has not been accompanied by a shake-up of trade regulations or radical market liberalization could upset the country's social and economic equilibrium. That is why Uzbekistan does not yet constitute a 'market' for foreign firms, especially small and medium-sized ones. There is no regular trade, and imports are limited to basic foodstuffs such as sugar and oil. Large companies, on the other hand, can find business opportunities if they come up with the necessary funds.

It should be noted that the government has decided to limit the sovereign guarantee facility to genuine priority areas. The country's debt-servicing capacity is, in fact, restricted by volatile export revenues based mainly on cotton and gold. Consequently, foreign business projects are very carefully vetted.

■ Means of entry

The terms of entry have been relaxed by a series of regulatory and legislative reforms, coupled with the easing of exchange controls. All sectors have been opened up, other than the strategic ones. There are no special restrictions on imported consumer and capital goods. Payments in hard currency are no longer limited by currency convertibility restrictions, but by the shortage of foreign currency at the banks of prospective customers. Firms based in Uzbekistan, however, usually manage to obtain foreign exchange in under a month.

■ Attitude towards foreign investors

Current Uzbek legislation offers safeguards against discrimination, nationalization and expropriation, and permits unrestricted repatriation of profits and capital. The only problem, as mentioned earlier, is the shortage of foreign exchange. Red tape remains an obstacle to entry in a country where the relevant regulations have never been revised.

Uzbekistan is in the process of privatizing its enterprises and has drawn up a list of companies for sale. However, the majority of these enterprises have either filed for insolvency or exist only on paper. The rules for buy-ins and buy-outs require foreign investors to renew the production apparatus, but do not require them to retain existing staff. In strategic sectors, such as cotton and its derivatives, gold, energy and aeronautics, foreign shareholdings are capped at 40 per cent, with the Uzbek government retaining a majority stake.

Uzbekistan is a member of the Islamic Development Bank and receives assistance from major multilateral financial institutions (IBRD, ADB, World Bank).

125

■ Foreign exchange regulations

As mentioned earlier, the currency is fully and freely convertible as of 15 October 2003. However, the country manages its currency flows with a great deal of caution. This may help to avert a crisis, but is not conducive to sweeping currency liberalization. The exchange rate seems to have steadied. The main problem faced by firms conducting business or investment transactions is the shortage of foreign exchange and the, hopefully no more than temporary, failure of the banks and customs service to deal with the situation.

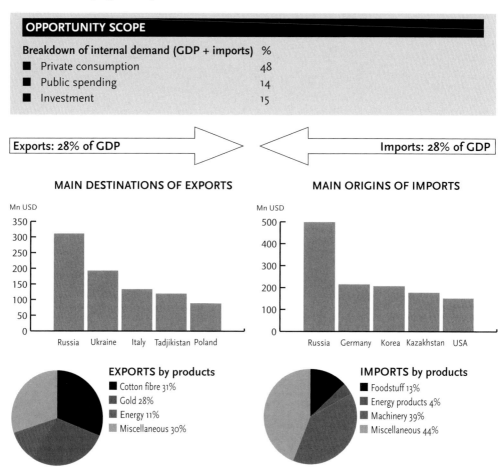

OPPORTUNITY SCOPE

Breakdown of internal demand (GDP + imports)	%
■ Private consumption	48
■ Public spending	14
■ Investment	15

Exports: 28% of GDP   Imports: 28% of GDP

MAIN DESTINATIONS OF EXPORTS

Mn USD

Russia · Ukraine · Italy · Tadjikistan · Poland

MAIN ORIGINS OF IMPORTS

Mn USD

Russia · Germany · Korea · Kazakhstan · USA

EXPORTS by products
- Cotton fibre 31%
- Gold 28%
- Energy 11%
- Miscellaneous 30%

IMPORTS by products
- Foodstuff 13%
- Energy products 4%
- Machinery 39%
- Miscellaneous 44%

STANDARD OF LIVING / PURCHASING POWER

Indicators	Uzbekistan	Regional average	DC average
GNP per capita (PPP dollars)	2410	8420	6778
GNP per capita (USD)	550	3544	3568
Human Development Index	0.729	0.810	0.708
Wealthiest 10% share of national income	22	25	33
Urban population percentage	37	61	60
Percentage under 15 years old	37	19	31
number of telephones per 1000 inhabitants	66	280	157
number of computers per 1000 inhabitants	n/a	101	66

The
Americas

2

The Economic Outlook for the Americas in 2004

Experts from Oxford Analytica, Oxford

Fiscal and monetary policy in the United States will remain accommodative in 2004, underpinning continued strong GDP growth. The resulting current account deficit suggests that 2004 could set the stage for a significant, broad dollar depreciation. In Brazil, some recovery in investment levels and economic growth may occur in 2004, but any dramatic and sustained improvement is unlikely in the light of institutional and decision-making stasis. Argentina's economic recovery, begun in 2003, will continue in 2004, albeit at a slower rate; political improvisation and disputes within the government and the ruling party may have an increasingly negative impact, with urgent structural reforms likely to be further delayed.

UNITED STATES

The US economy enters 2004 with strong momentum. Signs of growth are beginning to convince businesses to prepare for expansion. Such confidence should underpin modest growth in investment spending and moderation in the payroll cull. The OECD projects real GDP growth of 4.2 per cent in 2004, up from 2.9 per cent in 2003. The projection is based on a near-doubling in business investment growth and quadrupling in export growth.

Dollar weakness against Atlantic currencies is virtually assured, but there is no certainty that Asian policymakers will countenance more than the extremely limited appreciation they allowed in 2003. The outcome depends upon Beijing's renminbi policy. Even with a large dollar depreciation, strong

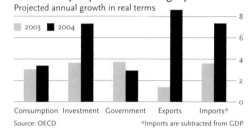

US GDP by expenditure category
Projected annual growth in real terms

2003 ■ 2004

Consumption Investment Government Exports Imports*
Source: OECD   *Imports are subtracted from GDP

export growth is a problematic prediction. On one hand, US industry is not well equipped to capitalize on a cheaper currency because of structural changes that have taken place during the post-1995 'strong dollar' period, such as overseas investment. On the other, import penetration is unlikely to respond much to a dollar fall. Canadian exporters to the United States, seeing their currency rise 20 per cent against the US dollar in 2003, reduced their profit margins, and managed to increase their exports by 5 per cent in volume terms.

■ Economic stimulus

Consumption growth should remain strong, and investment should pick up as the economy continues to benefit from accommodative monetary policy. The Federal Reserve has the luxury of keeping short rates low for a considerable period, due to a still-large output gap. Strong third-quarter 2003 growth notwithstanding, the economy has in this recovery (dating from November 2001) not grown at anything like its potential rate. This bequeaths significant slack. The OECD does not expect the output gap to be eliminated until the end of 2004 at the earliest.

Long-term rates depend upon Asian currency policy. A Chinese revaluation would produce at most a step-change in regional currency values against the dollar. This would reduce – but not end – Asian official flows into US Treasury securities, as policymakers defend a new level of dollar weakness. Thus, long-term interest rates are unlikely to rise precipitously in 2004, and could see at most a step-change as global capital flows adjust to new Asian currency values. A benign outlook for long-term rates underpins hopes for recovery in business investment.

It also facilitates a growing budget deficit. Fiscal stimulus should be bigger in 2004 than projected by the OECD, which credits lawmakers with significant budgetary restraint. A more realistic assessment suggests a still-growing budget deficit. The one fiscal drag will be state governments. Many have avoided drastic budget cuts by a variety of transitory means, including securitization of tobacco settlement payout revenues. Fewer such options will be available in 2004, and for the most part states are constitutionally prevented from engaging in deficit finance.

■ Uneven dollar

For any other country, this growth scenario would be difficult to manage in the absence of stronger growth in the rest of the world, due to the negative impact on the external balance. Strong US growth will bloat the external deficit, which is likely to finish 2004 at 6.0 per cent of GDP. The OECD's construction of time series data beginning in 1889 show the deficit has only once before breached 2 per cent of GDP – in the mid-1980s.

While not by definition unsustainable, this level of external deficit puts a large strain on the dollar. Asian central banks will probably continue to lean against dollar weakness – even after a one-time revaluation, should this come to pass – so the burden of currency adjustment will fall on Europe. This should provide a boost to parts of the import-competing sector of the US economy, but Europe will not provide a strong motor for US exports.

■ Employment challenge

This business cycle remains noteworthy for its job losses: payroll employment is still below the level of November 2001, the beginning of the current expansion. It would normally have risen 5 per cent at this stage, based on the average of five recoveries in the 1960–82 period. Even the 1991–93 'jobless recovery' generated a 1 per cent increase in payrolls by this stage. This statistic supports the finding of a US Federal Reserve study that the economy has undergone structural losses in the labour market. Rapid productivity growth means that impressive GDP growth does not necessarily create big gains in employment. However, it also creates little inflationary pressure, and hence the Fed's soft line on policy.

■ Growth questions

There is some reason for caution in interpreting real GDP results. Accelerating deflation in IT prices makes business spending look big in real terms; it is distinctly less so in nominal terms. A more broadly based recovery in business spending could become necessary should households begin to confront more binding limits on consumption growth:

- **Debt service.** As a percentage of income, household debt service has risen to 13 per cent. Because the principal of debt is increasing, the principal portion of debt service is growing. The benign outlook for short-term interest rates no longer provides relief in debt service; the debt burden continues to rise, eating a growing portion of disposable income.

- **Household wealth.** The property market could begin to show cracks in 2004, which would translate into question marks for household net wealth. Increases in net wealth have underpinned the resilience of consumer spending since the end of the 1993–2000 expansion. Any fall in home values will not be matched by a fall in the value of liabilities, creating a threat to net wealth. Home price growth was a reasonable 5.6 per cent in the third quarter of 2003, somewhat faster than the second quarter but much slower than in preceding years. However, the impact of strong growth in housing supply will eventually be felt

129

by the market. The rental market is already showing weakness, with rental income now falling in 80 per cent of US cities.

BRAZIL

Luiz Inacio Lula da Silva assumed the presidency on 1 January 2003 with a great store of goodwill and high expectations, but also with the considerable challenge of reconciling divergent interests among voters, his party, Congress, business and workers with regard to his economic and social policy agenda. General expectations that he would seek to balance economic discipline with social policy priorities, thus satisfying a range of interests, have been borne out. Barring some external shock, this should set the scene for a relatively tranquil year in economic terms, where the forthcoming municipal elections will be at the top of the political agenda.

■ Lula's second year

Predictions of a short honeymoon have proved false, at least in terms of public opinion. Nevertheless, the government cannot rely on this goodwill indefinitely and will have to start delivering on its promises of a 'growth spectacular': voters will not indefinitely ignore sluggish growth, failed promises on job creation, falling average incomes and growing violence and insecurity. Major efforts are being made to kick-start economic recovery – real interest rates are now at one-digit levels (9.49 per cent) and the nominal rate has fallen 9.5 percentage points in the past five months – and to clear the legislative agenda of the main reforms promised for the first year. However, these efforts are focused on the campaign for the municipal elections scheduled for October 2004. This type of short-term vision of policy reform is not conducive to longer-term sustainable growth or improvement in social indicators.

■ Positive economic signs

The last weeks of 2003 have set the stage for a relatively good start to 2004:

- The main stock market (BOVESPA) has attained record highs, with a 78 per cent gain in 2003, while C-bonds are trading at all-time highs at 97.5 per cent of face value.

- Country risk has fallen to around 500 basis points.
- The currency has stabilized at some 2.94 reals to the dollar.
- The trade surplus is expected to reach 23 billion dollars, while the current account is likely to end the year in surplus for the first time in 10 years.
- Moreover, the primary surplus has surpassed the IMF-set target, having reached over 5.8 per cent of GDP for the last 12 months.

On this basis, and despite the fact that GDP may expand by only 0.2 per cent this year, business and government are both predicting growth of about 3.5 per cent for 2004. This should be achievable, given that the economy is starting from a low base and the political imperatives of municipal elections will require some recovery, in part via public spending. However, consumption-led or government spending-led options are limited in the current situation, leaving exports or private investment as more probable sources of growth. It is still feasible to increase exports, and to stimulate infrastructure investment through better regulatory frameworks and government policy incentives, as well as offers of Public–Private Partnerships (PPP).

There is thus a growing expectation that foreign direct investment (FDI) will rise, especially in export-oriented sectors and infrastructure. This is reflected in forecasts predicting up to US$16 billion in FDI in 2004, up from less than US$9 billion this year – albeit still far below the US$30 billion recorded in 2000. In addition, export levels appear increasingly to reflect a structural shift, rather than the short-term market adjustment to demand slumps that has historically characterized Brazil's inwardly oriented business sectors. The industrial restructuring of the 1990s in response to trade liberalization also bodes well for future sustained improvement in export performance. The automotive industry, for example, has increased exports by over 25 per cent in the past year alone. However, these positive signs cannot be taken for granted.

■ Negative economic signals

Notwithstanding these positive indicators, other areas of economic performance will remain precarious. The net public debt-to-GDP ratio currently stands at

57.2 per cent; while this could drop to around 54 per cent next year, it is unlikely to fall below 50 per cent even in the best-case scenario. Brazil is likely to spend about 10 per cent of GDP on servicing public-sector debt in 2004 (similar to 2003 levels). The burden of public debt is the key obstacle both to growth and to resolving issues of social justice and policy flexibility, not least because it diverts banking sector resources away from credit creation and productive investment in the private sector. Despite this dismal picture, the debt profile is likely to improve over the course of 2004, with a lower percentage indexed to exchange rates and a higher percentage indexed to the falling benchmark Selic rate.

A major problem in both economic and political terms is the high level of unemployment, which is likely to remain stable at its current 13 per cent level in urban centres. This is made worse by low (and falling) levels of consumer confidence, declining real income – down 11.61 per cent year on year in 2003 – and low rates of gross fixed capital formation (under 18 per cent), all of which further dampen growth and make a quick recovery unlikely. This will provide ammunition for the opposition during the election campaign. However, it is still unclear whether the opposition will be sufficiently coherent in articulating this message to gain votes.

ARGENTINA

President Nestor Kirchner, having received only 22 per cent of the vote in the 27 April 2003 presidential election, enjoyed an approval rating of 86 per cent according to opinion polls in early December. This was due in large part to economic recovery during 2003 – although Kirchner and his government can claim only partial credit for this, having adopted a largely 'hands-off' approach – and ensures that political opposition will remain somewhat muted as long as his popularity remains high. However, the desire to maintain that popularity has encouraged Kirchner to delay unpopular but much-needed reforms, which may have a negative impact on future growth.

■ Economic prospects

In comparison with a year ago, the economy has improved substantially:

GDP growth, %

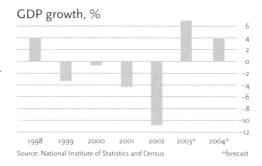

Source: National Institute of Statistics and Census   *forecast

- After a record contraction of 10.9 per cent in 2002, GDP will expand by at least 7.0 per cent in 2003.
- Inflation has fallen from 41 per cent in 2002 to an estimated 4 per cent in 2003, while the exchange rate – which reached nearly 4 pesos to the dollar in 2002 – has stabilized at just under 3.
- Unemployment fell from 21.5 per cent in May 2002 to 15.6 per cent in the same month of 2003, the last month for which official figures are available.

These figures are less impressive than they appear. Jobless figures declined in part because unemployed heads of household receiving a 150-peso (US$50) monthly subsidy are no longer classified as out of work. At the same time, if official growth forecasts for 2003 and 2004 are achieved, GDP in 2004 will only return to the level of 2001 – itself the third year of recession. Growth has depended to date on the use of idle capacity, increased consumer demand and buoyant agricultural and oil exports. However, lack of credit will not permit significant investment to expand capacity; commodity exports are vulnerable to

Unemployment rate, %

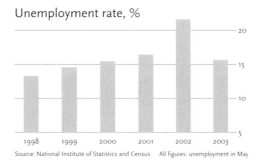

Source: National Institute of Statistics and Census   All figures: unemployment in May

weather conditions and international prices; and consumer demand remains repressed by high unemployment and low wages, despite the recently decreed rise in wages and pensions (50 and 20 pesos, respectively) that will take effect in January.

Macroeconomic forecasts in the 2004 budget – GDP growth of 4 per cent, an exchange rate of 3 pesos to the dollar and a primary surplus of 3 per cent of GDP – are largely realistic, although projected inflation of 9–11 per cent appears rather high and the level of recovery anticipated will do little to reduce jobless rates further. Moreover, there are doubts over the sustainability of fiscal performance in the absence of a serious reform; improved tax collection has depended on inflation, rising activity and export taxes, which the government has promised gradually to eliminate. At the same time, the impact of official proposals to stimulate growth through public works – virtually the only economic policy articulated to date – will be limited by spending constraints and the doubtful utility of planned projects.

■ Debt prospects

Pending debt restructuring negotiations will continue to constrain credit in 2004 and may have a more significant impact in 2005 if debt payments are restarted. The government's initial restructuring offer has met with strong resistance from bondholders, and further creditor lawsuits will follow. The government's strategy was to make an unacceptable initial offer in order to improve it thereafter, and it is anticipated that talks will take at least two years. If this is the case, the start of repayments on defaulted debt may coincide with the maturity of post-2001 debt – including 'Boden' bonds issued to compensate depositor losses and guaranteed loans – and 2005 debt payments are likely to prove unsustainable. At the same time, the renegotiation process could still be derailed if Kirchner decides to override Economy Ministry strategies, as he did in the course of IMF negotiations.

■ Reform prospects

The accord reached with the IMF in September did little to increase investor confidence, as it imposed macroeconomic targets only for 2004. At the same time, other 2004 goals demanded by the agreement

– a new revenue-sharing agreement with the provinces by August, completion of debt negotiations and banking reform – will not be met.

Banking reform to date has been largely market-driven, with banks reducing branch networks and beginning a limited process of mergers and acquisitions. Once compensation for post-devaluation losses is resolved, possibly by late 2004, further buy-outs and liquidations are likely, although solvency will remain an issue. The post-devaluation crisis led to a doubling of the market share of state-owned banks – especially the Banco Nacion and Banco Provincia – given the widespread perception that the government will not let these entities close. That share will increase in 2004, to the detriment of international banks in particular. At the same time, poor corporate governance at state banks implies that their increased market share may represent a systemic risk.

■ Political prospects

Populist rhetoric, improvisation and avoidance of unpopular decisions have characterized the Kirchner government to date. Unless these attitudes are reversed, they will have an impact on both the political and economic climate in future. The government has repeatedly postponed tariff negotiations with privatized utilities; however, advances will be crucial in 2004 to avoid the withdrawal of some operators and to ensure investments needed to maintain infrastructure. At the same time, government boasting of its 'aggressive' stance with foreign investors and governments – more muted in reality than in media reports – will tend to tarnish Argentina's image and reinforce the perception that Kirchner has failed to engage with investors. Kirchner's reliance on a small group of advisors will also continue to limit government efficiency and may lead to important cabinet changes in the short term.

US GDP growth in 2004 looks likely to be 4.0–4.2 per cent. Consumption and fiscal expansion will continue to dominate; exports and investment will probably underperform expectations, suggesting a less-than-sustainable growth composition for the medium term. The current account deficit, reaching

6.0 per cent of GDP, is likely to precipitate a broad dollar depreciation, which in subsequent years will shift some demand to the external sector, providing a more balanced composition of growth and repairing the US international investment position. While there will be some recovery in Brazilian economic growth, little progress is likely in removing structural bottlenecks, improving systemic competitiveness and reducing the debt-to-GDP ratio. The Argentinian political and economic situation is likely to remain relatively stable during 2004, although without significant advances as some important issues will have a visible impact only in 2005. However, slowing recovery and rising expectations may lead to an increase in social demands at a time when Kirchner's political support may prove ephemeral. There is a significant risk that the opportunity for reform will be lost.

2

The Range of Country @ratings in the Americas

Sylvia Greisman and Olivier Oechslin

Coface Country Risk and Economic Studies Department, Paris

COUNTRY @RATING SCALE

A regional country risk @rating represents an average of country @ratings weighted according to their contribution to the region's production.

A Country @rating measures the average level of short-term non-payment risk associated with companies in a particular country. It reflects the extent to which a country's economic, financial and political outlook influences financial commitments of local companies. It is thus complementary to @rating Credit Opinions on companies.

The quality of country risk has markedly improved in North America. In the United States, improvement in company profitability and solvency has accompanied robust economic activity. That situation should persist in 2004 and has prompted the upgrading of the Country @rating to A1.

In Latin America, the improvement has been less pronounced. The economic growth expected should remain moderate with the quality of risk in the region remaining below the emerging country average. Only Chile, with its positive-watchlisted A3 rating, has been benefiting from strong demand

from both the United States and Asia. Elsewhere in South America, improvement in the financial situation, progress on reforms and a brighter growth outlook have prompted the upgrading of Brazil's rating to B. Nonetheless, large economies like that of Venezuela (D) or Argentina (positive-watchlisted D rating) still present high levels of risk.

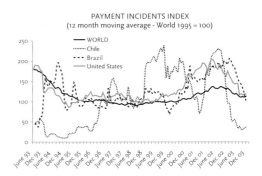

PAYMENT INCIDENTS INDEX
(12 month moving average - World 1995 = 100)

In **North America**, robust growth should persist in the United States at least until the upcoming presidential elections. Thereafter, the constraint associated with the country's 'twofold' deficit could result in a slowdown. With markedly improved profitability, however, companies will be ready this year to capitalize on the expansionary fiscal and monetary policies pursued by the public authorities. In this favourable context, the payment-incident decline initiated in the 2002 second half has been continuing with the Coface index almost matching the lowest levels reached in the 1990s.

Those favourable conditions only had a limited bandwagon effect on **Latin American** countries in 2003. Mexico has thus benefited little from the recovery while facing growing pressure from Asian competition on some products. Moreover, many countries are still contending with severe political crises or the constraints associated with financial discipline.

In 2004, the situation should be better. Many could finally benefit from the results of financial consolidation. The decline of domestic interest rates and emergence of fiscal room for manoeuvre could bolster internal demand. Acceleration of world demand, particularly from the United States and China, will contribute to sustaining high raw material prices. The continent's growth should thus be near 3 per cent. That recovery will nonetheless continue to depend on continued market confidence.

■ Countries rated A1

Very stable political and economic conditions favourably influence generally good company payment behaviour. Moreover, a satisfactory legal framework ensures protection of creditors and the effectiveness of collection procedures. That generally favourable environment nonetheless does not exclude either disparities in growth or occasional risks of payment default.

In the **United States**, activity should gain additional momentum amid continuing expansionary economic policy. Buoyed by the progressive decline of unemployment, household spending should remain robust even if the very high levels of automobile purchases and property investment have little chance of persisting. Companies will benefit from the lower dollar exchange rate to increase exports and reconquer the domestic market. The investment recovery should thus intensify.

In that more buoyant environment, the company situation should continue to improve with the Coface payment-incident index's sharp downward trend since the second half of 2002 confirming that outlook. However, the situation has remained difficult in sectors like civil aviation, electricity production and distribution,

telecommunications, metals and steel, as well as the car industry and textiles where, in many cases, foreign competition has been squeezing profits.

■ Countries rated A3

Company payment behaviour is poorer than in the two higher categories and could be affected by a change in the country's economic and political environment, although the likelihood of that leading to widespread payment defaults remains relatively low.

In **Chile** (with a positive-watchlisted rating), improved economic conditions in the United States, high growth in Asia, better copper prices and lower interest rates have spurred a substantial economic recovery since early 2003, causing a sharp improvement in company solvency. Part of the industrial sector has been nonetheless suffering from the renewed competitiveness of neighbouring countries. Thanks to the signature of free-trade agreements with its main trading partners and good fundamentals – essentially healthy public finances and very moderate public-sector debt – Chile should nonetheless benefit fully from the world growth upturn in 2004.

■ Countries rated A4

These countries often exhibit fairly mediocre payment behaviour that could be affected by an economic downturn, although the probability of that causing a large number of payment defaults remains moderate.

Although **Mexico**'s financial situation has remained relatively sound, its economy has remained sluggish. With the positive effects of recovery in the United States slow to materialize, a resumption of growth should nonetheless mark 2004. However, the capacity of Mexican companies to defend their market share against the competition will be a crucial factor with the restoration of competitiveness lost in recent years against countries like China constituting Mexico's main challenge. Although the peso depreciation will doubtless provide a short-term response, it has been undermining companies carrying dollar debt.

2

■ Countries rated B

A precarious economic environment could affect company payment behaviour, which is often poor.

In **Brazil**, with its @rating upgraded to B, the political and financial environment has improved thanks to the new government team's pragmatism. Economic growth has nonetheless remained sluggish amid restrictive fiscal and monetary policies. Weak demand has been hurting companies particularly in sectors focusing on the domestic market like the car industry or retail. The growth registered in the industrial sector and investment in late 2003 should nonetheless continue in 2004. The progressive interest-rate decline and strengthening local currency have been easing financial constraints, which has permitted a slight

COFACE MAP OF COUNTRY @RATINGS

improvement in company payment behaviour and concomitant decline in bankruptcies. The food and steel sectors have been particularly benefiting from new competitiveness gains linked to the real's weakness. A virtuous circle of growth could thus develop. Continued easing of monetary policy should permit more balanced and progressively more robust growth.

In **Colombia**, growth has accelerated since early in the 2003 second half due to export dynamism and a climate more conducive to consumer spending and investment. The construction, manufacturing, energy and financial services sectors have been benefiting from that dynamism. Company solvency and payment behaviour have been improving.

2

COFACE MAP OF MEDIUM- AND LONG-TERM COUNTRY RISK

Very low risk
Low risk
Quite low risk
Moderately high risk
High risk
Very high risk

Beyond restoring order, President Alvaro Uribe is seeking to overhaul the government completely. Total victory over the guerrillas will nonetheless be unlikely in the near term since they hold strong positions in difficult-to-access areas. Moreover, the public-sector debt burden has been limiting the president's room for manoeuvre to increase security spending. Finally, popular resistance to economic and popular reform has tended to outweigh concern about security.

Since the end of 2001, **Peru**'s growth has recovered strongly due essentially to development of the mineral and gas sector. Meanwhile, a substantial increase in exports has permitted the narrowing of the current account deficit and the reduction of debt ratios in relation to foreign currency earnings. Moreover, continuation of prudent fiscal policy coupled with IMF backing has been buoying investor confidence. However, the debt burden has remained high with the banking sector's substantial dollarization constituting a major source of vulnerability.

The country's main weakness is nonetheless still linked to political uncertainties that have been impeding reforms and deterring diversification of investments towards more labour-intensive sectors than mineral extraction.

■ Countries rated C

A very precarious economic and political environment could worsen payment behaviour that is already often poor.

In the **Dominican Republic**, the bankruptcy of the country's third bank, Baninter, in May 2003, had a negative impact that was as much political and social as it was economic and financial. In 2003, the country endured its first recession in 13 years. The government will only be able to rescue Baninter if it implements IMF reforms rapidly. However, the public violently opposes that reform programme. In that context and considering the low level of foreign

currency reserves and high degree of dollarization, the country has remained very vulnerable to sudden capital flight. The decline of the peso exchange rate has particularly undermined companies with dollar debt and revenues denominated only in the local currency. The outlook for 2004 has thus remained very uncertain.

■ Countries rated D

The economic and political environment presents a very high level of risk that exacerbates generally deplorable payment behaviour.

In **Argentina** (with a positive-watchlisted rating), growth has resumed since the economy collapsed in the 2002 first half. A low production capacity utilization rate has permitted companies to benefit from the peso's decline to reconquer the domestic market and, in some sectors, notably food, to develop exports. After the four crisis years that gripped the country, growth has thus been robust thanks to a catch-up effect. Strong growth should continue in 2004 with the 1988 production peak not yet reached. To permit growth to continue beyond that initial catch-up phase, restoration of financial flows to companies will nonetheless be essential. However, that will depend on implementation of painful reforms.

In **Venezuela**, political uncertainties are still the main risk element with tensions between President Chavez's supporters and opponents remaining very high. Stabilizing the political climate will nonetheless be essential since the Venezuelan crisis has triggered a deep recession. Capital flight has necessitated imposition of strict exchange controls that have been severely hindering companies as evidenced by deterioration of the Coface payment-incident index. Progressive recovery of oil production will thus be unlikely to permit a genuine economic upturn. Moreover, a possible oil-price decline in 2004 could further undermine the country. In such conditions and lacking political clarity, the company situation should remain very shaky.

Argentina

Population (million inhabitants)	37.5
GDP (million USD)	102,150

Short-term: **D**

Medium-term:
Very high risk

Coface analysis

2

STRENGTHS

- The country boasts many assets including substantial natural resources, a well-developed food sector and skilled labour.
- The structural reforms of the 1990s profoundly transformed the economy by bringing a long isolationist tradition to an end.
- The peso's weakness has permitted exports to recover and has benefited local production without generating excessive inflationary pressures.

WEAKNESSES

- Unsustainable external debt ratios have led to default with massive debt repudiation considered inevitable.
- Financial system solvency has remained shaky overall due to costs linked to the decision to let the peso float freely and the upsurge of bad debts.
- The authorities have little fiscal room for manoeuvre.
- The very high unemployment rate has been particularly affecting the middle and poorest classes.
- Despite the current president's popularity, the political outlook remains very uncertain.

RISK ASSESSMENT

The economy is progressing slowly after the economic collapse in the 2002 first half. Low production capacity utilization rates have permitted companies to capitalize on the peso's decline to reclaim domestic market share and, in some sectors, notably food, to develop exports. Restoration of financial flows towards industry will nonetheless be essential to sustain growth after an initial catch-up phase. Meanwhile, the return of investor confidence will depend on renegotiation of the foreign debt along with consolidation of public accounts and the banking system. The economic recovery, IMF agreement, and electoral successes registered in September 2003 have bolstered the authority of the new President, Nestor Kirchner, who will nonetheless have to make some painful choices. By obtaining adoption of unpopular financial reforms, he could displease a country where rioting contributed to driving two presidents from office in recent years. However, excessive hesitation and delay in implementing reforms could lead to gridlock.

MAIN ECONOMIC INDICATORS						
US$ billions	1999	2000	2001	2002	2003 (e)	2004 (f)
Economic growth (%)	-3.4	-0.8	-4.4	-10.9	5.8	3.5
Inflation (%)	-1.8	-0.7	-1.5	41.0	6.0	9.0
Public-sector balance/GDP (%)[1]	-4.2	-3.6	-5.7	-2.7	-2.7	-2.7
Exports	23.3	26.3	26.5	25.7	29.0	30.2
Imports	24.1	23.9	19.2	8.5	12.5	15.0
Trade balance	-0.8	2.5	7.4	17.2	16.5	15.2
Current account balance	-12.0	-9.0	-4.5	8.2	7.5	6.1
Current account balance/GDP (%)	-4.2	-3.2	-1.7	8.0	6.0	4.4
Foreign debt	145.4	146.5	141.5	142.0	145.6	148.5
Debt service/Exports (%)	75.2	76.9	96.6	63.4	69.2	59.9
Currency reserves (import months)	6.8	6.3	4.2	5.3	5.7	6.2

e = estimate, f = forecast

CONDITIONS OF ACCESS TO THE MARKET

■ Market overview

Since the second half of 1998, Argentina has been in the grip of a severe economic crisis. The economy shrank in 2001 and 2002, coupled with the country's withdrawal from the currency board, a sharp devaluation of the peso and a liquidity crisis in the banking sector. The risk of collapse of the banking system forced the Argentine government to introduce exchange controls and restrictions on foreign currency transfers. These should be gradually relaxed over the coming year especially in respect of foreign trade transactions.

The peso's devaluation has made the Argentine economy much more competitive, pushing up Argentine exports to US$14.5 billion in the first six months of 2003 despite export funding difficulties.

Argentine labour is among the cheapest in Latin America. The average monthly wage is US$450 (US$700 in Buenos Aires) and, since 1999, social security contributions have fallen from 33 per cent to 24 per cent.

■ Means of entry

The opening up of borders, privatization and the pegging of the peso to the dollar constituted the main pillars of government economic policy in the 1990s. In 2002, the government introduced an economic and financial emergency law abolishing the convertibility system and establishing a free currency market.

Since January 1995, goods from non-Mercosur countries have been subject to the common external tariff (CET), which ranges from 0 per cent to 28 per cent (average 15 per cent). A 3 per cent across-the-board increase in CET came into effect in December 1997. Although the founding treaty of Mercosur enshrines the principle of the free movement of goods, the four member countries maintain customs barriers for certain products, which they have undertaken gradually to lift.

Imports are liable to 0.5 per cent statistical tax on the CIF value, 21 per cent VAT (CIF value, plus customs duties, plus statistical tax), 9 per cent additional VAT on goods intended for sale as opposed to those directly used by the importer, and 30 per cent profits tax (CIF value, plus customs duties, plus statistical tax). Special procedures, eg clearance from the competent ministry, apply to pharmaceutical and agri-food imports.

■ Attitude towards foreign investors

The legal arrangements governing foreign investment in Argentina appear to be very liberal. The investment framework is defined by decree 1853/93, which lays down the principle of equal treatment of domestic and foreign investors and free repatriation of capital and profits. Foreigners may invest – on the same terms as local investors – in virtually any branch of the economy without seeking prior approval. Nevertheless, the stability of the legal and tax environment for foreign investment cannot be taken for granted, especially under the current state of economic and financial emergency.

PAYMENT INCIDENTS INDEX
(12 months moving average - base 100 : World 1995)

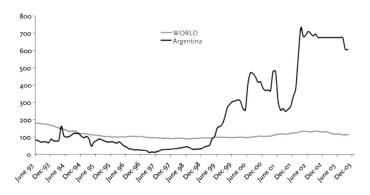

2

OPPORTUNITY SCOPE

Breakdown of internal demand (GDP + imports) %
- Private consumption   44
- Public spending   10
- Investment   12

Exports: 11% of GDP   Imports: 10% of GDP

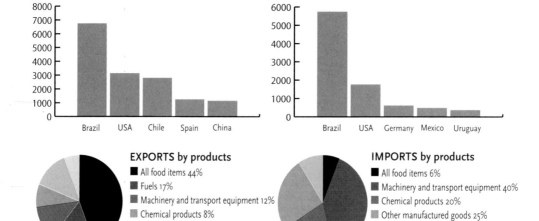

MAIN DESTINATIONS OF EXPORTS

Mn USD

Brazil · USA · Chile · Spain · China

MAIN ORIGINS OF IMPORTS

Mn USD

Brazil · USA · Germany · Mexico · Uruguay

EXPORTS by products
- All food items 44%
- Fuels 17%
- Machinery and transport equipment 12%
- Chemical products 8%
- Other manufactured goods 13%
- Miscellaneous 6%

IMPORTS by products
- All food items 6%
- Machinery and transport equipment 40%
- Chemical products 20%
- Other manufactured goods 25%
- Miscellaneous 9%

STANDARD OF LIVING / PURCHASING POWER

Indicators	Argentina	Regional average	DC average
GNP per capita (PPP dollars)	n/a	5819	6778
GNP per capita (USD)	2542	2928	3568
Human Development Index	0.849	0.770	0.708
Wealthiest 10% share of national income	n/a	41	33
Urban population percentage	88	74	60
Percentage under 15 years old	28	32	31
number of telephones per 1000 inhabitants	224	137	157
number of computers per 1000 inhabitants	91	52	66

Bolivia

Population (million inhabitants)	8.5
GDP (million USD)	7,812

Coface analysis

Short-term: **D**

Medium-term:
Very high risk

STRENGTHS

- Bolivia boasts abundant natural resources – minerals and especially hydrocarbons.
- The country has benefited from aid by multilateral institutions and concessional treatment of its debt by public-sector creditors.
- Association with Mercosur has enhanced its access to the Brazilian and Argentine markets.

WEAKNESSES

- The level of development is among the lowest in Latin America.
- Bolivia has remained heavily in debt despite the HIPC initiative for highly indebted poor countries.
- External accounts have remained structurally in deficit with exports resting on a limited number of staple commodities: soybeans, zinc, gold and natural gas represent half of total sales.
- The domestic savings rate is low.
- The political and social climate is very tense.

RISK ASSESSMENT

Bolivia's growth has been insufficient in recent years. Economic growth has essentially depended on the capital-intensive energy sector with fiscal restrictions and coca eradication affecting the purchasing power of the poorest population segments. Establishing durable growth will require diversification of the economy to reduce its vulnerability to fluctuations in world raw material prices and ensure more equitable distribution of wealth.

Despite debt reductions granted to the country, its debt ratios have remained very high in relation to currency earnings. Moreover, the banking sector's substantial dollarization would be a major source of vulnerability in a crisis of confidence. Nonetheless, the main uncertainties are linked to the grave deterioration of the social and political climate. The new president, Carlos Mesa, has only very limited room for manoeuvre in contending with the Indian movements that caused his predecessor's demise. The political uncertainties could undermine prospects for exploitation of oil fields and especially gas fields, which otherwise constitute promising vectors for growth in coming years.

MAIN ECONOMIC INDICATORS

US$ billions	1999	2000	2001	2002	2003 (e)	2004 (f)
Economic growth (%)	0.4	2.4	1.2	2.8	2.8	3.3
Inflation (%)	3.1	3.4	0.9	2.4	2.8	3.5
Public-sector balance/GDP (%)	-3.5	-3.7	-6.9	-8.9	-6.4	-4.6
Exports	1.1	1.2	1.3	1.3	1.4	1.6
Imports	1.8	1.8	1.7	1.8	1.7	1.8
Trade balance	-0.7	-0.6	-0.4	-0.5	-0.3	-0.3
Current account balance	-0.5	-0.4	-0.3	-0.3	-0.2	-0.2
Current account balance/GDP (%)	-5.9	-5.3	-3.4	-4.3	-2.8	-3.1
Foreign debt	5.5	5.8	4.7	4.9	5.2	5.6
Debt service/Exports (%)	24.3	24.5	28.1	22.5	20.9	20.4
Currency reserves (import months)	7.0	7.0	6.5	5.0	5.6	5.8

e = estimate, f = forecast

CONDITIONS OF ACCESS TO THE MARKET

■ Market overview

A small landlocked state surrounded by powerful neighbours, Bolivia has focused on opening up its borders and closer trade integration with other countries in the region. Since 1995, the five-tier Common External Tariff of the Andean Community of Nations (ACN) (0, 5, 10, 15 and 20 per cent) has been in force in the country. The other Community members have allowed Bolivia to apply *de facto* 10 per cent flat-rate *ad valorem* customs duty to all imports from non-ACN countries, excluding capital goods, which are liable to a reduced rate of duty. With the completion of key privatization-related development programmes, foreign investment has dropped to about US$750–800 million year on year and unfortunately remains concentrated in low job-growth sectors such as oil and gas, energy and telecommunications. Unskilled Bolivian labour is widely available and cheap. Wages can be fairly high for positions of responsibility. Employment of foreign staff is in principle limited to 15 per cent of a company's workforce.

■ Means of entry

Foodstuffs and crop and animal products require health certificates that comply with ACN standards. The national agency Senasag is responsible for enforcing all health standards relating to imported meats and meat products.

Imports in excess of US$3,000 are subject to inspection by one of two government-approved companies, Inspectorate and SGS. Under revised Bolivian customs legislation, a customs valuation department is to be set up shortly and outsourcing discontinued. Documentary credit is the most widely used means of payment for both cash and deferred settlements. Delivery against payment is also used, but is far less widespread. Where business relations are well established, payments are usually made by bank transfer. Corporate defaults have surged over the last two years. Against this background, irrevocable and confirmed documentary credit is strongly recommended if there is any doubt whatsoever about the buyer's creditworthiness.

■ Attitude towards foreign investors

There is no discrimination against foreign investors who are subject to the same rules as Bolivian nationals. Foreign investors are only required to register their investments with the Vice-Ministry of Foreign Trade and Investment and to submit various company incorporation documents. Despite political will and favourable legislation, foreign investors may still face serious problems caused by the lack of proper legal safeguards or events on the ground over which the government has little or no control.

■ Foreign exchange regulations

There are no foreign exchange controls and no restrictions on the buying and selling of currencies or capital transfers. Bolivia is a highly dollarized economy, with more than 95 per cent of bank deposits denominated in dollars.

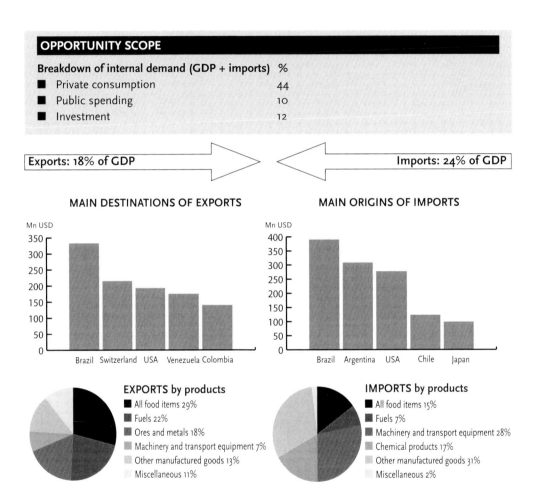

OPPORTUNITY SCOPE

Breakdown of internal demand (GDP + imports) %
- Private consumption — 44
- Public spending — 10
- Investment — 12

Exports: 18% of GDP   Imports: 24% of GDP

MAIN DESTINATIONS OF EXPORTS

Mn USD

Brazil Switzerland USA Venezuela Colombia

MAIN ORIGINS OF IMPORTS

Mn USD

Brazil Argentina USA Chile Japan

EXPORTS by products
- All food items 29%
- Fuels 22%
- Ores and metals 18%
- Machinery and transport equipment 7%
- Other manufactured goods 13%
- Miscellaneous 11%

IMPORTS by products
- All food items 15%
- Fuels 7%
- Machinery and transport equipment 28%
- Chemical products 17%
- Other manufactured goods 31%
- Miscellaneous 2%

STANDARD OF LIVING / PURCHASING POWER

Indicators	Bolivia	Regional average	DC average
GNP per capita (PPP dollars)	2240	5819	6778
GNP per capita (USD)	950	2928	3568
Human Development Index	0.672	0.770	0.708
Wealthiest 10% share of national income	32	41	33
Urban population percentage	63	74	60
Percentage under 15 years old	39	32	31
number of telephones per 1000 inhabitants	62	137	157
number of computers per 1000 inhabitants	21	52	66

Brazil

Population (million inhabitants)	172.4
GDP (million USD)	452,386

Coface analysis

Short-term: **B**

Medium-term:
High risk

STRENGTHS

- Brazil boasts abundant natural resources with a relatively diversified economy.
- Fiscal and monetary policy has been prudent and pragmatic.
- Domestic market potential and low labour costs have continued to attract foreign investors.
- The real's decline has permitted Brazilian companies to become more competitive.
- The country enjoys international financial community backing.

WEAKNESSES

- The public debt burden is very heavy with maturities too short.
- The external debt level is unsustainable over the long haul.
- External financing needs are too great in comparison to currency earnings due to the debt amortization burden.
- The low level of savings – which government financing needs essentially gobble up – has been impeding private company investment.
- The new president has little room for manoeuvre, squeezed by his electors' aspirations for change, the need to reach compromises with coalition partners, and economic restraints.

RISK ASSESSMENT

The financial environment has been improving thanks to the new government team's pragmatism. Economic growth has nonetheless remained sluggish so far due to restrictive fiscal and monetary policies. The weakness of demand has been hurting companies, particularly those like the car industry or retail sector focusing on the domestic market. Conversely, the progressive interest rate decline and strengthening of the real, which has been easing financial constraints, have caused a slight improvement in payment behaviour and a reduction in company bankruptcies. The food and steel sectors particularly have been benefiting from the new gains in competitiveness linked to the real's decline. Continued easing of monetary policy should permit more balanced and progressively more robust growth in 2004.

Despite improvement in the trade balance, the external financial situation will continue to be the main risk factor in the longer term. Financing needs have remained excessive due to very high amortization of external debt. With its pragmatic approach, the new president's team has been successful so far in reassuring lenders. Market sentiment could nonetheless rapidly turn sour if political tensions develop as could ultimately happen if the population's aspirations for change remain unsatisfied.

MAIN ECONOMIC INDICATORS

US$ billions	1999	2000	2001	2002	2003 (e)	2004 (f)
Economic growth (%)	0.8	4.4	1.4	1.5	0.5	3.7
Inflation (%)	8.4	5.3	9.4	14.7	9.1	5.2
Public-sector balance/GDP (%)	−5.8	−3.6	−3.6	−4.7	−4.7	−4.7
Exports	48.0	55.1	58.2	60.4	67.5	70.2
Imports	49.2	55.8	55.6	47.2	47.1	54.4
Trade balance	−1.2	−0.7	2.6	13.1	20.5	15.8
Current account balance	−25.3	−24.2	−23.2	−7.8	0.4	−8.6
Current account balance/GDP (%)	−4.7	−4.0	−4.6	−1.7	0.1	−1.7
Foreign debt	243.0	237.9	227.3	228.6	240.9	244.3
Debt service/Exports (%)	121.0	101.1	88.8	62.1	68.4	63.9
Currency reserves (import months)	4.8	4.2	4.5	5.4	7.5	7.2

e = estimate, f = forecast

2

CONDITIONS OF ACCESS TO THE MARKET

■ Market overview

Brazil's working population was estimated in 2002 by IBGE at 86 million out of a total of 140 million persons aged 10 years or more, ie an activity rate of 61.3 per cent. The minimum monthly wage is 240 reals (about 72 euros). Employer social security and compulsory benefit contributions amount to about 50 per cent of gross wages. Pension and tax reforms should lead to a reduction in contributions mainly for export firms.

■ Means of entry

The average rate of customs duty is approximately 11 per cent and the top rate 35 per cent. Having negotiated far higher duties with the WTO than it actually applies, Brazil is unlikely to call into question its multilateral commitments. The country is bound by Mercosur's Common External Tariff, which is riddled with exceptions. It maintains a number of non-tariff barriers to imports, including import licences, customs valuation inspections and prior registration. The most widely used means of payment are down-payments, prepayments, cash against documents, acceptance bills and irrevocable letters of credit confirmed by a Brazilian or foreign bank. Brazil places restrictions on the employment of foreigners. There are two types of work permit – permanent and temporary – both of which are issued on a restricted basis.

■ Attitude towards foreign investors

Foreign investors may set up a wholly owned subsidiary without a local partner. Restrictions on foreign investment are still in place, especially in the nuclear energy industry. The aeronautics sector is now open to foreign penetration (Dassault stake in Embraer). Once a company is set up, foreign investors are not subject to any regulatory restrictions, but must be represented by a lawyer in Brazil. Only foreigners having a permanent visa may be appointed directors of a subsidiary operating in the country. Foreign transfers for the purposes of capital repatriation, reinvestment or profit and dividend repatriation are authorized once the capital is registered. Such transfers must be handled by financial institutions trading on the currency market but are not subject to central bank clearance. Profit and dividend transfers are not taxed.

■ Foreign exchange regulations

Since January 1999, the exchange rate has been set freely by the interbank market. The central bank still intervenes on the markets, occasionally and indirectly, to counter erratic exchange-rate fluctuations. The new government formed after the October 2002 elections has honoured its pledge to maintain a flexible exchange rate. The central bank intervenes only occasionally when required to ensure liquidity in the market, but not to cut rates. Its sole aim is to control inflation in a manner that does not stunt growth. Brazilian commercial banks (Banco do Brazil) have, for some time, been making 'white interventions' or currency purchases on behalf of the Treasury, apparently in an effort to maintain the real at a level that guarantees export competitiveness.

PAYMENT INCIDENTS INDEX
(12 months moving average - base 100 : World 1995)

OPPORTUNITY SCOPE

Breakdown of internal demand (GDP + imports)   %
- Private consumption — 53
- Public spending — 18
- Investment — 18

Exports: 13% of GDP   Imports: 14% of GDP

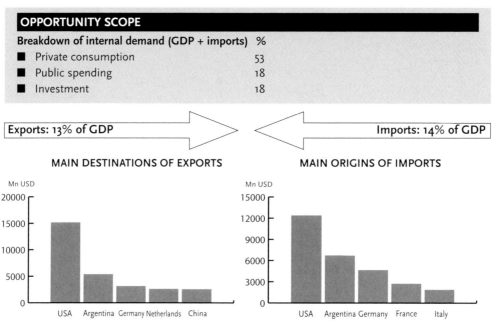

MAIN DESTINATIONS OF EXPORTS

Mn USD

USA   Argentina   Germany   Netherlands   China

MAIN ORIGINS OF IMPORTS

Mn USD

USA   Argentina   Germany   France   Italy

EXPORTS by products
- All food items 28%
- Ores and metals 9%
- Machinery and transport equipment 27%
- Chemical products 5%
- Other manufactured goods 22%
- Miscellaneous 9%

IMPORTS by products
- All food items 6%
- Fuels 15%
- Machinery and transport equipment 43%
- Chemical products 18%
- Other manufactured goods 14%
- Miscellaneous 4%

STANDARD OF LIVING / PURCHASING POWER

Indicators	Brazil	Regional average	DC average
GNP per capita (PPP dollars)	7070	5819	6778
GNP per capita (USD)	3070	2928	3568
Human Development Index	0.777	0.770	0.708
Wealthiest 10% share of national income	47	41	33
Urban population percentage	82	74	60
Percentage under 15 years old	28	32	31
number of telephones per 1000 inhabitants	218	137	157
number of computers per 1000 inhabitants	63	52	66

Canada

Population (million inhabitants)	31.4
GDP (million USD)	724,800
GDP per capita (USD)	23,073

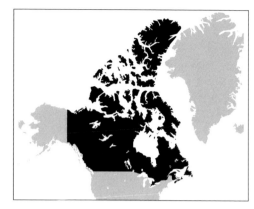

Coface analysis   Short-term: **A1**

RISK ASSESSMENT

Growth sagged in 2003 due to a series of negative shocks including the SARS pandemic, fires and electricity breakdowns. Moreover, both the sluggishness of the US economy during the first half and the Canadian dollar's appreciation, spurred by the rise of raw material prices, impeded expansion of trade with the United States, which absorbs over 80 per cent of Canadian exports. However, very steady private spending, buoyed by the decline of interest rates starting last summer and accommodating tax policy facilitated by the equilibrium of public finances, limited the extent of the slowdown.

Growth should accelerate again in 2004 due notably to the dynamism of the US economy, which will fuel exports despite probable continuation of the Canadian dollar's appreciation. Company investment should continue to expand thanks to an expected profit increase linked to the likely rise of export revenues. Despite continued high unemployment and progressive saturation of automobile and housing needs, household spending should remain buoyant.

The Coface company payment-incident index began to deteriorate in the 2003 second quarter, concomitantly with the economic slowdown. That deterioration should only be temporary due to the expected recovery. The clothing, wood, aviation and automobile sectors have weaknesses that an export upturn will only attenuate.

MAIN ECONOMIC INDICATORS

%	1999	2000	2001	2002	2003 (e)	2004 (f)
Economic growth	5.5	5.3	1.9	3.3	1.9	3
Consumer spending (% change)	3.8	4	2.6	3.4	3.5	3.3
Investment (% change)	7.2	6	1	−6	1.7	4.8
Inflation	1.7	2.2	1.8	1.9	2.8	2
Unemployment rate	7.6	6.8	7.2	7.6	7.7	7.6
Short-term interest rate	4.9	5.8	4	2.6	2.9	3.1
Public-sector balance/GDP (%)	1.6	3	1.4	0.8	0.5	0.6
Public-sector debt/GDP (%)	89.5	82	81	77.8	77	74
Exports (% change)	10.7	8	−3.1	−0.1	−2	5.8
Imports (% change)	7.8	8.1	−5	0.6	4	6
Current account balance/GDP (%)	0.3	2.9	2.4	2	1.7	1.9

e = estimate, f = forecast

PAYMENT AND COLLECTION PRACTICES

Reflecting its close historical ties with the Old World, Canada has a dual legal system: one, inspired by British common law, used in nine of the 10 provinces making up the federal state, and the other used by Quebec, whose legal traditions are based on the codified principles of the Napoleonic Code. Quebec's civil code, which came into force on 1 January 1994, is a completely revamped version of the Civil Code of Lower Canada dating back to 1 August 1866.

Canada was the first British colony to exercise executive and legislative powers as a federal state within the framework of the British North America Act of 1867.

■ Payment

Bills of exchange, promissory notes and cheques are governed by a single law throughout Canada. However, this law is interpreted according to common law precedents in the nine provinces and civil law principles in Quebec. Sellers are therefore advised to accept these instruments only where long-term commercial relations, based on mutual trust, have been established with the buyers.

Centralized accounts – which greatly simplify fund transfers by means of a centralized local collection system between buyers and sellers – are also used within Canada.

SWIFT transfers are the most widely used means of payment for international transactions. Leading Canadian banks use the SWIFT network, which offers a rapid and efficient fund transfer service. However, sellers should bear in mind that settlement by transfer is dependent upon the client's good faith as only the client decides whether or not to order payment.

The letter of credit (L/C) is also frequently used.

■ Debt collection

Canada's constitution divides judicial authority between the federal and provincial governments. Each province is responsible for administering justice, organizing provincial courts and implementing the rules of civil procedure in its territory. Though the names of courts may vary between provinces, the same legal system applies throughout the country, except in Quebec.

Within each province, provincial courts hear the vast majority of cases, however small, while superior courts hear more important cases, whether criminal or commercial. In Quebec, for example, all civil and commercial claims in excess of C$70,000 and criminal cases decided by jury are heard by the Superior Court of Quebec. Canadian superior courts are organized into two distinct divisions: a court of first instance and a court of appeal.

At federal level, the Supreme Court of Canada, based in Ottawa, and only with leave of the court itself (leave is granted if the case raises an important question of law), hears appeals against decisions handed down by the provincial appeal courts. The Supreme Court also hears appeals by the Canadian Federal Court (in appeal division), which has special jurisdiction in matters relating to maritime law, immigration, customs and excise, intellectual property and disputes between provinces, etc.

The right to bring cases before the Privy Council in London as the court of last resort was abolished in 1949.

The recovery process begins with the service of a final demand – or seven-day letter – by registered mail, reminding the debtor of his or her obligation to pay the outstanding debt plus any contractually agreed interest penalties.

In order to allow the court to determine the admissibility and foundation of the plaintiff's claim, ordinary proceedings take place in three phases: the writ of summons in which the plaintiff presents his or her claim against the defendant; the examination for discovery, which outlines the claim against the defendant and takes into account the evidence to be submitted to the court by each party; and the trial proper, during which the judge hears the adverse parties and their respective witnesses who are directly examined and cross-examined by the parties' legal counsels.

It should be noted that, although the vocabulary used to define the stages of proceedings is not standardized, this sequence of phases is generally applied throughout the country.

The reform of Quebec's code of civil procedure, enacted on 1 January 2003, aims to speed up and improve court proceedings by means of, for example, a writ of summons as the sole legal remedy and the introduction of a maximum time limit of 180 days within which the suit must be registered for 'examination of witnesses and hearing' (*pour enquête et audition*).

PAYMENT INCIDENTS INDEX
(12 months moving average - base 100 : World 1995)

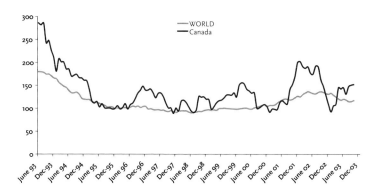

2

Chile

Population (million inhabitants) 15.4
GDP (million USD) 64,502

Coface analysis

Short-term: **A3**

Medium-term:
Low risk

STRENGTHS

- The absence of major economic imbalances coupled with the country's very solid financial situation has generally permitted the government and companies to benefit from the region's lowest-risk premiums.
- The political environment is stable amid a consensus on maintaining fundamental macroeconomic equilibriums.
- The banking system is the soundest in the region.
- Although copper still represents 40 per cent of exports, Chile has succeeded in developing other sectors including fruit, fish, wood and wood pulp.

WEAKNESSES

- The Chilean economy has remained too dependent on commodities or low value-added products.
- The high stock of foreign direct investment has been causing large foreign currency outflows.
- Some companies have been carrying heavy foreign debt.
- Severe social inequality has continued to mark the country.

RISK ASSESSMENT

Chile has had to contend with several shocks in recent years including the collapse of copper prices and sagging world demand, which affected the growth of a country very open to foreign trade. The economic upturn in the United States, high growth in Asia, recovery of copper prices and decline of interest rates have fuelled a substantial economic recovery since early 2003, which has caused a sharp improvement in company solvency and payment behaviour. Part of the industrial sector has nonetheless been suffering from the upsurge of competitiveness in neighbouring countries.

Thanks to the conclusion of free-trade agreements with its main trading partners and to its good fundamentals (essentially the public sector's sound finances and very moderate debt), Chile should benefit fully from the world growth recovery. Further out, however, the amount of foreign currency debt carried by some private companies will constitute a source of weakness. Moreover, the economy has remained too dependent on primary product exports. Economic diversification and shifting production toward higher value-added products will thus constitute essential goals.

MAIN ECONOMIC INDICATORS						
US$ billions	1999	2000	2001	2002	2003 (e)	2004 (f)
Economic growth (%)	−3.2	4.4	3.1	2.1	3.3	4.0
Inflation (%)	2.3	4.5	2.6	2.8	2.7	3.0
Public-sector balance/GDP (%)[1]	−1.4	0.1	−0.3	−0.8	−0.8	−0.7
Exports	17.2	19.2	18.5	18.3	20.3	22.3
Imports	14.7	17.0	16.4	15.8	17.4	18.7
Trade balance	2.4	2.2	2.1	2.5	2.9	3.7
Current account balance	−0.3	−1.0	−1.2	−0.6	−0.6	−0.2
Current account balance/GDP (%)	−0.5	−1.4	−1.7	−0.9	−0.9	−0.3
Foreign debt	36.1	37.5	38.8	42.5	42.6	43.3
Debt service/Exports (%)	17.5	20.7	24.1	27.4	26.3	20.3
Currency reserves (import months)	7.8	7.0	6.8	7.7	7.2	6.9

e = estimate, f = forecast

CONDITIONS OF ACCESS TO THE MARKET

■ Market overview

The Chilean market is secure and stable. The country's sound political and economic situation, satisfactory infrastructure and stable legislation create an attractive business environment, especially for small and medium-sized companies.

Chile has sought little or no tariff protection for many years, adopting unilateral measures to cut import duties backed by bilateral and regional trade agreements. Flat-rate customs duty was cut to 6 per cent with effect from 1 January 2003. Moreover, under the free-trade agreement with the EU, ratified by Congress and in force since 1 February 2003, customs duties for 99.8 per cent of industrial goods have been slashed to 0 per cent. From September 2003, the customs tariff applicable to the EU is 1.2 per cent.

Nevertheless, a number of measures operate in a similar manner to non-tariff barriers: a surtax on luxury goods, variable levies on edible oils, sugar, wheat and wheat flour and a super milk levy.

■ Means of entry

There are few non-tariff barriers. For food products, however, a number of health and plant health regulations with a similar effect are in place (type-approval and sampling procedures, etc).

The Intellectual Property Act 1991 provides inadequate protection for pharmaceuticals, especially with regard to formulae registered before 1991. The bill under review by Congress is designed to bring Chilean intellectual property legislation into line with WTO standards.

Chilean trademark and designation-of-origin laws are not yet fully WTO compliant.

All common means of payment are accepted in Chile.

■ Attitude towards foreign investors

There is equal treatment of foreign and local investors. Foreigners are not required to tie up with a local partner. Foreign investment status within the meaning of Decree-Law 600 applies to deals in excess of US$5 million. Capital inflows below this figure, but above US$10,000, must be declared to the Central Bank. Some regulations have been relaxed though. For instance, the one-year capital residence requirement has been scrapped, along with the mandatory zero-interest deposit scheme for foreign capital (encaje). The utilities privatization and concession programme continues to offer foreign investors start-up opportunities, even though most of the lucrative concessions have already been awarded.

Corporation tax is 15 per cent, but there is a 20 per cent surtax on profits repatriated abroad.

Labour legislation is not burdensome in terms of social security contributions. Despite the introduction of unemployment benefits in 2002 and the increase in severance pay provided for in the recently revised labour code, employer social security contributions are extremely low and limited to industrial accident protection.

To counter the decline in foreign investment inflows in 2002, the government is looking to enhance prospects for foreign start-ups in the country.

■ Foreign exchange regulations

The Central Bank abandoned the peso's crawling peg in September 1999. The exchange rate has since been determined solely by the market, with the monetary authorities intervening only on an exceptional basis.

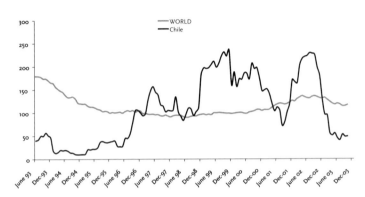

PAYMENT INCIDENTS INDEX
(12 months moving average - base 100 : World 1995)

OPPORTUNITY SCOPE

Breakdown of internal demand (GDP + imports) %
- Private consumption   49
- Public spending   9
- Investment   16

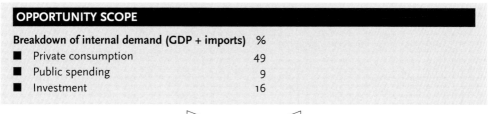

| Exports: 35% of GDP | Imports: 33% of GDP |

2

MAIN DESTINATIONS OF EXPORTS

Mn USD

USA   Japan   China   Mexico   Italy

MAIN ORIGINS OF IMPORTS

Mn USD

Argentina   USA   Brazil   China   Germany

EXPORTS by products
- All food items 24%
- Agricultural raw materials 11%
- Ores and metals 45%
- Chemical products 6%
- Other manufactured goods 7%
- Miscellaneous 7%

IMPORTS by products
- All food items 7%
- Fuels 18%
- Machinery and transport equipment 35%
- Chemical products 12%
- Other manufactured goods 24%
- Miscellaneous 4%

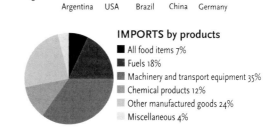

STANDARD OF LIVING / PURCHASING POWER

Indicators	Chile	Regional average	DC average
GNP per capita (PPP dollars)	8840	5819	6778
GNP per capita (USD)	4590	2928	3568
Human Development Index	0.831	0.770	0.708
Wealthiest 10% share of national income	45	41	33
Urban population percentage	90	74	60
Percentage under 15 years old	28	32	31
number of telephones per 1000 inhabitants	233	137	157
number of computers per 1000 inhabitants	107	52	66

Colombia

Population (million inhabitants)	43
GDP (million USD)	80,751

Short-term: **B**

Medium-term:
Coface analysis **High risk**

STRENGTHS

- Colombia, South America's third economic power, holds a central strategic position in the Andean Community.
- Its companies boast the highest productivity in the region.
- The country is well endowed with natural resources including agriculture, hydrocarbons and minerals.
- It has developed niche exports to reduce its dependence on raw material price trends.
- President Alvaro Uribe has continued to benefit from broad popular support.

WEAKNESSES

- Deep social inequalities along with geographic constraints may help explain Colombia's lack of unity and the central government's chronic incapacity to maintain control over the entire country.
- Attacks by guerrillas and drug traffickers and the exceptional level of violence have been deterring investment.
- Increased security spending must accompany the necessary consolidation of public accounts.
- Exports have remained too dependent on prices of staple commodities like coffee and oil.
- The foreign debt burden has been substantial.

RISK ASSESSMENT

Alvaro Uribe's election as president in May 2002 underscored yearnings for a radical solution to a conflict lasting since 1964 and that has already left over 200,000 dead. The president's strong personality and popular support have been assets in implementing reforms intended, beyond restoring order, profoundly to transform the country and reinstitute financial orthodoxy. Despite the electorate's expectations, however, total victory over the guerrillas will be very unlikely in the near term. The public debt burden has been limiting the president's limited room for manoeuvre in increasing security spending with the guerrillas continuing to hold strong positions in difficult-to-access areas. Moreover, the public's resistance to economic and social reforms has been stronger than its concern about security as evidenced by the failure of last October's referendum on government reform.

Growth has nonetheless accelerated since the 2003 second half began buoyed by export dynamism and a climate more conducive to consumption and investment. Construction, manufacturing, energy and financial services have been the most dynamic sectors.

MAIN ECONOMIC INDICATORS

US$ billions	1999	2000	2001	2002	2003 (e)	2004 (f)
Economic growth (%)	−4.2	2.9	1.4	1.6	2.7	3.3
Inflation (%)	9.2	8.8	7.7	7.0	6.1	5.6
Public-sector balance/GDP (%)	−6.2	−3.8	−3.8	−4.1	−4.1	−4.1
Exports	12.0	13.6	12.8	12.3	13.2	13.2
Imports	10.3	11.1	12.3	12.1	13.4	14.0
Trade balance	1.8	2.5	0.5	0.2	−0.2	−0.8
Current account balance	0.5	0.6	−1.2	−1.6	−1.9	−2.5
Current account balance/GDP (%)	0.6	0.8	−1.5	−2.0	−2.5	−3.2
Foreign debt	37.2	36.5	39.1	37.8	39.4	39.9
Debt service/Exports (%)	36.5	43.3	43.1	59.6	47.4	49.4
Currency reserves (import months)	6.1	6.0	6.3	6.9	6.4	6.1

e = estimate, f = forecast

CONDITIONS OF ACCESS TO THE MARKET

■ Market overview

Despite the economic recovery, the peso's devaluation prevents across-the-board increases in imported consumer goods. But steadily changing patterns of consumption act as a stimulus to imports. There are also high-growth niche markets, especially in mid-range agri-foodstuffs. The year 2004 should be a promising one for capital goods in particular due to firm demand and the government's temporary tax incentives for sectors such as textiles and garments, leather goods, automobiles, pharmaceuticals and food processing.

■ Means of entry

The few barriers to trade that remain mainly arise from the legal uncertainty created by frequent parliamentary changes as well as the plethora of government bodies and players operating without unified standards. This is especially true of taxation. In an effort to remedy the situation, the country's Congress is reviewing a bill to promote legal stability for foreign and domestic investment. Under this bill, investors will receive government compensation if specific legal provisions, whose stability is vital to investment decisions, are changed. Following the adoption of tax and labour law reforms in late 2002, other reforms in basic laws are due to come up for parliamentary review shortly. These include the administration of justice, arbitration procedures, public procurement, a tax evasion bill, devolution to local authorities and a corporate insolvency bill. Parliament is debating new tax reforms because the referendum – which primarily sought to introduce greater standards of morality in public life and freeze spending and wages for two years – turned out to be a near-total fiasco. The new bill, which will increase tax revenues to 7.5 per cent of GDP over a seven-year period, provides for an increase in the general rate of VAT from 16 to 17 per cent and the maintenance of the 10 per cent income tax surcharge, introduced under the last tax reform (law 788 of 2002) and due to be abolished in 2005.

■ Attitude towards foreign investors

All sectors of the economy are open to foreign investment, except for defence and the processing of toxic, hazardous or radioactive waste not produced in the country. Investment in financial

PAYMENT INCIDENTS INDEX
(12 months moving average - base 100 : World 1995)

services, oil and gas and mining is subject to prior government approval.

■ **Foreign exchange regulations**

The peso has been floating freely against the dollar since September 1999. So sharp was its rise at the end of 2002 that, despite levelling off in the following year, its average value in 2003 was up by 12–14 per cent on 2002, a rise of 6–8 per cent in real terms. A gain of 4–5 per cent in real terms is the target for 2004.

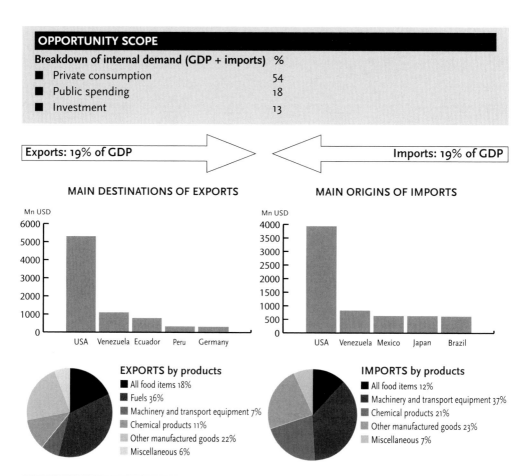

OPPORTUNITY SCOPE

Breakdown of internal demand (GDP + imports)	%
■ Private consumption	54
■ Public spending	18
■ Investment	13

Exports: 19% of GDP → ← Imports: 19% of GDP

MAIN DESTINATIONS OF EXPORTS

Mn USD

USA Venezuela Ecuador Peru Germany

MAIN ORIGINS OF IMPORTS

Mn USD

USA Venezuela Mexico Japan Brazil

EXPORTS by products
- ■ All food items 18%
- ■ Fuels 36%
- ■ Machinery and transport equipment 7%
- ■ Chemical products 11%
- ■ Other manufactured goods 22%
- ■ Miscellaneous 6%

IMPORTS by products
- ■ All food items 12%
- ■ Machinery and transport equipment 37%
- ■ Chemical products 21%
- ■ Other manufactured goods 23%
- ■ Miscellaneous 7%

STANDARD OF LIVING / PURCHASING POWER

Indicators	Colombia	Regional average	DC average
GNP per capita (PPP dollars)	6790	5819	6778
GNP per capita (USD)	1890	2928	3568
Human Development Index	0.779	0.770	0.708
Wealthiest 10% share of national income	48	41	33
Urban population percentage	75	74	60
Percentage under 15 years old	32	32	31
number of telephones per 1000 inhabitants	171	137	157
number of computers per 1000 inhabitants	42	52	66

Costa Rica

Population (million inhabitants)	3.9
GDP (million USD)	16,447
GDP per capita (USD)	4,217

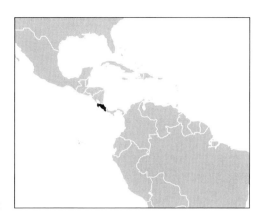

2

Short-term: **B**

Medium-term:

Coface analysis **Moderately high risk**

RISK ASSESSMENT

After three poor years of activity, the economy seems to have recovered since 2003, buoyed by tourism and a revival of demand for high-technology products. The technology upturn should benefit the US chipmaker Intel, which has operations in a customs-free area representing about 15 per cent of exports. The country has remained attractive to investors with enviable social indicators, a good level of education, and political stability offsetting a certain resistance to change by the population.

The public finances situation has nonetheless remained the country's Achilles heel with the slowdown of recent years accompanied by a substantial worsening of macroeconomic imbalances and an increase in public-sector debt. The high interest rate levels necessitated by near two-digit inflation and substantial government financing needs have also been responsible for a sharp increase in dollar-denominated deposits and loans. The extent of dollarization in comparison to the insufficient currency reserve levels has been undermining the banking sector. Although foreign debt has been rising, it has nonetheless remained relatively moderate in relation to export earnings.

MAIN ECONOMIC INDICATORS						
US$ billions	1999	2000	2001	2002	2003 (e)	2004 (f)
Economic growth (%)	8.2	2.2	0.9	2.8	5.0	5.5
Inflation (%)	10.0	11.0	11.3	9.2	9.4	8.9
Public-sector balance/GDP (%)	−2.9	−3.7	−3.8	−5.0	−4.0	−4.0
Exports	6.6	5.8	4.9	5.3	6.0	6.7
Imports	6.0	6.0	5.7	6.8	7.2	7.7
Trade balance	0.6	−0.2	−0.8	−1.5	−1.2	−1.0
Current account balance/GDP (%)	−4.3	−4.4	−4.6	−4.6	−2.0	−0.9
Foreign debt	3.9	4.0	4.2	4.7	5.0	5.2
Debt service/Exports (%)	8.3	10.0	11.3	9.7	10.0	6.8
Currency reserves (import months)	1.9	1.8	2.0	2.0	2.0	2.0

159

e = estimate, f = forecast

Cuba

Population (million inhabitants)	11.2
GDP (million USD)	50,000

Short-term: **D**

Coface analysis

Medium-term:
Very high risk

STRENGTHS

- Cuba boasts substantial economic assets including natural resources (nickel, oil), farming (sugar, tobacco), fishing and especially tourism.
- The country also benefits from a well-trained labour force.
- Incipient decentralization and the black market have permitted the partial overcoming of the handicaps of a centralized economy, notably in acquiring foreign currency.

WEAKNESSES

- Cuba's foreign trade has remained highly dependent on world raw material prices, particularly for sugar.
- By deterring foreign investment, the economy's centralized structure has been impeding Cuba's economic development.
- Access to less costly external financing, particularly long-term, will remain limited until the country settles arrears on debt.
- Hostile relations with the United States have remained a major obstacle to Cuba's integration into world trade.

RISK ASSESSMENT

A series of shocks have buffeted Cuba since 2001 including the 11 September attacks (which affected tourism), the increase of oil prices, hurricanes and the decline of nickel prices, as well as the overproduction and price collapse of sugar. These shocks have drained the foreign-exchange liquidities of a country whose currency reserves cover under a month of imports, and which does not have access to international financing. Despite a planned reduction of sugar production, a slight economic recovery could develop in 2004 should tourism rebound.

Even if the latter rebounds, however, the absence of reforms will limit Cuba's prospects. The country will need foreign capital to benefit from its economic assets including its tourism potential, mineral wealth and relatively well-trained population. Reconciliation with the international community appears nonetheless unlikely in the near term and relations with the United States should remain very strained due to the political situation.

MAIN ECONOMIC INDICATORS						
US$ billions	1999	2000	2001	2002	2003 (e)	2004 (f)
Economic growth (%)	6.2	5.6	3.0	1.1	1.3	3.4
Inflation (%)	−2.9	−2.3	−1.4	3.9	4.5	1.0
Public-sector balance/GDP (%)	−2.2	−2.2	−2.3	−3.1	−3.4	−3.0
Exports	1.5	1.8	1.8	1.6	1.6	1.7
Imports	4.4	4.9	4.8	4.6	4.6	4.7
Trade balance	−2.9	−3.1	−3.1	−3.0	−3.0	−3.0
Current account balance	−0.5	−0.8	−0.6	−0.8	−0.7	−0.6
Current account balance/GDP (%)	−2.1	−3.2	−2.2	−1.5	−1.4	−1.1
Foreign debt	11.0	10.9	10.8	11.6	12.2	12.4
Debt service/Exports (%)	14.8	15.0	15.0	15.3	16.4	16.9
Currency reserves (import months)	1.0	1.0	1.1	0.9	0.9	1.0

e = estimate, f = forecast

2

CONDITIONS OF ACCESS TO THE MARKET

■ Means of entry

Cuba is a founding member of the WTO and maintains trade relations with all the countries of the world, except the United States, which has maintained a trade embargo against it for the last 40 years. The Helms–Burton and Torricelli Acts have pushed up the price of imports. However, since late 2001, the US government has authorized a few agricultural and pharmaceutical goods to be traded against cash. The country's import regulations are very stringent and the market is only open to staples and goods meeting pre-defined government requirements. Price and funding are essential criteria, although quality, guarantees and after-sales service are gaining greater significance. Customs duties on the whole are fairly low, but have recently been raised for a number of products. The country has severe payment problems. Ineligible for funding from international institutions (World Bank, IDB), Cuba is forced to seek short-term loans (12 to 24 months) at rates that are 3 to 12 per cent higher than Libor. Payments are delayed due to the shortage of foreign currency. The preferred means of payment for foreign trade is the irrevocable documentary credit confirmed by a leading bank. As foreign payments cannot be legally made in dollars, other convertible currencies (euro, yen, etc) are used. Exchange controls in force since July 2003 require Cuban firms and agencies to seek central bank approval for foreign trade payments.

■ Attitude towards foreign investors

Cuba has encouraged foreign investment only for the last 10 years. It has concluded bilateral investment promotion and protection agreements with 53 countries, including France. The sectors benefiting from those agreements include tourism, basic industry, energy, telecommunications and banking. Education, healthcare and services in general are closed to foreigners. Bureaucratic and restrictive procedures regulate foreign investment, which must meet strict technology transfer, capital contribution and export development criteria. Economic difficulties, red tape and the Helms–Burton Act hamper foreign investment in the island. The government reserves the right to grant and renew import licences, which can be refused without explanation. The tax system does not discriminate against foreign investors and offers a number of incentives. Free zones award companies exemptions from business and labour taxes, customs duties and corporation tax. In exchange, companies must export 75 per cent of their production within three years of start-up. Labour on the whole is skilled but expensive and not highly motivated. The employing entity, necessarily Cuban, can decide pay rises unilaterally and lay off essential employees. Severance payments are compulsory and exorbitant.

■ Foreign exchange regulations

The exchange rate has steadied over the last two years at 26 pesos to the dollar. From July 2003, domestic commercial transactions previously conducted in dollars are carried out in convertible pesos (the Cuban peso is not recognized internationally) at the rate of one Cuban peso to the dollar. The dollar continues to be used in private business transactions.

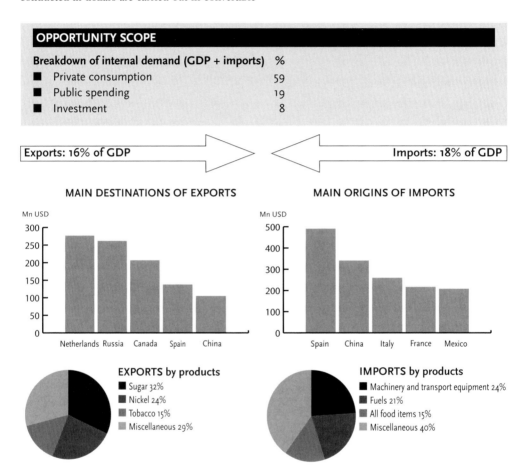

OPPORTUNITY SCOPE

Breakdown of internal demand (GDP + imports)	%
■ Private consumption	59
■ Public spending	19
■ Investment	8

Exports: 16% of GDP → ← Imports: 18% of GDP

MAIN DESTINATIONS OF EXPORTS

Mn USD

Netherlands, Russia, Canada, Spain, China

MAIN ORIGINS OF IMPORTS

Mn USD

Spain, China, Italy, France, Mexico

EXPORTS by products
- ■ Sugar 32%
- ■ Nickel 24%
- ▥ Tobacco 15%
- ▨ Miscellaneous 29%

IMPORTS by products
- ■ Machinery and transport equipment 24%
- ■ Fuels 21%
- ▥ All food items 15%
- ▨ Miscellaneous 40%

STANDARD OF LIVING / PURCHASING POWER

Indicators	Cuba	Regional average	DC average
GNP per capita (PPP dollars)	n/a	5819	6778
GNP per capita (USD)	4400	2928	3568
Human Development Index	0.806	0.770	0.708
Wealthiest 10% share of national income	n/a	41	33
Urban population percentage	75	74	60
Percentage under 15 years old	21	32	31
number of telephones per 1000 inhabitants	51	137	157
number of computers per 1000 inhabitants	20	52	66

Dominican Republic

Population (million inhabitants)	8.5
GDP (million USD)	21,651
GDP per capita (USD)	2,547

Short-term: **C**

Medium-term:

Coface analysis **High risk**

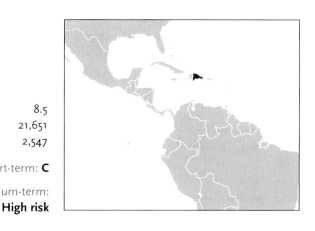

2

STRENGTHS

- The Dominican Republic boasts substantial natural resources (nickel) and agricultural potential (sugar, coffee, cocoa).
- The country has achieved a degree of diversification, combining manufactured product exports from customs-free areas and development of its tourist attractions.
- It benefits from its proximity to the North American market and participation in various regional and international trade agreements.

WEAKNESSES

- The country is vulnerable to external crises due notably to a chronic shortage of currency reserves.
- The Baninter Bank failure in 2003 undermined the financial system.
- Debt reimbursement and dividend repatriation linked to large foreign investments in infrastructure projects should ultimately affect the balance of payments.
- Social tensions have remained high in a context of persistent poverty gripping half the population, social indicators below the regional average, and substantial corruption.

RISK ASSESSMENT

The failure of the country's third bank, Baninter, in May 2003, had a negative impact that was as much political and social as it was economic and financial.

In 2003, the country endured its first recession in 13 years. The cost to the government of the Baninter rescuer widened the fiscal deficit and bloated the public debt, which will only be sustainable via rapid implementation of the IMF reform programme. Moreover, the short-term debt burden, notably in comparison to foreign exchange reserves, the extensive dollarization of banks, and the crisis of confidence triggered by the Baninter affair, has made the country very vulnerable to sudden capital flight. In that context, the peso's decline has particularly weakened companies carrying dollar debt, which focus on the domestic market and earn revenues only in the local currency.

Nonetheless, if confidence returns progressively in 2004, the combined potential of tourism and the customs-free areas could permit the country to benefit from the US recovery.

MAIN ECONOMIC INDICATORS						
US$ billions	1999	2000	2001	2002	2003 (e)	2004 (f)
Economic growth (%)	7.8	7.3	2.9	4.1	−3.0	0.1
Inflation (%)	5.1	9.0	4.4	10.5	35.0	9.0
Public-sector balance/GDP (%)	−3.0	−2.0	−2.1	−2.6	−3.5	−2.5
Exports	5.1	5.7	5.3	5.2	5.5	5.8
Imports	8.0	9.5	8.8	8.9	8.6	9.0
Trade balance	−2.9	−3.7	−3.5	−3.7	−3.1	−3.2
Current account balance/GDP (%)	−2.5	−5.2	−3.5	−4.0	1.0	1.0
Foreign debt	4.8	4.6	5.0	5.7	6.2	6.4
Debt service/Exports (%)	3.6	5.2	4.9	6.1	6.7	7.0
Currency reserves (import months)	0.8	0.6	1.2	0.6	0.8	1.2

e = estimate, f = forecast

Ecuador

Population (million inhabitants)	12.9
GDP (million USD)	20,105

Coface analysis

Short-term: **D**

Medium-term:
Very high risk

STRENGTHS

- With Ecuador possessing oil reserves, construction of a new pipeline should foster near-term development of oil exports.
- The country has been trying to diversify, notably via the sale of shrimp and flowers.
- The dollarization process has contributed to stabilizing the economy and the banking-sector situation.

WEAKNESSES

- The oil sector has been suffering from insufficient investment.
- External accounts and public finances have remained subject to oil prices.
- Dollarization has caused a loss of competitiveness by agriculture and industry.
- Debt ratios have remained high despite restructuring.
- The traditional opposition between coastal and mountain regions has undermined the country's unity.
- Severe political instability has been a major obstacle to implementing reforms.

RISK ASSESSMENT

Since taking office in January 2003, President Lucio Gutierrez's room for manoeuvre has been very limited due to the very heavy debt burden and lack of traditional monetary and fiscal-policy instruments due to dollarization. Dropping the local currency in favour of the dollar has doubtless contributed to stabilizing the economy after the 1999 crisis. Although the economy has nonetheless been stagnating since completion of the new pipeline, 2004 could be better due to the expected increase in oil sales volumes. However, the non-oil sector, which still represents most of the working population, has been suffering greatly from the loss of competitiveness by Ecuador's industries and agriculture since dollarization, with all the attendant social risks.

Major reforms have remained necessary, if only to obtain crucial IMF aid and modernize the oil sector. The political situation has nonetheless remained very shaky in a country that has had five presidents since 1996, including two forced to step down before the end of their term. With the government coalition representing only a very small minority, especially since the Pachakutik Indian movement's withdrawal, President Lucio Gutierrez – elected in the hope of an economic alternative – must contend with a parliament dominated by traditional parties.

MAIN ECONOMIC INDICATORS						
US$ billions	1999	2000	2001	2002	2003 (e)	2004 (f)
Economic growth (%)	−7.3	2.3	5.1	3.4	2.6	4.5
Inflation (%)	60.7	91.0	22.4	9.4	6.5	5.0
Public-sector balance/GDP (%)	−4.6	1.0	−0.5	1.0	1.5	1.6
Exports	4.6	5.1	4.8	5.2	5.5	5.8
Imports	3.0	3.7	5.2	6.2	5.9	6.4
Trade balance	1.6	1.4	−0.4	−1.0	−0.4	−0.6
Current account balance	0.9	0.9	−0.5	−1.2	−0.5	−0.7
Current account balance/GDP (%)	5.5	5.8	−2.6	−4.8	−2.0	−2.5
Foreign debt	16.3	13.6	14.4	16.3	17.1	17.3
Debt service/Exports (%)	33.2	23.4	20.5	20.5	19.6	21.4
Currency reserves (import months)	3.5	1.8	1.3	0.9	1.5	1.8

e = estimate, f = forecast

CONDITIONS OF ACCESS TO THE MARKET

■ Market overview

Ecuador is a founding member of the Andean Community of Nations and complies, in principle, with WTO rules since joining the organization in 1996. While trade between Ecuador and its three main ACN partners – Colombia, Bolivia and Venezuela (Peru will not become a full member until 2005) – has been fully exempt from customs duties since 1994, a host of ad hoc tariff and non-tariff barriers hamper intra-ACN trade. With regard to non-ACN tariff barriers, in 2002 Ecuador brought out a rehashed version of the old customs tariff. In this schedule, the rates of duty remain unchanged (0, 3, 5, 15, 20 and 35 per cent), but tariff item numbers have been changed and a range of tariff sub-items introduced. It should be noted that a new ACN common external tariff was due to replace the existing system on 31 December 2003. As well as the above-mentioned duties, a special consumer tax (ICE) ranging from 5.15 per cent and 15 per cent to 77.25 per cent, plus 12 per cent VAT, is levied on a number of so-called 'luxury' products. The 2–10 per cent surtax under the 'safeguard clause' has been abolished. Despite the introduction of a standard import declaration form (DUI: *Documento unico de importación*), recently replaced by the DAU (standard customs declaration), import procedures remain lengthy and constitute a major stumbling block to the free flow of trade. Ecuador runs a highly complex system of controls, prohibitions, authorizations and permits. Moreover, frequent changes in legislation create a high degree of legal uncertainty.

■ Attitude towards foreign investors

In theory, non-discrimination between domestic and foreign investors is the norm, except in so-called strategic sectors (such as the ban on property ownership along the borders). In practice, however, this liberalism is negated by the extreme complexity of the legal and judicial system, which breeds uncertainty. The high concentration of political, economic and financial power can also distort application of the law.

■ Foreign exchange regulations

The widespread use of the dollar provides a certain degree of monetary stability.

OPPORTUNITY SCOPE

Breakdown of internal demand (GDP + imports)	%
■ Private consumption	51
■ Public spending	7
■ Investment	19

Exports: 31% of GDP ⟹ ⟸ Imports: 34% of GDP

2

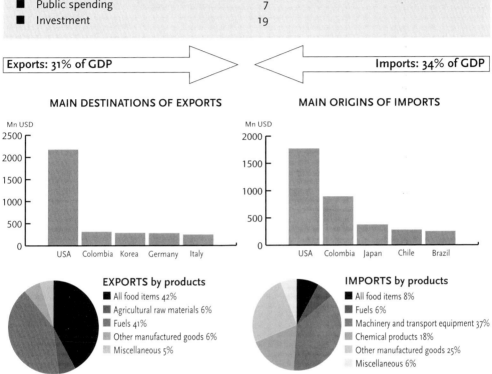

MAIN DESTINATIONS OF EXPORTS

Mn USD

USA   Colombia   Korea   Germany   Italy

MAIN ORIGINS OF IMPORTS

Mn USD

USA   Colombia   Japan   Chile   Brazil

EXPORTS by products
- ■ All food items 42%
- ■ Agricultural raw materials 6%
- ■ Fuels 41%
- ■ Other manufactured goods 6%
- ■ Miscellaneous 5%

IMPORTS by products
- ■ All food items 8%
- ■ Fuels 6%
- ■ Machinery and transport equipment 37%
- ■ Chemical products 18%
- ■ Other manufactured goods 25%
- ■ Miscellaneous 6%

STANDARD OF LIVING / PURCHASING POWER

Indicators	Ecuador	Regional average	DC average
GNP per capita (PPP dollars)	2960	5819	6778
GNP per capita (USD)	1080	2928	3568
Human Development Index	0.731	0.770	0.708
Wealthiest 10% share of national income	42	41	33
Urban population percentage	63	74	60
Percentage under 15 years old	33	32	31
number of telephones per 1000 inhabitants	104	137	157
number of computers per 1000 inhabitants	23	52	66

El Salvador

Population (million inhabitants)	6.4
GDP (million USD)	14,284
GDP per capita (USD)	2,232

Short-term: **B**

Medium-term:
Moderately high risk

Coface analysis

RISK ASSESSMENT

Growth sagged in 2003 amid declines in the farm and industrial sectors and reduced public investment spurred in recent years by reconstruction after the 1998 earthquake. Rising prices for products constituting the country's traditional exports (mainly coffee) and recovery of world demand should spur economic growth in 2004. Furthermore, the probable conclusion by the year-end of a free-trade agreement with the United States could energize sales to the North American market and reverse the trend towards a worsening current account deficit attributable to higher interest rates and oil prices.

The main source of concern has nonetheless remained rising debt amid a weak institutional environment, which has been contributing to deterioration of international investor confidence. In the run-up to legislative elections in March 2004, President Francisco Flores's government will have to contend with growing pressure not only from the main opposition party (FMLN) but also from within its own party (ARENA) to increase fiscal spending. This sensitive political context has not been conducive to deficit reduction by the government, although it has nonetheless remained essential to avert a further increase in public-sector debt.

MAIN ECONOMIC INDICATORS

US$ billions	1999	2000	2001	2002	2003 (e)	2004 (f)
Economic growth (%)	3.4	2.2	1.7	2.1	1.9	2.3
Inflation (%)	−1.0	4.3	1.4	2.8	3.0	2.5
Public-sector balance/GDP (%)	−2.6	−3.0	−4.3	−4.6	−4.1	−4.1
Exports	2.5	2.9	2.9	3.0	3.3	3.7
Imports	3.8	4.6	4.8	4.9	5.4	5.8
Trade balance	−1.4	−1.7	−1.9	−1.9	−2.1	−2.1
Current account balance/GDP (%)	−1.9	−3.3	−1.4	−2.7	−3.2	−3.4
Foreign debt	3.8	4.0	4.3	5.9	6.3	6.6
Debt service/Exports (%)	11.4	9.6	10.3	11.9	11.0	11.6
Currency reserves (import months)	5.7	4.5	4.1	3.5	3.3	2.6

e = estimate, f = forecast

Guatemala

Population (million inhabitants)	11.7
GDP (million USD)	23,257

Short-term: **B**

Medium-term:

Coface analysis   **High risk**

STRENGTHS

- Public-sector debt has remained at moderate levels for the region.
- Fiscal and monetary policies have been prudent.
- Guatemala has been benefiting from international financial aid.
- Tourist potential is substantial.

WEAKNESSES

- Exports have remained too focused on a few traditional agricultural products, mainly coffee, whose prices have remained depressed.
- Infrastructure has remained insufficiently developed amid low savings and investment rates.
- The country is still very inegalitarian with sharp differences that often reflect ethnic criteria and an Indian population often marginalized despite being a majority.
- There has been substantial political instability.

RISK ASSESSMENT

Growth remained relatively weak in 2003 amid sagging world demand, persistent difficulties in the coffee sector and uncertainties linked to the pre-electoral period, which have undermined household and investor confidence. The outlook should be somewhat better for 2004 with improved world economic conditions and the free-trade agreement with the United States likely to buoy the economy.

The new president elected on 28 December 2003 should continue to pursue his predecessor's orthodox economic policy. Debt levels have been relatively moderate for the region with inflation under control. The economy's structure has nonetheless remained archaic, not very diversified and very dependent on coffee sales. Growth has thus been quite insufficient to meet the immense social needs of a population subject to high demographics. Moreover, the political and social instability of a country still bearing the scars of violent civil war (that particularly victimized Indian farmers) along with corruption and drug-trafficking problems has been deterring foreign investors and lenders. Those weaknesses have also been impeding development of tourism, which nonetheless has high potential.

MAIN ECONOMIC INDICATORS						
US$ billions	1999	2000	2001	2002	2003 (e)	2004 (f)
Economic growth (%)	3.8	3.6	2.2	2.2	2.0	3.0
Inflation (%)	4.6	4.9	8.0	8.0	5.6	5.9
Public-sector balance/GDP (%)	–3.0	–2.2	–2.3	–0.8	–1.7	–1.0
Exports	2.8	3.1	2.9	2.6	2.8	2.9
Imports	4.6	5.2	5.6	6.1	5.7	5.9
Trade balance	–1.8	–2.1	–2.7	–3.5	–2.9	–3.0
Current account balance	–1.0	–1.0	–1.2	–1.2	–1.1	–1.2
Current account balance/GDP (%)	–5.5	–5.4	–5.9	–5.1	–4.5	–4.8
Foreign debt	4.6	4.6	4.5	4.8	4.9	4.9
Debt service/Exports (%)	10.1	9.4	8.2	8.8	10.0	10.0
Currency reserves (import months)	2.3	3.4	4.2	3.9	4.5	4.5

e = estimate, f = forecast

CONDITIONS OF ACCESS TO THE MARKET

■ Means of entry

Under the Common External Tariff (CET) of the Central American Common Market (CACM), the rates of duty are 0 per cent for commodities and capital goods, 15 per cent for finished goods and between 5 and 10 per cent for semi-finished goods. A certain degree of tariff protection remains in place for some agricultural products and locally manufactured goods, along with a system of temporary exceptions introduced under the state of emergency. The average rate of duty in the customs tariff is 7.6 per cent, compared with the WTO's consolidated rate of 40 per cent. Import licences are not required. Some tariff protection is provided for certain local industries (shoes) and staples. The new health regulations on wine and alcohol labelling are restrictive, but applied in a non-discriminatory manner. The two leading audit companies – SGS and Bureau Veritas – operate on a non-compulsory contractual basis at the request of the importer or exporter. In spite of the shaky banking sector, there are no difficulties with payments. Interest rates are very high. Letters of credit are the most widely used means of payment. Transfers are usually carried out in a timely manner.

■ Attitude towards foreign investors

Foreign investors benefit from non-discriminatory treatment and the most-favoured-nation clause and are subject to more or less the same procedures as national investors. There are no restrictions on investment, other than in so-called strategic sectors, such as domestic air and land transport, in which the minimum stake held by Guatemalans must be 60 per cent and 51 per cent respectively. This restriction will be gradually lifted for land transport firms by 2004. Post-establishment difficulties derive from the socio-cultural and political environment prevalent in Central America, rather than actual discrimination against foreign investors. At least 90 per cent of a firm's staff must be made up of Guatemalans, and wages paid to foreigners may not exceed 15 per cent of the total payroll. In principle, the legal system offers identical safeguards to foreign and national investors, but corruption and opaque administrative procedures often place foreigners at a disadvantage.

■ Foreign exchange regulations

There are no restrictions on capital, dividend and currency transfers, nor any exchange controls. The so-called 'Free Currency Trading' Act has legalized the circulation of the dollar within the economy and allows people to open dollar-denominated accounts and make all types of payment in that currency. There are no restrictions on the repatriation by foreign investors exercising their shareholder rights of capital invested or profit on retained earnings.

2

OPPORTUNITY SCOPE

Breakdown of internal demand (GDP + imports)	%
■ Private consumption	67
■ Public spending	6
■ Investment	12

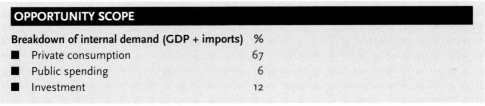

Exports: 19% of GDP   Imports: 28% of GDP

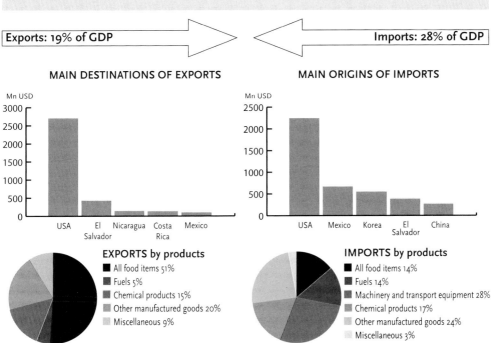

MAIN DESTINATIONS OF EXPORTS

Mn USD — USA, El Salvador, Nicaragua, Costa Rica, Mexico

EXPORTS by products
■ All food items 51%
■ Fuels 5%
▨ Chemical products 15%
▨ Other manufactured goods 20%
▨ Miscellaneous 9%

MAIN ORIGINS OF IMPORTS

Mn USD — USA, Mexico, Korea, El Salvador, China

IMPORTS by products
■ All food items 14%
■ Fuels 14%
▨ Machinery and transport equipment 28%
▨ Chemical products 17%
▨ Other manufactured goods 24%
▨ Miscellaneous 3%

STANDARD OF LIVING / PURCHASING POWER

Indicators	Guatemala	Regional average	DC average
GNP per capita (PPP dollars)	4380	5819	6778
GNP per capita (USD)	1680	2928	3568
Human Development Index	0.652	0.770	0.708
Wealthiest 10% share of national income	48	41	33
Urban population percentage	40	74	60
Percentage under 15 years old	43	32	31
number of telephones per 1000 inhabitants	65	137	157
number of computers per 1000 inhabitants	13	52	66

Haiti

Population (million inhabitants)	8.1
GDP (million USD)	3,737
GDP per capita (USD)	461

Short-term: **D**

Coface analysis

Medium-term:
Very high risk

RISK ASSESSMENT

Haiti is in a critical situation. The poorest Latin American country, it has been in recession for the past three years. The low level of its foreign exchange reserves has made the country dependent on emigrant worker remittances while the continued depreciation of its currency has spurred inflationary pressures. Moreover, the country's internal and external imbalances have been worsening despite fiscal consolidation and tight money policies implemented in an attempt to stabilize the economy and obtain the necessary international community backing.

An easing of political and social tensions will nonetheless constitute a prerequisite to obtaining that backing since the economic crisis is largely attributable to the current political instability, which has undermined investor confidence and limited international assistance essentially to humanitarian aid alone. The opposition has disputed the legitimacy of President Aristide's return to power in 2001 and the frequent breaches of the rule of law. That conflict has been impeding organization of the new parliamentary elections demanded by the international community.

MAIN ECONOMIC INDICATORS

US$ millions	1999	2000	2001	2002	2003 (e)	2004 (f)
Economic growth (%)	2.7	0.9	−1.1	−0.9	−0.1	1.0
Inflation (%)	9.9	15.3	12.3	10.1	41.8	10.0
Public-sector balance/GDP (%)[1]	−1.0	−2.5	−2.7	−3.1	−4.0	−1.9
Exports	339	331	305	273	321	351
Imports	1,018	1,087	1,055	983	1,028	1,149
Trade balance	−678	−756	−750	−709	−707	−798
Current account balance[1]	−298	−259	−224	−145	−147	−217
Current account balance/GDP (%)[1]	−7.2	−6.5	−6.3	−4.6	−4.9	−7.2
Foreign debt	1,200	1,207	1,209	1,233	1,169	1,244
Debt service/Exports (%)	4.8	3.7	3.7	3.4	3.1	3.4
Currency reserves (import months)	2.0	1.4	1.0	0.5	0.3	0.4

[1] excluding donations

e = estimate, f = forecast

Jamaica

Population (million inhabitants)	2.6
GDP (million USD)	8,000
GDP per capita (USD)	3,077

Short-term: **C**

Medium-term:

Coface analysis **High risk**

RISK ASSESSMENT

Severe imbalances in government finances and external accounts and their consequences for economic activity constitute major sources of concern with public-sector and current account deficits near 10 per cent of GDP. Although mostly domestic, public debt is almost 150 per cent of GDP, the highest level in the world. The lack of confidence in government finances has been driving interest rates up and thereby depressing economic activity. For over a decade, growth has thus remained sluggish due to a series of internal and external crises (with 11 September the latest one) in an economy very dependent on external flows, essentially tourism.

The US economic recovery should only moderately benefit Jamaica. Except in the mining sector, companies are often less competitive than their rivals in the region. The very high level of violence, often drug related, is even more disturbing, affecting tourism, the island's main resource, and spurring emigration of young graduates.

MAIN ECONOMIC INDICATORS						
US$ billions	1999	2000	2001	2002	2003 (e)	2004 (f)
Economic growth (%)	−0.4	0.7	1.7	1.0	2.2	1.6
Inflation (%)	6.0	8.2	6.9	7.1	10.1	10.7
Public-sector balance/GDP (%)[1]	−7.2	−5.6	−6.8	−10.0	−9.5	−9.0
Exports	1.5	1.5	1.5	1.4	1.4	1.4
Imports	2.7	2.9	3.0	2.9	3.3	3.3
Trade balance	−1.2	−1.4	−1.5	−1.5	−1.9	−1.9
Current account balance/GDP (%)	−2.9	−5.0	−10.1	−13.1	−11.1	−7.9
Foreign debt	3.9	4.3	4.9	5.1	4.9	5.8
Debt service/Exports (%)	13.5	13.8	13.9	18.2	14.8	14
Currency reserves (import months)	2.5	4.2	7.4	6.2	3.8	3.3

[1] March of year t and April of year t+1

e = estimate, f = forecast

Mexico

Population (million inhabitants)	99.4
GDP (million USD)	637,205

Coface analysis

Short-term: **A4**

Medium-term:
Quite low risk

STRENGTHS

- Mexico, which boasts abundant natural resources, has greatly developed its manufacturing industry.
- The country has benefited from its NAFTA (North American Free Trade Area) membership to consolidate its North American moorings.
- Its healthier fundamentals and a level of foreign debt more moderate than most regional countries have reassured international investors.
- Bank balance sheets have substantially improved since the 1994/95 crisis and the country has become much less vulnerable to financial crises.

WEAKNESSES

- The Mexican president has been encountering difficulties in implementing essential structural reforms.
- Mexico has been suffering from competitiveness problems against countries like China.
- Public finances have remained dependent on oil revenues.
- The banking system has not been playing its role in financing the economy.
- Heightened by inequalities, social tensions have remained strong.

RISK ASSESSMENT

Mexico's financial situation has not been giving much cause for concern with the country having made great strides since the 1980s and the 1994/95 crisis. Banks are now solid and currency reserves are relatively comfortable. Although public finance management has been prudent, government guarantees not counted in the public debt need watching.

Despite the relative stability of the country's financial situation, economic activity remains sluggish. Even though the positive effects of recovery in the United States have been slow to materialize, renewed growth should mark 2004. The capacity of Mexican companies to hold market share against competition will nonetheless constitute a crucial factor. Mexico's main challenge will thus be restoring a competitiveness eroded in recent years in face of countries like China. Although the peso's depreciation of course provides a short-term response, it weakens companies carrying dollar debt. In the longer term, modernization of both companies and infrastructures will be essential.

MAIN ECONOMIC INDICATORS

US$ billions	1999	2000	2001	2002	2003 (e)	2004 (f)
Economic growth (%)	3.6	6.6	−0.2	0.7	1.5	2.7
Inflation (%)	16.6	9.5	6.4	5.0	4.6	3.9
Public-sector balance/GDP (%)	−4.0	−3.7	−3.7	−3.4	−3.2	−3.2
Exports	136.4	166.5	158.4	160.8	164.6	170.3
Imports	142.0	174.5	168.4	168.7	171.7	179.5
Trade balance	−5.6	−8.0	−10.0	−7.9	−7.2	−9.2
Current account balance	−14.0	−18.2	−18.1	−13.9	−12.0	−14.5
Current account balance/GDP (%)	−2.9	−3.1	−2.9	−2.2	−1.9	−2.2
Foreign debt	167.3	159.4	162.8	175.6	188.5	200.7
Debt service/Exports (%)	22.9	19.8	16.4	13.3	16.4	15.5
Currency reserves (import months)	2.2	2.0	2.6	3.0	3.3	3.3

e = estimate, f = forecast

CONDITIONS OF ACCESS TO THE MARKET

■ Means of entry

Mexico's membership of the North American Free Trade Association (NAFTA) is coupled with incentives for foreign companies looking to gain a strategic foothold on the American continent. These include the gradual elimination of tariff barriers, industrial property protection and free movement of capital. Mexico has also signed 11 free-trade agreements with 32 other countries.

In late 2003, talks were under way to sign an agreement with Japan. The free-trade agreement concluded between the European Union and Mexico on 1 July 2000 has paved the way for European countries to win back market share and step up investment that has been declining under the impact of NAFTA and competition from Asian products. From 1 July 2000, 47 per cent of trade in industrial products with the EU was liberalized (0 per cent customs duty). A further 5 per cent has been liberalized from 1 January 2003. Customs duties for the remaining 48 per cent (mainly consumer goods) will be gradually lifted by 2007. It should be noted that, from 1 January 2003, no European industrial product is liable to more than 5 per cent duty. Government-licensed independent audit companies are responsible for checking compliance with Mexican Official Standards (NOM) and issuing certificates of conformity. The services of these companies are widely used but fairly expensive.

The most widely used invoicing currency is the US dollar. Payments are made within 30–45 days. This is fairly quick considering the high rates of interest and shortage of credit. Documentary credit is the safest means of payment for export firms, but expensive for the buyer.

■ Attitude towards foreign investors

As the economy gradually opens up to foreign investment, a certain number of strategic sectors remain the preserve of Mexican companies and are strictly off limits to foreign companies. Foreigners may invest in these sectors only through the 'neutral investment' mechanism (without decision-making powers). For sectors open to foreign investment, foreigners are required to obtain an authorization from the National Commission on Foreign Investment for investments above a certain

PAYMENT INCIDENTS INDEX
(12 months moving average - base 100 : World 1995)

threshold (currently 14 million euros). For investments below this amount, foreigners may acquire a 100 per cent stake in Mexican firms without seeking the Commission's approval . Since 1999, foreigners have been allowed to invest in commercial and merchant banks without a capital ceiling. The Mutual Investment Promotion and Protection Agreement (APPRI) between France and Mexico has reinforced the legal framework for French investment.

OPPORTUNITY SCOPE

Breakdown of internal demand (GDP + imports)	%
■ Private consumption	54
■ Public spending	9
■ Investment	16

Exports: 28% of GDP   Imports: 30% of GDP

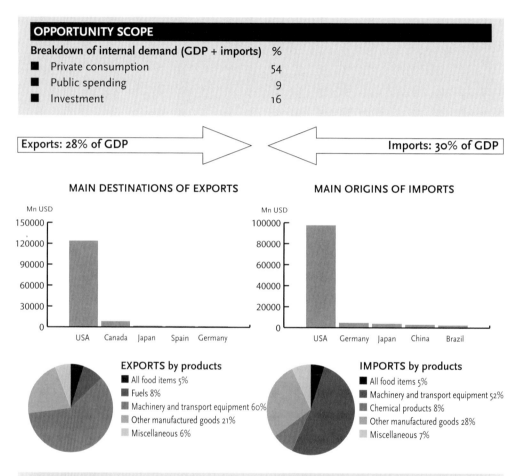

MAIN DESTINATIONS OF EXPORTS

Mn USD

USA   Canada   Japan   Spain   Germany

MAIN ORIGINS OF IMPORTS

Mn USD

USA   Germany   Japan   China   Brazil

EXPORTS by products
- ■ All food items 5%
- ■ Fuels 8%
- ■ Machinery and transport equipment 60%
- ■ Other manufactured goods 21%
- ■ Miscellaneous 6%

IMPORTS by products
- ■ All food items 5%
- ■ Machinery and transport equipment 52%
- ■ Chemical products 8%
- ■ Other manufactured goods 28%
- ■ Miscellaneous 7%

STANDARD OF LIVING / PURCHASING POWER

Indicators	Mexico	Regional average	DC average
GNP per capita (PPP dollars)	8240	5819	6778
GNP per capita (USD)	5530	2928	3568
Human Development Index	0.8	0.770	0.708
Wealthiest 10% share of national income	42	41	33
Urban population percentage	75	74	60
Percentage under 15 years old	34	32	31
number of telephones per 1000 inhabitants	137	137	157
number of computers per 1000 inhabitants	69	52	66

Nicaragua

Population (million inhabitants)	5.2
GDP (million USD)	4,003
GDP per capita (USD)	766

Short-term: **D**

Medium-term:
Very high risk

Coface analysis

2

RISK ASSESSMENT

Economic growth was sluggish again in 2003 due to the contraction of farm sector activity amid poor weather conditions. Rising coffee, sugar and marine-product prices along with the expected signature of a free-trade agreement with the United States and neighbouring countries should buoy exports in 2004 and bolster GDP growth. In early 2004, the country should also benefit from extensive debt cancellation under the HIPC programme for heavily indebted poor countries.

Although international financial community backing thus remains essential, political uncertainties could jeopardize it. Fratricidal conflict has persisted within the party in power since the imprisonment of the former president, Arnaldo Aleman, who continues to have supporters in parliament. This unstable climate has contributed to deterring foreign direct investment in one of Central America's poorest countries.

MAIN ECONOMIC INDICATORS						
US$ billions	1999	2000	2001	2002	2003 (e)	2004 (f)
Economic growth (%)	7.4	4.2	3.0	1.0	1.8	3.2
Inflation (%)	11.2	7.4	7.4	4.0	5.2	5.2
Public-sector balance/GDP (%)	−13.9	−9.5	−13.4	−10.5	−8.9	−7.4
Exports	0.6	0.6	0.6	0.6	0.6	0.7
Imports	1.7	1.6	1.6	1.6	1.6	1.7
Trade balance	−1.1	−1.0	−1.0	−1.0	−1.0	−1.0
Current account balance/GDP (%)	−17.9	−23.5	−24.1	−19.6	−17.7	−15.2
Foreign debt	6.9	6.9	6.4	6.1	5.8	5.8
Debt service/Exports (%)	16.2	28.1	34.2	40.6	25.8	23.0
Currency reserves (import months)	2.7	2.6	2.0	2.5	2.5	2.8

177

e = estimate, f = forecast

Panama

Population (million inhabitants)	2.9
GDP (million USD)	12,295
GDP per capita (USD)	4,240

Short-term: **A4**

Medium-term:

Coface analysis   **Moderately high risk**

RISK ASSESSMENT

After two years of stagnation, the Panamanian economy has been showing signs of recovery, buoyed by external demand and domestic spending, mainly by the public sector, in the run-up to the May 2004 presidential elections. However, the fiscal slippage along with the social security system's worsening deficit has been nullifying the results of the December 2002 tax reform and contributing to keeping the public-sector deficit at a relatively high level. Nonetheless, despite the increasing foreign debt burden (of which 75 per cent is public) that has resulted, the country's external financial situation has remained relatively sound.

In the longer term, the economy should demonstrate some dynamism considering the Panama Canal enlargement project, the upcoming conclusion of a free-trade agreement with the United States and the good performance of financial services. The country's weaknesses are mainly political and social in nature. Unemployment, inequality and allegations of corruption have been undermining the governmental team in the run-up to the next elections. Nonetheless, whatever elected team is in office, no major changes in the country's policies will be likely.

MAIN ECONOMIC INDICATORS

US$ billions	1999	2000	2001	2002	2003 (e)	2004 (f)
Economic growth (%)	4.2	3.3	0.3	0.8	2.5	2.9
Inflation (%)	1.5	0.7	0.0	1.8	1.5	1.8
Public-sector balance/GDP (%)	−1.2	−0.7	−2.4	−2.7	−2.7	−2.7
Exports[1]	0.7	0.8	0.8	0.8	0.8	0.8
Imports[1]	3.2	3.1	2.7	2.8	2.9	3.0
Trade balance	−2.5	−2.3	−1.9	−2.1	−2.1	−2.2
Current account balance/GDP (%)	−11.1	−6.0	−1.3	−1.3	−1.5	−2.0
Foreign debt	6.8	7.1	7.7	8.0	8.4	8.7
Debt service/Exports (%)	20.1	16.1	23.0	30.5	16.0	16.5
Currency reserves (import months)	1.8	1.6	2.7	3.0	3.0	3.0

[1] excluding Colon customs-free area   e = estimate, f = forecast

Paraguay

Population (million inhabitants)	5.6
GDP (million USD)	5,522

Coface analysis

Short-term: **D**

Medium-term:
Very high risk

STRENGTHS

- Agriculture, mainly soybeans, constitutes a major source of currency earnings.
- The country boasts substantial hydroelectric resources.
- Paraguay is situated in the heart of Mercosur.

WEAKNESSES

- The economy is too dependent on the primary sector, consumer goods and capital goods imports, and also economic conditions within Mercosur.
- This poor, landlocked country's narrow market, legal insecurity, extensive corruption and chronic political instability have been deterring foreign investors.
- A bloated and inefficient public sector and the lagging pace of structural reforms have also been hampering the country's development.
- Smuggling and drug trafficking have been spurring violence.

RISK ASSESSMENT

Good harvests coupled with a recovery of raw material prices permitted the country to emerge from recession in 2003. Export development, notably of soybeans (representing over half of sales abroad), has also permitted increasing trade balance surpluses and thus the stemming of depreciation of the local currency, the guarani. The persistence of strong world demand for soybeans should permit that trend to continue in 2004.

The election in August 2003 of Nicanor Duarte Frutos as president has also steadied Paraguay's previously very unstable political landscape. The political and financial situation has nonetheless remained very shaky. Although the country will need IMF backing to refinance some of its debt and thereby avoid payment default, that backing will continue to depend on reforming the bloated and often corrupt public sector. However, past attempts to bring about change in the civil service have always triggered violent resistance.

MAIN ECONOMIC INDICATORS						
US$ billions	1999	2000	2001	2002	2003 (e)	2004 (f)
Economic growth (%)	0.5	−0.4	2.7	−2.3	1.4	1.7
Inflation (%)	6.8	8.9	7.3	10.5	14.3	6.9
Public-sector balance/GDP (%)	−3.2	−4.1	−0.9	−3.9	−3.1	−3.2
Exports	2.3	2.2	2.0	2.3	2.6	2.6
Imports	2.8	2.9	2.5	2.4	2.4	2.4
Trade balance	−0.4	−0.7	−0.6	−0.1	0.2	0.2
Current account balance	−0.2	−0.3	−0.2	0.3	0.4	0.4
Current account balance/GDP (%)	−2.1	−3.8	−3.6	5.3	7.3	6.8
Foreign debt	3.4	3.1	2.8	2.8	2.9	2.9
Debt service/Exports (%)	8.2	11.6	12.4	14.0	13.0	12.8
Currency reserves (import months)	3.9	3.0	3.2	3.3	3.7	4.2

e = estimate, f = forecast

CONDITIONS OF ACCESS TO THE MARKET

■ Market overview

In general, Paraguay has a very open trade policy as its nascent industrial sector is unable to meet domestic demand. Membership of Mercosur in 1991 has forced it to raise customs duties on most products in line with the Common External Tariff gradually phased in by the four member countries.

Under Decree No. 13385, 10 per cent *ad valorem* additional duty was applied to a list of 332 Mercosur products (agri-foodstuffs, textiles, apparel, cast iron, etc) from 10 July 2001 to 31 December 2002. This decree was renewed for a year on 16 July 2003. The privatization of three public services – fixed telephones (Antelco), water/waste management (Corposana) and railways (FCP-CAL) – launched in October 2000 and due to be completed in 2002 has been indefinitely postponed by Law No. 1932/02 of 5 June 2002. The new government in power since 15 August 2003 has maintained this policy.

The most widely used invoicing currency is the US dollar. Documentary credit is only used for little-known importers, occasional sales or relatively large amounts.

■ Means of entry

An import ban is in place for certain products. The most restrictive non-tariff barrier is that erected by Law No. 194 involving unfair protection of the interests of Paraguayan agents, representatives and importers.

While mandatory inspections by an approved audit firm of goods exported to Paraguay were abolished in 1999, export documents must first be cleared with the Paraguayan consulate in the country of origin of the goods or the nearest consulate and the relevant stamp duty paid.

Copyright infringement and smuggling are rife in Paraguay. Despite repeated assurances from the government, the country's new intellectual property legislation lacks teeth.

■ Attitude towards foreign investors

There is no discrimination between national and foreign investors, except in the case of contractual relationships (Law No. 194). Foreign investment is not subject to approval or compulsory registration, except for investment covered by the Tax Incentives Act (No. 60/90) and the so-called 'Maquilla Act' (No. 1064 of 3 July 1997). Disputes between foreign investors and the government are heard by local courts.

A new Arbitration and Mediation Act (No. 1879/02) was passed in April 2002 based on the model proposed by Unsitral, which handles both domestic and international arbitration. The Act replaces Book V of the Code of Civil Procedure relating to disputes, particularly of a commercial nature.

Foreign exchange regulations

There are no exchange controls. In the first 10 months of 2003, the guarani rose by more than 10 per cent against the US dollar after having fallen by 50 per cent against the same currency in the previous year.

2

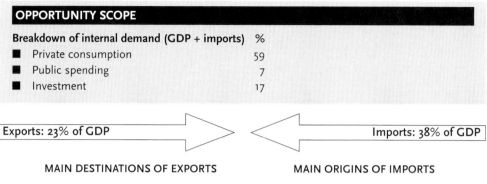

OPPORTUNITY SCOPE

Breakdown of internal demand (GDP + imports) %
- ■ Private consumption — 59
- ■ Public spending — 7
- ■ Investment — 17

Exports: 23% of GDP → ← Imports: 38% of GDP

MAIN DESTINATIONS OF EXPORTS

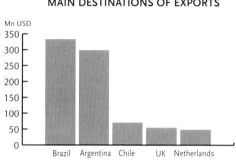

Mn USD
Brazil Argentina Chile UK Netherlands

MAIN ORIGINS OF IMPORTS

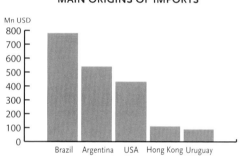

Mn USD
Brazil Argentina USA Hong Kong Uruguay

EXPORTS by products

- ■ All food items 69%
- ■ Agricultural raw materials 14%
- ■ Other manufactured goods 13%
- ■ Miscellaneous 4%

IMPORTS by products

- ■ All food items 14%
- ■ Fuels 16%
- ■ Machinery and transport equipment 27%
- ■ Chemical products 16%
- ■ Other manufactured goods 25%
- ■ Miscellaneous 2%

STANDARD OF LIVING / PURCHASING POWER

Indicators	Paraguay	Regional average	DC average
GNP per capita (PPP dollars)	5180	5819	6778
GNP per capita (USD)	1350	2928	3568
Human Development Index	0.751	0.770	0.708
Wealthiest 10% share of national income	44	41	33
Urban population percentage	57	74	60
Percentage under 15 years old	39	32	31
number of telephones per 1000 inhabitants	51	137	157
number of computers per 1000 inhabitants	14	52	66

Peru

Population (million inhabitants)	26.3
GDP (million USD)	56,870

Coface analysis

Short-term: **B**

Medium-term:
High risk

STRENGTHS

- The country is a major world producer of raw materials thanks to its mineral and fishing resources.
- Export earnings should continue to increase sharply in coming years buoyed notably by the many mining and gas projects, which should improve ratios of debt to currency earnings.
- Peru has made a commitment to pursue prudent monetary and fiscal policies and enjoys international financial institution backing.
- Its current account deficit has been declining with its foreign exchange reserves remaining at comfortable levels.

WEAKNESSES

- Peru's dependence on commodity exports could expose it to major crises in the event of a downturn in world prices and deterioration of weather conditions.
- External debt ratios, although falling, have remained high.
- There is substantial poverty and very unequal income distribution.
- Peru has a dual economy with a relatively modern sector in the coastal plains and a subsistence sector inland.
- President Toledo must contend with an increasingly hostile population, govern with a minority party in Congress and maintain fiscal discipline.

RISK ASSESSMENT

The undeniable improvement in Peru's economic and financial ratios in recent years has been in increasingly sharp contrast with the growing political risks associated with the country.

Robust growth has resumed since 2001 thanks essentially to development of the mining and gas sector. Meanwhile, substantial export growth has been reducing the current account deficit and improving ratios of debt to currency earnings. Moreover, the government's prudent fiscal policy and continued IMF backing have been bolstering investor confidence. The debt level has nonetheless remained high with the banking sector's extensive dollarization constituting a major source of vulnerability.

However, the country's main weakness is linked to political uncertainties that have tended to impede reforms and deter diversification of investments towards more labour-intensive sectors than mineral extraction. President Toledo is very unpopular since he must maintain financial discipline while responding to the expectations of the poorest population segments, mainly Indian, which had nonetheless massively supported his election.

MAIN ECONOMIC INDICATORS

US$ billions	1999	2000	2001	2002	2003 (e)	2004 (f)
Economic growth (%)	0.9	3.1	0.6	5.3	3.8	3.8
Inflation (%)	3.7	3.7	−0.1	1.5	1.5	1.9
Public-sector balance/GDP (%)	−3.1	−3.2	−2.5	−2.3	−2.1	−1.5
Exports	6.1	7.0	7.0	7.6	8.7	9.4
Imports	6.8	7.4	7.3	7.4	8.2	8.6
Trade balance	−0.7	−0.5	−0.3	0.2	0.4	0.7
Current account balance	−1.5	−1.6	−1.2	−1.2	−1.2	−1.1
Current account balance/GDP (%)	−2.9	−2.9	−2.2	−2.1	−1.9	−1.7
Foreign debt	29.3	28.5	27.6	28.7	29.5	30.3
Debt service/Exports (%)	40.4	40.0	36.7	34.0	31.3	30.3
Currency reserves (import months)	9.7	8.5	9.1	9.5	9.1	9.1

e = estimate, f = forecast

CONDITIONS OF ACCESS TO THE MARKET

■ Market overview

Key sectors include:

- The Camisea gas field where a US$1.4 billion gas development project is under way. This, along with a US$3 billion LNG export scheme, should help foster the growth of a large petrochemicals industry in the medium term. From 2004, Camisea will account for 1–1.5 per cent of GDP.
- Mining, which continues to grow on the back of Antamina, the world's largest copper and zinc mine commissioned in 2001, and firm gold prices.
- Construction, whose recovery is driven by a vast programme of low-cost housing and will be further boosted when the road network concessions are awarded.
- Textiles, which benefit from the inclusion of apparel in the generalized system of preferences (ATPDEA) granted by the United States to four Andean countries over a four-year period (2002–06).

■ Means of entry

The market is open and there are no payment difficulties in respect of imports. The average rate of customs duty is 10.9 per cent. An Andean Community of Nations common external tariff has been agreed for 62 per cent of tariff categories (four rates of duty: 0, 5, 10 and 20 per cent), but Peru has asked for it to be replaced by a more open system.

■ Attitude towards foreign investors

Peru's legislation offers foreign investors a wide range of incentives and safeguards, including equal rights with domestic investors, the option of signing legal stability agreements, unrestricted transfer of profits, dividends and capital, freedom of enterprise, freedom to import and export, etc.

Foreign investment is not subject to prior approval. However, investors seeking the benefit of the legal stability agreements must be registered with Proinversion.

Peru has signed the founding charter of the Multilateral Investment Guarantees Agency (MIGA) as well as the original act of the International Centre for Settlement of Investment Disputes (ICSID). It has also ratified the New York Convention on the Recognition and Enforcement of Arbitral Awards. A mutual investment promotion and protection agreement was signed with France on 6 October 1993 and ratified in February 1996.

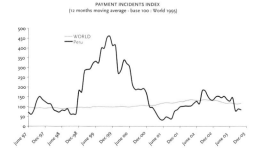

PAYMENT INCIDENTS INDEX
(12 months moving average - base 100 : World 1995)

In the field of taxation, Peru already has three dual taxation agreements (Sweden, Canada, Chile) and is engaged in talks to conclude a similar agreement with France.

Foreign investors may conclude a tax stability agreement with the authorities.

There is no difficulty in obtaining work or residence permits related to an investment.

Foreign exchange regulations

Peru has a floating, but managed, exchange rate.

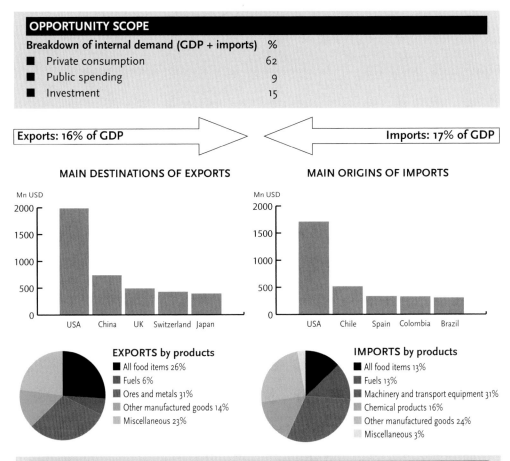

OPPORTUNITY SCOPE	
Breakdown of internal demand (GDP + imports)	**%**
■ Private consumption	62
■ Public spending	9
■ Investment	15

Exports: 16% of GDP   Imports: 17% of GDP

MAIN DESTINATIONS OF EXPORTS

Mn USD — USA, China, UK, Switzerland, Japan

MAIN ORIGINS OF IMPORTS

Mn USD — USA, Chile, Spain, Colombia, Brazil

EXPORTS by products
- ■ All food items 26%
- ■ Fuels 6%
- ■ Ores and metals 31%
- ■ Other manufactured goods 14%
- ■ Miscellaneous 23%

IMPORTS by products
- ■ All food items 13%
- ■ Fuels 13%
- ■ Machinery and transport equipment 31%
- ■ Chemical products 16%
- ■ Other manufactured goods 24%
- ■ Miscellaneous 3%

STANDARD OF LIVING / PURCHASING POWER			
Indicators	Peru	Regional average	DC average
GNP per capita (PPP dollars)	4470	5819	6778
GNP per capita (USD)	1980	2928	3568
Human Development Index	0.752	0.770	0.708
Wealthiest 10% share of national income	35	41	33
Urban population percentage	73	74	60
Percentage under 15 years old	33	32	31
number of telephones per 1000 inhabitants	78	137	157
number of computers per 1000 inhabitants	48	52	66

United States

Population (million inhabitants)   288.6
GDP (million USD)   10,383,100
GDP per capita (USD)   35,977

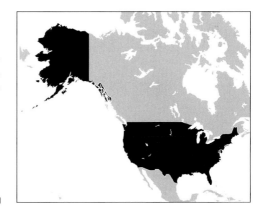

Coface analysis   Short-term: **A1**

STRENGTHS

- The reactivity and flexibility of companies and public authorities have tended to limit the duration of downturns.
- The dollar's predominance has facilitated financing public-sector and current account deficits.
- High immigration flows, high geographic mobility and flexible labour legislation have been conducive to balancing labour supply and demand.
- High levels of research and development and innovation have permitted companies to enjoy a technological lead beneficial to their productivity and renewal of their product and service offer.
- High growth potential has tended to hold foreign-investor interest over the long haul.

WEAKNESSES

- The continued worsening of public-sector and current account deficits for the past several years could ultimately trigger brutal economic and financial adjustments.
- With the size of both federal and state government deficits limiting public investment, notably in rail and road infrastructure, the dilapidated state of that infrastructure has hardly been conducive to balanced regional development.
- With the entire system of primary and secondary education, social protection and health remaining shaky despite the vote on Medicare reform, the ultimate ageing of the population will remain a challenge.
- Restructuring is still insufficient in many industrial sectors, moreover largely exposed to foreign competition.

RISK ASSESSMENT

After a difficult start in 2003, growth accelerated rapidly. Benefiting from favourable financing conditions and improved profitability, companies began increasing their investments in spring. Household spending remained buoyant throughout the year despite the war in Iraq and rising unemployment. Tax breaks and wage increases contributed to increasing disposable income with continued low interest rates spurring durable goods purchases on credit.

The economy should grow again in 2004, buoyed by still-expansionary economic policy.

Finally benefiting from declining unemployment, household spending should remain very robust, even if there is little chance that the very high levels of car purchases and property investments will persist. Companies will capitalize on lower dollar exchange rates to increase exports. In that context, the investment recovery should intensify.

In that more dynamic environment, the company situation should improve further as borne out by the Coface payment-incident index's sharply downward trend since late in the first quarter of 2003. The situation has nonetheless remained tense in sectors like civil aviation, electricity production and distribution, telecommunications, metallurgy and steel, or the car industry and textiles where foreign competition has been squeezing profits in many cases. Conversely, chemicals and paper have been faring better due to the greater control over prices resulting from production-capacity shutdowns.

MAIN ECONOMIC INDICATORS						
%	1999	2000	2001	2002	2003 (e)	2004 (f)
Economic growth	4.1	3.8	0.3	2.4	2.9	4.2
Consumer spending (% change)	4.9	4.3	2.5	3.1	3	3.5
Investment (% change)	8.1	7.8	−5.2	−5.7	2.5	9.0
Inflation	1.6	2.5	2	1.4	2.4	1.8
Unemployment rate	4.2	4	4.8	5.8	6	5.9
Short-term interest rate	5.4	6.5	3.7	1.8	1.1	1.2
Public-sector balance/GDP (%)	0.7	1.4	−0.5	−3.4	−5.1	−6.1
Public-sector debt/GDP (%)	64.5	58.8	58.9	61	65	68
Exports (% change)	3.4	9.7	−5.4	−1.6	0.3	5.2
Imports (% change)	10.9	13.2	−2.9	3.7	3.7	5.7
Current account balance/GDP (%)	−3.1	−4.2	−3.9	−4.6	−5.5	−5.4

e = estimate, f = forecast

MAIN ECONOMIC SECTORS

■ Telecommunications

In 2003, the telecommunications market registered a moderate recovery, concentrated in specialized services. Benefiting from that brighter period, operators increased their equipment purchases. Although the situation has remained uneven with fixed telephony in decline and mobile telephony continuing to expand moderately, operators and equipment makers have, in general, consolidated their financial situations and returned to profitability. Some actors faced with a lack of recovery in certain segments and unable to refinance their debt had to seek Chapter 11 bankruptcy protection. Although the recovery should gain momentum, 2004 will be a watershed for certain weakened players.

■ Computer equipment

Benefiting from increased household spending on computer equipment, the computer sector showed some clear signs of recovery in 2003. Personal computer sales resumed two-digit growth. While Dell, Apple and IBM quickly benefited from the improvement, HP should take longer to recover due to its special problems. The strengthening of that positive trend in 2004 and its extension to players like Sun Microsystems and Silicon Graphics, more specialized in high-end solutions (servers, graphics), will depend on confirmation of the company investment recovery.

■ Steel

US steel prices have been markedly higher than the 2001 low point even if they have sagged since the 2002 summer peak that followed introduction of protection measures by the government. They have nonetheless remained less below prices practised in other world regions. That is attributable to the influence of electric mills, sluggish domestic demand and a moderate import recovery. In 2004, strong demand from China and the fall of the dollar should ease pressure from imports. However, cancellation of the protectionist measures in December 2003, even if they no longer concerned more than a quarter of purchases, and continued high raw material and energy prices will continue to affect that industry, which still presents bankruptcy risks and will have to continue its restructuring.

■ Paper

In 2003, demand for cardboard remained sluggish. With tonnages below those of 2002, wood-pulp prices nonetheless rose slightly in the US market towards year-end. That increase is mainly attributable to Weyerhaeuser's decision to pass on high energy-prices with other producers following suit. However, as long as European wood-pulp prices remain below US prices, there will be little room for price increases. In 2004, the acceleration of economic activity and the dollar's sharp decline augurs improvement.

■ Retail

The retail sector posted moderate sales growth in 2003. Greater recourse to promotional offers has permitted maintaining sales prices although at the cost of margin erosion and stiff competition.

Specialists, including department stores and food wholesalers, have suffered most from competition from generalists like Wal-Mart. Only drug stores have registered good performance with the outlook remaining bright. Having exhausted their room for manoeuvre on cost reduction, retailers will only be able to develop leverage via increases in turnover, which appear possible based on forecasts for 2004.

■ Car industry

US carmakers have been in decline with their market share shrinking to the benefit mainly of Japanese competition. Their subsidiaries (notably European) have not been faring much better. The consequences have been grave: factory shutdowns and sell-offs, or lay-off programmes. Promotional campaigns, which have shown their limits in profitability terms, will be unlikely to disappear from the scene in 2003 due notably to the expected moderate sales decline.

PAYMENT AND COLLECTION PRACTICES

■ Payment

Exporters should be wary about the provisions of sales contracts payable on credit and ensure that the payment terms they obtain are appropriate to the context. Cheques and bills of exchange are very basic payment devices that do not allow creditors to bring actions for recovery in respect of exchange law (*droit cambiaire*).

Cheques are widely used but, as they are not required to be covered at their issue, offer relatively limited guarantees. Account holders may stop payment on a cheque by submitting a written request to the bank within 14 days of the cheque's issue. Moreover, in the event of default, payees must still provide proof of claim. Although more difficult to obtain, bank cheques drawn directly on a bank's own account provide greater security as they constitute a direct undertaking to pay from the bank.

Bills of exchange and promissory notes are less commonly used and offer no specific proof of debt.

SWIFT transfers are widespread and the majority of US banks are connected to the system. SWIFT funds transfers are fairly quick and easy to

make and are particularly suitable where trust exists between the contracting parties, as the seller is dependent on the buyer acting in good faith and ordering the transfer of funds (open account system).

■ Debt collection

Owing to the complexity and expensive nature of the US legal system, exporters are advised, wherever possible, to negotiate and settle out of court with clients. Parties can seek mediation through the relatively informal system of Alternative Dispute Resolution (ADR) and in so doing avoid costly and lengthy court cases.

The judicial system comprises two basic types of court: district courts, which fall under the federal court system, and circuit or county courts, which fall within the jurisdiction of the state. The vast majority of actions are heard by state courts, which apply state and federal law to disputes falling within their jurisdictions (ie actions concerning persons domiciled or resident in the state).

Federal courts, on the other hand, rule on disputes involving state governments, cases involving interpretations of the constitution or federal treaties, and claims above US$75,000 between citizens of different US states, or between a US citizen and a foreign national or foreign state body or, in some cases, between plaintiffs and defendants from foreign countries.

A key feature of the US judicial system is the pre-trial 'discovery' phase whereby each party may demand evidence and testimonies relating to the dispute from the adversary before the case is heard by the court. During the trial itself, judges give plaintiffs and their lawyers considerable leeway to produce pertinent documents at any time and conduct the trial in general (prosecution-orientated procedure).

Another feature of the US procedural system is that litigants may request a case to be heard by a jury, usually made up of 12 ordinary citizens, whose task is to deliver a verdict based overall on the facts of the case.

For especially complex, lengthy or expensive litigation, as in the case of insolvency actions, courts have been known to allow creditors to hold the professionals (eg auditors) counselling the defaulting party liable, where such advisors have demonstrably acted improperly.

PAYMENT INCIDENTS INDEX
(12 months moving average - base 100 : World 1995)

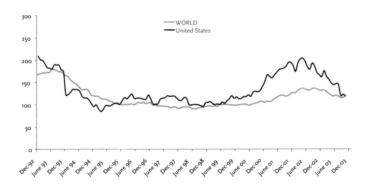

Uruguay

Population (million inhabitants)	3.4
GDP (million USD)	12,325

Short-term: **D**

Medium-term:

Coface analysis **High risk**

2

STRENGTHS

- Uruguay enjoys international financial community backing.
- Its democracy has deep roots.
- The country possesses rich agricultural land.
- Its social and educational indicators are high.

WEAKNESSES

- The 2002 banking crisis should long continue to affect the country's public finances and durably undermine Montevideo's role as a financial centre.
- Debt has grown substantially and, being essentially dollar denominated, the country's repayment capacity will be closely tied to exchange rate trends.
- Exports have remained dominated by agriculture with little diversification.
- Rising unemployment has caused some emigration of skilled labour.

RISK ASSESSMENT

The economy has slowly begun to improve after five years of recession on a scale comparable to that afflicting Argentina. The peso has stabilized and some deposits have been flowing back to financial institutions. Growth became positive again from the 2003 third quarter and could accelerate in 2004, fuelled mainly by farm-product exports. The need for restrictive fiscal policy should nonetheless durably undermine domestic demand.

The financial-system consolidation process has ultimately been weighing on public finances. The local currency's collapse in 2002 has notably undermined government and company solvency with public- and private-sector debt mainly dollar denominated. Uruguay's debt ratios now rank among the highest for emerging countries with the government only succeeding thus far in avoiding default on its bond debt thanks to rapid intervention by the public authorities and international financial institutions. The very unpopular current president has therefore had very limited room for manoeuvre in the run-up to presidential and legislative elections in October 2004.

MAIN ECONOMIC INDICATORS						
US$ billions	1999	2000	2001	2002	2003 (e)	2004 (f)
Economic growth (%)	−2.8	−1.4	−3.4	−10.8	−1.0	3.7
Inflation (%)	4.2	5.1	3.6	25.9	23.0	12.0
Public-sector balance/GDP (%)	−3.6	−3.8	−3.9	−4.1	−3.1	−3.1
Exports	2.3	2.4	2.1	1.9	2.1	2.2
Imports	3.2	3.3	2.9	1.9	1.7	1.8
Trade balance	−0.9	−0.9	−0.8	0.1	0.4	0.4
Current account balance	−0.5	−0.6	−0.5	0.2	0.4	0.3
Current account balance/GDP (%)	−2.4	−2.8	−2.9	1.5	3.9	2.7
Foreign debt	13.4	14.6	16.0	12.5	13.8	15.2
Debt service/Exports (%)	54.9	28.4	49.4	44.7	31.1	43.5
Currency reserves (import months)	5.2	5.9	8.0	3.1	5.8	7.1

e = estimate, f = forecast

CONDITIONS OF ACCESS TO THE MARKET

■ Market overview

A 20 per cent decline in the already-low reference wages has led many graduates to emigrate. Down 16 per cent in August 2003, unemployment has started to fall back to its 2001 levels.

Industrial output seems to be picking up again, mainly in the SME sector. Growth sectors, until recently limited to agri-foodstuffs and services, now include new technologies and software.

The approach of general elections at the end of the year creates a climate of uncertainty.

■ Means of entry

The Uruguayan market is open, although complex customs clearance procedures and a raft of duties delay the entry of luxury products. Goods may be freely imported into the country, with the exception of military equipment, second-hand vehicles, spare parts, meat and livestock.

A number of non-tariff barriers (eg strict health inspections for all foodstuffs) remain in place, but should be gradually lifted within the framework of Mercosur, whose customs union currently applies to 85 per cent of tariff items, except automobiles, spare parts and sugar. Customs duties and levies are calculated on the CIF value and vary between 0 per cent and 23 per cent. There is also a series of levies, including a port tax, a commission payable to the Bank of the Republic of Uruguay (BROU), VAT and an ad hoc domestic levy on non-essential goods. The most widely recommended means of payment is the documentary credit.

■ Attitude towards foreign investors

Foreign investment is unrestricted and does not require a declaration. All sectors are open to foreign investment, except for oil refining, fixed telephones, railways and electricity generation. The Foreign Investment Act 1998 offers significant financial incentives, including exemptions from tax and customs duties.

■ Foreign exchange regulations

There are no restrictions on currency inflows or outflows. The dollar is the *de facto* benchmark currency, with 85 per cent of loans and deposits denominated in dollars. The peso has been floating freely since July 2002. There are no exchange controls on import payments, but all foreign exchange transactions worth US$10,000 or more must be declared. Capital and profit transfers are not subject to any restrictions or authorizations.

OPPORTUNITY SCOPE

Breakdown of internal demand (GDP + imports) %
- Private consumption   62
- Public spending   11
- Investment   11

Exports: 19% of GDP   Imports: 20% of GDP

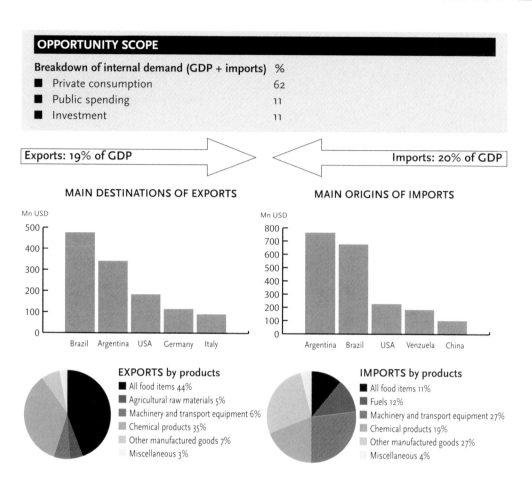

MAIN DESTINATIONS OF EXPORTS

Mn USD

Brazil   Argentina   USA   Germany   Italy

MAIN ORIGINS OF IMPORTS

Mn USD

Argentina   Brazil   USA   Venzuela   China

EXPORTS by products
- All food items 44%
- Agricultural raw materials 5%
- Machinery and transport equipment 6%
- Chemical products 35%
- Other manufactured goods 7%
- Miscellaneous 3%

IMPORTS by products
- All food items 11%
- Fuels 12%
- Machinery and transport equipment 27%
- Chemical products 19%
- Other manufactured goods 27%
- Miscellaneous 4%

STANDARD OF LIVING / PURCHASING POWER

Indicators	Uruguay	Regional average	DC average
GNP per capita (PPP dollars)	8250	5819	6778
GNP per capita (USD)	5710	2928	3568
Human Development Index	0.834	0.770	0.708
Wealthiest 10% share of national income	34	41	33
Urban population percentage	92	74	60
Percentage under 15 years old	25	32	31
number of telephones per 1000 inhabitants	283	137	157
number of computers per 1000 inhabitants	110	52	66

Venezuela

Population (million inhabitants) 24.6
GDP (million USD) 94,500

Coface analysis

Short-term: **D**

Medium-term:
High risk

STRENGTHS

- Venezuela boasts substantial oil, gas and mineral resources with North America constituting the primary market for its oil exports.
- Its external debt burden has remained moderate.

WEAKNESSES

- The economy has remained overly dependent on oil, which represents over 80 per cent of exports and half of fiscal revenues.
- The public sector is inefficient and poorly managed.
- Private investment has remained sluggish amid a lack of confidence in business circles.
- The establishment of exchange controls limiting access to foreign currency has severely impeded imports by companies.

RISK ASSESSMENT

Political uncertainties have been the main risk factor with tensions between President Chavez's supporters and opponents still running very high. Stabilizing the political climate would be crucially important, however, since the country's political crisis has caused a deep recession. To counter capital flight, the government has instituted strict exchange controls with very harsh effects on companies as evidenced by the Coface payment-incidents index. There is thus little likelihood that progressive resumption of oil production will permit fully fledged economic recovery. Moreover, a possible decline of oil prices in 2004 could further weaken the country. In such conditions and lacking clarification of the political landscape, the company situation should remain very shaky.

Further out, however, a durable solution to the political crisis would liberate the substantial economic potential of a country with vast oil-based wealth and relatively moderate external debt. The effects of the conflict are likely to linger on, however, considering the depth of the sociological and political cleavage between the two parties.

MAIN ECONOMIC INDICATORS

US$ billions	1999	2000	2001	2002	2003 (e)	2004 (f)
Economic growth (%)	−6.1	3.2	2.8	−8.9	−11.0	3.0
Inflation (%)	20.0	13.4	12.3	22.5	31.2	29.8
Public-sector balance/GDP (%)	−1.6	−1.6	−4.2	−3.3	−4.5	−4.0
Exports	20.8	33.0	26.7	26.2	23.2	24.0
Imports	13.2	15.5	17.4	12.3	9.0	11.6
Trade balance	7.6	17.5	9.3	13.9	14.2	12.4
Current account balance	3.6	13.0	3.9	7.6	10.2	7.7
Current account balance/GDP (%)	3.4	10.7	3.1	8.1	12.3	8.6
Foreign debt	39.6	38.6	40.4	40.3	40.1	41.8
Debt service/Exports (%)	26.2	19.4	21.2	28.2	32.3	33.7
Currency reserves (import months)	7.1	6.5	4.2	4.7	7.9	8.8

e = estimate, f = forecast

CONDITIONS OF ACCESS TO THE MARKET

■ Market overview

The political crisis – abortive *coup d'état* in April 2002 and a general strike between December 2002 and February 2003 – has had serious economic repercussions. Exchange and price controls have been in force since 5 February 2003 and the award of foreign exchange for imports at the preferential rate of 1,600 bolivars to the US dollar is subject to registration of goods on a so-called priority products list. This list has been revised on a number of occasions. After a laborious start, which saw imports all but grind to a halt, the commission in charge of the list has started to find its feet. The maximum retail price of food, consumer goods and cement remains more or less at its November, even August, 2002 levels, even though the consumer price index soared 25 per cent in 2003. Intellectual property protection remains patchy, especially for pharmaceuticals.

■ Means of entry

As well as exchange controls, a number of tariff and non-tariff barriers remain in place: multiple licensing procedures and discretionary licence awards (in particular for cheese and milk powder), fewer licences, blocking of containers at ports, stringent health restrictions on apples and potatoes, compulsory product labelling with mention of origin, and discrimination against imported products, including those originating in the ACN. Such an environment breeds corruption. In the field of government procurement, preferential measures have been adopted in favour of local companies that show a minimum of 20 per cent locally generated value added. This device is tantamount to knocking 20 per cent off the value of a local bid before it is compared with foreign bids.

■ Attitude towards foreign investors

The 2000 constitution gives foreign and domestic investors equal rights and duties . To date, only oil and gas, alumina and banking have seen major investment in the past three years. The poor law and order situation, government backtracking over utilities' privatization and the durability of the political crisis, marked nonetheless by a few rays of hope of a constitutional settlement, combine to keep investors away, with the notable exception of the gas and alumina sectors. A mutual investment promotion and protection agreement between France and Venezuela is in the final phase of ratification by the Venezuelan government.

PAYMENT INCIDENTS INDEX
(12 months moving average - base 100 : World 1995)

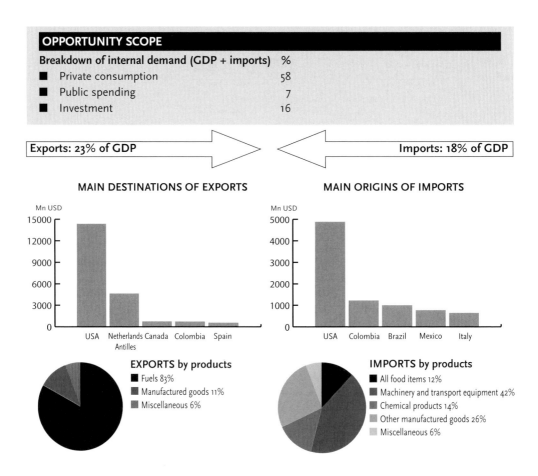

OPPORTUNITY SCOPE

Breakdown of internal demand (GDP + imports)   %
- Private consumption   58
- Public spending   7
- Investment   16

Exports: 23% of GDP   Imports: 18% of GDP

MAIN DESTINATIONS OF EXPORTS

Mn USD

USA, Netherlands Antilles, Canada, Colombia, Spain

MAIN ORIGINS OF IMPORTS

Mn USD

USA, Colombia, Brazil, Mexico, Italy

EXPORTS by products
- Fuels 83%
- Manufactured goods 11%
- Miscellaneous 6%

IMPORTS by products
- All food items 12%
- Machinery and transport equipment 42%
- Chemical products 14%
- Other manufactured goods 26%
- Miscellaneous 6%

STANDARD OF LIVING / PURCHASING POWER

Indicators	Venezuela	Regional average	DC average
GNP per capita (PPP dollars)	5590	5819	6778
GNP per capita (USD)	4760	2928	3568
Human Development Index	0.775	0.770	0.708
Wealthiest 10% share of national income	36	41	33
Urban population percentage	87	74	60
Percentage under 15 years old	34	32	31
number of telephones per 1000 inhabitants	109	137	157
number of computers per 1000 inhabitants	53	52	66

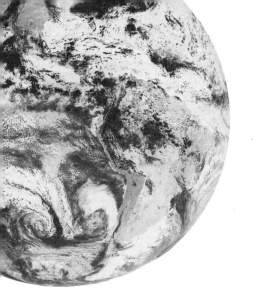

Asia

3

Economic Prospects for South and South-East Asia in 2004

Experts from Oxford Analytica, Oxford

SOUTH ASIA

Détente between India and Pakistan has given both states the opportunity to address issues of domestic development. India faces a closely fought general election, while instability in the smaller, neighbouring countries has increased.

The détente between India and Pakistan, initiated earlier this year by Indian Prime Minister Atal Behari Vajpayee, is likely to continue in 2004. Nevertheless, risks of an arms race, stemming from a spate of arms purchases by Delhi this year (the most notable being that of an early warning radar defence system from Israel), remain high. These have ensured high military budgets and may reduce the scope of possible peace dividends. Moreover, core issues – such as the status of Kashmir – are unlikely to be resolved. However, both sides now have too much at stake in maintaining US favour to revert to the tensions of 2002, when Delhi mobilized its troops along the border. As a result, an uneasy period of truce should persist.

■ Pakistan consolidation

In 2003, President Pervez Musharraf faced a turbulent domestic political climate. However, the opposition remains divided between secular and religious parties and has failed to influence Musharraf's policy agenda. Most recently, he appeared to have reached a compromise with the main Islamic opposition party – the Muttahida Majlis-i-Amal (MMA) – at the expense of the secularists. This move did not harm his ties with the United States. Indeed, the MMA may have recently toned down its anti-US rhetoric in return for domestic concessions in education, law and social policy. If this is the case, in 2004 Musharraf will be able to consolidate his authority through parliamentary approval for his constitutional reforms as set out in the Legal Framework Order, which the National Assembly has so far refused to pass. This could lead to a return of the military and Islamist alliance of the past, though this time it would take a moderate form.

■ Economic prospects

Delhi and Islamabad's desire for a faster pace of economic growth is another important driver of détente. With IMF and international assistance, the Pakistani economy has recovered from its precarious position before the 2001 US-led war in Afghanistan. Foreign exchange reserves have swelled, the Karachi stock exchange has doubled in value and GDP growth in 2002–03 reached 5.3 per cent. A similar level of growth is expected in 2003–04 and Pakistan has begun to seek a return to international capital markets. It is preparing a US$500 million eurobond issue and a number of privatizations for next year; how successful these prove will determine future economic strategy. Exceptional IMF (and US) support, along with economic reforms, has provided larger revenues (proportionate to GDP) than at any time in the last 15 years and has restrained debt accumulation. However, exports are narrowly concentrated, especially in cotton-related goods, and could be vulnerable to changes in WTO quota rules after 2005.

■ India Inc

India's GDP growth in 2003–04 – forecast at 7.3 per cent – is set to be one of the best in the world. Economic recovery (from GDP growth rates of around 4.5 per cent in each of the previous three years) has been a result of a doubling in the growth rate of manufacturing industry and a 15–20 per cent rise in exports across a broad range of goods. Services exports – such as computer software services, business process outsourcing, and research and development in the biotechnology sector – are set to grow rapidly over the medium term.

■ Slowing reform

Continuing liberal economic reform will support growth, though the impending general election may restrain progress in 2004. Liberalization of the financial sector, involving further foreign investment in the banking and pensions segments, will go ahead. However, the elections may lead the government to spend resources on key political constituencies, which could limit progress in tackling the fiscal deficit.

Nevertheless, dynamic economic growth has led to growing speculation that India may be on the cusp of achieving consistently high growth rates, which it has promised for a decade but thus far failed to deliver. Such speculation should be treated with caution. This year's boom has largely been the result of a successful monsoon, following three years of drought. It remains to be seen after next summer's monsoon whether the economy has achieved sufficient structural adjustment to shift growth to higher, sustainable levels or whether, as in the past, its fortunes continue to be dependent on climate conditions.

India and Pakistan appear set on the road to greater economic and political stability in 2004. The imperative to sustain such stability, and a need to ensure politically and economically important ties with the United States, will drive the current détente between the two sides.

SOUTH-EAST ASIA

In South-east Asia, accelerating domestic consumption and improving US demand should enable a moderate increase in growth in 2004. However, the pattern will be uneven due to sluggish investment, volatile oil prices and an over-dependency on export earnings.

Consensus forecasts suggest that GDP will expand by about 5.0 per cent within the Association of South-east Asian Nations (ASEAN) bloc, compared with an expected 4.5 per cent rise in 2003. Continuing their steady recovery from the 1997–98 financial crisis, the 10 nations will benefit from a stronger performance by industrialized economies as well as wider links with intra-Asian trade partners like China and India.

The World Bank expects the current cycle of growth to continue through to the end of 2004, underpinned by solid domestic demand and a broadly based recovery in world export markets. Capital inflows are expected to return gradually as confidence strengthens. Rising services income will play a critical role, as will the upward trend in commodity prices, especially in the farming sector. As in 2003, the prime focus will be on global conditions, though the region has displayed a surprising level of resilience to external shocks:

- SARS, the respiratory infection that afflicted much of South-east Asia in 2003, had less impact than expected, and lasting image problems are unlikely in Singapore, Malaysia and Thailand, which suffered the greatest losses. While tourism receipts fell by an average of 30 per cent at the height of the outbreak, airlines and hotels had mostly recovered by the third quarter, despite a loss of competitiveness from currency appreciations.

- An increased focus on regional export markets, coupled with robust domestic consumption, helped offset an anticipated decline in demand from advanced economies led by the United States, Japan and Western Europe. Shipments to China by the five leading ASEAN countries – Singapore, Indonesia, Malaysia, Thailand and the Philippines – surged by 40 per cent in July and accounted for 7 per cent of total export value. In January, China's share of total exports was 5.5 per cent.

- Swelling foreign reserves provided a buffer against exchange risks, erratic fuel prices and

3

fallout from the international campaign against terrorism, with the Iraqi war also having minimal impact. Malaysia, Thailand, Indonesia and the Philippines maintained average reserves of US$30.25 billion in June, sufficient for 5.4 months of import cover. At the onset of the 1997 crisis the average reserve was only US$23.25 billion.

■ Growth tests

The biggest challenge for the ASEAN countries in 2004 will be to achieve a balance between domestic and external demand that does not leave economies vulnerable to sudden reversals. Most indicators point to a revitalized global trade sector as the US recovery gathers steam. However, the failure of the Cancun multilateral forum could hurt Asian exporters if it leads to a protectionist backlash. At an industry level, there are lingering doubts over the sustainability of a recent revival in output of high technology goods, which provide the bulk of Southeast Asian export earnings. Indonesia, Thailand and the Philippines have sizeable local markets that can help spread the trade risks. In contrast, Singapore lacks the consumption bases to compensate for lower shipment values.

ASEAN's competitive edge will also be blunted by structural deficiencies that contributed to the 1997 crisis and have not yet been rectified. These include inefficient capital and labour markets, low productivity and weak banking sectors. Furthermore, inflows of direct foreign capital and portfolio funds are unlikely to return to pre-crisis levels until investor confidence in regulatory systems is restored, terrorism fears diminish and debt levels stabilize, leaving Indonesia, Malaysia and the Philippines especially disadvantaged.

In meeting these challenges, policymakers will have to contend with an unsettled business environment:

- **Monetary risks.** Low bank interest rates, which have kept credit flowing and boosted corporate profits, will come under pressure as monetary chiefs confront the twin threats of rising consumer activity and appreciating currencies. Inflation has been contained since 1999 by a mixture of excess industrial capacity, high debt levels and low commodity prices, but all of these indicators are likely to change in 2004–05. However, rate increases could still be deferred if oil prices, currently passing through a volatile phase, begin to stabilize. Widening the gap with US federal rates is also risky, as it could destabilize currencies by attracting speculative capital inflows.

- **Exchange risks.** Most Asian currencies are expected to make further gains against the dollar in the first half of the year due to US current account pressures, unless renewed terrorism attacks restore the dollar's haven appeal. ASEAN countries have used their offshore reserves to steady exchange rates and protect exporters, but steeper appreciations will be difficult to avoid if, as widely expected, the low dollar policy is sustained. Malaysia, which has fixed its currency to the dollar since 1998, will be the least affected. Singapore also has more durability due to its estimated US$100 billion of foreign reserves and a flexible interest rates policy.

- **Political risks.** Indonesia and the Philippines face crucial general elections in the next few months that appear likely to bring leadership changes and a possible reappraisal of government and economic policies. Malaysia has already seen a recent generational handover in its political system, and Thailand's government will go to the polls in early 2005. Singapore has indicated it is preparing for a leadership change. While it is unlikely there will be radical policy shifts, protectionism and other popularist campaign pledges traditionally dampen foreign investor interest and could impede capital inflows through much of the year.

■ Sectoral outlook

Countries with more diversified economic bases, embracing open trading environments and an ability to generate grassroots consumption, are likely to perform best during a challenging year. Closer integration through the ASEAN Free Trade Area (AFTA) will be accompanied by intensified competition for investment flows, putting a premium on industrial competitiveness, market openness and governance that will bring selective benefits.

■ Developing economies

Of the four less-advanced ASEAN members, only Vietnam has the growth fundamentals to attract substantial foreign capital, and it may also miss out unless a flagging reforms agenda is revived. All of these countries will benefit from strong commodity prices, but could be marginalized as the six mature economies warm to AFTA. Vietnam, helped by buoyant consumption, is expected to match this year's GDP growth of 7 per cent. Laos is forecast to expand by 6 per cent, slightly more than in 2003, and Cambodia by 5.5 per cent, which is also moderately higher. Data for Burma are unreliable, but slower growth is projected as economic sanctions bite. GDP is expected to expand by 3.5 per cent, compared with 3.8 per cent in 2003.

■ Mature economies

Thailand, with the broadest economic profile, healthy consumption growth and recovering investment, is expected to experience a second successive year of 6 per cent growth, but could be undermined by its energy dependency if oil prices firm. Indonesia, Malaysia and Brunei are net oil exporters, but suffer from weak investment, as does the Philippines. Malaysia is forecast to see 5 per cent growth, up from 4.3 per cent in 2003, Indonesia 4 per cent, rising from 3.8 per cent, and Brunei 4 per cent, unchanged. The Philippines, benefiting from stronger consumption, is expected to grow by 4.1 per cent, compared with 3.8 per cent in 2003. Singapore's impressive recovery is likely to continue, but could be slowed by an over-exposure to exports. GDP is forecast to rise by 4.7 per cent, after a paltry 0.8 per cent in 2003.

In South-east Asia the more stable external environment will ease growth barriers, enabling faster credit expansion and a recovery in income levels while corporate earnings rise. Maintaining this momentum will be difficult, however, without a greater commitment to structural reforms as currency and interest rate pressures expose uncompetitive industries.

3

The Range of Country @ratings in Asia

Sylvia Greisman and Pierre Paganelli
Coface Country Risk and Economic Studies Department, Paris

COUNTRY @RATING SCALE

A regional country risk @rating represents an average of country @ratings weighted according to their contribution to the region's production.

PAYMENT INCIDENTS INDEX
(12 month moving average - World 1995 = 100)

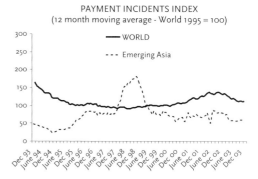

A Country @rating measures the average level of short-term non-payment risk associated with companies in a particular country. It reflects the extent to which a country's economic, financial and political outlook influences financial commitments of local companies. It is thus complementary to @rating Credit Opinions on companies.

In Asia, robust growth has been bolstering company solvency. The quality of risk on emerging countries in the region has been good and that favourable situation should persist in 2004. Coface has thus upgraded the ratings of Singapore and Taiwan to A1 and positive-watchlisted the ratings of Hong Kong (A2) and Indonesia (C). That regional dynamism has spread, moreover, to Japan where exports have spurred economic recovery. However, sluggish consumption has continued to affect the profitability of companies focusing on the domestic market while the process of reducing bad loans held by banks has remained incomplete. Coface has thus maintained Japan's A2 rating but placed it on the positive watchlist.

The unexpected SARS pandemic finally left few traces outside the tourism and air transport sectors where activity fell sharply in 2003. In 2004, emerging Asia should remain the world's main vector of economic growth.

Activity is benefiting from China's robust economy, which has been playing an increasing role in regional trade expansion buoyed by the electronics industry's dynamism and by domestic demand often stimulated by pursuit of accommodating economic policies.

Furthermore, despite the inadequate pace of structural reforms in the industrial and financial sectors, most regional countries have satisfactory external financial situations, which should permit them to withstand any economic or political shocks.

Japanese companies have been capitalizing on that environment thanks to their dynamic regional subsidiaries, which have been fostering exports including in sectors also facing sluggish domestic demand like steel, paper and chemicals.

■ Countries rated A1

Very stable political and economic conditions favourably influence generally good company payment behaviour. Moreover, a satisfactory legal framework ensures protection of creditors and the effectiveness of collection procedures. That generally favourable environment nonetheless does not exclude either disparities in growth or occasional risks of payment default.

With its rating upgraded in 2003, **Taiwan** is benefiting from growth driven by electronic-product exports and a domestic consumption recovery. Moreover, the economy boasts dynamic companies capable of adapting rapidly when conditions

COFACE MAP OF COUNTRY @RATINGS

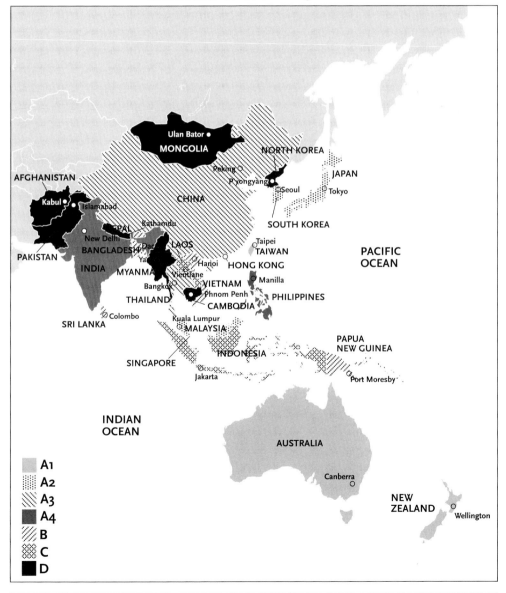

3

A1
A2
A3
A4
B
C
D

change. Their technological advance and delocalized production in China have permitted those companies to develop their sales, make profits and consolidate their solvency. Deteriorated public finances and a still excessively atomized banking sector are the island's two main weaknesses. With its economy nonetheless resting on sound foundations, Taiwan remains sheltered from any financial turbulence. Politically, although the upcoming presidential election in March 2004 has been the country's near-term focus, its relations with continental China will remain a source of tensions. Taiwan's growing economic ties with the mainland along with the pragmatism of China's new government team are nonetheless limiting risks of conflict.

After the economic slowdown linked to the bursting of the technological bubble and then last year's SARS crisis, **Singapore** has been enjoying strong growth. Expanding international demand for pharmaceutical and petrochemical products and a

COFACE MAP OF MEDIUM- AND LONG-TERM COUNTRY RISK

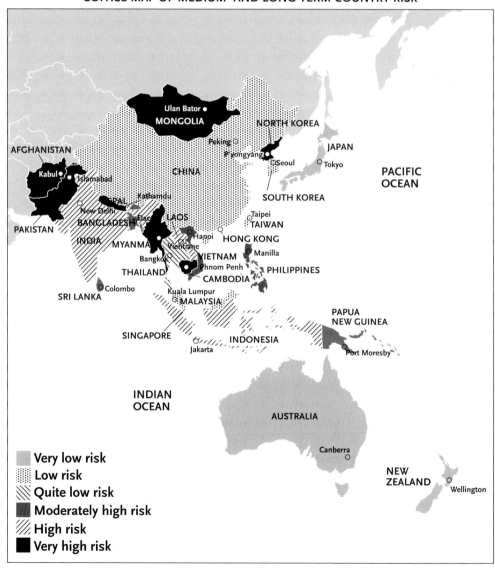

Very low risk
Low risk
Quite low risk
Moderately high risk
High risk
Very high risk

recovery in electronics are fuelling economic activity. In that context, company payment behaviour has remained satisfactory. Moreover, the country has been adapting its positioning notably by concluding numerous trade agreements with the main industrialized countries and diversifying its economy towards biotechnologies and high value-added services. Tax levy reductions have also been contributing to enhancing company competitiveness. Those positive trends permitted upgrading the country's rating in 2003.

■ Countries rated A2

Default likelihood has remained low on average even though the country's economic and political environment or local company payment behaviour is slightly less good than in countries rated A1.

In **Japan** (with a positive-watchlisted rating), strong foreign demand coupled with sharp improvement in company profitability after restructuring has spurred an industrial production recovery and an investment upsurge in export sectors like electronics, the car industry or steel. However, household spending has remained sluggish. In 2004, the upward trend of exports should be accompanied by more moderate growth due to an investment slowdown. Household spending will remain sluggish in an essentially restrictive fiscal context that should result in higher income taxes and value added tax. The decline of the Coface payment-incident index and bankruptcies, reflecting the improved economic conditions, thus warrants being considered with prudence, as structural reforms and consolidation of financial system accounts have remained incomplete. Moreover, exporting-company performance could suffer from an excessive yen appreciation.

Hong Kong (with a positive-watchlisted rating) has overcome the SARS crisis and is resuming stronger growth. Companies generally held up well during the slowdown as evidenced by the Coface payment-incident index. However, some companies operating solely in the local market are suffering from high production costs resulting from high wages and property prices. The territory is also striving to capitalize more on the ascendancy of China with which a bilateral free-trade agreement has just come into force. Although public finances, long in surplus,

are running structural deficits, Asia's second financial centre continues to boast major assets.

In **South Korea**, since the recession that developed in the 2003 first half, accommodating fiscal policy has been stimulating domestic demand. Exports nonetheless remain the main economic engine, buoyed by North American and Chinese demand. Export companies have not been very prone to payment incidents, unlike companies focusing on the domestic market. The country also continues to benefit from public finance surpluses and a sound external financial situation. Progress is still necessary, however, on the banking system and financial consolidation and governance of some conglomerates. Meanwhile, North Korea's nuclear machinations have been undermining relations with that country.

After Dr Mahathir's 20-year tenure, the transition has gone smoothly in **Malaysia**, with the new prime minister, Abdullah Ahmad Badawi, compelled to follow the same type of policy and his party appearing positioned to win the elections scheduled in November 2004. The economy remains robust and company payment behaviour has remained generally satisfactory. Malaysia will nonetheless have to adapt to world economic changes by focusing more on higher value-added products and services. Although the country has made progress on consolidating the banking sector, the level of bad debts has nonetheless remained high with industrial restructuring still incomplete.

■ Countries rated A3

Company payment behaviour is poorer than in the two higher categories and could be affected by a change in the country's economic and political environment, although the likelihood of that leading to widespread payment defaults remains relatively low.

In **China**, high levels of both household spending and investment as well as the expansion of exports continue to drive the economy. The country's admission to the WTO has been contributing to opening it up internationally and prompting foreign investors to delocalize production there and attempt to exploit the market's enormous potential. In that context, although the availability of financial information on companies has been improving, its reliability has not always been certain. Meanwhile, modernization of the public sector has been lagging and the commitment to propping up unprofitable state-owned companies has continued to nourish the flow of bad debts. Robust exports and bloated foreign currency reserves have been arguments serving to intensify pressure calling for re-evaluation of the yuan. At this stage, public authorities have been considering a move towards a flexible exchange rate but only after consolidating the banking system, progressing on structural reforms and fully integrating the country into the world economy.

Thailand's largely outward-looking economy has been benefiting from the world recovery. Domestic demand, buoyed by accommodating economic and monetary policies, nonetheless remains the main growth driver. With that favourable context benefiting companies, their solvency has been improving. However, they have been facing the twin problems of maintaining their competitiveness and moving upmarket to counter competition, particularly from China. Meanwhile, although improvement in the fiscal situation has appeared somewhat artificial, foreign debt has continued to decline. The banking sector consolidation remains inadequate amid a persistently high level of bad debts.

■ Countries rated A4

These countries often exhibit fairly mediocre payment behaviour that could be affected by an economic downturn, although the probability of that causing a large number of payment defaults remains moderate.

In the **Philippines**, strong household demand and expansion of electronic exports are driving growth. Company solvency has improved with large local groups or foreign-owned subsidiaries remaining less vulnerable. Public finances nonetheless remain in poor shape considering the high level of public-sector debt. However, insufficient domestic savings and foreign direct investment have made the country partly dependent on foreign capital to cover its financing needs. Moreover, the banking system has remained shaky. Even with market crisis risk remaining limited in the near term, the Philippines will nonetheless remain

one of Asia's most vulnerable countries. Moreover, despite President Arroyo's candidacy for the May 2004 presidential election, the political situation remains uncertain and difficult.

In **India**, although improvement of relations with Pakistan has marked the current political situation, the fundamental positions underlying the disagreement over Kashmir have not changed. Domestically, the BJP and Congress Party have been preparing for legislative elections. According to various regional elections, the BJP has been making gains, capitalizing on current good economic performance. India's economy continues to grow strongly buoyed by an expected investment upturn and steady household spending. It will nonetheless remain shaky due to the substantial dependence of consumption on the farm sector. The high level of the Coface payment-incident index has been reflecting the frequency of late payments by companies often linked to management deficiencies. Meanwhile, the public-sector deficit remains substantial. Public-sector internal debt thus continues to increase. However, foreign currency financing needs have been falling thanks to steady IT-service exports and private remittances.

■ Countries rated C

A very precarious economic and political environment could worsen payment behaviour that is already often poor.

In **Indonesia**, improvement in the economic environment has prompted the positive watchlisting of the country's rating. Domestic demand, fuelled by household spending, has been offsetting the tourism decline triggered by various terrorist attacks. The country's macroeconomic stability improved after resumption of IMF assistance in 2002 and new foreign debt rescheduling agreements. Although improving, the public finance situation remains shaky. Attracting little foreign investment outside privatizations, the country has to rely on official lenders to cover its substantial external financing needs. Politically, President Megawati seems assured of re-election in 2004 in the absence of a viable alternative and despite probable gains by moderate Islamic parties in the legislative elections.

Australia

Population (million inhabitants)   19.7
PIB (millions USD)   411,900
GDP per capita (USD)   20,948

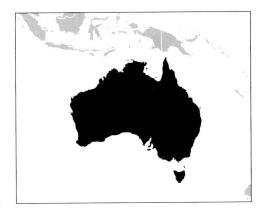

Coface analysis   Short-term: **A1**

3

RISK ASSESSMENT

Despite sagging exports affected by the strong Australian dollar and sluggish world economic conditions, growth has remained robust this year buoyed by dynamic household consumption, company investment and public spending. Benefiting from historically low unemployment, and notwithstanding the constant high interest rates in response to inflationary pressures, households have been financing their consumer spending and housing investments on credit, which has made them vulnerable to an economic downturn. Enjoying good financial health, companies have been eager to invest, notably in mining development or energy projects, whereas the government has been undertaking infrastructure projects.

An acceleration of growth in 2004 would depend on export recovery spurred by improvement in the international context with demand needing to steady at a more sustainable level for the economy in the wake of continued interest-rate hikes. The fiscal surplus should prompt the government to cut taxes.

This favourable economic environment will not preclude the occurrence of payment incidents, notably in distribution of telecommunications equipment to business customers, as evidenced by the increase in bankruptcies with an 11 per cent rise expected this year.

MAIN ECONOMIC INDICATORS						
%	1999	2000	2001	2002	2003 (e)	2004 (f)
Economic growth	4.4	3	2.7	3.3	3.0	3.4
Consumer spending (% change)	4.9	3.2	3.1	4.1	3.8	3.3
Investment (% change)	6.6	−3	1.5	12.4	10	6.1
Inflation	1	3.3	3.5	2.1	2.5	2.2
Unemployment rate	6.9	6.3	6.8	6.3	6.1	6.0
Short-term interest rate	5.0	6.2	4.9	4.8	4.8	5.4
Public-sector balance/GDP (%)	1.9	0.16	0	1.1	0.8	0.4
Public-sector debt/GDP (%)	26.8	23.5	21.5	19.4	18.9	18.4
Exports (% change)	4.6	10.8	1.4	−0.1	−0.8	4.5
Imports (% change)	9.2	7.1	−4.1	11.9	8.6	5.0
Current account balance/GDP (%)	−5.4	−3.4	−2	−4.1	−5.1	−4.7

e = estimate, f = forecast

PAYMENT AND COLLECTION PRACTICES

As a former colony of the British crown, Australia's legal system and legal precepts are broadly inspired by British common law and the British court system. Since 1901, the six states comprising Australia have formed an independent federated union within the Commonwealth.

■ Payment

Bills of exchange and promissory notes are not widely used in Australia and are considered, above all, to authenticate the existence of a claim. Cheques, which are defined as a 'bill of exchange drawn on a bank and payable on presentation', are commonly used for domestic and international transactions.

SWIFT bank transfers are the most commonly used payment method for international transactions. The majority of Australian banks are connected to the SWIFT network, offering a rapid, reliable and cost-effective means of payment.

Another fast-growing payment method enables sellers to request orders for payment, via the Internet site of their client's bank.

■ Debt collection

The recovery process starts with the issuance of final notice, or 'a seven days letter', reminding the client of his or her obligations to pay together with any contractually agreed interest penalties or, where no penalty clause has been provided for, the legal rate of interest applicable in each state.

Where no payment is received and the creditor's claim is undisputed (or where a judgment has already been handed down), the creditor may issue a summons demanding payment within 21 days. Unless the debtor settles the claim within the required timeframe, the creditor may lodge a petition for the winding up of the debtor's company, considered insolvent ('statutory demand under section 459E of the Corporations Law').

Under ordinary proceedings, once a statement of claim (summons) has been filed and where debtors have no grounds on which to dispute claims, creditors may solicit a fast-track procedure enabling them to obtain an executory order by issuing the debtor with an application for summary judgment. This petition must be accompanied by an affidavit (a sworn statement by the plaintiff attesting to the claim's existence) along with supporting documents authenticating the unpaid claim.

For more complex or disputed claims, creditors must instigate standard civil proceedings, an arduous, often lengthy process lasting up to two years given the fact that court systems vary from one state to the next.

During the preliminary phase, the proceedings are written insofar as the court examines the case documents authenticating the parties' respective claims. During the subsequent 'discovery phase', the parties' lawyers may request their adversaries to submit any proof or witness testimony that is relevant to the matter and duly examine the case documents thus submitted. Before handing down its judgment, the court examines the case and holds an adversarial hearing of the witnesses who may be cross-examined by the parties' lawyers.

Aside from the local courts, which hear minor claims not exceeding on average A$50,000, claims for amounts up to A$750,000 in New South Wales, A$250,000 in Queensland and Western Australia and A$200,000 in Victoria are heard by either a county or district court, depending on the state. Claims exceeding the aforementioned amounts are heard by the supreme court in each state.

As a general rule, appeals lodged against supreme court decisions, where a prior ruling in appeal instance has been handed down by a panel of judges, are heard by the High Court of Australia, in Canberra, which may decide, only with leave of the court itself, to examine cases of important legal subject. The right of final recourse before the Privy Council in London was abolished in 1986.

Lastly, though the Australian legal system does not have commercial courts per se, in certain states, such as New South Wales, commercial sections of the district or supreme courts offer fast-track proceedings for commercial disputes.

Since 1 February 1977, federal courts have been created alongside the state courts and established in each state capital. The federal courts have wide powers to hear civil and commercial cases (companies law, winding-up proceedings) in addition to matters concerning fiscal, maritime, intellectual property and consumer law. In certain cases, the jurisdictional boundaries between state and federal courts may be indistinct and this may lead to conflicts depending on the merits of each case.

Arbitration and mediation proceedings may also be used to resolve disputes and obtain out-of-court settlements, often at a lower cost than through the ordinary adversarial procedure.

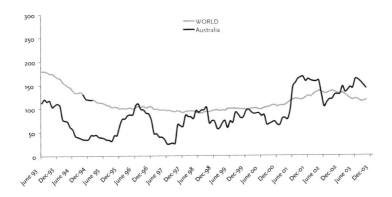

PAYMENT INCIDENTS INDEX
(12 months moving average - base 100 : World 1995)

3

Bangladesh

Population (million inhabitants)	133.3
GDP (million USD)	46,706
GDP per capita (USD)	350

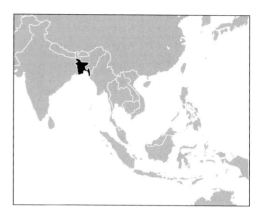

Coface analysis

Short-term: **B**

Medium-term:
High risk

RISK ASSESSMENT

The persistent conflict between the party leader of the governing coalition, the Bangladesh Nationalist Party (BNP) and the Awami League (AL) has continued to mark the political situation. That rivalry has been punctuated by many social movements and accompanied by an upsurge of political violence. Moreover, it has been spurring Islamic fundamentalism and slowing the reform process. The governing coalition could nonetheless hold on to power at least until the 2006 legislative elections but only in a context of recurrent confrontations.

Economic growth has remained high, sustained by strong domestic demand. Exports – with clothing articles representing 50 per cent of total sales – have increased remarkably. The slight deterioration of the current account balance is attributable to an increase in imports fuelled by steady domestic demand. Debt service, although far from negligible, has not really been a source of concern considering the large proportion of concessional loans. The public-sector deficit, however, has remained excessively high due to poor tax collection and the size of the grey economy. Strong demographic pressure and the country's extreme poverty have continued to weigh on the social situation. The very slow improvement of development indicators has tended to sustain political instability.

MAIN ECONOMIC INDICATORS

US$ millions	1999/ 00	2000/ 01	2001/ 02	2002/ 03 (e)	2003/ 04 (f)	2004/ 05 (f)
Economic growth (%)	5.9	5.3	4.4	5.2	5.5	6
Inflation (%)	3.4	1.6	2.4	5.2	4.5	4
Public-sector balance/GDP (%)	−5.1	−5.1	−4.7	−4.2	−4.8	−4.7
Exports	5,762	6,477	5,986	6,110	6,512	7,061
Imports	8,566	9,524	7,697	8,224	9,600	10,284
Trade balance	−2,804	−3,047	−1,711	−2,114	−3,088	−3,223
Current account balance/GDP (%)	−0.9	−2.4	0.6	0.4	−1.3	−1.6
Foreign debt	15,307	15,734	16,276	17,000	18,000	18,500
Debt service/Exports (%)	7.3	7.1	6.7	3.0	2.8	2.7
Currency reserves (import months)	2.24	1.64	2.47	3.06	3.21	3.57

e = estimate, f = forecast

Cambodia

Population (million inhabitants)	12.3
GDP (million USD)	3,404
GDP per capita (USD)	277

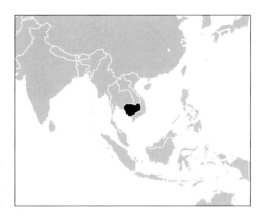

Coface analysis

Short-term: **D**

Medium-term:
Very high risk

3

RISK ASSESSMENT

After the July 2003 elections where his party obtained a relative majority, Prime Minister Hun Sen continued as head of a new coalition government. In 2002/03, Cambodia assumed the rotating annual presidency of ASEAN (which it joined in 1999) and thus attempted to improve both its diplomatic and economic image despite some tensions with Thailand and the United States.

The continuing economic take-off has been resting on the boom in textiles and tourism with the latter sector, which represents the country's main development potential, only temporarily affected by the SARS crisis in 2003. Moreover, the decent performance of the predominant farm sector has been bolstering growth, which has nonetheless been insufficient for one of the world's poorest countries.

Cambodia has thus remained very dependent on international aid to finance the substantial chronic deficit of its public-sector finances and external accounts. Meanwhile, with the country pursuing negotiations on WTO admission, the textile sector will have to contend with increased competition in the North American market from 2005 when the Multifibre Arrangement expires.

Reforms have been progressing slowly in the civil service and banking areas and on environmental protection. With the country continuing to face many challenges, the inadequacy of the rule of law, unrelenting corruption, continuation of illegal deforestation and various kinds of illicit trading could affect the attitude of many donor countries and deter many foreign investors.

MAIN ECONOMIC INDICATORS						
US$ millions	1999	2000	2001	2002	2003 (e)	2004 (f)
Economic growth (%)	6.9	7.7	6.3	4.5	5.0	5.5
Inflation (%)	4.0	−0.8	0.2	3.2	8.0	9.0
Public-sector balance/GDP (%)	−4.0	−5.2	−6.0	−6.8	−6.3	−6.5
Exports	1,099	1,394	1,475	1,605	1,745	1,901
Imports	1,373	1,846	1,951	2,046	2,210	2,415
Trade balance	−274	−452	−476	−441	−465	−514
Current account balance/GDP (%)	−8.4	−12.3	−13.4	−10.7	−10.4	−11.1
Foreign debt/GDP (%)	69	68	66	66	35	35
Debt service/Exports (%)	10.6	8.7	3.5	3.2	2.9	2.7
Currency reserves (import months)	3.5	3.1	3.3	3.6	3.7	3.6

e = estimate, f = forecast

China

Population (million inhabitants)	1,284
GDP (million USD)	1,237,144

Coface analysis

Short-term: **A3**

Medium-term:
Low risk

STRENGTHS

- The authorities have been demonstrating their commitment to pursuing structural reforms since the country's admission to the WTO.
- External debt has been very low in relation to foreign exchange reserves, with a relatively favourable structure (a moderate proportion of short-term debt).
- External accounts are in surplus thanks to the country's continued export dynamism.
- Large inflows of foreign direct investment have been boosting China's currency reserves, which rank second in the world after those of Japan.
- A very high savings rate has been benefiting the country.
- It boasts a relatively well-trained and low-cost labour pool.

WEAKNESSES

- Substantial industrial overcapacity has persisted with many obstacles impeding public-sector reform.
- The extent of non-performing loans on public companies has weakened the banking sector.
- A marked increase in fiscal resources will be necessary in restructuring the public banking and industrial sector, along with resolution of social and environmental problems.
- Development disparities have been fuelling tensions between rich coastal provinces and poor provinces.
- Excessive social inequality and rising unemployment have continued to mark Chinese society.
- Relations with Taiwan have remained tense.

RISK ASSESSMENT

Growth has remained high, even giving rise to fears of overheating in some sectors. Along with expansion of exports since China joined the WTO, sustained levels of household spending and investment have been driving economic activity. WTO membership has been contributing to opening the country and prompting foreign investors to transform it into the world's workshop while attempting, furthermore, to establish a commercial presence in a market with vast potential.

That catch-up phase has nonetheless not prevented persistent imbalances. Some inland regions, unlike most coastal provinces, have remained excluded from the growth along with the immense majority of the rural population. Modernization of the public industrial and banking sector has been progressing only slowly while the willingness to continue propping up public loss-making companies has maintained the flow of bad debts. Moreover, if obtaining financial information on companies has become increasingly possible, it is not always reliable, and the legal environment has remained hardly favourable for collecting claims in the event of non-payment.

Although the public finances situation will not constitute a source of concern in the near term, the

MAIN ECONOMIC INDICATORS

US$ billions	1999	2000	2001	2002	2003 (e)	2004 (f)
Economic growth (%)	7.1	8.0	7.5	8.0	8.1	8.2
Inflation (%)	−1.4	0.4	0.7	−0.8	0.4	0.4
Public-sector balance/GDP (%)	−3.0	−2.8	−2.6	−3.0	−2.9	−2.8
Exports	194.7	249.1	266.1	325.7	423.0	508.0
Imports	158.7	214.7	232.1	281.5	386.0	475.0
Trade balance	36.0	34.5	34.0	44.2	37.0	33.0
Current account balance	21.1	20.5	17.4	35.4	28.0	25.0
Current account balance/GDP (%)	2.1	1.9	1.5	2.9	2.1	1.7
Foreign debt/GDP (%)	17.6	16.2	14.5	13.8	12.9	12.1
Debt service/Exports (%)	10.0	8.2	7.5	6.4	4.3	3.8
Currency reserves (import months)	8.9	7.3	8.6	9.9	10.1	10.2

e = estimate, f = forecast

3

growing public-sector debt could affect the financing of economic and social reforms. External financial ratios have been satisfactory but, owing to the continued growth of reserves, international pressure calling for re-evaluation of the yuan has been intensifying.

The political environment has been stable. After the smooth changeovers in Communist Party and government leadership in November 2002 and March 2003, the new team headed by Hu Jintao and Wen Jiabao has been demonstrating its pragmatism. It will have to make progress on economic reforms to sustain the robust growth while striving to reduce regional and social inequalities.

CONDITIONS OF ACCESS TO THE MARKET

■ Means of entry

Access to the Chinese market is cluttered with obstacles that block, depress or mark up imports. As a full-time WTO member for the last two years, China has undertaken to open up its market. The average customs tariff was cut from 12.7 per cent to about 11.5 per cent on 1 January 2003 and will eventually be lowered to 10.9 per cent. Import licences and quotas will have been phased out by 2005.

Imported goods (foodstuffs, cosmetics, etc) are subject to restrictive and discriminatory health and technical standards, while new safety certification procedures (CCC) restrict the entry of cars, electrical appliances and electronic goods. Until 2005, only Chinese companies authorized to trade internationally may import goods. Moreover, foreign companies continue to be barred from setting up local entities to distribute their products in China.

■ Attitude towards foreign investors

The opening up of the Chinese market to foreign direct investment (FDI) has been skilfully handled by the government, with the pace of change quickening markedly since WTO entry.

The Chinese government has introduced four categories of FDI – encouraged, tolerated, restricted and prohibited – by sector. In March 2002, the main legislation in this field was amended in an attempt to honour China's WTO obligations. While FDI is prohibited in postal services, air traffic control, publishing and media, sectors such as telecommunications, construction and urban gas, water and central heating supply have been opened up. In addition, various undertakings in respect of the service sector are being phased in over a period of several years according to a pre-defined timetable. Foreigners, for example, will have practically unrestricted access to the retail sector by 2005. Every FDI scheme is subject to government approval. The level of government at which approval is given – municipal, provincial or central – is determined by the size of the investment. There is a trend towards granting more powers to local authorities, which are more flexible in the enforcement of national legislation. The centre retains the right to vet locally approved projects none the less. FDI projects are generally carried out via a foreign investment company (FIC), a somewhat unsophisticated entity eligible for tax incentives. There has been a flurry of acquisitions (asset purchases, buy-ins) of Chinese enterprises, especially in the public sector. Owing to the principle of public ownership of land, which can only be acquired leasehold (50 years for an industrial plant), investors are advised to check the status of land offered to them by the local authority. In principle, foreign investment companies are required to give job priority to locals, employing foreign workers only on an exceptional basis. The statutory working week is 40 hours and the duration of paid leave varies from 5 to 15 business days per year. China does not yet have a unified social welfare system.

■ **Foreign exchange regulations**

The yuan is freely convertible only for ordinary business transactions and is more or less pegged to the US dollar (around 8.28 yuan to the dollar).

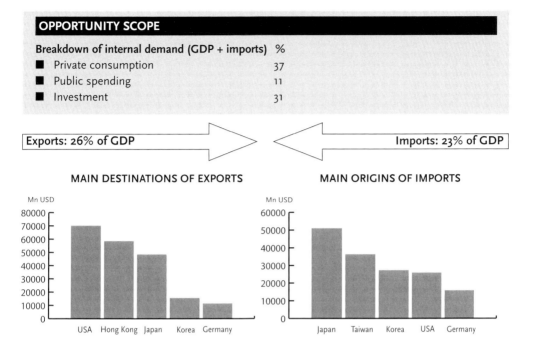

OPPORTUNITY SCOPE

Breakdown of internal demand (GDP + imports) %
- Private consumption   37
- Public spending   11
- Investment   31

Exports: 26% of GDP   Imports: 23% of GDP

MAIN DESTINATIONS OF EXPORTS

Mn USD

USA Hong Kong Japan Korea Germany

MAIN ORIGINS OF IMPORTS

Mn USD

Japan Taiwan Korea USA Germany

3

EXPORTS by products
- All food items 5%
- Machinery and transport equipment 33%
- Chemical products 5%
- Other manufactured goods 50%
- Miscellaneous 7%

IMPORTS by products
- Fuels 9%
- Ores and metals 6%
- Machinery and transport equipment 41%
- Chemical products 13%
- Other manufactured goods 22%
- Miscellaneous 9%

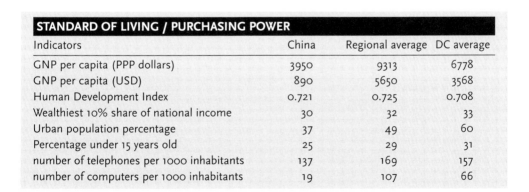

STANDARD OF LIVING / PURCHASING POWER

Indicators	China	Regional average	DC average
GNP per capita (PPP dollars)	3950	9313	6778
GNP per capita (USD)	890	5650	3568
Human Development Index	0.721	0.725	0.708
Wealthiest 10% share of national income	30	32	33
Urban population percentage	37	49	60
Percentage under 15 years old	25	29	31
number of telephones per 1000 inhabitants	137	169	157
number of computers per 1000 inhabitants	19	107	66

Hong Kong

Population (million inhabitants)   6.7
GDP (million USD)   161,896

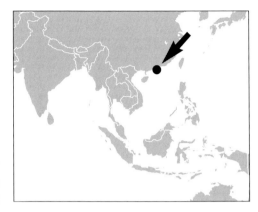

Short-term: **A2**

Medium-term:
Coface analysis   **Low risk**

STRENGTHS

- Hong Kong continues to afford privileged access to the Chinese market's enormous potential, a position strengthened by greater integration into the nearby Pearl River delta and the CEPA bilateral free-trade agreement effective from 2004.
- Preserving the Special Administrative Region's economic specificity is in China's interest.
- Asia's leading financial centre outside Japan, Hong Kong enjoys a favourable legal framework and a sound and effective banking sector.
- Its external financial situation remains comfortable.
- Benefiting from its expertise and leading position in services, particularly logistics and financial services, the territory has been focusing on the development of tourism and high technology.

WEAKNESSES

- With its very open economy, Hong Kong has remained sensitive to fluctuations in international economic conditions.
- The territory has been contending with a positioning and competitiveness problem, notably amid increased competition from Shanghai.
- Maintenance of an exchange system pegged to the US dollar could prompt some rethinking in the future although both local and Chinese authorities have insisted that it will not be called into question.
- The outlook for Hong Kong's political autonomy in relation to China remains uncertain.

RISK ASSESSMENT

Remaining very exposed to international economic conditions due to its very open economy, Hong Kong has overcome the SARS epidemic and should be resuming more sustained growth. Companies generally held up well during the 2003 slowdown as evidenced by the Coface payment-default index trend. High production costs resulting from high wages and property prices have nonetheless hampered some companies operating solely on the domestic market. The territory has also been working to redefine its positioning to capitalize better on China's ascendancy with a bilateral free-

trade agreement known as CEPA (Closer Economic Partnership Agreement) becoming effective in 2004.

Public finances, long in surplus, will henceforth be structurally in deficit due notably to a too-narrow tax base. The still-high level of fiscal reserves will nonetheless provide a solid safety net. Moreover, Asia's second-ranking financial centre has conserved many advantages including well-capitalized banks and a favourable legal framework along with comfortable current account surpluses, moderate foreign debt and substantial currency reserves.

Politically, the new 'accountability' system that provided the basis for the local executive's re-election

MAIN ECONOMIC INDICATORS						
US$ billions	1999	2000	2001	2002	2003 (e)	2004 (f)
Economic growth (%)	3.0	10.2	0.5	2.3	1.9	4.5
Inflation (%)	−4.0	−3.7	−1.6	−3.0	−2.9	−0.9
Public-sector balance/GDP (%)	0.8	−0.6	−5.0	−4.9	−6.8	−4.1
Exports	174.7	202.7	190.9	200.3	223.9	244.2
Imports	177.9	210.9	199.3	205.4	227.2	250.8
Trade balance	−3.2	−8.2	−8.3	−5.1	−3.3	−6.6
Current account balance	11.5	8.6	12.1	17.4	17.2	17.4
Current account balance/GDP (%)	7.3	5.2	7.4	10.8	10.7	10.2
Foreign debt/GDP (%)	24.2	25.7	35.4	35.8	38.8	37.8
Debt service/Exports (%)	1.2	1.6	2.4	3.0	3.1	2.9
Currency reserves (import months)	4.7	4.5	5.0	5.0	4.6	4.3

e = estimate, f = forecast

in July 2002 could ultimately undermine Hong Kong's autonomy in relation to China.

CONDITIONS OF ACCESS TO THE MARKET

■ Means of entry

Hong Kong's reputation is built on the effectiveness and transparency of its free-trade legislation and regulations. It is unquestionably the most open market in Asia and one of the most open in the world, even in the field of government procurement. Hong Kong's return to China on 1 July 1997 and its new status as a Special Administrative Region, which has allowed the former colony to maintain the same economic and legal system, has not affected its openness to international trade. Furthermore, Hong Kong remains a free port. There are no customs duties, and indirect taxes are levied on only a small number of products: cigarettes, wines and spirits, fuel and cars. Non-tariff barriers are scarce. A few foodstuffs are subject to health certification. For most imports, the only requirement is an import notification. By special arrangement and under certain conditions, it is possible to send in a monthly notification, rather than one for each shipment. Hong Kong has adopted standards that are in line with or similar to international standards. It is the second-largest financial centre after Tokyo and boasts a highly internationalized banking sector. Payments are usually made by ordinary letter of credit, but it is advisable to insist on payment by irrevocable letter of credit when dealing with small and medium-sized businesses, owing to the impact on many of them of the economic downturn between January 2001 and June 2003. However, the strong rebound since the second half of 2003 should lead to a marked improvement in the financial situation of SMEs.

■ Attitude towards foreign investors

The territory's free-trade principles inherited from the British have been followed by the government of the administrative region, without the mainland meddling in the territory's legal, financial and economic affairs. In keeping with its free-market philosophy, Hong Kong does not place any restrictions on the activities of foreign investors. There are no prior notification or approval formalities, but by the same token the territory does not offer any incentives or subsidies to foreign investors. Local monopolies have succeeded in driving out foreign competitors. In the absence of a competition law, the authorities only intervene when distortions damage consumer interests. The legal system is simple and company incorporation formalities rapid. Tax laws too are simple and tax rates fairly low (16 per cent income tax and 17.5 per cent corporation tax). On the other hand, the rules for the award of permanent work permits have been considerably tightened. Undeterred by the significant fall in office property prices and a moderate decline in nominal wages, Hong Kong continues to impose high start-up costs on potential investors.

■ Foreign exchange regulations

There are no exchange controls. The Hong Kong dollar is 'pegged' to the US dollar at the rate of HK$7.8 to US$1. This rate is guaranteed by a currency board system, which automatically links Hong Kong's foreign currency reserves to the monetary base.

PAYMENT INCIDENTS INDEX
(12 months moving average - base 100 : World 1995)

OPPORTUNITY SCOPE

Breakdown of internal demand (GDP + imports)	%
■ Private consumption	25
■ Public spending	4
■ Investment	11

Exports: 144% of GDP   Imports: 139% of GDP

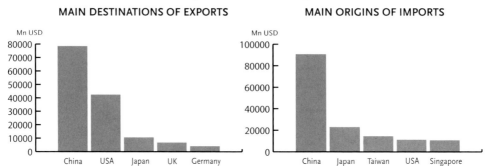

MAIN DESTINATIONS OF EXPORTS

Mn USD

China USA Japan UK Germany

MAIN ORIGINS OF IMPORTS

Mn USD

China Japan Taiwan USA Singapore

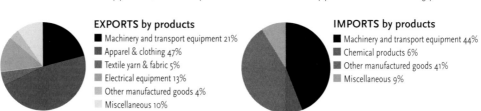

EXPORTS by products
- ■ Machinery and transport equipment 21%
- ■ Apparel & clothing 47%
- ■ Textile yarn & fabric 5%
- ■ Electrical equipment 13%
- ■ Other manufactured goods 4%
- ■ Miscellaneous 10%

IMPORTS by products
- ■ Machinery and transport equipment 44%
- ■ Chemical products 6%
- ■ Other manufactured goods 41%
- ■ Miscellaneous 9%

STANDARD OF LIVING / PURCHASING POWER

Indicators	Hong Kong	Regional average	DC average
GNP per capita (PPP dollars)	25560	9313	6778
GNP per capita (USD)	25330	5650	3568
Human Development Index	0.889	0.725	0.708
Wealthiest 10% share of national income	35	32	33
Urban population percentage	100	49	60
Percentage under 15 years old	17	29	31
number of telephones per 1000 inhabitants	580	169	157
number of computers per 1000 inhabitants	387	107	66

India

Population (million inhabitants)   1,032.4
GDP (million USD)   477,342

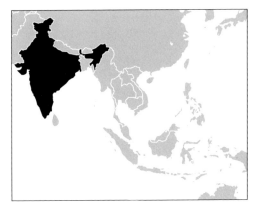

Short-term: **A4**

Medium-term:

Coface analysis   **Quite low risk**

3

STRENGTHS

- With 1 billion inhabitants, India offers substantial market potential.
- Structural reforms – the banking sector, trade liberalization, the tax system – have been steadily progressing.
- Its information and communication technology sectors are well developed.
- Currency reserves have been growing thanks to revenues from services and private remittances.
- Foreign debt has been high but manageable.

WEAKNESSES

- Public finances have been in poor shape amid high domestic debt.
- The country is still suffering from structural weaknesses, like under-investment, attributable to the low level of financial intermediation and inadequate infrastructure.
- Growth has been insufficient to ease the demographic constraint and reduce poverty.
- Relations with Pakistan have remained tense.

RISK ASSESSMENT

India's growth has been accelerating and should remain strong thanks to an expected investment upturn and firm household spending. Growth remains nonetheless shaky with consumption very dependent on the farm sector, which employs 65 per cent of the workforce and is itself dependent on weather conditions. The Coface payment-default index's high level reflects the frequency of late payments by companies, more often attributable to management deficiencies than to company insolvency. That index has been trending down in 2003 thanks to the robust growth recorded.

With the public deficit remaining very large, the long electoral period gripping the country – regional elections throughout the year and legislative elections in autumn 2004 – will not be conducive to fiscal adjustments. The public debt will thus continue to grow at a disturbing rate. Foreign-currency financing needs have been declining, however, thanks to the steadiness of IT-service exports and continued high level of private remittances. Moreover, favourable economic conditions have permitted the stabilizing of external debt ratios.

Politically, although relations with Pakistan have been progressively improving with diplomatic relations and transportation links restored, the fundamental disagreement over Kashmir has remained deadlocked. Domestically the BJP and Congress parties have been preparing for the legislative elections with exploitation of inter-religious conflicts by governing-party hardliners constituting a risk in the run-up to the elections.

MAIN ECONOMIC INDICATORS					
US$ billions	2000/ 01	2001/ 02	2002/ 03	2003/ 04 (e)	2004/ 05 (f)
Economic growth (%)	4.4	5.6	4.3	6.5	6
Inflation (%)	6.4	1.7	6	2.7	3.8
Public-sector balance/GDP (%)	−9.6	−10.2	−9.5	−9.6	−9.5
Exports	44.9	44.9	53.0	60.5	68.4
Imports	53.3	51.9	58.9	67.8	75.9
Trade balance	−8.4	−6.9	−5.9	−7.3	−7.5
Current account balance	−3.6	0.8	3.7	1.6	1.0
Current account balance/GDP (%)	−0.8	0.2	0.7	0.3	0.2
Foreign debt	113.0	113.8	117.9	121.0	125.0
Debt service/Exports (%)	15.7	14.6	13.5	14.6	10.1
Currency reserves (import months)	5.8	7.7	9.4	10.4	9.9

e = estimate, f = forecast

CONDITIONS OF ACCESS TO THE MARKET

■ Means of entry

Customs duties, though still high, are trending downwards. The median rate of duty was cut to 25 per cent in 2003, but additional duty (16 per cent in general) and special additional duty (4 per cent) drive up import levies. Numerous products, especially foodstuffs, continue to attract high rates of duty (wine: 150–264 per cent; spirits: 246–592 per cent). Conversely, certain products regarded as essential to the country's economic development benefit from reduced rates of duty (textile and computer equipment and semi-finished goods, certain uncut gems, drinking-water treatment equipment). Overall, India is taking action to lower customs duties. Under the information technologies agreement, it will have cut the rate of duty for 217 products to 0 per cent by 2005 and is committed to reducing and rationalizing its import duties over the next few years.

Complex non-tariff barriers remain in place. The phasing out of quantitative restrictions by 1 April 2001 has been accompanied by a proliferation of non-tariff barriers. Each shipment of imported foodstuffs is, in principle, subject to systematic inspections. Pre-packaged goods must bear on their label the maximum retail price (including local taxes and transport costs) prior to import. The product certification rules of the Bureau of Indian Standards are at times applied in a manner that places importers at a disadvantage. In some cases, firms exporting to India are required to open a subsidiary or a liaison office and pay ad hoc duties.

■ Attitude towards foreign investors

In contrast to the policy of economic self-sufficiency pursued by the government since independence, from 1991 India has been actively involved in opening up its economy to foreign investment mainly via the adoption of a 'negative list' of sectors, which makes automatic approval of FDI the norm. Nevertheless, a number of obstacles remain in place. These include restrictions on the manufacture of 750 goods, which remain the preserve of local small industry, ceilings on foreign shareholdings in a variety of fields and a ban on foreign investment in the retail sector. Similarly, a foreign company already based in India via a joint venture agreement may not open a subsidiary without the written consent of its Indian partner.

Corporation tax for companies incorporated under foreign law is 41 per cent, compared with 35 per cent for Indian companies. Indirect taxation is both complex and opaque. Notwithstanding the presence of these barriers, the government's reform programme continues to make headway. Key policy measures include planned abolition of barriers to domestic trade, reform of competition law, changes to intellectual property legislation, introduction of more transparent procedures for approving foreign investment applications, and convertibility of the rupee for ordinary business transactions.

PAYMENT INCIDENTS INDEX
(12 months moving average - base 100 : World 1995)

OPPORTUNITY SCOPE

Breakdown of internal demand (GDP + imports)	%
■ Private consumption	57
■ Public spending	11
■ Investment	20

Exports: 14% of GDP → ← **Imports: 15% of GDP**

MAIN DESTINATIONS OF EXPORTS

Mn USD

(bar chart)
- USA
- UK
- United Arab Emirates
- Hong Kong
- Germany

MAIN ORIGINS OF IMPORTS

Mn USD

(bar chart)
- USA
- Belgium
- China
- Singapore
- UK

EXPORTS by products
- ■ Gems and jewellery 17%
- ■ Engineering goods (incl. iron & steel) 16%
- ▦ Textiles 11%
- ▦ Readymade garments 10%
- ▢ Chemicals 9%
- ▢ Miscellaneous 37%

IMPORTS by products
- ■ Petroleum & petroleum products 27%
- ■ Capital goods 12%
- ▦ Precious & semi-precious stones 9%
- ▢ Electronic goods 8%
- ▢ Chemical & related products 7%
- ▢ Miscellaneous 37%

STANDARD OF LIVING / PURCHASING POWER

Indicators	India	Regional average	DC average
GNP per capita (PPP dollars)	2820	9313	6778
GNP per capita (USD)	460	5650	3568
Human Development Index	0.59	0.725	0.708
Wealthiest 10% share of national income	34	32	33
Urban population percentage	28	49	60
Percentage under 15 years old	33	29	31
number of telephones per 1000 inhabitants	38	169	157
number of computers per 1000 inhabitants	6	107	66

3

Indonesia

Population (million inhabitants)	215
GDP (million USD)	178,221

Coface analysis

Short-term: **C**

Medium-term:
High risk

STRENGTHS

- Indonesia boasts enormous natural resources (oil, gas, tin, copper, wood, rice and plantation agriculture) and has substantial demographic weight.
- The economy has been diversifying with external accounts remaining in surplus thanks notably to manufactured goods exports.
- Foreign exchange reserves have been at satisfactory levels.
- Institution of presidential elections via direct universal suffrage from June 2004 will strengthen the democratic process.

WEAKNESSES

- The external debt burden has necessitated rescheduling with the country remaining dependent on international financial aid.
- Structural reforms have been lagging (privatization, legal framework, campaign against extensive corruption).
- Public-sector debt has remained high due notably to restructuring of a still-shaky banking sector.
- The poverty level has remained very high with the education level remaining insufficient.
- The cohesiveness of the world's largest Muslim country has remained threatened by terrorist or separatist movements and conflicts in some parts of the archipelago.

RISK ASSESSMENT

Domestic demand, fuelled by household spending, has permitted Indonesia to maintain moderate growth and notably offset the drop in tourist revenues after the Bali (October 2002) and Jakarta (August 2003) terrorist attacks. Moreover, the country's macroeconomic stability increased after resumption of IMF aid in 2002 and new foreign-debt rescheduling agreements.

Although public finances have been improving, their management has remained a delicate process due to fiscal decentralization and fluctuating contribution of oil revenues. With its substantial external financing needs and inability to attract significant foreign direct investment outside privatizations, the country has to rely on official lenders. Continued reduction of excessive foreign debt remains, however, the main objective. Moreover, the comfortable level of foreign currency reserves would facilitate coping with an eventual market crisis, and the banking sector restructuring has been making progress.

Politically, President Megawati has been maintaining the regime's stability, but her room for manoeuvre has remained limited facing the Army and Islamic parties. Furthermore, the pace of economic reforms has been lagging in the run-up to legislative and presidential elections in 2004. The president has nonetheless appeared certain of re-election in the absence of a credible alternative and despite the likely gains of moderate Islamic parties in the coming legislative elections.

MAIN ECONOMIC INDICATORS

%	1999	2000	2001	2002	2003 (e)	2004 (f)
Economic growth (%)	0.8	4.8	3.5	3.6	3.8	4.0
Inflation (%)	20.4	3.7	11.5	11.9	6.6	6.1
Public-sector balance/GDP (%)	−1.6	−1.5	−3.6	−1.8	−1.9	−1.5
Exports	51.2	65.4	57.4	58.0	61.3	63.3
Imports	30.6	40.4	34.7	34.8	37.3	38.7
Trade balance	20.6	25.0	22.7	23.1	24.0	24.6
Current account balance	5.8	8.0	6.9	7.3	7.2	6.7
Current account balance/GDP (%)	4.1	5.2	4.7	4.1	3.5	2.9
Foreign debt/GDP (%)	105.0	92.4	90.3	75.1	60.9	52.6
Debt service/Exports (%)	39.1	23.0	25.4	30.1	27.4	27.6
Currency reserves (import months)	5.2	5.1	5.5	6.2	6.3	6.4

e = estimate, f = forecast

3

CONDITIONS OF ACCESS TO THE MARKET

■ Means of entry

A signatory to GATT since 1950 and a member of the WTO from the outset, Indonesia pursues a liberal, multilateral trade policy. Since the Marrakesh Agreement, customs duties have been slashed. The unweighted average MFN tariff was cut from 20 per cent in 1994 to 7.3 per cent in 2002. MFN tariff reductions were particularly significant between 1999 and 2001, with 72 per cent of tariff items now liable to 0–5 per cent duty, compared with 60 per cent in early 1999. While tariff peaks remain in force, particularly for imported manufactured goods, the liberalization programme continues apace in keeping with the commitments made at Marrakesh. Schedule XXI provides for the gradual lowering of maximum customs duty (ceiling rate) on imported manufactured goods to 40 per cent over the 1995–2004 period (except for 500 tariff items). As well as cutting customs duties, Indonesia is gradually lifting non-tariff barriers. The number of tariff items subject to import licences was reduced from 261 to 160 between 1994 and 1999. In the agricultural sector, the import monopoly of the National Logistics Agency (Bulog) has been abolished for all items except rice. Indonesia is liberalizing not only multilateral trade but also regional trade with its ASEAN partners under the Asian Free Trade Agreement (AFTA).

However, as it is once again structurally dependent on imported primary products (rice, sugar, etc), certain protectionist tendencies are beginning to emerge, underpinned by the recent failure of Cancun. The budget austerity programme resulted during 2003 in a number of barter transactions whose relative 'success' could act as a stimulus to development.

■ Attitude towards foreign investors

The Indonesian government has a tradition of openness to foreign direct investment. BKPM, the government investment coordination agency, is responsible for promoting direct investment opportunities in Indonesia. In the wake of the 1997–98 crisis, the government adopted a modest investment-friendly policy based on three- to five-year tax incentives. Since there are no exchange controls, investors may freely repatriate, without prior permission, capital gains on shares after dividend distribution and payment of local taxes. Notwithstanding this liberal legislation, investment is subject to prior government approval. BKPM is the gateway through which all foreign investment must pass, regardless of sector, with the exception of banking, financial services and insurance, and oil, gas and mining, which are overseen by the Ministry of Finance and the Ministry of Energy respectively. Simple in theory, the approvals procedure is both fastidious and bureaucratic. The new investment

221

bill containing proposals for revising the negative list of sectors subject to investment restrictions has been blocked by parliament since early 2002, along with every subsequent amendment. Clearly, one of the main challenges facing the government today is halting the sharp decline in FDI and domestic investment. Failure to do so would jeopardize the country's economic recovery and its chances of lifting growth rates above their current levels of 3.5 to 4 per cent.

PAYMENT INCIDENTS INDEX
(12 months moving average - base 100 : World 1995)

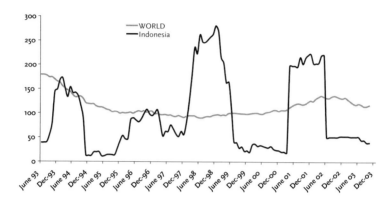

OPPORTUNITY SCOPE

Breakdown of internal demand (GDP + imports) %
- Private consumption 50
- Public spending 5
- Investment 13

Exports: 41% of GDP → ← Imports: 33% of GDP

MAIN DESTINATIONS OF EXPORTS

MAIN ORIGINS OF IMPORTS

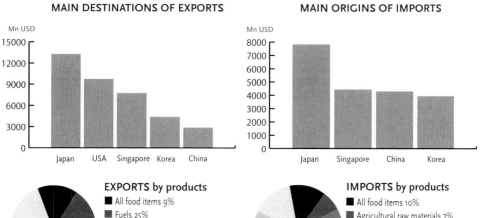

EXPORTS by products
- All food items 9%
- Fuels 25%
- Ores and metals 4%
- Machinery and transport equipment 16%
- Chemical products 5%
- Other manufactured goods 35%
- Miscellaneous 6%

IMPORTS by products
- All food items 10%
- Agricultural raw materials 7%
- Fuels 18%
- Machinery and transport equipment 30%
- Chemical products 17%
- Other manufactured goods 15%
- Miscellaneous 3%

STANDARD OF LIVING / PURCHASING POWER

Indicators	Indonesia	Regional average	DC average
GNP per capita (PPP dollars)	2830	9313	6778
GNP per capita (USD)	690	5650	3568
Human Development Index	0.682	0.725	0.708
Wealthiest 10% share of national income	29	32	33
Urban population percentage	42	49	60
Percentage under 15 years old	30	29	31
number of telephones per 1000 inhabitants	35	169	157
number of computers per 1000 inhabitants	11	107	66

Japan

Population (million inhabitants)	127.4
GDP (million USD)	3,993,400
GDP per capita (USD)	31,337

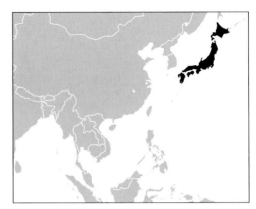

Coface analysis   Short-term: **A2**

STRENGTHS

- Industrial export sectors faced with international competition have proven capable of remaining competitive by restructuring themselves and particularly by undertaking partial delocalizations, but they represent only a small part of the economy.
- Despite still-high fixed costs and company-loan activity still in decline, banks have been exploiting capital gains resulting from rising stock prices to accelerate consolidation of their balance sheets and a return to profitability.
- Massive savings have been permitting households to maintain their spending levels.
- The appearance at last of credible political opposition with the Democratic Party of Japan's recent breakthrough could contribute to eliminating existing connivance between public authorities, government administration and some business circles.

WEAKNESSES

- The Japanese economy has remained essentially closed, not only with foreign trade representing a small share of production but also with foreign direct investment remaining limited due notably to regulations that continue to be unfavourable to new entrants.
- A rapidly ageing population already constitutes a major challenge that imposes a rapid return to public-account equilibrium.
- The social safety net has remained undersized with traditional family and professional solidarity crumbling in a context of decreasing job security and exacerbation of social and regional disparities.
- Increasing reliance on low-cost Asian imports, and productivity gains, as well as increasing competition within the retail sector, have been feeding deflation.

RISK ASSESSMENT

The Japanese economy benefited from a real but uneven recovery in 2003. Robust exports to the United States and Asia have been fuelling the upturn. The dynamic foreign demand, coupled with a sharp recovery of company profitability thanks to restructuring, has been responsible for an industrial production upturn and investment boom in export sectors like electronics, the car industry and even steel. However, despite a steadier employment market and an abrupt halt of

the wage decline, household spending has stagnated at the expense of a sharp savings-rate decline.

In 2004, growth should be more moderate due to an investment slowdown. Meanwhile, exports should demonstrate increased dynamism with continuing improvement in world economic conditions in advanced technology and increased resort to delocalization offsetting the negative effects of the strengthening yen. Finally, household spending could continue at the same pace in an

MAIN ECONOMIC INDICATORS

%	1999	2000	2001	2002	2003 (e)	2004 (f)
Economic growth	0.1	2.8	0.4	0.2	2.6	1.7
Consumer spending (% change)	0.2	1	1.7	1.3	1.1	1
Investment (% change)	−3.8	9.6	1.0	−4.7	10.0	4.0
Inflation	−0.7	−1.2	−1.5	−1.5	−1.4	−0.6
Unemployment rate	4.7	4.7	5	5.4	5.3	5.2
Short-term interest rate	0.2	0.2	0.1	0.1	0.1	0.1
Public-sector balance/GDP (%)	−7.2	−7.4	−6.1	−7.1	−7.7	−7.3
Public-sector debt/GDP (%)	124.9	133.0	141.5	147.2	155.0	162
Exports (% change)	1.4	12.4	−6.0	8.1	7.2	9.2
Imports (% change)	3.0	9.4	0.1	2.0	4.2	5.2
Current account balance/GDP (%)	2.6	2.5	2.1	2.8	2.8	3.4

e = estimate, f = forecast

3

essentially restrictive fiscal context with the likelihood of higher income taxes and VAT.

The Coface payment-incident index and bankruptcies have been in marked decline. That economic bright period should nonetheless be viewed with prudence considering the incomplete state of structural reforms and auditing of banking-sector accounts. Export sectors like information and communication technologies, the car industry, home electronics and even steel have been improving. Conversely, sectors relying on domestic demand like retail and even construction have been stagnating. Furthermore, the recovery has remained very dependent on exports, which could suffer in the event of excessive appreciation of the yen.

MAIN ECONOMIC SECTORS

■ Car industry

Japanese carmakers made large profits in 2003 thanks to dynamic sales abroad, the yen's temporary depreciation, and sales price reductions permitted by gains in productivity resulting from improved productivity. In 2004, sales will continue to benefit from dynamic economic conditions in Asia but also depend on developments in the US market.

■ Steel

The financial performance of large steelmakers benefited fully from the recovery of exports to Asia and strong demand from the car industry. The five main players now form only two major operators: Nippon Steel and JFE Holdings. In 2004, the market will benefit from steady prices and strong demand from Asia, notably China.

■ Construction

The construction market has continued to deteriorate due to the decline of local community investment and sagging industrial and commercial construction activity. Turnover and earnings declined across the sector last year. Medium-sized companies are still undergoing restructuring with additional bankruptcies expected, whereas the situation of larger actors has been improving.

■ Electronics

Despite the worldwide depression in this sector last year, the nine largest Japanese manufacturers continued to post operating profits thanks to restructuring and the take-off of the consumer electronics market. However, five of those companies had to contend with net losses due to the impact of capital losses suffered on interest holdings. In 2004, the electronics sector should benefit from the sector's strong recovery, provided that good economic conditions persist in the United States and Asia.

■ Retail

In the context of the sluggish consumer spending growth that has characterized the Japanese economy for several years now, retailer performance has continued to deteriorate. That has resulted from the sales price decline caused by stiff competition between chains. Department store and boutique chains have been posting very divergent performances. With Ito-Yokado C. and Ion Corporation posting good results, the Daiei and Seiyu department store chains are still undergoing restructuring. The Japanese economy's recovery has not been strong enough to ensure that the sector will emerge from its difficulties in 2004.

PAYMENT AND COLLECTION PRACTICES

■ Payment

Japan has ratified the international conventions of June 1930 on bills of exchange and promissory notes and of March 1931 on cheques. As a result, the validity of these instruments in Japan is subject to the same rules as in Europe. The bill of exchange and the widely used promissory note, when unpaid, allow creditors to initiate debt recovery proceedings via a fast-track procedure, subject to certain conditions. The fast-track procedure is available for unpaid cheques as well, although the use of cheques is far less common.

Clearing houses play an important role in the collective processing of the money supply arising from these instruments. The penalties for payment default act as a powerful deterrent. A debtor who, twice in six months, fails to honour a bill of exchange, a promissory note or a cheque liable to be settled in Japan is barred for a period of two years from undertaking business-related banking transactions (current account, loans) with financial establishments attached to the clearing house. In other words, the debtor is reduced to a *de facto* state of insolvency. These two defaults normally result in the calling in of any bank loans granted to the debtor.

Over the past few decades, bank transfers have become increasingly prominent in all fields of economic trade, thanks to the widespread use of electronic transfer systems by banks.

■ Debt collection

In principle, debt collection may only be undertaken by lawyers. However, the law of 16 October 1998, which came into force on 1 February 1999, creates the profession of 'servicer' as a way of facilitating the recovery of bad loans (NPL debts). Servicers are debt collection companies authorized to recover only certain types of debt (bank loans, loans by designated institutions, loans contracted under leasing arrangements, credit card repayments, etc).

Out-of-court settlement is always preferable and involves obtaining a signature from the debtor on a notarized deed that includes a clause acknowledging compulsory enforcement, which in the event of continued default is directly enforceable without requiring a court judgment.

The standard practice is for the creditor to send the debtor a registered letter with acknowledgement of receipt (*Naïyo Shomeï*), the content of which must be written in Japanese letters and certified by the post office. The effect of this letter is to set back the statute of limitation by six months (five years for commercial debts). If the debtor still fails to respond, the creditor must start legal action during this period in order to retain the benefit of interruption of the limitation period.

Summary proceedings (*Shiharaï Meireï*), comparable to an injunction to pay, apply to undisputed claims and allow creditors to obtain a court order within about three months. Court fees, payable by the plaintiff in duty stamps, vary according to the size of the claim. In the event of a dispute, these proceedings are converted into ordinary proceedings.

Ordinary proceedings are brought before the summary court (*kan-i saibansho*) for claims under 900,000 yen and before the district court (*chiho saibansho*) for claims above this amount. These proceedings, consisting of written and oral submissions, can take anything from one to three years and generate significant legal costs. Court fees, payable in duty stamps, depend on the size of the claim.

The chief characteristic of the Japanese legal system, it should be stressed, is the importance attached to reconciliation. The conciliation procedure (*chotei*) – conducted under review of the court – is made up of arbitration committee mediators, usually presided over by a judge and two assessors, whose role is to resolve civil and commercial disputes amicably. Any arbitration awards confirmed by the court become enforceable.

PAYMENT INCIDENTS INDEX

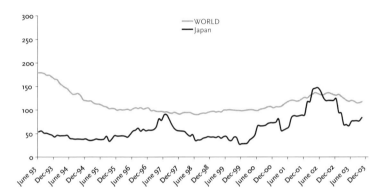

Malaysia

Population (million inhabitants)	24.5
GDP (million USD)	94,910

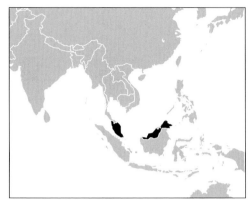

Short-term: **A2**

Medium-term:
Low risk

Coface analysis

STRENGTHS

- With a diversified economy, the country has given priority to training and technological development.
- A high savings rate has been benefiting the country.
- The external financial situation is favourable with reasonable levels of debt and, particularly, low short-term debt.
- A proactive financial sector consolidation programme is under way.
- Endowed with good infrastructure, the country is at the junction of the Malaysian, Chinese Indian and Western worlds.

WEAKNESSES

- The economy has remained dependent on exports, particularly electrical and electronic equipment.
- Overcapacity has persisted in some industrial sectors.
- The excessive debt carried by some industrial groups has undermined the banking sector.
- Domestic public-sector debt has been high.
- The upsurge of radical Islamist movements in the Malaysian community has created risks of ethnic and religious tension.

RISK ASSESSMENT

The new prime minister, Abdullah Ahmad Badawi, will have to meet serious challenges after the 20 years of coercive but controversial power exercised by his predecessor, Dr Mahathir. The transition has nonetheless gone smoothly with Abdullah compelled to pursue similar policies and his party appearing likely to win the elections normally scheduled in November 2004.

The economy has been dynamic in a more buoyant international environment. Malaysia will nonetheless have to adapt to changing regional and world economic conditions by giving greater emphasis to higher value-added outputs and by developing services. Meanwhile, the accumulation of fiscal deficits has given rise to substantial public-sector debt, nonetheless covered by the domestic savings rate. External accounts have continued to post surpluses with foreign debt at sustainable levels, particularly in relation to exports. Moreover, with little short-term debt in relation to currency reserves and the ringgit remaining pegged to the US dollar, the country is not very vulnerable to a crisis of confidence. Despite progress on banking-sector consolidation, the banks' situation has remained shaky due to the continuing high level of bad debts attributable to the incomplete status of company restructuring. Although their domestic debt has remained large, company payment behaviour has nonetheless remained satisfactory overall.

Finally, the upsurge of radical Islamism could strain inter-ethnic relations although the authorities have been pursuing policies intended to permit all communities to share in the fruits of growth.

MAIN ECONOMIC INDICATORS

US$ billions	1999	2000	2001	2002	2003 (e)	2004 (f)
Economic growth (%)	6.1	8.5	0.3	4.1	4.3	5.0
Inflation (%)	2.7	1.5	1.4	1.8	1.2	1.7
Public-sector balance/GDP (%)	−1.4	−4.5	−4.9	−5.6	−5.2	−4.2
Exports	84.1	98.4	88.0	93.4	99.0	105.0
Imports	61.5	77.6	69.6	75.2	79.3	87.0
Trade balance	22.6	20.8	18.4	18.1	19.7	18.0
Current account balance	12.5	8.4	7.3	7.2	7.3	5.5
Current account balance/GDP (%)	15.8	9.3	8.3	7.6	7.4	5.2
Foreign debt/GDP (%)	53.9	47.0	52.0	51.7	48.6	45.4
Debt service/Exports (%)	6.9	6.1	6.5	7.8	6.5	5.9
Currency reserves (import months)	4.3	3.3	3.8	4.0	4.3	4.2

e = estimate, f = forecast

3

CONDITIONS OF ACCESS TO THE MARKET

■ Means of entry

Malaysia has a long-standing free-trade policy. It is the world's 18th-largest trading nation, with foreign trade accounting for 190 per cent of GDP. Its pursuit of trade liberalization within the framework of the WTO and AFTA has resulted in the rapid dismantling of tariff barriers over the last few years. The average customs tariff for all goods is below 8 per cent, the average AFTA tariff is around 2 per cent, and over 99 per cent of tariff categories are liable to 0–5 per cent customs duty. Some tariff peaks remain in force, in particular for cars, steel and alcoholic beverages. The Malaysian government regulates the import and export of certain goods through automatic and discretionary licences. This hardly affects exporters and concerns 17 per cent of tariff categories mainly in forestry, agriculture, construction, chemicals, cars and metallurgical products.

■ Attitude towards foreign investors

In general, the Malaysian government welcomes foreign investment, especially if it generates export income and does not compete with Malaysian companies. The government seeks to encourage greater involvement of Malaysians, especially Bumiputras (the ethnic group comprising mainly Malays and natives) in the country's economic growth, by offering them a minimum 30 per cent

stake in companies operating in certain sectors. Faced with a slowdown in foreign investment, in May 2003 the government announced a series of measures designed to relax the rules for foreign shareholdings. Generally speaking, foreigners may now acquire a stake of up to 70 per cent in a local company and even wholly own manufacturing and high-tech companies. Foreign interests in companies operating in so-called strategic sectors (telecommunications, transport, defence, electricity and water supply), however, are capped at 49 per cent.

The Malaysian government has introduced a number of tax incentives aimed at encouraging the establishment of foreign businesses (Pioneer Status, Investment Tax Allowance, International Procurement Centre Status, Operational Headquarters Status). There is an offshore site in Labuan for financial services and 14 free zones where companies are exempt from taxes and customs duties.

PAYMENT INCIDENTS INDEX
(12 months moving average - base 100 : World 1995)

229

■ Foreign exchange regulations

In September 1998, the ringgit was pegged at 3.8 to the US dollar. In September 1999, the government introduced a more flexible exchange and capital control policy. Transfers are subject to the approval of the central bank, but this requirement, which has since been eased somewhat, does not in any way hamper business transactions and direct foreign investment.

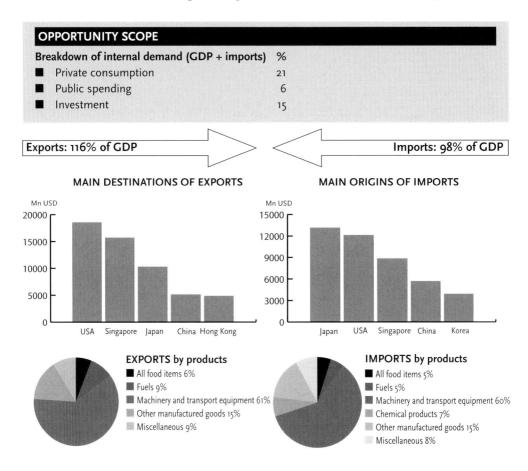

OPPORTUNITY SCOPE

Breakdown of internal demand (GDP + imports)	%
■ Private consumption	21
■ Public spending	6
■ Investment	15

Exports: 116% of GDP   Imports: 98% of GDP

MAIN DESTINATIONS OF EXPORTS

Mn USD

USA Singapore Japan China Hong Kong

MAIN ORIGINS OF IMPORTS

Mn USD

Japan USA Singapore China Korea

EXPORTS by products
- ■ All food items 6%
- ■ Fuels 9%
- ■ Machinery and transport equipment 61%
- ■ Other manufactured goods 15%
- ■ Miscellaneous 9%

IMPORTS by products
- ■ All food items 5%
- ■ Fuels 5%
- ■ Machinery and transport equipment 60%
- ■ Chemical products 7%
- ■ Other manufactured goods 15%
- ■ Miscellaneous 8%

STANDARD OF LIVING / PURCHASING POWER

Indicators	Malaysia	Regional average	DC average
GNP per capita (PPP dollars)	7910	9313	6778
GNP per capita (USD)	3330	5650	3568
Human Development Index	0.79	0.725	0.708
Wealthiest 10% share of national income	38	32	33
Urban population percentage	58	49	60
Percentage under 15 years old	34	29	31
number of telephones per 1000 inhabitants	196	169	157
number of computers per 1000 inhabitants	126	107	66

Mongolia

Population (million inhabitants)	2.4
GDP (million USD)	1,049
GDP per capita (USD)	437

Short-term: **D**

Medium-term:

Coface analysis **Very high risk**

3

RISK ASSESSMENT

The People's Revolutionary Party in power since 2001 could win the June 2004 elections despite formation of an opposition coalition, some popular discontent and lagging progress on poverty reduction.

Farm activity has been benefiting from better weather conditions after suffering two harsh winters that severely reduced livestock. Industrial and mining production has been expanding meanwhile with tourism beginning to develop. The economic situation has nonetheless remained linked to fluctuations in world prices for exported raw materials (copper, gold, cashmere), which, along with imports of equipment needed by the mining sector, have been negatively affecting external accounts.

Moreover, the authorities' room for manoeuvre has remained limited by the size of fiscal deficits (whose reduction has been planned) and public external debt (roughly equivalent to GDP). Settlement of the debt contracted before 1991 with Russia seems nonetheless to be under way. Under IMF auspices, meanwhile, the government has been pursuing reform of property ownership, the public and social sectors and the banking system.

Mongolia's development has nonetheless remained very dependent on international aid with foreign investors deterred – apart from in the promising mining sector – by the domestic market's narrowness and the country's landlocked situation.

MAIN ECONOMIC INDICATORS						
US$ millions	1999	2000	2001	2002	2003 (e)	2004 (f)
Economic growth (%)	3.2	1.1	1.0	3.9	5.0	5.3
Inflation (%)	7.6	11.6	6.3	1.0	5.0	5.0
Public-sector balance/GDP (%)	−12.2	−6.8	−5.4	−6.0	−6.0	−5.9
Exports	454	536	523	524	596	654
Imports	567	676	693	753	812	853
Trade balance	−113	−140	−170	−229	−215	−199
Current account balance/GDP (%)	−14.0	−15.8	−16.6	−16.1	−15.0	−12.8
Foreign debt/GDP (%)	90.9	86.3	88.7	88.8	92.6	91.8
Debt service/Exports (%)	7.0	5.2	4.8	4.7	4.7	4.7
Currency reserves (import months)	2.4	2.7	3.0	3.4	3.6	3.8

e = estimate, f = forecast

Myanmar

Population (million inhabitants)	48.3
GDP (million USD)	8,474

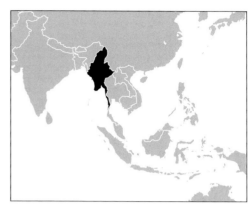

Coface analysis

Short-term: **D**

Medium-term:
Very high risk

STRENGTHS

- Myanmar boasts abundant mineral (oil, gas, gemstones), forest and agricultural resources (rice, seafood) as well as substantial hydroelectricity potential.
- The country is well situated geographically in a dynamic region near China and India.
- Myanmar has been a member of ASEAN since 1997.
- It is endowed with a vast cultural heritage.

WEAKNESSES

- In 2003, Western countries strengthened the economic sanctions they imposed in 1989 due to human rights violations.
- The various ethnic groups in conflict with the central government have been a chronic cause of instability.
- Infrastructure deficiencies and the manufacturing industry's embryonic state have been impeding economic development of one of the world's poorest countries.
- Major structural reforms have been lacking.
- The country has been suffering from persistently large fiscal deficits, insufficient foreign exchange reserves and high external debt.

RISK ASSESSMENT

The unwillingness of the State Peace and Development Council – the ruling military junta, reshuffled in mid-2003 but still divided – to accept meaningful negotiations with the NLD democratic opposition (the National League for Democracy) has prompted a toughening of Western economic sanctions and continued to deprive Myanmar of the backing of international financial institutions. Meanwhile, the junta has been keeping intense pressure on NLD leader Aung San Suu Kyi, ranging from detention to house arrest. The country has nonetheless been benefiting from backing by ASEAN – which has hailed the recent 'roadmap' supposed to engage the junta on the path to democracy and national

reconciliation – as well as from economic aid from China and India.

Despite increased gas exports and firm prices for its main raw material exports, Myanmar is likely to suffer from the ban on sales to the United States. Remaining one of the world's poorest countries, it has been contending with persistent, major macroeconomic imbalances while lacking a coherent economic policy. Its external financial situation has also remained difficult with inflation remaining at high levels and the local currency continuing to depreciate.

Moreover, insecurity and severe structural handicaps have been impeding a real economic take-off. Those problems have been preventing the country from capitalizing on its assets, which

MAIN ECONOMIC INDICATORS						
US$ millions	1999	2000	2001	2002	2003 (e)	2004 (f)
Economic growth (%)	5.5	5.0	5.4	5.2	0.8	1.1
Inflation (%)	49.1	11.4	21.1	57.1	52.8	44.4
Public-sector balance/GDP (%)	−4.6	−8.3	−4.9	−4.9	−5.0	−5.0
Exports	1,281	1,619	2,225	2,886	3,067	3,031
Imports	2,160	2,135	2,625	2,184	2,367	2,406
Trade balance	−879	−516	−400	702	700	625
Current account balance/GDP (%)	−3.0	−3.3	−4.0	1.2	−0.6	−2.1
Foreign debt/GDP (%)	65.1	60.7	78.7	71.9	69.5	68.2
Debt service/Exports (%)	14.7	16.1	11.5	11.9	11.4	11.7
Currency reserves (import months)	1.3	1.0	1.4	1.7	1.8	1.8

e = estimate, f = forecast

3

include a favourable geographic situation, abundant forest and mineral resources and substantial tourist potential.

CONDITIONS OF ACCESS TO THE MARKET

■ Means of entry
The problem with the country's trade is not really one of tariff barriers, as customs duties on the vast majority of imports vary between 1 and 40 per cent. The main obstacles blocking access to the market are non-tariff barriers, lack of transparency of the local business environment and obsolete, unsuitable, changeable and unpredictable regulations, often applied retroactively in the absence of an official publication.

As with other impoverished countries, Burma's non-tariff barriers to trade include a restrictive system of import licences under which goods are listed as essential, non-essential or prohibited. Since 1998, imports of wines and spirits and canned food have been banned.

These restrictions, never enforced with great zeal, are circumvented by means of a thriving border trade with mainly Thailand and China. This explains why contraband goods are so freely available in most Rangoon shops. Since 1998, importers have been required to generate, or 'purchase' from an export firm, hard currency for the payment of imported goods. But from March 2002, only Burmese export companies are allowed to import. The value of their imports is prorated to their export income. Foreign companies are denied import–export licences.

■ Attitude towards foreign investors
The Foreign Investment Law of 1991, which looks highly investment-friendly on paper, provides the legal framework for majority foreign-held companies in Burma. But its somewhat restrictive and rigid interpretation by the Myanmar Investment Commission, coupled with the imposition of lengthy approval formalities (two years on average), contradicts its very spirit and explains why, in the last few years, growing numbers of rogue Asian investors have decided to circumvent it altogether.

A dozen or so sectors are closed to foreign investors. With notable exceptions, such as Total and airline companies, foreign companies are barred by the Myanmar Investment Commission from 12 sectors of the country's economy. Burmese intellectual property legislation is woefully inadequate. The present system is a legacy of the colonial past (Burma Copyright Act 1914 for copyright protection and Indian Patent Act 1911 for trademark and patent protection) and provides few safeguards or remedies for foreign rights.

As a result of the US embargo and European sanctions, Myanmar has not received any international aid for the past 12 years. Its hand-to-mouth existence forces it to adopt expedients that push it further towards China – the country's main trading partner with which it carries out probably more than 50 per

233

cent of its 'real' trade – which undoubtedly sees it as a cheap source of raw materials for its own fast-growing economy. Alternative outlets for Burmese manufactured goods usually require financing.

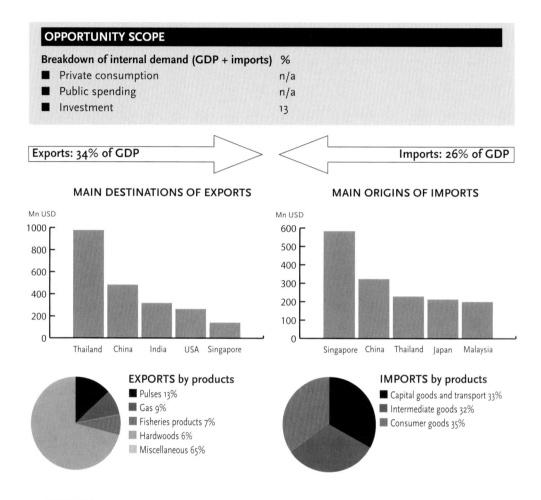

OPPORTUNITY SCOPE

Breakdown of internal demand (GDP + imports) %
- Private consumption — n/a
- Public spending — n/a
- Investment — 13

Exports: 34% of GDP → ← Imports: 26% of GDP

MAIN DESTINATIONS OF EXPORTS

Mn USD

Thailand · China · India · USA · Singapore

MAIN ORIGINS OF IMPORTS

Mn USD

Singapore · China · Thailand · Japan · Malaysia

EXPORTS by products
- Pulses 13%
- Gas 9%
- Fisheries products 7%
- Hardwoods 6%
- Miscellaneous 65%

IMPORTS by products
- Capital goods and transport 33%
- Intermediate goods 32%
- Consumer goods 35%

STANDARD OF LIVING / PURCHASING POWER

Indicators	Myanmar	Regional average	DC average
GNP per capita (PPP dollars)	n/a	9313	6778
GNP per capita (USD)	169	5650	3568
Human Development Index	0.549	0.725	0.708
Wealthiest 10% share of national income	n/a	32	33
Urban population percentage	28	49	60
Percentage under 15 years old	33	29	31
number of telephones per 1000 inhabitants	6	169	157
number of computers per 1000 inhabitants	1	107	66

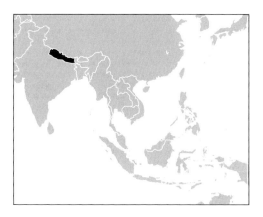

Nepal

Population (million inhabitants)	23.6
GDP (million USD)	5,562
GDP per capita (USD)	236

Coface analysis

Short-term: **D**

Medium-term:
Very high risk

RISK ASSESSMENT

Nepal's political outlook has remained uncertain with the Maoist rebels having broken in August 2003 the seven-month truce concluded with the authorities, after the failure of negotiations. The renewed violence in the country is attributable to the growing influence of the Maoists who now control nearly 40 per cent of the territory. Furthermore, political parties have continued to protest against irregularities in the way the king took power and the peremptory appointment of a new prime minister after dissolution of the assembly in May 2002.

The economic situation thus remains shaky. The reduction of political tensions had permitted a modest recovery in early 2003 buoyed by a progressive return of tourists and the energy sector's rebound thanks to implementation of hydroelectric projects. However, renewed turmoil, very unfavourable to tourism, has compromised the upturn. Moreover, growth has remained too dependent on the farm sector (39 per cent of GDP). Financially, although remaining dependent on expatriate worker remittances and international aid, the country benefits from IMF backing and an external financial situation nearly in balance.

3

MAIN ECONOMIC INDICATORS						
US$ millions	1999/ 00	2000/ 01	2001/ 02 (e)	2002/ 03 (f)	2003/ 04 (f)	2004/ 05 (f)
Economic growth (%)	6.2	4.8	−0.5	2.3	1.5	2
Inflation (%)	0.6	2.4	2.9	4.7	5.3	4.3
Public-sector balance/GDP (%)	−5	−6.2	−5.7	−4	−6.3	−5.7
Exports	971	942	754	633	680	883
Imports	1,713	1,773	1,496	1,630	1,777	2,024
Trade balance	−742	−831	−742	−997	−1,097	−1,141
Current account balance/GDP (%)	0.5	1.2	2.6	−1.0	−1.7	−1.8
Foreign debt	2,890	2,785	2,935	2,995	3,025	3,052
Debt service/Exports (%)	4.7	4.7	5.3	5.6	6.0	6.3
Currency reserves (import months)	5.6	7	6.7	6.8	6.4	6.3

e = estimate, f = forecast

New Zealand

Population (million inhabitants)	3.9
PIB (millions USD)	59,300
GDP per capita (USD)	15,055

Coface analysis   Short-term: **A1**

RISK ASSESSMENT

Growth sagged in 2003 due to less-dynamic export performance hampered by the strong New Zealand dollar and sluggish international economic conditions. While drought affected agriculture, the country's main exporting sector, it also drove up electricity prices and thus production costs. However, by keeping inflationary pressures under control, the Central Bank has been able to cut its key rates and thus reduce upward pressure on the currency. Residential construction, benefiting from that relative easing of interest rates and from heavy immigration, has remained the main growth driver. Moreover, companies have capitalized on the New

Zealand dollar's strength to accelerate capital goods imports.

In 2004, the fiscal surplus should encourage the government to increase public spending and pursue accommodating fiscal policy. Conversely, inflationary pressures intensified by the prolonged property boom should prompt a tightening of monetary policy. The limited export recovery, the decline of farm production, and expected consumption slowdown will affect investment.

Despite the growth slowdown, company bankruptcies and payment defaults have remained relatively low. Considering the economy's soundness, the upward trend should persist in 2004.

MAIN ECONOMIC INDICATORS

%	1999	2000	2001	2002	2003 (e)	2004 (f)
Economic growth	4.7	3.7	2.2	4.2	2.5	2.7
Consumer spending (% change)	3.9	2.0	2.2	3.8	3.4	2.6
Investment (% change)	−1.5	17.5	2.0	5.2	9.0	7
Inflation	0.3	2.0	2.1	1.5	1.7	1.9
Unemployment rate	6.8	6.0	5.3	5.2	5.3	5.2
Short-term interest rate	4.8	6.5	5.7	5.7	4.8	5.1
Public-sector balance/GDP (%)	0.6	1.5	1.2	2.7	2.4	2.6
Public-sector debt/GDP (%)	47.4	45.1	42.8	40.5	37.0	35.0
Exports (% change)	8.0	6.5	2.4	5.8	3.3	3.9
Imports (% change)	11.8	0.2	1.6	8.8	5.7	3.3
Current account balance/GDP (%)	−6.2	−4.8	−2.6	−3.7	−4.5	−4.8

e = estimate, f = forecast

PAYMENT AND COLLECTION PRACTICES

As a former British colony in the 19th century and a Commonwealth member since 1907, New Zealand's legal code and precepts are largely inspired by British common law and the British court system.

■ Payment

Bills of exchange and promissory notes are not frequently used for commercial transactions in New Zealand and are considered, above all, to authenticate the existence of a claim. Conversely, cheques are relatively widely used for domestic transactions. Wire transfers or SWIFT bank transfers are the most commonly used payment method for international transactions. Most of the country's banks are connected to the SWIFT network, which offers a rapid, cost-efficient means of effecting payments.

■ Debt collection

The recovery process starts with the issuance of final notice, or a 'seven days letter', by registered mail in which the creditor notifies the debtor of his or her payment obligations.

Where no payment is received and where claims are undisputed (or once a judgment has been obtained), the creditor may summons the debtor to settle the debt within 15 days or to face a winding-up petition (statutory demand under section 289 of the 1993 Companies Act). If no response is received within the required timeframe, the debtor's company is considered insolvent.

Under ordinary proceedings, once a statement of claim (summons) has been filed and where debtors have no grounds on which to dispute claims, creditors may solicit a fast-track procedure enabling them to obtain an executory order by issuing the debtor with an application for summary judgment. This petition must be accompanied by an affidavit (a sworn statement by the plaintiff attesting to the claim's existence) along with supporting documents authenticating the unpaid claim.

For more complex or disputed claims, creditors must instigate standard civil proceedings, an arduous, often lengthy process lasting up to two years. Proceedings are heard by the district courts or by the High Court, for claims exceeding NZ$200,000.

Under New Zealand's constitution, the Privy Council in London has jurisdiction to hear appeals filed against decisions made by the New Zealand Court of Appeal in Wellington, concerning claims for NZ$5,000 or more. In addition, the High Court may hold summary proceedings for commercial disputes that concern the fields of insurance, banking, finance, intellectual property and goods transport, and which are enumerated in its 'commercial list'.

During the preliminary phase, proceedings are written insofar as the court examines the case documents authenticating the parties' respective claims. During the subsequent 'discovery phase', the parties' lawyers may request their adversaries to submit any proof or witness testimony that is relevant to the case and duly examine the case documents thus submitted. Before handing down its judgment, the court examines the case and holds an adversarial hearing of the witnesses who may be cross-examined by the parties' lawyers.

Arbitration and mediation proceedings may also be used to resolve disputes and obtain out-of-court settlements, often at a lower cost than through the ordinary adversarial procedure.

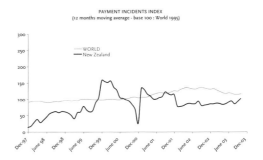

PAYMENT INCIDENTS INDEX
(12 months moving average - base 100 : World 1995)

Pakistan

Population (million inhabitants)	141.5
GDP (million USD)	58,668

Coface analysis

Short-term: **D**

Medium-term:
Very high risk

STRENGTHS

- The country's nuclear-power status and the risk of it switching to an anti-Western camp have placed Pakistan at the centre of US strategic concerns.
- The financial situation has benefited from the granting of aid and debt rescheduling.
- Several structural reforms concerning public tariffs and taxation have progressed under IMF auspices.
- Expatriate worker remittances have been bolstering the country's foreign exchange position.

WEAKNESSES

- The economy is very dependent on low value-added sectors like textiles and cotton.
- Private foreign investment has been slow to take over from official financing due to political risks.
- Recurrent tensions with India have been generating considerable risk of regional destabilization.
- Foreign policy options are far from attracting a consensus among the population.

RISK ASSESSMENT

The country's financial situation has continued to improve as evidenced by the high level of currency reserves and reduction of debt ratios. Furthermore, exports have been dynamic, buoyed by the US recovery and higher textile import quotas. Meanwhile, relatively expansionary fiscal policy has also been boosting growth, which has remained high.

The durability of the good performance nonetheless remains uncertain. Above all, the government has to reduce its deficit, which could impede economic activity. Moreover, there are still structural obstacles to growth. The dominant economic sectors have remained shaky. With

textiles (including the cotton industry) representing 60 per cent of exports and agriculture representing 24 per cent of GDP, economic performance will continue to be dependent on weather conditions. The country has been lagging increasingly on health and education with demographics constituting a major constraint.

Furthermore, political risk has remained high. The influence of Islamist movements has been growing, spurred by increasingly widespread anti-US sentiment. In foreign affairs, although Indo-Pakistani relations have been easing and a dialogue developing, the two countries have not modified their official positions on the Kashmir issue.

MAIN ECONOMIC INDICATORS

US$ billions	1999/ 2000	2000/ 01	2001/ 02	2002/ 03	2003/ 04 (f)	2004/ 05 (f)
Economic growth (%)	4.3	2.2	3.4	5.1	5.3	5.1
Inflation (%)	5.1	4.4	2.7	3.1	4.0	4.0
Public-sector balance/GDP (%)	−5.5	−5.2	−6.7	−4.5	−4.5	−4.5
Exports	8.2	8.9	9.1	10.9	11.8	11.9
Imports	9.6	10.2	9.4	11.4	12.9	13.7
Trade balance	−1.4	−1.3	−0.3	−0.5	−1.1	−1.8
Current account balance	−1.1	0.1	0.1	3.0	0.4	0.5
Current account balance/GDP (%)	−2.1	0.2	0.2	4.4	0.6	0.8
Foreign debt	34.0	36.1	36.0	35.2	35.5	35.6
Debt service/Exports (%)	44.0	35.9	29.2	26.1	25.9	25.0
Currency reserves (import months)	1.2	1.1	3.8	7.1	7.3	7.6

e = estimate, f = forecast

3

CONDITIONS OF ACCESS TO THE MARKET

■ Means of entry

The country's economy is gradually opening up. Customs duties in the industrial sector are trending downwards. The maximum rate of *ad valorem* custom duty (CIF value) is 25 per cent, except for products subject to a separate system of taxation, such as cars. The maximum rate of duty in the service sector is 10 per cent.

As a rule, Pakistani customs use the World Customs Organization's harmonized international nomenclature. However, the practice in the customs service of reclassifying imported goods in a higher duty category places local importers at a disadvantage and, sometimes, results in disputes. Excise duty of 2–3 per cent and maximum general sales tax of 25 per cent are imposed on all goods and transactions in addition to customs duties. Capital transfers are not subject to major constraints. The Central Bank now permits full convertibility and unrestricted capital transfers and there is a free currency market. In a crisis , however, the bank may intervene to regulate foreign currency flows with foreign countries.

■ Attitude towards foreign investors

Foreign investment is governed by special legislation. The Pakistani government takes an extremely positive view of foreign investment – which remains small in volume terms – and hopes to attract investors by means of a far more investment-friendly legal environment.

There are no restrictions on the form of company constituted by foreign investors or foreign property rights, nor any requirement for foreigners to tie up with a local partner, except for projects in the services and agricultural sectors, where foreign investors must take in a local partner after five years and cap their shareholding at 60 per cent.

Once established, resident firms are liable to the same taxation as local enterprises (45 per cent corporation tax in 2003). Moreover, the Pakistani government has signed bilateral investment protection treaties with 36 countries, which provide investors with effective safeguards against nationalization or unlawful expropriation and unrestricted capital and profit repatriation rights.

Pakistan has signed, ratified and implemented the Convention on the Settlement of Investment Disputes and is a signatory to the founding treaty of the Multilateral Investment Guarantee Agency, MIGA, an arm of the World Bank.

239

OPPORTUNITY SCOPE

Breakdown of internal demand (GDP + imports) %
- Private consumption   63
- Public spending   8
- Investment   13

Exports: 18% of GDP   Imports: 19% of GDP

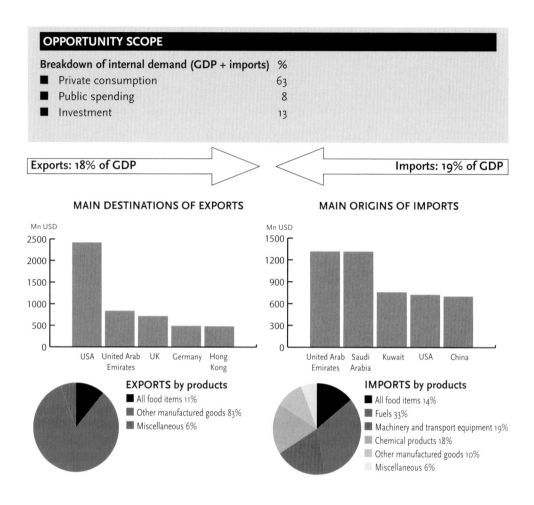

MAIN DESTINATIONS OF EXPORTS

Mn USD

USA | United Arab Emirates | UK | Germany | Hong Kong

MAIN ORIGINS OF IMPORTS

Mn USD

United Arab Emirates | Saudi Arabia | Kuwait | USA | China

EXPORTS by products
- All food items 11%
- Other manufactured goods 83%
- Miscellaneous 6%

IMPORTS by products
- All food items 14%
- Fuels 33%
- Machinery and transport equipment 19%
- Chemical products 18%
- Other manufactured goods 10%
- Miscellaneous 6%

STANDARD OF LIVING / PURCHASING POWER

Indicators	Pakistan	Regional average	DC average
GNP per capita (PPP dollars)	1860	9313	6778
GNP per capita (USD)	420	5650	3568
Human Development Index	0.499	0.725	0.708
Wealthiest 10% share of national income	28	32	33
Urban population percentage	33	49	60
Percentage under 15 years old	41	29	31
number of telephones per 1000 inhabitants	23	169	157
number of computers per 1000 inhabitants	4	107	66

Papua New Guinea

Population (million inhabitants)	5.3
GDP (million USD)	2,959
GDP per capita (USD)	558

Short-term: **B**

Coface analysis

Medium-term:
Moderately high risk

3

RISK ASSESSMENT

With Papua New Guinea enjoying political stability since the June 2002 elections, the prime minister, Sir Michael Somare, has initiated a five-year 'improvement and development' programme focused on export sectors. However, implementation of that plan by a 10-party coalition government hampered by corruption problems has proven difficult. The country has nonetheless emerged from three recession years (2000–02) during which political uncertainties, poor weather conditions, depletion of oil reserves and postponement of mining projects all impeded economic activity. In any case, it will be necessary to restore fundamental macroeconomic equilibriums and, in particular, consolidate public finances and undertake structural reforms. This would also permit the country to maintain the essential backing of the main donors and international financial institutions.

Fragmented geographically, ethnically and linguistically, Papua New Guinea has remained hampered by archaic infrastructure. Moreover, to benefit from durable development, the country must diversify its currently dual economy with large mining operations and farms generating 80 per cent of foreign currency earnings. It must also reduce its exposure to world raw-material price fluctuations. However, the Moran oil field's production start-up contributed to a modest growth recovery in 2003. Moreover, the Kainantu gold mine and Ramu nickel and cobalt mine start-ups in 2004 along with possible realization of the gas pipeline to Queensland in Australia should spur economic activity.

MAIN ECONOMIC INDICATORS						
US$ millions	1999	2000	2001	2002	2003 (e)	2004 (f)
Economic growth (%)	7.5	−1.2	−3.4	−3.1	1.2	2.0
Inflation (%)	13.2	10	10.3	11.7	17.5	13.5
Public-sector balance/GDP (%)	−2.5	−1.4	−4.1	−5.5	−3.4	−2.0
Exports	1,927	2,094	1,813	1,640	1,785	1,751
Imports	1,071	1,000	933	960	965	1,001
Trade balance	856	1,094	880	680	820	750
Current account balance/GDP (%)	2.8	10.0	9.7	0.4	−0.3	−2.1
Foreign debt/GDP (%)	78.6	73.7	89.2	92.2	82.6	77.9
Debt service/Exports (%)	31.3	18.4	24.7	25.7	26.5	28.2
Currency reserves (import months)	1.3	2.1	3.1	2.2	2.1	2.4

e = estimate, f = forecast

Philippines

Population (million inhabitants)	79.6
GDP (million USD)	77,887

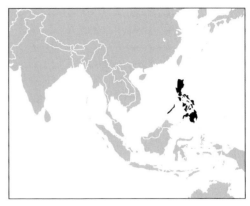

Coface analysis

Short-term: **A4**

Medium-term:
Moderately high risk

STRENGTHS

- Satisfactory training and productivity levels in conjunction with low-cost labour are beneficial to multinational firms.
- The regional economic environment is favourable.
- Exports are dynamic, particularly in special economic areas and the electronic sector.
- External accounts remain in surplus due notably to the scale of expatriate remittances.

WEAKNESSES

- Growth rates are insufficient in relation to demographic development and do not permit a reduction of the increasing poverty levels that constitute a source of social tensions.
- Unlike the situation in most Asian countries, domestic savings are insufficient.
- With public finances in poor shape amid excessive public-sector debt, reducing the substantial fiscal imbalances will require firmer political commitment.
- The poor condition of the banking sector has been crying out for reform.
- Insecurity, due notably to Islamist separatist movements in the south of the archipelago, has been deterring tourism and foreign investment.

RISK ASSESSMENT

Sustained household demand and increasing electronics-sector exports have been bolstering growth despite sagging farm production. In that context, the Coface payment-incident index remains at satisfactory levels with large domestic groups and subsidiaries of foreign companies less exposed than other enterprises.

Public finances nonetheless remain in poor shape due to tax collection problems with the balanced-budget objective postponed until 2009. Public-sector debt thus remains substantial with an increasing share of fiscal revenues devoted to debt service at the expense of productive spending. Unlike the situation of other Asian countries, however, the insufficiency of domestic savings and foreign direct investments is making the country dependent on foreign capital to cover its needs. Although that has not posed a problem thus far, it has caused spreads to increase and kept foreign debt at high levels in relation to GDP. Moreover, the banking system remains in poor shape with insufficient reform and oversight of the sector. Although near-term market crisis risk nonetheless remains low due to the small proportion of short-maturity financing, the Philippines is still one of Asia's most vulnerable countries.

MAIN ECONOMIC INDICATORS						
US$ billions	1999	2000	2001	2002	2003 (e)	2004 (f)
Economic growth (%)	3.4	6.0	3.0	4.4	3.8	4.5
Inflation (%)	6.7	4.3	6.1	3.1	3.0	3.5
Public-sector balance/GDP (%)	−3.5	−4.7	−4.6	−5.8	−4.7	−4.2
Exports	34.2	37.3	31.2	34.4	36.5	39.7
Imports	29.3	33.5	32.0	34.0	37.5	41.0
Trade balance	5.0	3.8	−0.7	0.4	−1.0	−1.2
Current account balance	7.0	6.3	1.3	4.2	2.0	1.9
Current account balance/GDP (%)	9.1	8.2	1.8	5.4	2.5	2.3
Foreign debt (% GDP)	76.2	75.7	80.3	76.2	73.4	69.0
Debt service (% Exports)	16.6	17.3	21.4	19.5	19.2	17.1
Currency reserves (import months)	3.9	3.6	4.0	3.8	3.4	3.2

e = estimate, f = forecast

3

Politically, despite President Arroyo's decision to run again for president in May 2004, the situation remains uncertain and difficult. Persistently high levels of corruption and poverty with their negative impact on social tensions have been compounding the security problems.

CONDITIONS OF ACCESS TO THE MARKET

■ Market overview

On the whole, the market is very open and whatever import restrictions there are consist mainly of non-tariff barriers. It is difficult, even impossible, for foreigners to enter certain sectors (utilities) protected by the constitution. Imports of certain products are subject to stringent regulatory restrictions involving the award of certificates by an inefficient and often corrupt administrative service. The government has already met its tariff reduction targets for 2003, agreed with the WTO, in respect of 85 per cent of tariff items. Accordingly, duty on finished products has been cut to 10 per cent and on commodities to 3 per cent. By 2004, a single rate of 5 per cent will apply, although some exceptional protective tariffs will remain in force. At present, there are six rates of duty: 0, 3, 5, 10, 15 and 20 per cent. Products subject to preferential tariff quotas, such as agricultural goods, are taxable outside the quota system at rates as high as 45, 50 or even 60 per cent.

Payment by irrevocable documentary letter of credit is strongly recommended.

While a legal framework has been set in place to enhance intellectual property protection, the slowness of administrative procedures and the lack of resources at the disposal of judges for the enforcement of legal decisions limit its effectiveness.

■ Attitude towards foreign investors

A 'one-stop action centre' is responsible for disseminating practical information and facilitating registration formalities. Foreign companies are advised to use the services of a local lawyer. The Security and Exchange Commission, a government agency, has responsibility for the registration, regulation and monitoring of all companies and partnerships established in the Philippines. Registration with the SEC can take anything from one to four weeks. A fast-track system, based on the filing of applications in English, allows registration formalities to be completed within three days against cash payment of the invoice. By easing foreign investment regulations, the Foreign Investments Act of 1991, amended in 1996 and again in 1998, has greatly boosted investment over the last 10 years. Foreign investors interested in infrastructure development can avail themselves of certain provisions of the Build-Operate-Transfer Act (1990). Another law allows foreign investors to lease land for the purposes of establishing a

243

manufacturing facility. The Philippines constitution also allows foreign businesses to repatriate their investment, together with any profits earned, in the original currency, and to raise loans on the local financial market. Foreign firms are provided with safeguards against expropriation and confiscation of their investment. Various types of incentive are also available. The Philippines is one of the most open countries in the region, even though some sectors of activity remain the preserve of local investors.

■ Foreign exchange regulations

There are no exchange controls, but all imports in excess of US$1,000 are subject to a foreign exchange application being filed by the importer. Similarly, when the currency is under strong pressure, local banks may, on the instructions of the central bank, require clients to document their request for foreign currency. The exchange rate is floating.

PAYMENT INCIDENTS INDEX
(12 months moving average - base 100 : World 1995)

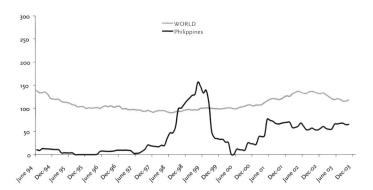

OPPORTUNITY SCOPE

Breakdown of internal demand (GDP + imports) %
■ Private consumption   46
■ Public spending   8
■ Investment   12

Exports: 49% of GDP   Imports: 47% of GDP

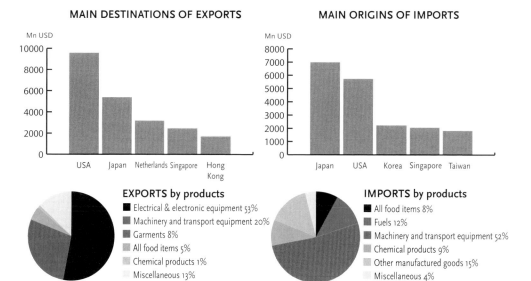

MAIN DESTINATIONS OF EXPORTS

Mn USD

USA   Japan   Netherlands   Singapore   Hong Kong

EXPORTS by products
■ Electrical & electronic equipment 53%
■ Machinery and transport equipment 20%
▦ Garments 8%
▦ All food items 5%
▦ Chemical products 1%
▦ Miscellaneous 13%

MAIN ORIGINS OF IMPORTS

Mn USD

Japan   USA   Korea   Singapore   Taiwan

IMPORTS by products
■ All food items 8%
■ Fuels 12%
▦ Machinery and transport equipment 52%
▦ Chemical products 9%
▦ Other manufactured goods 15%
▦ Miscellaneous 4%

STANDARD OF LIVING / PURCHASING POWER

Indicators	Philippines	Regional average	DC average
GNP per capita (PPP dollars)	4070	9313	6778
GNP per capita (USD)	1030	5650	3568
Human Development Index	0.751	0.725	0.708
Wealthiest 10% share of national income	36	32	33
Urban population percentage	59	49	60
Percentage under 15 years old	37	29	31
number of telephones per 1000 inhabitants	42	169	157
number of computers per 1000 inhabitants	22	107	66

3

Singapore

Population (million inhabitants)   3.9
GDP (million USD)   90,291

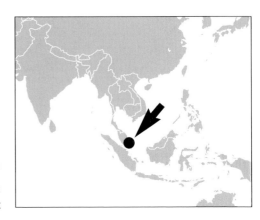

Short-term: **A1**

Coface analysis

Medium-term:
Very low risk

***STRENGTHS

- Singapore constitutes a major regional platform thanks to the quality of its infrastructure and financial system.
- Labour is well trained and highly skilled.
- The economic success has been founded on a policy of inviting foreign capital and promoting exports.
- The city-state benefits from a comfortable financial situation thanks to the accumulation of fiscal and current account surpluses and to ample foreign exchange reserves.
- It enjoys remarkable political stability.

WEAKNESSES

- The economy's extreme sensitivity to fluctuations in world economic conditions has increased due to its specialization in electronics.
- The rigidity of the education system and government framework has tended to stifle entrepreneurial and innovative spirit.
- To remain competitive, the country will have to adjust to a rapidly changing regional environment.

RISK ASSESSMENT

After enduring an economic slowdown in 2003, partly attributable to the SARS pandemic's negative impact on sectors involved in distribution or linked to tourism, Singapore has been benefiting from more sustained growth. The economic recovery has been depending on growing international demand for pharmaceutical and petrochemical products and an upturn in the electronics sector, which represents two-thirds of exports. In that framework, the Coface payment experience on most companies has remained satisfactory with the only incidents registered remaining concentrated in small trading companies.

The accumulation of fiscal surpluses has afforded the country considerable leverage in spurring domestic demand via stimulatory policy. External accounts have continued to post large surpluses with foreign debt remaining very low and foreign currency reserves ample. The banking system has remained the soundest in the region, especially with banks continuing to reduce their non-performing loans.

With its extreme sectoral specialization, Singapore has been diversifying its economy focusing on biotechnologies and high value-added services. Moreover, it has been reducing tax levies to offset a loss of competitiveness in relation to other countries in the region as well as to China and India. Singapore has also been concluding numerous trade agreements with major industrialized countries.

MAIN ECONOMIC INDICATORS

US$ billions	1999	2000	2001	2002	2003 (e)	2004 (f)
Economic growth (%)	5.4	9.9	−2.0	2.2	0.8	4.9
Inflation (%)	0	1.4	1.0	−0.4	0.5	1.1
Public-sector balance/GDP (%)	0.5	2.0	1.6	−1.1	−1.2	0.7
Exports	115.6	138.9	122.5	128.4	142.1	152.0
Imports	104.4	127.5	109.6	109.8	121.5	134.8
Trade balance	11.2	11.4	12.9	18.5	20.6	17.2
Current account balance/GDP (%)	19.4	17.2	20.9	20.7	22.9	20.1
Foreign debt/GDP (%)	12.6	14.9	19.7	18.3	15.3	14.8
Debt service (% Exports)	0.9	0.6	0.8	0.9	0.9	0.8
Currency reserves (import months)	6.7	6.0	6.4	6.8	7.0	6.9

e = estimate, f = forecast

3

CONDITIONS OF ACCESS TO THE MARKET

■ Market overview

A fervent advocate of multilateral trade through international institutions such as the WTO and regional bodies such as ASEAN and APEC, Singapore is engaged in an ambitious programme of free-trade talks aimed at strengthening its links with the most vibrant markets. In 2003, Singapore signed free-trade agreements with the United States and Australia. Agreements with Canada, India, Mexico, South Korea, Jordan and other countries are under negotiation. The failure of the Cancun conference has led Singapore to speed up the negotiation of bilateral and regional free-trade agreements.

■ Means of entry

The city-state's openness to the outside world is one of the keys to its economic success. Foreign trade accounted for 277 per cent of GDP in 2002. Despite the international economic downturn, Singapore continues to pursue liberal trade and investment policies, without the slightest inclination towards protectionism. Singapore's trade policy is characterized by the absence of all but a few tariff and non-tariff barriers. With a few exceptions, customs duties are zero.

■ Attitude towards foreign investors

Singapore keenly welcomes foreign investment and offers a very open and well-planned economic and political environment. The government uses foreign direct investment to develop priority sectors (electronics, chemicals, biotechnology). The aim is to encourage the growth of high added-value activities and turn the island into a regional hub for foreign investors looking to do business in Asia. The Economic and Development Board (EDB) is a key actor in the development and promotion of investment in Singapore. However, certain sectors (media, legal and financial services, energy generation and distribution, water supply) are only partially open to foreign investment. The government has started to open them up, but progress is slow.

■ Foreign exchange regulations

The exchange rate is the key instrument of government monetary policy. The main feature of this policy is a flexible exchange rate within an adjustable fluctuation band. The declared aim of the Monetary Authority of Singapore is to steady the Singapore dollar's nominal effective exchange rate against a basket of currencies of its main trading partners, the main component of which is the US dollar. After adjusting the fluctuation band's central rate in July 2003, the government reverted to its policy of neutrality towards exchange rate moves of the Singapore dollar.

PAYMENT INCIDENTS INDEX
(12 months moving average - base 100 : World 1995)

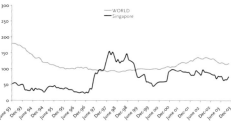

OPPORTUNITY SCOPE

Breakdown of internal demand (GDP + imports)	%
■ Private consumption	17
■ Public spending	5
■ Investment	10

Exports: 174% of GDP → ← Imports: 152% of GDP

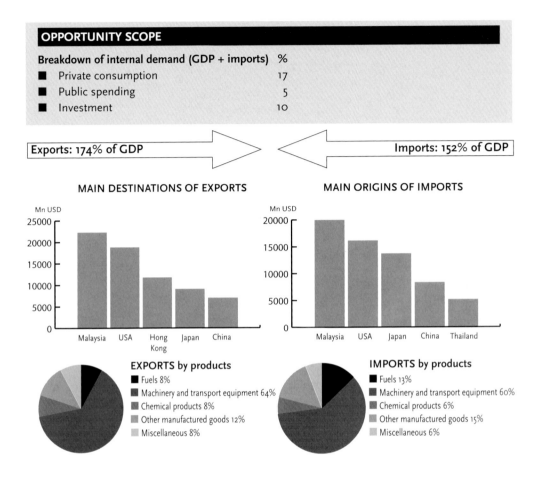

MAIN DESTINATIONS OF EXPORTS

Mn USD

Malaysia · USA · Hong Kong · Japan · China

MAIN ORIGINS OF IMPORTS

Mn USD

Malaysia · USA · Japan · China · Thailand

EXPORTS by products
- ■ Fuels 8%
- ■ Machinery and transport equipment 64%
- ■ Chemical products 8%
- ■ Other manufactured goods 12%
- ■ Miscellaneous 8%

IMPORTS by products
- ■ Fuels 13%
- ■ Machinery and transport equipment 60%
- ■ Chemical products 6%
- ■ Other manufactured goods 15%
- ■ Miscellaneous 6%

STANDARD OF LIVING / PURCHASING POWER

Indicators	Singapore	Regional average	DC average
GNP per capita (PPP dollars)	22850	9313	6778
GNP per capita (USD)	21500	5650	3568
Human Development Index	0.884	0.725	0.708
Wealthiest 10% share of national income	33	32	33
Urban population percentage	100	49	60
Percentage under 15 years old	22	29	31
number of telephones per 1000 inhabitants	471	169	157
number of computers per 1000 inhabitants	508	107	66

South Korea

Population (million inhabitants)   52.5
GDP (million USD)   476,690

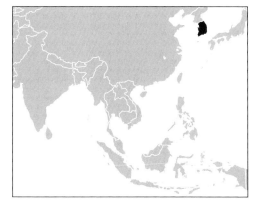

Short-term: **A2**

Medium-term:

Coface analysis   **Low risk**

3

STRENGTHS

- The country's industrial fabric is diversified and efficient.
- The quality of its education system is excellent.
- The savings rate has remained high.
- Public accounts have been in surplus.
- The external financial situation remains sound.
- The public authorities have continued to act resolutely to consolidate the financial system.

WEAKNESSES

- Very export focused, the economy has remained sensitive to exogenous shocks.
- Financial-system consolidation and good governance of certain conglomerates (chaebols) will be essential in modernizing the economy.
- Progress is still needed in restructuring and privatizing the banking sector.
- Uncertainties about North Korea's future have persisted with ultimate reunification of the two Koreas appearing ineluctable.

RISK ASSESSMENT

After the sharp slowdown in ballooning consumer credit in 2003, a domestic demand recovery is emerging, buoyed notably by accommodating fiscal policy. Exports nonetheless remain the main economic driver thanks to strengthening demand in the United States and continued growth of sales in China. In that context, companies operating on the domestic market have been more exposed than exporting companies to payment incidents.

Meanwhile, the country has continued to post public finance and external account surpluses. Furthermore, the external financial situation has been solid with a moderate external debt burden in relative terms, ample foreign currency reserves and the won in satisfactory shape. Progress is nonetheless still needed in the banking system with privatizations in process and the strategy for diversifying loans to private individuals having created problems. Still unresolved, moreover, is the question of the financial consolidation, transparency and governance of certain conglomerates along with that of measures to ease social tensions.

The centre-left President Roh, in office since February 2003, has been working to maintain the continuity of policies pursued by his predecessor Kim. However, North Korea's nuclear machinations have been hampering dialogue with that country while the conservative party, holding a parliamentary majority, has been impeding chaebol reform. Exacerbated by social problems, that situation has been seriously undermining the president's credibility, with the opposition likely to retain a majority after the April 2004 legislative elections.

MAIN ECONOMIC INDICATORS						
US$ billions	1999	2000	2001	2002	2003 (e)	2004 (f)
Economic growth (%)	10.9	9.3	3.1	6.3	2.6	5.0
Inflation (%)	0.8	2.3	4.1	2.8	3.3	2.8
Public-sector balance/GDP (%)	−2.7	1.3	1.3	3.8	0.7	1.1
Exports	145.2	175.9	151.3	162.6	192.0	222.0
Imports	116.8	159.1	137.8	148.4	174.0	206.0
Trade balance	28.4	16.9	13.5	14.2	18.0	16.0
Current account balance	24.5	12.2	8.2	6.1	7.0	5.0
Current account balance/GDP (%)	6.0	2.7	1.9	1.3	1.3	0.9
Foreign debt (% GDP)	32.9	28.4	27.7	28.1	27.3	27.2
Debt service (% Exports)	24.4	11.2	14.0	9.0	9.3	7.3
Currency reserves (import months)	5.8	5.7	6.9	7.6	7.5	7.0

e = estimate, f = forecast

CONDITIONS OF ACCESS TO THE MARKET

■ Means of entry

South Korea's import arrangements are very open. The vast majority of imports have been liberalized in recent years, particularly since OECD membership in 1996. The average rate of customs duty is 8 per cent, although tariff peaks remain in place, especially in the agricultural sector. Obstacles to trade placed in the way of foreign companies consist mainly of non-tariff barriers, such as health and technical standards.

Intellectual property remains poorly protected and there is widespread abuse despite reforms aimed at harmonizing legislation with international standards. The legal system today may appear satisfactory, but the overall application of laws leaves a lot to be desired.

Business relations with a Korean partner are not quite as difficult as they are made out to be. For ordinary business transactions, not always within the financial reach of Korean buyers, it is customary for the exporter, at least early on in a relationship, to ask for partial or total payment before shipment. For small buyers in any case the irrevocable letter of credit is recommended.

■ Attitude towards foreign investors

Since joining the OECD in 1996, South Korea has adopted a particularly dynamic FDI promotion strategy and opened up almost all sectors to foreign investment. The few restrictions that remain are often also found in the legislation of other OECD countries (utilities, defence, agriculture). Foreign direct investment inflows increased eightfold to US$15.7 billion between 1995 and 2000, but seem to have dried up since. President Roh Moo-hyun's government, which came to power in February 2003, has responded by introducing a series of measures designed to enhance South Korea's attractiveness to foreign investors and ultimately to turn the country into the hub of North-east Asia.

■ Foreign exchange regulations

The parity of the won is determined by the currency market and since January 2001 – the date of abolition of exchange controls introduced in the wake of the 1997 financial crisis – the currency has been fully convertible and freely transferable. Korean residents, however, are required to declare capital exports.

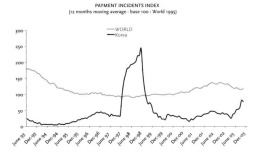

PAYMENT INCIDENTS INDEX
(12 months moving average - base 100 : World 1995)

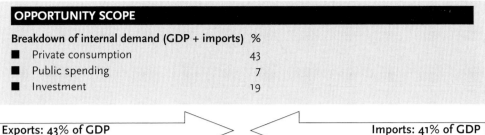

OPPORTUNITY SCOPE

Breakdown of internal demand (GDP + imports) %	
■ Private consumption	43
■ Public spending	7
■ Investment	19

Exports: 43% of GDP → ← Imports: 41% of GDP

3

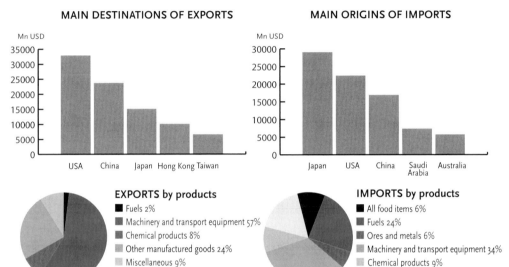

MAIN DESTINATIONS OF EXPORTS

Mn USD

USA China Japan Hong Kong Taiwan

MAIN ORIGINS OF IMPORTS

Mn USD

Japan USA China Saudi Arabia Australia

EXPORTS by products
- ■ Fuels 2%
- ■ Machinery and transport equipment 57%
- ■ Chemical products 8%
- ■ Other manufactured goods 24%
- ■ Miscellaneous 9%

IMPORTS by products
- ■ All food items 6%
- ■ Fuels 24%
- ■ Ores and metals 6%
- ■ Machinery and transport equipment 34%
- ■ Chemical products 9%
- ■ Other manufactured goods 17%
- ■ Miscellaneous 4%

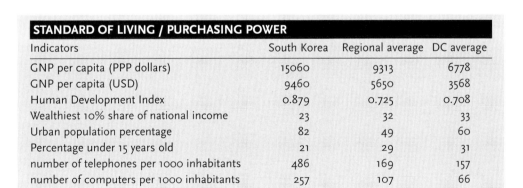

STANDARD OF LIVING / PURCHASING POWER

Indicators	South Korea	Regional average	DC average
GNP per capita (PPP dollars)	15060	9313	6778
GNP per capita (USD)	9460	5650	3568
Human Development Index	0.879	0.725	0.708
Wealthiest 10% share of national income	23	32	33
Urban population percentage	82	49	60
Percentage under 15 years old	21	29	31
number of telephones per 1000 inhabitants	486	169	157
number of computers per 1000 inhabitants	257	107	66

Sri Lanka

Population (million inhabitants)	18.7
GDP (million USD)	15,911

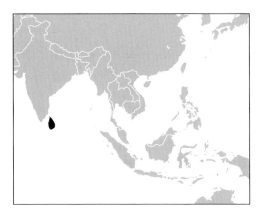

Short-term: **B**

Coface analysis

Medium-term:
Moderately high risk

STRENGTHS

- The country has emerged from 20 years of civil war between the Tamil Tigers and Singhalese authorities, which left 60,000 dead.
- In the areas of health and education, Sri Lanka has been posting indicators far above the average for South Asia.
- The economy's diversification has been progressing with the manufacturing and services sectors making an increasingly important contribution to growth.
- The country's tourist potential is high.

WEAKNESSES

- The economy has remained very dependent on weather conditions with agriculture representing 19 per cent of GDP and hydroelectricity contributing 70 per cent of energy.
- The country's international specialization centred on the textile sector is subject to fierce competition from China and India.
- Deterioration of public accounts has tended to inflate the public-sector debt burden, whose high proportion of securities constitutes a source of vulnerability.

RISK ASSESSMENT

In November 2003, President Kumaratunga announced the suspension of parliament and dismissal of three ministers. The improvement in the political climate observed since the cease-fire between the Tamil rebels and the government – in force since February 2002 – could thus come to an end with possible effects on the peace negotiations between the authorities and Tamil representatives. That announcement was an outgrowth of the rivalry between the president – opposed to the idea of an autonomous Tamil entity situated in the country's north-east region – and a prime minister much involved in the peace talks. It also reflects the divisions within the population on the question of concession-making to the Tamils.

Although the improved political climate has permitted a return to growth buoyed by a domestic demand recovery, this upturn may not last considering the recent tensions. The fiscal deficit has remained high spurring a very burdensome level of public-sector debt (104 per cent of GDP). An adjustment of spending (especially military) and disciplined policies under IMF auspices will be essential in making the public-sector debt sustainable. The current account deficit has been increasing due to a loss of price competitiveness. Conversely, external debt – almost entirely concessional – has not been a source of concern.

MAIN ECONOMIC INDICATORS

US$ billions	1999	2000	2001	2002	2003 (e)	2004 (f)
Economic growth (%)	4.3	6	−1.4	3.3	5	4.5
Inflation (%)	4.7	6.2	14.2	9.6	8.9	8.9
Public-sector balance/GDP (%)	−7.5	−9.9	−10.9	−8.9	−7.5	−7.5
Exports	4.6	5.5	4.8	4.6	5.1	5.7
Imports	6.0	7.3	6.0	6.0	6.9	7.6
Trade balance	−1.4	−1.8	−1.2	−1.4	−1.8	−1.9
Current account balance/GDP (%)	−3.8	−6.4	−2.5	−3.3	−3.3	−2.3
Foreign debt	9.97	10.09	9.86	9.84	10.39	10.39
Debt service/Exports (%)	15.2	14.7	15.5	13.5	11.7	11.7
Currency reserves (import months)	2.2	1.3	1.9	2.6	2.8	3.1

e = estimate, f = forecast

3

CONDITIONS OF ACCESS TO THE MARKET

■ Means of entry

Sri Lanka remains one of the most open countries in South-east Asia, with 70 per cent of imports exempt from customs duties. Its system of incentives for foreign direct investment, simplified customs tariff arrangements and trade practices modelled on the US and the UK make the island a relatively free and attractive market.

The 20 per cent surcharge on imports has been temporarily renewed. From 1 May 2002, stamp duty on imports is abolished and replaced by 1 per cent across-the-board import duty calculated on the CIF value.

The gradual implementation of the various clauses of the Indo-Sri Lankan free-trade agreement concluded in 2000 has made India one of the main trading partners of its southern neighbour (number one supplier and fifth-largest customer). Sri Lanka too hopes to use the clauses of this agreement to attract foreign investors looking to take advantage of the terms offered by the country, while targeting the Indian market.

■ Attitude towards foreign investors

The Board of Investment (BOI) is responsible for promoting and monitoring investment. Sri Lanka has adopted a number of measures to attract foreign investors. These should continue to bear fruit if the peace process is consolidated. The 2002 budget abolished restrictions on foreign investment in the transport, construction, road-building, energy, water supply, banking and financial services sectors. In April 2002, the 100 per cent tax on land acquisitions by foreigners was also abolished.

The government is currently reviewing a bill aimed at opening up the labour market. Sri Lanka maintains a policy of non-discrimination between foreigners and nationals. However, preferential treatment is given to companies prepared to invest over US$5.5 million in the form of flagship status and tax exemptions.

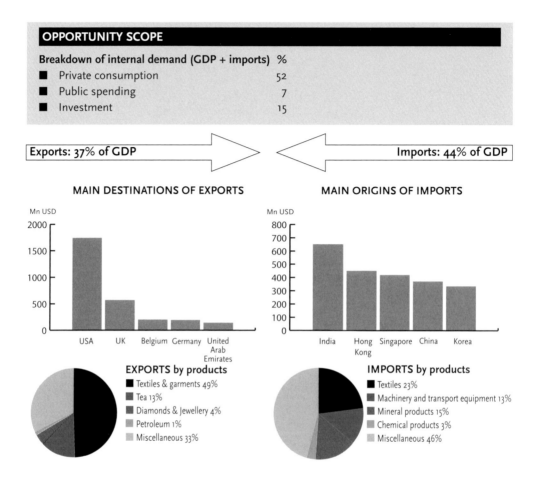

OPPORTUNITY SCOPE

Breakdown of internal demand (GDP + imports) %
- Private consumption 52
- Public spending 7
- Investment 15

Exports: 37% of GDP   Imports: 44% of GDP

MAIN DESTINATIONS OF EXPORTS   **MAIN ORIGINS OF IMPORTS**

EXPORTS by products
- Textiles & garments 49%
- Tea 13%
- Diamonds & Jewellery 4%
- Petroleum 1%
- Miscellaneous 33%

IMPORTS by products
- Textiles 23%
- Machinery and transport equipment 13%
- Mineral products 15%
- Chemical products 3%
- Miscellaneous 46%

STANDARD OF LIVING / PURCHASING POWER

Indicators	Sri Lanka	Regional average	DC average
GNP per capita (PPP dollars)	3260	9313	6778
GNP per capita (USD)	880	5650	3568
Human Development Index	0.73	0.725	0.708
Wealthiest 10% share of national income	28	32	33
Urban population percentage	23	49	60
Percentage under 15 years old	26	29	31
number of telephones per 1000 inhabitants	44	169	157
number of computers per 1000 inhabitants	9	107	66

Taiwan

Population (million inhabitants)   22.3
GDP (million USD)   281,900

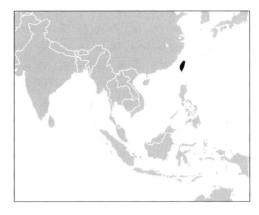

Short-term: **A1**

Medium-term:

Coface analysis   **Low risk**

3

STRENGTHS

- The economy continues to rest on solid foundations with an excellent level of education and companies positioned on growth markets like high technology.
- Taiwan has been a WTO member since 2002.
- High savings and productive-investment rates have benefited the country.
- Foreign debt has been low particularly in relation to substantial foreign exchange reserves.
- The country has consolidated its democracy.

WEAKNESSES

- Political tensions with the People's Republic of China, upon which the Taiwanese economy increasingly depends, can undermine foreign investor confidence.
- Progress on adopting and implementing structural reforms has been slow.
- The deterioration of public finances has made tax reform necessary.
- The country has remained very dependent on oil imports.

RISK ASSESSMENT

Taiwan has been benefiting from a domestic consumer spending recovery, buoyed by low interest rates, firm stock-market prices and declining unemployment, as well as the start of a pre-electoral period. Exports have also continued to fuel growth with their dynamism largely depending on an upturn in the electronics sector. Moreover, the economy has been benefiting from the dynamism of companies able to adapt rapidly to changing regional and world conditions. By preserving their technological lead and delocalizing their production to China, those companies have been able to develop their turnover, generate profits and consolidate their solvency.

The island's two main weaknesses derive from shaky public finances in need of tax reform and a banking sector hampered by too many institutions. Taiwan has nonetheless remained sheltered from financial turbulence thanks to its very substantial currency reserves exceeding its foreign debt by a wide margin.

Politically, although the presidential election scheduled for March 2004 may dominate Taiwan's near future, its relations with mainland China will remain the main source of uncertainty. However, the island's growing economic ties with the continent have reduced risks of conflict. Moreover, the backing of the United States and the pragmatism of the People's Republic of China's new leadership will be conducive to maintaining the status quo.

MAIN ECONOMIC INDICATORS						
US$ billions	1999	2000	2001	2002	2003 (e)	2004 (f)
Economic growth (%)	5.4	5.9	-2.2	3.5	3.2	4.3
Inflation (%)	0.2	1.3	0.0	-0.2	-0.2	0.5
Public-sector balance/GDP (%)	-5.9	-4.5	-6.6	-4.9	-4.7	-4.6
Exports	121.1	147.6	122.1	129.9	137.7	145.1
Imports	106.1	133.6	101.9	105.1	115.2	126.4
Trade balance	15.0	14.0	20.2	24.8	22.5	18.7
Current account balance	8.4	9.0	17.9	25.7	23.7	20.3
Current account balance/GDP (%)	2.9	2.9	6.4	9.1	8.4	6.7
Foreign debt/GDP (%)	9.4	11.8	12.6	16.0	18.3	18.2
Debt service/Exports (%)	2.0	2.0	2.6	1.8	2.3	2.4
Currency reserves (import months)	9.5	7.5	10.8	13.7	14.5	14.3

e = estimate, f = forecast

CONDITIONS OF ACCESS TO THE MARKET

■ Market overview

There are no major restrictions on imports of goods and services into Taiwan. For the last 10 years, the Taiwanese government has focused on opening up the country's market and harmonizing its regulations with international standards in order to pave the way for WTO accession. Its membership of the organization on 1 January 2002 provides foreign companies with an added incentive to invest in the country. Under the terms of accession, customs duties, low by comparison with other countries in the region, will be slashed and tariff barriers dismantled even further. The average nominal tariff was cut from 8.25 per cent prior to accession to 7.2 per cent on 1 January 2002, and will be lowered to 5.5 per cent by 2005. Tariff reductions for almost 4,500 imported products will be spread over a 10-year period from 2002 to 2011. The first series of cuts took effect from 1 January 2002. The biggest reductions concern agricultural products. In 2002, their average tariff was cut from 20.02 per cent to 14.01 per cent. By 2005, it will be lowered to 12.9 per cent. The obstacles identified by French firms concern the tightly regulated nature of certain sectors (agri-foodstuffs, pharmaceuticals) and the sort of business practices prevalent in sectors little orientated towards export (construction, environment, utilities). Numerous business persons point to the shortcomings of the legal environment, especially in matters of public procurement and intellectual property.

The letter of credit generally valid for 180 days is the most widely used means of payment in Taiwan. To a lesser degree, open accounts are also used for settlements between companies. Instruments other than the letter of credit should be used with caution because of the difficulties in enforcing court judgments against defaulters. Taiwan is not a member of major international organizations or a signatory to international treaties and so applies the principle of bilateral reciprocity, especially in matters of enforcement.

■ Attitude towards foreign investors

Foreign companies encounter few administrative obstacles to establishment. Most companies are involved in marketing and so look to open a sales office or branch in the country. Those involved in a heavier activity such as manufacturing set up subsidiaries in the form of capital companies having their own legal personality and commercial capacity. Taiwan's

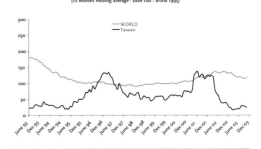

PAYMENT INCIDENTS INDEX
(12 months moving average - base 100 : World 1995)

ordinary company law contains discriminatory provisions against foreign-held subsidiaries, which can be waived by obtaining foreign investment approval.

Foreign exchange regulations

In theory, the Taiwanese currency (new Taiwanese dollar) has a floating exchange rate. In practice, however, the central bank intervenes very actively on the currency market to control the currency's value. Investors should note that Taiwan's foreign exchange regulations are fairly strict, but the foreign investment approval requirement has recently been relaxed.

3

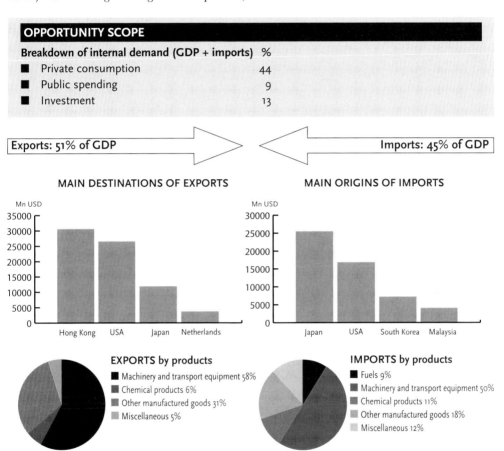

OPPORTUNITY SCOPE

Breakdown of internal demand (GDP + imports)	%
■ Private consumption	44
■ Public spending	9
■ Investment	13

Exports: 51% of GDP   Imports: 45% of GDP

MAIN DESTINATIONS OF EXPORTS

Mn USD (Hong Kong, USA, Japan, Netherlands)

MAIN ORIGINS OF IMPORTS

Mn USD (Japan, USA, South Korea, Malaysia)

EXPORTS by products
- Machinery and transport equipment 58%
- Chemical products 6%
- Other manufactured goods 31%
- Miscellaneous 5%

IMPORTS by products
- Fuels 9%
- Machinery and transport equipment 50%
- Chemical products 11%
- Other manufactured goods 18%
- Miscellaneous 12%

STANDARD OF LIVING / PURCHASING POWER

Indicators	Taiwan	Regional average	DC average
GNP per capita (PPP dollars)	22604	9313	6778
GNP per capita (USD)	12586	5650	3568
Human Development Index	n/a	0.725	0.708
Wealthiest 10% share of national income	n/a	32	33
Urban population percentage	n/a	49	60
Percentage under 15 years old	n/a	29	31
number of telephones per 1000 inhabitants	n/a	169	157
number of computers per 1000 inhabitants	n/a	107	66

Thailand

Population (million inhabitants)	63
GDP (million USD)	125,601

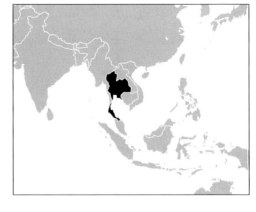

Coface analysis

Short-term: **A3**

Medium-term:
Quite low risk

STRENGTHS

- The economy has become diversified thanks to the performance of agriculture (notably rice and fish farming), tourism and some industrial sectors (automobile, electronics).
- The savings rate has been high and external accounts in surplus.
- A regional strategic crossroads, Thailand has continued to attract foreign investors.
- The country has benefited from ethnic and religious cohesiveness and a stable political system.

WEAKNESSES

- Industrial and financial sector restructuring is still incomplete.
- Resistance to implementing structural reforms and opening the economy to foreign capital has persisted.
- The economy has continued to face competitiveness problems and a need for production to move up the value chain.
- Progress is still needed in the areas of education, health and rural development.
- The country has remained dependent on its main trading partners, the United States and Japan.

RISK ASSESSMENT

The largely outward-looking Thai economy has benefited from the world economic upturn. However, domestic demand buoyed by accommodating fiscal and monetary policies has remained the main growth engine. That favourable context has been benefiting companies whose solvency has been improving as evidenced by a low Coface payment-incident index. Nonetheless, they are still facing the problem of maintaining their competitiveness and shifting to higher-value activities notably to meet Chinese competition. Restructuring will thus have to continue. Moreover, a major effort on education and professional training will be necessary.

The improvement achieved in the fiscal situation has been somewhat artificial with expenses transferred to public financial institutions. Meanwhile, public-sector debt has continued to rise even if abundant domestic savings have been covering the necessary financing. The country has kept its external accounts in surplus and has continued to reduce foreign debt, notably via early repayment of IMF loans in 2003. Short-term debt has been declining amid ample foreign exchange reserves. The consolidation programme under way in the banking sector has nonetheless remained insufficient due to the persistently high bad-debt level.

Although Thaksin Shiwanatra's government has been slow to implement privatizations and some reforms, he has continued to enjoy popular backing and seems sure to win the legislative elections scheduled in January 2005.

MAIN ECONOMIC INDICATORS

US$ billions	1999	2000	2001	2002	2003 (e)	2004 (f)
Economic growth (%)	4.4	4.6	1.9	5.3	5.8	6.0
Inflation (%)	0.3	1.6	1.7	0.6	1.9	2.3
Public-sector balance/GDP (%)	-6.0	-4.1	-2.0	-3.0	-0.5	-0.4
Exports	56.8	67.9	63.2	66.9	75.8	82.7
Imports	42.8	56.2	54.6	57.1	63.6	72.8
Trade balance	14.0	11.7	8.6	9.8	12.2	9.9
Current account balance	12.5	9.3	6.2	7.6	8.8	6.5
Current account balance/GDP (%)	10.2	7.6	5.4	6.1	6.3	4.0
Foreign debt/GDP (%)	77.7	65.1	58.5	48.4	37.6	30.3
Debt service/Exports (%)	19.6	12.9	19.3	17.4	10.4	8.8
Currency reserves (import months)	6.5	5.0	5.2	5.8	5.6	5.1

e = estimate, f = forecast

3

CONDITIONS OF ACCESS TO THE MARKET

■ Market overview
Spurred by its remarkable economic performance since 2002, Thailand aims to be the leading economic power in South-east Asia. This situation clearly opens up interesting prospects for consumer demand and investment, underpinned by the rapid emergence of an urban middle class.

■ Means of entry
In accordance with its WTO commitments, Thailand is gradually reducing import quotas and steadily replacing them with customs duties and tariff quotas, which for consumer goods remain on the high side. However, the government plans to cut customs duties on many semi-finished and capital goods. Thailand's active involvement in the construction of the South-east Asian Free Trade Area (AFTA) has resulted in customs duties being slashed for goods traded with its ASEAN partners.

■ Attitude towards foreign investors
The government's legal reform programme continues apace. The reforms aim to improve the business environment in the country. Although government rhetoric vacillates between protectionism and liberalization, Thailand's multiple strengths continue to attract investors. The Board of Investment, a government investment promotion agency, is responsible for facilitating foreign start-ups and awarding incentives (total or partial exemption from corporation tax and import duties for inputs) based on sector of activity and place of establishment.

■ Foreign exchange regulations
From the onset of the Asian crisis on 2 July 1997, the baht has been floating against the dollar. Keen to maintain the stability of the local currency as well as its foreign currency reserves, the central bank only intervenes on an ad hoc basis to cushion sharp fluctuations and limit off-shore transactions of the baht. While Thai legislation does not restrict foreign currency transactions relating to the trade of goods and services, it has recently been tightened to stop purely speculative activity.

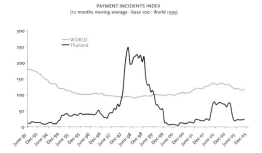

PAYMENT INCIDENTS INDEX
(12 months moving average - base 100 : World 1995)

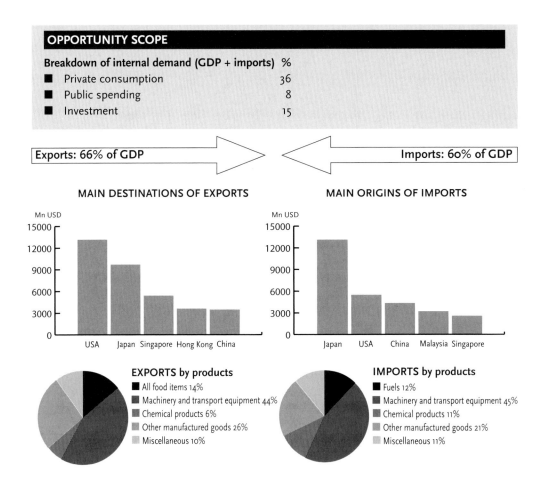

OPPORTUNITY SCOPE

Breakdown of internal demand (GDP + imports) %
■ Private consumption   36
■ Public spending   8
■ Investment   15

Exports: 66% of GDP   Imports: 60% of GDP

MAIN DESTINATIONS OF EXPORTS

Mn USD

15000 / 12000 / 9000 / 6000 / 3000 / 0

USA   Japan   Singapore   Hong Kong   China

MAIN ORIGINS OF IMPORTS

Mn USD

15000 / 12000 / 9000 / 6000 / 3000 / 0

Japan   USA   China   Malaysia   Singapore

EXPORTS by products
■ All food items 14%
■ Machinery and transport equipment 44%
■ Chemical products 6%
■ Other manufactured goods 26%
■ Miscellaneous 10%

IMPORTS by products
■ Fuels 12%
■ Machinery and transport equipment 45%
■ Chemical products 11%
■ Other manufactured goods 21%
■ Miscellaneous 11%

STANDARD OF LIVING / PURCHASING POWER

Indicators	Thailand	Regional average	DC average
GNP per capita (PPP dollars)	6230	9313	6778
GNP per capita (USD)	1940	5650	3568
Human Development Index	0.768	0.725	0.708
Wealthiest 10% share of national income	34	32	33
Urban population percentage	20	49	60
Percentage under 15 years old	24	29	31
number of telephones per 1000 inhabitants	99	169	157
number of computers per 1000 inhabitants	28	107	66

Vietnam

Population (million inhabitants)	80.1
GDP (million USD)	35,344

Short-term: **B**

Medium-term:

Coface analysis **Moderately high risk**

3

STRENGTHS

- The will to reform economic structures has gained momentum since the Communist Party's leadership changeover in 2001.
- The growing private sector is proving dynamic.
- With Vietnam's ASEAN membership furthering its integration in a dynamic region, WTO membership has become the country's new objective.
- It has normalized relations with the United States since the lifting of the embargo in 1994 and conclusion of a trade agreement with that country, effective since the end of 2001.
- The quality and low cost of its workforce have permitted multinational companies to be attracted.

WEAKNESSES

- Most state-owned enterprises and banks have remained in poor financial shape with attempts to reform them meeting with resistance.
- Public sector restructuring has been causing government debt to increase.
- Foreign exchange reserve levels have been insufficient.
- The administrative and legal environment has remained ill suited to meet foreign-investor needs despite improved legislation.
- Social inequalities have been worsening, notably between urban and rural regions.
- In per capita income terms, the country ranks among Asia's poorest.

RISK ASSESSMENT

Vietnam should continue to enjoy strong growth. Dynamic domestic demand, stimulated by accommodating fiscal policy, as well as a dynamic private sector and the generally positive effects of the trade agreement with the United States will be conducive to continuation of that expansion. Acceleration of the transition process will nonetheless depend on a profound change of mentalities and major overhaul of the business environment. Moreover, contract and bankruptcy law has remained virtually non-existent with the banking sector strained by its bad-debt burden. The process of opening the economy nonetheless appears irreversible with the country's trade liberalization and prospective WTO membership.

Intensifying reform efforts will be essential to accelerate the private sector's rapid expansion and continue to attract foreign investors. The authorities have been pursuing an ambitious economic reform programme since 2001 after the Communist Party leadership changes and implementation of IMF backing. The cost of consolidating the public industrial and banking sector will nonetheless be high and cause a sharp increase in public-sector debt, financed easily, however, by abundant domestic savings and recourse to international financial institutions. Meanwhile, modernization of

MAIN ECONOMIC INDICATORS						
US$ billions	1999	2000	2001	2002	2003 (e)	2004 (f)
Economic growth (%)	4.8	6.8	6.8	6.9	7.0	7.1
Inflation (%)	4.1	−1.7	−0.4	3.8	3.0	4.5
Public-sector balance/GDP (%)	−2.8	−2.8	−2.9	−1.9	−2.3	−2.8
Exports	11.5	14.4	15.0	16.7	19.9	22.0
Imports	10.6	14.1	14.4	17.6	21.9	24.2
Trade balance	1.0	0.4	0.6	−0.9	−2.0	−2.2
Current account balance	1.2	1.1	0.8	−0.4	−1.3	−1.3
Current account balance/GDP (%)	4.1	3.5	2.5	−1.1	−3.4	−3.1
Foreign debt/GDP (%)	40.7	39.7	36.9	38.9	38.3	39.7
Debt service/Exports (%)	11.9	9.7	9.6	9.0	7.6	6.7
Currency reserves (import months)	2.8	2.3	2.4	2.1	2.2	2.2

e = estimate, f = forecast

the economy has been increasing capital goods imports and causing deterioration of the external accounts, nonetheless without posing financing problems. However, the low level of currency reserves could prove an inadequate safety net should external-account deficits widen further.

CONDITIONS OF ACCESS TO THE MARKET

■ Means of entry

There is no doubt that Vietnam has been striving for several years to liberalize its trade. The first step was membership of AFTA in 1995 as part of the country's regional commitments to ASEAN. In December 2001, Vietnam committed itself to a broader programme of liberalization under a bilateral trade agreement with the United States. These two agreements, along with the cooperation agreement with the European Union, should pave the way for Vietnam's WTO accession, which the government has scheduled for 2005 despite the failure of the Cancun ministerial conference.

Vietnam's membership of AFTA creates the framework for tariff reductions. From July 2003, most ASEAN products are liable to less than 20 per cent customs duty (with the notable exception of agri-foodstuffs and cars). The rate of duty will have been cut to below 5 per cent by the end of 2005.

The 'minimum price scheme' though remains in place as an import control measure. This considerably undermines the transparency of customs procedures. As a candidate for WTO membership, Vietnam will need to address this question more vigorously.

■ Attitude towards foreign investors

The legal environment is in a state of flux. The country's basic law lays down very investment-friendly principles. The constitution, amended in 1992, encourages private investment and perceives free enterprise as private ownership of the means of production, with the exception of land and mineral resources. Moreover, the country's foreign investment law, amended on several occasions, most importantly in 2000, is one of the most liberal in the region.

The government, however, exercises de facto control over investment via the prior approval requirement for all foreign investment projects. While the legal framework is attractive and relatively liberal, it is incomplete, unstable and ambiguous. Investments via joint ventures are often difficult to manage if the Vietnamese partner proves to be uncooperative. In matters of litigation and jurisdiction, trial procedures and inadequate enforcement of court decisions remain a problem. National arbitration is limited and there is little or no recourse to international arbitration. Yet, licensed foreign investment during the first nine months of 2003 rose by 36.6 per cent to US$1,194.3 million, compared to the same period in 2002. Ongoing investment projects increased funding by US$523 million. In all, Vietnam has attracted an estimated US$1.7 billion in foreign capital since the beginning of the year.

■ **Foreign exchange regulations**

Foreign-held companies may acquire foreign exchange from commercial banks in connection with their business. There are no cash guarantees, but the law provides for government guarantees in respect of 'very important' projects. Foreign-held companies may now open a foreign account. In the past, central bank approval was required to hold such accounts, which had to be used for foreign loan repayments. Changes in currency legislation have abolished the provision requiring companies to convert a proportion of their income earned in foreign exchange into the local currency.

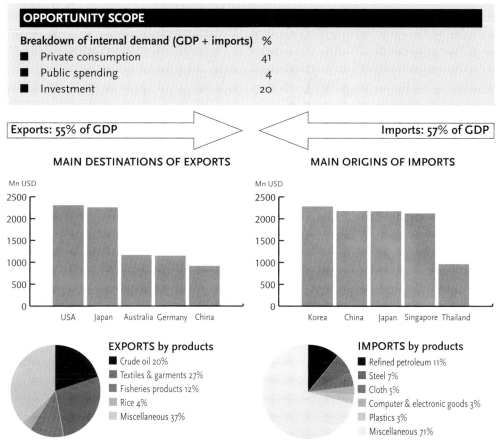

OPPORTUNITY SCOPE

Breakdown of internal demand (GDP + imports)	%
■ Private consumption	41
■ Public spending	4
■ Investment	20

3

Exports: 55% of GDP → ← Imports: 57% of GDP

MAIN DESTINATIONS OF EXPORTS

Mn USD

USA | Japan | Australia | Germany | China

MAIN ORIGINS OF IMPORTS

Mn USD

Korea | China | Japan | Singapore | Thailand

EXPORTS by products
■ Crude oil 20%
■ Textiles & garments 27%
■ Fisheries products 12%
■ Rice 4%
■ Miscellaneous 37%

IMPORTS by products
■ Refined petroleum 11%
■ Steel 7%
■ Cloth 5%
■ Computer & electronic goods 3%
■ Plastics 3%
■ Miscellaneous 71%

STANDARD OF LIVING / PURCHASING POWER

Indicators	Vietnam	Regional average	DC average
GNP per capita (PPP dollars)	2070	9313	6778
GNP per capita (USD)	410	5650	3568
Human Development Index	0.688	0.725	0.708
Wealthiest 10% share of national income	30	32	33
Urban population percentage	25	49	60
Percentage under 15 years old	32	29	31
number of telephones per 1000 inhabitants	38	169	157
number of computers per 1000 inhabitants	12	107	66

The Middle East and North Africa

4

Prospects for the Middle East and North Africa Region

Experts from Oxford Analytica, Oxford

The oil price remains a key economic variable for the Middle East, but prospects for oil markets and prices have rarely been so uncertain as they are for 2004. In Iran, Majlis elections will dominate the domestic political scene in 2004. The economy performed well in 2003 and will continue to do so in 2004 if oil prices remain firm.

OIL MARKET OUTLOOK

In 2003, an unusual set of circumstances was generated in oil markets. Prices were relatively strong throughout the year; at the end of October, the OPEC reference basket averaged US$27.91 per barrel for the year compared to US$24.60 per barrel in 2002. However, OPEC discipline was relatively poor, with most producers (except Saudi Arabia) producing close to capacity. Up to late 2003, OPEC had increased its production by some 1.4 million barrels per day. Cuts of 900,000 barrels per day agreed in September and due on 1 November appeared to have been virtually ignored.

■ 2004 framework

Demand looks set to continue strengthening as the US recovery gathers strength and Asia continues to grow. Chinese demand looks particularly strong, especially for gasoline. Car sales in the first seven months of 2003 were twice the level of the previous year. On the other hand, if the Chinese economy is indeed overheating, the authorities might use oil access as a means of macroeconomic tightening, thus tempering demand expectations. Moreover, Japanese nuclear capacity is back online and US

natural gas markets are rebalancing, with lower prices reducing substitution into oil. In late 2003, the IEA estimated oil demand in 2004 at 1.1 million barrels per day.

Encouraged by continuing high oil prices, non-OPEC supply is expected to have a good year in 2004, with the IEA estimating production at 1.4 million barrels per day. Russia will continue to be the main source of growth, particularly as export constraints are reduced as new pipeline capacity comes on-stream. However, there are some uncertainties as relations between the government and the oil giants appear strained. Other sources of growth include the United States, Brazil, Chad and Angola. The numbers clearly suggest that the oil market will be oversupplied in the second quarter of 2004 – a seasonal period of demand weakness – to the extent of 2 to 2.5 million barrels per day. OPEC will thus be forced to cut, and may well announce the cut at its 4 December 2003 meeting. Two uncertainties hang over the market:

- **OPEC calculus.** OPEC will have a challenge in managing cuts when some members, notably Venezuela and Indonesia, are producing well below existing quotas. Some members, notably Nigeria and Iran, with parliamentary and presidential elections looming, could struggle to meet existing quotas given political uncertainties. Other members, notably Algeria and Libya, are expanding capacity and are already producing well over quota. A pro rata cut will be controversial and probably ignored.

OPEC will increasingly suffer from overcapacity arising from upstream investments by the international oil companies. Estimates suggest that, during 2004, capacity in the OPEC 10 (which excludes Iraq) will grow by 800,000 barrels per day, and by the end of 2004 excess capacity in OPEC 10 could reach 5 million barrels per day. During 2003, OPEC 10 produced at capacity and still experienced high prices. In October 2003, the IEA put OPEC 10 output at 26.1 million barrels per day, compared to a quota level of 25.4 million barrels per day, falling to 24.5 million barrels per day on 1 November 2003. A repeat performance will be difficult in 2004, and a key uncertainty will be OPEC discipline in a world where Saudi Arabia seems determined to defend a minimum price of US$25 per barrel. Such a price may encourage non-OPEC to take ever greater market share away from OPEC.

- **Iraq.** Oil exports from southern Iraq have been growing and were estimated by the Coalition Provisional Authority (CPA) to be at 1.2 million barrels per day in October 2003. Such claims should be treated with great caution, given the political sensitivity of the numbers and the CPA's desperation to show an improving situation. The problem is that the southern export terminal – the Basra Terminal (formerly Mina Al Bakr) – is reaching capacity. The CPA has not allocated a capital budget for the oil sector in 2004 and only US$1 billion in 2005 and 2006. The Bush administration has asked Congress for US$2.1 billion for the Iraqi oil sector, but almost half of this is for oil product imports.

The key to any significant expansion of exports lies in reopening the northern export pipeline through Turkey, which has been out of action since the US invasion and has been subjected to regular attacks. The deteriorating security situation means it is unlikely to open in the foreseeable future. Significantly, the CPA itself estimates an overall export level of only 1.6 million barrels per day in its 2004 budget. Even this might be optimistic if the security situation worsens. The insurgents have made it clear that they regard oil export facilities as a high-priority target.

■ Geopolitics points to tightness

The year 2004 will see OPEC overcapacity and probable indiscipline in a context of higher inventories, creating downward pressure on prices and possibly forcing OPEC to make decisions it would rather not make for fear of creating serious divisions within the organization. However, the price could well continue to receive support from geopolitics, with the situation in Iraq, Venezuela, Nigeria and Iran uncertain. The political situation in Saudi Arabia itself could pose the biggest problem both for oil supply and for policy. These factors, and the 'war on terror' itself, probably tip the balance in the direction of tightness. Prices should remain in the middle to top of the OPEC price band of US$22–28 per barrel.

THE PARTICULAR CASE OF IRAN
■ Growing economy

Thanks to high oil prices, a second year of good harvests, and some reform measures, the economy performed well in the past year in a number of sectors and should continue to do so. It is expected to grow at a slightly slower average of 5.2 per cent in the next three years, but much depends on sustained high oil prices and restraint on non-development spending.

Key reforms in tax and customs administration and foreign exchange controls are likely to continue in 2004. A new foreign investment law has considerably eased restrictions on foreign investment. Four private banks have been licensed, and more licences should be forthcoming. Two mid-sized state-owned banks should be privatized in 2004. A law permitting private insurance companies was enacted in 2003 and will be implemented in the coming year.

However, serious structural problems remain:

- Inflation remains high and is rising.
- No more than a dent has been made in the high rate of unemployment, and productive private-sector investment is still not rising rapidly

enough to absorb the huge number of annual new entrants into the job market.

- The Khatami government has failed in its attempt to subject the bonyads (parastatal bodies) to greater public accountability, and the privatization of state-owned industrial enterprises proceeds at a snail's pace.
- The government is hoping to reduce subsidies, but the issue is politically sensitive.
- A small number of well-connected bazaar merchants monopolize important sectors of the import–export trade, quashing competition and industry.

Reforms are likely to continue. However, fear of political unrest, the power of entrenched interests, an inflated civil service, continued declared and hidden subsidies, and reluctance to privatize and reduce the role of the state will continue to distort the economy and hamper growth. The economy continues to be overly dependent on oil revenues, particularly for foreign exchange earnings. Substantial foreign exchange reserves provide a cushion of sorts, but a significant drop in oil prices could still deal it a severe shock.

Oil market fundamentals point to oversupply in 2004, which would lead to lower prices if all else were equal. As in 2003, however, geopolitics looks set to lend assistance to high prices, suggesting that price will remain in the middle to top of the OPEC price band of US$22–28 per barrel. This will aid Iran, whose economy continues to be overly dependent on oil revenues, particularly for foreign exchange earnings.

NORTH AFRICA: THREATS TO THE EURO-MEDITERRANEAN PARTNERSHIP

Efforts to build multilateral cooperation in the Mediterranean remain stalled at the Naples conference, owing to the Israeli–Palestinian conflict and regional rivalries, principally between Morocco and Algeria; such efforts may not be able to provide anything more than fragile frameworks for dialogue.

Late 2003 saw a flurry of diplomatic activity in the western Mediterranean, including the sixth foreign ministers' conference of the Euro-Mediterranean Partnership (EMP), also known as the 'Barcelona Process', launched in 1995, which was held in Naples (2–3 December). The Naples conference, contrary to announced decisions, actually did no more than implement or embellish decisions already agreed at the previous EMP conference, held in Valencia in April 2002. Indeed, there was a disappointment for Euro-Mediterranean enthusiasts in that the conference failed to reach agreement on where the new foundation would be based, neither Alexandria, Rome nor Valetta attracting a consensus. The decision on its location was left to the Euro-Med Committee of senior officials. Meanwhile, Israeli opposition prevented a mention of the Geneva Accords in the 'conclusions' issued at the end of the event.

The lack of progress is likely to feed growing perceptions that the EMP is moribund. With Malta and Cyprus joining the EU next year, Turkey aspiring to membership before long and Morocco focusing more on using the new EU Neighbourhood Policy as a framework within which to realize its aspirations, the EMP is in decline. Even in the event of an Israeli–Palestinian breakthrough, it seems unlikely to survive in its current format. Within some Mediterranean countries there is increased advocacy of an alternative Euro-Arab partnership (extending to Gulf states) and/or of enhanced western Mediterranean cooperation through the 5 + 5 grouping.

The Range of Country @ratings in the Middle East and North Africa

Sylvia Greisman and Catherine Monteil

Coface Country Risk and Economic Studies Department, Paris

COUNTRY @RATING SCALE

PAYMENT INCIDENTS INDEX
(12 month moving average - World 1995 = 100)

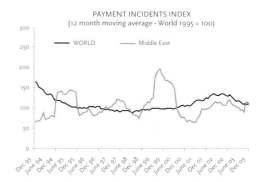

A regional country risk @rating represents an average of country @ratings weighted according to their contribution to the region's production.

A Country @rating measures the average level of short-term non-payment risk associated with companies in a particular country. It reflects the extent to which a country's economic, financial and political outlook influences financial commitments of local companies. It is thus complementary to @rating Credit Opinions on companies.

The quality of country risk in the Middle East and North Africa has been improving only moderately. Having benefited from financial market confidence and sustained economic growth, Turkey is the only country to have been upgraded to category B in 2003. Despite this upgrade, the quality of country risk in the region remains below its December 2000 level and the emerging-country average. The business climate has thus not been very conducive to improvement in company payment behaviour. Although high barrel prices have been benefiting the oil sector, other economic sectors have been registering only weak growth amid regional political instability. Any limitation on production instituted to bolster oil prices in 2004 would have little chance of improving the region's economic outlook.

In the Middle East, political instability has continued to affect most countries in the region. It has remained the main risk factor for economic activity, tourism and investment, delaying furthermore implementation of structural reform programmes. A worst-case scenario, which cannot yet be entirely excluded, would entail the Iraq situation degenerating into civil war and thus opening the door to demands for independence along ethnic or religious lines, which would in turn create risks of regional conflict. Moreover, al-Qaeda's destabilizing influence should not be underestimated. Although resolution of the Israeli–Palestinian conflict could contribute to easing regional tensions, there has been little cause for optimism on that score.

269

Economically, the main oil-exporting countries, all OPEC members, will probably reduce their production to bolster prices with non-cartel member countries increasing production. They should thus experience slower growth and some deterioration of their external and fiscal balances after the exceptionally favourable situation they enjoyed in 2003. Outside the oil sector and exporting countries, economic recovery will remain dependent on an easing of political tensions, which alone can reassure investors and permit a real tourism upturn.

■ Countries rated A2

Default likelihood has remained low on average even though the country's economic and political environment or local company payment behaviour is slightly less good than in countries rated A1.

The **United Arab Emirates'** economy is the most diversified among regional countries. Non-oil sector dynamism and public spending should thus permit partly offsetting a reduction of oil production in accordance with OPEC recommendations. Although the public-sector deficit is of course structurally high and its revenues vulnerable to oil market fluctuations, the country's financial situation has been giving no cause for concern. Despite the

COFACE MAP OF COUNTRY @RATINGS

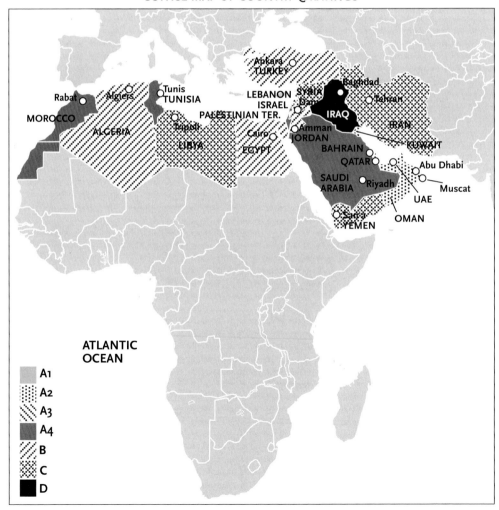

expected decline of barrel prices and export volumes, external accounts should remain largely in surplus. Furthermore, the external debt burden has remained modest in relation to the country's foreign currency earnings and reserves and its substantial holdings abroad.

Qatar's investment strategy has been successful with the emirate now on a sounder financial foundation as it undertakes a second phase of development of its gas reserves and downstream industry segments. Continuing to enjoy a bright development outlook, Qatar should remain sheltered from turmoil due notably to the US military presence. Rising living standards in

conjunction with the government's options – it has instituted a process of economic liberalization and democratization – will foster political stability and an investment-friendly environment.

■ Countries rated A3

Company payment behaviour is poorer than in the two higher categories and could be affected by a change in the country's economic and political environment, although the likelihood of that leading to widespread payment defaults remains relatively low.

Bahrain has been benefiting from economic activity underpinned by public spending including

COFACE MAP OF MEDIUM- AND LONG-TERM COUNTRY RISK

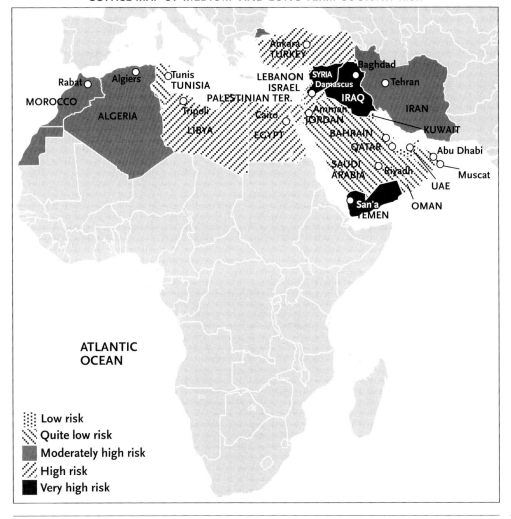

ATLANTIC
OCEAN

Low risk
Quite low risk
Moderately high risk
High risk
Very high risk

4

both productive investments in large industrial projects and social spending intended to contain tensions within the Shiite population. Nonetheless, the expected oil-price decline should worsen fiscal and external deficits. With the external debt burden still representing a moderate constraint at this stage, the financial situation should not constitute a source of difficulty. Although the economic liberalization policy and structural reforms intended to attract foreign investors constitute a step in the right direction, the social component and resistance from conservative quarters have nonetheless been impeding progress. Moreover, regional instability could affect the economy and social climate. Those weaknesses prompted the downgrading of the country's rating in 2003.

■ Countries rated A4

Countries rated A4 often exhibit fairly mediocre payment behaviour that could be affected by an economic downturn, although the probability of that causing a large number of payment defaults remains moderate.

Oil market trends in 2003 benefited **Saudi Arabia** permitting it substantially to increase its production while oil prices were high. That exceptional situation spurred economic activity, permitted the reduction of public-sector debt and bolstered the country's financial situation. However, the relative sluggishness of other economic sectors has progressively undermined company solvency and increased late-payment frequency. Moreover, the kingdom's commitment to sustaining oil prices could prompt it to reduce production in 2004, which could result in an economic downturn, resumption of fiscal deficits and deterioration of external accounts. The external financial situation has nonetheless not been a source of concern with foreign debt low in relation to foreign currency earnings. The country remains vulnerable to an oil market downturn with a loss of market share a by-product of its price-support policy. Reforms will be necessary to attract foreign investment, diversify the economy, foster durable growth and balance public-sector accounts. The reform process has nonetheless been lagging due to resistance from conservative quarters and an

unstable social climate exacerbated by political uncertainties.

In **Israel** (with a negative-watchlisted rating), an economic slowdown linked to the international downturn in 2001 and then to aggravation of political tensions has been accompanied by rising unemployment, deterioration of living standards, a worsening public-sector deficit, and social tensions. That situation has affected company solvency, payment-incident frequency and the number of bankruptcies, which has been increasing significantly for several years. In the near term, robust economic activity in the United States and the electronics sector's improved performance could fuel recovery. It will nonetheless remain limited by the political climate, which has been deterring consumer spending, tourism and investment, and fiscal austerity policy. Further out, the country's development will essentially depend on resolution of the conflict with the Palestinians.

In **Morocco**, the farm sector's steadiness has permitted the economy to resume growing at high rates. The brighter economic conditions have nonetheless failed to cause an improvement in company payment behaviour notably in the textile and food sectors, very subject to late payments. External financing needs have remained modest, which has contributed to reducing the foreign debt burden. Furthermore, Morocco still enjoys the confidence of international capital markets and the political and financial backing of Western countries and multilateral institutions. Nonetheless, the government resulting from the 2002 elections has to contend with two major challenges. It must consolidate public-sector accounts whose deficits have been generating large public debt. It must also undertake vigorous programmes to combat poverty despite its limited room for manoeuvre. The aggravation of social tensions and their drift towards political extremism could have a negative impact on foreign investment and tourism revenues.

Tunisia's growth outlook for 2004 is bright. The country has continued to pursue its prudent policy of modernization, diversification and public-sector debt reduction. The political stability and international community backing enjoyed by Tunisia have been facilitating that policy. The main risk will concern trends on exports and tourism whose recovery has remained uncertain. However, with investment inflows increasing, debt ratios remaining reasonable and the country continuing to enjoy ready access to international capital markets, balance-of-payment crisis risks will remain limited. Company payment behaviour, notably in textiles, has deteriorated amid a credit squeeze and competition from countries with weaker currencies. However, the Coface payment-incident index's high level has been more a reflection of late payments than actual instances of insolvency.

■ Countries rated B

A precarious economic environment could affect company payment behaviour, which is often poor.

In **Algeria**, after the economy's good performance in 2003 buoyed by exceptional oil market conditions, the economic trend should be more moderate in 2004 amid the expected hydrocarbon-sector slowdown. High oil prices since 2000 have strengthened the country's financial situation, affording it the means to stimulate non-oil-sector growth through public spending. In the private sector, the application of new laws to companies and banks concerning capitalization and prudential regulations should consolidate the sector and reduce payment default risk. The economy has nonetheless remained vulnerable to exogenous shocks. Structural reforms are still necessary to foster durable growth, attract investors and reduce unemployment. Although announced by successive governments, reforms have been slow to materialize due to the political and social context.

In **Turkey**, the wave of terrorist attacks in Istanbul in November 2003 does not appear to have destabilized the climate of confidence restored thanks to renewed backing by the IMF and US authorities. Despite their great sensitivity to political risk, financial indicators have continued to improve. Interest rates have fallen sharply, which has facilitated the financing of public-sector debt. The country appears to have covered its short-term foreign exchange financing needs. Meanwhile, growth has been high, buoyed by robust consumer spending and investment with disinflation

continuing. This favourable economic context and good company payment behaviour prompted the upgrading of the country's rating late last year.

In **Egypt** (with a negative-watchlisted rating), after a slowdown lasting several years, a moderate recovery could develop in a still uncertain regional context thanks to improved export competitiveness attributable to the pound's depreciation and progressive resumption of tourism. The growth rate has nonetheless remained very insufficient to improve per capita income levels. Sluggish demand has been affecting company solvency. Furthermore, limited access to foreign currency has caused an increase in payment defaults. The accumulation of fiscal deficits attributable to the weighty government apparatus along with interest on the debt has been generating increased public-sector debt, now a source of concern. The lack of a foreign direct investment recovery coupled with more difficult access to capital markets could undermine the balance of payments. A financial crisis has nonetheless remained unlikely since international aid should not be lacking considering the country's strategic position.

■ Countries rated C

A very precarious economic and political environment could worsen payment behaviour that is already often poor.

In **Iran**, the opacity of company financial information always makes risk-taking a haphazard affair. Public spending and progressive implementation of reforms have been benefiting the non-oil sector. High oil prices since 2000 have enhanced the country's financial situation with foreign debt remaining relatively low. In the near term, the economy should grow at a more moderate pace amid the expected decline of oil revenues. External accounts could go into deficit again, which should nonetheless not pose a problem considering the country's comfortable level of foreign currency reserves. The economy is still very dependent on the oil sector, and the public sector has remained preponderant. Although continuation of the structural reform programme will be essential, progress has been lagging in a difficult political context.

4

■ Countries rated D

The economic and political environment presents a very high level of risk, which exacerbates generally deplorable payment behaviour.

After the overthrow of Saddam Hussein's regime and the lifting of United Nations sanctions, **Iraq** has remained a poor country in need of political and economic reconstruction, its immense natural resources notwithstanding. Sabotage and terrorism have been increasing the cost of reconstruction and delaying the process of restarting the government administration and economy. In coming years, oil revenues will be insufficient to cover the operating costs of the administrative apparatus, service the debt and finance reconstruction costs. Although restructuring of foreign debt and mobilization of international aid will be necessary, they will nonetheless remain subordinate to normalization of the political situation, which is precisely the main element of uncertainty. Insecurity has been exacerbating tensions among the population amid increasing political, ethnic, religious and tribal cleavages. Risks of civil war will remain substantial until the political situation is normalized.

Algeria

Population (million inhabitants)   30.8
GDP (million USD)   54,680

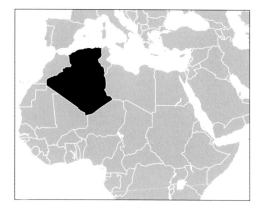

Short-term: **B**

Medium-term:
Coface analysis   **Moderately high risk**

STRENGTHS

- The country boasts substantial natural wealth (oil, gas).
- Considering the foreign interests in the hydrocarbon sector and Europe's dependence on Algerian oil and gas, the country can rely on Western country backing.
- The country has set up an oil stabilization fund to permit it to cope with oil-market trend reversals.
- The country has initiated a process of economic liberalization and diversification.

WEAKNESSES

- The economy has remained dependent on the oil and agriculture sectors, both vulnerable to external crises.
- Although in decline, foreign debt remains constraining.
- The equilibrium of public-sector accounts, undermined by inflexible expenses (wages and debt), has remained very dependent on oil revenues.
- Improvement in living standards has remained barely perceptible, with high unemployment spurring social tensions.

RISK ASSESSMENT

Oil-price steadiness since 2000 has strengthened the country's financial situation, affording it the means to pursue stimulatory economic policy via public-sector spending to create jobs and satisfy expectations on infrastructure improvement.

After good economic performance in 2003 thanks to exceptional oil market conditions, economic growth should be more moderate in 2004 amid the expected hydrocarbon-sector slowdown. Despite the anticipated oil-price decline, the external financial situation is giving little cause for concern considering the accumulated currency reserves whose total currently exceeds that of external debt.

The cost of reconstruction after the 21 May 2003 earthquake in conjunction with the prospect of declining oil revenues should increase the fiscal deficit in 2004 and probably in the two following years as well.

Further out, the economy will remain vulnerable to external crises and undermined by public company inefficiency and the banking sector's weakness. Structural reforms will be necessary to sustain economic growth durably, attract investors and reduce unemployment. Although announced by successive governments, they have been slow to materialize due to social and political tensions. Moreover, the precarious security situation has tended to deter investors.

4

MAIN ECONOMIC INDICATORS						
US$ billions	1999	2000	2001	2002	2003 (e)	2004 (f)
Economic growth (%)	3.2	2.2	2.1	4.1	5.5	4.5
Inflation (%)	2.7	0.3	4.2	1.4	4.0	3.5
Public-sector balance/GDP (%)	−2.0	9.8	3.8	0.2	0.2	−4.0
Exports	12.3	21.7	19.1	18.8	21.4	17.3
Imports	9.0	9.4	9.5	11.1	12.3	13.1
Trade balance	3.4	12.3	9.6	7.7	9.1	4.2
Current account balance/GDP (%)	0.0	16.5	12.9	8.5	10.7	4.2
Foreign debt/GDP (%)	59.5	46.9	41.7	41.1	35.1	33.2
Debt service/Exports (%)	36.9	20.5	20.8	18.6	17.4	19.5
Currency reserves (import months)	3.9	9.7	15.0	16.6	19.7	19.6

e = estimate, f = forecast

CONDITIONS OF ACCESS TO THE MARKET

■ Market overview

Algeria has made sweeping changes to its customs tariff by streamlining and slashing customs duties (three rates are now applicable: 30, 15 and 5 per cent) and abolishing the administered prices system. The new tariff, which came into force in January 2002, lowers the average weighted rate of duty to below the 9 per cent mark. Duties are levied on the transaction value in line with the most-favoured-nation principle, pending enforcement of the association agreement with the European Union concluded in April 2002. Certain branches of the country's manufacturing industry will continue to enjoy extra protection via an additional duty (24 per cent in 2004) due to be abolished by 2006. There are no longer special import restrictions, licences or quotas, except for pharmaceuticals, where imports are subject to a subsequent investment commitment in plant. More than 25 per cent of Algeria's imports come from France and close to 66 per cent from the EU.

■ Attitude towards foreign investors

Algeria does not discriminate between local and foreign investment in manufacturing and services (development, extension of capacity, privatization-related buy-ins or buy-outs) or investments made in connection with the award of concessions and/or licences (Decree No. 01-03 of 20 August 2001).

Similar tariff preferences and tax concessions are granted to locals and foreigners to encourage investment. Foreign-held subsidiaries are permitted to operate in most sectors open to private investment, including financial services. The law guarantees repatriation of all principal and earnings. A certain number of sectors (telecommunications, sea and air transport, electricity and gas supply, mining) have been opened up to private investment in the last two years.

As a rule, investment in plant is welcome. Conversely, trade and retailing do not qualify as investment sectors. Fee transfers relating to services and intangible investments (royalties, etc) continue to pose problems. Investment in the oil and gas sector is subject to specific regulations.

■ Foreign exchange regulations

The dinar is fully convertible for the import of goods and equipment and, with foreign exchange reserves in excess of US$31 billion at the end of 2003, the risk of default is limited. However, given the low capitalization of many recently established Algerian companies and the lack of transparency of balance sheets, which hampers the work of the few audit firms in the marketplace, the most widely recommended means of payment is the bill of exchange and, in its absence, the documentary bill. People doing business with Algeria should also be aware of the reputation of their customer's bank. The country's cumbersome banking procedures continue to pose problems. The dinar is convertible but exchange controls are in place for the settlement of service contracts invoiced in foreign currency for which Central Bank permission is required.

OPPORTUNITY SCOPE

Breakdown of internal demand (GDP + imports) %
- Private consumption   36
- Public spending   12
- Investment   21

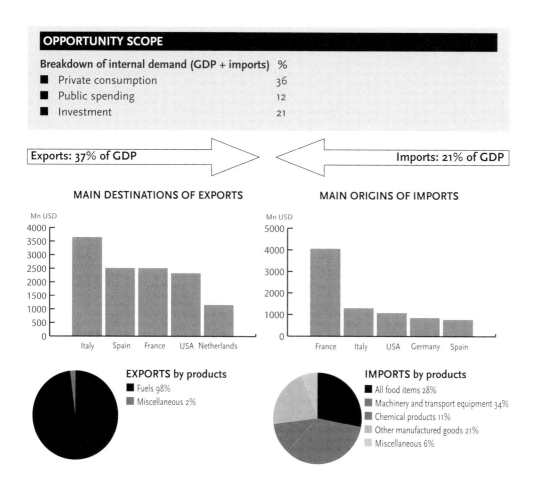

Exports: 37% of GDP   Imports: 21% of GDP

MAIN DESTINATIONS OF EXPORTS

Mn USD
(Italy, Spain, France, USA, Netherlands)

MAIN ORIGINS OF IMPORTS

Mn USD
(France, Italy, USA, Germany, Spain)

EXPORTS by products
- Fuels 98%
- Miscellaneous 2%

IMPORTS by products
- All food items 28%
- Machinery and transport equipment 34%
- Chemical products 11%
- Other manufactured goods 21%
- Miscellaneous 6%

STANDARD OF LIVING / PURCHASING POWER

Indicators	Algeria	Regional average	DC average
GNP per capita (PPP dollars)	5910	7496	6778
GNP per capita (USD)	1650	4722	3568
Human Development Index	0.704	0.740	0.708
Wealthiest 10% share of national income	27	30	33
Urban population percentage	58	70	60
Percentage under 15 years old	35	35	31
number of telephones per 1000 inhabitants	61	164	157
number of computers per 1000 inhabitants	7	56	66

4

Bahrain

Population (million inhabitants)	0.71
GDP (million USD)	8,045

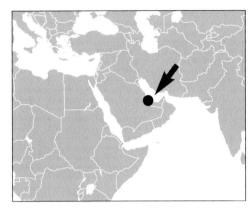

Short-term: **A3**

Coface analysis

Medium-term:
Quite low risk

STRENGTHS

- The economy boasts diversified industrial (oil/gas, aluminium) and services sectors (banks, tourism).
- It is open to foreign investment.
- Well situated geographically and open to offshore banks, Bahrain has become the region's leading financial centre.
- The archipelago has benefited from the financial backing of neighbouring countries.
- The country has been engaged in a democratization process.

WEAKNESSES

- The country has only very limited oil reserves of its own.
- Despite its diversification, the economy has remained very dependent on the oil sector.
- Foreign debt has been increasing.
- The country's Shiite majority has been a destabilizing factor in a monarchy controlled by the Sunnite minority.
- Rising unemployment among nationals has been stoking tensions.

RISK ASSESSMENT

Public spending should continue to sustain economic activity. That spending has included both productive investments in large industrial projects and spending for social purposes intended to stem tensions among the Shiite majority. The expected oil-price decline should nonetheless worsen fiscal and external deficits. With the foreign-debt burden remaining a moderate constraint at this stage, the external debt situation should not constitute a difficulty. The kingdom enjoys access to financial markets and also counts on foreign investments, which could nonetheless be further affected by regional geopolitical uncertainties.

The economy has remained vulnerable to a sudden oil-price downturn with rising foreign debt tending to increase its vulnerability. Although the economic liberalization policy and structural reforms intended to attract foreign investors have been moving the country in the right direction, the social component and resistance from the more conservative quarters have been impeding progress. Moreover, regional instability could affect economic activity and the social climate.

MAIN ECONOMIC INDICATORS

US$ billions	1999	2000	2001	2002(e)	2003 (e)	2004 (f)
Economic growth (%)	4.3	5.3	4.8	5.1	4.9	5.4
Inflation (%)	–1.3	–0.7	–1.2	0.5	–0.2	0.7
Public-sector balance/GDP (%)	–7.6	0.6	–2.2	–3.7	–2.1	–5.2
Exports	4.4	6.2	5.5	5.8	6.3	5.6
Imports	3.5	4.4	4.0	4.5	5.1	4.8
Trade balance	0.9	1.8	1.5	1.3	1.3	0.8
Current account balance/GDP (%)	–0.5	10.3	2.1	–1.6	–1.8	–9.7
Foreign debt/GDP (%)	42.3	38.1	39.9	49.4	64.9	76.6
Debt service/Exports (%)	9.5	7.4	7.0	7.1	7.0	10.5
Currency reserves (import months)	3.1	2.9	3.2	3.0	3.2	3.1

e = estimate, f = forecast

CONDITIONS OF ACCESS TO THE MARKET

■ Market overview

The Kingdom of Bahrain has a liberal trade policy designed to attract maximum direct foreign investment, diversify the economy and reduce the country's dependence on oil and gas. Bahrain is by virtue of its long trading tradition one of the most open countries in the Gulf. Since 2001, it has overtaken its GCC neighbours in matters of economic liberalization by adopting a number of measures to free up the economy, including permission for foreign companies to acquire a 100 per cent stake in a Bahraini company, adoption of anti-money-laundering regulations and harmonization of customs duties with the GCC common external tariff in 2003.

Customs duties on imports from non-GCC countries are 5 per cent for all but 53 duty-free products, and alcohol and cigarettes, which are liable to 125 per cent and 100 per cent duty respectively. Imports of goods intended for local manufacture are exempt from duty. Under the GCC free-trade agreement, any product with a 40 per cent GCC component is admitted duty-free by member countries. The Mina Salman port contains a free zone providing duty-free access to all GCC markets.

Under the law of 13 March 1998, foreign companies are no longer required to use the services of an agent. Bahrain's highly flexible regulations and attractive tax laws, administered by a well-respected body, encourage the establishment of financial institutions and banks. A single GCC currency pegged to the dollar will be introduced in 2010. A public procurement committee responsible for ensuring transparency in the award of tenders has been operational since 2002. The country has signed the trade secrets agreement and launched a large-scale energy privatization programme.

■ Attitude towards foreign investors

Bahrain offers foreign companies a highly attractive legal and tax environment, including:

● no corporation tax, income tax, fund transfer tax or VAT;
● unrestricted foreign investment in projects;
● 100 per cent ownership of local companies by foreigners in certain sectors (information and communication technologies, healthcare, tourism, training, services, manufacturing);
● easy movement of persons (simplified visa formalities, relatively free social customs for the region);
● duty-free access for goods intended for re-export and manufacturing equipment and machinery;
● acquisition of land by foreigners in delimited areas.

4

As well as these benefits, in 2001 the foreign-investment-friendly Bahrain government set up an Economic Development Board (EDB) to facilitate and speed up administrative formalities. Acting in cooperation with the Business Department and agencies attached to the Ministry of Trade and Industry, the EDB has set in place a fast-track registration system for companies.

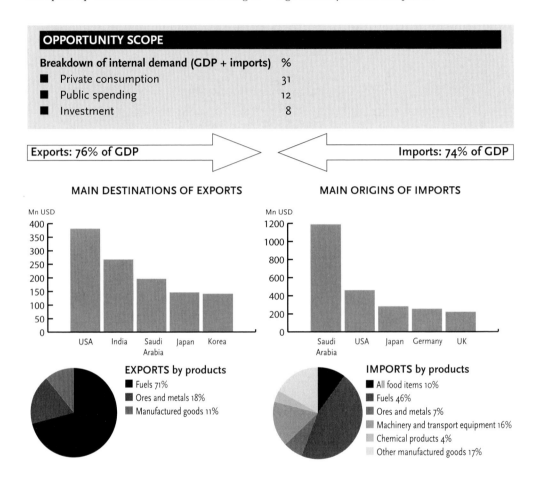

OPPORTUNITY SCOPE

Breakdown of internal demand (GDP + imports)	%
■ Private consumption	31
■ Public spending	12
■ Investment	8

Exports: 76% of GDP   Imports: 74% of GDP

MAIN DESTINATIONS OF EXPORTS

Mn USD

USA, India, Saudi Arabia, Japan, Korea

MAIN ORIGINS OF IMPORTS

Mn USD

Saudi Arabia, USA, Japan, Germany, UK

EXPORTS by products
- ■ Fuels 71%
- ■ Ores and metals 18%
- ■ Manufactured goods 11%

IMPORTS by products
- ■ All food items 10%
- ■ Fuels 46%
- ■ Ores and metals 7%
- ■ Machinery and transport equipment 16%
- ■ Chemical products 4%
- ■ Other manufactured goods 17%

STANDARD OF LIVING / PURCHASING POWER

Indicators	Bahrain	Regional average	DC average
GNP per capita (PPP dollars)	n/a	7496	6778
GNP per capita (USD)	n/a	4722	3568
Human Development Index	0.839	0.740	0.708
Wealthiest 10% share of national income	n/a	30	33
Urban population percentage	n/a	70	60
Percentage under 15 years old	n/a	35	31
number of telephones per 1000 inhabitants	n/a	164	157
number of computers per 1000 inhabitants	n/a	56	66

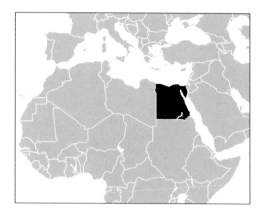

Egypt

Population (million inhabitants)	65.2
GDP (million USD)	98,476

Short-term: **B**

Medium-term:
High risk

Coface analysis

STRENGTHS

- Egypt's diversified sources of foreign currency include the Suez Canal, tourism and private remittances with the possibility of gas ultimately picking up the slack for declining oil production.
- The country has been implementing a structural reform programme since 1991 intended to foster conditions for economic growth.
- The level of foreign currency reserves is still ample with foreign debt remaining moderate.
- Considering its regional mediator role, Egypt can rely on Western country political and financial backing.

WEAKNESSES

- Regional uncertainties have undermined the tourism sector whose earnings are crucial to the country's current account balance.
- The public sector has remained predominant and progress on reforms has been slow.
- The domestic debt level constitutes a rigidity factor in an economy with substantial infrastructure needs.
- The uncertainties surrounding Egypt's currency policy have been deterring investment, and foreign exchange controls have been impeding growth.
- The investment rate has remained low in relation to the country's development needs.

RISK ASSESSMENT

After a slowdown lasting several years, a moderate recovery could develop in a still-shaky regional context thanks to greater competitiveness on exports resulting from the pound's depreciation and to progressive resumption of tourism. The growth rate has nonetheless remained very insufficient to raise per capita income. Sluggish demand has been affecting companies' solvency. Moreover, the limited access to foreign currency has sometimes caused payment incidents.

The accumulation of fiscal deficits attributable to the weight of state machinery and interest on the debt has been spurring growth of public-sector debt to worrisome levels. The absence of a foreign direct investment recovery and the more difficult access to capital markets could affect the balance of payments. A financial crisis has nonetheless remained unlikely since international aid should not be lacking considering the country's strategic position.

4

MAIN ECONOMIC INDICATORS						
US$ billions	1998/ 99	1999/ 00	2000/ 01	2001/ 02	2002/ 03 (e)	2003/ 04 (f)
Economic growth (%)	6.3	5.1	3.5	3	2	2.8
Inflation (%)	3.8	2.9	2.4	2.4	4.5	4.4
Public-sector balance/GDP (%)	−3.5	−4.4	−5.9	−6.8	−7.5	−9.7
Exports	4.4	6.4	7.1	6.6	7.0	7.2
Imports	17.0	17.9	16.4	14.6	15.1	16.4
Trade balance	−12.6	−11.5	−9.4	−8.0	−8.1	−9.2
Current account balance/GDP (%)	−3.2	−2.1	−0.8	−1.3	−2.2	−2.8
Foreign debt/GDP (%)	35.1	29.8	29.8	34.0	37.4	42.3
Debt service/Exports (%)	9.7	9.1	13.7	9.5	14.6	9.7
Currency reserves (import months)	9.1	7.1	6.9	7.7	7.5	7.4

e = estimate, f = forecast

CONDITIONS OF ACCESS TO THE MARKET

■ Market overview

Since 1994, Egypt has been engaged in slashing its customs tariffs. The maximum rate of duty rarely exceeds 40 per cent today, with the average rate standing at around 24 per cent.

Rates, however, vary greatly from product to product. Customs duties may be very high for certain foodstuffs, cars, chemicals and textiles (especially after the decision to raise duties for ready-to-wear at the end of 2001 in contradiction to Egypt's commitments to the WTO), but those levied on wines and spirits, which can be charged up to 2,000 per cent or more duty, are positively swingeing. On the other hand, sectors such as computer products enjoy extremely low duties. From May 2001, 2–3 per cent supplementary duty plus 10 per cent general sales tax applies to retailers and wholesalers, and not just to manufacturers, service providers and importers.

Often, actual rate setting is haphazard and arbitrary and the definition of product categories questionable. Moreover, the basis for calculating customs value remains arbitrary, despite the Customs Valuation Act of 25 June 2001, which aims to rationalize procedures in line with international standards.

■ Means of entry

Numerous non-tariff barriers remain in place, despite a programme to streamline customs organization financed by the EU and USAID. Government departments and agencies are required to meet their procurement requirements through local suppliers for a number of products (telephone equipment, furniture, cars, tyres, bulbs, pipes, etc), as imports are only permitted where there is no local substitute.

The merging, in 2000, of the various inspection agencies into the General Organization for Import and Export Control (G0EIS), responsible for coordinating inspection procedures for imports and exports, as well as the approval granted to international certification firms recently, should undoubtedly help to simplify procedures. Exporters and importers can also qualify for simplified inspections by applying for registration on 'white lists'.

The commitments contracted by Egypt to the WTO and the conclusion in June 2001 of an association agreement with the European Union, ratified by the Egyptian parliament in April 2003, should also open up numerous sectors in the medium term.

■ Attitude towards foreign investors

Law No. 8 of 1997 guarantees the transfer and repatriation of capital and offers investors longer-term tax incentives if their businesses are located in a new industrial town or in the high or middle Nile Valley. Plans are under way to privatize a number of sectors, including telecommunications and banking.

In furtherance of investment law No. 8/1997, the prime minister promulgated a decree (OJ No. 39a of 27 September 2001) on 24 September 2001 setting up a new interministerial committee for the settlement of investor disputes. The committee is charged with resolving disputes relating to the application of the investment Act and ensuring coordination between the various ministries and GAFI (General Authority for Investment).

A circular issued in 2001 significantly raises the equity threshold for foreign managers and partners of an Egyptian-based company applying for a work permit in Egypt.

■ Foreign exchange regulations

The Egyptian pound is officially convertible. There are no legal restrictions on the repatriation by foreign companies of income and profits, though access to the currency market has often been restricted in the recent past. The depreciation and successive devaluations of the pound (which lost 50 per cent of its value against the US dollar in the last two years) have not eroded demand for hard currency on the unofficial market against a background of economic and regional political uncertainty. The use of irrevocable and confirmed documentary letters of credit for payments is recommended and widespread in Egypt.

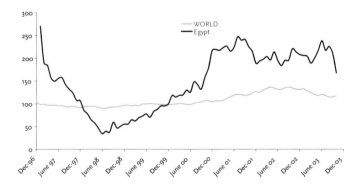

PAYMENT INCIDENTS INDEX
(12 months moving average - base 100 : World 1995)

OPPORTUNITY SCOPE

Breakdown of internal demand (GDP + imports) %
- Private consumption — 63
- Public spending — 10
- Investment — 12

Exports: 18% of GDP   Imports: 23% of GDP

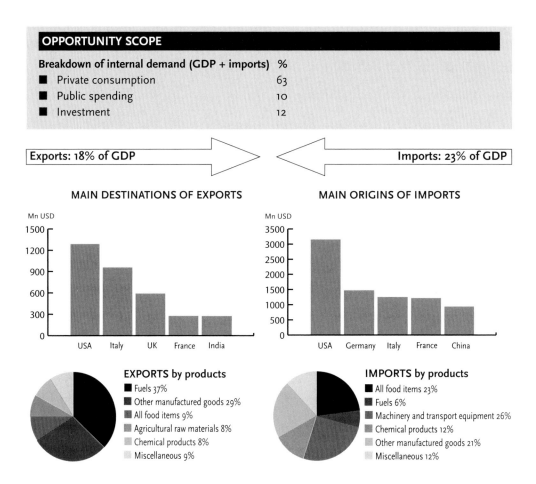

MAIN DESTINATIONS OF EXPORTS

Mn USD — USA, Italy, UK, France, India

MAIN ORIGINS OF IMPORTS

Mn USD — USA, Germany, Italy, France, China

EXPORTS by products
- Fuels 37%
- Other manufactured goods 29%
- All food items 9%
- Agricultural raw materials 8%
- Chemical products 8%
- Miscellaneous 9%

IMPORTS by products
- All food items 23%
- Fuels 6%
- Machinery and transport equipment 26%
- Chemical products 12%
- Other manufactured goods 21%
- Miscellaneous 12%

STANDARD OF LIVING / PURCHASING POWER

Indicators	Egypt	Regional average	DC average
GNP per capita (PPP dollars)	3560	7496	6778
GNP per capita (USD)	1530	4722	3568
Human Development Index	0.648	0.740	0.708
Wealthiest 10% share of national income	30	30	33
Urban population percentage	43	70	60
Percentage under 15 years old	35	35	31
number of telephones per 1000 inhabitants	104	164	157
number of computers per 1000 inhabitants	16	56	66

Iran

Population (million inhabitants)	64.5
GDP (million USD)	114,052

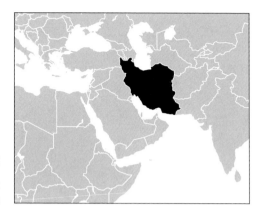

Coface analysis

Short-term: **C**

Medium-term:
Moderately high risk

STRENGTHS

- Iran is the second-largest OPEC producer and its gas reserves are the world's largest after Russia.
- During the 1992 and 1998 financial crises, the authorities demonstrated their capacity to restore external-account equilibrium quickly.
- The country has made progress on structural reforms.
- Debt has remained at low levels.

WEAKNESSES

- The United States has branded the country as part of an axis of evil.
- The continuing nuclear programme has undermined relations with the international community.
- Iran has remained excessively dependent on oil, which generates most of external and fiscal revenues.
- The current legal and political framework has not been conducive to partnerships with foreign companies or to direct investment.
- The deadlock between reformers and conservatives has impeded progress on reforms.

RISK ASSESSMENT

The good conditions on the oil market since 2000 have afforded the country the means to pursue expansionary fiscal policy that has spurred the growth rate of a non-oil sector also benefiting from progressively implemented reforms. The financial situation has improved with foreign debt remaining relatively low. In a context of declining oil prices, more prudent fiscal policy should impede growth of the non-oil sector, also affected by the regional instability likely to persist. Although external accounts are likely to begin to show deficits again, they should not pose a problem considering the comfortable level of currency reserves.

Despite progress made, the economy is still very dependent on oil-sector revenues, and the public sector has remained predominant. Continued efforts on the structural reform plan will be necessary to foster conditions conducive to growth and contain unemployment, although progress is slow in a difficult political context.

4

MAIN ECONOMIC INDICATORS

US$ billions	1999/ 00	2000/ 01	2001/ 02	2002/ 03 (e)	2003/ 04 (f)	2004/ 05 (f)
Economic growth (%)	2.0	5.2	5.8	7.6	5.8	4.0
Inflation (%)	20.1	12.6	11.4	15.8	17.0	13.5
Public-sector balance/GDP (%)	−0.6	0.6	−0.7	−4.0	−3.0	−4.0
Exports	21.0	28.5	23.9	27.4	28.9	26.8
Imports	13.4	15.1	18.1	23.2	26.9	28.6
Trade balance	7.6	13.4	5.8	4.2	2.0	−1.8
Current account balance/GDP (%)	6.4	13.2	6.0	3.9	2.3	−1.3
Foreign debt/GDP (%)	10.1	8.4	7.2	8.0	7.9	7.6
Debt service/Exports (%)	21.6	12.3	12.9	7.1	6.3	7.8
Currency reserves (import months)	4.1	7.9	9.2	8.7	8.2	7.0

e = estimate, f = forecast

CONDITIONS OF ACCESS TO THE MARKET

■ Market overview

Iran's customs tariff, whose *raison d'être* remains the protection of local producers, is undergoing gradual revision to facilitate the country's transition from a non-tariff system to a tariff-based one in accordance with WTO membership criteria. Revised tariff levels were introduced on 21 March 2002 along with a new exchange rate. In certain cases, this has led to a reduction in duties. The import of non-Islamic products is banned. Payments made in connection with imports are handled primarily by Iranian banks.

■ Attitude towards foreign investors

A new law to attract foreign investment was passed in summer 2002. Its main provisions include:

● Maintenance of the system of government approval for all investments. The sole body in charge of foreign investment is OIATEI (Iranian Economic and Technical Assistance and Investment Organization), headed by the Deputy Minister of Economic Affairs. Investment applications are the responsibility of an inter-ministerial body known as the Foreign Investment Commission.

● Establishment of two categories of foreign investment: direct investment in areas open to the private sector, and buy-back or BOT.

● A ceiling on foreign operations in the country. Foreign investment's share of total turnover in the manufacturing and service sectors may not exceed 25 per cent and 35 per cent respectively.

● The award of the right to foreigners to hold a 100 per cent stake in Iranian companies. On 12 May 2003, France and Iran signed an investment promotion and protection agreement due to be ratified shortly. The retroactive nature of the agreement in respect of disputes will help offset the lag between the signature of the agreement and its ratification. The agreement also provides for international arbitration. Tax reforms were introduced on 21 March 2003. The new tax rates, which have cut corporation tax from 54 to 25 per cent, offer much encouragement to local and foreign firms.

■ Foreign exchange regulations

On 21 March 2002, the two exchange rates were unified into a single market rate (US$1 = 8,000 rials). The administered exchange rate has been abolished. Subsidies are now included in the accounts published by recipient firms.

OPPORTUNITY SCOPE

Breakdown of internal demand (GDP + imports) %
- Private consumption   42
- Public spending   11
- Investment   24

Exports: 28% of GDP   Imports: 21% of GDP

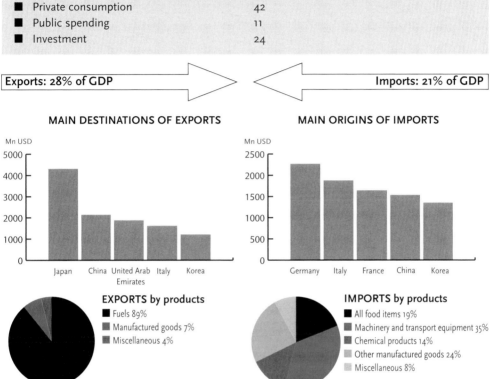

MAIN DESTINATIONS OF EXPORTS

Mn USD

Japan, China, United Arab Emirates, Italy, Korea

MAIN ORIGINS OF IMPORTS

Mn USD

Germany, Italy, France, China, Korea

EXPORTS by products
- Fuels 89%
- Manufactured goods 7%
- Miscellaneous 4%

IMPORTS by products
- All food items 19%
- Machinery and transport equipment 35%
- Chemical products 14%
- Other manufactured goods 24%
- Miscellaneous 8%

4

STANDARD OF LIVING / PURCHASING POWER

Indicators	Iran	Regional average	DC average
GNP per capita (PPP dollars)	5940	7496	6778
GNP per capita (USD)	1680	4722	3568
Human Development Index	0.719	0.740	0.708
Wealthiest 10% share of national income	34	30	33
Urban population percentage	65	70	60
Percentage under 15 years old	33	35	31
number of telephones per 1000 inhabitants	169	164	157
number of computers per 1000 inhabitants	70	56	66

Iraq

Population (million inhabitants)	24.8
GDP (million USD)	19,100
GDP per capita (USD)	909

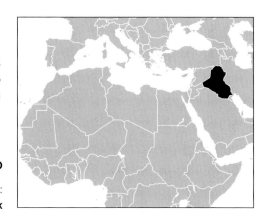

Short-term: **D**

Medium-term:
Very high risk

Coface analysis

RISK ASSESSMENT

Since the demise of Saddam Hussein's regime and the lifting of United Nations sanctions, Iraq has remained a poor country in need of political and economic reconstruction despite its immense natural resources. The official end of the war has given way to acts of sabotage and terrorism that have been increasing the cost of reconstruction and delaying revival of government administration and the economy under Coalition Provisional Authority auspices. In coming years, oil revenues will not suffice to cover operating expenses of government machinery, service the debt and finance the cost of reconstruction. Although rescheduling the external debt and mobilizing international aid will be essential, they will nonetheless depend on prior normalization of the country's political and legal situation.

Achieving such normalization is precisely the main factor of uncertainty. Insecurity has been exacerbating tensions within the population, and political, ethnic, religious and tribal cleavages have been intensifying. Until the political situation is normalized, risks of civil war will remain substantial.

MAIN ECONOMIC INDICATORS

US$ billions	2000 (e)	2001 (e)	2002 (e)	2003 (e)	2004 (f)
Economic growth (%)	4	−12.3	−20.5	−22.2	29.9
Inflation (%)	n/a	29	15	15	n/a
Public sector balance/GDP (%)	n/a	n/a	n/a	−42	−55
Exports	20.6	15.8	12.5	9.3	12.1
Imports	11.1	10.8	9.4	7.3	17.8
Trade balance	9.5	4.9	3.0	1.9	−5.6
Current account balance/GDP (%)	22.7	3.3	−2.5	20.8	−39.4
Foreign debt/GDP (%)	455	550	724	974	782

e = estimate, f = forecast

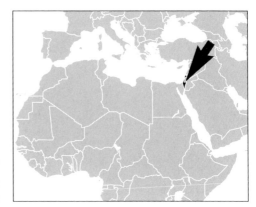

Israel

Population (million inhabitants)   6.4
GDP (million USD)   108,325

Coface analysis

Short-term: **A4**

Medium-term:
Quite low risk

STRENGTHS

- The economy is diversified and open.
- Development of high-technology industries is a growth factor nonetheless dependent on the US market.
- Israel can rely on the United States and the diaspora for political and financial backing.

WEAKNESSES

- The security situation has been impeding economic activity.
- Social and military spending has been weighing on public finances and causing debt to grow.
- Rising unemployment, falling living standards, fiscal constraints and pervasive insecurity have been undermining the social climate.

RISK ASSESSMENT

The economic slowdown, attributable to a sagging international economy and worsening political tensions, has developed amid rising unemployment, a falling standard of living, growing public-sector deficit and increasing social tensions. That situation has affected company solvency as evidenced by an increase in bankruptcies and deterioration of the Coface payment-incident index.

Although exports may fuel recovery in the near term buoyed by the economic rebound in the United States, the political climate will limit the upturn by deterring consumer spending, tourism and investment.

In the longer term, the country's development will essentially depend on resolution of the conflict with the Palestinians with prospects for that seeming to be waning. In this unfavourable context, the climate of insecurity could continue to undermine the country's economic and financial situation.

Regarding the government's payment capacity, reduced fiscal revenues, affected by the sagging economy and increased defence spending, have been increasing deficits and causing further increases in already-high debt levels. However, risks are limited due to the United States' guarantee, affording Israel privileged access to capital markets.

4

MAIN ECONOMIC INDICATORS

US$ billions	1999	2000	2001	2002	2003 (e)	2004 (f)
Economic growth (%)	2.6	7.4	−0.9	−1.0	0.5	2.5
Inflation (%)	5.2	1.1	1.1	5.7	2.6	2.1
Public-sector balance/GDP (%)	−2.2	−0.6	−4.4	−4.0	−6.0	−4.0
Exports	25.6	30.9	27.7	27.4	30.0	32.5
Imports	30.0	34.0	30.9	31.2	33.2	35.8
Trade balance	−4.5	−3.1	−3.3	−3.8	−3.2	−3.3
Current account balance/GDP (%)	−2.0	−0.9	−2.0	−2.1	−1.0	−1.2
Foreign debt/GDP (%)	60.0	56.0	57.3	64.4	63.1	63.2
Debt service/Exports (%)	16.5	14.4	18.6	13.9	17.0	16.5
Currency reserves (import months)	5.6	4.9	5.5	5.9	5.6	5.2

e = estimate, f = forecast

CONDITIONS OF ACCESS TO THE MARKET

■ Market overview

With per capita GDP around US$16,000, the Israeli market remains sizeable, solvent and growth-driven, despite the economic recession in 2001 and 2002. The market's current and future export potential is large with significant joint venture opportunities available to the vast majority of French firms, both big and small, regardless of field of activity. The Israeli government is set to pursue its policy of economic liberalization (privatization of banks, telecommunications and transport), tax reform and BOT infrastructure development.

■ Means of entry

Israel is one of only two countries in the world, along with Mexico, to have signed a free-trade agreement with the European Union and the United States. Similar agreements have been concluded with EFTA, Turkey, Canada, the Czech Republic, Poland, Hungary, Slovenia and Mexico. Except for some agricultural products, goods covered by the major free-trade agreements may be imported into Israel duty-free. They remain, however, liable to 18 per cent VAT. A variable sales tax is levied on some consumer goods. Under the Public Tender Act, foreign bidders are required to comply with offsetting arrangements amounting to at least 30 per cent of the tender's total value.

■ Attitude towards foreign investors

Israeli legislation contains various measures designed to encourage investment, whether local or foreign. Foreign investment is unrestricted (subject to the filing of an application for the release of benefits) except in protected sectors such as defence and some utilities. There are no restrictions on commercial payments between Israel and foreign countries, nor on the transfer or repatriation of profits, dividends and financial receivables, after payment of Israeli taxes. However, current regulations in respect of foreign workers have become more restrictive. The cost of living in Israel is high and comparable, even superior in some cases (consumer goods), to the European average.

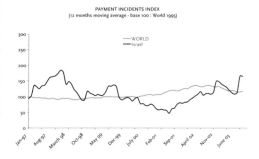

PAYMENT INCIDENTS INDEX
(12 months moving average - base 100 : World 1995)

OPPORTUNITY SCOPE

Breakdown of internal demand (GDP + imports)	%
■ Private consumption	40
■ Public spending	20
■ Investment	13

Exports: 40% of GDP   Imports: 47% of GDP

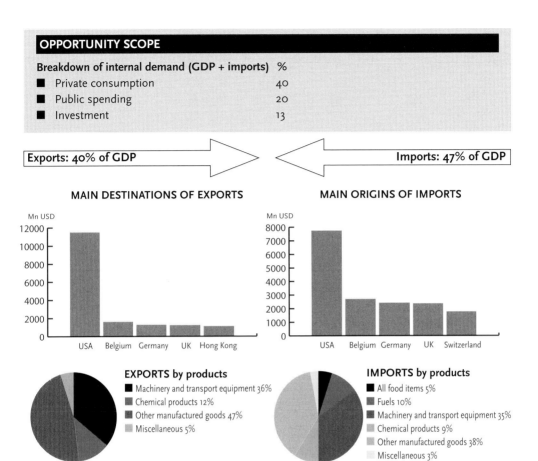

MAIN DESTINATIONS OF EXPORTS
Mn USD — USA, Belgium, Germany, UK, Hong Kong

MAIN ORIGINS OF IMPORTS
Mn USD — USA, Belgium, Germany, UK, Switzerland

EXPORTS by products
- ■ Machinery and transport equipment 36%
- ■ Chemical products 12%
- ■ Other manufactured goods 47%
- ■ Miscellaneous 5%

IMPORTS by products
- ■ All food items 5%
- ■ Fuels 10%
- ■ Machinery and transport equipment 35%
- ■ Chemical products 9%
- ■ Other manufactured goods 38%
- ■ Miscellaneous 3%

4

STANDARD OF LIVING / PURCHASING POWER

Indicators	Israel	Regional average	DC average
GNP per capita (PPP dollars)	19630	7496	6778
GNP per capita (USD)	16750	4722	3568
Human Development Index	0.905	0.740	0.708
Wealthiest 10% share of national income	28	30	33
Urban population percentage	92	70	60
Percentage under 15 years old	28	35	31
number of telephones per 1000 inhabitants	476	164	157
number of computers per 1000 inhabitants	246	56	66

Jordan

Population (million inhabitants)	5
GDP (million USD)	8,829

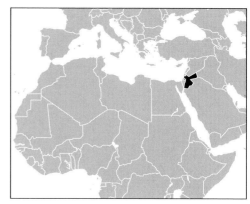

Coface analysis

Short-term: **B**

Medium-term:
High risk

STRENGTHS

- Jordan has enjoyed political and financial backing by Western countries and Arab Gulf states.
- That backing has permitted the country's integration into international trade (WTO membership, free-trade agreements with the United States and association agreements with the European Union) and the easing of its foreign debt burden.
- Development of customs-free areas has buoyed manufactured-product exports and attracted investors.
- Tourism and transportation have been development focuses.

WEAKNESSES

- The country has few natural resources (phosphate and potassium), a narrow industrial base and large water deficit.
- It has been dependent on international aid to cover its internal and external financing needs.
- Jordan suffers from the unstable regional environment (Israeli–Palestinian conflict, Iraq, Syria), which has been deterring tourism and reducing the country's attractiveness to investors.
- It has been contending with grave social problems including strong demographic pressure, Palestinian refugees, severe poverty and high unemployment (especially unemployed youth).

RISK ASSESSMENT

Despite an economic slowdown, Jordan ultimately suffered less than expected from the war in Iraq, its second trading partner. The international community has granted Jordan substantial additional aid – both financial and oil – to offset the interruption of the preferentially priced Iraqi oil supply.

The outlook for recovery in 2004 will depend on stabilization of the regional context with the continuing Israeli–Palestinian conflict and uncertainties in Iraq and Syria notably limiting tourism revenues and investments. Moreover, although consolidating public and external accounts has remained imperative, that would entail a speed-up of economic restructuring and an austerity policy difficult to implement in a social context marked by high levels of poverty and unemployment.

Nonetheless, the international aid and external debt reduction obtained via successive Paris Club agreements have consolidated the country's financial situation and permitted the limiting of its financing needs.

MAIN ECONOMIC INDICATORS

US$ billions	1999	2000	2001	2002	2003 (e)	2004 (f)
Economic growth (%)	3.1	4.1	4.2	5	3	4.8
Inflation (%)	0.6	0.7	1.8	1.8	2.1	2.5
Public-sector balance/GDP (%)[1]	−7	−8.9	−8.1	−8.1	−8.7	−9.6
Exports	1.8	1.9	2.3	2.8	2.9	3.1
Imports	3.3	4.1	4.3	4.5	4.9	5.1
Trade balance	−1.5	−2.2	−2	−1.7	−2	−2
Current account balance/GDP (%)[1]	0.2	−4.1	−5.2	−0.4	−4.6	−3.8
Foreign debt/GDP (%)	106.3	93.4	86.5	88.0	84.6	76.1
Debt service/Exports (%)	15.2	16.5	11.5	13.5	13.5	12.8
Currency reserves (import months)	5.8	6.3	5.7	7.3	9	9.3

[1] excluding donations

e = estimate, f = forecast

CONDITIONS OF ACCESS TO THE MARKET

■ Means of entry

While the banking system as a whole is solid and many first-rate financial institutions continued to improve profitability in 2003, with 22 banks it remains oversized. The Central Bank is striving to encourage concentration in the industry without much success. Since the introduction of the new Banking Act in 2000, the Bank of Issue has strengthened prudential measures mainly by increasing bad debt provisions (90 days instead of 180) and increasing bank capitalization. By 2007, the minimum capital requirement for banks should be 40 million dinars (approximately US$56.4 million), compared with 20 million dinars today.

In the hotel sector, where investment has been particularly heavy, consolidation agreements with banks are in place to enable hotels to offset the loss of business caused by the regional political situation. Caution is called for when dealing with private Jordanian customers.

Although bankruptcies remain few and far between, cases of late payment exist. Also, information on local firms is scarce, despite recent moves towards greater transparency. In 2002,

Jordan's credit insurer merged Coface @rating companies into its database. To avoid unreasonable risk, exporters should check the credit history of potential customers and gather key information about them from local market sources.

■ Attitude towards foreign investors

Apart from the first wave of privatizations that saw France become the leading investor in Jordan in terms of inventory, recent moves to open up the economy (banks, mobile telephony, potassium, retail) have facilitated the influx of new foreign businesses that exercise a stabilizing influence and play a market-leading role. Foreign and local investors receive equal treatment.

Moreover, Jordan's membership of the WTO, the implementation of a free-trade agreement with the United States and an association agreement with the EU, and the structural reforms undertaken to modernize the economy (Amman Stock Exchange, introduction of VAT, intellectual property protection) are helping to bring the country into line with Western standards.

The deteriorating regional political situation has led Jordan to redouble efforts to attract foreign investors via tax benefits and preferential access to the US and European markets.

4

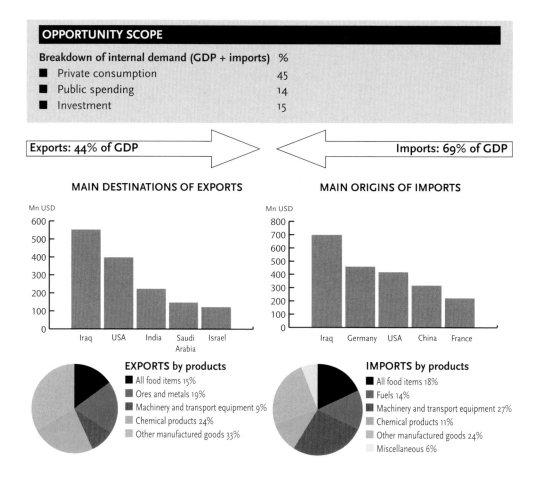

OPPORTUNITY SCOPE

Breakdown of internal demand (GDP + imports) %
- Private consumption   45
- Public spending   14
- Investment   15

Exports: 44% of GDP   Imports: 69% of GDP

MAIN DESTINATIONS OF EXPORTS

Mn USD

Iraq   USA   India   Saudi   Israel
                     Arabia

MAIN ORIGINS OF IMPORTS

Mn USD

Iraq   Germany   USA   China   France

EXPORTS by products
- All food items 15%
- Ores and metals 19%
- Machinery and transport equipment 9%
- Chemical products 24%
- Other manufactured goods 33%

IMPORTS by products
- All food items 18%
- Fuels 14%
- Machinery and transport equipment 27%
- Chemical products 11%
- Other manufactured goods 24%
- Miscellaneous 6%

STANDARD OF LIVING / PURCHASING POWER

Indicators	Jordan	Regional average	DC average
GNP per capita (PPP dollars)	3880	7496	6778
GNP per capita (USD)	1750	4722	3568
Human Development Index	0.743	0.740	0.708
Wealthiest 10% share of national income	30	30	33
Urban population percentage	79	70	60
Percentage under 15 years old	38	35	31
number of telephones per 1000 inhabitants	127	164	157
number of computers per 1000 inhabitants	33	56	66

Kuwait

Population (million inhabitants)	2
GDP (million USD)	32,806

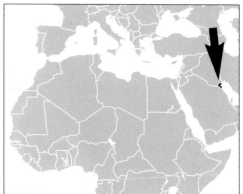

Short-term: **A2**

Medium-term:
Low risk

Coface analysis

STRENGTHS

- Kuwait boasts very extensive oil reserves.
- The country has a very solid financial position, with comfortable external and fiscal surpluses that have permitted accumulating considerable holdings abroad capable of cushioning external shocks.
- Foreign debt has been moderate.
- The banking system is sound and well supervised.
- The country enjoys strategic alliances not only with the United States but also with France, the United Kingdom and Russia.

WEAKNESSES

- The economy has remained dependent on the oil sector with little diversification.
- Despite the demise of Saddam Hussein's regime, political instability in Iraq could affect investments.
- Growth of the working population has been jeopardizing the welfare state.
- Remittances abroad by foreign labour have been undermining the invisibles balance.
- Political cleavages have been impeding reforms.

RISK ASSESSMENT

The Iraq war finally caused little damage to Kuwait's oil rigs. On the contrary, it spurred the country's economy and bolstered its financial situation thanks to increased oil production and high barrel prices. The presence of more foreign troops also temporarily spurred the non-oil sector. After those exceptional events, the economy could fall back into recession in 2004 amid the expected decline of oil production and sagging domestic demand. Moreover, a drop in barrel prices should affect the external and internal account balances.

The country's financial situation will still give little cause for concern considering its modest foreign debt burden and the extent of holdings abroad denominated in foreign currencies.

Further out, consolidating the conditions for growth will require structural reforms to diversify the economy and develop the private sector. Although reforms have been planned, a still-conservative parliament with a capacity for obstruction could impede progress. Furthermore, the unstable Iraq situation could undermine Kuwait's capacity to attract foreign investments.

4

MAIN ECONOMIC INDICATORS						
US$ billions	1999	2000	2001	2002 (e)	2003 (e)	2004 (f)
Economic growth (%)	−4.9	7.5	−1.0	−4.1	12.5	−4.4
Inflation (%)	3.0	1.8	1.7	1.4	1.6	2.0
Public-sector balance/GDP (%)	0.9	30.1	38.2	21.1	22.6	20.8
Exports	12.3	19.5	16.2	15.4	20.0	15.6
Imports	6.7	6.5	7.0	8.1	9.0	9.1
Trade balance	5.6	13.0	9.2	7.3	11.0	6.5
Current account balance/GDP (%)	26.0	39.7	24.3	12.0	15.3	5.6
Foreign debt/GDP (%)	34.4	26.9	32.4	36.7	32.3	36.6
Debt service/Exports (%)	12.1	8.2	8.4	9.1	8.1	11.1
Currency reserves (import months)	4.7	6.1	7.9	6.7	5.0	5.1

e = estimate, f = forecast

CONDITIONS OF ACCESS TO THE MARKET

■ Means of entry

Kuwait is a free market with one of the highest import-to-consumption ratios in the world (90 per cent). In line with the decision by the six member countries of the Gulf Cooperation Council to standardize their customs duties, from September 2003 Kuwait applies customs duty at a standard rate of 5 per cent *ad valorem*, with duty-free admission for 417 imported goods, including numerous pharmaceuticals and food staples.

Per capita income is high and demand for capital and consumer goods disproportionately large for a country of its size. But Kuwait is a highly coveted market demanding special knowledge and perseverance, backed by close contact with ordering customers. Companies exporting to Kuwait are not required to have a sole local partner and may sell directly to several Kuwaiti importers.

Now that relations with Iraq have been restored, Kuwait should regain its role as a hub serving both the vast Iraqi market with its 25 million consumers and Iran, with its large towns facing the Kuwaiti coast.

■ Attitude towards foreign investors

Under the FDI Act No. 8/2001, which handed the Kuwaiti government powers to introduce practical regulatory measures in connection with its enforcement, foreigners may now hold up to 100 per cent of a company's capital and obtain 10-year tax exemption.

The government has also drawn up a positive list of sectors open to FDI, with the exception of oil exploration and production, which remain closed. Sectors open to foreigners include light processing industries, tourism, hotels, leisure (foreigners may acquire real estate for their projects), culture, information, marketing, livestock breeding and farming, banking, investment and currency management (subject to approval of the central bank), insurance (subject to approval of the Ministry of Trade and Industry) and data processing. At the same time, tax reforms have been announced in a bid to cut corporation tax for foreign companies from 55 to 25 per cent. Recent moves to open up the country's economy to foreign investment offer investors attractive opportunities in this solvent and growing market.

OPPORTUNITY SCOPE

Breakdown of internal demand (GDP + imports)   %
- Private consumption   35
- Public spending   19
- Investment   7

Exports: 55% of GDP	Imports: 37% of GDP

MAIN DESTINATIONS OF EXPORTS

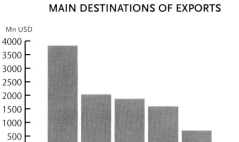

Mn USD — Japan, Korea, USA, Singapore, Netherlands

MAIN ORIGINS OF IMPORTS

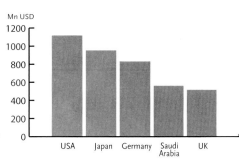

Mn USD — USA, Japan, Germany, Saudi Arabia, UK

EXPORTS by products
- Fuels 91%
- Manufactured goods 9%

IMPORTS by products
- All food items 17%
- Machinery and transport equipment 40%
- Chemical products 9%
- Other manufactured good 30%
- Miscellaneous 4%

STANDARD OF LIVING / PURCHASING POWER

Indicators	Kuwait	Regional average	DC average
GNP per capita (PPP dollars)	21530	7496	6778
GNP per capita (USD)	18270	4722	3568
Human Development Index	0.82	0.740	0.708
Wealthiest 10% share of national income	n/a	30	33
Urban population percentage	96	70	60
Percentage under 15 years old	32	35	31
number of telephones per 1000 inhabitants	240	164	157
number of computers per 1000 inhabitants	132	56	66

4

Lebanon

Population (million inhabitants)	4.4
GDP (million USD)	16,709

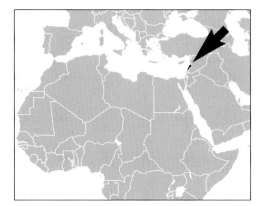

Short-term: **C**

Coface analysis

Medium-term:
Very high risk

STRENGTHS

- The financial backing of the diaspora and international community has permitted the cushioning of the country's economic and financial difficulties.
- The authorities have undertaken a structural reform programme.
- Tourism and financial services continue to play pivotal roles in the economy.

WEAKNESSES

- With the country very dependent on imports, its trade balance is structurally in deficit.
- Moreover, the domestic political landscape has been impeding rapid implementation of policies that would permit the absorbing of Lebanon's massive internal and external debt.
- Uncertainties linked to the regional environment have been weighing on the country's outlook and thus on its capacity to attract foreign direct investment.
- The banking sector is very exposed to sovereign risk.

RISK ASSESSMENT

Since the Paris Conference afforded breathing space in November 2002, Lebanon's situation has become critical again, exacerbated by a deteriorating regional environment and difficult domestic economic situation. The growth rate has remained weak, the level of investment insufficient and the public-finance situation shaky.

Regarding public finances, efforts made to increase revenues and reduce spending have permitted a reduction of deficits, which have nonetheless remained very large and could increase even more with elections approaching in 2004. The already-unsustainable public debt burden would thus continue to grow.

Meanwhile, the external account situation has remained very precarious with external financing needs likely to increase considerably. Through lack of foreign direct investment inflows or revenues from privatizations, the country might have to draw again on its reserves or resort to borrowing with its external debt ratios already very high.

MAIN ECONOMIC INDICATORS						
US$ billions	1999	2000	2001	2002	2003 (e)	2004 (f)
Economic growth (%)	1	−0.5	1	1.5	2	2
Inflation (%)	0.3	−0.4	−0.4	1.8	2.8	1.9
Public-sector balance/GDP (%)	−13.6	−22.5	−16.1	−15.8	−13.7	−14.9
Exports	0.7	0.7	0.9	1.0	1.3	1.5
Imports	5.8	5.8	6.8	6.0	6.2	6.3
Trade balance	−5.1	−5.1	−5.9	−5.0	−4.9	−4.8
Current account balance/GDP (%)	−30.5	−29	−33.3	−30.1	−27.2	−27.1
Foreign debt	13.7	14.3	13.8	15.3	17.9	18.5
Debt service/Exports (%)	187.6	161.8	160.6	175.7	147.9	130.9
Currency reserves (import months)	12.5	9.2	6.4	8	12.0	10.2

e = estimate, f = forecast

CONDITIONS OF ACCESS TO THE MARKET

■ Market overview

Lebanon, which direly needs real investment to revive its economy and retain the skilled labour flowing out of the country due to lack of job opportunities, has over the years developed a legal system that protects the rights and property of Lebanese and foreign investors alike.

■ Means of entry

Lebanon stands out from its neighbours by virtue of a highly developed and reliable banking system that is well governed by the Bank of Lebanon, full currency convertibility, a free currency market and the absence of restrictions on capital movements. In late 2000, the rates of customs duty were drastically cut from 6 per cent and 105 per cent to 0 per cent and 70 per cent. A new customs code based on the Brussels Nomenclature was adopted in April 2001 in line with WTO and World Customs Organization requirements. The customs service has also adopted an automated data-logging system (CAJM) for online transactions (NOOR) that enables buyers to pay customs duties on the spot. However, the cuts in customs duties introduced in 2002 for a large number of products were accompanied by a strengthening both of tariff barriers (rejection of amounts declared and their revaluation by reference to local transaction values) and of non-tariff barriers (in particular inspections)

in respect of imports. Non-tariff barriers mainly include an import ban on some 326 products or product categories, import licences and permits for 261 other product categories and technical inspections based on changing specifications. Health regulations, though based on somewhat vague legal principles, are fairly liberal and comply with the recommendations of leading international organizations. All means of payment are accepted, although the irrevocable and confirmed letter of credit is the most widely used guarantee for the payment of imported goods.

Exporters should note that the central bank requires a cash bank guarantee equal to 15 per cent of the LC's value. Due to the unpredictability of the legal system and the lack of transparency of court procedures, companies usually avoid litigation. The problem of bad debt is often sorted out amicably. For large contracts, the best way of resolving disputes is through the Lebanese code of civil procedure. Revised in August 2002, it provides for international arbitration outside Lebanon and for an arbitration clause in contracts signed with the government.

■ Attitude towards foreign investors

While Lebanon does not have special legislation to protect foreign investment, its regulatory framework for investments contains few stumbling blocks to the establishment of foreign businesses in the country, other than certain nationality and permit

4

299

requirements. In the absence of specific investment legislation, foreign joint ventures are automatically subject to common law in matters of taxation, labour law, etc. Such companies are eligible for benefits under the country's Investment Promotion Act of August 2001, which among other things empowers the government one-stop shop, IDAL (Investment Development Authority in Lebanon), to handle and facilitate investor formalities in certain sectors or specially designated underprivileged regions. Liable to fairly low ordinary taxation (15 per cent), foreign companies can in addition obtain tax exemptions in respect of investments having a recognized economic, social and environmental impact.

As the legal machinery is strengthened and adjusted to comply with WTO trade requirements, the investment environment continues to be undermined by the absence and repeated postponement of administrative reforms, the arbitrary enforcement of laws, legal uncertainty and lack of transparency of administrative procedures.

OPPORTUNITY SCOPE

Breakdown of internal demand (GDP + imports) %
- ■ Private consumption   66
- ■ Public spending   13
- ■ Investment   13

Exports: 12% of GDP   Imports: 42% of GDP

MAIN DESTINATIONS OF EXPORTS

Mn USD

Switzerland, Saudi Arabia, United Arab Emirates, USA, Jordan

MAIN ORIGINS OF IMPORTS

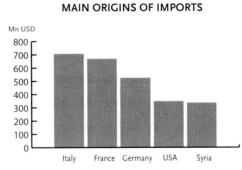

Mn USD

Italy, France, Germany, USA, Syria

EXPORTS by products
- ■ All food items 18%
- ■ Machinery and transport equipment 14%
- ■ Chemical products 22%
- ■ Other manufactured goods 40%
- ■ Miscellaneous 6%

IMPORTS by products
- ■ All food items 17%
- ■ Fuels 18%
- ■ Machinery and transport equipment 24%
- ■ Chemical products 10%
- ■ Other manufactured goods 25%
- ■ Miscellaneous 6%

4

STANDARD OF LIVING / PURCHASING POWER

Indicators	Lebanon	Regional average	DC average
GNP per capita (PPP dollars)	4400	7496	6778
GNP per capita (USD)	4010	4722	3568
Human Development Index	0.752	0.740	0.708
Wealthiest 10% share of national income	n/a	30	33
Urban population percentage	90	70	60
Percentage under 15 years old	32	35	31
number of telephones per 1000 inhabitants	195	164	157
number of computers per 1000 inhabitants	56	56	66

Libya

Population (million inhabitants)   5.4
GDP (million USD)   34,137

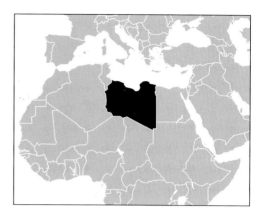

Short-term: **C**

Medium-term:
High risk

Coface analysis

STRENGTHS

- The country possesses substantial natural oil and gas resources.
- Faced with the need to attract foreign capital, the authorities have been demonstrating their commitment to reforms to consolidate the public sector.
- The level of currency reserves has been high.
- The debt level is moderate, despite the country's payment behaviour concerning old debts remaining poor.

WEAKNESSES

- The unpredictability of economic policy and lack of an adequate legal and financial framework have been deterring investors.
- A plethoric and inefficient public sector, which has been undermining public accounts, has continued to dominate the Libyan economy.
- With its dependence on the oil sector, the economy has remained vulnerable to external shocks.
- Its centralized management and a United Nations embargo, lifted in 2003, have undermined the economy.

RISK ASSESSMENT

After the oil sector's good performance spurred the economy in 2003, the expected decline of oil prices and probably of export volumes should cause an economic slowdown and reduction of external and internal balances. Such developments should not, however, affect the external financial situation (likely to remain steady considering the level of foreign currency reserves) or public accounts, which have remained in surplus.

The country's economic and financial situation has nonetheless remained very dependent on the oil sector with oil export income generating little benefit for the rest of the economy where growth has been feeble. In that context, development prospects have remained poor and insufficient to absorb the population reaching working age. Structural reforms will be necessary to encourage private investors, raise living standards and establish durable growth. Considering the social cost, however, the reform process will take time.

The system's opacity and unpredictability have remained the main risk factors.

MAIN ECONOMIC INDICATORS						
US$ billions	1999	2000	2001	2002 (e)	2003 (e)	2004 (f)
Economic growth (%)	0.7	2.3	0.5	−0.2	5.6	1.8
Inflation (%)	2.6	−3	−8.8	−9.8	2.8	2.9
Public-sector balance/GDP (%)	5.5	9.5	−0.3	3.9	14.2	6.5
Exports	7.2	12.1	9.0	8.3	10.1	8.6
Imports	4.7	4.1	5.3	7.4	6.3	6.7
Trade balance	2.5	8.0	3.6	0.9	3.8	1.9
Current account balance/GDP (%)	5.4	20.5	8.6	−1.2	10.4	0.6
Foreign debt	5.8	5.3	5.4	5.6	5.6	5.6
Debt service/Exports (%)	3.1	7.1	9.0	6.6	8.7	10.3
Currency reserves (import months)	13.3	24.7	23.3	17.4	21.7	20.8

e = estimate, f = forecast

CONDITIONS OF ACCESS TO THE MARKET

■ Market overview

Foreign investment is encouraged by amended Law No. 5, which provides for foreign majority shareholdings in the agricultural, fisheries, services, industrial and tourism sectors.

Significant investment programmes have been launched to improve transport infrastructure and equipment (air, land, rail), telecommunications (extension of the landline network from 0.7 to 1 million lines and of the GSM network to 0.5 million lines), electricity (extension of generating capacity from 4,500 MW to 10,000 MW over five years), oil and gas production and exploration (award of new licences with a view to increasing output from 2 to 2.5 million barrels daily), large-scale river development (water supply), desalination (installation of 11 desalination plants), environment, radio and television (digitalization of equipment and training), food supply, etc.

Libya therefore offers a host of new business opportunities, despite the widespread system of state controls, characterized by cumbersome, slow and inconsistent administrative practices.

■ Means of entry

From early 2003, licences are no longer required to import goods into the country. All shipments must be accompanied by a certificate of origin. Since January 1998 the Libyan customs tariff has been based on the simplified harmonized nomenclature. An import ban is in place on so-called 'luxury' and locally manufactured products, a list of which is available. Sales contracts are settled exclusively by irrevocable letter of credit, which can take six months or more to open. The law governing contracts with Libyan government agencies requires foreign suppliers to pay 2 per cent stamp duty on the total value of contracts (1 per cent for subcontracting agreements). Companies should factor in the cost of this duty when preparing bids. The Libyan market should only be approached by financially solid companies used to long and arduous negotiations. SMEs can usefully engage in ordinary business that does not require funding. Firms wishing to sell goods in Libya must henceforth sign a representation agreement with a Libyan agent responsible for after-sales service.

■ Foreign exchange regulations

The country's foreign exchange regulations, far more flexible than in the past, are overseen by the Exchange Control Department, an arm of the Central Bank. Since 16 June 2003, the Libyan government has succeeded in setting a single and free exchange rate on the capital market by abolishing the tax on external financial and currency transactions and carrying out a 15 per cent devaluation of the Libyan dinar. The current exchange rate is 1.6 dinars to the euro.

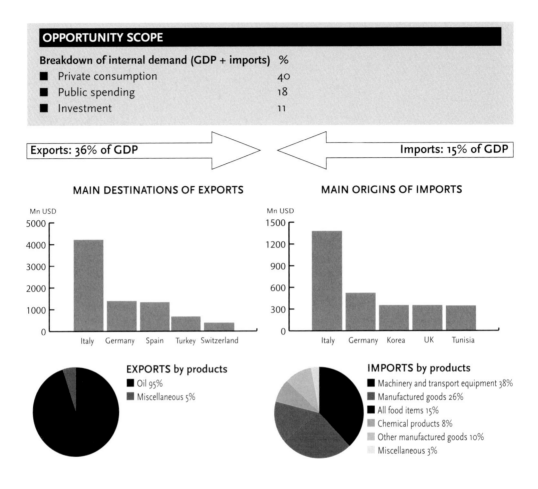

OPPORTUNITY SCOPE

Breakdown of internal demand (GDP + imports) %
- Private consumption 40
- Public spending 18
- Investment 11

Exports: 36% of GDP Imports: 15% of GDP

MAIN DESTINATIONS OF EXPORTS

Mn USD

5000 | 4000 | 3000 | 2000 | 1000 | 0

Italy Germany Spain Turkey Switzerland

MAIN ORIGINS OF IMPORTS

Mn USD

1500 | 1200 | 900 | 600 | 300 | 0

Italy Germany Korea UK Tunisia

EXPORTS by products
- Oil 95%
- Miscellaneous 5%

IMPORTS by products
- Machinery and transport equipment 38%
- Manufactured goods 26%
- All food items 15%
- Chemical products 8%
- Other manufactured goods 10%
- Miscellaneous 3%

STANDARD OF LIVING / PURCHASING POWER

Indicators	Libya	Regional average	DC average
GNP per capita (PPP dollars)	n/a	7496	6778
GNP per capita (USD)	n/a	4722	3568
Human Development Index	0.783	0.740	0.708
Wealthiest 10% share of national income	n/a	30	33
Urban population percentage	88	70	60
Percentage under 15 years old	34	35	31
number of telephones per 1000 inhabitants	109	164	157
number of computers per 1000 inhabitants	n/a	56	66

Morocco

Population (million inhabitants)   29.2
GDP (million USD)   34,219

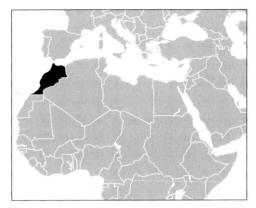

Short-term: **A4**

Medium-term:

Coface analysis   **Moderately high risk**

STRENGTHS

- The country's potential wealth (natural resources, tourism, population) in conjunction with the accelerated pace of structural reforms has been attracting investors.
- Morocco's political, economic and financial proximity to the European Union has contributed to its economic dynamism.
- The external constraint has had moderate impact with financing needs tending to decline and the policy pursued by authorities having reduced external debt.
- With its political stability and democratic development, the country has earned the support of financial backers.

WEAKNESSES

- Still too dependent on farming (20 per cent of GDP, 40 per cent of jobs), the Moroccan economy has remained vulnerable to weather conditions.
- Demographic trends, unemployment (particularly among young people) and poverty could be sources of social unrest, which constitute a formidable challenge for the authorities.
- The tighter the public finance situation, the more difficult it will be to respond to those challenges.
- The unresolved West Sahara problem has continued to affect relations with Algeria.

RISK ASSESSMENT

The farm sector's steadiness has permitted the Moroccan economy to resume high growth. Those more favourable conditions have nonetheless not led to an improvement of company payment behaviour, notably in the textile and food sectors where late payments have remained commonplace.

External financing needs have remained at modest levels and that has contributed to reducing the external debt burden. Moreover, Morocco continues to enjoy the confidence of international capital markets and political and financial backing of Western countries and multilateral institutions.

Besides the pursuit of structural reforms (including privatizations, banking reform and a labour code overhaul), the government resulting from the 2002 elections must contend with two major challenges. It must consolidate public accounts whose deficits have been generating substantial public debt. With little room for manoeuvre, furthermore, it must also undertake bold programmes to combat poverty. The risk exists that the aggravation of social tensions and their drift towards political extremism could have a negative impact on foreign investment and tourism revenues.

4

MAIN ECONOMIC INDICATORS						
US$ billions	1999	2000	2001	2002	2003 (e)	2004 (f)
Economic growth (%)	−0.7	1	6.3	3.2	5.2	4.7
Inflation (%)	0.7	1.9	0.6	2.8	1.6	1.7
Public-sector balance/GDP (%)	−4.2	−6.4	−5.7	−4.3	−4.5	−4.5
Exports	7.5	7.4	7.1	7.9	8.4	9.3
Imports	10	10.7	10.2	10.9	12.4	13
Trade balance	−2.4	−3.2	−3.0	−3.0	−3.9	−3.7
Current account balance/GDP (%)	−0.5	−1.6	4.4	3.7	0.7	1.4
Foreign debt	19.2	17.9	17.0	17.1	17.1	16.4
Debt service/Exports (%)	23.5	19.6	17.5	15.6	15.3	14.2
Currency reserves (import months)	5.2	4.2	7.5	8.3	8	8.5

e = estimate, f = forecast

CONDITIONS OF ACCESS TO THE MARKET

■ Market overview

Customs duties range from 0 to 50 per cent. Tariff peaks remain in place in agriculture and agri-foodstuffs, especially for food staples. In the third year of application of the association agreement with the European Union, in force since 1 March 2000, customs duties for half the tariff categories – raw materials, spare parts, inputs and goods not produced in Morocco – have been cut to zero. The agreement will lead to the establishment of a free-trade area by 2012.

The last few years have seen wide-ranging reforms aimed at stabilizing the business environment. The measures adopted thus far include: a new Trade Code (1996); a Private Limited Liability Company, Partnership and Joint Venture Law (1997); new government procurement legislation modelled on the French code (1998); a new Customs Code (2000) that crowns the modernization programme so ably conducted by the government; a Competition and Price Act; an Intellectual and Industrial Property Protection Act whose implementing decrees have yet to be published; and a Literary and Artistic Property Act, which came into force on 1 January 2001. The Public Limited Companies Act, adopted in 1996, finally came into force in January 2001. An Insurance Code Bill abolishing all caps on foreign investment in the sector was passed by parliament in November 2002 and is due to come into force shortly.

■ Attitude towards foreign investors

The setting up of 16 regional investment centres (CRI), overseen by walis (prefects), significantly simplifies start-up procedures by offering a one-stop shop to investors. This measure, long awaited by the business community, cuts start-up formalities to under a week. The general provisions of the investment charter are also quite favourable.

■ Foreign exchange regulations

A supervised foreign exchange market remains in place. The exchange rate is set by the central bank, Bank Al Maghrib, on the basis of a basket of currencies. A currency convertibility system set up in 1992 encourages hard-currency investment in Morocco by guaranteeing profit repatriation.

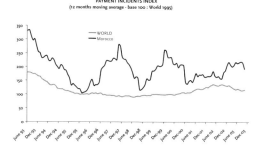

PAYMENT INCIDENTS INDEX
(12 months moving average - base 100 : World 1995)

OPPORTUNITY SCOPE

Breakdown of internal demand (GDP + imports) %
- Private consumption   46
- Public spending   13
- Investment   18

Exports: 30% of GDP ⟩ ⟨ Imports: 36% of GDP

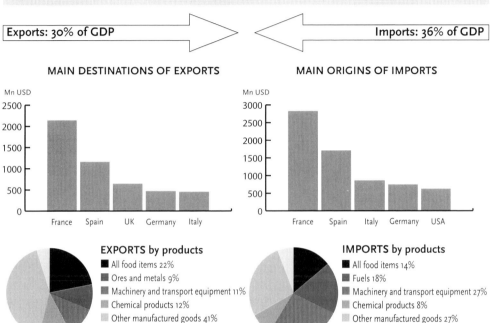

MAIN DESTINATIONS OF EXPORTS

Mn USD — France, Spain, UK, Germany, Italy

MAIN ORIGINS OF IMPORTS

Mn USD — France, Spain, Italy, Germany, USA

EXPORTS by products
- All food items 22%
- Ores and metals 9%
- Machinery and transport equipment 11%
- Chemical products 12%
- Other manufactured goods 41%
- Miscellaneous 5%

IMPORTS by products
- All food items 14%
- Fuels 18%
- Machinery and transport equipment 27%
- Chemical products 8%
- Other manufactured goods 27%
- Miscellaneous 6%

4

STANDARD OF LIVING / PURCHASING POWER

Indicators	Morocco	Regional average	DC average
GNP per capita (PPP dollars)	3500	7496	6778
GNP per capita (USD)	1190	4722	3568
Human Development Index	0.606	0.740	0.708
Wealthiest 10% share of national income	31	30	33
Urban population percentage	56	70	60
Percentage under 15 years old	34	35	31
number of telephones per 1000 inhabitants	41	164	157
number of computers per 1000 inhabitants	14	56	66

Oman

Population (million inhabitants)   2.5
GDP (million USD)   19,826

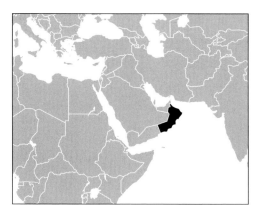

Coface analysis

Short-term: **A2**

Medium-term:
Quite low risk

STRENGTHS

- The country enjoys natural wealth (gas and oil).
- It has been engaged in diversifying its economy (gas, petrochemicals, aluminium, tourism) and developing the private sector.
- Its WTO membership favours foreign investments.
- Restructuring measures and strengthened prudential regulations have consolidated the banking sector.

WEAKNESSES

- The economy has remained vulnerable to a trend reversal in the oil sector.
- Considering its ageing oil fields, the sector needs large investments to bolster production capacity.
- Investment outlays, payroll costs and military spending have strained public accounts.
- Foreign worker remittances have been undermining the invisibles balance.

RISK ASSESSMENT

After a two-year slowdown caused by technical oil-production problems linked to the age of the fields, the economy should recover in 2004. With the oil-production decline likely to be under control, the non-oil sector's continued dynamism stimulated by public spending should buoy the recovery. The expected oil-price decline could cause the Sultanate of Oman's external and public accounts to sink back into deficit. The external financial situation should not be a source of difficulty considering the relatively modest debt burden. In the near term, financial assets accumulated in recent years thanks to high oil prices will cover the government's financing needs. Further out, continued deficits in a context of downward-trending oil prices could undermine the government's financial situation. A consolidation of public accounts will be necessary and depend on continuation of the reform programme, itself nonetheless dependent on substantial foreign direct investment that regional geopolitical uncertainties could deter.

MAIN ECONOMIC INDICATORS

US$ billions	1999	2000	2001	2002 (e)	2003 (e)	2004 (f)
Economic growth (%)	−0.2	5.5	9.3	2.3	2.2	4.8
Inflation (%)	0.5	−1.2	−1.0	−0.7	1.0	1.1
Public-sector balance/GDP (%)	0.8	9.7	3.8	3.7	3.1	−0.6
Exports	7.2	11.3	11.1	11.3	11.6	10.9
Imports	4.3	4.6	5.3	5.6	6.6	7.4
Trade balance	2.9	6.7	5.8	5.6	5.0	3.5
Current account balance/GDP (%)	−1.5	17.7	11.1	10.0	6.9	−0.6
Foreign debt/GDP (%)	43.1	33.0	30.3	28.2	25.1	29.3
Debt service/Exports (%)	8.8	10.8	11.5	8.4	6.1	6.8
Currency reserves (import months)	4.1	3.3	3.0	3.8	3.9	3.5

e = estimate, f = forecast

CONDITIONS OF ACCESS TO THE MARKET

■ Market overview

Oman remains highly dependent on the oil sector. The government continues to pursue its five-year plan, which focuses on economic diversification via industrial development, in particular the development of natural gas as a source of energy or raw material for large-scale industrial schemes and the promotion of the private sector's role in the economy through privatization of state-owned companies and utilities. The last plank of government policy concerns the Omanization of jobs.

■ Means of entry

For private contracts, exporters of consumer goods that do not demand any after-sales service are not required to have a local agent. For public tenders open to foreign companies, the foreign supplier must have a local office or be represented by an Omani company. General customs duty for the majority of products is 5 per cent of the CIF value. However, a prior licence is mandatory for some products on grounds of health, religion or protection of local manufacture. There are no exchange controls and foreign currency may be sold freely. There are no restrictions on the transfer of corporate profits and no barriers to the free movement of capital.

■ Attitude towards foreign investors

Omani legislation tends to encourage foreign investment but has kept in place a number of restrictions in order to channel funds into industrial and infrastructure projects, especially those linked to the country's privatization programme. As a result, foreigners can now acquire a stake in manufacturing, trading and service companies, whereas in the past they were rarely allowed to own shares in the latter two. From 2000, foreign companies that have operated for more than 10 years and possess at least three foreign subsidiaries may open a local sales office without local sponsorship.

Tax incentive schemes have been introduced to reduce discrimination against foreign companies and encourage local companies to open their capital to foreigners.

4

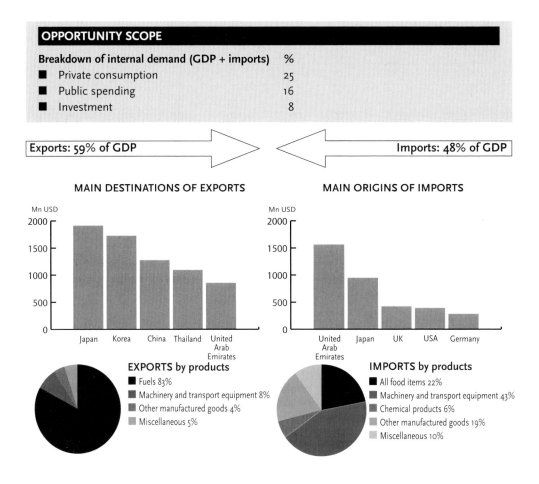

OPPORTUNITY SCOPE

Breakdown of internal demand (GDP + imports)   %
- Private consumption   25
- Public spending   16
- Investment   8

Exports: 59% of GDP   Imports: 48% of GDP

MAIN DESTINATIONS OF EXPORTS

Mn USD

Japan, Korea, China, Thailand, United Arab Emirates

MAIN ORIGINS OF IMPORTS

Mn USD

United Arab Emirates, Japan, UK, USA, Germany

EXPORTS by products
- Fuels 83%
- Machinery and transport equipment 8%
- Other manufactured goods 4%
- Miscellaneous 5%

IMPORTS by products
- All food items 22%
- Machinery and transport equipment 43%
- Chemical products 6%
- Other manufactured goods 19%
- Miscellaneous 10%

STANDARD OF LIVING / PURCHASING POWER

Indicators	Oman	Regional average	DC average
GNP per capita (PPP dollars)	n/a	7496	6778
GNP per capita (USD)	n/a	4722	3568
Human Development Index	0.755	0.740	0.708
Wealthiest 10% share of national income	n/a	30	33
Urban population percentage	76	70	60
Percentage under 15 years old	43	35	31
number of telephones per 1000 inhabitants	90	164	157
number of computers per 1000 inhabitants	32	56	66

Palestinian Territories

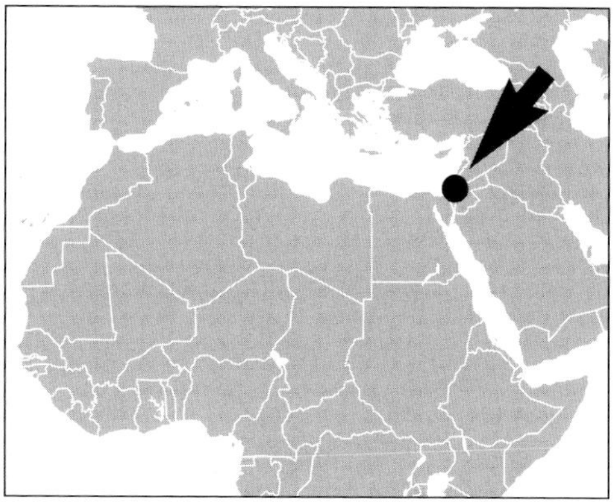

Population (million inhabitants)	3.4
GDP (million USD)	3,700
GDP per capita (USD)	1,095

Coface analysis

RISK ASSESSMENT

Although the situation of conflict with Israel since the current intifada began in September 2000 has left the Palestinian Territories' economy in shambles, it has held up better than expected thanks to international community and expatriate backing and the dynamism of some companies. The Palestinian economy is very dependent on the Hebrew state, and economic activity and employment have suffered from the blocking of road traffic. The insecurity has notably affected tourism, construction and investment. Although public-sector balances have deteriorated sharply since 2001, international aid has permitted the partial financing of the fiscal deficits. After three recession years, the economy has been slowly recovering. Restitution since 2003 of taxes collected by Israel should permit the stemming of the accumulation of payment arrears and the limiting of fiscal deficits. The Palestinian Authority has taken pains to bolster its institutional framework with the consolidation of financial channels likely to reassure donor countries whose contributions have been declining. With the Palestinian economy's health remaining inexorably tied to resolution of the conflict with Israel, the prospects for peace still seem remote.

4

MAIN ECONOMIC INDICATORS						
US$ billions	1998	1999	2000	2001	2002	2003 (e)
Economic growth (%)	11.8	8.9	−5.4	−15	−14.5	4
Inflation (%)	5.6	5.5	2.8	1.2	5.7	n/a
Public-sector balance/GDP (%)	−4.9	−5.3	−6.2	−22.5	−25.7	−15
Unemployment rate (%)	14.4	11.8	14.1	25.5	31.3	31.0
Imports	3.3	3.8	3.4	3.2	2.8	3.0
Exports	0.9	0.9	0.9	0.5	0.4	0.5
Trade balance	−2.4	−2.9	−2.5	−2.7	−2.4	−2.5
Current account balance/GDP (%)	−26.3	−34.9	−25.2	−23.4	−5.6	n/a

311

e = estimate

Qatar

Population (million inhabitants)	0.61
GDP (million USD)	16,200

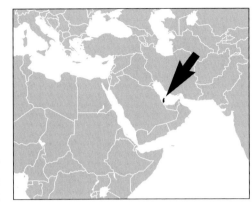

Coface analysis

Short-term: **A2**

Medium-term:
Quite low risk

STRENGTHS

- Enormous gas resources (ranked third in world reserves) continue to offer substantial development and growth prospects.
- Diversification of energy-intensive activities (steel and petrochemicals) will enhance the country's external position.
- The emirate has enjoyed the backing of the United States.
- The Al-Jazeera television channel has been promoting the country's image of openness and efficiency.

WEAKNESSES

- Although the financing of gas and industrial projects has generated heavy foreign debt, that has only represented a moderate constraint due to the growth of foreign currency earnings.
- Fiscal revenues have remained very dependent on conditions in the oil sector.
- Foreign worker remittances have been undermining the invisibles balance.

RISK ASSESSMENT

Qatar's investment strategy has been successful with the emirate now undertaking, on sounder financial foundations, a second phase of development of its gas reserves as well as of downstream activities. The increased production resulting from those investments coupled with steady oil prices has spurred growth and, in recent years, permitted the restoring of the public account balance and the posting of substantial external account surpluses. That trend should persist despite forecasts of declining oil prices. The debt burden has been a relatively limited constraint in comparison to foreign currency earnings. Qatar should continue to accumulate foreign currency reserves and build up reserve funds.

Politically, Qatar should remain sheltered from external or domestic turmoil. With the regional situation still uncertain after the demise of Saddam Hussein's regime in Iraq, the US army's strengthened presence has been protecting the country and its natural wealth.

Rising living standards along with the government's options – its initiation of an economic liberalization and democratization process – have been fostering political stability and an investment-friendly environment.

MAIN ECONOMIC INDICATORS						
US$ billions	1999	2000	2001	2002 (e)	2003 (e)	2004 (f)
Economic growth (%)	7	7.8	6.5	5.4	9	6
Inflation (%)	2.2	−1	1.4	1	2	1.9
Public-sector balance/GDP (%)	−4.3	8.6	0.1	4.8	4.6	2.8
Exports	7.2	11.6	10.9	11.4	13.0	10.8
Imports	2.3	2.9	3.4	3.8	4.0	4.1
Trade balance	5.0	8.7	7.5	7.6	9.0	6.7
Current account balance/GDP (%)	17.5	33.2	26.5	24.3	28.2	18.3
Foreign debt/GDP (%)	94.4	87.9	93.8	91.8	85.9	93.1
Debt service/Exports (%)	18.0	14.1	19.6	21.0	20.0	22.3
Currency reserves (import months)	2.9	2.1	2.1	2.4	4.2	4.5

e = estimate, f = forecast

CONDITIONS OF ACCESS TO THE MARKET

■ Market overview

The Qatari market is free and open to trade. Imports, however, are subject to rules of origin that vary from country to country. The distribution of imported goods in the market is subject to the prior conclusion of a contract with a local sponsor, except for public tenders. Trademark and intellectual property protection legislation is relatively recent. Qatar has been a signatory to the Geneva Convention (industrial property) and the Bern Convention (intellectual property) only since 5 July 2000. Consequently, the country still lacks the means to enforce and implement this legislation on a systematic basis.

■ Means of entry

From 1 January 2003, all goods are liable to 5 per cent *ad valorem* duty under the GCC customs union, except for products directly competing with local manufacture (steel: 20 per cent), products taxed on grounds of health (cigarettes: 100 per cent) and those banned by Islam (wines and spirits: 100 per cent).

Exporters are advised to demand the irrevocable and confirmed letter of credit, the most widely used means of payment in Qatar, for transactions with local customers.

■ Attitude towards foreign investors

Regulations governing foreign investment were relaxed under a new law passed on 16 October 2000. Foreign investors are now permitted to own 100 per cent of a company in the agricultural, manufacturing, healthcare, education, tourism and energy sectors, subject to the approval of the Ministry of Economic Affairs and Trade.

There is only one precondition: that foreign investments comply with the government's development plans. Sectors falling outside the scope of this legislation include banking, insurance, property and retail. Foreigners investing in these sectors are required to have a majority Qatari partner with a minimum 51 per cent stake. Foreign investors may acquire leaseholds for a maximum period of 50 years on a renewable basis, but are barred from acquiring freehold property. Disputes between a foreign investor and a local party are referred to local or international arbitration. Foreigners are required to have a Qatari sponsor when applying for a residence permit tied to a work permit. Plans to allow foreign investors to access the stock market via mutual funds are under review and a decision on this matter is due shortly. The Ministry of Finance, Economic Affairs and Trade grants wholly foreign-funded projects 10 years' tax relief as well as exemption from customs duties for imported equipment, raw materials and semi-finished goods that are not available locally.

4

313

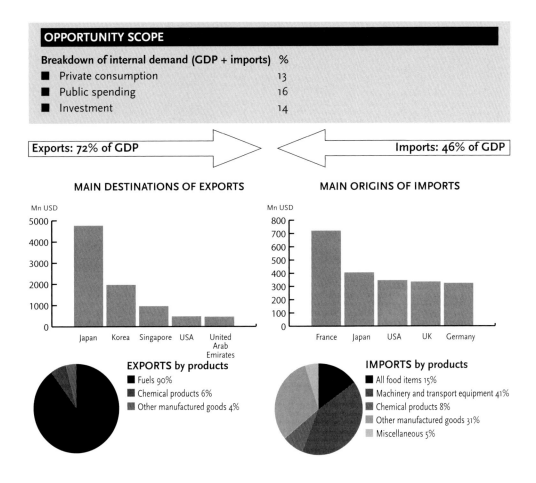

OPPORTUNITY SCOPE

Breakdown of internal demand (GDP + imports)   %
- Private consumption   13
- Public spending   16
- Investment   14

Exports: 72% of GDP   Imports: 46% of GDP

MAIN DESTINATIONS OF EXPORTS

Mn USD

Japan · Korea · Singapore · USA · United Arab Emirates

MAIN ORIGINS OF IMPORTS

Mn USD

France · Japan · USA · UK · Germany

EXPORTS by products
- Fuels 90%
- Chemical products 6%
- Other manufactured goods 4%

IMPORTS by products
- All food items 15%
- Machinery and transport equipment 41%
- Chemical products 8%
- Other manufactured goods 31%
- Miscellaneous 5%

STANDARD OF LIVING / PURCHASING POWER

Indicators	Qatar	Regional average	DC average
GNP per capita (PPP dollars)	n/a	7496	6778
GNP per capita (USD)	n/a	4722	3568
Human Development Index	0.826	0.740	0.708
Wealthiest 10% share of national income	n/a	30	33
Urban population percentage	n/a	70	60
Percentage under 15 years old	n/a	35	31
number of telephones per 1000 inhabitants	n/a	164	157
number of computers per 1000 inhabitants	n/a	56	66

Saudi Arabia

Population (million inhabitants)	21.4
GDP (million USD)	186,489

Coface analysis

Short-term: **A4**

Medium-term:
Quite low risk

STRENGTHS

- The leading OPEC oil-producing country with one-quarter of world oil reserves, Saudi Arabia holds a strategic position in oil markets.
- The need to attract foreign investment coupled with the prospect of upcoming WTO membership has revived the reform process.
- Development of the gas industry will enhance growth prospects.
- The country will continue to enjoy a privileged relationship with the United States in the region although relations have become more complicated since 11 September 2001.
- Prince Abdallah has been maintaining political continuity.

WEAKNESSES

- Very dependent on oil revenues, the economy has remained vulnerable to exogenous shocks.
- Public accounts have been running structural imbalances due to spending rigidities (subsidies, wages and interest on domestic debt).
- Payment times the government imposes on suppliers have tended to hurt the private sector's development potential.
- Immigrant worker remittances have been undermining the balance of payments.
- Terrorist threats have been increasing.

4

RISK ASSESSMENT

Oil market trends benefited Saudi Arabia in 2003 with the country able to increase production significantly while the price per barrel remained high. Those exceptional conditions thus spurred the country's economy, permitted the reduction of public-sector debt and bolstered its financial situation. A desire to support crude prices should prompt the kingdom to cut production in 2004, which could cause an economic slowdown, re-emergence of a fiscal deficit and deterioration of external accounts. The external financial situation has nonetheless been giving little cause for concern

with the debt burden low in relation to foreign currency earnings.

The country remains vulnerable to an oil market downturn and the consequence of its price-support policy is a reduction of its market share. Reforms will be necessary to attract the foreign investment needed to diversify the economy, establish durable growth and balance public accounts. The reform process has nonetheless been lagging due to resistance from conservative quarters and to the unstable social climate exacerbated by geopolitical uncertainties.

MAIN ECONOMIC INDICATORS

US$ billions	1999	2000	2001	2002	2003 (e)	2004 (f)
Economic growth (%)	−0.8	4.9	1.2	1.0	4.7	−1.5
Inflation (%)	−1.6	−0.6	−0.8	0.6	1.1	1.0
Public-sector balance/GDP (%)	−6.0	3.2	−3.9	−6.0	1.6	−3.5
Exports	50.7	77.5	67.9	71.5	82.0	71.0
Imports	25.7	27.7	28.6	29.6	30.4	33.1
Trade balance	25.0	49.8	39.3	41.9	51.6	37.9
Current account balance/GDP (%)	0.3	7.6	5.1	6.2	10.6	3.8
Foreign debt/GDP (%)	20.8	21.1	19.7	19.9	18.2	18.5
Debt service/Exports (%)	9.4	8.2	8.4	7.2	6.3	7.5
Currency reserves (import months)	3.3	3.3	3.1	3.6	3.8	3.9
Public-sector debt/GDP (%)	119.0	87.0	92.1	94.0	83.0	86.0

e = estimate, f = forecast

CONDITIONS OF ACCESS TO THE MARKET

■ Market overview

Saudi households spend the bulk of their income on non-durable goods despite the continued decline in purchasing power. The Saudization of jobs by 5 per cent a year remains a difficult prospect due to the lack of local human resources with adequate business training. Rising unemployment (15–20 per cent of the male working population) has a destabilizing effect on the 200,000 young Saudis who arrive on the job market each year. Consequently, spending on education and vocational training is a government priority in every budget.

■ Means of entry

Although member states of the Gulf Cooperation Council (Saudi Arabia, Bahrain, United Arab Emirates, Kuwait, Oman and Qatar) introduced a customs union on 1 January 2003, Saudi Arabia continues to apply differential duties to some 900 products. Actual customs duties are 0 per cent for basic foodstuffs and staple commodities, 5 per cent for 80 per cent of imported goods, 12 or 20 per cent for some locally produced goods, 25 per cent for some fruit and vegetables, and 100 per cent for milk, wheat, cigarettes and dates.

Import bans are in force on mostly religious grounds. Variable and reduced rates of duty apply to products from Jordan, Egypt, Morocco and Syria. Some goods (electrical appliances, cars, chemicals) are automatically subject to pre-shipment inspection. All public procurement contracts are subject to the national-preference rule. Entry and residence requirements for foreigners are very strict (compulsory Saudi sponsor). The legal environment is fairly unstable and intellectual property protection inadequate. In general, government agencies are slow to pay (7 to 30 months), but payment defaults in the oil and petrochemical industries are rare.

■ Attitude towards foreign investors

A new Investment Code was adopted in April 2000. Its key features include: issue of licences within 30 days, establishment of a one-stop shop for processing applications (SAGIA), acquisition of facilities and staff accommodation as freehold, self-sponsorship for foreign companies, and access to concessional Saudi financing. However, given the monopoly barring foreigners from holding shares in the country, foreign companies may only set up Saudi law subsidiaries incorporated as private limited liability companies or branches. A negative

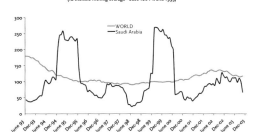

PAYMENT INCIDENTS INDEX
(12 months moving average - base 100 : World 1995)

list of sectors from which foreign investors are barred, published on 11 February 2001, was shortened in February 2003. The marginal rate of corporation tax applicable to foreign companies has been cut to 30 per cent and should be lowered to 25 per cent in due course. Losses can now be carried forward over an indefinite number of years. A reciprocal investment protection and promotion agreement with France, concluded in June 2002, is due to come into force shortly.

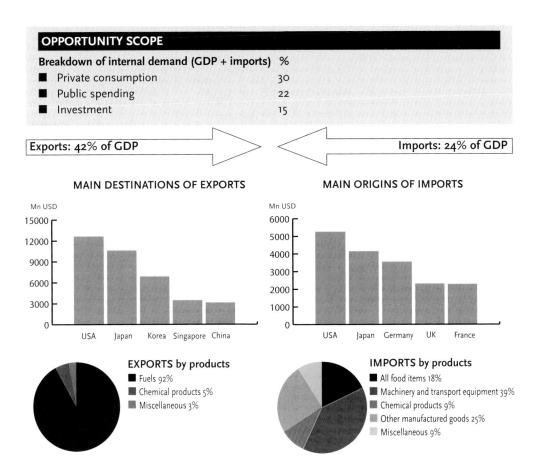

OPPORTUNITY SCOPE

Breakdown of internal demand (GDP + imports) %

■ Private consumption   30
■ Public spending   22
■ Investment   15

Exports: 42% of GDP   Imports: 24% of GDP

MAIN DESTINATIONS OF EXPORTS

Mn USD: USA, Japan, Korea, Singapore, China

MAIN ORIGINS OF IMPORTS

Mn USD: USA, Japan, Germany, UK, France

EXPORTS by products
■ Fuels 92%
■ Chemical products 5%
■ Miscellaneous 3%

IMPORTS by products
■ All food items 18%
■ Machinery and transport equipment 39%
■ Chemical products 9%
■ Other manufactured goods 25%
■ Miscellaneous 9%

STANDARD OF LIVING / PURCHASING POWER

Indicators	Saudi Arabia	Regional average	DC average
GNP per capita (PPP dollars)	13290	7496	6778
GNP per capita (USD)	8460	4722	3568
Human Development Index	0.769	0.740	0.708
Wealthiest 10% share of national income	n/a	30	33
Urban population percentage	87	70	60
Percentage under 15 years old	41	35	31
number of telephones per 1000 inhabitants	145	164	157
number of computers per 1000 inhabitants	63	56	66

4

Syria

Population (million inhabitants)	16.6
GDP (million USD)	19,495

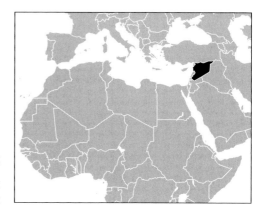

Short-term: **C**

Coface analysis

Medium-term:
Very high risk

STRENGTHS

- Syria has initiated an economic liberalization process intended to encourage investments and thereby fuel growth and create jobs. Progress remains nonetheless slow.
- The agricultural sector has been assuring food self-sufficiency.
- The tourism sector offers substantial development potential.
- Rising gas production should permit sustaining exportable oil volumes.
- Efforts made to settle payment arrears should permit Syria to rehabilitate its image with international financial backers.

WEAKNESSES

- Continued tight government supervision over the entire economy including banks has stymied emergence of a dynamic private sector with progress lagging on reforms.
- The economy is still dependent on the farm and oil sectors, which are vulnerable to exogenous shocks.
- Oil reserves have been dwindling.
- Sanctions imposed by the United States are having a negative effect on the country's image despite their likely limited economic consequences.
- Persistent regional instability has been affecting tourism and investment.
- Statistical data have been opaque.

RISK ASSESSMENT

Public spending and good farm-sector performance have been buoying growth, which has nonetheless remained weak. The fiscal deficit has been growing. With the prospect of falling oil revenues amid a downward price trend, continued expansionary policy could exacerbate imbalances. External accounts could also deteriorate. Debt ratios have remained high despite rescheduling agreements concluded with some countries. They are likely to rise even more with the expected decline of oil prices.

The economy has remained exposed to exogenous shocks affecting not only agriculture and the oil sector but also tourism and investment. Further out, improved conditions for growth will depend on implementation of necessary structural reforms. A centralized and inefficient economy continues to mark the country. Despite President Assad's evident willingness to move the country towards a market economy, internal resistance has been impeding the transition process and fostering a wait-and-see attitude among investors, intensified by regional tensions.

MAIN ECONOMIC INDICATORS						
US$ billions	1999	2000	2001	2002 (e)	2003 (e)	2004 (f)
Economic growth (%)	−0.9	0.6	7.2	2.7	0.9	2.5
Inflation (%)	−2.1	−0.6	0.5	1.5	2.5	3
Public-sector balance/GDP (%)	−1	−2.4	−1.6	−3	−4.4	−5.2
Exports	3.8	5.1	5.7	6.0	6.0	5.0
Imports	3.6	3.7	4.3	4.5	4.9	5.1
Trade balance	0.2	1.4	1.4	1.5	1.1	−0.1
Current account balance/GDP (%)	0.6	5.5	5.9	4.2	2.6	−2.1
Foreign debt/PIB	129.5	112.8	103.4	96.6	91.6	87.1
Debt service/Exports (%)	40.9	37.6	32.9	30.6	30.8	33.7
Currency reserves (import months)	4.1	5.0	5.8	6.7	6.5	6.4

e = estimate, f = forecast

CONDITIONS OF ACCESS TO THE MARKET

■ Means of entry

Syria has carried out customs reform and gradually liberalized its foreign trade. It is engaged in numerous free-trade negotiations and has concluded a series of free-trade agreements with Lebanon, Iraq, the United Arab Emirates and Jordan. The agreement with Saudi Arabia came into force in January 2003. It has also been involved since 1996 in negotiations over an association agreement with the European Union. These talks are now in their final phase. Under the terms of this agreement, trade between Europe and Syria will be exempt from customs duties at the end of a period of gradual tariff dismantlement.

There are 10 rates of customs duty from 1 per cent (agricultural and industrial raw materials) to 200 per cent (cars). The weighted average rate of duty is 30 per cent. As well as customs duties, there are various taxes (war effort, taxes on consumer and luxury goods) whose rates vary between 5 and 30 per cent of the value of the imported product. As part of the Syrian government's current policy on customs reform, the Ministry of Economic Affairs and Foreign Trade issued a series of decrees in December 2002 aimed at facilitating customs clearance, freeing up certain imports and listing banned products under eight customs nomenclatures. Syria follows the European Union's tariff nomenclature.

The risk of default in budgeted public transactions is, in the short term, minimal.

The means of payment normally used in transactions between foreign suppliers and Syrian buyers from both the public and private sectors is the letter of credit. Most Syrian private import firms have funds with foreign banks, especially in Lebanon. Export credit agencies are slowly reviving their medium-term guarantees for Syria.

■ Attitude towards foreign investors

In 1991, Syria introduced a series of tax and legal regulations, collectively known as Law No. 10, to encourage investment, regardless of the origin of funds or the nationality of investors. This law was later relaxed by a raft of measures, including:

● A decree law passed in June 2000 authorizing foreign currency transfers for companies divesting after five years of business, and extending the tax-exemption period. The government is currently studying ways of further relaxing the provisions of this decree to include profit transfers.

● An amendment to Law No. 10 in 2001 offering private investors greater incentives and encouraging long-term projects. The amendment also grants investors property ownership rights where this is required for business.

There are also seven free zones in Syria (Decree 84 of 1972) offering companies based there a number of tax breaks and exemptions.

4

The main restrictions concern trade with Israel or with Israeli-held companies in accordance with Arab boycott legislation, reactivated since the intifada in the Palestinian Territories.

Foreign exchange regulations

The exchange rate of the Syrian pound against the US dollar has been unified since 2000 (46 pounds to the dollar for exports and 46.5 pounds for imports). The pound is a non-convertible currency pegged to the dollar. According to a statement issued by the Ministry of Finance in October 2003, the current system of exchange controls could soon be abolished.

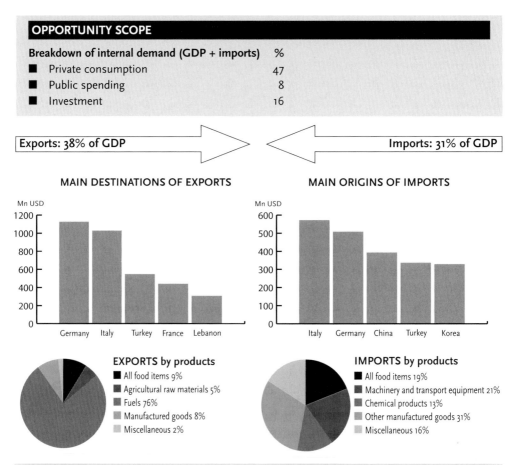

OPPORTUNITY SCOPE

Breakdown of internal demand (GDP + imports)	%
■ Private consumption	47
■ Public spending	8
■ Investment	16

Exports: 38% of GDP

Imports: 31% of GDP

MAIN DESTINATIONS OF EXPORTS

Mn USD — Germany, Italy, Turkey, France, Lebanon

MAIN ORIGINS OF IMPORTS

Mn USD — Italy, Germany, China, Turkey, Korea

EXPORTS by products
- ■ All food items 9%
- ■ Agricultural raw materials 5%
- ■ Fuels 76%
- ■ Manufactured goods 8%
- ■ Miscellaneous 2%

IMPORTS by products
- ■ All food items 19%
- ■ Machinery and transport equipment 21%
- ■ Chemical products 13%
- ■ Other manufactured goods 31%
- ■ Miscellaneous 16%

STANDARD OF LIVING / PURCHASING POWER

Indicators	Syria	Regional average	DC average
GNP per capita (PPP dollars)	3160	7496	6778
GNP per capita (USD)	1040	4722	3568
Human Development Index	0.685	0.740	0.708
Wealthiest 10% share of national income	n/a	30	33
Urban population percentage	52	70	60
Percentage under 15 years old	40	35	31
number of telephones per 1000 inhabitants	103	164	157
number of computers per 1000 inhabitants	16	56	66

Tunisia

Population (million inhabitants)   9.7
GDP (million USD)   19,980

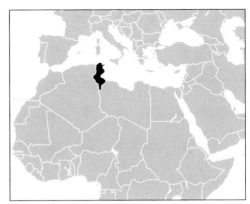

Coface analysis

Short-term: **A4**

Medium-term:
Quite low risk

STRENGTHS

- With its stability and policy of diversifying and opening its economy, Tunisia has earned the international community's political and financial backing.
- The partnership agreement with the European Union has spurred industrial, infrastructure and financial-sector upgrading.
- The country's prudent economic policy has facilitated access to international capital markets.
- Access to education and a developed social system have contributed to reducing inequality and fostering emergence of a dynamic middle class.

WEAKNESSES

- The country possesses only modest natural resources and its economy has remained subject to exogenous factors (weather conditions, European demand, tourism).
- Its increasingly open economy and the end of the Multifibres Arrangement in 2005 will compel Tunisia to improve the competitiveness of its industrial product offer.
- The unsteady pace of structural reforms has affected foreign direct investment inflows.
- Unemployment has remained relatively high (15 per cent of the overall working population but 30 per cent of the youngest segment).

RISK ASSESSMENT

The bright growth outlook for 2004 will be subject to many uncertainties (tourism, weather conditions, economic activity in Europe). The country has nonetheless continued to pursue its prudent policy of modernization, diversification and public-sector deficit reduction. The country's political stability and the international community backing it enjoys have been facilitating that policy.

The main risks will concern trends on exports and tourism where recovery has remained uncertain.

However, provided investment flows continue to increase, debt ratios remain reasonable and the country retains easy access to international capital markets, there will be little risk of a balance-of-payments crisis.

Company payment behaviour, notably in the textile sector, has deteriorated, however, amid tightening credit and competition from countries with weaker currencies. The high Coface payment-incident index has nonetheless been more a reflection of late payments than actual defaults and insolvency.

4

MAIN ECONOMIC INDICATORS						
US$ billions	1999	2000	2001	2002	2003 (e)	2004 (f)
Economic growth (%)	6.1	4.7	4.9	1.7	6	5.6
Inflation (%)	2.7	3.0	1.9	2.8	2.7	2.5
Public-sector balance/GDP (%)	–3.6	–3.7	–3.5	–2.4	–1.9	–2.1
Exports	5.9	5.8	6.6	6.9	8.1	8.7
Imports	8	8.1	9	9	10.1	10.7
Trade balance	–2.1	–2.3	–2.4	–2.1	–2	–1.9
Current account balance/GDP (%)	–2.2	–4.2	–4.3	–3.5	–3	–1.9
Foreign debt	11.8	11.2	12.9	14.8	15.8	16
Debt service/Exports (%)	17.7	20.4	14	14.2	12.6	12.9
Currency reserves (import months)	2.7	2.1	2.1	2.7	2.6	2.7

e = estimate, f = forecast

CONDITIONS OF ACCESS TO THE MARKET

■ Means of entry

Ninety per cent of foreign products can be freely imported. Authorization must be obtained from the Ministry of Trade or the competent ministry to import products considered sensitive on grounds of security, public order, health, hygiene and morality, or essential for the protection of wild life, plants and cultural heritage.

Despite the conclusion of a free-trade agreement with the European Union, the average level of tariff protection in Tunisia remains high. Consequently, duties on a large number of foodstuffs exceed 100 per cent, as do duties on imported products that compete with local manufacture and so-called luxury goods. Since 1 January 2000, duties on luxury goods have been gradually cut and are due to be abolished by 2008. Tunisian import firms are able to pay their suppliers directly in foreign exchange and hold hard-currency accounts for that purpose.

Since 1993, payments for ordinary transactions have been made through approved financial institutions (banks) without prior central bank approval. Disputes over contracts entered into with Tunisian companies are usually brought before Tunisian courts.

■ Attitude towards foreign investors

Under the Investment Incentive Code (CII) of December 1993, foreigners are free to invest in all sectors, except mining, energy, domestic trade and financial services, all of which are governed by specific regulations. The conditions regulating foreign business activity in the country, however, are governed by the decree law of 1961. Foreigners may not invest in industries in which the state has a monopoly (water supply, post office, cigarettes), unless they are awarded a concession. This area has been opened up since the deregulation of electricity generation, mobile telephone services and, more recently, banking.

Foreign investment is treated on an equal footing with domestic investment. However, prior authorization must be obtained for certain service activities that are not entirely export related and in which the foreign interest exceeds 50 per cent. Investments that are totally export related are granted tax incentives. The acquisition by foreigners of marketable securities with attached voting rights or of shareholdings in existing Tunisian companies is subject to the approval of the

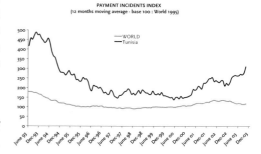

PAYMENT INCIDENTS INDEX
(12 months moving average - base 100 : World 1995)

Higher Investment Commission where the overall foreign interest exceeds 49 per cent. Foreign investors are barred from owning farmland.

There is very little red tape for offshore banks, totally export-orientated firms and non-profit organizations. But, despite the opening of a one-stop shop for foreign investors, administrative formalities often take longer than expected.

On the whole, attitudes towards foreign business people are open. However, investors should give their fullest attention to the management of risks relating to wider issues of governance (legal stability, legal certainty, clarity of administrative procedures).

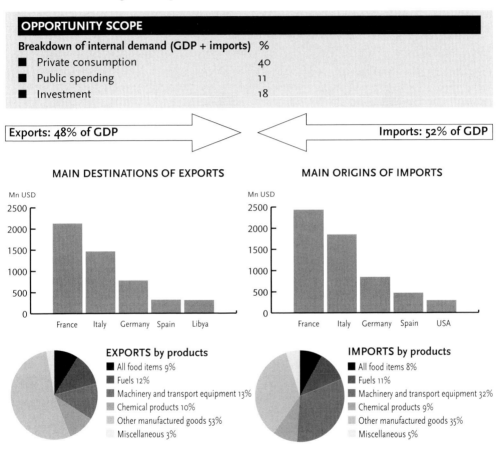

OPPORTUNITY SCOPE

Breakdown of internal demand (GDP + imports)	%
■ Private consumption	40
■ Public spending	11
■ Investment	18

Exports: 48% of GDP ⟹ ⟸ Imports: 52% of GDP

4

MAIN DESTINATIONS OF EXPORTS

Mn USD

France, Italy, Germany, Spain, Libya

MAIN ORIGINS OF IMPORTS

Mn USD

France, Italy, Germany, Spain, USA

EXPORTS by products
- ■ All food items 9%
- ■ Fuels 12%
- ■ Machinery and transport equipment 13%
- ■ Chemical products 10%
- ■ Other manufactured goods 53%
- ■ Miscellaneous 3%

IMPORTS by products
- ■ All food items 8%
- ■ Fuels 11%
- ■ Machinery and transport equipment 32%
- ■ Chemical products 9%
- ■ Other manufactured goods 35%
- ■ Miscellaneous 5%

STANDARD OF LIVING / PURCHASING POWER

Indicators	Tunisia	Regional average	DC average
GNP per capita (PPP dollars)	6090	7496	6778
GNP per capita (USD)	2070	4722	3568
Human Development Index	0.74	0.740	0.708
Wealthiest 10% share of national income	32	30	33
Urban population percentage	66	70	60
Percentage under 15 years old	29	35	31
number of telephones per 1000 inhabitants	109	164	157
number of computers per 1000 inhabitants	24	56	66

Turkey

Population (million inhabitants)	66.2
GDP (million USD)	147,683

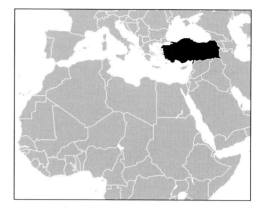

Coface analysis

Short-term: **B**

Medium-term:
High risk

STRENGTHS

- A diversified and dynamic private sector has been adapting rapidly to an unstable environment.
- Several laws recently adopted to improve the political framework are intended to permit Turkey to comply with political criteria for European Union admission.
- Progress made on banking reforms, despite a high level of risk, could provide the basis for durable growth and disinflation.
- With its NATO membership and European partner status, Turkey has continued to enjoy international community backing.

WEAKNESSES

- Public finance imbalances sustained by debt-linked interest expense whose weight depends on financial market confidence have remained a major source of weakness.
- Absent political commitment, public sector privatization and streamlining have been slow to materialize.
- The Cyprus status question and Kurdish minority situation (with emergence of an autonomous Kurdish state possible in Iraq) have remained potential sources of conflict.
- The secularism debate could ultimately destabilize the Turkish political situation.

RISK ASSESSMENT

The Turkish economy has resumed high growth buoyed by consumption and investment amid continued disinflation. The climate of confidence has returned thanks to renewed backing by the IMF and US authorities. Interest rates have fallen in consequence, which facilitates refinancing the public debt. For the short term, the country appears to have covered its foreign exchange financing needs. In such favourable economic conditions, the Coface payment-incident index has remained far below the world average, reflecting the good payment behaviour of Turkish companies.

The wave of confidence observed is nonetheless shaky, remaining vulnerable to swings in market sentiment. The exchange rate has thus been excessively volatile. Moreover, confidence has remained dependent on compliance with IMF-imposed conditions whereas the AKP government's record on reforms has been inconsistent. Politically, Turkish–US relations have warmed again. However, the Kurdish question has re-emerged with internal and regional unrest remaining possible. The evolution of Turkey's candidacy to the European Union is also likely to influence market confidence.

MAIN ECONOMIC INDICATORS

US$ billions	1999	2000	2001	2002	2003 (e)	2004 (f)
Economic growth (%)	−5	7.2	−7.4	7.8	5	4.5
Inflation (%)	68.7	39.0	68.4	29.8	21.0	14.4
Public-sector balance/GDP (%)	−24.2	−17.8	−19	−14	−13.8	−13.6
Exports	29.3	31.7	35.3	39.8	47.6	54.3
Imports	39.8	54.0	39.7	48.2	60.5	68.6
Trade balance	−10.4	−22.4	−4.5	−8.4	−12.9	−14.3
Current account balance	−1.4	−9.8	3.4	−1.5	−7.0	−7.5
Current account balance/GDP (%)	−0.7	−5	2.3	−0.8	−2.9	−2.8
Foreign debt	103.3	120.0	115.0	135.0	143.0	149.0
wherein short-term debt (%)	24.2	24.6	16.3	13.8	15.9	17.6
Debt service/Exports (%)	41.2	41.7	61.3	58.5	46.8	38.5
Currency reserves (import months)	5.1	4.0	4.2	5.2	4.6	4.3

e = estimate, f = forecast

CONDITIONS OF ACCESS TO THE MARKET

■ Means of entry

The Turkish market is by and large open to imported goods and services. The country's economic system has largely been harmonized with that of the European Union, except for certain agricultural products. Turkish companies are particularly keen to conclude partnership agreements and joint ventures. All means of payment are used and accepted. Documentary credit is strongly recommended for initial transactions and during periods of economic instability. It should preferably be opened with a foreign bank, although Turkish companies generally prefer to work with their own banks. Acceptance credit letters are the most widely used means of payment but, because of their cost, cash against documents or payment against goods is usually preferred by Turkish importers.

Several audit companies of international standing have offices in Turkey.

■ Attitude towards foreign investors

On 5 June 2003, the Grand National Assembly of Turkey voted a law regulating foreign direct investment in Turkey. The new law, in force since its publication in the *Official Journal of the Republic of Turkey* No. 25141 on 17 June 2003, replaces Law No. 6224 on Foreign Investment Incentives. It relaxes administrative restrictions and authorizations, while protecting the rights of foreign investors. It also reaffirms freedom of investment, equality of treatment between foreign investors and Turks, and unrestricted transfer of profits. Article 1 of this law aims to encourage foreign direct investment, protect the rights of foreign investors, harmonize the definitions of 'investment' and 'investor' with international standards and replace the system of prior authorizations and approvals with a new information system.

Article 3 of Law No. 4875 reaffirms the principles of equality and freedom of investment. This provision waives the requirement that foreign investors contribute a minimum of US$50,000 in equity and obtain prior approval from the Directorate-General for Foreign Investment (DGIE) attached to the Office of the Under-Secretary of State for the Treasury. This last formality has been replaced by a duty to inform the competent authorities. However, the opening of a branch office remains subject to the approval of the DGIE.

4

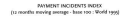

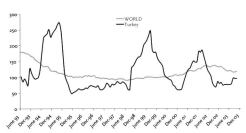

PAYMENT INCIDENTS INDEX
(12 months moving average - base 100 : World 1995)

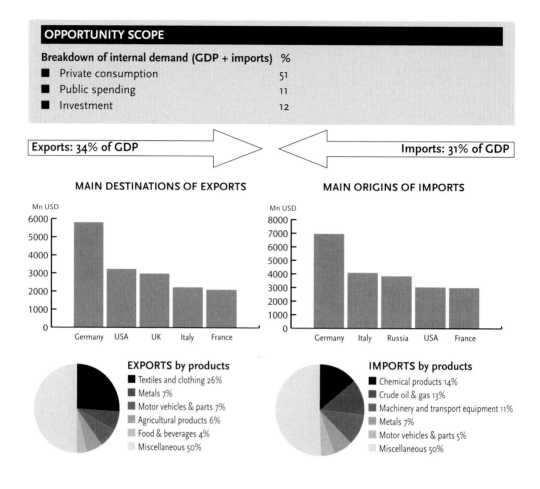

OPPORTUNITY SCOPE

Breakdown of internal demand (GDP + imports) %
- Private consumption — 51
- Public spending — 11
- Investment — 12

Exports: 34% of GDP   Imports: 31% of GDP

MAIN DESTINATIONS OF EXPORTS

Mn USD

Germany, USA, UK, Italy, France

MAIN ORIGINS OF IMPORTS

Mn USD

Germany, Italy, Russia, USA, France

EXPORTS by products
- Textiles and clothing 26%
- Metals 7%
- Motor vehicles & parts 7%
- Agricultural products 6%
- Food & beverages 4%
- Miscellaneous 50%

IMPORTS by products
- Chemical products 14%
- Crude oil & gas 13%
- Machinery and transport equipment 11%
- Metals 7%
- Motor vehicles & parts 5%
- Miscellaneous 50%

STANDARD OF LIVING / PURCHASING POWER

Indicators	Turkey	Regional average	DC average
GNP per capita (PPP dollars)	5830	7496	6778
GNP per capita (USD)	2530	4722	3568
Human Development Index	0.734	0.740	0.708
Wealthiest 10% share of national income	31	30	33
Urban population percentage	66	70	60
Percentage under 15 years old	28	35	31
number of telephones per 1000 inhabitants	285	164	157
number of computers per 1000 inhabitants	41	56	66

United Arab Emirates

Population (million inhabitants)	3.2
GDP (million USD)	67,600

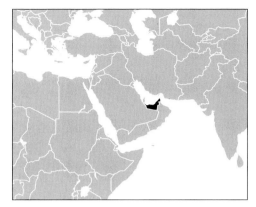

Short-term: **A2**

Medium-term:

Coface analysis

Low risk

STRENGTHS

- The economy is open and diversified.
- Dubai has been vigorously developing the non-oil sector (aluminium, financial services, tourism).
- Abu Dhabi boasts substantial oil and gas reserves.
- Sustained efforts have been made to attract foreign investments.
- The country's considerable holdings abroad constitute a guarantee of its financial solidity.

WEAKNESSES

- Amid opaque public accounts, continuing high fiscal deficits have contributed to reduction of holdings abroad.
- Although diversified, the economy has remained dependent on oil revenues and exposed to external crises.
- Remittances abroad by immigrant foreign workers have been undermining external accounts.
- Disagreement has persisted with Iran over that country's occupation of the Lesser Tumbs, Greater Tumbs and Abu Mousa islands since 1971.

RISK ASSESSMENT

Reduction of oil production according to OPEC recommendations should retard growth in 2004. Non-oil-sector dynamism and public spending could partially offset that slowdown. Investment and tourism could nonetheless suffer further from regional uncertainties.

Despite the expected decline of oil prices and volumes, external accounts should continue to post large surpluses. The financial situation is giving no particular cause for concern. The external debt burden remains modest in relation to foreign currency earnings and reserves and the country's considerable holdings abroad. The public-sector deficit should nonetheless remain high and financing it via earnings from those holdings abroad could eventually undermine the Emirates' financial situation. Consolidating the public accounts will necessitate continuation of the reform programme (privatizations, public service concessions, subsidy reductions, tax system improvements), which will nonetheless depend on substantial foreign direct investments that regional uncertainties could deter.

4

MAIN ECONOMIC INDICATORS						
US$ billions	1999	2000	2001	2002 (e)	2003 (e)	2004 (f)
Economic growth (%)	4.4	10.0	3.8	1.8	5	4
Inflation (%)	2.2	1.4	2.2	2.8	2.9	2.2
Public-sector balance/GDP (%)	−5.6	6.0	−5.3	−8.9	−7.8	−7.6
Exports	36.5	49.6	48.2	49.6	53.5	52.3
Imports	27.9	30.8	32.8	34.8	36.9	37.8
Trade balance	8.6	18.8	15.4	14.8	16.6	14.5
Current account balance/GDP (%)	11.1	25.8	15.0	8.4	11.9	9.9
Foreign debt/GDP (%)	31.2	23.5	27.7	27.2	30.0	30.9
Debt service/Exports (%)	8.6	7.0	6.9	6.5	6.4	7.4
Currency reserves (import months)	3.4	4.0	3.9	3.9	3.6	3.8

e = estimate, f = forecast

CONDITIONS OF ACCESS TO THE MARKET

■ Market overview

In spite of a number of restrictive practices (local majority partner requirement, closing off of certain sectors to foreigners, local agent requirement, local sponsorship requirement for obtaining a resident visa), the United Arab Emirates market is very open and thus highly competitive. In the last 10 years, UAE imports have grown at an average rate of 6 per cent per annum. The UAE is a member of the WTO and, through the GCC, party to talks on a free-trade agreement with the European Union.

■ Means of entry

Customs duties in force in the UAE as of 1 January 2003, the date of introduction of the customs union of the Cooperation Council for the Arab States of the Gulf, are 0 per cent for 417 customs nomenclatures and 5 per cent of the CIF value for other goods.

The UAE's standards policy is based on that of the GCC. In the first six months of 2003, a national agency, ESMA (Emirates Authority for Standardization and Metrology), was set up to establish nationwide standards and, above all, to play an active role in the harmonization of regulations within the GCC.

All modern means of payment are available in the United Arab Emirates. The cheque, documentary credit collection, promissory note and bill of exchange are not recommended.

■ Attitude towards foreign investors

The Emirate of Abu Dhabi has actively sought FDI both to develop the oil and gas sector and, more recently, to improve management of some of its public services. The Emirate of Dubai, in the face of gradual depletion of its resources, is striving to attract foreign investment aimed at stepping up and consolidating economic diversification, particularly in the property, tourism and service sectors.

The absence in the UAE of direct taxation of companies (excluding banks and oil companies) and people, of exchange controls and of restrictions on the repatriation of capital acts as a magnet for investment. On the whole, the country's legislation and legal practices are investment-friendly (adoption of new intellectual property protection laws, progress in Dubai on ownership of land by foreigners). However, a number of obstacles to FDI remain. These include the requirement for foreign companies outside the free zones to have a local majority partner in a joint venture, stringent restrictions on property ownership by foreigners, and a sponsorship requirement for non-nationals residing in the Emirates.

■ Foreign exchange regulations

There are no exchange controls in the UAE. The UAE dirham enjoys fixed parity with the dollar (US$1 = 3.6725 dirham). There are no restrictions on capital transfers.

OPPORTUNITY SCOPE

Breakdown of internal demand (GDP + imports) %
- Private consumption 29
- Public spending 10
- Investment 14

Exports: 80% of GDP ➤ ◁ **Imports: 65% of GDP**

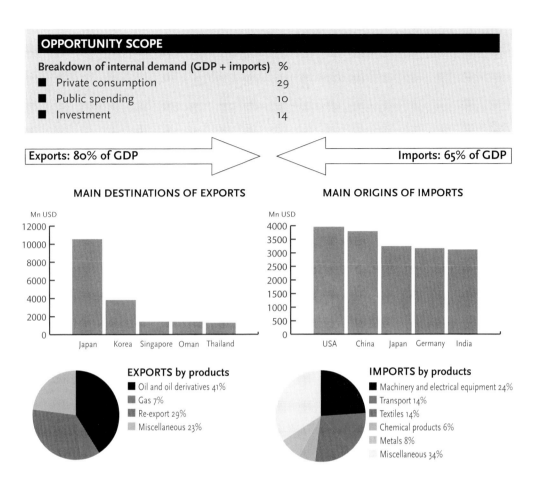

MAIN DESTINATIONS OF EXPORTS

Mn USD

Japan, Korea, Singapore, Oman, Thailand

MAIN ORIGINS OF IMPORTS

Mn USD

USA, China, Japan, Germany, India

EXPORTS by products
- Oil and oil derivatives 41%
- Gas 7%
- Re-export 29%
- Miscellaneous 23%

IMPORTS by products
- Machinery and electrical equipment 24%
- Transport 14%
- Textiles 14%
- Chemical products 6%
- Metals 8%
- Miscellaneous 34%

4

STANDARD OF LIVING / PURCHASING POWER

Indicators	United Arab Emirates	Regional average	DC average
GNP per capita (PPP dollars)	n/a	7496	6778
GNP per capita (USD)	n/a	4722	3568
Human Development Index	0.816	0.740	0.708
Wealthiest 10% share of national income	n/a	30	33
Urban population percentage	87	70	60
Percentage under 15 years old	26	35	31
number of telephones per 1000 inhabitants	340	164	157
number of computers per 1000 inhabitants	136	56	66

Yemen

Population (million inhabitants)	18
GDP (million USD)	9,276

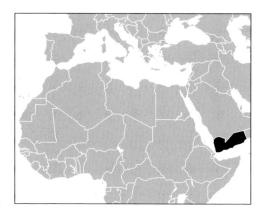

Short-term: **C**

Medium-term:
Very high risk

Coface analysis

STRENGTHS

- Yemen boasts substantial and still little exploited natural gas reserves.
- It has been benefiting from international community backing with its progress on reforms under scrutiny.
- Foreign debt has been a mild constraint considering the reductions obtained from the Paris Club.
- The country has strengthened its cooperation with the United States and Saudi Arabia.
- It is a candidate for the Gulf Cooperation Council.

WEAKNESSES

- The economy has remained dependent on the oil sector with the decline of known reserves, estimated at 20 years of production, making structural reforms essential.
- Oil-product subsidies have not only fostered waste, smuggling and corruption but they have also contributed to public finance imbalances.
- Insecurity has been affecting investment and tourism.
- Water is scarce.

RISK ASSESSMENT

The decline of oil production and prices should contribute to a growth slowdown and deterioration of public and external balances. However, the external financial situation has been giving little near-term cause for concern due to the relatively limited amount of debt in relation to foreign currency earnings and to the comfortable level of official currency reserves.

Further out, Yemen will have to meet a major challenge. Barring new discoveries, the scheduled oil production decline from 2004, in conjunction with downward-trending oil prices, should progressively worsen the external and fiscal deficits. Structural reforms will thus be essential in fostering durable non-oil-sector growth and consolidating public accounts. To achieve that, the country will be counting on private investments. However, the climate of insecurity, social tensions and extensive corruption could continue to impede the process and deter foreign investment.

Politically, although President Saleh strengthened his position in the last elections, the country's cooperation with the United States in combating terrorism could spur opposition movements.

MAIN ECONOMIC INDICATORS						
US$ billions	1999	2000	2001	2002	2003 (e)	2004 (f)
Economic growth (%)	3.5	4.4	4.6	3.9	3.8	3.3
Inflation (%)	8	10.9	10.7	6.8	12.1	11.9
Public-sector balance/GDP (%)¹	−1	6.7	2.3	−2.8	−2.5	−2.9
Exports	2.5	3.8	3.3	3.6	4.1	3.5
Imports	2.4	2.6	2.8	3.1	3.5	3.7
Trade balance	0.0	1.2	0.5	0.5	0.6	−0.2
Current account balance/GDP (%)¹	2.7	13.2	5.3	3.9	0.5	−2.4
Foreign debt/GDP (%)	73.2	50.3	51.3	49.0	45.1	43.4
Debt service/Exports (%)	9.2	4.7	4.9	3.6	3.3	4.2
Currency reserves (import months)	4.5	8.6	10.5	10.6	9.8	10.4

¹ excluding donations   e = estimate, f = forecast

CONDITIONS OF ACCESS TO THE MARKET

■ Market overview

The Yemeni market can be deemed an open market, as there are few restrictions and no discrimination between supplier countries.

■ Means of entry

There are several categories of taxes on imported goods:

- 'duties and levies' on all authorized imports based on the CIF value: 5 per cent, 10 per cent, 15 per cent and 20 per cent;
- a freight tax calculated on the volume and length of storage;
- 1 per cent tax on net trading profits.

Customs tariff reform is under study.

Only irrevocable and confirmed letters of credit should be used, guaranteed by a first-rate, preferably foreign bank. Advance payment is also acceptable as some Yemeni traders have financial assets abroad and can use them to pay for imports into Yemen. If a letter of credit is opened with Crédit Agricole Indosuez (the only Western financial institution with branches in Yemen), it does not need to be confirmed, as long as the seller

is prepared to cover the risk of non-transfer. Some foreign audit companies (SGS, but not Véritas) are represented in Yemen, but do not have offices there. As a result, caution is called for when dealing with inspections.

■ Attitude towards foreign investors

Foreign investment is governed by Law No. 22 of 2002.

There are also ad hoc laws offering special terms for oil exploration and production and major contracts. In general, investors are granted tax breaks and exemptions from customs duty. Capital invested and profits can be freely repatriated at the market rate. The law enshrines the principle of equality between Yemenis and foreigners. Foreigners can hold a majority, or even 100 per cent, stake in local companies. The Labour Code, written in Arabic, covers key issues, but a number of points are open to interpretation. Social protection is poor. Some companies take out private insurance cover for their employees, but are not required to do so.

■ Foreign exchange regulations

The dollar serves as a benchmark. The rial floats against the dollar and in October 2003 the exchange rate was 182 rials to the dollar.

4

OPPORTUNITY SCOPE

Breakdown of internal demand (GDP + imports)	%
■ Private consumption	47
■ Public spending	10
■ Investment	15

Exports: 51% of GDP

Imports: 46% of GDP

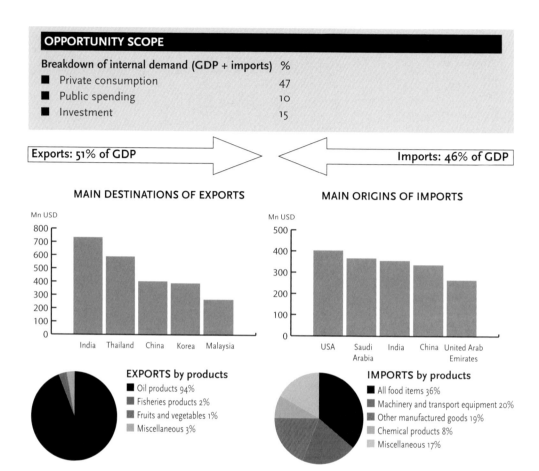

MAIN DESTINATIONS OF EXPORTS

Mn USD

India, Thailand, China, Korea, Malaysia

EXPORTS by products
- ■ Oil products 94%
- ■ Fisheries products 2%
- ▥ Fruits and vegetables 1%
- ▨ Miscellaneous 3%

MAIN ORIGINS OF IMPORTS

Mn USD

USA, Saudi Arabia, India, China, United Arab Emirates

IMPORTS by products
- ■ All food items 36%
- ■ Machinery and transport equipment 20%
- ▥ Other manufactured goods 19%
- ▨ Chemical products 8%
- ▨ Miscellaneous 17%

STANDARD OF LIVING / PURCHASING POWER

Indicators	Yemen	Regional average	DC average
GNP per capita (PPP dollars)	730	7496	6778
GNP per capita (USD)	450	4722	3568
Human Development Index	0.47	0.740	0.708
Wealthiest 10% share of national income	26	30	33
Urban population percentage	25	70	60
Percentage under 15 years old	46	35	31
number of telephones per 1000 inhabitants	22	164	157
number of computers per 1000 inhabitants	2	56	66

Sub-Saharan Africa

5

Economic Prospects for Southern Africa and Oil Stakes in 2004

Experts from Oxford Analytica, Oxford

SOUTHERN AFRICA

■ South Africa: unemployment and poverty

Modest economic growth, highly capital-intensive investment projects and continued job shedding in existing enterprises have combined to push unemployment levels continuously upward to 40 per cent, possibly higher. There has been strong growth of a black middle class – in part the result of affirmative action and black economic empowerment (BEE) policies – and the government has delivered significant improvements in access to housing, water and sanitation services. However, survey evidence suggests that poverty levels are increasing among the poorer underclasses, with an estimated 17 million people (around 37 per cent of the population) currently living in absolute poverty. Opposition from the left wing of the ANC alliance to the government's neo-liberal economic policies – allegedly the source of the increased poverty – continues unabated.

■ South Africa: economic outlook

GDP growth in 2003 is unlikely to exceed 2 per cent – well below the government's target of more than 3 per cent. A big drop in agricultural output (partly drought-related) and declining manufacturing output (largely the result of the continuing extraordinary appreciation of the rand) have been the main sources of disappointment.

However, domestic demand has picked up in recent months as a result of the combination of rising pre-election government spending, rapidly falling inflation and the recent sharp cuts in interest rates. Consequently, there has been an output surge in the construction, retail trade and transport and communication sectors. In addition, the recovery in global growth, coupled with expanding Chinese demand for resources, is now benefiting mining-sector export volumes. Against this, the still-appreciating rand – the result of the current worldwide flight from dollar-denominated assets – is squeezing profits in exporting and import-competing firms. However, despite indications that some mining expansion projects are being put on hold on account of the rand's current strength, fixed investment levels on the whole appear to be holding up.

Domestic demand will be underpinned by further cuts in interest rates in the near term. However, the economic outlook depends crucially on both global trends and the direction of the exchange rate. Given continuing buoyancy in global demand for – and prices of – resources and continuing dollar weakness, South Africa's balance of payments should be able to sustain the domestic recovery during 2004, provided there is no dramatic turnaround in the exchange rate. However, further appreciation of the rand would imply structural distortions as manufacturing competitiveness would be further undermined. The challenge for the monetary authorities is to achieve a combination of interest rate cuts and dollar purchases (for the reserves) that will weaken the rand, while keeping inflation within the target 3–6 per cent range and avoiding a capital exodus. This balancing act could be upset domestically by policy errors (such as excessive interest rate cuts) or unexpected political problems, and externally by dollar collapse, rising US interest rates and/or Chinese revaluation.

■ The Zimbabwe dilemma

The seemingly inexorable downward spiral towards implosion in Zimbabwe continues to threaten to destabilize the region. Accelerating economic contraction has severely curtailed Zimbabwe's normal bilateral trade relations with its neighbours. In addition, the growing flood of migrants and refugees across Zimbabwe's borders is creating serious social – and in some cases political – problems for the neighbouring states.

■ Socio-economic issues

All the Southern African states will continue to suffer from the ravages of the HIV/AIDS pandemic, which in some cases is becoming increasingly interconnected with drought- and policy-induced famine. A shortfall in funding for the region's food-aid needs appears likely. However, the combination of increasing global funding, reducing drug prices and more focused policy initiatives offers hope of improved efforts to limit the spread of the virus and extend the duration and quality of life of those already infected. Whether real progress towards these objectives will be realized will depend on the strength of political will and institutional implementation capacity.

A further threat to the region's long-term stability is posed by the growing incidence of organized crime, including drug smuggling and money laundering. Increased international assistance has been made available for combating international crime, especially since the terrorist attacks of 11 September 2001, but progress is likely to remain limited, not least because of the large scale of unregulated and illegal border crossings.

■ Trade negotiations

A plethora of trade negotiations, currently under way, will pose challenges for the achievement of regional cohesion in economic policies. Aside from SADC's own free-trade protocol, towards which only slow progress has been made, the negotiations include:

- economic partnership agreements (EPAs) between the EU and regional states under the Cotonou treaty arrangements;
- free-trade area (FTA) negotiations between the United States and the five countries – Botswana, Lesotho, Namibia, South Africa and Swaziland – of the Southern African Customs Union (SACU); and
- FTA negotiations between SACU and the European Free Trade Association (EFTA) countries.

These negotiations are further complicated by overlapping memberships of SACU, SADC and the Common Market for Eastern and Southern Africa (COMESA), and by the different preferential treatments accorded to individual Southern African countries by the EU and by the American Growth and Opportunity Act (AGOA). These differences are a potential source of divisions among the regional states, and of major new bureaucratic complexities.

A delicate policy balancing act is needed to protect the South African economy from the impact of adverse global developments. Progress in meeting socio-economic challenges will depend on the political will and institutional capacities for devising and implementing new policy initiatives.

OIL OUTLOOK

In September 2003 the share of Sub-Saharan Africa in world oil production (crude, natural gas liquids and condensate) of 78.2 million barrels per day was 4.72 million barrels per day, or 6 per cent. Of this African total, 2.24 million barrels per day (including condensate) came from Nigeria and 910,000 barrels per day from Angola. The remainder was principally contributed by Equatorial Guinea, Sudan, Congo-Brazzaville and Gabon.

Upstream expansion

Although critically important for these producing countries, with respect especially to public revenues, Sub-Saharan oil is therefore not of great significance in world markets. The prospects for

5

increases in African production are, however, strong. The increases depend partly on further development of onshore resources, but more importantly reflect access to fields in deep and ultra-deep water as a result of advances in 3D seismic surveying and deep-water drilling techniques.

From Nigeria the first deep-water production is expected in April 2004 at Shell's Bonga field. Total producing capacity in 2004 has been forecast to reach 3 million barrels per day, and 4 million barrels per day by 2006 is held to be a realistic target. Angolan production will trend upward in 2004 and is expected to exceed 1.5 million barrels per day by 2006. Crude exports from both countries are largely to the United States.

Production from Equatorial Guinea is expected to reach 350,000 barrels per day in 2004. Revenues from fields overlapping its maritime boundary with Nigeria are shared 60:40 in Nigeria's favour. Nigeria has agreed a similar arrangement with Sao Tome and Principe, where bids for offshore blocs have recently been made, but from which production is unlikely for four or five years. Chadian exports by the pipeline through Cameroon have begun and are expected to reach 225,000 barrels per day in 2004. Sudanese output will be about 300,000 barrels per day in 2004 and is planned to reach 450,000 barrels per day by 2005.

■ US interests

Increases in oil production along the west coast are warmly supported by lobbies in the United States and by plans for US corporate investment in the region's oil and gas upstream totalling US$35 billion over the next five years. An increase from the current 15 per cent to 25 per cent in the African share of US oil imports is targeted by 2005, with further increases thereafter, at the expense of Middle Eastern oil supplies. Not only does West Africa have an advantage in proximity to US markets, but also it is held to be a more reliable source of supply than the Middle East. This reliability is relative. Nigerian production is interrupted or curtailed from time to time by popular disturbances in the Niger Delta, from which as yet all the production comes. Angolan production so far is mostly from the near offshore of

the Cabinda enclave, in which there is an active separatist movement. Exploitation of the Doba oil field in Chad was long delayed by political uncertainties, and the area in which it is located remains highly unstable. Beyond West Africa, the distribution of oil revenues between the north and south of Sudan remains an outstanding issue in a settlement of the civil war.

■ Overcapacity

World demand for oil is unlikely to grow at much more than 1 million barrels per day per annum. It follows from expectations of increases in producing capacity in Africa (and elsewhere) that excess capacity at current prices is likely to increase next year. The burden of shutting in capacity falls, at least initially, on OPEC. Nigeria is the only SSA member of OPEC. It is from Nigeria, however, that the largest early production increase from Africa is expected. Nigeria might therefore leave OPEC, but it has an overriding fiscal interest in the maintenance of oil prices within the OPEC target. There is a tension, therefore – which other SSA producing countries are likely also eventually to experience – between rising production capacity and the defence of prices.

■ Natural gas

Very large pools of natural gas are also to be found along the west coast, both associated (with oil deposits) and non-associated. Limited local use of this resource has been made, but the greater part of the associated gas was for long flared. The Nigerian LNG plant at Bonny, operated by Shell, initially used non-associated gas, but in 2003 use began to be made also of associated gas. The original two-train plant has been expanded to five, completion of which is expected in 2004 with an annual capacity of 16.7 million tonnes of LNG and 2.2 million of liquefied petroleum gas.

By Chevron's proposed West African gas pipeline, associated gas will be conveyed by pipeline from Nigeria to Benin, Togo and Ghana, for use primarily in power generation. A final investment decision on this project is now expected in April next year, but initial gas deliveries will not be until 2005.

A single-train LNG plant is planned in Angola to utilize associated offshore gas. It will be operated by Chevron-Texaco. Next year is the start date for construction and the plant is expected to come on-stream in 2007. Liquefaction of natural gas in Equatorial Guinea has also been mooted.

The growth curve in demand for natural gas is expected to be steeper than that for oil over the next 20 years, and the appearance of excess capacity is therefore less likely. LNG projects and other processes of gas conversion in SSA create local employment and provide opportunities for local contractors, but these benefits are limited by the highly capital-intensive nature of the operations. Further, the returns in revenue from natural gas are more problematic than those from oil, the price of which is upheld by output restrictions. LNG has not so far reduced the dependence of the Nigerian budget on oil.

Significant increase in oil-producing capacity will occur in Nigeria in 2004, with increases also in Angola, Sudan, Chad and Equatorial Guinea. The excess of world capacity over demand at current prices may, however, confront Nigeria with the choice of leaving OPEC or shutting in part of its greater capacity. Exports of LNG from Nigeria will rise substantially in 2004 but the local benefits are limited relative to oil.

5

The Range of Country @ratings in Sub-Saharan Africa

Sylvia Greisman and Bernard Lignereux

Coface Country Risk and Economic Studies Department, Paris

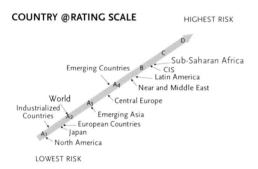

COUNTRY @RATING SCALE — HIGHEST RISK / LOWEST RISK

PAYMENT INCIDENTS INDEX
(12 month moving average - World 1995 = 100)

A regional country risk @rating represents an average of country @ratings weighted according to their contribution to the region's production.

A Country @rating measures the average level of short-term non-payment risk associated with companies in a particular country. It is thus complementary to @rating Credit Opinions on companies.

Although stable, the quality of African risk has remained the poorest among emerging countries with company solvency and payments affected by a very shaky economic and political environment. In 2003, despite steady raw material prices, payment-incident frequency linked to the Ivory Coast crisis increased. The ratings assigned to countries in the region reflect that high-risk level since – except for Botswana (A2), Mauritius and Namibia (A3) and South Africa (A4) – they are confined to categories B, C and D.

In 2003, Sub-Saharan Africa benefited from generally firm raw material prices. Prices trended up for oil as well as for minerals like gold, platinum and copper or even for some farm products like cotton. Moreover, with the notable exceptions of the Ivory Coast and Zimbabwe, African countries benefited from a relative political stability, which has nonetheless remained shaky.

The impact of those positive factors was nonetheless undermined by persistent weather and humanitarian disasters like the drought gripping the continent's eastern and southern regions, famines, AIDS and other epidemics. In total, Sub-Saharan Africa's growth rate remained near 3 per cent, or essentially the same level as the previous year and very insufficient in relation to the population's needs.

Many countries have continued to face very shaky financial situations despite debt reductions granted under the HIPC programme for highly indebted poor countries. International aid still represents an important source of financing for those countries, except for South Africa and a few other southern African countries. Moreover, the region has remained vulnerable to political, ethnic and social tensions and to exogenous shocks capable of undermining economic activity.

■ Countries rated A4

These countries often exhibit fairly mediocre payment behaviour that could be affected by an economic downturn, although the probability of that causing a large number of payment defaults remains moderate.

In **South Africa**, improvement in fundamental macroeconomic and financial equilibriums has fostered steady growth, although modest in relation to the population's needs. Public finance management has been disciplined and the foreign debt level has remained low. Furthermore, the country's political stability, which should persist after this year's elections, could permit it to cope

with any future challenges, notably the uncertain outcome of the Zimbabwe crisis and the black population's social and economic demands. Good company payment behaviour and a lower bankruptcy rate have been reflecting the country's firm economy. Weaknesses have nonetheless persisted. The rand's continued appreciation since 2002 has constituted an obstacle to growth, affecting exporting company competitiveness. Moreover, despite moderate financing needs, South Africa has remained vulnerable to capital market fluctuations due to its high short-term debt and limited foreign currency reserves. Further out, sustaining the growth rate and indeed increasing it will depend on both continued restructuring and investment, hampered by the low domestic savings rate, scarcity of skilled labour, a brain drain and the AIDS pandemic.

COFACE MAP OF COUNTRY @RATINGS

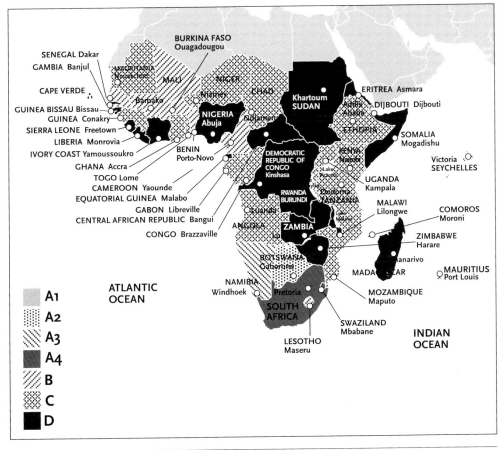

5

■ Countries rated B

A precarious economic environment could affect company payment behaviour, which is often poor.

In **Senegal**, growth has resumed at a sustained pace, attributable to development of the mineral and chemical sectors, steadier food and electricity supplies, and dynamic civil engineering and services sectors. Meanwhile, fiscal and external accounts have continued to run high deficits, which should nonetheless stabilize with the country benefiting this year from cancellation of its public-sector debt under the HIPC programme for highly indebted poor countries. However, the poverty and unemployment rates have remained high with the expected acceleration of structural reforms in socio-economic areas likely to intensify social tensions. The deterioration of company payment behaviour registered in 2003 has been a reflection more of late

payments than of actual defaults and has particularly concerned the electrical capital goods and tools sector. Continued strong growth in 2004 should permit stabilization of payment incidents.

Cameroon's growth outlook has suffered from completion of the Doba/Kribi pipeline construction, declining oil production, and a recurrent electricity deficit that has been affecting industrial production. Several factors should nonetheless continue to buoy economic activity including the start-up of major infrastructure projects in the transportation and energy sectors, the dynamism of services, and continuation of structural reforms essential in coping with the oil production decline and diversifying the economic fabric. In spring 2004, furthermore, the country should reach the completion point in the HIPC programme reserved for highly indebted poor

COFACE MAP OF MEDIUM- AND LONG-TERM COUNTRY RISK

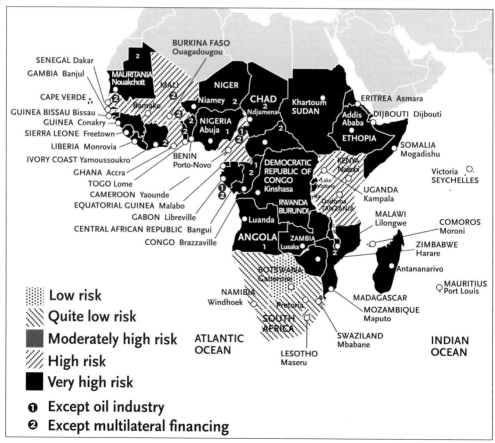

Low risk
Quite low risk
Moderately high risk
High risk
Very high risk

❶ Except oil industry
❷ Except multilateral financing

countries, which will bolster public-sector and external accounts by reducing the external debt burden.

■ Countries rated C

A very precarious economic and political environment could worsen payment behaviour that is already often poor.

Despite its assets, and the renewed confidence inspired by the smooth political changeover after the December 2002 elections, **Kenya** has not succeeded in generating a growth rate sufficient to permit its development and reduce poverty. However, intensification of the anti-corruption campaign has paved the way for resumption of support by financial backers under a new programme that will ultimately permit debt cancellation based on the HIPC initiative reserved for highly indebted poor countries. Although that support will be essential in improving the country's solvency and reducing its domestic and foreign debt burden, the capacity of the new public authorities to continue the effort to consolidate public accounts and restructure state-owned companies remains uncertain.

Tanzania has been benefiting from strong growth fuelled by development of the mineral sector, particularly gold-bearing. On structural reforms, the country has made notable but still insufficient progress to meet the many challenges it has been facing: poverty, unemployment, AIDS, infrastructure development. Those challenges have been weighing heavily on public finances, which the authorities have been unable to consolidate. Despite efforts to develop more revenues, the tax base has remained narrow with the financing of development spending continuing to depend on international aid, which has notably resulted in cancellation of public foreign debt based on the HIPC initiative reserved for highly indebted poor countries.

■ Countries rated D

The economic and political environment presents a very high level of risk, which exacerbates generally deplorable payment behaviour.

In **Nigeria**, after re-election in April 2003, President Obasanjo's new term in office appears to be off to an inauspicious start. Political, ethnic and religious tensions, which have remained high, could limit the authorities' ability to define and implement policy capable of attracting the investments needed to revive the country's economy. The economic and financial situation has nonetheless remained dependent on oil price and extraction levels. However, the oil price decline expected in 2004 will reduce the government's revenues accordingly, worsening public and external account deficits. In those conditions, settlement of foreign debt and accumulated arrears, which have represented a sizeable burden, will certainly be difficult.

In **Ivory Coast**, the September 2002 rebellion, which resulted in *de facto* partition of the country and economic paralysis in the north, sharply undermined the economic outlook and produced a recession for the fourth consecutive year. Despite a financial situation less catastrophic than initially expected, the country has been unable to avoid recourse to payment arrears with cancellation of its public foreign debt under the HIPC initiative thus postponed indefinitely. The level of the Coface payment-incident index reflects the crisis's impact on company behaviour and solvency. A growth recovery will depend on restoring political stability, which would reassure national and foreign economic actors. However, the progress made since conclusion of the Linas-Marcoussis agreement in January 2003 has been sporadic, making the outlook for 2004 all the more uncertain with the tensions that have gripped the political landscape for several years only easing slowly.

5

Angola

Population (million inhabitants)	13.5
GDP (million USD)	9,471

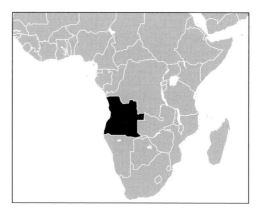

Coface analysis

Short-term: **C**

Medium-term:
Very high risk

STRENGTHS

- Angola boasts considerable natural resources (oil, diamonds, hydroelectricity, diverse minerals, as well as farming and fishing potential).

- Sub-Saharan Africa's second oil-producing country (900,000 barrels a day), the country attracts substantial direct foreign investment and represents a strategic interest for Western countries.

- The peace treaty signed with UNITA in 2002 has permitted the country to redeploy resources towards spending on economic development and combating poverty.

WEAKNESSES

- The impact of oil wealth has not spread throughout the economy, whose restructuring has been lagging.

- The civil war's aftermath has been weighing heavily on the country's demographic, economic and financial outlook.

- The opacity of public accounts has been deterring international financial community backing.

- Besides the oil sector, the business environment has not been very attractive to foreign investment.

RISK ASSESSMENT

The pace of economic growth is essentially attributable to oil production trends. This should not obscure the country's substantial macroeconomic imbalances, which have been generating high inflation and accounts with large deficits.

This situation and the deadlock on structural reforms have tended to impede implementation of a support programme by the international financial community. That support will be essential, however, in consolidating external accounts affected by the weight of imports and a very negative invisibles balance. It will also be crucial in reducing both the internal and external public debt burden, which has been causing substantial payment arrears.

Without financial aid, the country would not have sufficient resources to rebuild infrastructure and diversify the economic fabric. The political calm spell that began with the end of the civil war (except in the Cabinda enclave) has not been accompanied by enough growth to make up for major social deficiencies.

MAIN ECONOMIC INDICATORS						
US$ millions	1999	2000	2001	2002	2003 (e)	2004 (f)
Economic growth (%)	3.3	3	3.2	9.7	5.6	7.3
Inflation (%)	248	325	153	109	115	125
Public-sector balance/GDP (%)	−35.5	−8.6	−3.7	−9	−8.9	−8.9
Exports	5,344	7,921	6,534	8,359	8,742	9,618
Imports	3,270	3,040	3,179	3,709	4,320	4,813
Trade balance	2,074	4,881	3,355	4,650	4,422	4,805
Current account balance/GDP (%)	−27.8	9.0	−15.1	−5.8	−8.2	−4.2
Foreign debt	10,311	10,200	9,600	10,500	11,000	11,500
Debt service/Exports (%)	43.6	38.7	48.8	25.1	22.9	20.0
Currency reserves (import months)	0.8	1.9	1.1	0.5	0.6	1.1

e = estimate, f = forecast

CONDITIONS OF ACCESS TO THE MARKET

■ Market overview

The cease-fire agreements signed in April 2002 following the death of Jonas Savimbi have altered Angola's fundamentals and the economic landscape. While the country looks like remaining basically a mono-sector economy for a long time yet, there is already evidence of productive investment in basic consumer and small industrial goods. Angola has opened up its market to international trade by cutting customs duties, simplifying its international trading arrangements (establishment of a single customs document) and revising its foreign direct investment (FDI) code for the economy as a whole and not just the dominant oil sector. But growth sectors such as agriculture and mining (with the exception of diamonds) are on the brink of collapse and struggling to make headway despite their potential. Corruption, mainly bred by arms purchases, has in the course of time spread to all branches of the economy and is delaying a fairer distribution of wealth across the country. There is still no clear national socio-economic programme and the much-vaunted privatization programme has yet to be implemented. International companies drawn by the country's strong multi-sector potential remain unwilling to invest in a big way, while Angola's trading partners, in particular the Europeans, South Africans, Americans and Chinese, jockey for position in preparation for the future.

■ Means of entry

Customs duties vary between 0 and 35 per cent. Angola does not apply a preferential customs tariff to member countries of the Preferential Trade Area (PTA) and the Southern Africa Development Community (SADC). However, two exemptions are due to be introduced for foreign investment-related imports: duty-free admission for some products, and 50 per cent reduction in customs duties for imported capital goods and raw materials intended for investment projects undertaken in priority areas.

■ Attitude towards foreign investors

The Foreign Investment Act underwent root-and-branch reforms in 2003, with investment regulations being liberalized and brought into line with those of the other SADC member countries. The setting up of the National Foreign Investment Agency (ANIP) – a one-stop shop that brings together the main government departments – is a step in the right direction. Angola is the largest recipient of foreign direct investment in Africa, along with Egypt and Algeria, largely due to the boom in the off-shore oil sector. Despite the survival of an outdated ideology, administrative bottlenecks, the power of patronage at all levels of government and a lack of transparency in public- as well as oil- and diamond-sector accounting, which slows administration to a crawl, a

5

343

new investment-friendly language has emerged since 2002. When an agreement with international lenders is concluded, Angola will become a sought-after trade destination.

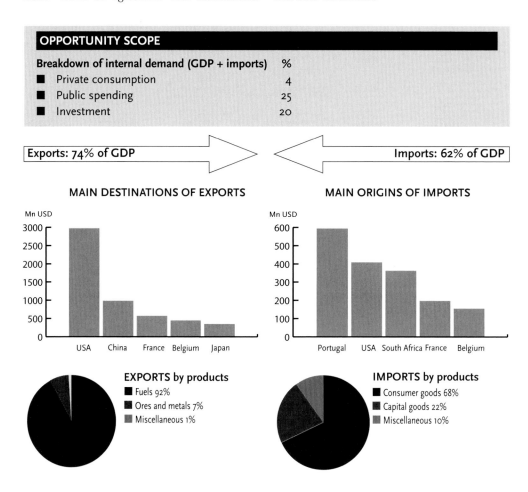

OPPORTUNITY SCOPE

Breakdown of internal demand (GDP + imports)	%
■ Private consumption	4
■ Public spending	25
■ Investment	20

Exports: 74% of GDP   Imports: 62% of GDP

MAIN DESTINATIONS OF EXPORTS

Mn USD

USA   China   France   Belgium   Japan

MAIN ORIGINS OF IMPORTS

Mn USD

Portugal   USA   South Africa   France   Belgium

EXPORTS by products
- ■ Fuels 92%
- ■ Ores and metals 7%
- ▓ Miscellaneous 1%

IMPORTS by products
- ■ Consumer goods 68%
- ■ Capital goods 22%
- ▓ Miscellaneous 10%

STANDARD OF LIVING / PURCHASING POWER

Indicators	Angola	Regional average	DC average
GNP per capita (PPP dollars)	1690	2841	6778
GNP per capita (USD)	500	999	3568
Human Development Index	0.377	0.498	0.708
Wealthiest 10% share of national income	n/a	36	33
Urban population percentage	35	44	60
Percentage under 15 years old	47	42	31
number of telephones per 1000 inhabitants	6	33	157
number of computers per 1000 inhabitants	1	17	66

Benin

Population (million inhabitants)	6.4
GDP (million USD)	2,372
GDP per capita (USD)	371

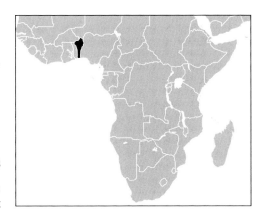

Short-term: **B**

Medium-term:

Coface analysis **High risk**

RISK ASSESSMENT

The current economic situation and outlook for 2004 have remained favourable amid a good cotton harvest, the level of economic activity in Nigeria (Benin derives much of its resources from the transit of merchandise toward that country) and buoyant domestic demand likely to spur high growth.

In March 2003, moreover, the country reached the 'completion point' in the HIPC programme for highly indebted poor countries, prompting a sharp reduction in its external debt burden, which has permitted the freeing up of additional resources for infrastructure investment (transportation, health, education) thereby facilitating the economy's diversification.

Meanwhile, the outcome of the March 2003 legislative elections will permit the government to benefit henceforth from a solid parliamentary majority. That should help accelerate the pace of structural reforms and regional integration, which has been taking shape, notably, in the energy area. The country could thus be headed toward sustained growth in the longer term.

In the near term, however, the country will still have to meet major challenges. Public accounts have been proving difficult to consolidate due to spending linked to the size of public administration and to support afforded to cotton producers. Concurrently, fiscal evasion has been reducing the authorities' capacity to generate revenues. External accounts have also remained in deficit and particularly dependent on world cotton prices with that commodity representing 45 per cent of export revenues. With the international community nonetheless expected to maintain its backing, there are no significant fears of a balance-of-payments crisis.

5

MAIN ECONOMIC INDICATORS						
US$ millions	1999	2000	2001	2002	2003 (e)	2004 (f)
Economic growth (%)	4.7	5.8	5	6	5.5	6.3
Inflation (%)	0.3	4.2	4.0	2.4	2.5	2.4
Public-sector balance/GDP (%)	−1.6	−5.5	−4.1	−4.6	−4.7	−4.2
Exports	223	189	210	214	288	325
Imports	474	447	467	491	635	680
Trade balance	−251	−258	−256	−277	−347	−356
Current account balance/GDP (%)	−10.3	−9.8	−10.2	−10.2	−10.9	−10.2
Foreign debt	1,686	1,565	1,600	1,535	1,526	1,625
Debt service/Exports (%)	15.4	13.7	8.6	8.5	7.3	5.7
Currency reserves (import months)	7	8.4	10.1	10.1	7.1	6.7

e = estimate, f = forecast

Botswana

Population (million inhabitants)	1.7
GDP (million USD)	5,196

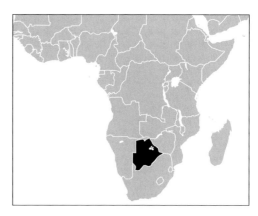

Short-term: **A2**

Medium-term:
Low risk

Coface analysis

STRENGTHS

- The country boasts substantial natural resources including diamonds (second world producer), copper and nickel.
- Its political stability, low level of corruption and the quality of its transportation and financial infrastructures are attractive to foreign investors.
- The economy's diversification (textiles, information technologies) is well under way.
- Botswana's low level of debt and substantial currency reserves would afford ample room for manoeuvre to withstand economic shocks.

WEAKNESSES

- Representing a small landlocked market with 1.6 million inhabitants, the country is heavily dependent on South Africa (75 per cent of imports) and has also been suffering from the crisis in Zimbabwe, which has been deterring tourism (second source of currency revenues).
- Diamond mining still represents too large a share of the economy (50 per cent of fiscal revenues and 80 per cent of export earnings).
- The AIDS pandemic, which afflicts 40 per cent of the adult population, has been affecting growth and fiscal spending (health, social impact) and will ultimately generate considerable demographic and economic imbalances.

RISK ASSESSMENT

Despite the manufacturing sector's dynamism, the general pace of economic activity has continued to depend on trends in diamond production whose 11 per cent increase in 2003 fuelled the economy's strong growth, which should ease in 2004.

Both external accounts and public finances have been reflecting those trends. Burdened by large increases in health and social spending linked to the AIDS pandemic, public accounts have developed deficits likely to persist in the future. Conversely, external accounts have been showing substantial surpluses, which explain the country's limited foreign debt and relatively abundant currency reserves. Assessed favourably by rating agencies, furthermore, the country has continued to enjoy access to international capital markets.

Further out, despite evident assets like political stability, the country will have to focus on coping with the AIDS pandemic's impact on its economic development and diversification programme.

MAIN ECONOMIC INDICATORS

US$ millions	1999	2000	2001	2002	2003 (e)	2004 (f)
Economic growth (%)	8.1	9.2	4.7	4.2	7.6	3.5
Inflation (%)	7.8	8.5	6.6	8.1	9.7	6.1
Public-sector balance/GDP (%)	5.8	8.9	−2.5	−5.1	−2.8	−2.8
Exports	2,658	2,683	2,326	2,443	2,587	2,610
Imports	1,874	1,778	1,663	1,704	1,753	1,786
Trade balance	784	905	663	739	834	824
Current account balance/GDP (%)	12.2	10.2	8.2	11.1	7.9	8.5
Foreign debt	1,105	1,053	1,042	960	991	984
Debt service/Exports (%)	3.8	3.4	3.8	3.5	2.9	3.0
Currency reserves (import months)	31.4	31.9	32.1	28.1	23.6	23.3

e = estimate, f = forecast

CONDITIONS OF ACCESS TO THE MARKET

■ Market overview

Botswana is a member of the Southern Africa Customs Union (SACU), which also comprises Lesotho, Swaziland, Namibia and South Africa. *Ad valorem* common external tariffs and excise duties are applicable to third countries. The renewed Lomé Convention, the Generalized System of Preferences and the extension of the Trade, Development and Cooperation Agreement between the EU and South Africa to SACU member countries grant Botswanan products preferential access to European and North American markets in line with AGOA rules. In October 2002, Botswana teamed up with other SACU members to sign a fresh customs protocol establishing a new system for resolving commercial disputes and setting customs duties. Botswana is also an active member of the South African Development Community (14 countries in Southern Africa), headquartered in the capital Gaborone. The local market, however, remains narrow and mainly concentrated in towns to the east of the country.

■ Means of entry

Botswana's customs regulations grant duty-free admission to raw materials and machinery imported for the manufacture of products intended for export. Other tax measures include exemption from sales tax on raw materials used in exported products.

Sales agents of any nationality are allowed to operate, though local agents and representatives predominate. Public invitations to tender and large-scale works contracts comply with internationally recognized standards. Imports are usually invoiced in rands, US dollars or pounds sterling. The euro is starting to gain acceptance as legal tender in trade, albeit to a limited degree. Botswana uses similar means of payments to those used in Europe and the United States.

■ Attitude towards foreign investors

Botswana possesses numerous investment-grade assets and is one of the most competitive countries in Africa. It has a liberal economy, no exchange controls, a convertible currency, attractive tax laws (15 per cent corporation tax for manufacturing companies and 25 per cent for others, 10 per cent VAT from July 2002) and peaceful social relations. The Botswana Export Development and Investment Authority (BEDIA) encourages investment in the country, especially through export-related projects and import substitution. The focus is on industrial diversification to reduce the country's dependence on the mining sector (diamonds) and on partnerships between foreign investors and local players with a view to facilitating technology transfers. Priority sectors include manufacturing (glass, tanneries, textiles, etc), information and communication technologies, tourism and financial services (international financial centre).

5

347

Botswana's legal system is founded on the principles of common law. Consequently, its judicial procedures are highly liberal and similar to those in developed countries.

As the country is a signatory to both the World Bank's MIGA Agreement and the OPIC Agreement with the United States, it provides investment safeguards. A reciprocal promotion and investment protection agreement is under negotiation with France and due to be finalized in 2004.

■ Foreign exchange regulations

Botswana's foreign exchange reserves – over US$5 billion or nearly 100 per cent of GDP – enable it to pursue a highly flexible foreign exchange policy. There are no exchange controls. The fully convertible local currency, the pula, was introduced after the country's withdrawal from the rand area in 1976. There are no restrictions on the repatriation of capital by non-residents. Both dividends and capital can be freely transferred by a foreign investor upon payment of 15 per cent withholding tax.

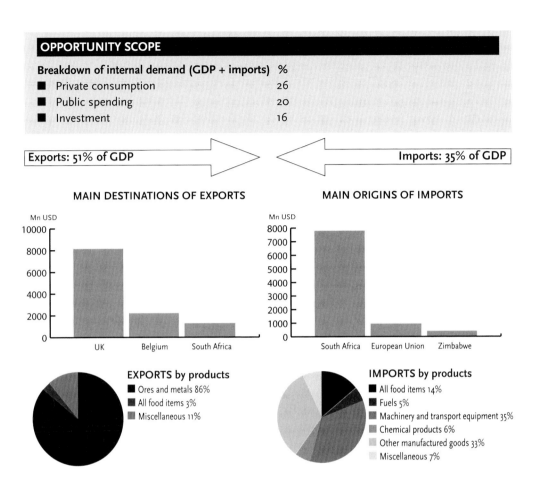

OPPORTUNITY SCOPE

Breakdown of internal demand (GDP + imports)	%
■ Private consumption	26
■ Public spending	20
■ Investment	16

Exports: 51% of GDP → ← Imports: 35% of GDP

MAIN DESTINATIONS OF EXPORTS

Mn USD

UK, Belgium, South Africa

MAIN ORIGINS OF IMPORTS

Mn USD

South Africa, European Union, Zimbabwe

EXPORTS by products
- ■ Ores and metals 86%
- ■ All food items 3%
- ▥ Miscellaneous 11%

IMPORTS by products
- ■ All food items 14%
- ■ Fuels 5%
- ▦ Machinery and transport equipment 35%
- ▦ Chemical products 6%
- ▥ Other manufactured goods 33%
- ▤ Miscellaneous 7%

5

STANDARD OF LIVING / PURCHASING POWER

Indicators	Botswana	Regional average	DC average
GNP per capita (PPP dollars)	7410	2841	6778
GNP per capita (USD)	3100	999	3568
Human Development Index	0.614	0.498	0.708
Wealthiest 10% share of national income	57	36	33
Urban population percentage	49	44	60
Percentage under 15 years old	42	42	31
number of telephones per 1000 inhabitants	91	33	157
number of computers per 1000 inhabitants	39	17	66

Burkina Faso

Population (million inhabitants)	11.6
GDP (million USD)	2,486
GDP per capita (USD)	214

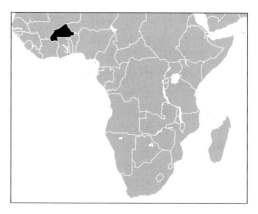

Short-term: **B**

Coface analysis

Medium-term:
High risk

RISK ASSESSMENT

Economic activity sagged in 2003, affected by fallout from the Ivory Coast crisis with the closing of rail and roadway links to that country affecting most economic sectors, notably industry, and reducing expatriate-worker remittances. The slowdown now appears likely to be less severe than initially expected provided the normalization process under way stays on track with the good cotton harvests of recent years and their effect on household incomes continuing to buoy domestic demand.

However, the slowdown has contributed to reducing government revenues further and thus worsening the public finance deficit. Moreover, the loss of the Ivory Coast market, the increased cost of imports and exports to circumvent that country, and the decline of private remittances have been sharply inflating the current account deficit. Burkina has thus remained dependent on international community aid, which has notably permitted an easing of its foreign debt burden, the country having reached the 'point of completion' in the HIPC programme for highly indebted poor countries. Provided structural reforms continue to progress, the country should nonetheless continue to enjoy international community backing.

MAIN ECONOMIC INDICATORS						
US$ millions	1999	2000	2001	2002	2003 (e)	2004 (f)
Economic growth (%)	6.3	1.6	4.6	4.6	2.7	4
Inflation (%)	−1.1	−0.3	4.9	2.3	3	2.5
Public-sector balance/GDP (%)	−13.3	−10.9	−11.3	−10.4	−11	−9.9
Exports	254	206	222	239	291	313
Imports	580	518	524	517	698	711
Trade balance	−327	−312	−302	−278	−407	−398
Current account balance/GDP (%)	−15.6	−15.0	−13.6	−12.9	−14.2	−12.6
Foreign debt	1,522	1,807	1,585	1,404	1,329	1,262
Debt service/Exports (%)	16.7	19.2	13.6	17.1	8.1	7.7
Currency reserves (import months)	5.2	4.5	4.9	5.3	4.4	4.4

e = estimate, f = forecast

Cameroon

Population (million inhabitants)	15.2
GDP (million USD)	8,501

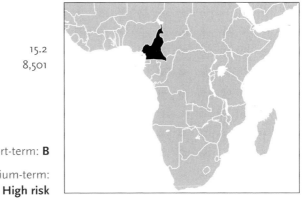

Short-term: **B**

Medium-term:
Coface analysis   **High risk**

STRENGTHS

- Cameroon boasts one of Central Africa's most diversified economies as well as substantial resources including agriculture, wood and energy (oil, gas, hydroelectricity).
- The structural reform policy, which has been attracting foreign investment, has received the support of financial backers (restructuring and ultimately debt reduction).
- The Chad–Cameroon pipeline should enhance regional integration and improve the country's economic outlook.
- Franc-zone membership and disciplined fiscal policy have contributed to its monetary stability.

WEAKNESSES

- Cameroon has remained dependent on exogenous factors including weather conditions and world raw material prices.
- Its proven oil reserves have been dwindling.
- The business environment has remained difficult.
- The problems in neighbouring countries (Central African Republic and Nigeria) could affect Cameroon.
- The war against poverty has remained a major challenge for the authorities.

5

RISK ASSESSMENT

Completion of the Doba/Kribi pipeline construction, declining oil production and a recurrent electricity deficit, which has been affecting industrial production, have tempered the country's growth outlook. Several factors should nonetheless continue to buoy growth including implementation of major infrastructure projects (transportation, energy), the dynamism of the services sector, and continuation of structural reforms needed to contend with the oil production decline and further diversify the economy.

In spring 2004, furthermore, the country should reach the completion point in the HIPC programme established for highly indebted poor countries in 2000, which should bolster Cameroon's public-sector finances and external accounts by reducing external debt.

Its attractiveness to investors could further benefit from prospects for greater regional integration, peaceful settlement of the dispute with Nigeria over the Bakassi Peninsula, and the country's continued political stability despite persistent regional tensions. The presidential elections scheduled for autumn 2004 will be unlikely to jeopardize that stability.

MAIN ECONOMIC INDICATORS

US$ millions	1999	2000	2001	2002	2003 (e)	2004 (f)
Economic growth (%)	4.4	4.2	4.8	4	3.6	3
Inflation (%)	3.1	−1.3	1.2	2.5	2.5	2
Public-sector balance/GDP (%)	1	2.4	−1.2	−3.6	1.1	0.9
Exports	1,713	1,992	2,128	1,798	1,857	1,784
Imports	1,484	1,542	1,635	1,858	1,959	2,119
Trade balance	229	450	493	−60	−102	−335
Current account balance/GDP (%)	−4.4	0.2	0.5	−4.9	−4.9	−4.3
Foreign debt	9,444	9,241	8,996	7,334	7,563	7,650
Debt service/Exports (%)	23.0	29.3	15.3	14.8	10.1	8.4
Currency reserves (import months)	0	0.9	1.4	2.5	2.9	2.7

e = estimate, f = forecast

CONDITIONS OF ACCESS TO THE MARKET

■ Market overview

The Cameroon market is open to imports and the authorities apply no special protectionist measures or tariff barriers. Customs duties on imports from within the CEMAC area range from 5 per cent for staple commodities, 10 per cent for raw materials and capital goods and 20 per cent for semi-finished products and miscellaneous items to 30 per cent for certain consumer products. There is 18.7 per cent VAT from which staple commodities are exempt and an excise duty for so-called luxury products. Red tape, however, remains a problem, with customs clearance taking several weeks. Foreign companies are strongly advised to check that funds are available for the project, to ensure that partners are solvent and to respond to invitations to tender only when they are financed by foreign funding agencies. They are also advised to demand cash payment upon confirmation of the order or payment by irrevocable letter of credit confirmed by a first-rate bank.

■ Attitude towards foreign investors

A developing country heavily dependent on foreign capital and incapable of raising funds locally since returning to growth almost 10 years ago, Cameroon has an open policy towards foreign investment. The Investment Code was replaced in 2002 by an Investment Charter offering greater incentives. The tax structure has been simplified. A bilateral double taxation agreement between France and Cameroon came into force on 1 January 2003. The country also has an Investment Code Management Unit designed to promote investment and inform and assist investors. In actual fact, a number of factors, in particular rampant corruption (the country is the second-most-corrupt African country after Nigeria according to Transparency International) at all levels of the economy, hamper foreign investment. The inadequacy of the country's transport infrastructure is also a major obstacle to the development of the private sector. Moreover, companies based in the country have to cope with a heavy tax burden and a largely ineffectual legal and judicial system characterized by widespread circumvention of laws and regulations.

OPPORTUNITY SCOPE

Breakdown of internal demand (GDP + imports)	%
■Private consumption	53
■Public spending	9
■Investment	14

Exports: 32% of GDP   Imports: 29% of GDP

MAIN DESTINATIONS OF EXPORTS

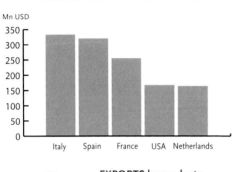

Mn USD

Italy   Spain   France   USA   Netherlands

MAIN ORIGINS OF IMPORTS

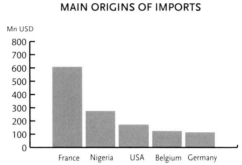

Mn USD

France   Nigeria   USA   Belgium   Germany

EXPORTS by products
- ■ All food items 17%
- ■ Agricultural raw materials 21%
- ▨ Manufactured goods 5%
- ▨ Fuels 52%
- ▨ Ores and metals 5%

IMPORTS by products
- ■ All food items 16%
- ■ Fuels 18%
- ▨ Machinery and transport equipment 26%
- ▨ Chemical products 11%
- ▨ Other manufactured goods 25%
- ▨ Miscellaneous 4%

5

STANDARD OF LIVING / PURCHASING POWER

Indicators	Cameroon	Regional average	DC average
GNP per capita (PPP dollars)	1580	2841	6778
GNP per capita (USD)	580	999	3568
Human Development Index	0.499	0.498	0.708
Wealthiest 10% share of national income	37	36	33
Urban population percentage	5	44	60
Percentage under 15 years old	42	42	31
number of telephones per 1000 inhabitants	7	33	157
number of computers per 1000 inhabitants	4	17	66

Cape Verde

Population (inhabitants)	442,000
GDP (million USD)	550
GDP per capita (USD)	1,243

Short-term: **B**

Medium-term:

Coface analysis **Very high risk**

RISK ASSESSMENT

The country's limited energy and food resources have hampered its economy as reflected in severe external account imbalances financed by expatriate remittances, recourse to debt, international aid and frequent accumulation of payment arrears.

Under the IMF's triennial poverty reduction and growth facility set up in 2002, the authorities have succeeded in limiting the public-sector deficit despite the precarious situation of many state-owned companies. Concurrently, they have continued, albeit slowly, to implement structural reforms. The run-up to elections in 2004 and 2005 could nonetheless prompt a slackening of those efforts.

Further out, the country could attract more foreign investment, notably for development of its deep-water ports. The stability deriving from the local currency's euro peg should also bolster investor confidence.

MAIN ECONOMIC INDICATORS						
US$ millions	1999	2000	2001	2002	2003 (e)	2004 (f)
Economic growth (%)	8.9	6.6	3.8	4.6	5	5
Inflation (%)	4.4	−2.4	3.8	1.8	3	2
Public-sector balance/GDP (%)	−20.2	−25.9	−10.8	−10.6	−9.2	−8
Exports	26	40	37	42	46	51
Imports	242	233	232	277	300	317
Trade balance	−215	−194	−194	−236	−254	−265
Current account balance/GDP (%)	−21.3	−14.7	−14.2	−17	−17.8	−16.8
Foreign debt	315	359	521	520	534	537
Debt service/Exports (%)	15.0	5.9	17.2	9.1	8.2	7.9
Currency reserves (import months)	1.4	1	1.5	2.2	2.2	2.4

e = estimate, f = forecast

Central African Republic

Population (million inhabitants)	3.8
GDP (million USD)	967
GDP per capita (USD)	254

Short-term: **D**

Medium-term:

Coface analysis **Very high risk**

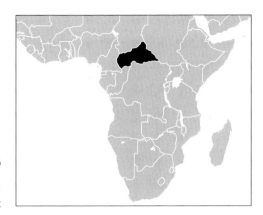

RISK ASSESSMENT

After several years marked by repeated coup attempts and by substantial border, social and political tensions, which have sorely affected the country's economic and financial situation, the authorities emanating from the March 2003 coup have yet to demonstrate their capability of righting the situation. The challenges are substantial: to manage the political transition, make the country secure and settle wage arrears that have been accumulating for over a year.

In this context, defining an improvement programme in cooperation with international financial institutions represents, at this stage, an unavoidable step. However, the country will not be able to negotiate such a programme until tangible signs of durable stabilization appear.

As a matter of fact, the Central African Republic will need that backing to revive its economy and stem the slippage of its public-sector accounts, which the narrow tax base linked to the country's poverty has made even shakier. Consolidation of public finances would also help the country to agree with financial backers on new foreign debt restructuring.

Further out, the country will need to implement major reforms to capitalize on its mineral (diamonds, gold) and forest resources. Those resources could attract foreign investments and permit the development of a large farming area, which could spur food exports to neighbouring countries (Sudan, Chad).

5

MAIN ECONOMIC INDICATORS						
US$ millions	1999	2000	2001	2002	2003 (e)	2004 (f)
Economic growth (%)	3.6	2.3	−0.4	0.6	−0.4	1.5
Inflation (%)	−1.5	3.1	3.8	2.3	7	3
Public-sector balance/GDP (%)	−11	−7	−4.2	−3.7	−5.6	n/a
Exports	138	162	137	158	173	188
Imports	124	118	111	121	131	142
Trade balance	14	44	26	37	42	45
Current account balance/GDP (%)	−5.9	−5.4	−6.1	−3.9	−5.3	−6
Foreign debt	966	911	863	1,040	1,153	1,254
Debt service/Exports (%)	20.2	19.5	18.3	17.5	16.4	15.5
Currency reserves (import months)	6.6	6.4	6.1	5.4	4.9	n/a

e = estimate, f = forecast

Chad

Population (million inhabitants)	7.9
GDP (million USD)	1,600
GDP per capita (USD)	203

Short-term: **C**

Medium-term:

Coface analysis **Very high risk**

RISK ASSESSMENT

Chad's economy has reached a turning point. The first flow of oil from the Doba oil fields and its routing to the Cameroonian port of Kribi will considerably increase the country's national production and currency earnings starting notably in 2004. Oil will then represent 40 per cent of GDP. Transformation of a now essentially agricultural economy into an oil power could cause new structural imbalances.

Management of the oil manna, although subject to thorough World Bank oversight, and the lagging pace of reforms could spur tensions with international financial institutions. Thanks to improvement in its debt ratios, however, the country has become less dependent on their backing. Moreover, oil could become a new source of domestic tensions.

MAIN ECONOMIC INDICATORS

US$ millions	1999	2000	2001	2002	2003 (e)	2004 (f)
Economic growth (%)	−3.6	0.6	8.5	5.4	9.3	45.2
Inflation (%)	−8	3.8	12.4	5.2	4.3	4
Public-sector balance/GDP (%)	−10.9	−12.3	−11	−12.2	−11.7	−4.7
Exports	197	177	178	176	342	1,673
Imports	255	237	539	872	788	588
Trade balance	−58	−60	−361	−695	−446	1,085
Current account balance/GDP (%)	−15	−16	−41	−58	−36	−11
Foreign debt	993	1,059	1,266	1,455	1,530	1,633
Debt service/Exports (%)	11.2	12.3	14.5	18.1	9.8	2.6
Currency reserves (import months)	2.2	3.0	1.7	1.7	2.5	2.1

e = estimate, f = forecast

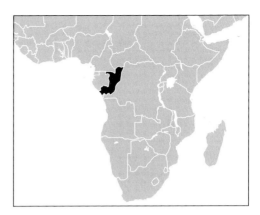

Congo

Population (million inhabitants)   3.1
GDP (million USD)   2,751

Short-term: **C**

Medium-term:
Coface analysis   **Very high risk**

STRENGTHS

- An oil- and wood-producing country, Congo also boasts other major resources (hydroelectricity, copper, potassium).
- Stabilization of the political situation should permit implementation of an economic improvement programme.
- Restoration of links to the international financial community will brighten the economic outlook (progress on structural reforms, processing of the debt under the HIPC programme for highly indebted poor countries).

WEAKNESSES

- The country is still too dependent on oil revenues (87 per cent of exports) whereas reserves have been declining.
- With manufacturing industries still only in an embryonic state and the farm sector incapable of feeding the population, the country has recurrent needs to import consumer goods and food.
- External debt, secured by the oil resources, has remained very high while giving rise to payment arrears.
- The business environment is very difficult.
- Three years of civil war (1997–99) destroyed much of the country's infrastructure.

RISK ASSESSMENT

The structural decline of oil production, a shaky external financial situation (marked by persistent payment arrears and low currency reserves despite firm oil prices) and a necessary dose of fiscal austerity after the 2002 slippage have impeded economic activity in 2003. Although the outlook for 2004 has remained modest, that should not obscure the more robust growth of non-oil GDP (5.5 per cent).

This trend reflects confirmation of the stabilization policy as well as implementation of structural and oil-sector reforms. Acceleration of the pace of those reforms appears nonetheless essential to facilitate the signing of an agreement with international financial institutions, which would permit the reduction of the public-sector external debt burden thereby freeing up more resources to combat poverty and increase infrastructure investments.

5

MAIN ECONOMIC INDICATORS						
US$ millions	1999	2000	2001	2002	2003 (e)	2004 (f)
Economic growth (%)	−3.3	7.5	3.6	3.5	2.0	3.0
Inflation (%)	3.1	3.0	0.8	3.3	2.0	2.0
Public-sector balance/GDP (%)	−5.9	1.2	−0.9	−8.3	7.1	3.7
Exports	1,556	2,519	2,055	2,325	2,560	2,315
Imports	523	597	681	706	856	886
Trade balance	1,033	1,922	1,374	1,619	1,704	1,430
Current account balance/GDP (%)	−16.6	9.8	−3.4	2.0	4.8	1.1
Foreign debt	6,833	6,703	5,741	5,427	5,381	5,276
Debt service/Exports (%)	46.1	24.2	24.8	21.6	17.2	18.8
Currency reserves (import months)	0.2	1.2	0.4	0.2	0.2	0.2

e = estimate, f = forecast

CONDITIONS OF ACCESS TO THE MARKET

■ Market overview

Congo is a member of CEMAC – the Economic and Monetary Community of Central Africa (formerly UDEAC). In this capacity, the Congolese government is aware of the need to bring its business laws into line with those applicable at the sub-regional level (CEMAC) and apply the guidelines laid down by OHADA.

There are no tariff barriers as such, except for products such as cigarettes, sugar (manufactured locally) and those that are restricted or prohibited on humanitarian, security or health grounds.

■ Means of entry

Since 1999, the task of carrying out pre-shipment quality and quantity audits of goods has been entrusted to BIVAC (Bureau Veritas Group). Under Amendment No. 1 signed with the Congolese government in July 2002, goods valued at 1 million Central African francs or more are subject to inspections from 1 October 2002. Previously, the ceiling was 3 million Central African francs. Imports valued at over 500,000 Central African francs have to be registered with BIVAC.

New CEMAC provisions require that:

- all imports must be notified for statistical purposes;
- imports valued at 5 million Central African francs or more must be domiciled with a Congolese bank;
- imports valued at 100 million Central African francs or more must undergo inspections closely monitored by the bank ordering payment.

CEMAC's common external tariff applies to all goods entering Congo, which are divided into four dutiable categories: staples (5 per cent), capital goods and raw materials (10 per cent), semi-finished goods (20 per cent) and ordinary consumer goods (30 per cent).

■ Attitude towards foreign investors

A national investment charter, currently under review by parliament, will replace Law No. 008/92 of 10 April 1992 and Law No. 7/96 of 6 March 1996.

Congolese legislation places foreign investors on an equal footing with local investors. There are no restrictions on the repatriation of profits.

OPPORTUNITY SCOPE

Breakdown of internal demand (GDP + imports)	%
◼ Private consumption	19
◼ Public spending	7
◼ Investment	18

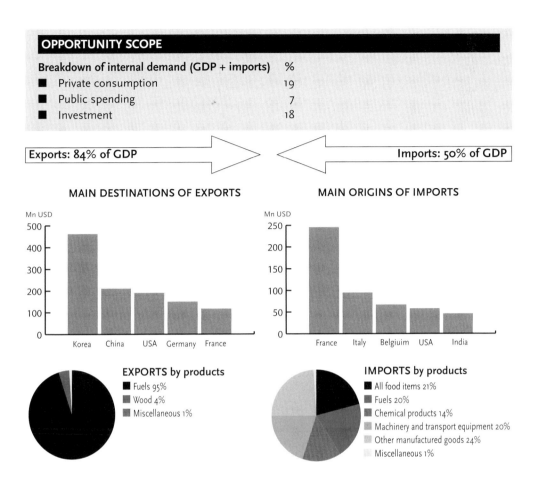

Exports: 84% of GDP → ← Imports: 50% of GDP

MAIN DESTINATIONS OF EXPORTS

Mn USD

Korea China USA Germany France

MAIN ORIGINS OF IMPORTS

Mn USD

France Italy Belgiuim USA India

EXPORTS by products
- ◼ Fuels 95%
- ◼ Wood 4%
- ◼ Miscellaneous 1%

IMPORTS by products
- ◼ All food items 21%
- ◼ Fuels 20%
- ◼ Chemical products 14%
- ◼ Machinery and transport equipment 20%
- ◼ Other manufactured goods 24%
- ◼ Miscellaneous 1%

5

STANDARD OF LIVING / PURCHASING POWER

Indicators	Congo	Regional average	DC average
GNP per capita (PPP dollars)	680	2841	6778
GNP per capita (USD)	640	999	3568
Human Development Index	0.502	0.498	0.708
Wealthiest 10% share of national income	n/a	36	33
Urban population percentage	66	44	60
Percentage under 15 years old	46	42	31
number of telephones per 1000 inhabitants	7	33	157
number of computers per 1000 inhabitants	4	17	66

Eritrea

Population (million inhabitants)	4.2
GDP (million USD)	688
GDP per capita (USD)	164

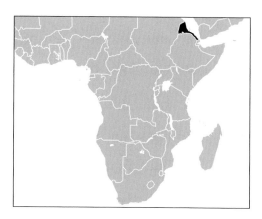

Short-term: **D**

Medium-term:
Very high risk

Coface analysis

RISK ASSESSMENT

The aftermath of the conflict with Ethiopia compounded by a long drought has profoundly affected the economy. Public-sector accounts have been posting substantial deficits with unsustainable public debt (190 per cent of GDP) and external accounts heavily in the red. The country has thus remained dependent on international aid.

Economic growth could accelerate in 2004 provided weather conditions improve. However modest, recovery prospects will nonetheless remain subject to many uncertainties. The volume of international backing could depend on the present government's future behaviour, with increasing repression of the opposition and the press together with indefinite postponement of elections harming relations with the West, particularly the European Union. Moreover, tensions with Ethiopia have been rising again over demarcation of the border between the two countries. Besides the risk of renewed hostilities, that situation has been depriving the country of revenues previously derived from transit of Ethiopian merchandise towards its ports, whereas revenues linked to mineral extraction and development of tourism are still remote prospects.

MAIN ECONOMIC INDICATORS

US$ millions	1999	2000	2001	2002	2003 (e)	2004 (f)
Economic growth (%)	0.3	−12	8.7	−1.2	2.0	4
Inflation (%)	8.4	19.9	14.6	16.9	18.8	12.4
Public-sector balance/GDP (%)	−62.1	−51.5	−52.5	−42.5	−43.7	n/a
Exports	20	37	20	52	35	36
Imports	495	470	537	533	574	575
Trade balance	−475	−434	−517	−482	−539	−539
Current account balance/GDP (%)	−38.4	−32	−35.4	−27.8	−29.3	−29.3
Foreign debt	275	332	434	509	509	509
Debt service/Exports (%)	5.7	3.8	5.3	15.1	12.9	10.8
Currency reserves (import months)	1.1	0.9	1.0	0.7	0.6	1.3

e = estimate, f = forecast

Ethiopia

Population (million inhabitants)	65.8
GDP (million USD)	6,233
GDP per capita (USD)	95

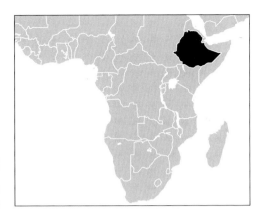

Short-term: **C**

Medium-term:
Coface analysis   **Very high risk**

RISK ASSESSMENT

Ethiopia suffered greatly from two consecutive drought years that affected economic growth and further undermined already seriously out-of-balance public and external accounts.

International financial community backing has nonetheless materialized, notably with reduction of foreign debt via the HIPC initiative for highly indebted poor countries, which should ultimately permit debt cancellation. Moreover, the currently favourable coffee prices and better weather outlook should permit a sharp upturn in 2004 and modest improvement in the country's accounts.

Major uncertainties have nonetheless persisted. International backing could decline unless the country makes more progress on structural reforms (privatizing, financial sector). Furthermore, the regional environment has remained unstable. Tensions with Eritrea, which have been affecting the country's domestic political affairs, have remained high as evidenced by Ethiopia's reluctance to accept the border demarcation decided in April 2002 by the International Court of Justice in The Hague.

5

MAIN ECONOMIC INDICATORS						
US$ millions	1999	2000	2001	2002	2003 (e)	2004 (f)
Economic growth (%)	6.3	5.4	7.7	1.2	−3.8	6.7
Inflation (%)	3.9	4.2	−7.2	−7.2	14.6	5.5
Public-sector balance/GDP (%)	−12.9	−14.8	−10.3	−14	−17.4	−15.9
Exports	484	486	441	431	468	514
Imports	1,558	1,611	1,556	1,696	1,976	2,103
Trade balance	−1,074	−1,125	−1,115	−1,265	−1,508	−1,589
Current account balance/GDP (%)	−11.2	−9.8	−10.1	−13.2	−15.2	−14.4
Foreign debt	5,544	5,483	5,697	6,793	6,180	6,234
Debt service/Exports (%)	48.3	36.9	16.6	12.3	10.9	11.5
Currency reserves (import months)	2.9	1.8	2	3.8	4.2	4.5

e = estimate, f = forecast

Gabon

Population (million inhabitants)	1.3
GDP (million USD)	4,334

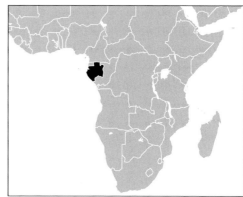

Short-term: **C**

Medium-term:
Very high risk

Coface analysis

STRENGTHS

- Gabon boasts a wealth of minerals, notably oil and manganese (second world producer), and vast hydroelectric and forest resources.
- Gabon's oil resources have permitted it to become a middle-income country and finance its infrastructure development.
- It has made great strides in diversifying domestic production and adding value (notably wood processing).
- Its political stability has been attractive to foreign investors.

WEAKNESSES

- Gabon's market is very narrow with only 1.3 million inhabitants.
- The farm sector has been meeting under 20 per cent of the country's food needs, generating unavoidable inflows of imports.
- The economy has remained very dependent on oil (55 per cent of tax receipts and 80 per cent of export earnings) with proven reserves tending to decline.
- Inadequate reforms and restructuring costs have been weighing on economic growth and public-sector accounts.
- The external debt burden is heavy and financing needs high.

RISK ASSESSMENT

The progressive oil production decline has continued to impede growth, which should remain modest in 2004 despite steady non-oil production (wood, manganese, services) and efforts to diversify the economy. Moreover, faced with internal and external public-sector debt burdens, the authorities have adopted more restrictive fiscal policy, thereby limiting their capacity to sustain economic activity via public spending. They have also settled a large proportion of their domestic arrears, which has contributed to improving company payment behaviour.

The country's financial situation could nonetheless begin to improve in 2004. The letter of intention signed in June 2003 with the IMF should permit implementation of a new loan and especially facilitate negotiation of new foreign-debt rescheduling with the Paris Club. In return, it has imposed acceleration of structural reforms, notably privatizations, and disciplined management of public finances.

Social tensions linked to those reforms and the decline of the population's purchasing power should not jeopardize the country's political stability, which should continue to be attractive to foreign investors.

MAIN ECONOMIC INDICATORS						
US$ millions	1999	2000	2001	2002	2003 (e)	2004 (f)
Economic growth (%)	−6.2	−1.9	2	0	0.1	1.8
Inflation (%)	−0.7	0.4	2.1	0.2	2	2
Public-sector balance/GDP (%)	1.2	11.6	3.2	3.4	6.6	3.5
Exports	2,359	3,218	2,620	2,695	2,984	3,128
Imports	798	807	902	987	1,263	1,404
Trade balance	1,561	2,412	1,718	1,708	1,720	1,724
Current account balance	−8.8	6.2	0.3	0.7	−2.9	−4.7
Foreign debt	5,301	4,941	4,332	4,346	4,371	4,345
Debt service/Exports (%)	28.0	16.6	26.2	16.7	15	18.1
Currency reserves (import months)	0.1	0.8	0.1	0.5	0.4	0.8

e = estimate, f = forecast

CONDITIONS OF ACCESS TO THE MARKET

■ Market overview

The Gabonese market is very open. The system of customs duties in place is operated by the Economic and Monetary Community of Central Africa (CEMAC). Its main features are duty-free admission of goods from within CEMAC (though the volume of goods traded is extremely limited), zero rate of duty for special products such as medical equipment and stationery, 6 per cent for staple commodities, 11 per cent for raw materials and capital goods, 21 per cent for semi-finished goods and 31 per cent for consumer goods.

The most strongly recommended means of payment is the irrevocable and confirmed letter of credit. Documentary collection upon presentation of a complete set of bills of lading and bills of exchange should only be used if the customer is well known to the exporter. Bank transfers and cheques, for which the customer is not liable, should be avoided. Exporters should be cautious when dealing with government agencies. For all government orders, it is necessary to obtain a copy of the official purchase order issued by the Budget Expenditure Office at the Ministry of Finance. Orders placed by the government with a foreign supplier have to be countersigned by the Director-General of Public Accounts. Suppliers are advised to check the relevant tax clauses with the departments concerned.

■ Attitude towards foreign investors

The legislative and regulatory environment is extremely liberal and the attitude of government officials generally positive. Investors enjoy free trade through CEMAC, modern instruments of business law through OHADA (Organization for the Harmonization of Business Law), investment security through the Multilateral Investment Guarantee Agency (MIGA) and a guaranteed appeals procedure through the International Centre for the Settlement of International Disputes (CIRDI).

An Investment Charter provides for freedom of enterprise, the right to property (including intellectual property), unrestricted access to foreign currency, free movement of capital, etc. From time to time, it is supplemented by special laws (Forestry Code adopted in December 2001, Investment Code, Mining Act, Oil Act, Labour Code, Competition Act). A one-stop shop, the Private Investment Promotion Agency (APIP), was set up in 2002 to provide investors with practical information. The Gabonese Employers Federation (CPG) gives entrepreneurs proper support and is proactive rather than reactive.

Customs duties and VAT are negotiable for large industrial schemes. In 2005, the Mandji Free Zone (Port-Gentil) is due to open its doors to companies engaged in the processing of natural

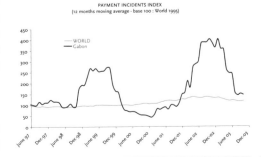

PAYMENT INCIDENTS INDEX
(12 months moving average - base 100 : World 1995)

5]

resources, the provision of services and the assembly and distribution of finished goods. These companies will be eligible for extremely attractive tax incentives and capital transfer provisions (10-year tax exemption, investment- and job-related tax credits, etc).

Wood processing, regulated by the new Forestry Code, offers tremendous growth potential. Libreville too offers real comparative advantages as a site for the development of services on a regional scale, especially as a regional headquarters for international corporations.

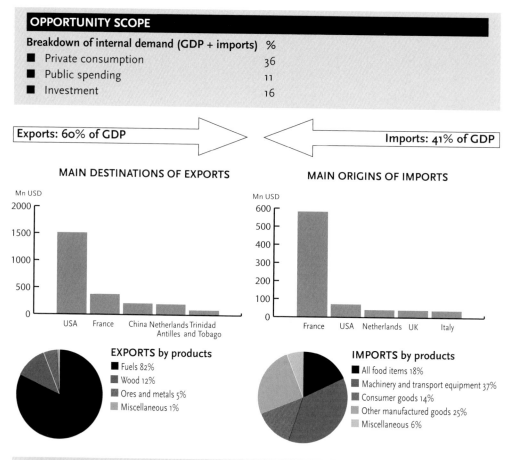

OPPORTUNITY SCOPE

Breakdown of internal demand (GDP + imports) %
- Private consumption — 36
- Public spending — 11
- Investment — 16

Exports: 60% of GDP

Imports: 41% of GDP

MAIN DESTINATIONS OF EXPORTS

Mn USD

USA France China Netherlands Trinidad Antilles and Tobago

EXPORTS by products
- Fuels 82%
- Wood 12%
- Ores and metals 5%
- Miscellaneous 1%

MAIN ORIGINS OF IMPORTS

Mn USD

France USA Netherlands UK Italy

IMPORTS by products
- All food items 18%
- Machinery and transport equipment 37%
- Consumer goods 14%
- Other manufactured goods 25%
- Miscellaneous 6%

STANDARD OF LIVING / PURCHASING POWER

Indicators	Gabon	Regional average	DC average
GNP per capita (PPP dollars)	5190	2841	6778
GNP per capita (USD)	3160	999	3568
Human Development Index	0.653	0.498	0.708
Wealthiest 10% share of national income	n/a	36	33
Urban population percentage	82	44	60
Percentage under 15 years old	40	42	31
number of telephones per 1000 inhabitants	30	33	157
number of computers per 1000 inhabitants	12	17	66

Ghana

Population (million inhabitants)   19.7
GDP (million USD)   5,301

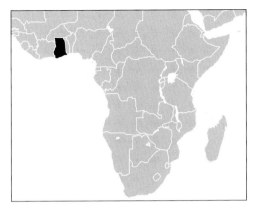

Short-term: **C**

Medium-term:

Coface analysis   **High risk**

STRENGTHS

- The country's political stability and the development of regional economic and monetary integration within ECOWAS constitute assets for investors.
- Long engaged in structural reforms, the country has enjoyed the support of financial backers.
- That backing should lead to cancellation of its public external debt under the HIPC programme for highly indebted poor countries.

WEAKNESSES

- Insufficiently diversified with gold and cocoa representing two-thirds of export revenues, the economy has remained vulnerable to external shocks (climate, world prices).
- The public-accounts situation has generated a large debt burden, an accumulation of arrears and high inflation.
- The pace of privatization has been slow, limiting the foreign investments needed to diversify the economy.
- The country has remained very dependent on international aid.

RISK ASSESSMENT

With good weather conditions, Ghana's growth outlook should remain positive. Nonetheless, to maintain the current pace of growth and further diversify its economic fabric, the country must intensify its structural reform programme.

After years of deterioration that has generated heavy public-sector debt (150 per cent of GDP in 2003), overhauling government accounts and public-sector companies has remained a major challenge for authorities. As the run-up to general elections in December 2004 will limit the authorities' room for manoeuvre in curtailing public spending, the improvement expected in 2004 will particularly reflect the substantial external-debt-burden reduction from which the country will benefit once it reaches the point of completion under the HIPC programme for highly indebted poor countries.

Moreover, after a good year in 2003 attributable to firm cocoa and gold prices, the expected decline of those raw material prices in 2004 should again undermine external accounts, which have remained structurally vulnerable to exogenous factors. Financing needs have remained substantial and foreign direct investment inflows insufficient. The country will thus remain dependent on international backing.

5

MAIN ECONOMIC INDICATORS						
US$ millions	1999	2000	2001	2002	2003 (e)	2004 (f)
Economic growth (%)	4.4	3.7	4.2	4.5	4.7	4.9
Inflation (%)	12.4	25.2	32.9	14.8	27.5	14.5
Public-sector balance/GDP (%)	−9.8	−10	−14.6	−8.1	−7.5	−5.7
Exports	2,006	1,936	1,867	2,061	2,664	2,629
Imports	3,252	2,759	2,968	2,705	3,226	3,457
Trade balance	−1,246	−823	−1,101	−644	−562	−828
Current account balance/GDP (%)	−11.8	−7.8	−10.8	−4.1	−1.5	−6.6
Foreign debt	7,214	7,020	7,332	7,032	7,446	7,198
Debt service/Exports (%)	17.1	17.9	12.6	11.2	11.6	13.1
Currency reserves (import months)	1.4	0.9	1.1	2.1	2.8	3.2

e = estimate, f = forecast

CONDITIONS OF ACCESS TO THE MARKET

■ Market overview

There are no import licences or exchange controls. The country has comprehensive copyright protection laws, though these are not properly enforced. Industrial property is better protected. Trademarks and company logos receive proper and adequate protection, provided they have been registered beforehand.

Customs duties vary between 0 and 25 per cent. Some products from the Economic Community of West African States (ECOWAS) are exempt from customs duty. Products from non-ECOWAS countries are subject to 0.5 per cent duty (ECOWAS levy). A new 0.5 per cent tax has also been introduced to provision the Export Development Investment Fund (EDIF). Since 1 April 2000, goods inspections at the point of entry have been carried out by GSBV (a Bureau Veritas/ Ghana Standards Board joint venture) and by Gateway Services Limited (GSL – a Cotecna/ Ghanian Customs joint venture). GSBV inspects goods at airports and land borders, whereas GSL conducts inspections at the ports of Tema and Takoradi.

VAT is applicable at a flat rate of 12.5 per cent on the customs value of goods, in addition to customs duties and levies. Foreign companies, however, face a number of difficulties, including a stifling bureaucracy, a somewhat arbitrary legal and judicial system subject to outside interference (even if it can be said to be adequate for the job) and poor financing (the banking system is not interested in industrial and business investment).

■ Attitude towards foreign investors

To set up a joint venture with a local partner, a minimum investment of US$10,000 is required. The equity requirement is five times greater for wholly foreign-owned companies. Purchasing and sales groups are required to invest US$300,000 and employ at least 10 local staff. These conditions do not apply to investment or fund management firms or to companies engaged in the export of Ghanaian products.

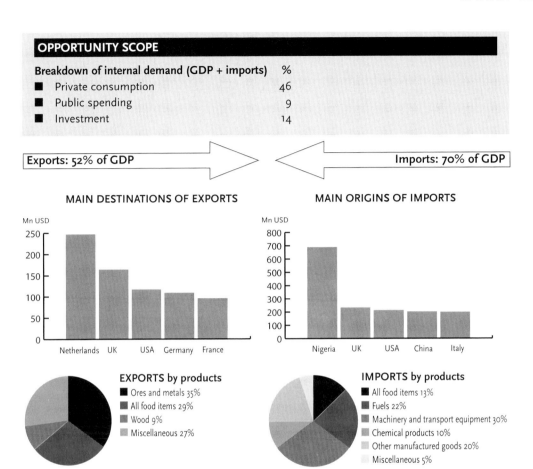

OPPORTUNITY SCOPE

Breakdown of internal demand (GDP + imports)	%
■ Private consumption	46
■ Public spending	9
■ Investment	14

Exports: 52% of GDP   Imports: 70% of GDP

MAIN DESTINATIONS OF EXPORTS

Mn USD

Netherlands   UK   USA   Germany   France

MAIN ORIGINS OF IMPORTS

Mn USD

Nigeria   UK   USA   China   Italy

EXPORTS by products
- ■ Ores and metals 35%
- ■ All food items 29%
- ■ Wood 9%
- ■ Miscellaneous 27%

IMPORTS by products
- ■ All food items 13%
- ■ Fuels 22%
- ■ Machinery and transport equipment 30%
- ■ Chemical products 10%
- □ Other manufactured goods 20%
- □ Miscellaneous 5%

5

STANDARD OF LIVING / PURCHASING POWER

Indicators	Ghana	Regional average	DC average
GNP per capita (PPP dollars)	2170	2841	6778
GNP per capita (USD)	290	999	3568
Human Development Index	0.567	0.498	0.708
Wealthiest 10% share of national income	30	36	33
Urban population percentage	36	44	60
Percentage under 15 years old	43	42	31
number of telephones per 1000 inhabitants	12	33	157
number of computers per 1000 inhabitants	3	17	66

Guinea

Population (million inhabitants)	7.6
GDP (million USD)	2,989

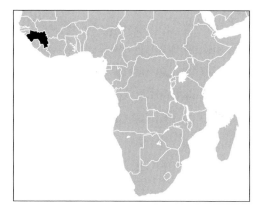

Coface analysis

Short-term: **D**

Medium-term:
Very high risk

STRENGTHS

- Guinea boasts substantial mineral resources – bauxite (second world producer and exporter), iron, gold and diamonds – and considerable hydroelectric, farming and tourist potential.
- Structural reforms have been progressing, albeit slowly.
- Guinea's customs and monetary integration into ECOWAS should enhance its attractiveness to investors.

WEAKNESSES

- The country's environment has spawned refugee, guerrilla and smuggling problems, which, although partially resolved, have remained risk factors.
- That situation and a tense political and financial context have been limiting foreign investments.
- Inadequate investment has been impeding the transportation and energy infrastructure construction, economic diversification and agricultural development (65 per cent of the working population) needed to reduce poverty.
- The country's resources have thus remained very dependent on its bauxite exports.

RISK ASSESSMENT

The internal and external political context has remained uncertain. The Guinea-Bissau, Liberia and Ivory Coast situations could still destabilize the region and thus trigger new refugee flows.

Domestically, with the problem of President Conte's succession approaching, implementation of the structural policies demanded by financial backers via the Poverty Reduction and Growth Facility has appeared paralysed, which could prompt interruption of the programme. That would be all the more damaging with the country's public and external account deficits remaining large and generating substantial financing needs.

In that context, Guinea's solvency will continue to depend on maintaining investment inflows in the minerals sector and on cancellation of its external debt under the HIPC programme for highly indebted poor countries. However, that cancellation will depend on political stability and renewed progress on public sector restructuring.

MAIN ECONOMIC INDICATORS						
US$ millions	1999	2000	2001	2002	2003 (e)	2004 (f)
Economic growth (%)	4.6	1.9	3.8	4.2	3	2.5
Inflation (%)	4.6	6.8	5.4	3	8	12
Public-sector balance/GDP (%)	−5.4	−5.6	−7.5	−8.2	−7.2	−6.3
Exports	646	667	723	700	776	833
Imports	582	583	562	650	686	702
Trade balance	64	83	161	51	90	131
Current account balance/GDP (%)	−7.2	−8.2	−3.8	−7.8	−6.1	−5.2
Foreign debt	3,655	3,483	3,391	3,270	3,165	3,045
Debt service/Exports (%)	33.4	21.6	22.7	20.8	23.8	20.8
Currency reserves (import months)	2.5	1.8	2.6	2.0	1.8	2.7

e = estimate, f = forecast

CONDITIONS OF ACCESS TO THE MARKET

■ Market overview

Guinea is a WTO member and the country's market is very open. Average import duty (excluding internal levies, at times high for certain products) is around 16 per cent. The maximum rate of duty is 32 per cent plus 18 per cent VAT.

Import regulations do not pose any special problems, although there is a vast and thriving grey market. The banking sector is active and largely made up of foreign banks. But its growth is checked by the narrowness of the official currency market and the poor creditworthiness of importers. There are no restrictions on currency transfers. However, the shortage of foreign currency on the official market often causes importers to turn to the grey market. The 20 per cent discount at which the local currency trades on this market marks up the price of imported products proportionately.

■ Attitude towards foreign investors

Guinea has adopted and ratified the Organization for the Harmonization of Business Law in Africa (OHADA) treaty and plans to adopt the WAEMU's liberal common external tariff in the medium term. This should enhance investment security, while

OHADA's harmonization drive should help promote investment safeguards. An Arbitration Board and a new Penal Code were established in 1999. While the Investment Code has been amended, in practice the legal system offers few safeguards. Appeals are difficult to obtain and rarely successful. Industrial property protection exists but the system is ineffective in the face of unfair competition from products imported through the grey market. The legacy of the past and the power wielded by the bureaucracy are everyday obstacles, despite the introduction of incentives encouraging foreign investors to set up in business alone or with a Guinean partner.

■ Foreign exchange regulations

Guinea is not a member of the franc area, but is a member of IMAO (West Africa Monetary Institute). The Guinean franc is not convertible, though it is *de facto* pegged to the US dollar and moves in response to fluctuations in the value of the dollar. Since 1 September 1999, the Guinean franc's exchange rate has been set by an auction market located at the central bank. Auctions are attended both by the country's key financial players and by international financial institutions and conducted on the basis of supply and demand.

5

OPPORTUNITY SCOPE

Breakdown of internal demand (GDP + imports) %
- Private consumption 58
- Public spending 4
- Investment 17

Exports: 28% of GDP · Imports: 29% of GDP

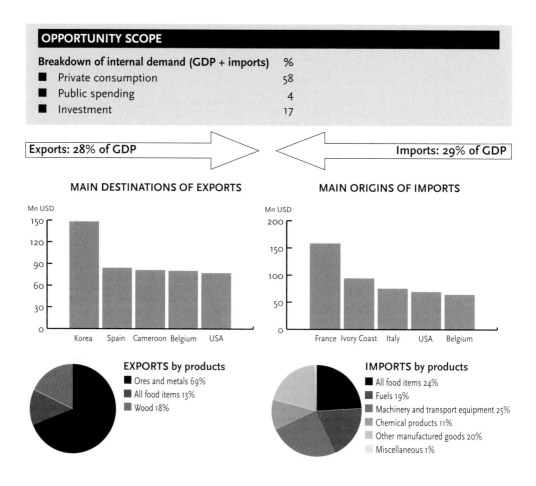

MAIN DESTINATIONS OF EXPORTS

Mn USD

Korea · Spain · Cameroon · Belgium · USA

MAIN ORIGINS OF IMPORTS

Mn USD

France · Ivory Coast · Italy · USA · Belgium

EXPORTS by products
- Ores and metals 69%
- All food items 13%
- Wood 18%

IMPORTS by products
- All food items 24%
- Fuels 19%
- Machinery and transport equipment 25%
- Chemical products 11%
- Other manufactured goods 20%
- Miscellaneous 1%

STANDARD OF LIVING / PURCHASING POWER

Indicators	Guinea	Regional average	DC average
GNP per capita (PPP dollars)	1900	2841	6778
GNP per capita (USD)	410	999	3568
Human Development Index	0.425	0.498	0.708
Wealthiest 10% share of national income	32	36	33
Urban population percentage	28	44	60
Percentage under 15 years old	44	42	31
number of telephones per 1000 inhabitants	3	33	157
number of computers per 1000 inhabitants	4	17	66

Ivory Coast

Population (million inhabitants)   16.4
GDP (million USD)   10,411

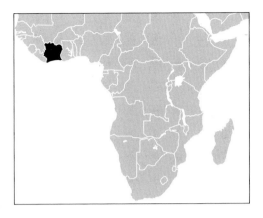

Short-term: **D**

Medium-term:

Coface analysis   **Very high risk**

STRENGTHS

- The Ivory Coast economy boasts substantial agricultural and mineral potential in West Africa, enhanced by a significant processing industry and good transportation infrastructure.
- It is a very important transit country for Burkina Faso, Mali and Niger.
- West African Economic and Monetary Union (WAEMU) membership has contributed to monetary stability.

WEAKNESSES

- The country has remained dependent on farm production – cocoa (leading world producer), coffee, cotton – and thus on exogenous factors (climate, world prices), which has always threatened to undermine its public and external accounts.
- The recurrent political, social and ethnic tensions that have disrupted the country could durably deter foreign investors.
- Structural reforms have continued to lag.

5

RISK ASSESSMENT

The September 2002 rebellion that resulted in the country's de facto partition and in economic paralysis in the north has severely deteriorated prospects for the Ivory Coast economy, mired in a fourth consecutive recession year.

Nonetheless, steady cocoa prices, revenues stemming from hydrocarbon exports, and an import slowdown permitted the posting of external account surpluses in 2003. In conjunction with interruption of the public investment programme, those revenues have contributed to avoiding a public finances drift. However, with recourse to payment arrears having proven unavoidable, cancellation of external public-sector debt under the HIPC programme for highly indebted poor countries has been postponed indefinitely.

A growth recovery will depend on restoring durable political stability, which would reassure both domestic and foreign economic actors. However, only sporadic progress has resulted since the Linas-Marcoussis agreement concluded in January 2003. The 2004 outlook is all the more uncertain with the tensions disrupting the country for the past several years only easing slowly. Moreover, with cocoa revenues expected to fall (with declines in production and prices) and resumption of international aid depending on a durable stabilization of the political situation, the country's financial situation could become even worse.

The high Coface payment-incident index reflects the impact of the crisis on company behaviour.

MAIN ECONOMIC INDICATORS

US$ millions	1999	2000	2001	2002	2003 (e)	2004 (f)
Economic growth (%)	1.6	−2.3	−0.8	−1.2	−4	n/a
Inflation (%)	0.7	2.5	4.4	3.1	3.7	2.7
Public-sector balance/GDP (%)	−3.7	−1.5	0.4	−1.1	−1.1	n/a
Exports	4.5	3.8	3.9	5.2	5.1	4.8
Imports	2.6	2.3	2.4	2.4	2.8	2.9
Trade balance	1.8	1.5	1.5	2.7	2.2	1.9
Current account balance/GDP (%)	−2.9	−3.5	−3.9	6.5	4.9	−0.7
Foreign debt	14.6	13.0	13.6	13.8	13.5	13.2
Debt service/Exports (%)	31.1	36.6	30.1	24.2	24	n/a
Currency reserves (import months)	1.4	1.7	2.6	2.6	2.5	n/a

e = estimate, f = forecast

CONDITIONS OF ACCESS TO THE MARKET

■ Means of entry

From 1 January 2000, the date of introduction of the common external tariff, all WAEMU countries have had the same customs procedures. Member states enjoy total exemption from customs duties, while non-members are liable to four rates of duty: 0, 5, 10 and 20 per cent. There is also a statistical tax (1 per cent of the CIF value), a community solidarity tax (1 per cent), an ECOWAS levy (0.5 per cent) and 18 per cent single-rate VAT, cut from 20 per cent by the Finance Act 2003. Special taxes are levied ad hoc on a number of products such as fish, rice, alcoholic beverages, tobacco, cigarettes and petroleum products. Protectionist measures include an import licence for cottons and 100 per cent cotton products (eg wax and bazin). Products are quantity- and quality-controlled prior to shipment by Bivac and Cotecna. Under the law of 2 April 2002, a certificate of conformity is required to commercialize some 80 products from 2 June 2003.

■ Attitude towards foreign investors

Since 1995, Ivory Coast has had a new Investment Code generally regarded as investment-friendly. The Code lays down two separate procedures according to the size and type of investment. Both offer five- to eight-year tax exemptions. Under the approval procedure (for investments over 762,000 euros), investors are liable to only 5 per cent flat-rate import duty on machinery, material and the first batch of spares. The Code does not differentiate between origins of investment and applies to both local and foreign investment. Legal uncertainty and customs and tax maladministration continue to be a major cause for concern among companies. There are no special restrictions on the employment of foreign workers in the Ivory Coast. However, foreigners can be hired only if the corresponding vacancy has been advertised for two months and prior approval has been obtained from the Ministry of Labour.

■ Foreign exchange regulations

Financial flows between Ivory Coast and non-ECOWAS member states (excluding France) are subject to the approval of the Ministry of Economic Affairs and Finance (Finex Department). In principle, there are no restrictions on the free movement of capital between Ivory Coast and other member countries (including France).

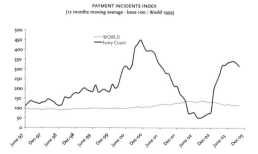

PAYMENT INCIDENTS INDEX
(12 months moving average - base 100 : World 1995)

OPPORTUNITY SCOPE

Breakdown of internal demand (GDP + imports)	%
■ Private consumption	56
■ Public spending	7
■ Investment	8

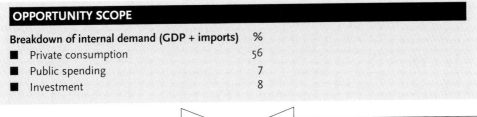

Exports: 39% of GDP → ← Imports: 32% of GDP

MAIN DESTINATIONS OF EXPORTS	MAIN ORIGINS OF IMPORTS

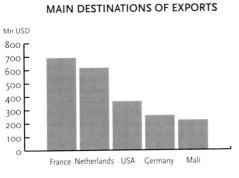

Mn USD — France, Netherlands, USA, Germany, Mali

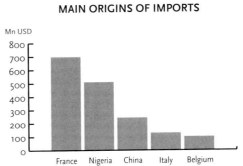

Mn USD — France, Nigeria, China, Italy, Belgium

EXPORTS by products
- ■ All food items 50%
- ■ Agricultural raw materials 14%
- ■ Manufactured goods 14%
- ■ Fuels 20%
- ■ Miscellaneous 2%

IMPORTS by products
- ■ All food items 17%
- ■ Fuels 34%
- ■ Machinery and transport equipment 16%
- ■ Chemical products 14%
- ■ Other manufactured goods 16%
- ■ Miscellaneous 3%

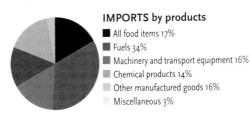

5

STANDARD OF LIVING / PURCHASING POWER

Indicators	Ivory Coast	Regional average	DC average
GNP per capita (PPP dollars)	1400	2841	6778
GNP per capita (USD)	630	999	3568
Human Development Index	0.396	0.498	0.708
Wealthiest 10% share of national income	29	36	33
Urban population percentage	44	44	60
Percentage under 15 years old	42	42	31
number of telephones per 1000 inhabitants	18	33	157
number of computers per 1000 inhabitants	7	17	66

Kenya

Population (million inhabitants)	30.7
GDP (million USD)	11,396

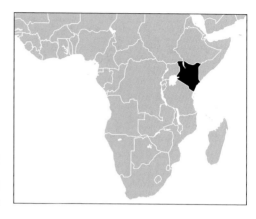

Coface analysis

Short-term: **C**

Medium-term:
High risk

STRENGTHS

- Endowed with a more diversified economy than most African countries, Kenya benefits from agricultural (tea, coffee) and tourism resources.
- It is a crucial player in East Africa (transportation, finance, regional headquarters for many institutions and companies).
- The strengthening of regional integration (EAC, COMESA) represents an asset for investors.

WEAKNESSES

- The economy has remained very dependent on weather conditions, which affect agriculture and hydroelectric production, and thus industrial activity.
- The country's relations with the international financial community have been unsteady with anti-corruption measures imposed by financial backers meeting with strong resistance.
- In this context, the level of investments has been insufficient to generate sustained growth.
- Poverty, unemployment and the AIDS pandemic will continue to pose major challenges for the country.

RISK ASSESSMENT

Despite its assets, and the renewed confidence inspired by the smooth political changeover after the December 2002 elections, Kenya has not succeeded in generating a high enough growth rate to ensure its development and reduce poverty.

The outlook appears nonetheless encouraging. Reforms demanded by international financial institutions aimed at strengthening anti-corruption measures have been adopted. They have paved the way for resumption of financial backing via a new programme that will ultimately permit debt cancellation under the HIPC initiative for highly indebted poor countries.

Although that backing will be essential in improving the country's solvency and reducing its domestic and foreign debt, the new authorities' capacity to continue the effort of consolidating public accounts and restructuring state-owned companies has remained uncertain. The near-term social cost of those measures could notably trigger substantial social and political tensions leading to a new deadlock on reforms.

MAIN ECONOMIC INDICATORS

US$ billions	1999	2000	2001	2002	2003 (e)	2004 (f)
Inflation (%)	5.7	10	5.7	2.0	6.6	4.5
Public-sector balance/GDP (%)	0.1	−5	−3.4	−4.6	−6.6	−5.0
Exports	1.8	1.8	1.9	2.0	2.2	2.4
Imports	2.7	3.0	3.2	3.2	3.6	3.9
Trade balance	−0.9	−1.3	−1.3	−1.2	−1.4	−1.5
Current account balance/GDP (%)	−2.2	−3.6	−4.3	−4.2	−6.2	−7.3
Foreign debt	6.2	5.9	5.4	5.5	6.1	6.9
Debt service/Exports (%)	30.9	20.6	22.1	16.4	13.3	10.7
Currency reserves (import months)	2.7	2.7	3.0	3.0	2.7	2.7

e = estimate, f = forecast

CONDITIONS OF ACCESS TO THE MARKET

■ Market overview

The Kenyan market is open to various types of investment and capital or consumer goods that meet the country's standards. Only some products (arms, pesticides, animal and plant seed, etc) are banned or restricted. There are few protectionist measures and those that exist do so mainly in connection with foreign ownership of farmland, the acquisition of shares in utilities, and restrictions on insurance and investment management companies.

Tariff barriers mainly consist of suspended duties (temporary surcharges) regularly levied on maize, sugar, wheat, rice, natural fibres (cotton), etc. These duties vary between 20 and 80 per cent and are applicable along with other duties and levies. Import duties on goods that undergo transformation in Kenya (eg car assembly) are fairly low. There is a system of exemption for products processed in a free zone and intended for export. The structure of customs duties has been simplified to facilitate assessment and collection. There are six rates of customs duty: 0, 3, 5, 15, 25 and 35 per cent. From July 2003, the standard rate of VAT is 16 per cent. Moves are also under way to conclude a customs union agreement between the three East African countries. Since the liberalization of trade and the currency market in the early 1990s, payment difficulties in the private sector have become a rare occurrence and are usually due to poor choice of a local partner and failure to take elementary precautions.

■ Means of entry

Some formalities, such as pre-inspection of imports, must be complied with. The US dollar and the pound sterling are the most widely used international units of account, although the euro is rapidly gaining ground on the back of the fact that the EU is the country's largest trading partner and biggest lender. In any case, it is advisable to take certain precautions with regard to payments and use tested procedures such as presentation of documents against payment, guaranteed bank cheques, international transfers and confirmed letters of credit.

■ Attitude towards foreign investors

The Kenyan government is torn between its desire to attract foreign investment and its determination to Africanize an economy largely in the hands of Kenyans of Indian and British origin and

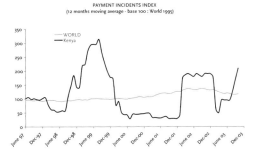

PAYMENT INCIDENTS INDEX
(12 months moving average - base 100 : World 1995)

multinationals. Foreign investment is keenly welcomed by the Kenyan government, especially where it helps to promote exports, technology transfers and jobs.

Growth sectors include agriculture (horticulture), telecommunications, energy and utilities earmarked for privatization (certain road concessions, water supply, railways, port terminal). There are few restrictive or discriminatory measures, though there are ad hoc regulations limiting access to specific sectors and stricter restrictions on obtaining work permits.

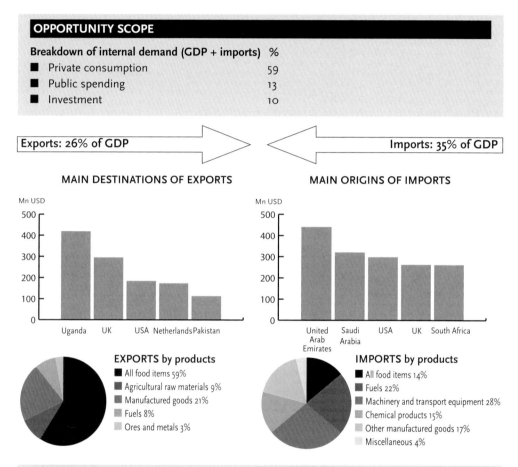

OPPORTUNITY SCOPE

Breakdown of internal demand (GDP + imports)	%
■ Private consumption	59
■ Public spending	13
■ Investment	10

Exports: 26% of GDP

Imports: 35% of GDP

MAIN DESTINATIONS OF EXPORTS

Mn USD

(Uganda, UK, USA, Netherlands, Pakistan)

MAIN ORIGINS OF IMPORTS

Mn USD

(United Arab Emirates, Saudi Arabia, USA, UK, South Africa)

EXPORTS by products
- ■ All food items 59%
- ■ Agricultural raw materials 9%
- ■ Manufactured goods 21%
- ■ Fuels 8%
- ■ Ores and metals 3%

IMPORTS by products
- ■ All food items 14%
- ■ Fuels 22%
- ■ Machinery and transport equipment 28%
- ■ Chemical products 15%
- ■ Other manufactured goods 17%
- ■ Miscellaneous 4%

STANDARD OF LIVING / PURCHASING POWER

Indicators	Kenya	Regional average	DC average
GNP per capita (PPP dollars)	970	2841	6778
GNP per capita (USD)	350	999	3568
Human Development Index	0.489	0.498	0.708
Wealthiest 10% share of national income	36	36	33
Urban population percentage	34	44	60
Percentage under 15 years old	43	42	31
number of telephones per 1000 inhabitants	10	33	157
number of computers per 1000 inhabitants	6	17	66

Madagascar

Population (million inhabitants)   16.0
GDP (million USD)   4,604
GDP per capita (USD)   288

Short-term: **D**

Medium-term:
Coface analysis   **Very high risk**

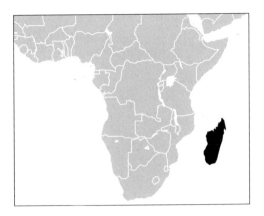

RISK ASSESSMENT

The political crisis that resulted from the contested election outcome in 2001 and lasted until July 2002 led to economic paralysis and a sharp activity decline. The institutional stabilization that culminated with the December 2002 legislative elections facilitated negotiation of a new arrangement with the IMF and implementation of a reconstruction programme that has permitted the revitalizing of the economy.

However, with public spending essentially driving the rebound, recovery will only materialize progressively in the tourist and industrial sectors, which also depend on developments in US and European economic conditions.

In this context, consolidating public and external accounts will constitute a major challenge for the new authorities whose promises will be difficult to finance. New tensions will thus remain possible.

5

MAIN ECONOMIC INDICATORS						
US$ millions	1999	2000	2001	2002	2003 (e)	2004 (f)
Economic growth (%)	4.7	4.8	6	−12.7	6	6
Inflation (%)	9.9	11.9	7.4	15.8	8	5
Public-sector balance/GDP (%)	−6.4	−6.4	−8.2	−7.7	−7.6	−6.9
Exports	582	839	1,011	505	788	915
Imports	749	943	995	628	910	1,004
Trade balance	−167	−104	16	−123	−121	−89
Current account balance/GDP (%)	−6.6	−6.5	−2.0	−6.1	−7.3	−5.6
Foreign debt	4,551	4,117	4,147	4,229	4,335	4,479
Debt service/Exports (%)	16.2	12.4	10.2	19.6	14.1	12.4
Currency reserves (import months)	2.1	2.2	3.0	4.0	2.9	2.7

e = estimate, f = forecast

Malawi

Population (million inhabitants)	10.5
GDP (million USD)	1,749
GDP per capita (USD)	167

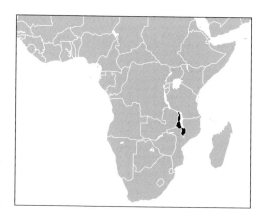

Short-term: **D**

Coface analysis

Medium-term:
Very high risk

RISK ASSESSMENT

Landlocked, densely populated and lacking natural resources other than agricultural ones, Malawi has been undergoing a difficult period marked by the after-affects of a large-scale food crisis. This context has further complicated matters for the authorities in contending with many challenges.

Their room for manoeuvre is constrained by the need to consolidate relations with the international financial community, which renewed its backing in late 2003 after a three-year credit freeze despite continued fiscal-policy laxity in the

run-up to the 2004 general elections. This renewed backing should facilitate the covering of the country's external financing needs and the restructuring of its domestic and foreign debt.

Those prospects in conjunction with a revival of farm production, notably of tobacco, should enhance the likelihood of a growth recovery, although at a rate that will remain insufficient in relation to demographic growth. In the longer term, the pace of structural reforms will have to accelerate to meet the challenges of combating poverty and AIDS, diversifying the economy and attracting foreign investors.

MAIN ECONOMIC INDICATORS						
US$ millions	1999	2000	2001	2002	2003 (e)	2004 (f)
Economic growth (%)	4	1.7	−1.5	−1.3	1.7	2.6
Inflation (%)	44.8	29.6	27.2	16	11.6	13
Public-sector balance/GDP (%)	−12.6	−15.0	−15.9	−13.4	−10.7	−10.8
Exports	447	406	407	397	454	472
Imports	673	563	582	635	623	636
Trade balance	−226	−157	−175	−238	−169	−164
Current account balance/GDP (%)	−17.1	−14.2	−12.9	−26.2	−14.4	−13.8
Foreign debt	2,608	2,674	2,736	2,858	2,963	3,019
Debt service/Exports (%)	16.7	21.2	20.9	19.8	19.5	20.3
Currency reserves (import months)	3.5	4.2	3.6	2.3	1.8	4.3

e = estimate, f = forecast

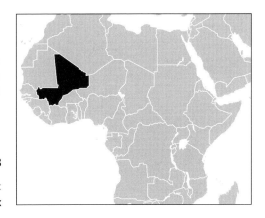

Mali

Population (million inhabitants)	11.1
GDP (million USD)	2,647
GDP per capita (USD)	238

Short-term: **B**

Medium-term:

Coface analysis

High risk

RISK ASSESSMENT

The good results of 2002 have given way to mediocre performance in 2003. Neither the cotton and cereal harvests nor gold extraction have reached the previous year's levels despite steady world prices. Moreover, the Ivory Coast crisis has been hampering activity in the transportation, industrial and construction sectors. In this context, the deficits of the public and external accounts grew, underscoring the country's dependence on expatriate-worker remittances and international aid.

However, despite those difficulties and a political landscape marked by the absence of a parliamentary majority, the authorities have persisted with their policies of economic liberalization, tax base consolidation and structural reforms. Mali was thus able to reach the point of completion in the HIPC programme for highly indebted poor countries in March 2003, paving the way for cancellation of public external debt.

The outlook for 2004 thus appears brighter although remaining subject to external factors like rainfall, cotton and gold prices, and stabilization of the Ivory Coast situation.

5

MAIN ECONOMIC INDICATORS

US$ millions	1999	2000	2001	2002	2003 (e)	2004 (f)
Economic growth (%)	6.7	3.7	3.5	9.7	0.5	5.7
Inflation (%)	−1.2	−0.7	5.2	5	4.5	2.5
Public-sector balance/GDP (%)	−8.7	−9.7	−8	−7.7	−9.1	−8.3
Exports	597	530	725	939	1,005	1,095
Imports	633	576	735	716	845	905
Trade balance	−36	−46	−10	224	160	190
Current account balance/GDP (%)	−10.8	−13.0	−14.2	−6.3	−8.2	−6.7
Foreign debt	3,230	3,001	3,000	3,005	3,030	3,067
Debt service/Exports (%)	13.8	15.6	9.3	9.0	9.4	9.1
Currency reserves (import months)	4.7	5.1	1.5	4.9	5.2	6.7

e = estimate, f = forecast

Mauritania

| Population (million inhabitants) | 2.7 |
| GDP (million USD) | 1,007 |

Coface analysis

Short-term: **C**

Medium-term:
Very high risk

STRENGTHS

- The country's mineral resources (high-quality iron, copper, cobalt, gypsum) and development potential (oil, diamonds) have been attracting foreign investors.
- With implementation of structural reforms, the country has earned international financial community backing.
- That backing has resulted in broad debt cancellation under the HIPC programme for highly indebted poor countries.
- The strengthening of regional cooperation (Morocco, Senegal) has been an encouraging development.

WEAKNESSES

- With 2.7 million inhabitants, Mauritania constitutes a small market where iron and fish exports generate nearly all currency earnings.
- The economy's insufficient diversification has made it vulnerable to exogenous factors (weather, world prices).
- The country's geographic situation (desert) and weather conditions have made it dependent on food imports.
- Inadequate infrastructure has been hampering development of its resources.
- Recurrent intercommunity tensions have remained a source of risk.

RISK ASSESSMENT

In a context of disciplined fiscal and monetary policy, economic growth, spurred by public and private investment, has benefited from implementation of important structural reforms. Those reforms have also permitted the country to reach the point of completion in the HIPC programme for highly indebted poor countries in June 2002 and benefit from debt cancellation.

The authorities will nonetheless still have to meet major challenges. The economy's diversification beyond iron ore and fishing has remained insufficient and the oil prospecting under way will not go into production before 2005 at best.

The functioning of the banking system and the foreign exchange market has been a source of difficulty for companies. Meanwhile, the poverty level (50 per cent of the population) has remained high.

Mauritania continues to be dependent on foreign capital to cover its external financing needs, which have remained substantial. However, investors will be likely to exercise more caution amid risks of an increase in social or political tensions. The attempted coup in June 2003 and the turmoil accompanying the presidential elections in November 2003, won by the incumbent president, reflect the underlying tensions.

MAIN ECONOMIC INDICATORS						
US$ millions	1999	2000	2001	2002	2003 (e)	2004 (f)
Economic growth (%)	5.2	5.2	4.0	3.3	5.4	6.1
Inflation (%)	4.1	3.3	4.7	3.9	6.4	3.7
Public-sector balance/GDP (%)	2.1	−4.4	−5.5	6.2	−2.1	−2.7
Exports	333	345	339	330	341	368
Imports	305	336	372	418	472	500
Trade balance	28	9	−34	−88	−131	−133
Current account balance/GDP (%)	−4.2	−5.8	−10.4	−0.6	−9.5	−8
Foreign debt	2,456	2,456	2,603	1,451	1,401	1,532
Debt service/Exports (%)	33.3	33.6	31.6	14.9	12.3	12.8
Currency reserves (import months)	6.2	7	6.1	7.8	5.8	5.0

e = estimate, f = forecast

CONDITIONS OF ACCESS TO THE MARKET

■ Attitude towards foreign investors

The legal environment is fairly well endowed in terms of both the quantity and quality of the country's laws (trade code, investment code, taxation code, etc). Property ownership laws, however, tend to be fairly vague in some cases and need to be improved in respect of urban areas, industrial areas, ports, airports and their surroundings, and land adjacent to major roads. A foreign company can win an action against a local partner belonging to the dominant tribe. It is even possible to win an action against the government and have the ruling enforced. On the other hand, it may be difficult, even impossible, for a foreigner to enforce a ruling against a business person belonging to the dominant Smacid tribe or an allied tribe (Ouled Bousba or Idawali).

There exists a double taxation treaty about which nobody has complained so far. However, the relationship between parent and subsidiary companies should be re-examined as there appear to be cases of double taxation that could be detrimental to investment.

The financial environment gives the greatest cause for concern. Mauritanian banks perform none of the functions normally expected of a banking system: savings collection, provision of credit for investment, etc. Their only role is to serve a limited number of interest groups as providers of foreign exchange and lately the national currency. Business persons not linked to these groups turn to bureaux de change to meet their foreign currency requirements in the exercise of their activities, but have to pay a surcharge for this service. As both business and non-business people keep cash savings in the local currency at home or at their workplace, there is a thriving grey market.

5

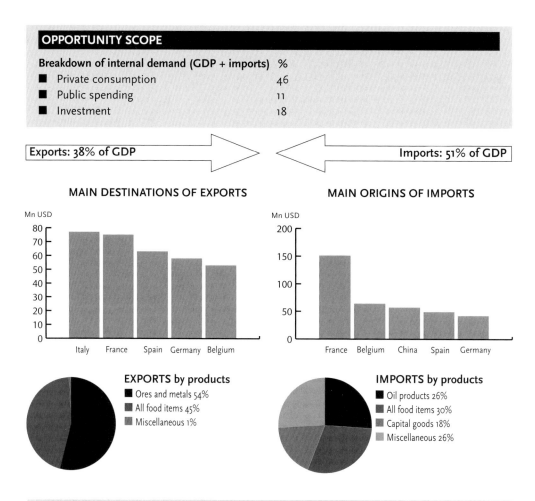

OPPORTUNITY SCOPE

Breakdown of internal demand (GDP + imports) %
- Private consumption — 46
- Public spending — 11
- Investment — 18

Exports: 38% of GDP   Imports: 51% of GDP

MAIN DESTINATIONS OF EXPORTS

Mn USD

Italy, France, Spain, Germany, Belgium

MAIN ORIGINS OF IMPORTS

Mn USD

France, Belgium, China, Spain, Germany

EXPORTS by products
- Ores and metals 54%
- All food items 45%
- Miscellaneous 1%

IMPORTS by products
- Oil products 26%
- All food items 30%
- Capital goods 18%
- Miscellaneous 26%

STANDARD OF LIVING / PURCHASING POWER

Indicators	Mauritania	Regional average	DC average
GNP per capita (PPP dollars)	1940	2841	6778
GNP per capita (USD)	360	999	3568
Human Development Index	0.454	0.498	0.708
Wealthiest 10% share of national income	28	36	33
Urban population percentage	59	44	60
Percentage under 15 years old	44	42	31
number of telephones per 1000 inhabitants	7	33	157
number of computers per 1000 inhabitants	10	17	66

Mauritius

Population (million inhabitants)	1.2
GDP (million USD)	4,500

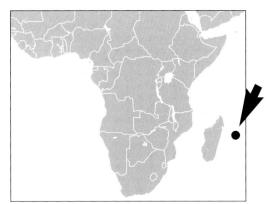

Coface analysis

Short-term: **A3**

Medium-term:
Quite low risk

STRENGTHS

- GDP per capita and the human development index are among the African continent's highest.
- The economy has been opening up to high value-added activities like new technologies and finance.
- Customs-free areas have permitted the attracting of foreign investment and the developing of exports.
- External financing needs are low with a consequently reasonable level of external debt.
- Besides enjoying good relations with Western countries and Africa, Mauritius has been developing its relations with India and China.

WEAKNESSES

- The pace of economic activity has remained sensitive to developments in the sugar sector (production, processing and effects on household consumption) and thus to weather conditions (notably cyclones).
- The rising level of unemployment has underscored the need to develop technical skills in the labour force.
- The investment needed to achieve that development (education, professional training) has been straining public accounts already squeezed by a narrow tax base.
- In this context, internal public debt has been steadily increasing.

RISK ASSESSMENT

After the 2002 slowdown, economic activity has resumed at a more sustained pace in 2003 with the sugar economy returning to normal conditions and public investment offsetting sluggish textile exports affected by the world slowdown and competition from lower-production-cost countries. Considering the need to consolidate public finances, growth prospects for 2004 will be more dependent on world recovery, tourism and the sugar harvest. In any case, the country's firm external accounts and low external debt burden with no hint of default risk have left the authorities with ample room for manoeuvre.

Except for payment incidents affecting the textile sector, company payment behaviour has remained acceptable.

5

MAIN ECONOMIC INDICATORS						
US$ millions	1999	2000	2001	2002	2003 (e)	2004 (f)
Economic growth (%)	5.4	2.7	7	2.6	4.1	5.6
Inflation (%)	7.9	4.4	6	6.7	5.3	5
Public-sector balance/GDP (%)	−4.6	−4.3	−7.1	−6.5	−5.7	−4.9
Unemployment rate (%)	1,680	1,523	1,639	1,583	1,676	1,742
Exports	2,046	2,007	1,892	1,802	1,943	2,026
Trade balance	−366	−483	−252	−219	−266	−284
Current account balance/GDP (%)	−1.5	−1.6	3.4	5.2	4.6	3.5
Foreign debt	1,780	1,870	1,780	1,784	1,700	1,626
Debt service/Exports (%)	11.3	12	15.2	7.9	7.1	7.6
Currency reserves (import months)	3.6	4.0	5	6.7	8.2	9.3

e = estimate, f = forecast

CONDITIONS OF ACCESS TO THE MARKET

■ Market overview

Mauritius has been a full member of the WTO since the 1994 Marrakesh Summit. It signed the New York Convention on International Arbitration in June 1996 and ratified it in October 2002. It has dismantled tariff barriers under a series of regional trade agreements and in 1998 introduced 10 per cent flat-rate VAT, which was raised to 15 per cent in the 2002–03 budget.

Import licences remain in force for only three product categories: prohibited (dangerous items such as arms and explosives, and vehicle spare parts); supervised or subject to government approval (foodstuffs, energy and pharmaceuticals); unrestricted or formality-free.

Adopted in 1994, the system of customs duties differentiates between exporting countries benefiting from a preferential tariff (EU, USA, COMESA, SADC) and the 25 or so countries that are subject to a general tariff. Import duties under this system vary between 0 and 80 per cent. Regional agreements permit tariff reductions for certain products with a view to establishing free-trade areas. Excise duties are levied on four broad imported and/or locally manufactured product categories (wines and spirits, cigarettes, petrol and motor vehicles). Ranging from 15 to 400 per cent *ad valorem* for imported products, excise duties can be as high as 255 per cent for locally manufactured products (cigarettes). Some products (staples and pharmaceuticals) and services (education, transport, electricity and water) are exempt from VAT. Customs duties on imports, which vary between 0 and 80 per cent, have been cut significantly since 1998.

Import licences and price controls apply to staples, 30 of which are also subject to administered pricing or profit control. Government monopolies enjoy exclusive powers to import so-called 'strategic' products. The two biggest monopolies are:

- STC (State Trading Corporation), which imports almost all the rice, wheat flour, petroleum products and cement (up to 50 per cent of requirements). Rice also enjoys a subsidy.
- AMB (Agricultural Marketing Board), which holds an import monopoly for onions, garlic, maize, certain seeds, soya, cotton seeds and certain animal feeds. However, since 1998, approved private agents have been allowed to import potatoes subject to certain conditions but not to price controls. The task of AMB is to regulate markets and protect local producers.

■ Attitude towards foreign investors

While Mauritius has over the years sought to attract the largest possible number of foreign investors, as attested by the numerous incentive schemes offered by the Board of Investment – a one-stop shop set up in 2001 for investments of 300,000 euros or more – and the investment protection agreements concluded with the country's main trading partners, it is very selective about FDI and ensures that the funds are channelled only into certain sectors. The country's legislation and laws reflect this will to channel FDI flows towards specific sectors.

■ **Foreign exchange regulations**

There are no exchange controls in Mauritius. The Mauritian rupee is fully convertible against the main currencies and may be transferred without restriction upon the sender providing proof of the origin of the funds.

PAYMENT INCIDENTS INDEX
(12 months moving average - base 100 : World 1995)

OPPORTUNITY SCOPE

Breakdown of internal demand (GDP + imports)	%
■ Private consumption	38
■ Public spending	8
■ Investment	15

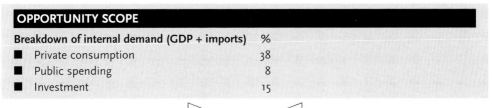

Exports: 64% of GDP Imports: 63% of GDP

MAIN DESTINATIONS OF EXPORTS

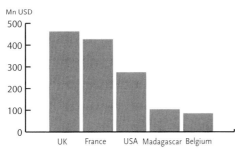

MAIN ORIGINS OF IMPORTS

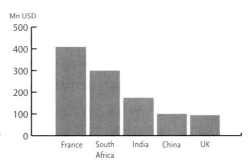

EXPORTS by products

■ All food items 24%
■ Manufactured goods 72%
▓ Miscellaneous 4%

IMPORTS by products

■ All food items 16%
■ Fuels 11%
▓ Machinery and transport equipment 23%
▓ Chemical products 8%
▓ Other manufactured goods 39%
▓ Miscellaneous 3%

STANDARD OF LIVING / PURCHASING POWER

Indicators	Mauritius	Regional average	DC average
GNP per capita (PPP dollars)	9860	2841	6778
GNP per capita (USD)	3830	999	3568
Human Development Index	0.779	0.498	0.708
Wealthiest 10% share of national income	n/a	36	33
Urban population percentage	42	44	60
Percentage under 15 years old	26	42	31
number of telephones per 1000 inhabitants	257	33	157
number of computers per 1000 inhabitants	109	17	66

Mozambique

Population (million inhabitants)	18.1
GDP (million USD)	3,607

Coface analysis

Short-term: **C**

Medium-term:
Very high risk

STRENGTHS

- The country boasts still relatively unexploited natural resources (coal, hydroelectricity, gas, tourist potential) that have been attracting foreign investors.
- It has also been benefiting from its solid financial and economic ties to South Africa.
- With its ambitious structural reform programme, Mozambique has earned international financial community backing.
- One of the first admitted to the HIPC programme for highly indebted poor countries, it has benefited from a very substantial reduction of its public-sector debt.

WEAKNESSES

- The economy still bears the scars of 30 years of war (refugees, displaced persons, extreme poverty).
- The predominance of agriculture (80 per cent of the population, 34 per cent of GDP) goes hand in hand with great dependence on weather conditions.
- Its infrastructure (transportation, energy) is still insufficiently developed.
- Development has remained limited to the Maputo region, generating regional inequalities that could heighten the underlying political tensions lingering since the civil war ended in 1994.
- The country continues to be very dependent on international aid.

RISK ASSESSMENT

Mozambique is continuing to post robust growth fuelled by foreign investment, although the economy has remained too concentrated geographically and dependent on large projects. Further out, major infrastructure problems and financing capacities limited by a low domestic saving rate will hamper development prospects.

The country's solvency will thus remain dependent on international community backing. Despite notable efforts to consolidate public accounts, they continue to show severe imbalances.

However, the external accounts (which will remain heavily in deficit) should begin coming back into balance with completion of the Mozal II and Sasol projects, which could generate increased export earnings. Moreover, the country has benefited from debt cancellation granted under the HIPC initiative reserved for highly indebted poor countries (Mozambique was one of the first countries to reach the completion point).

Meanwhile, the country's political stability and increasing economic integration into Southern Africa represent plus factors for investors.

MAIN ECONOMIC INDICATORS						
US$ millions	1999	2000	2001	2002	2003 (e)	2004 (f)
Economic growth (%)	7.5	1.5	13	7.7	7	8.4
Inflation (%)	2.9	12.7	9	16.8	13	9.2
Public-sector balance/GDP (%)	−13.2	−14	−21.4	−19.7	−13.5	−13.1
Exports	284	364	703	682	896	1,259
Imports	1,200	1,163	1,063	1,263	1,602	1,488
Trade balance	−916	−799	−360	−581	−706	−229
Current account balance/GDP (%)	−28.1	−28.9	−28.4	−23.3	−26.8	−17.3
Foreign debt	6,982	7,135	4,102	4,639	5,154	5,312
Debt service/Exports (%)	15.3	2.5	3.5	4.3	3.8	3.7
Currency reserves (import months)	4.5	4.9	4.4	4.7	4.1	4.1

e = estimate, f = forecast

CONDITIONS OF ACCESS TO THE MARKET

■ Market overview

Customs duties currently range from 0 per cent for pharmaceuticals, 2.5 per cent for commodities, 5 per cent for raw materials and 7.5 per cent for semi-finished goods to 25 per cent for luxury and similar products. There can be different rates of duty for the same product category (eg 5–25 per cent for passenger cars). According to foreign companies based in Mozambique, the fact that the country's grey market is large and not subject to import duties, levies or VAT hampers fair competition and exports of their products.

Customs procedures are so long-winded and complex that it is essential to hire the services of a special Mozambican agent, in addition to a shipping agent. For payments, other than credit from international lenders, the irrevocable and confirmed documentary letter of credit is strongly recommended. Even where central bank and Ministry of Finance approval is obtained, foreign capital may be repatriated only if the investment project has been authorized beforehand by the Investment Promotion Centre (CPI). Since 1998, customs management has been satisfactorily handled by Crown Agents of the UK and goods inspection by the UK firm Intertek Testing Services (ITS).

■ Attitude towards foreign investors

An Investment Promotion Centre was set up to facilitate and coordinate the direct investment decision-making process. While there is no legal requirement to consult this body, foreign investors are strongly recommended to do so. The government guarantees legal certainty and protection of property and other rights. A tax benefits code and industrial free zone legislation offer many incentives for FDI. The minimum level of foreign direct investment is US$50,000 in equity. While the country's legislation provides for the establishment of wholly foreign-owned businesses, joint ventures with local partners are encouraged by the government. Living conditions for expatriates are very suitable in the capital and major towns, but hygiene in some regions is still far from satisfactory.

■ Foreign exchange regulations

An interbank currency market regulating purchases and sales of foreign currency has been set up. This market is closed to everyone but the central bank and approved financial institutions. The value of the metical is determined daily on the basis of supply and demand. Foreigners are strongly advised to carry out all foreign exchange transactions via approved banks and bureaux de change. Banks may carry out currency transactions up to the value of their hard-currency holdings. There are no restrictions on capital transactions.

5

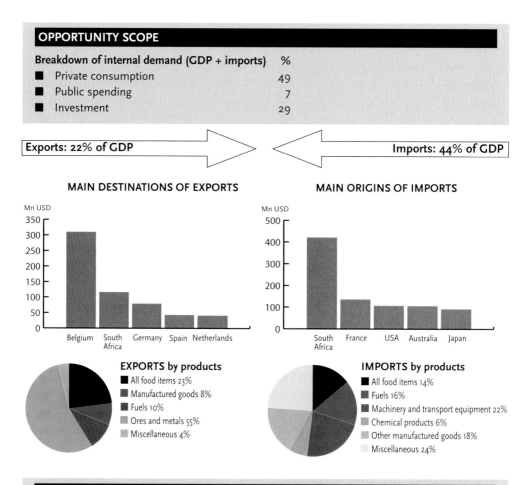

OPPORTUNITY SCOPE

Breakdown of internal demand (GDP + imports)	%
■ Private consumption	49
■ Public spending	7
■ Investment	29

Exports: 22% of GDP → ← Imports: 44% of GDP

MAIN DESTINATIONS OF EXPORTS

Mn USD

Belgium, South Africa, Germany, Spain, Netherlands

MAIN ORIGINS OF IMPORTS

Mn USD

South Africa, France, USA, Australia, Japan

EXPORTS by products
- ■ All food items 23%
- ■ Manufactured goods 8%
- ■ Fuels 10%
- ■ Ores and metals 55%
- ■ Miscellaneous 4%

IMPORTS by products
- ■ All food items 14%
- ■ Fuels 16%
- ■ Machinery and transport equipment 22%
- ■ Chemical products 6%
- ■ Other manufactured goods 18%
- ■ Miscellaneous 24%

STANDARD OF LIVING / PURCHASING POWER

Indicators	Mozambique	Regional average	DC average
GNP per capita (PPP dollars)	1050	2841	6778
GNP per capita (USD)	210	999	3568
Human Development Index	0.356	0.498	0.708
Wealthiest 10% share of national income	32	36	33
Urban population percentage	33	44	60
Percentage under 15 years old	43	42	31
number of telephones per 1000 inhabitants	4	33	157
number of computers per 1000 inhabitants	4	17	66

Namibia

Population (million inhabitants) 1.8
GDP (million USD) 3,100
GDP per capita (USD) 1,722

Coface analysis

Short-term: **A3**

Medium-term:
Quite low risk

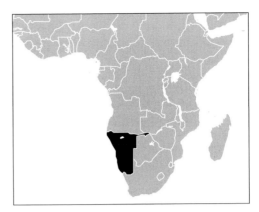

RISK ASSESSMENT

The country's outlook has been encouraging. With the political context remaining stable, Namibia's economic fabric and exports have begun to diversify (metals, textiles, development of tourism), buoyed by investment in communication, transportation and energy infrastructure. However, although the country's external solvency has remained at comfortable levels, steady deterioration of public accounts and the increase of domestic debt will ultimately constitute risk factors.

Weaknesses have persisted. With agriculture, fishing and mineral extraction (diamonds) still representing its main resources, the country has remained vulnerable to exogenous shocks. Moreover, its economy is still very dependent on South Africa, not only for export sales and imports but also for investment inflows. And the Namibian dollar is pegged to the South African rand.

Finally, the inadequacy of economic growth to meet the country's needs could exacerbate its underlying weaknesses: demographic pressure, poverty, land allocation and water supply problems, and the spread of AIDS.

5

MAIN ECONOMIC INDICATORS						
US$ millions	1999	2000	2001	2002	2003 (e)	2004 (f)
Economic growth (%)	3.3	3.3	2.4	2.3	3.3	4.3
Inflation (%)	8.7	9.3	9.3	11.3	8.0	6.3
Public-sector balance/GDP (%)	−2.2	−1.0	−4.8	−4.4	−4.9	−6.0
Exports	1,196	1,313	1,142	1,162	1,154	1,333
Imports	1,396	1,432	1,325	1,190	1,373	1,423
Trade balance	−200	−119	−183	−28	−219	−90
Current account balance/GDP (%)	4.0	6.5	2.1	2.1	2.9	3.1
Foreign debt	158	160	390	623	678	714
Debt service/Exports (%)	1.4	1.4	3.9	2.3	2.8	2.9
Currency reserves (import months)	2.1	1.8	1.7	2.5	3.4	3.8

e = estimate, f = forecast

Niger

Population (million inhabitants)	11.2
GDP (million USD)	1,954
GDP per capita (USD)	174

Short-term: **C**

Medium-term:
Coface analysis **Very high risk**

RISK ASSESSMENT

Niger is one of the world's poorest countries with an economy very dependent on trends in the agricultural sector, particularly in livestock breeding (Niger's second source of export revenues after uranium), and on international-financial-community backing.

Growth forecasts for 2004 only marginally surpass demographic expansion. Moreover, they will depend on the precipitation outlook as well as the situation in Ivory Coast and Nigeria, the country's two main African trading partners. The

authorities will also have to consolidate public finances, hampered by a large grey market, settle accumulated arrears and accelerate the privatization programme, which has been generating social tensions further heightened by the prospect of legislative and presidential elections in late 2004.

Those measures will be essential in keeping IMF backing, covering its still-substantial external financing needs and reaching the point of completion in the HIPC programme for highly indebted poor countries, which should permit further foreign-debt reduction in 2004.

MAIN ECONOMIC INDICATORS						
US$ millions	1999	2000	2001	2002	2003 (e)	2004 (f)
Economic growth (%)	−0.6	−1.4	7.1	3	4	4.1
Inflation (%)	−2.3	2.9	4	2.7	−0.7	0.9
Public-sector balance/GDP (%)	−9.9	−8.1	−7.9	−7.7	−8.6	−8.2
Exports	270	283	273	295	375	438
Imports	299	331	332	415	533	609
Trade balance	−28	−48	−59	−121	−159	−171
Current account balance	−7.5	−7.9	−6.6	−8.4	−8.8	−8
Foreign debt	1,685	1,772	1,809	1,684	1,859	1,988
Debt service/Exports (%)	21.6	28.2	34.1	34.7	25.2	13
Currency reserves (import months)	1.1	2.2	2.9	3	2	1.8

e = estimate, f = forecast

Nigeria

Population (million inhabitants)	129.9
GDP (million USD)	41,373

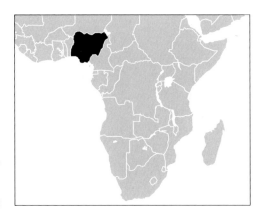

Coface analysis

Short-term: **D**

Medium-term:
Very high risk

STRENGTHS

- With half West Africa's population, Nigeria boasts substantial oil resources, attractive to foreign investors, and farming potential.
- It is thus expected to play a leading political and economic role regionally and on the African continent.
- Its transition to democracy has permitted resumption of a dialogue with the international financial community.
- The country has undertaken structural reforms.
- The prospect of economic and monetary integration within ECOWAS will ultimately encourage investors.

WEAKNESSES

- Nigeria has remained very dependent on oil, which represents 98 per cent of exports and three-quarters of fiscal revenues.
- The constitutional and political climate obstructs implementation of reforms required by foreign lenders.
- Foreign debt has been a very heavy burden for public finances, which suffer from recurrent imbalances.
- The business climate has tended to deter investor interest.
- Ethnic and religious differences, inequalities between north and south, poverty and unemployment have been constant sources of unrest.

RISK ASSESSMENT

The new term in office of President Obasanjo, who was re-elected in April 2003, appears to have got off to an inauspicious start. Political, ethnic and religious tensions, which have remained high, could ultimately inhibit the authorities' capacity to define and implement policy apt to attract the investment needed to diversify the country's economy.

The economic and financial situation has remained dependent on oil price and extraction levels. The foreseeable oil-price decline in 2004 will reduce the government's revenues accordingly and thus worsen the public and external account deficits. In such conditions, settling the external debt and accumulated arrears will certainly prove difficult.

To obtain a new rescheduling of its debt, Nigeria will need international financial community backing. However, such backing will depend on acceleration of structural reforms and privatizations, which have been spurring severe social tensions.

MAIN ECONOMIC INDICATORS						
US$ billions	1999	2000	2001	2002	2003 (e)	2004 (f)
Economic growth (%)	1	4.1	2.8	0.5	5.2	3.8
Inflation (%)	6.6	6.9	18	13.7	12.3	10.6
Public-sector balance/GDP (%)	−4.4	6.4	−3.3	−5	−4	−13.5
Exports	11.9	21.4	17.9	15.9	18.1	16.3
Imports	10.5	11.1	12.3	13.3	14.8	15.0
Trade balance	1.4	10.3	5.6	2.6	3.3	1.3
Current account balance/GDP (%)	−9.5	9.9	2.8	−6.3	−3.5	−5.7
Foreign debt	28.7	30.2	29.7	29.8	29.9	30.3
Debt service/Exports (%)	20.9	14.9	17.8	15.3	15.8	17.1
Currency reserves (import months)	3.6	5.7	6.1	4.1	3.9	3.8

e = estimate, f = forecast

CONDITIONS OF ACCESS TO THE MARKET

■ Market overview

The Nigerian economy is very open to foreign trade. Imports are extremely varied and liable to customs duty ranging from 5 to 100 per cent of the CIF value. There is an import ban on a number of products, including re-treaded and second-hand tyres, second-hand clothes, cars that are more than five years old, frozen foods, mineral water, pasta and biscuits.

The Nigerian government has adopted a growing number of protectionist measures in favour of local products such as finished goods, but has cut customs duties for raw materials and industrial goods. Labour is fairly cheap. A skilled worker earns about 150 euros a month, and an English-speaking local secretary earns about 245 euros. Employees usually receive one month's extra pay.

■ Attitude towards foreign investors

The Nigerian Investment Promotion Commission (NIPC), headquartered in Abuja, regularly publishes a list of priority investment sectors and incentives

(financial, tax, etc) granted by the government to companies. The repatriation of capital, dividends and profit is unrestricted, though extremely slow.

Nigeria encourages oil companies to develop their exploration and production activities. The country's long-term output target is 4 million barrels daily. The country is set to develop its deep-sea oil fields. Gas output is rising sharply. Furthermore, the majors are promoting the growth of the gas group NLNG, which is setting up new production facilities.

■ Foreign exchange regulations

The Central Bank of Nigeria (CBN) uses the Dutch auction system to supply the local market with currency. Under this system, twice a week the CBN announces the volume of currency (dollars) it is prepared to sell against nairas and invites importers and foreign currency end-users to put in purchase bids for nairas through their banks. Exporters are strongly advised to obtain payment for all orders before shipment either by irrevocable and confirmed letter of credit or in cash in a hard currency. French banks no longer operate in the country.

OPPORTUNITY SCOPE

Breakdown of internal demand (GDP + imports)	%
■ Private consumption	32
■ Public spending	17
■ Investment	19

Exports: 48% of GDP   Imports: 49% of GDP

MAIN DESTINATIONS OF EXPORTS

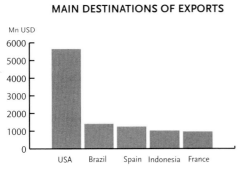

MAIN ORIGINS OF IMPORTS

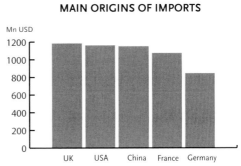

EXPORTS by products

■ Fuels 100%

IMPORTS by products

■ All food items 20%
■ Machinery and transport equipment 34%
■ Chemical products 20%
□ Other manufactured goods 21%
□ Miscellaneous 5%

5

STANDARD OF LIVING / PURCHASING POWER

Indicators	Nigeria	Regional average	DC average
GNP per capita (PPP dollars)	790	2841	6778
GNP per capita (USD)	290	999	3568
Human Development Index	0.463	0.498	0.708
Wealthiest 10% share of national income	41	36	33
Urban population percentage	45	44	60
Percentage under 15 years old	44	42	31
number of telephones per 1000 inhabitants	5	33	157
number of computers per 1000 inhabitants	7	17	66

Senegal

Population (million inhabitants)	9.8
GDP (million USD)	4,645

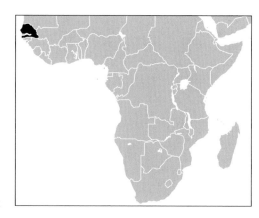

Coface analysis

Short-term: **B**

Medium-term:
High risk

STRENGTHS

- The country's political stability and image have been assets.
- It enjoys international community backing (multilateral bodies, European Union, United States), which has contributed to easing its foreign debt.
- The economy has continued its diversification (pisciculture, chemicals, tourism, information technology), posting high growth since 1995.
- Accelerated regional integration (energy, transportation) has represented an additional factor of economic dynamism attractive to foreign investors.

WEAKNESSES

- Three-fifths of the working population are still dependent on the farm sector (20 per cent of GDP) and thus on weather conditions.
- Strong demographic growth, unemployment and poverty (65 per cent of the population) constitute persistent weaknesses contributing to social tensions.
- The restructuring of public companies – heavily in debt – has been lagging.
- The country has remained dependent on the international community to cover its financing needs.
- The country has yet to settle the separatist problem of the southern province of Casamance, which is affecting tourism.

RISK ASSESSMENT

After the effects of drought and disorganization in the groundnut sector, which caused a 20 per cent reduction in farm production in 2002, growth has resumed at a sustained pace buoyed notably by development of the mining and chemicals sectors, a steadier electricity supply and dynamic civil engineering and services sectors. Rising private and public-sector investment should drive economic activity even though the public sector's investments have contributed to the undermining of public finances despite notable tax-collection successes.

Concurrently, external accounts have continued to suffer from high deficits, which should nonetheless stabilize in 2004 with the country benefiting from cancellation of its public-sector debt under the HIPC programme for highly indebted poor countries.

Although the current government has enough time at its disposal with the next elections not until 2006, the confidence accorded to it by the public seems to be waning amid continued high levels of poverty and unemployment. Meanwhile, the expected speed-up of structural reforms in sensitive socio-economic areas could accentuate social tensions.

In this context, the deterioration of company payment behaviour registered in 2003 has been more a reflection of late payments than actual default claims and has particularly concerned the electrical capital goods and equipment sector. Continued strong growth in 2004 should permit a stabilization of payment incidents.

MAIN ECONOMIC INDICATORS

US$ millions	1999	2000	2001	2002	2003 (e)	2004 (f)
Economic growth (%)	5	5.6	5.6	2.4	4.8	5
Inflation (%)	0.8	0.7	3	2.3	0.7	2.1
Public-sector balance/GDP (%)	–3.5	–2	–3.9	–1.6	–4	–3.7
Exports	1,028	922	1,004	1,098	1,363	1,516
Imports	1,374	1,341	1,430	1,557	2,052	2,212
Trade balance	–346	–418	–426	–459	–689	–696
Current account balance/GDP (%)	–7.9	–8.5	–6.5	–6.3	–7.6	–6.7
Foreign debt	3,639	3,626	3,641	3,141	3,062	2,938
Debt service/Exports (%)	12.0	11.6	9.3	11.6	6.1	4.6
Currency reserves (import months)	2.4	2.4	2.7	2.9	2.2	2.1

e = estimate, f = forecast

CONDITIONS OF ACCESS TO THE MARKET

■ Market overview

The customs union established by the member states of WAEMU (West African Economic and Monetary Union) is simple and non-discriminatory. Customs duties vary between 0 and 20 per cent according to product category. Imports are also liable to some token surtaxes (usually around 2.5 per cent) and 18 per cent flat-rate VAT. All importers and exporters are required to register with the Foreign Trade Department (Comex) and to obtain a trading and import/export licence. The main restrictions concern arms and drugs.

The Senegalese government has appointed Cotecna Inspection to carry out goods inspections under the Import Verification Programme. An Advance Import Notification must be submitted for all imported goods with a CIF value of 1 million CFA francs or more. From 15 October 2001, imports with a CIF value of 3 million CFA francs or more are subject to pre-shipment inspection.

■ Attitude towards foreign investors

To provide improved terms of access to investors, Senegal is focusing on a number of long-term improvements, including modernization of production facilities primarily through wider availability of electricity (power supply from Mali, emergency plan for Senelec), land transport (railways, roads, motorways) worthy of the name and cement for construction purposes (commissioning of a new cement works in 2002); better penetration of European and US markets by means of the preferential benefits it receives along with other African countries (especially LDCs); rapid expansion of West African financial markets and the regional stock market BRVN (38 listed companies, including Sonatel, which accounts for 25 per cent of the market's 1 billion-plus capitalization); and continued support for WAEMU as guarantor of economic and monetary stability and economic openness (Community Investment Code under preparation). In the field of domestic policy, changes to the tax code, in particular the suspension of company registration duties, will provide tax relief for start-ups, while a new mining bill, under discussion in parliament, also seeks to grant tax breaks in this sector. However, foreign investment continues to be hampered by red tape.

■ Foreign exchange regulations

There are no restrictions on business-related transfers within the franc area, provided they are handled by approved intermediaries such as banks. Fund transfers in excess of 300,000 CFA francs outside the franc area are subject to presentation of either an invoice, a pro forma, a contract or a documentary letter of credit. Dividend transfers are permitted, but must be handled by approved intermediaries (banks) and supported by proof of

5

payment. Companies incorporated under local law are free to hold foreign currency accounts in Senegal subject to the approval of the Ministry of Finance. Since 8 October 2001, the Central Bank for West African States (BCEAO) has been responsible for handling euro account opening applications.

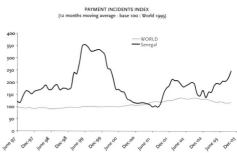

PAYMENT INCIDENTS INDEX
(12 months moving average - base 100 : World 1995)

OPPORTUNITY SCOPE

Breakdown of internal demand (GDP + imports)	%
■ Private consumption	57
■ Public spending	7
■ Investment	14

Exports: 30% of GDP → ← Imports: 38% of GDP

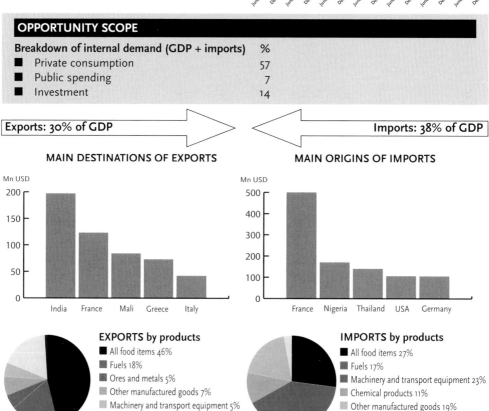

MAIN DESTINATIONS OF EXPORTS

Mn USD

India, France, Mali, Greece, Italy

MAIN ORIGINS OF IMPORTS

Mn USD

France, Nigeria, Thailand, USA, Germany

EXPORTS by products
- ■ All food items 46%
- ■ Fuels 18%
- ■ Ores and metals 5%
- ■ Other manufactured goods 7%
- ■ Machinery and transport equipment 5%
- ■ Chemical products 18%
- ■ Miscellaneous 1%

IMPORTS by products
- ■ All food items 27%
- ■ Fuels 17%
- ■ Machinery and transport equipment 23%
- ■ Chemical products 11%
- ■ Other manufactured goods 19%
- ■ Miscellaneous 3%

STANDARD OF LIVING / PURCHASING POWER

Indicators	Senegal	Regional average	DC average
GNP per capita (PPP dollars)	1480	2841	6778
GNP per capita (USD)	490	999	3568
Human Development Index	0.43	0.498	0.708
Wealthiest 10% share of national income	34	36	33
Urban population percentage	48	44	60
Percentage under 15 years old	44	42	31
number of telephones per 1000 inhabitants	25	33	157
number of computers per 1000 inhabitants	19	17	66

South Africa

Population (million inhabitants)　　43.2
GDP (million USD)　　113,274

Coface analysis

Short-term: **A4**

Medium-term:
Quite low risk

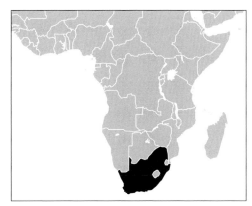

STRENGTHS

- Representing 40 per cent of Africa's GDP, South Africa's political and economic role on the continent has been growing.
- It boasts substantial mining resources, diversified industry and a very effective service sector (banks, telecommunications, transportation).
- Public accounts are under control, external debt is low and external financing needs are moderate.
- Despite domestic tensions, the current macroeconomic-stability policy has remained intact.

WEAKNESSES

- With low savings and investment rates, the domestic resources needed to finance the country's development have been lacking.
- Considering the public's aspirations and the extent of the needs, insufficient growth could spark social and political tensions.
- The country has remained vulnerable to a crisis of confidence on capital markets.
- The AIDS pandemic will continue to represent a major challenge in coming years.

5

RISK ASSESSMENT

Although modest considering the population's needs, South Africa's economic growth seems to be maintaining a steady pace, buoyed by improvement in fundamental macroeconomic equilibriums. Disciplined public-finance management and the low foreign-debt level have been giving no cause to fear a solvency crisis. Meanwhile, the country's political stability, which should persist after the elections in 2004, could permit it to contend with possible future challenges (the black population's social and economic demands, uncertain outcome of the Zimbabwe crisis).

Coface's payment-incident index and the decline of bankruptcies registered in the country reflect the steady economic conditions.

Despite South Africa's moderate financing needs, it has nonetheless remained very vulnerable to a loss of confidence on capital markets, which could compromise the country's positive outlook. Such a loss of confidence could generate a liquidity crisis considering the low level of its currency reserves, the volatility of its external financing and particularly the high level of short-term debt. In that regard, the continuing rand appreciation since 2002, which has affected exporting company earning, has remained a factor of uncertainty.

Further out, the growth rate's durability, if not its acceleration, will depend on both continuation of restructuring and a major investment effort, hampered however by the low domestic savings rate, scarcity of skilled labour, the brain-drain and the AIDS pandemic.

MAIN ECONOMIC INDICATORS

US$ billions	1999	2000	2001	2002	2003 (e)	2004 (f)
Economic growth (%)	2.0	3.5	2.8	3.0	2.1	3.5
Inflation (%)	5.0	5.3	5.7	9.2	6.3	3.6
Public-sector balance/GDP (%)	-2	-2	-1.5	-1.2	-2.4	-3.2
Exports	28.6	31.7	30.5	30.9	33.4	35.3
Imports	24.6	27.4	25.7	26.5	30.3	32.6
Trade balance	4.1	4.4	4.8	4.4	3.1	2.7
Current account balance/GDP (%)	-0.5	-0.4	-0.3	0.3	-0.9	-1.4
Foreign debt	38.9	36.9	30.8	32.7	37	38.3
Debt service/Exports (%)	15.5	13.8	14.6	13.8	13.8	12.9
Currency reserves (import months)	2.1	1.9	2.0	1.9	1.9	2.0

e = estimate, f = forecast

CONDITIONS OF ACCESS TO THE MARKET

■ Market overview

South Africa's trade liberalization programme, which began in 1990, has come a long way since the country's membership of the WTO in 1995.

South Africa uses the World Customs Organization's harmonized international nomenclature. Customs duties have been significantly reduced in the last five years and tariff reforms completed in late 1999.

■ Means of entry

Under the free-trade agreement signed with the European Union in October 1999, and that came in to effect in 2000, some 86 per cent of products imported from the European Union will be exempt from customs duty by 2012. South Africa is not a signatory to the WTO agreement on the award of government procurement contracts. Up until now, tenders have been overseen at the central level by the State Tender Board and at the local level by one of nine provincial tender boards. In the near future, a common service provider is due to replace the tender boards for the purposes of putting in place a uniform policy in the field of government procurement. The Preferential Procurement Policy Framework Act, in force since February 2000, creates a points system that favours companies whose shareholders or managers comprise 'historically underprivileged people' (blacks, mixed-race, Indian), women and the disabled. South African public tender legislation consequently favours South African or foreign companies that team up with black partners (BEE – Black Economic Empowerment).

Where a public tender exceeds US$10 million, foreign companies are required to pay 30 per cent compensation on the total value of imports under the National Industrial Participation Programme. A Black Economic Empowerment Charter has been adopted by the financial services industry. Under the provisions of the charter, 25 per cent of a company's equity must be held by blacks by 2010.

The South African Bureau of Standards cooperates with a large number of similar international bodies to harmonize technical standards and regulations. International standards such as IEC and ISO are recognized by the bureau, but still require clearance.

■ Attitude towards foreign investors

Foreign companies are subject to numerous statutory provisions and orders that limit their decision-making powers. The administrative environment in which they operate at times lacks transparency and predictability, as in the case of privatizations and public tenders. Invoicing of imported goods is generally done in US dollars. Also used are the euro, the pound sterling, the Japanese yen and the South African rand.

PAYMENT INCIDENTS INDEX
(12 months moving average - base 100 : World 1995)
— WORLD
— South Africa

■ Foreign exchange regulations

Exchange controls, which are governed by the 1961 Act and its manifold subsequent amendments, have been considerably relaxed in the last few years. The provisions governing transfers of capital related to ordinary business transactions have been liberalized. Currency traders believe there are no more *de facto* exchange controls for non-residents, with a few notable exceptions (borrowings in local currency, loans from a parent company to a South African subsidiary, etc).

The rand's sharp volatility over the last few years – falls in 2001 and 2002 and a rally in 2003 – has introduced a great deal of uncertainty in investors' minds.

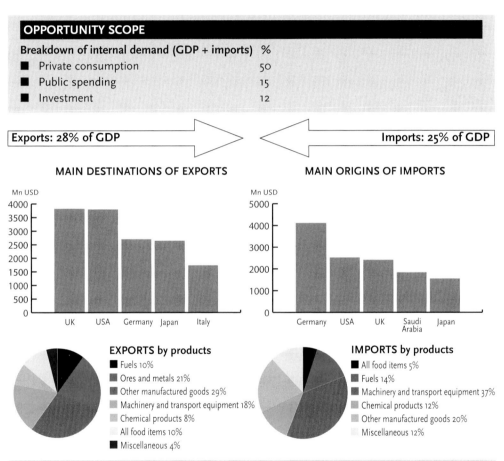

OPPORTUNITY SCOPE

Breakdown of internal demand (GDP + imports)	%
■ Private consumption	50
■ Public spending	15
■ Investment	12

Exports: 28% of GDP   Imports: 25% of GDP

MAIN DESTINATIONS OF EXPORTS

Mn USD (bars): UK, USA, Germany, Japan, Italy

MAIN ORIGINS OF IMPORTS

Mn USD (bars): Germany, USA, UK, Saudi Arabia, Japan

EXPORTS by products
- ■ Fuels 10%
- ■ Ores and metals 21%
- ■ Other manufactured goods 29%
- ■ Machinery and transport equipment 18%
- ■ Chemical products 8%
- ■ All food items 10%
- ■ Miscellaneous 4%

IMPORTS by products
- ■ All food items 5%
- ■ Fuels 14%
- ■ Machinery and transport equipment 37%
- ■ Chemical products 12%
- ■ Other manufactured goods 20%
- ■ Miscellaneous 12%

STANDARD OF LIVING / PURCHASING POWER

Indicators	South Africa	Regional average	DC average
GNP per capita (PPP dollars)	10910	2841	6778
GNP per capita (USD)	2820	999	3568
Human Development Index	0.684	0.498	0.708
Wealthiest 10% share of national income	47	36	33
Urban population percentage	58	44	60
Percentage under 15 years old	32	42	31
number of telephones per 1000 inhabitants	112	33	157
number of computers per 1000 inhabitants	69	17	66

5

Sudan

Population (million inhabitants)	31.7
GDP (million USD)	12,525
GDP per capita (USD)	395

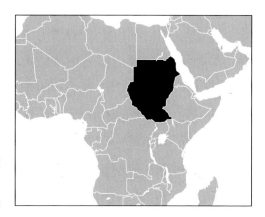

Short-term: **C**

Medium-term:
Very high risk

Coface analysis

RISK ASSESSMENT

Several positive factors have benefited Sudan's economy. Increased oil production and exports in conjunction with investments linked to that sector have been underpinning strong growth. Disciplined fiscal and monetary policy as well as implementation of a vast structural reform programme since 1997 have contributed to improving the business environment.

Those encouraging results should nonetheless not obscure certain weaknesses. Despite steady oil prices, external-account imbalances have persisted and the expected oil price decline in 2004 will weigh on the country's financing needs. Furthermore, the external debt burden has been heavy and the country has not yet been able to clear its payment arrears.

Moreover, with those favourable prospects remaining too dependent on the oil sector, the country will have to continue its efforts to diversify the economic fabric. The outlook will also depend on the success of the negotiation process under way since the agreement concluded in July 2002 between the government and the secessionist movement in the south after nearly 20 years of war. After a six-year transition period, those negotiations are supposed to settle the problems of secession by the south and the sharing of the country's wealth and thereby establish durable peace. After initial difficulties, they have made definite progress like the September 2003 agreement on security and distribution of the armed forces.

MAIN ECONOMIC INDICATORS

US$ millions	1999	2000	2001	2002	2003 (e)	2004 (f)
Economic growth (%)	6.9	6.9	6.2	5.5	6.1	6.4
Inflation (%)	16.0	8.0	4.9	8.4	8.8	9.0
Public-sector balance/GDP (%)	−0.9	−0.8	−1.0	−0.9	−0.9	−1.0
Exports	780	1,864	1,699	1,948	2,334	2,055
Imports	1,500	1,553	2,031	2,153	2,353	2,564
Trade balance	−720	311	−332	−205	−19	−509
Current account balance/GDP (%)	−15.4	−14.3	−10.6	−11.2	−11.9	−12.6
Foreign debt	23,900	19,970	20,950	23,470	24,180	25,100
Debt service/Exports (%)	108.9	68.6	49.4	28.5	29.1	32.8
Currency reserves (import months)	0.2	0.5	0.1	0.8	1.2	1.4

e = estimate, f = forecast

Tanzania

Population (million inhabitants) 34.4
GDP (million USD) 9,341

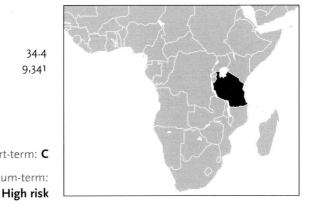

Short-term: **C**

Medium-term:

Coface analysis **High risk**

STRENGTHS

- Tanzania enjoys remarkable economic potential (cultivable land, mineral wealth, tourism) capable of attracting more foreign investment.
- Its political stability has facilitated implementation of major structural reforms.
- Support by financial backers has permitted cancellation of its external public debt under the HIPC programme for highly indebted poor countries.
- The strengthening of regional integration (East African Community, Southern African Development Community) has been beneficial to the country's economy.

WEAKNESSES

- The economic fabric has remained insufficiently diversified (farm products, gold) and very exposed to exogenous factors.
- Poverty still afflicts over half the population.
- Tanzania remains one of the countries most dependent on international aid.
- Inadequate infrastructure development (transportation, energy) and the shaky financial situation of public companies have been hampering the economy.
- The business environment remains difficult.
- Relations with the autonomous island of Zanzibar, where the economic situation has been very poor, have been unstable.

RISK ASSESSMENT

Tanzania's progress (strong growth, sustained implementation of structural reforms, and development of the mineral sector, notably gold-bearing) has nonetheless remained insufficient to meet the many challenges facing the country: poverty, unemployment, AIDS, infrastructure development.

Meeting those challenges has been weighing heavily on public finances, which authorities have been unable to consolidate. Despite efforts to develop more revenues, the tax base remains narrow with the financing of development spending still dependent on international aid.

Similarly, despite cancellation of its public external debt via the HIPC initiative reserved for highly indebted poor countries since 2001, the rise of capital goods imports linked to ongoing investment projects has contributed to inflating the country's external financing needs. Further out, however, the expected increase of gold and gas exports (in addition to the production start-up of the Songo Songo field in 2004) as well as tourism revenues should generate more currency earnings.

In any case, the country's political stability will permit counting on continued restructuring of its economic fabric, thus facilitating relations with the international financial community.

MAIN ECONOMIC INDICATORS						
US$ millions	1999	2000	2001	2002	2003 (e)	2004 (f)
Economic growth (%)	4.7	4.9	5.7	6.2	5.2	5.5
Inflation (%)	7.9	5.9	5.2	4.6	5	4.5
Public-sector balance/GDP (%)	−7.8	−5.3	−5.6	−7.9	−9.3	−8.4
Exports	543	715	816	953	1,170	1,279
Imports	1,573	1,439	1,554	1,708	2,128	2,211
Trade balance	−1,030	−724	−738	−755	−958	−932
Current account balance/GDP (%)	−12.9	−9.4	−8.9	−9.3	−11.7	−10.5
Foreign debt	6,622	7,386	6,676	5,063	5,390	5,625
Debt service/Exports (%)	33.4	30.2	31	6.2	5.8	6.8
Currency reserves (import months)	3.9	5.2	6.1	7.8	7.1	7.4

e = estimate, f = forecast

CONDITIONS OF ACCESS TO THE MARKET

■ Market overview

The open general licence system or the system of import licensing administered by the Republic of Tanzania has been abolished since 1994. As a rule, there are no import controls other than pre-shipment inspection under customs supervision. On 1 March 1995, the Tanzania Revenue Authority appointed Cotecna Inspection SA to carry out pre-shipment inspections (PSI). Commercial imports with an FOB value in excess of US$5,000 are subject to inspection, as are goods shipped in containers, whatever their FOB value. The Customs and Excise Department is responsible for collecting international trade levies. Import duties have been cut since 1996 and the ceiling rate lowered from 40 per cent to 25 per cent. Tariff categories have been gradually reduced from seven to four. Import duties are calculated on the CIF value (cost, insurance and freight) of goods imported into the country. A number of priority products are admitted duty-free.

All exchange controls have been abolished in Tanzania. There are no restrictions on the availability of hard currency. However, the notification requirement for large transactions remains in place.

The means of payment are decided by the contracting parties. SWIFT transfers are the most widespread means of payment for trade transactions with countries having this facility. However, transactions are still carried out by telex, letter of credit and guaranteed bank cheques. Transactions are usually denominated in Tanzanian shillings or US dollars, although the euro is slowly gaining acceptance.

■ Attitude towards foreign investors

As well as its economic liberalization and privatization programme, Tanzania has adopted a strategy to promote direct foreign investment spearheaded by the Tanzania Investment Act 1997. This Act sets up a national investment promotion agency, the Tanzania Investment Centre (TIC), which serves as a one-stop shop for both foreign and domestic investors whose investments are above the thresholds set under the Act (US$300,000 for foreign investors). The TIC issues an acknowledgement certificate or certificate of incentives to investors who meet the legal requirements. This certificate entitles them to statutory tax breaks, including exemption from import duties, VAT and corporation tax during the first five years of business.

In 2002, the Tanzanian government set up free zones. While the legislation governing these zones offers additional incentives, it imposes an export requirement in respect of finished goods.

OPPORTUNITY SCOPE

Breakdown of internal demand (GDP + imports)	%
■ Private consumption	59
■ Public spending	5
■ Investment	14

Exports: 16% of GDP   Imports: 24% of GDP

MAIN DESTINATIONS OF EXPORTS

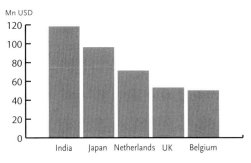

MAIN ORIGINS OF IMPORTS

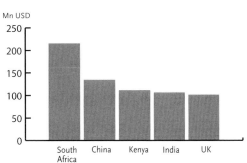

EXPORTS by products
- ■ Ores and metals 33%
- ■ All food items 32%
- ■ Agricultural raw materials 9%
- ■ Manufactured goods 7%
- ■ Miscellaneous 19%

IMPORTS by products
- ■ Capital goods 32%
- ■ Transport equipment 11%
- ■ Oil products 13%
- ■ Consumer goods 31%
- ■ Miscellaneous 13%

STANDARD OF LIVING / PURCHASING POWER

Indicators	Tanzania	Regional average	DC average
GNP per capita (PPP dollars)	520	2841	6778
GNP per capita (USD)	270	999	3568
Human Development Index	0.4	0.498	0.708
Wealthiest 10% share of national income	30	36	33
Urban population percentage	33	44	60
Percentage under 15 years old	45	42	31
number of telephones per 1000 inhabitants	4	33	157
number of computers per 1000 inhabitants	3	17	66

5

Togo

Population (million inhabitants)	4.7
GDP (million USD)	1,259
GDP per capita (USD)	268

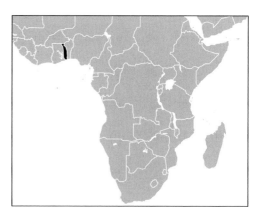

Short-term: **C**

Medium-term:

Coface analysis   **Very high risk**

RISK ASSESSMENT

The high level of cotton prices and increased phosphate production should benefit Togo's economy. The country's prospects have nonetheless remained below its potential and will not permit a response to the challenge of poverty.

The reduction of international aid since 1998 has limited the government's capacity for infrastructure investment and social spending and has undermined hopes for near-term cancellation of its public-sector debt. The conditions in which recent elections were held – the December 2002 parliamentary elections and those in May 2003 that permitted President Eyadema's re-election – have not helped to restore the confidence of financial backers.

However, their backing has remained essential to cover the country's internal and external financing needs and avoid an accumulation of payment arrears.

MAIN ECONOMIC INDICATORS						
US$ millions	1999	2000	2001	2002	2003 (e)	2004 (f)
Economic growth (%)	2.7	−0.5	1.1	4.2	3.1	3.5
Inflation (%)	−0.1	1.9	3.9	3.1	−0.6	2
Public-sector balance/GDP (%)	−4.6	−5	0.1	−1	−3.6	n/a
Exports	392	363	358	415	462	486
Imports	490	486	517	566	649	793
Trade balance	−98	−123	−159	−152	−186	−307
Current account balance/GDP (%)	−11.3	−12.7	−14.3	−11.6	−9.3	−8.7
Foreign debt	1,522	1,432	1,406	1,581	1,553	1,536
Debt service/Exports (%)	19.9	18.8	18.1	17.7	14.5	13.3
Currency reserves (import months)	3	3.7	2.9	4	3.5	2.8

404

e = estimate, f = forecast

Uganda

Population (million inhabitants)	22.8
GDP (million USD)	5,675

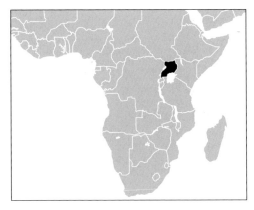

Short-term: **C**

Medium-term:

Coface analysis　　　　**High risk**

STRENGTHS

- Uganda has great potential with diversification of its economic fabric well under way.
- Increased regional integration will represent a further asset.
- With its structural reform policy, the country has earned broad international-financial-community backing.
- That international backing has permitted it to benefit from the HIPC initiative reserved for highly indebted poor countries.
- Uganda has made encouraging progress on education and in combating poverty and improving public health conditions.

WEAKNESSES

- The country is still very dependent on agriculture (40 per cent of GDP) and thus on weather conditions and world price trends.
- It has continued to depend on international aid to cover its deficits.
- An inadequate civil-service framework and unfavourable business environment have been impeding investment and implementation of the programme to combat poverty and the AIDS pandemic.
- Persistent regional and domestic tensions have damaged the country's image.

RISK ASSESSMENT

Bolstered by implementation of disciplined economic policy, Uganda has continued to enjoy respectable growth rates. After a slight slowdown in 2003 that particularly reflected the impact of bad weather conditions on farm production, economic activity should recover in 2004. That outlook should nonetheless not obscure the persistence of either large regional disparities or major weaknesses.

The country's public and external accounts have remained very shaky. Security spending and difficulties encountered in widening the country's tax base have been straining public accounts.

Meanwhile, persistent external-account deficits have been underscoring Uganda's difficulties in developing sufficient foreign currency revenues despite considerable reduction of its foreign debt burden.

In that context, with foreign direct investment inflows below expectations, the country will continue to depend on international aid to cover both its internal and external financing needs. However, the level of that backing will depend on continued easing of the regional situation (notably in the Democratic Republic of Congo) and liberalization of the regime.

MAIN ECONOMIC INDICATORS						
US$ millions	1999	2000	2001	2002	2003 (e)	2004 (f)
Economic growth (%)	7.9	5.3	5.5	6.6	4.4	5
Inflation (%)	0.2	5.8	4.5	-2	7.7	6.5
Public-sector balance/GDP (%)	-7.7	-15.5	-8.9	-12.7	-11.4	-11.3
Exports	549	453	446	472	549	604
Imports	1,039	978	973	1,083	1,170	1,252
Trade balance	-490	-525	-527	-611	-621	-648
Current account balance/GDP (%)	-10.8	-13.0	-14.5	-13.4	-13.3	-13.7
Foreign debt	3,708	3,494	3,733	3,945	4,183	4,358
Debt service/Exports (%)	13.9	16.3	7.9	6.5	6.2	6.8
Currency reserves (import months)	5.6	5.5	5.5	5.9	5.8	5.4

e = estimate, f = forecast

CONDITIONS OF ACCESS TO THE MARKET

■ Market overview

Piecemeal customs and tax (VAT) management is the main problem faced by importers and investors. Customs declarations must be supported by an import certificate, an invoice and a certificate of origin. Where applicable, a health certificate for live animals, a health certificate and import licence for plants (fresh fruits, plants and seeds) and a disinfection certificate for second-hand clothes, bedding and similar articles intended for sale must also be produced. Customs clearance takes about a week.

Following cuts in Ugandan customs duties, henceforth the lowest in East Africa, three rates of duty remain in force: 0, 7 and 15 per cent. COMESA member countries are granted a preferential tariff consisting of three rates of duty: 0, 4 and 6 per cent. Production equipment and essential staples are admitted duty-free. All duties are *ad valorem* and calculated on the CIF value of goods transported by road, and on the insured value of goods transported by air. In addition to customs duties and a 4 per cent levy calculated on the CIF value (warehousing duty), all imports are liable to 0.8 per cent import duty on the FOB value (in respect of inspection fees), a 2 per cent import charge on the CIF value (Import Licence Commission) and, where applicable, 17 per cent VAT plus excise duties.

Three standard rates of duty – 0, 10 and 25 per cent – will apply when the customs union of EAC member states (Kenya, Tanzania and Uganda) comes into force.

■ Attitude towards foreign investors

Despite the government's determination to open up the market, foreign direct investment (FDI) in Uganda is governed by the outdated 1991 Investment Code, whose restrictions deter a good many potential investors. The changes to the Code demanded time and again by the business community are still under examination.

In a pragmatic move, the government has given the Ugandan Investment Authority (UIA), the body responsible for issuing licences and promoting investment, wide powers of initiative to reduce discrimination between foreigners and nationals pending introduction of a more liberal-minded code. To obtain a licence, foreign investors must submit to the UIA a business plan along with a detailed financial statement of their company's activities. The accounts do not have to be infallibly accurate as licences for a minimum period of five years are granted automatically if the investment complies with the Code. The UIA is required to draw up a report on each investment application within 30 days and reach its decision within an additional 14 days. The Ugandan Investment Code does not guarantee foreign investors equal treatment with local ones. Foreign investors are subject to a number of requirements not applicable to domestic investors, including a minimum investment of US$100,000, the establishment of a local office, the purchase of locally manufactured goods and environmental protection. Moreover, foreign investors have restricted access to local credit, although this measure is not enforced in practice. The main problems faced by the vast majority of foreign investors following start-up are, in descending order, the slowness of the legal system, government corruption and unequal treatment by the Uganda Revenue Authority.

The Investment Code provides for international arbitration of disputes in a form mutually acceptable to both parties. Uganda has ratified the New York Convention on International Arbitration and the International Centre for Settlement of Investment Disputes (ICSID) convention.

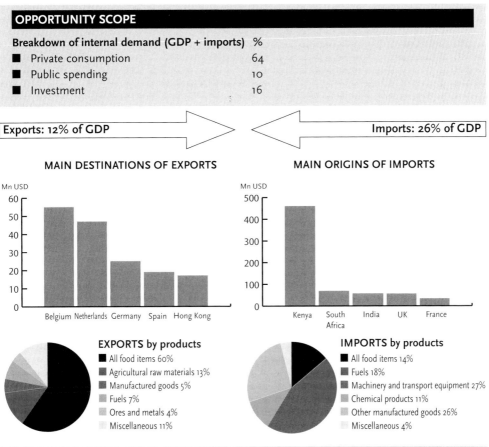

OPPORTUNITY SCOPE

Breakdown of internal demand (GDP + imports) %
- Private consumption — 64
- Public spending — 10
- Investment — 16

Exports: 12% of GDP → ← Imports: 26% of GDP

MAIN DESTINATIONS OF EXPORTS
Mn USD (Belgium, Netherlands, Germany, Spain, Hong Kong)

MAIN ORIGINS OF IMPORTS
Mn USD (Kenya, South Africa, India, UK, France)

EXPORTS by products
- All food items 60%
- Agricultural raw materials 13%
- Manufactured goods 5%
- Fuels 7%
- Ores and metals 4%
- Miscellaneous 11%

IMPORTS by products
- All food items 14%
- Fuels 18%
- Machinery and transport equipment 27%
- Chemical products 11%
- Other manufactured goods 26%
- Miscellaneous 4%

STANDARD OF LIVING / PURCHASING POWER

Indicators	Uganda	Regional average	DC average
GNP per capita (PPP dollars)	1460	2841	6778
GNP per capita (USD)	260	999	3568
Human Development Index	0.489	0.498	0.708
Wealthiest 10% share of national income	30	36	33
Urban population percentage	15	44	60
Percentage under 15 years old	49	42	31
number of telephones per 1000 inhabitants	3	33	157
number of computers per 1000 inhabitants	3	17	66

Zambia

Population (million inhabitants)	10.3
GDP (million USD)	3,639

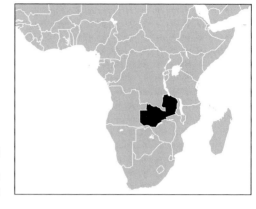

Coface analysis

Short-term: **D**

Medium-term:
Very high risk

STRENGTHS

- Zambia boasts substantial mining resources (world cobalt production leader, Africa's copper production leader).
- Its large agricultural and tourism potential has been the focus of development policy intended to foster the economy's necessary diversification.
- The country's assets and the structural reforms undertaken will be apt to attract foreign investors.
- The country has been benefiting from international financial community backing and the HIPC foreign-debt reduction programme reserved for highly indebted poor countries.

WEAKNESSES

- The economy has remained very exposed to exogenous shocks (copper prices, weather conditions).
- Zambia is a landlocked country, and its exports have suffered from inadequate transportation infrastructure and been sensitive to increases in shipping costs.
- With a very heavy foreign debt burden and limited currency reserves, the country's external constraint has been very severe.
- Poverty has been affecting large segments of the population, also very affected by the AIDS pandemic.
- The unstable regional environment (Zimbabwe, Democratic Republic of Congo) could generate tensions (smuggling, refugees).

RISK ASSESSMENT

Zambia has been going through a difficult period. Despite brighter aspects attributable to the impact on growth of good harvests and increased copper and cobalt production, these will not suffice to meet the challenges of combating poverty and modernizing the country's infrastructure.

Moreover, the political climate has remained tense. The conditions of President Mwanawasa's election are being contested in court, anti-corruption measures have been threatening many vested interests, and the authorities have been tempted by populist measures (suspension of privatizations, sharp increases in public-sector wages) that worsen public-sector deficits and deter international-financial-community backing.

Considering the country's substantial financing needs, however, that backing will remain essential, notably to permit reduction of its foreign debt via the HIPC programme for highly indebted poor countries.

MAIN ECONOMIC INDICATORS						
US$ millions	1999	2000	2001	2002	2003 (e)	2004 (f)
Economic growth (%)	2.4	3.6	4	2.3	3.1	3.4
Inflation (%)	26.8	26.1	21.7	22.2	21.7	19.9
Public-sector balance/GDP (%)	−11.6	−11.6	−13	−13.9	−13.9	−11.5
Exports	756	746	884	916	1,051	1,185
Imports	922	978	1,253	1,204	1,387	1,456
Trade balance	−166	−232	−369	−288	−336	−271
Current account balance/GDP (%)	−17.0	−18.8	−20.8	−17.3	−16.7	−14.8
Foreign debt	6,237	6,259	7,294	7,228	7,190	7,187
Debt service/Exports (%)	14.9	17.2	23.6	27.2	24.8	30.2
Currency reserves (import months)	0.4	0.9	0.8	2	1	1.6

e = estimate, f = forecast

CONDITIONS OF ACCESS TO THE MARKET

■ Means of entry

Goods can be exchanged freely and some agricultural and mining products are exempt from import duties. ATA carnets are accepted. Customs clearance usually takes about 72 hours after presentation of the products, and consolidated import shipments are allowed. For preferential treatment of products, a COMESA or SADC certificate of origin is required. Excise duties vary between 5 and 125 per cent of the product's value and customs duties between 0 and 25 per cent. There is 17.5 per cent VAT as well as a refund scheme under the so-called duty drawback system. All means of payment are available, but documentary credit is recommended.

■ Attitude towards foreign investors

The Investment Act 1993, amended in 1998, guarantees freedom of investment in Zambia. Certain sectors – tourism, mining, air and road transport and financial services – require an additional operating licence. There are no restrictions on the repatriation of profits. The free zones (EPZ) set up in 2003 provide foreign investors with tax breaks, including exemptions from corporation tax and excise duties. Zambia has mutual investment protection and double taxation agreements with numerous countries, including France. All disputes between foreign investors and local parties are subject to local or international arbitration (ICSIO and UNICITRAL). Zambian law makes it difficult to employ expatriates and 50 per cent of company directors must be Zambian.

■ Foreign exchange regulations

There are no exchange controls in Zambia. A foreign resident may open a foreign currency account with a local bank. However, there is no provision for exchange rate cover. Financial transaction costs are high.

5

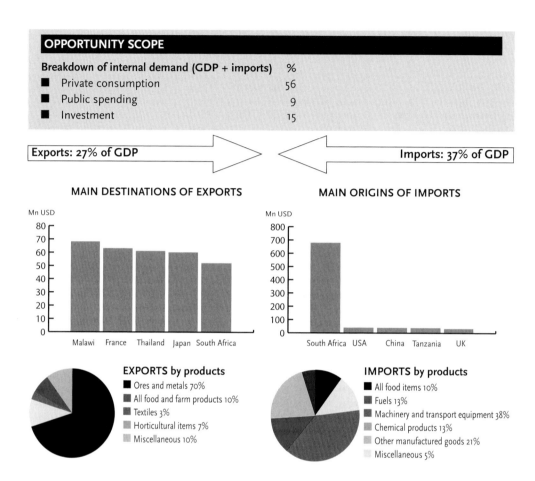

OPPORTUNITY SCOPE

Breakdown of internal demand (GDP + imports)	%
■ Private consumption	56
■ Public spending	9
■ Investment	15

Exports: 27% of GDP → ← Imports: 37% of GDP

MAIN DESTINATIONS OF EXPORTS

Mn USD

Malawi, France, Thailand, Japan, South Africa

MAIN ORIGINS OF IMPORTS

Mn USD

South Africa, USA, China, Tanzania, UK

EXPORTS by products
- ■ Ores and metals 70%
- ■ All food and farm products 10%
- ■ Textiles 3%
- ■ Horticultural items 7%
- ■ Miscellaneous 10%

IMPORTS by products
- ■ All food items 10%
- ■ Fuels 13%
- ■ Machinery and transport equipment 38%
- ■ Chemical products 13%
- ■ Other manufactured goods 21%
- ■ Miscellaneous 5%

STANDARD OF LIVING / PURCHASING POWER

Indicators	Zambia	Regional average	DC average
GNP per capita (PPP dollars)	750	2841	6778
GNP per capita (USD)	320	999	3568
Human Development Index	0.386	0.498	0.708
Wealthiest 10% share of national income	41	36	33
Urban population percentage	4	44	60
Percentage under 15 years old	45	42	31
number of telephones per 1000 inhabitants	8	33	157
number of computers per 1000 inhabitants	7	17	66

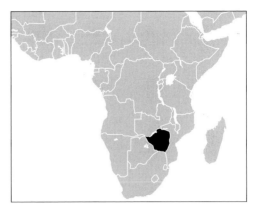

Zimbabwe

Population (million inhabitants)	12.8
GDP (million USD)	9,057

Coface analysis

Short-term: **D**

Medium-term:
Very high risk

STRENGTHS

- Zimbabwe enjoys substantial economic potential with mineral and agricultural resources, a diversified industrial fabric and a well-educated labour force.
- The quality of its transportation and financial infrastructures could facilitate an economic upturn.
- With South Africa, the country could constitute an economic and political engine for Southern Africa.

WEAKNESSES

- The crisis has had disastrous effects on the country's economic situation and its effects will be difficult to overcome.
- Zimbabwe is in default on payments to international financial organizations and its creditors.
- It is increasingly ostracized by the international community.
- The economic crisis has severely strained the social and political climate.
- The AIDS infection rate is among the highest in Africa and the world.

RISK ASSESSMENT

Zimbabwe has continued to sink into a grave crisis affecting all economic sectors and personal incomes. The farm sector's disorganization has amplified the drought's effects causing scarcity of food products and famine. A dearth of credit has been preventing companies from procuring energy and intermediate goods. Moreover, unable to meet international commitments, owing to a lack of currency earnings, the country has been at odds with the IMF and international financial community.

The outlook for 2004 has thus remained gloomy with the country's deficits continuing to grow. With a very strained political and social situation, an economic turnaround seems difficult to imagine.

Should a turnaround develop, however, improving the country's situation would nonetheless take time. Its dependence on international backing should thus persist for several years.

5

MAIN ECONOMIC INDICATORS

US$ millions	1999	2000	2001	2002	2003 (e)	2004 (f)
Economic growth (%)	−4.1	−6.8	−8.8	−12.8	−13.6	−6.2
Inflation (%)	58	56	77	140	352	432
Public-sector balance/GDP (%)	−9.8	−23	−10.8	−10	−17.7	−10.6
Exports	1,930	2,190	1,610	1,418	1,170	1,049
Imports	1,680	1,850	1,780	1,822	1,586	1,513
Trade balance	250	340	−170	−404	−416	−464
Current account balance/GDP (%)	0.2	0.5	−4.9	−6.7	−7.5	−8.1
Foreign debt	5,045	5,114	5,137	5,177	5,274	n/a
Debt service/Exports (%)	22.8	24.3	29.5	31.0	28.1	n/a
Currency reserves (import months)	0.2	0.1	0.1	0.1	0.1	n/a

e = estimate, f = forecast

CONDITIONS OF ACCESS TO THE MARKET

■ Market overview
Zimbabwe's economic and financial situation makes it a high-risk country for foreign investors.

■ Means of entry
Goods can be freely exchanged, although a certificate of origin is required for imports. Customs duties vary between 0 and 138 per cent according to the type of import, except for goods from COMESA, which are exempt from duties on the basis of reciprocity. Exporters are also required to pay 15 per cent or 25 per cent import duty – replaced by VAT from 1 January 2004 – along with a 10 per cent surtax. All means of payment are accepted. Credit cards are not widely used.

■ Attitude towards foreign investors
In principle, the 1989 Investment Act guarantees foreign investors free access to the local market. The government allows foreign majority stakes in the mining and manufacturing sectors. Foreign investors may not hold more than 70 per cent of a service company or 35 per cent of an agricultural, armaments or water supply company. From 1 January 1995, all profits and dividends are repatriable after tax. Disputes between a foreign investor and a local party are subject to local or international arbitration. Corporation tax is 30 per cent, and foreign companies are liable to 15 per cent tax on 56 per cent of the taxable income of their subsidiaries in addition to corporation tax. They are also liable to a 3 per cent AIDS levy. The country has double taxation agreements, including one with France. Foreign enterprises can be sited in the so-called 'Export Processing Zones', which offer among other things tax breaks and more flexible wage arrangements. The stock exchange is open to foreign capital, but a listed company may not be more than 40 per cent held by foreign interests, and no foreign shareholder may singly hold more than 10 per cent of a listed company. Investors can obtain a three-year work permit. It is possible to employ foreigners where equivalent local skills are unavailable.

■ Foreign exchange regulations
Foreign exchange transactions in Zimbabwe are subject to strict controls due to a shortage of hard currency. The official exchange rate is 826 Zimbabwean dollars to one US dollar. The exchange rate on the grey market varies between 6,000 Zimbabwean dollars (buy) and 7,000 Zimbabwean dollars (sell) to the US dollar. Exporters must exchange 50 per cent of their foreign currency earnings with the central bank at the official rate and may keep the remaining 50 per cent in a foreign currency account for 60 days.

OPPORTUNITY SCOPE

Breakdown of internal demand (GDP + imports)   %
■   Private consumption   60
■   Public spending   16
■   Investment   7

Exports: 22% of GDP   Imports: 21% of GDP

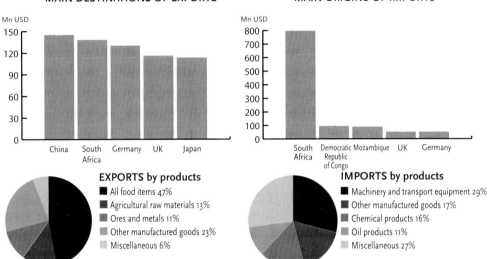

MAIN DESTINATIONS OF EXPORTS

Mn USD

China, South Africa, Germany, UK, Japan

EXPORTS by products
■ All food items 47%
■ Agricultural raw materials 13%
■ Ores and metals 11%
■ Other manufactured goods 23%
■ Miscellaneous 6%

MAIN ORIGINS OF IMPORTS

Mn USD

South Africa, Democratic Republic of Congo, Mozambique, UK, Germany

IMPORTS by products
■ Machinery and transport equipment 29%
■ Other manufactured goods 17%
■ Chemical products 16%
■ Oil products 11%
■ Miscellaneous 27%

5

STANDARD OF LIVING / PURCHASING POWER

Indicators	Zimbabwe	Regional average	DC average
GNP per capita (PPP dollars)	2220	2841	6778
GNP per capita (USD)	480	999	3568
Human Development Index	0.496	0.498	0.708
Wealthiest 10% share of national income	40	36	33
Urban population percentage	36	44	60
Percentage under 15 years old	45	42	31
number of telephones per 1000 inhabitants	19	33	157
number of computers per 1000 inhabitants	12	17	66

ACRONYM TABLE AND LEXICON

AKP Turkey: the Justice and Development Party running the Turkish government since November 2002

BJP (India): Bharatiya Janata Party, the Indian nationalist party leading the coalition in power since 1999

CEPA (Hong Kong): Closer Economic Partnership Association (with mainland China)

CIS: Community of Independent States

COMESA: Common Market for Eastern and Southern Africa

currency board: system whereby a country pegs its currency to a foreign currency (generally the US dollar or euro) with a currency board supplanting the central bank

EAC: East African Community

ECOWAS: Economic Community of West African States

FDI: foreign direct investment

FMLN and ARENA (El Salvador): major political parties – Frente Farabundo Marti para la Liberacion Nacional and Alianza Republicana Nacionalista

GDP: gross domestic product

GNP: gross national product

HIPC: a joint IMF/World Bank initiative in favour of heavily indebted poor countries, which can permit cancellation of their public external debt once they meet specified conditions and thus reach the HIPC 'completion point'

ILSA (USA): Iran–Libya Sanctions Act approved by Congress in August 1996 to punish Iran and Libya notably via trade sanctions

IMF: International Monetary Fund

NATO: North Atlantic Treaty Organization

NICT: new information and communication technologies

OPEC: Organization of Petroleum Exporting Countries

Paris Club: an informal group of official creditors devoted to finding sustainable solutions to payment difficulties experienced by debtor nations

PPP: purchasing power parity

PRGF: Poverty Reduction and Growth Facility, the IMF's special low-interest lending programme for poor countries with structural balance-of-payments difficulties

R&D: research and development

SADC: Southern African Development Community

SWIFT: Society for Worldwide Interbank Financial Telecommunication, which runs a worldwide network whereby messages concerning financial transactions can be exchanged between banks and other financial institutions in 194 countries

UNITA (Angola): União para a Indepêndencia Total de Angola, rebel movement defeated in 2002 after nearly 30 years of civil war

WAEMU: West African Economic and Monetary Union